Investing
in
Development

Family bagging swamp rice, Liberia

Investing
in
Development

Lessons of World Bank Experience

Warren C. Baum and Stokes M. Tolbert

PUBLISHED FOR THE WORLD BANK • OXFORD UNIVERSITY PRESS

Oxford University Press

NEW YORK OXFORD LONDON GLASGOW
TORONTO MELBOURNE WELLINGTON HONG KONG
TOKYO KUALA LUMPUR SINGAPORE JAKARTA
DELHI BOMBAY CALCUTTA MADRAS KARACHI
NAIROBI DAR ES SALAAM CAPE TOWN

First printing of hardcover and paperback editions July 1985

Photo credits: All illustrations are World Bank photos unless otherwise specified. Betsy Bumgarner, chapters 2, 9, 21; Kay Chernush, chapter 10; John Courtney, chapter 12; FAO, frontispiece; Yosef Hadar, chapters 8, 19; Inter-American Development Bank, chapter 18; David Mangurian, Inter-American Development Bank, chapter 24; Ivan Massar, chapter 13; Yutaka Nagata, chapter 7; James Pickerell, chapters 14, 16, 25; Reynolds, UNICEF, chapter 5; Tomas Sennett, chapters 11, 15, 22; United Nations, chapter 27; Ray Witlin, chapters 1, 3, 4, 6, 17, 20, 23, 26, index.

Library of Congress Cataloging in Publication Data

Baum, Warren C.
   Investing in development.

   Includes index.
   1. World Bank—Developing countries.   2. Investments,
Foreign—Developing countries.   I. Tolbert, Stokes M.,
1923–   .   II. International Bank for Reconstruction and
Development.   III. Title.
HG3881.5.W57B38   1985   332.1'532'091724   85-8830
ISBN 0-19-520475-1
ISBN 0-19-520476-X (pbk.)

Foreword

INVESTING IN DEVELOPMENT has been the central activity of The World Bank for more than thirty-five years.

In close partnership with its developing members—which number well over a hundred separate, sovereign, culturally diverse societies—the Bank has acquired a rich store of experience. It has worked on every continent. It has faced a wide range of local conditions. It has helped search for solutions to an evolving mixture of complex development problems.

In recent years the global economy has been swept by the energy crisis, the persistent recession, the international debt problem, and the natural catastrophe of prolonged drought. The Bank has responded to these events through an array of new lending instruments, and it will continue to look for innovative and catalytic approaches as new challenges arise. But assisting countries to invest in development—planning investments, designing projects, building institutions, and devising appropriate policies—is where the Bank's traditional strength lies. There is a consensus among the Bank's shareholder governments that investing in development should be the mainstay of future operations as well.

Over the years the Bank has published a wide selection of materials on various aspects of its work. But the present volume represents the first time we have sought to portray the full scope of the investment process. It provides a detailed and comprehensive overview of the process that none of our previous publications has attempted.

The book has been a major undertaking, and for it the Bank has called on the services of two senior World Bank officials who between them have nearly forty years of project experience. Warren C. Baum has served as vice president of the Central Projects Staff and of the Operations Policy Staff, and Stokes M. Tolbert as director of the Industrial Development and Finance Department and of the Tourism Projects Department. They, in turn, have drawn upon a group of experts in the Bank for contributions in their specialized fields.

What, then, is the goal of this volume?

It is, quite simply, to share the central lessons that The World Bank has learned during the almost four decades it has been assisting its developing member countries to achieve their investment objectives. It is an effort to distill the Bank's experience as a hands-on lender and make it available to others in as helpful a form as possible.

Foremost among the intended readers are the officials in developing countries who have the critical task of managing their societies' resources. But the book is relevant to the interests of many other groups as well: staff of development institutions and aid agencies, consultants, researchers— indeed to all those who are working in the field of development.

Let me emphasize that this book is not about how The World Bank "does" development projects. It is, rather, about what the Bank has learned, through both successes and failures, that can prove useful to developing countries in their own investment and project work. It is about what these countries—through more effective investment in development—can do to enhance their economic growth and to improve their quality of life. The Bank can help in this effort by making the knowledge and insights that it has gained available to those officials who bear the heavy burden of hastening their countries' economic and social advance.

We will go on learning from, and with, our member countries as they proceed along the path of development. The Bank's relationship with its members is characterized as much by a lively and fruitful dialogue as by the transfer of financial resources. This book, by increasing the area of common ground, should enrich and deepen that dialogue.

A. W. CLAUSEN
President, The World Bank

June 1985

Contents

Preface

THE WORLD BANK'S approach to investment lending is an integral part of its wider role as a development institution working in close relationship with its developing member countries to help promote their economic growth and social welfare. This relationship takes many forms, ranging from giving broad advice on macroeconomic policies and development strategies based on a comprehensive program of country economic and sector work, to conducting economic research and special studies on development issues, to providing technical assistance for investment planning or for any of the myriad tasks of development, to engaging in the "nuts and bolts" of project lending.

The origins of this book can be traced to an article written by one of the authors called "The Project Cycle," which appeared in *Finance & Development* in 1968. It provided, for the first time, a brief summary of how the Bank goes about its project work. In several editions and languages, it has reached a wide audience. From time to time requests have been made, both within and outside the Bank, that the project cycle be described from the viewpoint of a developing country carrying out its own projects. This we initially set out to do in this book.

It soon became apparent, however, that the usefulness of our account would be limited if we did not set project work in its proper context of investment planning and management at the national and sector levels. The World Bank has been one of the pioneers in the study of national economies as a whole and in the systematic analysis of their main sectors, which together provide an indispensable basis for selecting sound projects and determining appropriate policies. In expanding the coverage of the book to reflect these activities, we have increased its bulk greatly, but it now, we hope, constitutes a guide to the entire process of managing a country's investment resources wisely. We have had to omit many important specialized topics because of space restrictions. Our aim has been to achieve the virtues of broad, if not always deep, coverage of the investment process as a whole.

Many studies that seek to explain one aspect or another of the development process rely on—or build—theoretical models that are presumed to have not only explanatory but also predictive powers. This book takes a different tack. It is based entirely on the World Bank's observation of, and participation in, the actual successes and failures of investment efforts over the past thirty-five years in its developing member countries—which comprise most of the world's developing countries except for some of the centrally planned economies of Eastern Europe. The authors believe that a book thus firmly anchored in experience can provide a practical guide for officials and others in these countries. It has long been recognized that the knowledge and example of the developed countries constitute an invaluable resource for the developing countries to draw upon, enabling them to leapfrog some steps toward development. It is a thesis of this book that the vast accumulation of experience with the development process in the developing countries themselves is an even more fruitful resource. This book attempts to pull together some of that experience and make it readily available.

In writing about the investment process from the point of view of officials in developing countries, who are our primary audience, we have kept in mind that they have a wide variety of backgrounds and professional experience. For this reason, and especially to make the discussion accessible to those without formal training in economics, we have tried to keep the theoretical concepts and analytical techniques as simple as possible and to avoid technical jargon. We have also sought to make our advice practical and to present it in a way that is directly applicable and as unambiguous as the complexity of development problems permits.

In the discussion we have recognized explicitly that economic development depends in large measure on noneconomic factors. Although social, cultural, and institutional factors have been examined, we have not been able—because of limitations of time and space and of our own knowledge—to give systematic treatment to the political aspects of development. We allude to what is often the ultimately political nature of choices to be made; for example, in the allocation of resources among sectors and in the size and timing of price adjustments in the public sector. But it has not been possible to portray adequately the political pressures that officials in developing countries constantly face. Most economic decisions—certainly the important ones—involve a competition for scarce resources and a balancing of conflicting claims put forward by various sectoral, regional, commercial, or other interests. The decisionmaker is at the center of these pressures, which may delay or significantly compromise sound decisions, and indeed may sometimes overwhelm rational economic choice.

We have tried to avoid giving the impression that we believe the decisionmaker can always accept and act on sound economic advice if only he chooses to do so. But it would have been impossible, without excessive repetition, to note this at every turn. Suffice it to say that underlying the arguments presented here is an appreciation of the multiplicity of competing interests and priorities that give the decisionmaking process its real flavor. We have sought to provide a guide not toward ideal but toward better decisions, recognizing that less than optimal decisions are not simply shortfalls from an ideal but sometimes the best possible solution to complex problems amid multiple constraints.

We have not tried to minimize the persistent obstacles on the path to development. At the same time, we hope we have reflected the conviction that World Bank staff share with officials of many of our member countries: not only that the old ways must go but also that the needed new ways can be found; that the prospect of degrading poverty can be tempered with hope of a reasonable degree of shared prosperity. This book conveys the message that the economic development process, which is spreading a technological revolution to many parts of the globe, can be nurtured and hastened through the application of some relatively simple lessons.

Much of the Bank's experience has remained in the form of internal studies, reports, and memoranda or in the minds of its professional staff. The book has attempted to compile and synthesize this experience in a form usable by development practitioners. The source material for the book has accordingly come almost entirely from within the Bank. This explains the relatively few references given, especially since the only Bank documents we have cited are those available to the general public.

This analysis of the substantive lessons of the Bank's experience has drawn extensively on the competence of many other people; our heavy debt to them is acknowledged separately. We also benefited greatly from the advice and comments of others in and outside the Bank who reviewed all or most of the book in draft, including Colin Bruce, Ram Chopra, Anthony Churchill, Ernesto Fontaine, S. S. Kirmani, A. M. A. Muhith, Guy Pfefferman, Robert Picciotto, Robert Sadove, Wilfried Thalwitz, and Mervyn Weiner. Herman van der Tak undertook an especially painstaking and searching review of the entire draft. In addition, we received helpful comments on various chapters of the book from Hans Adler, George Baldwin, Michael Bamberger, Esra Bennathan, Hans Binswanger, Michael Cernea, Cynthia Cook, Maurice Dickerson, Nancy Farmer, Aklilu Habte, Clifford Hardy, Clell Harral, Ernesto Henriod, John Holsen, Ian Hume, Tariq Hussain, Keith Marsden, Katherine Marshall, Maurice Mould, Al Raizen, Visvanathan Rajagopalan, Anandarup Ray, Gloria Scott, Raghavan Srinivasan, Donald Strombom, Jeremy Warford, Larry Westphal, Christopher Willoughby, and Montague Yudelman. Peter Richardson played an important role in shaping the initial concept of the book. The two authors are responsible for the content of the book, however, including the errors that doubtless still remain.

Jeanne Rosen, our tireless editor, devoted many hours to improving our drafts, in the process making not only our writing but also our thinking clearer; her contribution was indispensable, and if the reader finds his way through the analysis with relative ease, much of the credit goes to her. Our gratitude to our secretaries, Moreen Tolerton and Virginia Acio, cannot be measured; they toiled through innumerable drafts, giving word processing new dimensions of cheerfulness, precision, and celerity, and were as committed as we to the quality of the book.

Acknowledgment to Contributors

This book would not have been possible without the contributions of many other World Bank staff members and some consultants long associated with the Bank. These contributors provided authoritative and up-to-date material that reflected the range of Bank experience in their particular areas of expertise. They entered into a unique form of collaboration with the two authors, in which they prepared draft chapters, or background papers for chapters, while accepting that we would retain full editorial control. The intent was to produce not a collection of readings by individual authors, with the duplications in coverage and differences in approach and style that such a collection inevitably entails, but rather a unified treatment of the subject from a single viewpoint. A few of the contributions required little change, but most were, in varying degree, revised, reorganized, expanded, or reduced to fit the requirements of the book. The contributors, with notable grace and patience, often prepared revised drafts, reviewed our redrafts, and filled gaps in data or analysis.

A special note of appreciation is due to Shirley Boskey, who in addition to participating in the drafting of two chapters, as noted below, did extensive editing of several other chapters.

We gratefully acknowledge, for the following chapters or sections of chapters, our extensive debt to these contributors:

PART I. NATIONAL INVESTMENT MANAGEMENT

Development Planning   *Ramgopal Agarwala*
Pricing Policy   *Ramgopal Agarwala*
Public Investment Programs and Budgets   *Ramgopal Agarwala*

PART II. SECTOR ANALYSIS AND MANAGEMENT

Agriculture   *Graham Donaldson, Graeme Donovan, and Peter Hopcraft*
Education   *Stephen Heyneman*
Energy   *Richard Dosik*
Population, Health, and Nutrition   *David de Ferranti and Lauren Chester*
Transport   *Vincent Hogg and Edward Holland*
Urbanization   *Michael Cohen*
Water and Sanitation   *John Kalbermatten*

PART III. THE PROJECT CYCLE

Project Implementation   *Arturo Israel*
Ex Post Evaluation   *Shirley Boskey*

PART IV. PROJECT ANALYSIS

Technical Analysis (section on Scientific
  and Technological Development)   *Charles Weiss*
Economic Analysis   *Prem Garg*
Social Analysis   *Jasper Ingersoll and Fern Ingersoll*
Social Analysis (section on
  Women in Development)   *Shirley Boskey*
Institutional Analysis   *Geoffrey Lamb*
Environmental Analysis   *Robert Goodland and George Ledec*
Procurement   *Charles Morse*
Use of Consultants   *Charles Morse*

Abbreviations and Definitions

DFC   Development finance company
EEC   European Economic Community
FAO   Food and Agriculture Organization
GDP   Gross domestic product
GNP   Gross national product
IBRD   International Bank for Reconstruction and Development
IDA   International Development Association
ILO   International Labour Organisation
IMF   International Monetary Fund
OECD   Organisation for Economic Co-operation and Development
OED   Operations Evaluation Department (World Bank)
UNDP   United Nations Development Programme
UNEP   United Nations Environment Programme
Unesco United Nations Educational, Scientific, and Cultural
       Organization
UNICEF United Nations International Children's Emergency Fund
UNIDO United Nations Industrial Development Organization
WHO   World Health Organization

Billion is 1,000 million.
Dollars are U.S. dollars.
Hectare is 10,000 square meters or approximately 2.47 acres.

Investing
in
Development

Woman carrying water, Ethiopia

1

Introduction

ECONOMIC DEVELOPMENT is transforming the lives of millions of people throughout the developing world. The character of development, its direction and pace, and the way people share in its benefits are largely determined by how a country manages its investment resources. This book is about that investment process, viewed from the experience of the World Bank, which has been a leading source of finance for development for more than thirty-five years.[1]

Much of the book is concerned with investments in the form of specific projects: how to identify the most promising projects in each sector, how to prepare them, how to carry them through to successful completion, how to operate and maintain them afterward. The project, sometimes described as the "cutting edge of development," has become an important means of marshaling a country's resources, human and material, for investing in development.

But this book is about more than projects; to put it another way, it treats the project approach to investment in the broadest context. The approach comprises analyses and decisions at the *national* level, where projects are aggregated into a national investment plan and a framework of macroeconomic policies is put in place; at the *sector* level, where sector investment strategies and priorities, along with supporting policies, are elaborated; and at the *project* level, where specific projects are identified, prepared, and implemented.

In the years after World War II, a new-found concern with raising the living standards of the two-thirds of mankind in the developing world led to international cooperation for development on an unprecedented scale. International lending agencies were established and programs of bilateral aid launched to transfer resources and provide technical assistance to developing countries. In conjunction with these efforts, development economics emerged as a major field of intellectual endeavor, seeking to identify the factors that stimulate economic growth and to design techniques to overcome constraints to that growth. Theories and doctrines of development appeared rapidly: physical capital formation, balanced growth, and the "big push"; dependency theories; backward linkages; industrialization or rural development; import substitution or export promotion; structuralism or market-based development; and, recently, investment in human capital with an emphasis on basic needs. In retrospect, it is clear that these offered not so much a comprehensive theory of development as a guide to a better understanding of one aspect or another of the complex process of development.

THE PROJECT APPROACH

Amid this ferment and the frequent changes of emphasis that it encouraged, the project approach has endured as a disciplined way to

---

1. For convenience or variety, we shall also refer to the World Bank as "the Bank." Its formal name is the International Bank for Reconstruction and Development.

manage the use of resources to achieve important development objectives. This approach has assisted developing countries to establish the viable institutions indispensable for orderly economic growth, to effect the policy changes needed for good project performance, and to make investments that are properly engineered, financially feasible, and economically sound.

The project approach accords well with the increasingly pragmatic view of development found in many countries today. The international community has become much more knowledgeable about the development process, recognizing that there is no single blueprint or prescription for overcoming the problems of underdevelopment. Economic development is now perceived as a long, slow, and often painful process of learning from experience. The complexity and interdependence of the modern global economy have imposed discipline and realism on policymakers; this has been reinforced by recent vicissitudes—recession, reduction in foreign aid, debt crisis. Instead of constructing elaborate models for central planning, governments are concentrating more of their efforts on the two primary means within their control for guiding the growth process: a sound public sector investment program that allocates scarce resources to high-priority public needs, and a policy framework that elicits the desired behavior from both public and private entities. The emphasis is on being practical rather than doctrinaire, on learning by doing, and on using what works and abandoning what does not. This is increasingly true of centrally planned as well as market economies. In this context, the project approach has proved a flexible, useful tool—regardless of a country's economic system, type of government, or stage of development.

Origins of the Project Concept

The notion that investment can and should be planned and executed in the form of specific projects is itself relatively new. Although the use of the term project, in the general sense of a plan, design, or scheme for doing something, can be traced back for several centuries,[2] it is only in the postwar period, beginning in the 1950s, that development practitioners and academics have focused on projects as the units into which investments could be packaged.

It is fair to say that the World Bank has played a key role in developing and applying the project concept. The Articles of Agreement adopted at the Bretton Woods conference in 1944, on which the work of the Bank rests, stipulate that "loans made or guaranteed by the Bank shall, except in special circumstances, be for the purpose of specific projects of reconstruction or development." No doubt specific projects were regarded as a way of ensuring that capital was invested only for "productive" purposes, in accordance with the primary objective of the Bank as set forth in the first Article. This was a reaction to the experience of

---

2. In 1711, Addison wrote that "new projects were every day set on foot for money, which served only to offend and incense the people." (Addison, Spectator no. 5 [1711], p. 13, cited in the *Compact Edition of the Oxford English Dictionary* [1981 ed.], vol. 2, p. 2320.)

international lending in the 1920s and 1930s, when the proceeds of international loans had often been used improperly, wastefully, and without adequate supervision; the resulting defaults had generated ill will and a sense of frustration in the entire international community. A different kind of lending was necessary to restore investors' confidence.[3]

The United Kingdom delegation to the Bretton Woods conference first introduced the language that loans should generally be made for "specific projects," and the phrase survived the successive rounds of drafting that eventuated in the Articles. No attempt was made at an explicit definition of a project, but a reference was added to "special circumstances" under which other types of loans could be made. This compromise language, according to a principal member of the United States delegation, was intended to give the Bank "wider discretion."[4]

With latitude for differing interpretations built into the Articles, it is not surprising that this matter preoccupied the Bank's Executive Directors and management at the outset. An early review by Bank legal staff of the use of the term "project" in various places in the Articles concluded that it was ambiguous. The Executive Directors debated whether the Bank's first three loans, made for general reconstruction purposes to France, the Netherlands, and Denmark in the late 1940s, constituted specific projects or had to be justified under special circumstances. (In the end, it was concluded that they were not specific projects.) During occasional discussions of the clause on specific projects over the years, however, the Executive Directors and management have been concerned more with identifying the conditions that could constitute a special circumstance than with defining a specific project. As is sometimes the case, the exceptions received more attention than the rule. Nevertheless, it was apparent from the beginning that the Bank intended to interpret the concept of a project broadly to mean the use of resources for a specific productive purpose. This continues to be the prevailing view.

What a Project Is

This pragmatic and flexible approach to project lending has served the Bank in good stead. In the course of time, the concept of a project has evolved and the range of activities embraced within it has expanded and become more diversified. A project can be a multibillion dollar investment in a large and capital-intensive hydroelectric dam and power plant; or one or more years of the investment program of a national railway or telecommunications enterprise; or the strengthening of a country's agricultural research or extension service; or the development of curricula and textbooks and the training of teachers for primary education; or the provision of equipment and facilities to reorganize and improve the maintenance of a highway system; or the building of health clinics, the training of paramedics, and the provision of information and education programs to promote family planning.

3. See the address by John J. McCloy, President, to the Board of Governors of the World Bank, 1948.

4. See the testimony of Harry D. White before the House Committee on Banking and Currency, *Hearings on H.R. 2211*, 79th Congress, 1st Session (1945), p. 78.

The project concept essentially provides a disciplined and systematic approach to analyzing and managing a set of investment activities. However diverse the specific activities they embrace, projects are likely to include several or all of the following elements, although in varying proportions and with different emphases:

- Capital investment in civil works, equipment, or both (the so-called bricks and mortar of the project)
- Provision of services for design and engineering, supervision of construction, and improvement of operations and maintenance
- Strengthening of local institutions concerned with implementing and operating the project, including the training of local managers and staff
- Improvements in policies—such as those on pricing, subsidies, and cost recovery—that affect project performance and the relationship of the project both to the sector in which it falls and to broader national development objectives
- A plan for implementing the above activities to achieve the project's objectives within a given time.

These common elements suggest a way to define a project that captures its essential features. In this book, a project is taken to be a discrete package of investments, policy measures, and institutional and other actions designed to achieve a specific development objective (or set of objectives) within a designated period.

Building the Project Tradition

After the Bank had granted its first three loans for general reconstruction in the late 1940s, it was displaced in this role by the advent of the Marshall Plan. The Bank made its first loans for specific projects in 1948: two concurrent loans to Chile, one of $13.5 million for electric power and one of $2.5 million for agricultural credit to buy farm machinery. A few years later, project lending for development purposes began in earnest. Since then, with the growing volume of Bank loans and with the addition in 1961 of the International Development Association (IDA) as an affiliate to provide credits on softer terms, lending for projects has reached impressive proportions. Through the end of the 1984 fiscal year, the Bank has made 2,429 loans and IDA has granted 1,515 credits. These operations, close to 4,000 in number, have together provided $135 billion in development funds. Since the Bank and IDA finance on the average only about a third of the cost of a project, the total investment under these projects is roughly $400 billion. Although the boundary line between project and nonproject lending is not always easy to draw in practice, the overwhelming proportion of the loans and credits—in excess of 90 percent—have been for projects, broadly defined. The World Bank has become the largest lender for development projects on the international scene.[5]

---

5. Unless the context indicates otherwise, references to the World Bank or to the Bank should be taken to include the International Development Association.

Over the years, as the Bank has continually refined its approach to project lending, a strong project tradition has been established. From the outset, the Bank recognized the need to build up its own qualified technical staff so that the projects it financed would be sound and thereby retain the confidence of the banking community. First to be recruited were engineers and financial analysts; the need for project economists was not identified until a later date. Today, the Bank's project staff is unique in its size and diversity of nationality, background, and experience. At the end of the 1984 fiscal year, it comprised 1,275 people from about a hundred countries, representing more than eighty specialized disciplines and ranging from agronomists, anthropologists, and architects to urban planners, veterinarians, and water engineers. The project staff accounts for two-thirds of the professional staff engaged in operational work.

As befits its role as a development agency, the Bank has been a "hands on" lender; that is, it has been closely involved at all stages of what it calls the project cycle, from assisting borrowers in the initial selection of projects through to completion and the evaluation of results. In the process, project lending has been forged into a potent instrument for promoting economic growth. Some other lending agencies, both multilateral and bilateral, have followed the Bank's policies and procedures in their own project work or have used Bank-appraised projects for their lending. There are those, the present authors among them, who believe that the project approach—combining sound investments with project-related policy and institutional reforms—has been the Bank's most important single contribution to the development process around the world.

There are others who would question this assessment, their argument running essentially as follows. External lenders (including the World Bank) tend to select the best or highest-priority projects in a borrowing country's investment program. But these are the projects that the country itself would be most likely to finance even in the absence of foreign aid. Since financial resources are fungible, what the lending agencies are really financing through the additional resources they make available are the marginal or lowest-priority projects in a country's investment program.

Several points can be made in response. First, the projects that the Bank helps to finance are invariably changed as a result of the Bank's close involvement in their preparation, appraisal, and implementation. Some of the Bank's most experienced borrowers regard the technical assistance provided by the Bank through the advice and counsel that it gives in the course of project work to be as important as the transfer of resources. This "value added" by the Bank varies from project to project, but it is usually substantial. Indeed, the Bank avoids projects to which it cannot make such a contribution, since it sees this as the heart of its development role. Second, some large projects could not be undertaken at all without financial and technical assistance from abroad. Third, as we have already emphasized, the Bank's project approach does not focus solely on individual projects but generally extends to a review of the national investment program as a whole—in part to eliminate projects of low return—and to assistance in setting investment priorities at the sector level.

Finally, from the point of view of officials in developing countries who, as we explain below, are the principal audience of this book, the argument has no relevance. They must be concerned with the proper analysis of all the projects that make up their country's investment program, not just with those financed by external agencies.

Responding to the Economic Crisis

The worldwide economic crisis of the late 1970s and early 1980s has led the Bank to introduce even greater flexibility and variety into its lending operations. Structural adjustment loans—clearly of a nonproject nature—were made through the end of fiscal year 1984 to sixteen countries to assist them in carrying out comprehensive but concrete programs of policy and institutional reform to adapt their economies to new and difficult conditions. Several countries received two or more structural adjustment loans. The loans are disbursed quickly for urgently needed imports but in accordance with performance on the measures agreed to be necessary to achieve the structural objectives. Structural adjustment loans account for 10 percent of the Bank's current lending operations. In addition, a growing number of loans have been concerned primarily with achieving policy and institutional reform of individual sectors, or specific policy objectives such as improvements in fertilizer pricing or the accelerated liberalization of international trade; in part these are new types of lending, in part shifts of emphasis within existing types. They further blur the distinction between project and nonproject lending and make such a distinction even less relevant to Bank operations. The Bank does not view this as a sudden sea change in its role, but rather as a gradual, evolutionary process that preserves its traditional strengths as a lender for long-term development investment while affording it greater flexibility to respond to the evolving needs of its member countries.[6] It is expected that support for investment will continue to be the mainstay of Bank operations in future years.

The need for developing countries to adjust to the recent economic crisis has caused them to focus even greater attention on managing the national economy. Some countries have found it necessary to cut back on their investment programs. This makes it all the more important that their scarce investment resources be used wisely and that their project work, which must continue regardless of the form in which international assistance is provided, be done as effectively as possible so that it makes the maximum contribution to economic recovery and growth. Indeed, the fact that the great upsurge in commercial bank lending and suppliers' credits to developing countries—which helped provoke the debt crisis—was often not linked to sound and productive investments undoubtedly aggravated the severity of the adjustment process.

Nowhere is the need to give greater attention to sound investment planning more evident than in sub-Saharan Africa, which emerged in the

6. See the address by A. W. Clausen, President, to the Board of Governors of the World Bank and the International Finance Corporation, 1984.

early 1980s as the region of greatest concern to the development community because of its poverty, rapidly rising population, and declining living standards. The Bank's most recent study of the region stresses that "the better use of investment—both domestic and foreign—is the key issue." It notes:

> Experience demonstrates that too much investment has gone into projects that have failed to generate significant increases in output. Genuine mistakes and misfortunes cannot explain the excessive number of "white elephants." Too many projects have been selected either on the basis of political prestige or on the basis of inadequate regard for their likely economic and financial rate of return. Changing the structure of an economy still requires strict adherence to criteria for project selection and design in order to maximize the return on investment. External financial agencies have shared the responsibility for this inadequate discipline over the use of investment resources.[7]

LEARNING FROM EXPERIENCE

As part of its project activities, the Bank closely supervises the projects it finances while they are being implemented. Moreover, each completed project is subject to an evaluation by an independent department of the Bank—the Operations Evaluation Department. Supervision of ongoing projects accounts for a high proportion—about 40 percent—of the resources devoted to project work, and evaluation of completed projects for an additional 5 percent. Those projects classified as problem projects receive most attention in the course of project supervision.

Supervision and evaluation activities continually yield lessons about what does and does not work well in particular circumstances. These lessons, in turn, are built into the design, preparation, and implementation of subsequent projects. It is not realistic to expect that mistakes will not be made, and the Bank has made its share. But a premium is placed on learning from them, so as to reduce the likelihood that they will be repeated.

In the course of more than thirty-five years, the Bank has accumulated a vast experience in project lending. The lessons of this experience have been internalized, through the supervision and evaluation procedures to which we have referred, in a continual quest for better projects. The Bank has been much less systematic, however, in sharing this experience with the outside world. Annual reports of the Operations Evaluation Department are made public, and numerous research papers, sector policy papers, and other reports are published on different aspects of project work. But there remains a large gap between what the Bank has learned and what it has taken the time to communicate. This book is intended to help fill that gap.

---

7. World Bank, *Toward Sustained Development in Sub-Saharan Africa: A Joint Program of Action* (Washington, D.C., 1984), pp. 1, 24.

PURPOSE OF THE BOOK

This, then, is a book about the World Bank's experience in investment and project work. In a sense the book is inward-looking, being about the Bank's experience, written by two staff members with the collaboration of many others, and financed by the Bank. We have not attempted to study the experience of other lending agencies, which certainly contains valuable lessons, nor have we surveyed the large non-Bank literature that exists on various aspects of project work.

In another and very important sense, however, the book is outward-looking. It is not about the Bank as such—not about how the Bank goes about its project work, nor about its internal organization, policies, and procedures, nor about how to apply for a loan. Rather, it is about what the Bank has learned and, above all, about how these lessons of experience can be used by officials of developing countries in planning, designing, and executing their own projects. By the same token, we have been concerned not with the relatively small proportion of developing countries' investment resources coming from abroad, nor with the even smaller proportion accounted for by the World Bank, but with the total resources at their disposal. Our goal, simply put, has been to assist developing countries to manage their investment resources better.

The primary audience we have had in mind are the middle- and senior-level officials of government departments and agencies in developing countries: the directors, deputy directors, and senior staff of finance and planning ministries, and of operating ministries such as agriculture, education, transport, and so forth. While we trust that others in the development community will find the book of value, it is not written with their concerns primarily in mind.

This is not, however, either a textbook or a detailed manual on how to do project work. The discussion of cost-benefit analysis, for example, is not designed to instruct the neophyte on how to perform a discounted cash flow analysis or to calculate an internal rate of return; it is intended to inform officials who have to review and understand the work of others about the meaning and significance of cost-benefit analysis, its advantages and pitfalls, and how it should and should not be used. The emphasis is on how to use project analysis, not on how to do it.

We had originally intended to make extensive use of case studies of specific projects, but this has not proved feasible. Since presenting case studies in sufficient detail requires considerable space, we have had to sacrifice most of them in order to treat more adequately the broader issues within a book of manageable size. For the same reason, we have been unable to treat as fully as we would have liked the wide diversity of country circumstances. Nevertheless, the general discussions and the illustrative examples are firmly rooted in the rich experience of several thousand Bank-assisted projects in developing countries throughout the world.

Authors inevitably bring some ideological baggage to a work like this. In the pragmatic spirit that is the tradition of the World Bank, we have tried to let the lessons speak for themselves. The values that we have stressed throughout, implicitly or explicitly, are essentially two: *efficiency* in the use of scarce resources, so that they can be stretched as far as possible; and *equity* in the treatment of people, with particular concern for improving the distribution of income to the poorest members of society. We believe that these are values that most governments share, whatever their political orientation.

The reader will no doubt detect a bias in favor of letting the marketplace do its job whenever possible. This is undoubtedly true, but it is a preference arrived at through experience rather than ideological preconception. The market has many imperfections, but the "invisible hand" that Adam Smith observed in operation through the competing forces of the marketplace will often produce the desired results more effectively than public administrators, however well intentioned. Reasonably efficient and responsive government leadership is critical to successful development, and there are many services that the government alone can provide. But the legitimate demands on the public sector are very large, while the capacity for public management is among the scarcest of development resources. This capacity should, therefore, be devoted to those activities where it is most needed and most likely to be efficacious.

How to Read the Book

This book is divided into five parts, which trace a logical sequence. Part I, on managing national investment, discusses development planning, establishing the macroeconomic policy framework—and especially the pricing policy—that conditions the environment in which both public and private investment take place, preparing a public investment program, and integrating it with the budget. Part II, on sector analysis, covers eight principal sectors of the economy: agriculture; education; energy; industry; population, health, and nutrition; transport; urbanization; and water and sanitation. It seeks to provide background knowledge on the main policy, institutional, and investment issues in each sector, knowledge that is essential to the conduct of project work. Sector and project analyses interact in two principal ways: priorities among individual projects can be established only in the context of the objectives, needs, and priorities of the sector as a whole; and the institutions, policies, and people in the sector have a major impact on how projects are designed and how they are carried out.

Parts III and IV focus on the design and implementation of projects. Part III covers the various stages of the project cycle, from identification of potential projects through to evaluation of completed projects. The principal dimensions of project analysis, which apply in varying degrees at different stages of the project cycle, receive separate treatment in part IV; these include technical, economic, financial, social, institutional, and environmental analysis. Two specialized subjects are also treated: procurement and the use of consultants. Finally, part V summarizes the highlights of the Bank's experience.

No way of organizing a book of this kind is ideal, and the way we have selected is not without its problems. On the one hand, the reader might find it advantageous to be more conversant with the project cycle and the several dimensions of project analysis before reading about the various sectors in part II. On the other hand, the sector discussions provide background for and contribute to a better understanding of the project issues dealt with in parts III and IV. In the end, we have had to choose, and the organization we have adopted incorporates, in itself, an important lesson of experience: that project work must be approached as a continuum, extending from the formulation of a public investment program and the macroeconomic policy framework, through the analysis of policies, issues, and investment priorities of particular sectors, to detailed work on individual projects. These three levels interact through what is, in practice, a continuing process of iteration, the plans and analyses developed at one level feeding into and affecting those at each of the other levels.

We do not expect that even the most diligent reader will peruse this volume from cover to cover. Our recommendation is that part I be read as a whole, since national investment management is an essential prelude to the sector and project discussions. As for part II, except for the introductory chapter on sector analysis, each chapter is likely to be of primary interest to those concerned with the particular sector in question; reading all of them in sequence could cause the reader to lose the continuity of the discussion. The reader would do well, therefore, to focus on chapter 5 and the sector chapter or chapters of immediate interest and then proceed to part III. Similarly, although all of the chapters on the project cycle in part III may be of general interest, some of the more specialized topics covered in part IV may not. Since many readers will not read the book in its entirety, except perhaps over an extended period of time, we have tried to make most of the chapters self-contained, at the expense of some repetition.

This book is a record of both successes and failures. Doing project work well is not an easy task even under the most favorable circumstances, and these seldom exist. But properly designed and executed investment projects can make an indispensable contribution to economic growth. If developing countries learn and apply the lessons of the Bank's experience, their economic growth can be more rapid and the benefits of that growth shared more equitably among their people.

PART I
National Investment Management

Farmer bringing hay to market near Beijing, China

2

Development Planning

IN THE PAST three decades, governments in most developing countries have taken an activist role in development—setting macroeconomic policies, investing to build infrastructure and expand basic services, fostering and sometimes engaging directly in productive activities. Some form of national planning to guide the use of the country's investment resources has been considered an essential part of the development effort. Developing countries have gone about this task in quite different ways, however, and many of them have changed their approach over time. This chapter reviews briefly some aspects of the postwar experience with development planning in order to identify emerging trends and lessons.

We look first at the enthusiasm of developing countries for comprehensive economic planning in the 1950s and also at some of its inherent problems. We next examine the shift in many of these countries toward concentrating their efforts on devising a policy framework that provides incentives to elicit desired behavior from both private and public entities, and on planning an appropriate public sector investment program, rather than on trying to plan the inputs and outputs of the entire economy. Finally, we identify some approaches that have been found to make development planning more effective. The succeeding chapters in part I elaborate upon two main issues in this evolving approach. Chapter 3 deals with the central role of prices within the policy framework for national investment management, while chapter 4 focuses on designing a public investment program and integrating it with annual budgets.

During the past thirty years, more than 300 plans have been formulated in developing countries. They have varied widely in their intentions and achievements, from comprehensive plans with heavy emphasis on physical quantities and on centralized control, to indicative plans that do little more than forecast the future state of the economy as a means of guiding the investment choices of independent decisionmakers. Many socialist economies of Eastern Europe and Asia drew their inspiration for planning from the U.S.S.R., as did other countries in Asia as well as in northern Africa. These plans generally sought to be comprehensive and, particularly in India, *dirigiste* (that is, with large elements of direction and control). Plans in sub-Saharan Africa and the Caribbean, in contrast, were often inspired by colonial or former colonial governments and managed largely by expatriates; moreover, external aid agencies often played a prominent role. Except in a few of these countries, such as Botswana and Malawi, the plans lacked domestic political support and remained largely ceremonial. Similarly, plans in Latin American countries, which were slowest to embrace formal planning, were little heeded in practice.

In the East Asia region, Japan, Korea, Taiwan, and Singapore developed their own brand of planning, perhaps best characterized as comprehensive cooperative planning. As in South Asia, the approach was geared to managing national resources—thus the focus was on comprehensiveness. However, the traditions of these economies allowed the government to develop a unique partnership with the private sector, which cooperated in designing a long-term strategy as well as short-term action programs. These economies managed to be pragmatic about the role of prices, of

the private sector, and of foreign investment. Their plans were characterized neither by technical sophistication nor by strict adherence to targets,
but by consultation and flexibility. Other economies, among them Mexico, Thailand, and Hong Kong, put even less emphasis on central planning
and relied even more heavily on the functioning of the marketplace, and
on the price signals arising from it, to guide investment.

These plans have had many purposes, some stated and some unstated.
To the extent that the purpose was to attract foreign aid, many plans have
served well even when not fully implemented. In addition, plans have
often generated public support for national goals, fostered interministerial coordination of policies and programs, and emphasized an economic
rationale for investment—so that the process of planning itself has often
achieved important purposes, irrespective of any other results. Lack of
adherence to targets does not necessarily indicate failure, because changing circumstances might have made a departure from the original targets
desirable, or because the targets might have been unrealistic in the first
place. In fact, in many successful instances of development planning, as
in Japan, plans were neither detailed nor adhered to rigidly.

EXPERIENCE WITH COMPREHENSIVE PLANNING

Within this broad array of types of development plans and of purposes
to which they have been put, some notable trends can be discerned. By
the time the World Bank made its first loan outside Europe in 1948, it
found many developing countries committed to or already engaged in
some form of centralized economic planning. The surge of enthusiasm
for comprehensive planning probably reached its peak in the 1950s.
Among the factors contributing to this enthusiasm were the apparent
success of the Russian five-year plans, the wartime experience of national
planning in Europe and the United States, and the success of postwar
European recovery programs, which relied heavily on national planning
efforts orchestrated by governments. The case for planning was further
strengthened by the development of computers, along with modeling and
programming techniques, which appeared to make it feasible to exercise
detailed centralized economic direction. Additional impetus came from
international aid agencies, which believed that the effectiveness of their
assistance would be increased if it fitted into an overall development
program.

Probably the most important factor, however, was the structuralist
view of development that prevailed from the 1940s until the early 1960s.[1]
This view holds that developing countries are characterized by accumulated cultural, social, and institutional rigidities, which inhibit or prevent

1. See Hollis Chenery, "The Structuralist Approach to Development Policy," *American
Economic Review*, vol. 65, no. 2 (May 1975), pp. 310 ff. This term first came into use in
the 1950s with reference to structuralist explanations of inflation in Latin America—as
opposed to monetarist explanations and policies largely identified with the International
Monetary Fund (IMF)—but it has been broadened by Chenery to characterize the approach
described in the text. See also the discussion in I. M. D. Little, *Economic Development:
Theory, Policy, and International Relations* (New York: Basic Books, 1982), pp. 19–26.

change; that resources tend to be "stuck" (or, in economic terms, that the supply of most goods and services is inelastic); and that only determined government action to change the structures of production and trade, and to reallocate resources within the economy, can bring about modernization and development. Furthermore, this view stresses managing quantities rather than prices, since it is implicitly assumed that price signals are not adequate tools for allocating resources. Any distortions in prices that arise in the course of managing quantities are regarded as innocuous or else necessary for achieving social objectives.

The structuralist view represents a sharp divergence from the neoclassical view, which has been mainstream economics for more than a century. In the neoclassical view, quantities are in fact flexible and resources mobile, producers and consumers do respond to price signals, businessmen seek to maximize profits by shifting their production methods when input prices change—and, despite particular failures, markets do generally work if allowed to do so. Few economists accept that the underlying assumptions of the neoclassical view—namely, the prevalence of free competitive markets that allocate resources efficiently and establish prices reflecting true economic values—correspond fully to reality. Nevertheless, the neoclassical position is generally regarded as an indispensable starting point for the analysis of the workings of developed economies, and as an essential frame of reference for understanding the role of prices.

But in much of the developing world in the 1940s and 1950s, the neoclassical view seemed so remote from the realities of those economies that it appeared irrelevant even as a point of departure for analysis. The wide acceptance of the structuralist view was understandable. Most developing countries felt mired in a condition of underdevelopment, and government activism appeared to be the only available tool for achieving rapid economic and social progress. Government, it was felt, must not only employ various inducements and restrictions to control the private sector, but must also take decisive steps to remove structural disequilibria in the economy and bring about a massive reallocation of resources. It should invest, promote, often act as entrepreneur, and through its own actions spur and guide development. A logical corollary was that governments should develop comprehensive plans for coordinating the investment programs, policies, and projects needed to achieve rapid development.

During the 1950s and 1960s, detailed and comprehensive planning, based on the structuralist approach, was put to a severe test in a number of countries, and results generally failed to live up to expectations. Sometimes the targets were achieved, but more often implementation was poor and accomplishment limited. Overambitious planning often favored launching large public sector projects and guiding the private sector by administrative fiat, and these biases proved costly. Experience revealed some inherent limitations of highly detailed planning in a rapidly changing environment. Neither the analytical techniques nor the administrative apparatus proved able to cope with the complexity of economic change and keep comprehensive plans up-to-date and relevant. An obsession with efforts to improve comprehensive plans—which typically demand extensive data—diverted attention and resources from more pressing issues. Moreover, most countries simply did not have the administrative capacity or "reach" to implement comprehensive plans.

A SHIFT IN APPROACH

An alternative approach, closer to neoclassical thinking and making greater use of markets and prices while concentrating on programming of public rather than total investment, has encountered less formidable problems and allowed more efficient adjustment. Indeed, the history of planning efforts in the developing countries since World War II can be traced in terms of the competition between the two contrasting views of the development process—the structuralist and the neoclassical—with the former favoring a combination of positive commands and negative controls to guide and direct the economy and the latter relying more heavily on markets and the price mechanism. In the early postwar years, as we have seen, many developing countries adopted plans oriented toward the structuralist view; more recently, with wider recognition of the indispensable role of prices, more and more countries have been moving toward the neoclassical view. Neither alone is a fully satisfactory guide to development planning. The structuralist approach assumes greater availability of data, more wisdom as to what government measures are needed, and much greater administrative capacity to devise and implement those measures than exist in most developing countries. The neoclassical approach suffers from the weakness of its basic assumptions about the existence and the efficacy of free competitive markets in developing countries.

It is clear that, to maximize economic output, resources must be allocated by a mechanism that takes full account of their relative scarcity and costs. In theory, this can be accomplished, at one extreme, by centralized planning, which determines allocations administratively; or, at the other extreme, by an unregulated market system. But in practice, no planning organization is capable of calculating and managing relative scarcities for all goods and services, while no government can afford to place unqualified reliance on free markets. The best economic performance has come neither in countries with comprehensive central planning (such as India, Bangladesh, Turkey, Ethiopia, and Sri Lanka) nor in countries where both the planning effort and economic management were weak (such as Nigeria, Senegal, Argentina, Ghana, and Jamaica). Instead, it has come in countries (such as Korea, Malawi, Malaysia, Colombia, and Kenya) that chose to concentrate their efforts on devising a framework of price and other incentives to guide both public and private activity and on designing an appropriate public investment program. These countries do not necessarily do less planning, but rather planning of a different kind.

Prices and Markets

For price and incentive policies to serve their intended role, supporting measures are often called for to make markets work better. These may include, for example, improving the flow of information or reducing monopoly elements and restrictions on entry of new firms. Markets may perform imperfectly, however, not only because they lack adequate information or sufficient competition, but also because they do not take account of indirect costs and benefits (so-called externalities, such as pollution or demonstration and training effects). Nor can free markets handle certain public needs, such as national defense, or natural monopolies, where the overwhelming advantages from the economies of large-scale operations make competition infeasible. And, of course, markets do not act to correct inequalities in income and wealth, a major concern of many societies. Some form of market regulation may also be needed for reasons of public interest: for example, traffic control and safety, public health, or protection of the environment cannot be left exclusively to market forces. Thus, there will always be legitimate economic and noneconomic objectives that governments can pursue only by intervention. All countries must and do rely on a combination of government intervention and market forces. The challenge for every government, whatever its political orientation, is to intervene in ways that minimize the economic costs of achieving the desired goals.

To illustrate, there may be strong reasons of public interest for governments to act to limit fluctuations in the prices of basic commodities, especially foodstuffs. Most South Asian governments, for example, consider that allowing rice prices to fluctuate freely with world market forces could lessen producer incentives and jeopardize political stability. World trade in rice is small relative to production and consumption, and world rice prices can vary substantially from year to year. Accordingly, governments in these countries intervene in an attempt to insulate the domestic rice market from the world market—while still allowing some price fluctuations in response to seasonal trends so that, for example, price variations between harvests cover the cost of on-farm and commercial storage. Of crucial importance, however, is the nature of the intervention. If the government intervenes by buying for or selling from official stocks to smooth fluctuations, while using the market mechanism as a tool for setting actual prices, then the price system can continue to perform its essential functions. But if the government intervenes by fixing prices directly, trouble begins—especially if an attempt is made to set prices over the long term at a level above or below what the market would set.

Even seemingly simple economies are complex. It is exceedingly difficult to affect directly the economic choices of large numbers of widely dispersed decisionmakers. The advantage of price and other incentives is that they can stimulate action on a decentralized basis, in a cost-effective manner, and with minimal bureaucratic involvement. Even in the imperfect markets usually found in developing countries, greater reliance on prices would prove useful to governments desiring to improve the way resources are allocated. A market need not be purely competitive, as assumed in neoclassical economics, in order to justify more reliance on the prices it produces. When no overriding public reason dictates the contrary, the presumption ought generally to be in favor of accepting the prices arising from the free working of even an imperfect market, given the unlikelihood that a more economic price can be established by administrative fiat.

Many recent national plans do, in fact, give more attention to prices and markets. For example, Korea's fifth plan (1982–86) focuses on greater use of price incentives. Investment and output projections, and even export projections, are treated more as background scenarios to aid in decision-making than as targets. A number of centrally planned economies have also switched in varying degrees to greater reliance on prices and markets. Yugoslavia started the process in the 1950s, Hungary in the 1960s, and China in the late 1970s. In recent years, even the U.S.S.R. has been moving away from its earlier emphasis on balancing physical quantities and on allocating resources by administrative action. With some ups and downs, comprehensive planning continued in India until the 1970s, but recently there has been some movement toward allowing a greater role for the price mechanism in the allocation of resources, and India's sixth plan (1981–85) includes an extensive discussion of price policy.

Public Investment Programs

In focusing their planning efforts on an investment program for the public sector, rather than for the economy as a whole, countries have adopted approaches which vary in detail but have several common elements. The starting point is preparation of macroeconomic forecasts to provide a framework for making decisions, including those about feasible growth patterns for the economy and feasible annual levels of investment. This is followed by identification of public investment needs in individual sectors, along with an assessment of the consistency among the various sector programs. Countries are learning the value of avoiding overly complex and sophisticated forecasting exercises, not only when preparing macroeconomic forecasts but also when planning for individual sectors, since knowledge about the relationship between investment and output at the sector level is limited. They therefore reserve detailed forecasting and analytical efforts for key infrastructure sectors, such as transport and power, in which the market alone cannot provide the basis for investment decisions, and also for examining whether the proposed outputs of these sectors are consistent with the likely requirements of the productive sectors.

Experience has shown the advantages of combining programming of public investment with forecasting (not targeting) for the private sector. Such "indicative forecasting" has been used in a number of countries as an alternative to the detailed targeting attempted by some planning agencies. Even Korea, which has used detailed export targets so successfully, is now moving away from that approach toward reliance on indicative forecasting. These points and others relating to the preparation of national investment programs are taken up at greater length in chapter 4.

ELEMENTS OF EFFECTIVE PLANNING

In planning, accordingly, as in other aspects of development, many countries have gone through a process of learning by doing. To perform their investment planning and policy tasks most effectively, governments have found it advisable to adopt approaches that embody consultation, flexibility, selectivity, policy coordination, and information and monitoring.

Consultation

Whether for formulating the right incentives or for designing sound public investment programs, close consultation among the groups concerned is vital. Given all the complexities and uncertainties of the economy, analytical techniques are in themselves inadequate to arrive at optimal solutions; qualitative judgments are required. These judgments are more likely to be sound if planners emphasize consultation, not only among different parts of the government but also with representatives of other groups in the economy. Japan, Korea, and Brazil have for some time used the process of consultation in managing investment. Such a process has proved most effective when it seeks to inform and to build a consensus rather than to achieve unanimity. An interesting example is Yugoslavia's "self-management planning," which is intended to coordinate investment decisions by facilitating an exchange of information about basic assumptions, with a view to strengthening eventual contractual agreements among enterprises. The Yugoslav experience demonstrates that such consultations must be carefully managed if they are not to become as cumbersome and time-consuming as central planning.

If indicative forecasting for the private sector is to be effective, the government must make its plans, policies, and macroeconomic projections widely known. The public investment program cannot, of course, be sensibly drawn up without at least some broad assumptions about the direction of growth and location of new investments in the private sector. But at the same time, so that it can forecast demand and make its own decisions, the private sector must know what are the national priorities, the intended public sector investments, and the policies that will affect the returns to private investment. The government, consequently, needs to devote considerable effort to explaining the public investment program, and to consulting with private sector representatives both during and after the preparation of the program.

Flexibility

Experience during the economic turmoil following the oil crises of the 1970s has shown that the best-designed policies and programs can quickly become outdated with changing circumstances. Flexibility is therefore essential. The ability to make a quick policy response to a change in circumstances is something too few governments possess. Those that have developed the means to do so have fared much better in the face of the vicissitudes of the 1970s. Willingness to adjust plans and policies as circumstances change or new information becomes available has been more effective than a fixed blueprint. The experience of Chile in the late 1970s shows how rigid adherence to a set of policies in the face of changing circumstances can be counterproductive. Morocco, Ivory Coast, Mexico, Venezuela, and Turkey in the late 1970s or the early 1980s illustrate how a country's inability to modify its public investment program to reflect reduced resource availability can lead to a balance of payments crisis and disruption in the growth process.

Selectivity

Reconciling consultation with flexibility is not easy; consultation is time-consuming, whereas flexibility requires quick response. Given this dilemma, two approaches have been found useful. First, governments need to be selective in the goals and instruments they emphasize. Theoretically, everything depends on everything else, and a comprehensive approach is intellectually attractive; however, policymakers cannot solve all problems simultaneously, and selectivity is essential. In Japan, both the national plans and the programs of the Ministry of International Trade and Industry concentrated on selected themes. In Korea, export promotion became a focal point for the development effort. Planning was improved in Bangladesh when it was directed at key issues such as increasing food production. In Malaysia, improving the distribution of income and wealth between Malays and non-Malays has been the central concern for the past ten years. In mineral-based economies such as Botswana, planning has concentrated on trying to convert mineral wealth into human and physical capital while minimizing the adverse side effects on the rest of the economy. The practice of preparing papers on important policy or investment issues for cabinet consideration has proved useful in Kenya.

Policy Coordination

Second, in seeking to combine consultation with flexibility, one developing country after another has found it helpful to designate a central authority for coordinating policy efforts. In Korea, planning, budgeting, and policy functions have been integrated under a deputy prime minister, who is also the chairman of a policy committee consisting of various economic ministries. In Brazil and Japan, the finance and industry ministries have played an active part in coordinating policies. In Hungary, that role has been assumed by an economic policy committee. In both India and Pakistan, policy review capacity has recently been strengthened in the planning agencies and in the office of the prime minister and the president. While the specific arrangements depend upon the circumstances of each country, an authoritative coordinating agency is clearly desirable.

Information and Monitoring

Many countries have come to recognize that they need to know not only where they want to go but also where they have been and where they are. The preparation of a development plan is intellectually stimulating and has received much emphasis; less attention has been paid to the problems of gathering basic data and of monitoring progress toward the plan's objectives. A good information system will provide an accurate reading of the status of implementation and of the results being achieved. This is essential for making the adjustments in policies and programs that are always necessary in a fast-changing world. Better information, especially on the main performance indicators, often brings larger dividends than do sophisticated techniques of long-term forecasting.

Effective monitoring depends on the adequacy of basic data-gathering systems. Without reasonably systematic data, governments cannot adequately address important issues as they arise. When oil prices rose sharply in the 1970s, for example, few developing countries had the data they needed to reassess their energy requirements and to develop conservation programs. In many countries heavily dependent on agriculture, the lack of reliable, up-to-date agricultural statistics has seriously handicapped monitoring activities and the formulation of appropriate policies and development plans.

Since it is expensive to collect information, governments need to set priorities. This often requires adoption of a medium-term plan for statistical development. Greater use can be made of sample surveys, which are relatively cheap, impose less of a burden on the statistical office, and, if well designed, can produce reliable and up-to-date information. Recent advances in microcomputers, which are cheap, portable, and versatile, and the growing library of associated software have multiplied the potential for providing planners with current analyses of relevant data.

Three main points emerge from this brief survey of three decades of experience with planning and set the stage for the discussion in the next two chapters. First, comprehensive planning failed to live up to expectations in most developing countries; no clear association can be established between a high degree of planning effort and good growth performance. Countries that performed best were those that combined effective planning for the public sector with avoidance of price distortions for the economy as a whole. Second, the technical and administrative deficiencies of comprehensive planning are inherent in the process and are unlikely to be remedied by more strenuous efforts to strengthen the planning machinery. Third, planning in developing countries must be reoriented toward new goals.

- More attention should be devoted to improving the system of prices and incentives and the performance of markets.
- Instead of preparing a long-term blueprint for development, with detailed quantitative targets for public and private investments and outputs, effort should be focused on programming public investment.
- Governments need to be selective and address only the most important policy issues and public investment concerns.
- Emphasis should be placed on coordination and consultation—both within government and with the private sector.
- Governments must be able to respond quickly to changing events by modifying their policies and programs. This requires a much improved information and data base and some centralized responsibility for policy coordination.

Adult literacy class for farm women, Ethiopia

3

Pricing Policy

AS WAS DESCRIBED in chapter 2, attempts by developing countries to carry out detailed physical planning of an entire economy have encountered serious technical and administrative difficulties, with problematic results at best. Many of these countries, consequently, have come to recognize the advantage of concentrating their analytical and planning efforts on two essential tasks—devising a sound public investment program and establishing an appropriate macroeconomic policy framework. These tasks are the most feasible, given the limitations of manpower and of data; they are the most likely to be useful in accelerating growth; and they are, in any event, the unavoidable responsibility of government.

The macroeconomic framework is composed of a series of interlocking policies—including fiscal, monetary, foreign exchange, trade, and wage policies—that affect all aspects of economic behavior. They affect the rate and pattern of capital accumulation and resource utilization, the amount of foreign exchange earnings, the maintenance of balance of payments equilibrium, the need for foreign borrowing, the rate of domestic inflation, and, ultimately, the pace of economic activity and growth. A country's policy framework should be flexible enough to provide adequate incentives for long-term growth, to foster the social objectives that the country sets for itself, and to permit the economy to adjust to external and internal disturbances. In this chapter, we focus on one aspect of the macroeconomic framework—price policy—which has a profound influence on how economic agents function and on how economic benefits are allocated.

ROLE OF THE PRICE SYSTEM

The role of prices is central to any macroeconomic policy framework. Many of the policies mentioned above revolve around prices—wage rates, interest rates, exchange rates. Whether they are determined in free markets, or established by a central planning agency, or modified by government policies, prices have a powerful influence on any country's rate and pattern of development. As one observer has noted, "Perhaps the most useful knowledge that economics can convey to the development manager is an understanding of the means by which prices allocate resources and mobilize resources."[1] This chapter analyzes the recent experience of developing countries with key pricing policies in order to demonstrate their impact on national and sectoral output and efficiency. The record shows the high cost of departing from a sound price structure. Before examining this record, however, it is useful to look briefly at the functions of a price system and at how prices are or should be set.

The most basic questions of economic analysis and policy concern the allocation of scarce resources to alternative uses. This necessarily involves choice, and choice requires valuation. Prices provide a basis for this

1. Gerald M. Meier, ed., *Pricing Policy for Development Management* (Baltimore, Md.: Johns Hopkins University Press for the World Bank, 1983), p. 5.

valuation. A price system is thus essential for dealing with the universal problem of scarcity; accordingly, the need for a price system is not restricted to any particular type of economy. Prices are as crucial to the operation of a state-owned, centrally planned economy as to a private-property, market economy. In a centrally planned economy, prices may not be determined by the free play of the market forces of supply and demand, but they must then be established by an official authority if the economy is to function.

The price system performs several basic functions. First, it is a highly cost-effective information system, providing signals that harmonize a multitude of individual production and consumption decisions. Second, changes in supply and demand lead to changes in prices—and in profitability—so that resources are attracted to an expanding sector away from a stable or declining sector. Price changes thus induce efficiency in the allocation of resources among competing goals within an economy. Third, when a scarce commodity or factor rises in price, the increase performs a rationing function: only buyers who place the higher value on the commodity or factor exercise their demand, while other buyers withdraw. Fourth, the price system has a resource mobilization function. While a price increase rations a scarce commodity, it also stimulates an increase in supply. New producers with higher costs can enter the market, and existing producers can increase their investment and scale of output.

As to the appropriate level of prices, the basic principle, dictated by the need to make the most efficient use of the economy's resources, is that the price of any product should equal the marginal cost of producing the last unit sold.[2] A free competitive market would achieve the desired result of bringing prices into line with marginal costs, thereby allocating resources efficiently. In the real world, however, market conditions nearly always diverge from the competitive ideal. Even where there is a high degree of competition, the results produced by the market are efficient only for a given distribution of income. They may, therefore, not be consonant with other objectives, such as greater equity or social justice. Governments can intervene to improve the distribution of income by such means as imposing taxes or providing subsidies. The price system, if it is functioning properly, will then help to establish an allocation of resources which again is broadly efficient, but with a greater degree of social justice. In general, the best results will be obtained when producers face prices based on efficiency criteria, with indirect taxes and subsidies applied to consumer prices to achieve social objectives.

Where the market does not set prices, as is the case for most goods and services produced by the public sector—power, water, rail transport, and so on—governments must do so. If the only objective were economic efficiency, the rule for pricing would be clear: to duplicate to the extent

2. The concept of cost is crucial; marginal cost must measure the true opportunity cost (see chapter 20, Economic Analysis). A full discussion of marginal cost pricing and of the many practical issues that arise, both in market determination of prices and in government establishment of prices for public sector goods and services, is contained in Meier, *Pricing Policy*, chap. 4.

possible the results of a free competitive market, by setting price equal to marginal cost. But, as noted above, other objectives—such as concern for distributive justice—may call for departures from this rule. Moreover, when a revenue-earning enterprise (such as a power company) is involved, price policy must accommodate its financial objectives. The enterprise should generate enough revenue to cover all its costs—not only because it may be considered equitable in many cases that the beneficiaries of a good or service pay for it, but also because full cost recovery would ensure the viability of the enterprise, including its ability to generate cash and raise capital for system expansion. Recovery of costs from beneficiaries also provides the revenue to enable a government agency to extend the service to others, as in the case of irrigation water or low-cost housing.

Thus, public pricing policy must embody at least three dimensions— efficiency, equity, and revenue generation. The latter two will often justify departures from a rigorous marginal pricing rule. Public policy may, therefore, require some carefully designed intervention in the market to achieve the various objectives of development.

Such intervention is not easy; the fact is that it is not always possible to know what the "right" price is in a particular sector or activity. Calculating marginal costs is often difficult in practice—although a rough approximation may suffice for many purposes—while determining the most desirable tradeoff among efficiency, equity, and revenue considerations may entail difficult matters of judgment. But even when the "right" prices are known, they are often not adopted for political reasons. Economic planners have to recognize the political pressures operating on decisionmakers, and to understand that policies the economist perceives as irrational are often perfectly rational from a political point of view; such necessary wisdom brings greater realism to the process of devising policies and programs. However, political considerations are all too often used as an excuse for failure to analyze fully the costs of departing from sound pricing policies, to see to it that the costs are adequately examined at the proper level of authority, or to ascertain whether the efficiency benefits forgone are clearly compensated by the political benefits obtained. Even when these steps are taken, implementing the "right" decisions may be painful and call for political will of a high order. But, as we shall see below, the rewards can be substantial.

PRICE DISTORTIONS

Many developing countries in the past thirty years have experienced a persistent—in some cases massive—distortion of prices as the result of a multiplicity of government actions or policies, many of them ill-considered. The adverse effects are only now coming to be fully recognized. A recent World Bank review has shown that price distortions during the 1970s have been very costly in terms of growth, resource mobilization, and efficiency of investment, often without any offsetting benefits. These findings are discussed below for each of the major areas of price distortion.

Overvalued Exchange Rate

The exchange rate is the main variable affecting the relation between domestic and foreign prices. If allowed to reflect underlying economic factors, it can act as a powerful aid in allocating resources in line with a country's comparative advantage. Changing the real exchange rate can be a highly effective tool for balancing trade—by simultaneously promoting exports and discouraging imports—without burdening the administrative system and without distorting domestic incentives. Yet many of the Bank's member countries, even those with large balance of payments deficits, have maintained overvalued exchange rates for long periods. This has been particularly serious in sub-Saharan Africa, where the average real effective exchange rate appreciated by 44 percent between 1973 and 1981.[3] As a result, several African countries have found that producers of traditional export crops cannot be paid enough to cover their costs of production, even though these are crops in which the countries have a strong comparative advantage. Losses in production, in exports, and in foreign exchange earnings have followed, the last two aggravated when crops are smuggled to neighboring countries for export.

The marked reluctance of governments to devalue their currencies to appropriate levels, even when overvaluation is causing serious trade and payments problems, appears to have several causes. These include the difficulty of raising prices of imports demanded by politically powerful groups, concern for national prestige, a fear that devaluation will lead to capital flight and pressures for further devaluation, and knowledge that the benefits of a devaluation can easily be wiped out by a rise in domestic prices. When it becomes clear, however, that adjustment will be forced upon the economy in one way or another, then devaluation, properly supported by other policy measures, has usually been found to be the course of action that is the least costly because it least distorts domestic price incentives. Many governments are now keeping the exchange rate under more regular review as an important development policy variable. This is a step forward since, in the past, incorrectly valued exchange rates have often resulted less from active policy decisions than from a failure to adjust exchange rates when conditions altered.

It is increasingly recognized that an overvalued exchange rate harms not only the short-term balance of payments position but also long-term growth. Even in those countries that initiated programs of economic reform during the 1970s—such as Argentina, Chile, Sri Lanka, and Uruguay—the real exchange rate was subsequently allowed to appreciate, and this weakened the reform effort. If exporters and importers, producers and consumers are to make the desired responses to adjustments in the exchange rate, then the government's exchange rate policy must be publicly known and consistently followed.

Overpricing of Industrial Products

Tariffs and other measures designed to protect domestic industries have allowed the prices of certain industrial products to remain above

---

3. World Bank, *World Development Report 1983* (New York: Oxford University Press, 1983), p. 58.

world market levels. The price distortion is increased when the level of protection varies greatly among different manufacturing industries, as it frequently does.

In the 1950s and early 1960s, import substitution strategies were ubiquitous in developing countries. Several currents of thought, economic and political, contributed to this trend. Development was generally equated with industrialization, and free trade was regarded as a colonial legacy. For former colonies, reliance on export earnings appeared to carry the risk of substituting economic dependence for their earlier political dependence, whereas replacing imports by domestic production seemed to avoid economic dependence as well. Pessimism about the possibility of expanding exports, along with fluctuations in export earnings, further strengthened arguments for measures to reduce imports of manufactures. Another compelling reason in many countries was the desire to protect infant industries during the necessary growing-up period. Some of these reasons, especially the infant industry argument, have merit. Import substitution (as discussed in chapter 9, Industry) is the logical first step in industrialization.

Although import controls can indeed protect infant industries, they are rarely geared to promoting an industry's long-run growth potential and are often not reduced after the industry has reached adolescence or even maturity. The loss of efficiency resulting from the price distortions such policies introduce can be considerable: in extreme cases—steel in Bangladesh, tin cans in Kenya, and cars in Thailand—the foreign exchange cost of importing raw materials and capital significantly exceeds the foreign exchange cost of importing the finished products.

Import restrictions have generally led to high-cost domestic industry that penalizes consumers. Those lucky enough to obtain an import license have reaped windfall gains from the scarcities that were created. One estimate for Turkey in 1968 suggests that the windfall gains associated with import restrictions alone amounted to about 15 percent of GNP.[4] Quantitative import restrictions have been especially discriminatory and have presented strong temptations for corruption. Efforts to prevent corruption, in turn, have led to mechanical methods of allocating import licenses on the basis of "past shares"; this has tended to shelter existing firms (some of which are inefficient), to hamper entry of new firms into the market, and to reduce the speed of adjustment in the economy. Since an import substitution strategy does not involve budgetary costs for the treasury (in fact, it generally produces budgetary revenues), and since the national welfare costs noted above are diffuse, distortions have often been carried to extremes without being detected. An export-oriented strategy, in contrast, because it pushes industry to compete in world markets, reduces the use of restrictions and the price distortions that accompany them, and forces governments to recognize and rectify policy mistakes that would be hidden by an import substitution strategy.

Underpricing of Agricultural Products

While industry has been protected, agriculture has often been penalized—through instruments such as taxes on output and on exports,

4. *World Development Report 1983*, p. 52.

compulsory sale of agricultural products by farmers to government procurement agencies at low prices, and subsidized sale of these products to consumers through government channels for marketing and distribution. The strategy of underpricing agricultural output is based on three assumptions: first, that higher prices of food would have adverse effects on low-income urban consumers (who have substantial political power); second, that agricultural production is not very responsive to price changes; and third, that rapid growth requires rapid industrialization, which in turn requires a transfer of income from agriculture to industry.

This reasoning ignores the adverse effects of low agricultural prices on the much larger number of rural poor, as well as the accumulating evidence that farmers do in fact respond to price changes as long as they feel some degree of assurance that a new set of prices will prevail for a reasonable period. As for industrialization, it is true that in the early stages of development, when agriculture dominates the economy, some resources for industrial development must inevitably come from agriculture. But paying artificially low prices to agricultural producers and taxing agricultural exports—frequently in conjunction with maintaining an overvalued exchange rate and heavy protection for manufactured goods—turn the domestic terms of trade (that is, relative prices) against agriculture and discourage agricultural production. Land taxation and the mobilization of rural savings through financial institutions are economically more desirable means of transferring resources from agriculture to industry. These played a significant role in Japan's early development; more recently, Taiwan, Korea, and the Indian state of Punjab, among others, have successfully used financial institutions to channel rural savings to other sectors.

Underpricing of agricultural products was a common phenomenon in developing countries in the 1950s. In many cases, compensation was attempted through countervailing underpricing (that is, subsidizing) of agricultural credit and of inputs such as fertilizers. These subsidies were generally inadequate, however, to compensate for the discrimination in the product market. In addition, they forced governments to resort to rationing and led to multiple distortions, inequities, and inefficiencies—demonstrating the general difficulty of trying to offset one set of distortions by another.

By the 1960s, it was beginning to be recognized that underpricing of agriculture slowed agricultural growth and that this slowdown, in turn, adversely affected overall growth and equity. On the project level, it was found that inadequate prices for agricultural inputs and products led to poor utilization of agricultural investments in irrigation, extension services, and input distribution. Some countries, including India and Pakistan, switched to policies that reduced discrimination against agriculture. Nevertheless, many developing countries, particularly in sub-Saharan Africa, were still underpricing agricultural output in the 1970s.

A particularly arresting example is the experience in Ghana with the Cocoa Marketing Board. Set up in 1947 to market and export cocoa and to stimulate production by smallholders, the board was later assigned additional functions, including taxation of export earnings. The objective of raising revenue eventually prevailed over the others. The government's share of sales revenue increased from 3 percent in 1947–48 to 60 percent in 1978–79. As a result of this policy and the overvalued exchange rate, the price received by Ghana's cocoa farmers declined in real terms (that is, after adjusting for price inflation) beginning in the early 1960s: it reached half the 1953 level in 1979. As cocoa production in Ghana became less profitable, it fell dramatically. In 1979, less than half as much cocoa was produced as in 1965; the volume officially exported declined by 80 percent over the same period. Foreign exchange earnings were also lost because about one-sixth of the total output was smuggled to neighboring countries for export. By 1979, Ghana was no longer the leading world producer and exporter of cocoa. Many farmers had switched to other crops, whose real returns to the economy were only a fraction of those of cocoa.[5]

Underpricing of Capital

During most of the postwar period, governments in many developing countries have favored low and controlled interest rates along with credit rationing. Among the reasons have been a desire to stimulate industrial and agricultural investment (which, it was believed, would not be adequate to accelerate growth unless interest rates were kept low); a desire to keep down the costs of servicing public sector debt; the suspicion that free markets charged usurious rates that were harmful for smaller borrowers; the concern that higher interest rates were inflationary through their effects on costs; and the "second best" argument that low interest rates would offset other distortions in the economy, such as low prices for agricultural products. In centrally planned economies, in particular, interest rates have not been regarded as an instrument for the allocation of resources.

The attempt to target particular beneficiaries of subsidized interest rates—whether farmers or small investors—has almost universally backfired. The artificially low rates have encouraged excess demand, and in the ensuing rationing process the cleverer or stronger or more influential—that is, the richer—have obtained the available funds. There have also been leakages of subsidized funds to unintended uses, depending in part on the ingenuity of operators in the credit market. Moreover, because of the high risks involved in lending to small borrowers, nonsubsidized sources of funds have tended to dry up, unable to compete with the low interest rates from official sources. As a result, there has often been less rather than more lending to the target groups.

The policy of low (and relatively stable) nominal interest rates became increasingly untenable as inflation accelerated, particularly in the 1970s. In many countries, interest rates were significantly lower than inflation rates, not just temporarily but for a decade or more. Low or even negative interest rates in real terms penalize savers and discourage savings. They prompt the public to hold a larger proportion of their savings in real estate and other physical assets such as gems and precious metals and, where possible, in foreign currency deposits. As a result, both financial savings and foreign exchange for domestic investment are reduced, and credit rationing—with its attendant administrative problems—is encouraged.

5. *World Development Report 1983*, p. 77.

In addition to the effects on savers, the impact on investment decisions generally, and on the design and implementation of development
projects, has also been adverse. Low or negative real interest rates, by
lowering the cost of capital, have permitted investment to take place
when marginal rates of return were low or even negative. This has often
led to unduly large inventories and high capital intensity, along with
excess capacity and slow project implementation; all these, in turn, have
lowered the average efficiency of investment. Efficiency of investment has
also suffered because negative real interest rates have severely hampered
the development of the financial sector, especially the financial intermediaries, such as commercial and development banks, needed to help
allocate savings according to productivity. Furthermore, to the extent that
real income has been transferred from low-income savers to high-income
investors, low real interest rates have also been inequitable.

During the 1970s, financial savers in some countries lost an average of
at least 10 percent a year in real terms (some of these savers, of course,
were also borrowing from the banking system at similarly low real rates).
In some countries, particularly in Latin America, real interest rates were
–20 percent a year or even lower. Initially, the highly negative rates were
seldom the result of a deliberate policy decision, but were rather the
consequence of high inflation rates unmatched by corresponding rises in
interest rates. To raise interest rates to a positive real level in such
circumstances required political will of a high order. Such a decision
proved so difficult that very few countries with rapid inflation managed
to have even slightly positive real interest rates during the 1970s.

In some countries with relatively high inflation and uncertain expectations, however—for example, those in the Southern Cone of Latin
America—the freeing of short-term interest rates has consistently led to
very high real rates. Such high rates create their own distortions, unduly
discourage investment, and weaken the financial position of many businesses. In general, the governments that have fared best are those that
have achieved a stable, moderate real rate for savers and a stable and
somewhat higher real rate for borrowers.

Overpricing of Labor

While the cost of capital has been distorted primarily because of
inflexible interest rate policies, the cost of labor has been distorted
primarily because of well-intentioned efforts to raise wages. Many developing-country governments in the 1950s believed strongly in encouraging
trade union activities and promoting minimum wage legislation to provide an "adequate" income for workers. The official minimum wage was
often fixed at a level well above the marginal productivity of labor. That
organized labor formed only a small part of the total labor force, and that
underdevelopment unfortunately did not permit "adequate" income for
all laborers, were facts largely unheeded by urban-oriented governments.
Concern with the adverse effects of high wages was further muted by the
structuralist view that the relative demand for labor and capital was not
sensitive to their respective costs.

In the 1960s, as a result of government measures, real wages in the
modern or organized sector increased far more rapidly than productivity

in many developing countries. In addition, high wages in protected industrial sectors as well as in privileged mining or other foreign enclaves pushed up wages elsewhere. In many mineral-based economies, especially in Africa and Latin America, the drive for higher mining wages not only spread to other sectors, but also raised mining labor costs far above those in competitor countries. Econometric studies, engineering data, and specific industry studies (for example, in Korea) as well as anecdotal evidence have shown that capital-labor ratios are in fact—contrary to the structuralist view—responsive to the relative costs of labor and capital.[6] Capital-intensive investment has been encouraged where the price of labor has been increased by unrealistic minimum wage laws and social security taxes. In addition, people in rural areas have been encouraged to leave the land in pursuit of the high wages paid to those lucky enough to find jobs in the modern urban sector. Distortions in labor markets have tended, therefore, to reduce international competitiveness and to hurt both economic growth and its labor intensity; by impeding the growth of employment they have contributed, in particular, to urban unemployment.

Underpricing of Infrastructural Services

The pricing of infrastructural services such as power and transport has presented difficult problems in the developing countries. Since an increasing scale of operations brings greater returns, these services tend to be natural monopolies. This means that prices for such services, rather than being determined by the market, are almost invariably fixed or controlled by a public authority. The generally accepted criterion of economic efficiency, as we have noted earlier, is that price be set equal to the marginal cost of production unless equity or revenue considerations rule otherwise. In most developing countries, however, the concern for greater distributive justice has often prevailed over strict efficiency objectives or revenue considerations. Electricity, water, public transport, and other infrastructural services have been underpriced in order to provide benefits to various groups. In many cases, prices have not covered the average costs of production, and the agencies supplying these services have consequently been unable to meet operating costs and to undertake adequate investment without extensive subsidies, which constitute a heavy drain on the public budget and are themselves a disincentive to efficient operation. The usual result, as with underpricing of capital, has been excess demand and rationing, with its attendant problems. Ample evidence on these points is presented in the sector chapters of part II.

The rapid increases in international prices of energy and capital in the 1970s should have led to corresponding increases in the costs of infrastructural services, which generally require large inputs of both energy and capital. With the exception of some oil-exporting countries and some energy products, most developing countries have adjusted domestic energy prices to international levels. Infrastructure prices have been raised too slowly, however, to judge by the low rate of return on capital achieved by power utilities. A review of sixty countries conducted by the

6. See, for example, I. M. D. Little, *Economic Development: Theory, Policy, and International Relations* (New York: Basic Books, 1982), pp. 176–81.

World Bank in 1980 showed that about half of the power companies had low (less than 4 percent) rates of return, while several incurred losses. In transport and water supply, rates of return are not available for any sizable sample, but the indications are that many countries fail to recover the full costs of these services. Such underpricing not only undermines the financial viability of the agencies, but also increases demand for their services—and thus for the resources employed in them—beyond what is economically justified.

High and Accelerating Inflation

The 1970s was a decade of rising inflation the world over, with most developing countries experiencing double-digit rates. Nearly all the countries that had high—15 percent a year or more—inflation in the 1960s continued in that category in the 1970s, and many others joined their ranks. In several countries (such as Argentina, Bolivia, Chile, Ghana, Mexico, Nigeria, and Turkey), the rate of inflation in the 1970s was several times that in the 1960s.

Overall price inflation, particularly when high and even more so when accelerating, strongly affects the efficiency of resource allocation. First, it creates uncertainty about future prices—both absolute and relative—and this uncertainty hurts investment. Second, as with low or negative interest rates, it increases the attractiveness of investing in nonproductive assets (real estate, precious metals, and other hedges against inflation) in search of windfall gains, and so diverts resources from productive activities. For those without access to such assets or whose assets yield negative returns in real terms, inflation gives an incentive for greater consumption.

Even though in principle it is possible to index wages, interest rates, exchange rates, and other important prices, in practice it has proved difficult to implement a system of comprehensive indexation. Moreover, such a system has often spurred inflation, and those not covered by indexation—mostly the poor—have experienced substantial social and economic injustice.

Price Distortions, Growth, and Equity

Price distortions invariably result in a loss of efficiency. Studies of Brazil, Chile, Pakistan, the Philippines, and Turkey in the 1960s estimate that the costs of distorted prices caused by trade restrictions alone may have amounted to 4 to 10 percent of GNP.[7] Countries such as Brazil, Colombia, and Korea that embarked on programs to correct prices in the 1960s also showed significant gains in output and employment as a result of their liberalization efforts. Those countries that avoided price-distorting trade policies were typically more successful in adjusting to external shocks in the 1970s than those with such policies.[8]

A more recent statistical analysis of the relationship between price distortion and growth in the 1970s for thirty-one developing countries

7. Bela Balassa, "Disequilibrium Analysis in Developing Economies: An Overview," *World Development*, vol. 10, no. 12 (1982), pp. 1027–38; also available as World Bank Reprint Series no. 241.

8. World Bank, *World Development Report 1981* (New York: Oxford University Press, 1981), chaps. 3 and 6.

Table 3-1. _Indices of Price Distortions and Various Components of Growth in the 1970s: Thirty-One Countries_
(percent)

Price distortion index	Average annual growth rate				Average savings-income ratio	Average return on investment	Average percentage of income going to poorest 40 percent
	GDP	Agriculture	Industry	Export volume			
Low	6.8	4.4	9.1	6.7	21.4	27.6	14.9
Medium	5.7	2.9	6.8	3.9	17.8	26.9	14.0
High	3.1	1.8	3.2	0.7	13.8	16.8	13.6

Note: See tables 3-2 and 3-3 for more details.
Source: Based on data in Ramgopal Agarwala, _Price Distortions and Growth in Developing Countries,_ World Bank Staff Working Paper no. 575 (Washington, D.C., 1983).

confirms these earlier findings.[9] Those countries with a _low_ price distortion index[10] had an average growth rate of 7 percent a year—2 percentage points higher than the average for the entire sample. Those countries with _high_ price distortion had an average growth of about 3 percent a year, 2 percentage points lower than the overall average (see table 3-1 above and table 3-3 and figure 3-1 at the end of this chapter). The relation between price distortion and the various components of growth is presented in table 3-2 at the end of this chapter: high distortion is associated with low domestic savings in relation to GDP and with low value added per unit of investment. Distortion also affects growth rates in agriculture and industry, with a marked influence on exports. In short, the statistical analysis clearly shows that prices do matter for growth.

Price distortions alone, however, explain less than half the variation in growth among countries; the rest is the result of other economic, social, political, and institutional factors. A country well endowed with natural resources (such as Nigeria) or with a fully mobilized labor force (such as China) could still grow relatively fast even if its price structure were distorted. With fewer price distortions, however, its growth could be significantly faster.

In many countries, price-distorting policies have been defended on the basis of their presumed beneficial impact on income distribution. For

9. _World Development Report 1983_, pp. 59–63.

10. The method used for deriving an index of price distortion is described in Ramgopal Agarwala, _Price Distortions and Growth in Developing Countries_, World Bank Staff Working Paper no. 575 (Washington, D.C., 1983) pp. 7–10, 33–38. See also _World Development Report 1983_, pp. 59–63. For individual goods and services, the degree of distortion is measured by the extent to which their prices fail to reflect correctly their scarcity, that is, their true opportunity cost (see chapter 20, Economic Analysis). Distortion is calculated for the prices of capital, labor, infrastructure services (particularly power), and foreign exchange. To arrive at a composite index of these price distortions, three different statistical approaches were used; since all three led to the same basic conclusion, the simplest—an unweighted average of the various distortions—was employed in the tables in this chapter.

example, it has often been argued that low interest rates, high wages, low infrastructure prices, and import restrictions were designed to help low-income groups. Recent studies, however, have found no evidence of a positive association between protectionist policies and equitable income distribution. In the case of Pakistan, for example, there is evidence that credit and exchange rate distortions in the 1960s may have actually increased inequality in income distribution.[11]

The data presented in table 3-1 confirm these findings. For twenty-seven countries for which figures on income distribution are available, regression analysis shows that the price distortion index explains barely 3 percent of the variation in equity (measured by the proportion of income going to the poorest 40 percent of the population). And even this low association goes in the opposite direction to that claimed to justify distortions. If anything, high distortion seems to be associated with less, not greater, equity.

DIFFICULTIES OF POLICY REFORM

Even when the importance of reforming price and other policies has been recognized, the process of adjustment has by no means been easy. In the 1970s, major changes were initiated in the Southern Cone countries of Latin America, starting in 1974 in Uruguay, in 1975–76 in Chile, and in 1976 in Argentina. About the same time, Sri Lanka also embarked on a program of adjustment. More recently, other developing countries, including the Ivory Coast, Jamaica, Kenya, Peru, the Philippines, and Turkey, have attempted varying degrees of adjustment. These programs have usually included a lower exchange rate, greater export incentives, less (and more uniform) industrial protection, tighter monetary policy with higher real interest rates, fewer controls over credit, higher energy prices, and smaller consumer subsidies. In addition, these programs usually have sought to restrain public sector spending and to increase the scope for the private sector and market forces. Similar reform programs were also introduced in some socialist economies, such as China and Hungary, in the 1970s and early 1980s.

These reforms have had an uneven course. Chile, faced with widespread distortions, made dramatic changes over a remarkably short period; this adjustment was followed by rapid growth in GNP and considerable success in controlling inflation. But distortions subsequently re-emerged in certain areas, followed by a rise in unemployment and a weakening in the financial position of many enterprises. In Sri Lanka, investment, employment, and GNP grew faster after 1977 when the adjustment program had taken effect, although the balance of payments and inflation worsened. Turkey's case is particularly interesting; it achieved rapid growth in exports and brought inflation down sharply, but managed only modest growth in private investment and employment. On the average, those countries where adjustment led to low price distortion managed a significantly better growth performance in 1979–82 than did those with persisting high distortion.

11. See Agarwala, *Price Distortions and Growth in Developing Countries,* and references cited there.

Many other countries are now showing interest in adjusting their price structures. For them, the question is not whether to adjust, but how. Experience suggests that the process of adjustment has to be managed carefully with regard to timing, pace, and scope. Countries have encountered difficulty, for example, in liberalizing trade and financial markets while simultaneously trying to moderate inflation through restrictive monetary and fiscal policies. The benefits of liberalization operate primarily through changes in relative prices, with resultant changes in the flows of new investment, and they are easier to bring about when economic growth is rapid. The pace of adjustment has also to be tailored to the circumstances of each country—its political resilience, the degree of distortion in its pricing system, and the resources (especially foreign exchange) it has available during adjustment. Korea's successful reforms in the early 1960s were bold and were greatly helped by a favorable external environment. Turkey's reforms in the late 1970s—less comprehensive and more gradual, though nonetheless radical—were initiated in much more difficult circumstances, yet were largely successful.

What the evidence presented in this chapter shows is that the countries that have enjoyed relatively high growth rates are those that have managed to follow most of these policies for most of the time:

- Avoid an overvalued exchange rate
- Keep the rate of effective protection for manufacturing industry low and uniform among products
- Avoid underpricing agricultural products
- Keep interest rates positive in real terms
- Avoid real wage increases not justified by rising productivity
- Apply cost recovery principles in pricing infrastructure services
- Avoid high and accelerating inflation.

The empirical evidence of the past two decades strongly suggests that few things are more critical for economic progress than the skillful management of this interconnected system of prices and incentives.

It is also clear from the experience of the Bank's member countries that, once major distortions have occurred, the transitional problems associated with price adjustment programs are considerable and that no single prescription for effective adjustment exists. The successes of Korea, Brazil, and Colombia in the 1960s, and of China and Turkey in the 1970s and early 1980s, indicate that both pragmatism and flexibility are needed to deal with complex and changing circumstances. What is equally clear is that, regardless of the economic system, interference with prices—of whatever nature, in whatever sector, and even when done for the laudable purpose of increasing benefits to the poor—is problematic. It calls for great care in analyzing the ramifications for the economy as a whole and in evaluating the tradeoffs in order to determine whether the benefits exceed the costs. The lessons of the experience with price distortions described in this chapter can be ignored by developing countries only at the risk of reducing their rates of growth.

Table 3-2. *Indices of Price Distortions and Various Components of Growth in the 1970s*

Country	Distortion index	Simple group average	Annual GDP growth rate (percent)	Simple group average	Domestic savings income ratio (percent)	Simple group average
Malawi	1.14		6.3		14	
Thailand	1.43		7.2		21	
Cameroon	1.57		5.6		18	
Korea, Rep. of	1.57		9.5		22	
Malaysia	1.57	1.56	7.8	6.8	20	21.4
Philippines	1.57		6.3		24	
Tunisia	1.57		7.5		27	
Kenya	1.71		6.5		19	
Yugoslavia	1.71		5.8		27	
Colombia	1.71		5.9		22	
Ethiopia	1.86		2.0		8	
Indonesia	1.86		7.6		22	
India	1.86		3.6		20	
Sri Lanka	1.86		4.1		13	
Brazil	1.86	1.95	8.4	5.7	22	17.8
Mexico	1.86		5.2		22	
Ivory Coast	2.14		6.7		24	
Egypt	2.14		7.4		12	
Turkey	2.14		5.9		17	
Senegal	2.29		2.5		8	
Pakistan	2.29		4.7		7	
Jamaica	2.29		−1.1		16	
Uruguay	2.29		3.5		14	
Bolivia	2.29		4.8		20	
Peru	2.29	2.44	3.0	3.1	21	13.8
Argentina	2.43		2.2		22	
Chile	2.43		2.4		14	
Tanzania	2.57		4.9		12	
Bangladesh	2.57		3.9		2	
Nigeria	2.71		6.5		21	
Ghana	2.86		−0.1		9	
Overall average	2.01		5.0		17.4	

a. Increase in real GDP valued at current prices divided by investment at current prices. This is the reciprocal of the incremental-capital-output ratio, adjusted for different rates of inflation in investment goods and GDP. It is thus equivalent to income rate of return on revalued capital.

b. GDP growth rates were negative.

Source: World Bank, *World Development Report 1983* (New York: Oxford University Press, 1983), p. 60.

Additional output per unit of investment[a] (percent)	Simple group average	Annual growth rate of agriculture (percent)	Simple group average	Annual growth rate of industry (percent)	Simple group average	Annual growth rate of export volume (percent)	Simple group average
25.3		4.1		7.0		5.7	
27.6		4.7		10.0		11.8	
26.3		3.8		8.6		2.5	
31.1		3.2		15.4		23.0	
32.6	27.6	5.1	4.4	9.7	9.1	7.4	6.7
23.1		4.9		8.7		7.0	
31.4		4.9		9.0		4.8	
32.7		5.4		10.2		−1.0	
18.4		2.8		7.1		3.9	
27.4		4.9		4.9		1.9	
30.7		0.7		1.4		−1.7	
40.1		3.8		11.1		8.7	
15.6		1.9		4.5		3.7	
22.2		2.8		4.0		−2.4	
35.5	26.9	4.9	2.9	9.3	6.8	7.5	3.9
23.4		2.3		6.6		13.4	
25.5		3.4		10.5		4.6	
24.2		2.7		6.8		−0.7	
24.5		3.4		6.6		1.7	
12.8		3.7		3.7		1.2	
28.1		2.3		5.2		1.2	
—[b]		0.7		−3.5		−6.8	
20.9		0.2		5.2		4.8	
22.7		3.1		4.3		−1.6	
21.5	16.8	0.0	1.8	3.7	3.2	3.9	0.7
10.7		2.6		1.8		9.3	
15.1		2.3		0.2		10.9	
23.9		4.9		1.9		−7.3	
22.3		2.2		9.5		−1.9	
23.8		0.8		8.1		2.6	
—[b]		−1.2		−1.2		−8.4	
23.2		3.0		6.1		3.5	

Table 3-3. *Cross-Classification of Countries by Growth and Price Distortion*

Annual rate of growth of GDP in 1970s	Distortion index			
	Below 1.8	1.8–2.2	Above 2.2	Row average
6 percent and above	Korea (9.5) Malaysia (7.8) Tunisia (7.5) Thailand (7.2) Kenya (6.5) Malawi (6.3) Philippines (6.3)	Brazil (8.4) Indonesia (7.6) Egypt (7.4) Ivory Coast (6.7)	Nigeria (6.5)	(1.77)
4 to 6 percent	Colombia (5.9) Yugoslavia (5.8) Cameroon (5.6)	Turkey (5.9) Mexico (5.2) Sri Lanka (4.1)	Tanzania (4.9) Bolivia (4.8) Pakistan (4.7)	(2.0)
4 percent and below		India (3.6) Ethiopia (2.0)	Bangladesh (3.9) Uruguay (3.5) Peru (3.0) Senegal (2.5) Chile (2.4) Argentina (2.2) Ghana (–0.1) Jamaica (–1.1)	(2.32)
Column average	(6.8)	(5.7)	(3.1)	(5.0)
Row average				(2.01)

Note: Figures in parentheses are annual GDP growth.

Source: Ramgopal Agarwala, *Price Distortions and Growth in Developing Countries,* World Bank Staff Working Paper no. 575 (Washington, D.C., 1983), p. 42.

Figure 3-1. *Price Distortions and Growth in the 1970s*

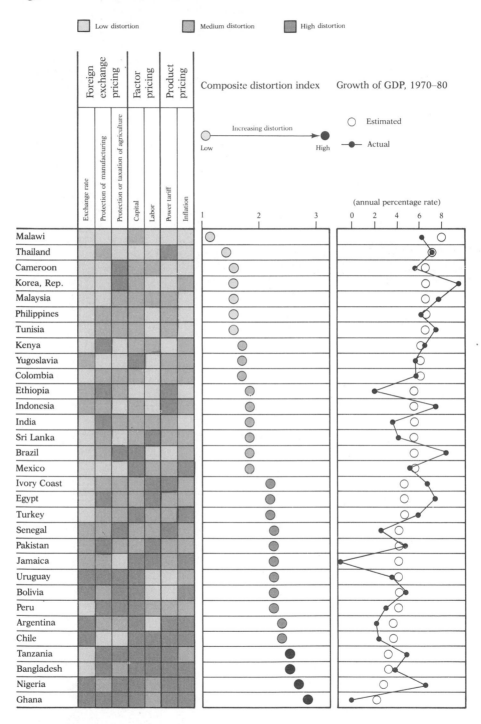

In this figure countries are listed in order of increasing degree of distortion in prices. In the first section, the shading of the squares indicates the degree of distortion in the principal categories of prices. The middle section is a composite index of price distortion for each country: as a country's distortion index increases, the shading of the circle changes from light to dark. In the right-hand section, the small circles show the actual annual rate of growth of GDP; the large circles are estimates of the GDP growth obtained by a regression relating growth to the distortion index.

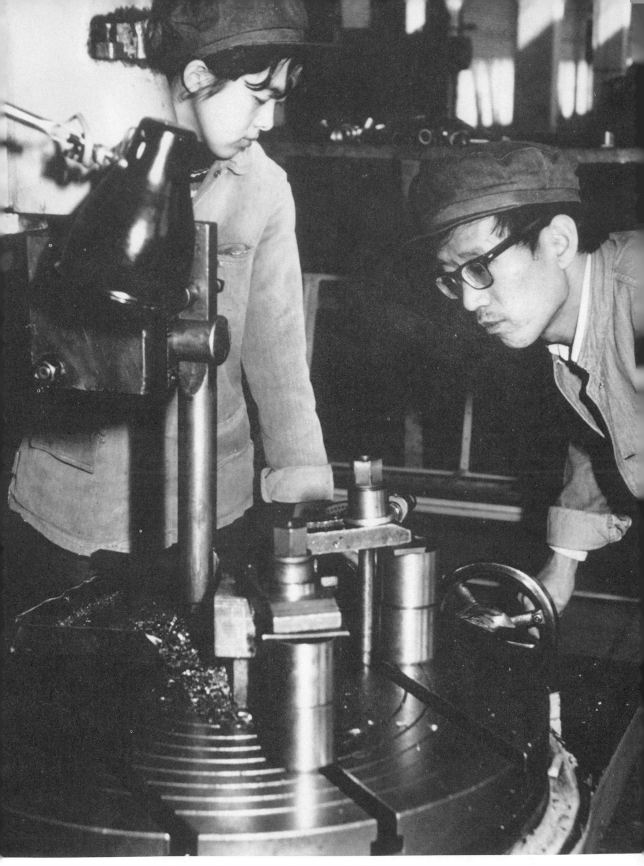

Machine tool operators at locomotive depot, Baoji, China

4

Public Investment Programs and Budgets

IN ADDITION TO ensuring that correct prices play their role in allocating resources efficiently, governments need to plan public investment carefully. The public sector in most developing countries accounts for 15 to 25 percent of value added in gross domestic product (GDP) and for roughly half of total investment. (For the developed countries as a group, the public sector's contribution to value added is a little higher, but its share of investment is lower.) While the dividing line between public and private investment varies from one type of economy to another, in virtually every country it is the public sector that provides basic education and health services as well as the infrastructure for transport, power, water supply, and major irrigation systems. The public investment program thus involves governments deeply in the kind of investment projects discussed in this book. In this chapter, we examine what experience has taught about formulating and implementing public investment programs in developing countries, and about integrating these with national budgets.

Designing Public Investment Programs

Most countries will have achieved a degree of consensus at the national level on broad economic and social objectives—such as raising national income and improving its distribution, increasing employment, or reducing dependence on external assistance. These objectives guide and inform economic policy choices and the general direction of public investment, and they serve as goals against which progress can be assessed from time to time. But they offer little guidance for plotting the details of a specific medium-term public investment program. For that task, governments must, as an initial step, rely on forecasts of the principal macroeconomic magnitudes. Forecasts of such variables as GDP, savings, investment, public revenue, public expenditure, exports, imports, and foreign capital inflow are needed to provide an informed framework for decisionmaking. By forecasting both the resources for and the constraints on overall economic growth, this macroeconomic framework permits planners to project a feasible growth pattern for the economy. Furthermore, after assumptions about proposed tax and other revenue policies, the growth of recurrent expenditures, and similar factors are incorporated, this framework also supplies a basis for estimating the financial resources, both domestic and external, likely to be available for public sector investment in a given year.

Detailed and overly sophisticated forecasting exercises are generally counterproductive, however, because of inadequacies in the data and a lack of understanding of how the variables interact. Alternative scenarios, for example a "high" and a "low" case based on different assumptions, are a useful means of dealing with the uncertainty that such forecasts inevitably face. These scenarios also provide useful guidance to private decisionmakers.

At the sector level, the typical comprehensive planning approach was to formulate medium- and long-term output targets in each sector, calculate the investment requirements to achieve them, and then assign these investments to either the public or private sector. This exercise often proved of little use in practical decisionmaking because the planners' knowledge of sectoral investment-output coefficients and time lags was limited. The art here lies in identifying the minimum amount of forecasting and analysis necessary to arrive at judgments about the appropriate level and types of investment in each sector. Forecasts are needed in the key infrastructure sectors such as transport and power, where markets cannot provide adequate guidance for investment decisions; and the expected outputs should be subjected to consistency checks (discussed further below) to determine whether they are broadly in line with likely demands from the productive sectors of agriculture and industry. But it is neither necessary nor feasible to forecast in detail all sectoral outputs and investments.

For the productive sectors, the response of output to investment is difficult to calculate at any level of aggregation above the individual farm or firm. Forecasts of output trends must, therefore, be based on past performance and on general assumptions about investment levels, preferably formulated after extensive consultation with private sector representatives. Obtaining precision in such forecasts is less important, however, than taking steps to encourage the free working of prices and markets to guide investment decisions in the productive sectors. In the social sectors, the calculation of investment requirements will hinge largely on the size of groups not yet adequately served and on judgments about what is an administratively and financially feasible rate at which services can be expanded to reach new recipients.

Drawing up the public sector investment program requires several rounds of iteration, that is, feedback from one phase to another, to obtain a satisfactory fit among the variables. The time frame for public investment programming may vary among sectors. There may be a ten- or fifteen-year program in some sectors (for example, in energy, where least-cost electric power programs to meet anticipated demand must look far ahead), while in other sectors with smaller investments requiring less lead time, the planning period may be much shorter. The overall public investment program for a given year, therefore, may include elements from a ten-year power program, an eight-year railway program, a three-year rural road program, and so on. Countries have adopted different time frames for their overall programs: some retain the five-year period that has been traditional for development plans, while others have adopted shorter or even longer periods. For most countries, three years is about as far ahead as is practicable to prepare an overall investment program. The macroeconomic forecasts are usually made for a three- to five-year period.

Once a multiyear program consistent with the macroeconomic framework is approved, the planners must phase it for implementation in the form of annual programs that can be integrated with the annual budget. Many countries have also found it useful to update the macroeconomic framework at the time each annual program is prepared, and to revise and extend the public investment program by one more year, thereby making it a "rolling" program.

An essential step in preparing the investment program is to identify the supporting policies, at both macroeconomic and sector levels, that are necessary to stimulate the desired responses from both private and public entities. These should include especially the policies on pricing and incentives discussed in chapter 3. It is also important to identify and plan the institutional changes that are necessary to achieve the results envisaged by the program.

Though they have gone about these tasks in different ways, developing countries have encountered many common problems and have learned similar lessons about what works best. Some of the more significant of these are recounted in the following sections.

Overall Resource Balance

Public investment programs that exceeded by a wide margin the resources that could be devoted to them have been a common feature in developing countries, as indicated by reviews by the World Bank of public investment programs in many of its member countries during the 1970s. Some deliberate overprogramming of investment may be a useful strategy insofar as it is intended to stimulate resource mobilization, as well as to allow for slippages in some programs. In many cases, however, the planners had not systematically worked out the resource implications of proposed investment programs—and in some cases overprogramming reflected an unwillingness or inability to make hard decisions as to priorities. Costs were routinely underestimated, as was the length of time required to bring projects through the various stages to completion.

In some countries, expectations about resource availability were clearly unrealistic. For example, a World Bank review of the public investment program in Turkey for 1982–85 estimated that if all the projects in various agency pipelines were scheduled for implementation, it would call for an annual public sector investment almost twice what macroeconomic analysis established as the maximum feasible level. In Bolivia, the public investment program for 1983–85 was wholly incompatible with the domestic savings and foreign transfers that could reasonably be expected. The overall cost of $983 million (17 percent of GDP) was far out of line with the zero public sector savings in recent years, and the foreign exchange requirement of about $500 million was excessive in view of prevailing attitudes of foreign lenders to Bolivia. In Sri Lanka during the 1970s, very large gaps between identified financial resources and planned capital outlays year after year underscored the lack of realistic planning and of an orderly budgetary process. Similar problems were experienced in Morocco. In these and other countries, the launching of excessively ambitious programs led to too many projects being started at the same time. This, in turn, led to an excessive dispersal of available skills, slowdowns in project implementation, and lower returns from investment.

Funding for Ongoing and Completed Projects

Furthermore, ambitious programs for new investment, to which politicians, planners, and others tend to give priority, have often been carried out at the expense of adequate funds for completion of projects still being constructed, and for operation and maintenance of completed projects. A recent survey by the World Bank has shown that in six out of ten of the Bank's borrowers, underfunding of both the construction of ongoing projects and the maintenance of completed projects had assumed serious proportions. This is not to imply that all the completed projects or those under construction were sound and should always have been given priority over new projects. Nevertheless, an outright waste of resources occurs when capital lies idle because investment is spread too thinly among too many projects. Strong reasons exist for giving priority to completing ongoing projects (since the sunk costs—that is, the costs already incurred—usually mean a high return on the additional investment needed for completion) and to using and safeguarding existing capital stock by proper operation and maintenance.

Examples of underfunding of both ongoing and completed projects are numerous. A review of Turkey's investment program showed that annual expenditure on projects under construction was only about 5 percent of the total cost of the projects. This implied an average completion time of twenty years—which was clearly excessive. It was found that by proper screening, many of the projects could be temporarily shelved to allow more expeditious completion of priority projects. In Nigeria, following a review of the proposed public investment program for 1984–86, the World Bank recommended rephasing the ongoing projects because of their vast number and large funding requirements; only three projects not yet started were given priority, and these were also subject to substantial scaling down of capital costs. In Pakistan's sixth plan (1983–88), shortfalls in the allocations for several of the power plants raise the possibility of delays in commissioning the plants, which would aggravate an already critical power shortage.

The planning of public investment programs must also give much greater recognition to the need for adequate and timely maintenance. Deferring maintenance eventually becomes extremely expensive. In many countries, especially those of sub-Saharan Africa, past neglect has now made maintenance and rehabilitation of paramount importance. We will return to this point frequently in the sector discussions in part II.

Calculation of "Free" Resources

In view of the serious consequences of neglecting ongoing and completed projects, it is highly advisable to adopt a systematic approach to deciding how much funding can be devoted to new projects in a given budget year. A useful technique is to calculate the funding needs of ongoing and completed projects, explicitly including operation and maintenance needs, in order to determine the "free" public sector resources remaining for new projects.

Ideally, this analysis should be done in the context not only of a multiyear investment program, but also of a multiyear budget. Adding this dimension to the budgeting process where it does not already exist would enable planners to be aware of and take into account the full resource implications—including both capital costs and future recurrent costs for operation and maintenance—before deciding to embark on a new investment. Botswana's National Development Plan, for example, contains projections of recurrent budget costs arising from each project in the public investment program. These are consolidated into revenue and spending projections for the next three years, which are periodically updated and rolled forward.

Many countries find that, when operation and maintenance needs are taken fully into account, free resources are very limited. Such calculations are essential to signal when resource limitations require the central planning agency to scale down or postpone projects proposed by various sector ministries. Planning agencies, as well as sector ministries, have often not been sufficiently sensitive to their responsibility for ensuring adequate funding of operation and maintenance.

Economic Analysis

The planning agency must both "shoot down" bad projects and, often more important when resources are especially scarce, select carefully among good projects those to be initiated in a particular budget year. For these purposes, strengthening the capacity to appraise projects is essential in most developing countries. This calls for greater use of cost-benefit analysis and economic rates of return (using shadow prices where appropriate; see chapter 20, Economic Analysis). More rigorous application of economic criteria would make a major contribution to the better use of resources by pointing up the need to abandon, scale down, or postpone the large and unaffordable "white elephants"—typically projects with low economic returns—that appear in almost every country's investment plan.

Public-Private Balance

Reviews by the World Bank of investment programs show that in many countries (including Pakistan, Bangladesh, Turkey, Morocco, Peru, and the Ivory Coast) capacity and intentions have been seriously mismatched with regard to the balance between the public and private sectors. The financial resources and the managerial capacity of the public sector have become overloaded. Greater efficiency of the public sector is essential in most countries, and some improvement can be achieved by better training and stronger incentives, points discussed more fully in chapter 23, Institutional Analysis. There are limits to this process, however, and it is necessary to be realistic about what can be expected of the public sector in the constrained circumstances of a developing country. In a growing number of countries, the trend is toward divesting public sector enterprises and confining the public sector to the provision of those services (education, infrastructure, and so on) that are almost universally regarded as belonging in the public domain. At the same time, although in some countries the private sector (outside of agriculture) is a largely untapped resource with considerable development potential, it is necessary to be realistic about its capabilities also. The private sector is sometimes burdened with problems similar to those of the public sector: scarcity of technical and financial competence, poor management, inadequate training programs—plus, in many instances, a lack of entrepreneurial spirit and an aversion to competition. On balance, however, in many developing countries, the public sector has been overextended and the private sector unduly restricted, given their respective capabilities and potential.

In Pakistan in recent years, recognition of the need for improved government policies and liberal incentives to promote recovery of the private sector has led to a surge in private investment, which increased, albeit from a low base, by 14 percent a year in real terms between 1979 and 1981. The measures used included denationalization and constitutional safeguards against arbitrary government acquisition, the opening up of more areas to private investment, incentives such as tax holidays and excise and import duty concessions, easier access to imported raw materials, concessional credit, and streamlined procedures for sanctioning investment. In Sudan, the private sector rapidly built up road transport capacity for both freight and passengers when the necessary roads were put in place in the 1970s. When Bangladesh put the supply of agricultural inputs such as fertilizer and irrigation pumps into private hands in 1979, it freed substantial public resources that had previously been used for this purpose. The experience of these and many other countries supports the view that the limited management capacity of the public sector should be focused on activities that require it, not on those that are better left to the private sector.

Sectoral Balances and Priorities

A large amount of investment planning effort has traditionally been devoted to achieving sectoral balances and determining sectoral priorities—that is, to the question of how investment should be allocated among sectors so as to ensure that supply in each sector is adequate to meet at least the high-priority demands for its goods and services. Achievement of sectoral balances is difficult because of changing technical coefficients (such as input-output ratios) and demand patterns, and the emphasis on balances has sometimes resulted in neglect of economic analysis of the justification of individual projects.

With respect to tradables (that is, goods which enter into international trade), it appears that appropriate pricing of output is more effective than investment programming for obtaining the desired level of output and of efficiency. For key nontradables such as power, transport, water supply, and telecommunications, although appropriate pricing is essential, governments must also directly address the issue of balance between supply and demand. It is, therefore, on the nontradables that governments' efforts to avoid or overcome bottlenecks should be concentrated. In recent years, investment programming in India, for example, has increasingly directed attention to such critical sectoral issues as the availability of electric power in amounts and at locations necessary to serve industry and agriculture. Investment reviews by the Bank have demonstrated the considerable scope for avoiding wasteful investment that exists—even in a country such as Korea, with its substantial growth rate—when the focus on these key issues is sharpened.

Consistency checks are necessary to ensure that sectoral balances are in fact achieved, that is, that the outputs expected from a sector tally with the likely demands from other sectors for those outputs. For example, on the basis of an analysis of expected demand by other sectors for, say, transport, investment plans can be developed for meeting the anticipated requirements for expanded road or rail services at the least cost. If the proposed investment exceeds the financial or implementation capacity, it becomes necessary to reassess the estimated requirements and the feasibility of the initially assumed growth rate. A series of iterations may be required to arrive at reasonably consistent projections. Such analyses can be complex and demand considerable data—but where data are not available for sophisticated analysis, some simple, commonsense consistency checks can still be useful. Efforts must be devoted not only to seeking consistency among sectoral investment programs, but also to identifying and making provision for essential links between projects, in order to ensure the availability of power for specific irrigation projects, for example, or of transport for major industrial undertakings.

Beyond the issue of sectoral balances, the question of investment priorities among sectors is particularly difficult. The relative attention to be given, for example, to programs that will benefit the poorest groups in areas such as food, health, education, and housing cannot be decided by an economic calculus; nor can the appropriate balance between investment in these social sectors and in the productive or infrastructure sectors (agriculture, power, and so on). It is often advisable to put these questions to the decisionmakers as ultimately political choices. The contribution that economists can make may be limited because their analytical tools are inadequate and because value judgments are required, but they may still be crucial in delineating the costs of alternatives and in providing the relevant data on which informed judgments can be made. These data might include, for example, the size and location of poverty groups, the number of people without access to safe water or electricity, the levels of health and nutrition in different parts of the population, or the proportion of school-age children not yet reached by the education system. Adequate information may itself go a long way toward guiding decisions on priorities among sectors. As to investment priorities within a sector, much can be done with the tools of cost-benefit analysis to improve choices.

Flexibility in Adjusting Programs

Experience to date as well as the uncertainty of future prospects suggest that investment programs need to be modified repeatedly as economic conditions, resource availabilities, and other circumstances change. To assist this process of adjustment, India, Bangladesh, Nigeria, and several other countries have found it useful to identify a "core program" of high-priority investments so that, in case of resource shortfalls, program cuts can be selective rather than across the board.

Another technique, noted earlier, that has been found useful in Botswana, Korea, Ivory Coast, and many other countries is to have a rolling public investment program that is updated at regular intervals—most often, a three-year program updated each year. This program is usually calculated in expected current prices (as opposed to the five-year plan expressed in constant prices that was once common). For this technique to be successful, an effective system must be established for monitoring implementation of the investment program so that the annual revisions can be based on reliable and up-to-date information. The system should monitor both physical and financial progress, since it often happens that project funds are spent more or less on schedule while physical progress falls behind, so that upcoming cost overruns are not perceived until too late. Causes of delays in implementation need to be identified and the problems brought to the attention of the responsible officials. The investment program, or portions of it, may have to be revised even more frequently than annually if the economic environment changes sharply. The ability to respond rapidly to these changes by adjusting both the investment program and the policies related to it is central to the success of a country's economic management.

Elements of a Sound Public Investment Program: An Illustration

A specific example may help to illustrate some important elements in designing a successful public investment program. The case of the Ivory Coast demonstrates both common pitfalls to be avoided and desirable features to be adopted.

After a decade of impressive growth performance, the economy of the Ivory Coast faced a grave internal and external crisis in the late 1970s. Encouraged by exceptionally high international prices for coffee and cocoa that led to an 80 percent improvement in the terms of trade between 1975 and 1977, the government rapidly increased public expenditures (financed, to a large extent, by external borrowing) to about 41 percent of GDP by 1978. Financial and budgetary discipline as well as the system of project selection and screening were weakened. Even when international prices for coffee and cocoa fell and the country faced deteriorating terms of trade, the momentum of the large public expenditure program did not abate. The combination of an excessive and inefficient investment program, large external debt-servicing requirements, declining public savings, a worsening external economic climate, and generally poor economic management saddled the country with large current account deficits in the balance of payments and the budget. When these problems were recognized, the Ivorian government embarked in late 1980 on an economic recovery plan supported by two structural adjustment loans from the World Bank.

A high-priority item in the package of policies needed to bring about stabilization and restructuring was the redesign of the public investment program. Much of the program comprised projects in the social sectors; many were poorly planned, with the result that they had low rates of return and high recurrent costs. Expenditures in education had been devoted to several overdesigned facilities for higher education; at the same time, the education sector was beset with growing inefficiency, increasing irrelevance to the needs of the economy, and escalating recurrent costs absorbing as much as 46 percent of the government's recurrent budget. Capital and recurrent expenditures in the housing sector were substantial, with about one-third of civil servants receiving free housing in 1981. Building specifications were also set at very high standards. The main problem in the transport sector was the excessive scale of highway investment. In the directly productive sectors, large and poorly designed projects dominated. For example, in agriculture, six completed sugar complexes had unit operating costs two to three times above world market prices. In energy, the local oil refinery suffered from the consequences of lagging demand and high cost overruns. The World Bank estimated that, because of inadequate project selection standards, the rate of return on the $8 billion of public investment undertaken in 1976–80 was approximately 40 percent lower than that on investment undertaken in 1970–75.

The economic recovery plan addressed some of these issues by canceling or deferring many low-priority projects, scaling down and restructuring many others, lowering design standards, and instituting better cost recovery through reduced subsidies. But most important, the plan recognized the need for proper project selection. It set up mechanisms for better evaluation and screening at the sector level to ensure the financial, technical, and economic soundness of funded projects and the government's capacity to pay future operating and maintenance costs. With increased vigilance, projects of doubtful viability were halted and the sugar complexes limited to the six already completed.

One factor behind the bloated public expenditure program in the Ivory Coast was the existence of decentralized parastatal agencies, among them the Agricultural Exports Stabilization Fund, which had access to vast surpluses during the coffee and cocoa price boom and which independently pursued its own expenditure and investment program. A consolidated picture of overall resources in the public sector was thus not available to guide resource allocation. The recovery plan fully integrated all receipts into the treasury. Institutionally, a centralized Committee for Financial Coordination and Investment Control was charged with assessing available resources and setting priorities. It produced a five-year framework for structural adjustment as well as shorter-term (three-year) macroeconomic plans balancing resource availability and investment requirements. These were translated into three-year rolling public investment programs. To permit better adjustment to future uncertainties, these rolling investment programs were to be evaluated at short intervals to realign available resources with priorities.

INTEGRATING INVESTMENT PROGRAMS AND BUDGETS

Government budgets are the principal administrative instrument through which public investment programs are transformed into tangible achievements. Only one developing country in ten, however, has a system of multiyear budgeting that would facilitate the integration of multiyear plans with budgets. It is also discouragingly true in many countries that, after great effort has been devoted to formulating an investment plan, the budget for the first year following adoption of the plan bears little or no resemblance to it. Over the past thirty years, many governments have attempted to strengthen the links between budgets and investment plans; success, however, has been uneven and much remains to be done. Important issues in this context are the coverage of the budget, the organization of the budget and planning office, the classification of budget items, the control system for implementation and monitoring, and the evaluation of results. In the following sections, we discuss each of these in turn.

Coverage of the Budget

A major shortcoming in the budgetary systems of many developing countries is the failure to prepare a consolidated public sector budget. This places severe limitations on investment programming and its full integration with the budget (and also reduces the possibility of using fiscal policies for stabilization purposes). A study of Costa Rica's economic administration in 1980 found that some 550 autonomous institutions enjoyed legal, sometimes constitutional, guarantees of financial independence and operated outside the control of the central administration; about 10 percent of central expenditure functions was performed by the treasury outside the budget; some specialized ministries also had independent budgets; and fully half of tax collections were earmarked for specific purposes. In Ecuador, the national budget in 1979 covered only 62 percent of public revenues and 43 percent of expenditures; the balance was accounted for by special funds, by autonomous agencies such as the social security institution, and by state enterprises. In Brazil, where historically the treasury budget covered all federal tax revenues and their allocation, central surveillance was progressively weakened in the 1970s by the growth of the public sector and the earmarking of an increasing proportion of tax revenues. Egypt's budgetary reform in 1980 brought a number of special funds and separate accounts into the state budget, and budgets of public sector companies were explicitly linked with it. The current budget was thus unified, but responsibility for financing public investments was transferred to the newly established National Investment Bank, which meant in effect there were then two central budgeting agencies.

While these and other countries have made efforts, with more or less success, to improve budgetary administration, in many countries the fragmentation of budgetary responsibility makes allocation of resources according to central priorities very difficult. Where the financial system is essentially modeled on either British or French practice, a consolidated fund is the general rule and earmarking of taxes is exceptional. But in both eastern and western Africa, the area covered by the central budget has steadily been reduced by the growth of public enterprises and other autonomous agencies, such as commodity marketing boards, state commercial agencies, development finance institutions, and area development authorities, which have varying degrees of budgetary independence.

A consolidated public sector budget for purposes of investment programming would include all agencies and organizations that either invest or save significant amounts. The investment side of the budget would include government funds for industrial and agricultural credit programs channeled through development banks or other intermediaries, as well as net government lending to state-owned enterprises. The resources side of the budget would include savings being mobilized through social security, pension funds, and the like, as well as resources accruing to commodity boards and other parastatal operations, and project financing expected from external agencies. The aim is to prepare a comprehensive budget that enables the government to obtain a full picture of resource mobilization as well as of expenditure (though not to exercise detailed central supervision of expenditure; see below, "Budget Control"). When this is done, it is often found that public investment is occurring in areas or in proportions that are not in accordance with the priorities expressed in the public sector investment program, and that there is scope for substantial reallocation of resources in desired directions.

Organization of Budget and Plan Offices

The approaches taken to integrate budgeting and investment planning functions are basically of three types: the planning agency takes over the budgeting function; the budgeting office takes over the planning function; or these two functions are taken over by a national ministry of finance and planning. Variants of the first approach are found in Brazil and Korea, where performance under this arrangement has been quite good. The second approach, found mostly in developed countries, seeks to put into practice various programming and budgeting systems. The third approach was tried in the Bahamas, Bahrain, Pakistan, Singapore, Tanzania, and Zambia, among others. These organizational mergers have faced difficulties that have grown mainly out of the fact that each agency had developed an administrative style of its own and did not lose its identity even when integrated with others. Several countries, consequently, reverted to separate budget and planning agencies; others, notably Pakistan, Tanzania, and Zambia, have gone through a cyclical process, with the separation of functions followed by integration and eventually by reversion to separate agencies again.

In light of this experience, generalization is obviously difficult. On balance, it would appear that combining planning and budget offices under one ministry is likely to improve coordination of expenditure programs. It may be, however, that having enough properly trained staff, linked to a decisionmaking authority, is as important as where the integrated function is located—especially since integration of plans and budgets can be tackled through procedural measures instead of organizational mergers. In Chile, for example, the budget cannot include any capital investment funds not related to projects appraised according to methods established by the Planning Ministry and reviewed by that ministry.

Classification of Budget Items

Irrespective of organizational structure, conformity of budget and investment program categories is important for their integration. Reclassification of budget items is generally necessary for that purpose. In earlier days, budget classifications were established primarily as a basis for legislative oversight and a source of information about what each unit was spending money for. Toward this end, classifications were devised to show the item of expenditure—salaries, equipment, and so on—in addition to the organization responsible for incurring it (that is, the point of administrative or financial control). These classifications proved inadequate since they yielded no information on the objectives of an expenditure, such as providing irrigation to a specified area. Alternative budget classification schemes were developed to make possible a division of government receipts and expenditures into functions, programs, and economic categories. Within this broad framework, several variations in practice are observed in developing countries. A commonly used variant is classification into a current and a capital budget. Supporters of the dual budget claim that it enables a clear identification of borrowing and its utilization, and focuses attention on balancing the current account as a key element of economic policy. Opponents of the dual budget argue that it contributes to needless emphasis on brick-and-mortar projects and, conversely, to a neglect of necessary recurring expenditures for operations and maintenance. In addition, controversies abound on the merits of different ways of classifying and measuring capital outlays.

Budget items can also be classified by functions or programs (see the discussion of program budgeting under "Evaluation of Results" below). This is especially helpful when various parts of a program are administered by several agencies. Bringing these parts under one classification shows the links among them and gives a better understanding of the objectives of each expenditure. Yet another approach is to classify government transactions into categories that facilitate the assessment of the budget's impact on the economy—consumption expenditures, subsidies, transfer payments, capital formation, and so on.

While these budget classifications are improvements over traditional practices, they still leave much to be desired. First, the basis for division of expenditures into current and capital items is not always clearly delineated, and expenditures are frequently switched from one category to another. Second, the functional and program classifications are often too broad to serve either planning or managerial purposes. Third, classifications used for the budget and for investment programs may be quite different. Budget classifications should meet the basic requirement of making it possible to track the public investment program through line items of budget appropriation and expenditure. This is seldom achieved—though some countries, such as India, have developed link documents providing a crosswalk between budget and plan categories. Classifications should be frequently reassessed or updated to reflect the changing tasks of government. Although any simple generalization is risky, it is usually helpful to classify budgets into current and capital expenditures—but any implication that only capital expenditures help raise productivity must be avoided.

Budget Control

The implementation of many development plans, experience reveals, has been hindered by excessive use of negative controls by the finance and planning agencies. In principle, once budget allocations are made, the responsibility for implementing the budget, along with the requisite freedom to do so, should be entrusted to the spending departments. The central agencies, for their part, should depend on various accounting reports to monitor overall financial progress and its implications for national economic policies. Budgetary uncertainties, however, have contributed to a situation in which central agencies in many countries have been reluctant to allow spending agencies any freedom; over the years, the dependence of spending agencies on central agencies has steadily increased. Frequent delays in making funds available to project authorities have been a major weakness in project implementation.

To some extent, this problem has been recognized and attempts made to mitigate it by appointing financial advisors, who are in effect nominees of the finance ministry, to help selected spending ministries with their financial management; Bangladesh, India, and Pakistan have taken this approach. On the whole, however, progress in building up adequate financial management capability within spending agencies has been limited. Even in countries where some progress has been made, it has often been offset by reimposition of highly centralized controls during periods of financial austerity.

This reflects the fact that the process of decentralization has to take into account the responsibility of central agencies for overall fiscal and monetary policy, including any short-term stabilization programs, as well as for orderly financial management. Nevertheless, the need to give the spending departments greater financial authority, along with greater operational freedom to carry out their assigned tasks, is so clear that it requires no special advocacy. Tight central control can have only limited success, even under carefully defined conditions. Its persistence over prolonged periods is bound to be counterproductive, because central agencies do not have the capability to comprehend and control the full spectrum of government operations. Effective implementation of government policies and programs requires that those responsible for formulating and administering them also be able to manage the related finances, and this can be accomplished only by the integration of administrative and financial responsibilities.

As a corollary, once resources are allocated by a centralized agency after adequate scrutiny of the programs involved, the spending agencies should be made accountable not merely for routine observance of accounting requirements but, above all, for achievement of results. The resources allocated need to be viewed as contractual obligations on the part of the spending agencies to deliver specified performance. This, in turn, requires that the spending agencies have the financial management capability to estimate and monitor costs and to fulfill program tasks within specified cost ceilings. As a preliminary step, governments need to review the status of financial management in spending agencies and then, in selected major spending agencies, to begin to organize and staff appropriate financial units and devise measures to ensure accountability. The process of decentralization is likely to be a long, slow journey, but it can begin only when the first, decisive steps are taken.

Financial Information Systems

Further progress in integrating investment programs and budgets depends not only on building up financial management capabilities in spending agencies, but also on strengthening financial information systems. Development of financial information systems, however, has been hampered by the lack of modern government accounting systems. Public accounts are frequently maintained by a central office, and the need to build up proper accounts within spending agencies, although recognized, has not been met. The classification used in accounts has been geared more to traditional legislative concerns than to the measurement of operational results. The growth of too many special accounts, including those of autonomous entities, that must frequently be reconciled slows the timely processing of accounts. As a result, government accounts are published in many countries with a considerable time lag after the close of the financial year.

To deal with these problems, several governments have installed electronic data processing (EDP) systems to speed up the compilation and consolidation of data. Some countries, notably India and Korea, have also installed improved financial reporting systems, with coverage wider than that of government accounts.

The use of EDP systems requires, however, well-organized payment procedures—whether on a centralized or decentralized model—along with standardized bookkeeping practices and an efficient communications system. A few countries (among them Bahrain, Saudi Arabia, and Kenya) have successfully implemented computerized systems and have up-to-date financial information. In others (Guyana, Liberia, Papua New Guinea, and Tanzania) the introduction of EDP systems was followed by many problems, typically because accounting systems and procedures were not rationalized in advance. Even where this was done, problems were encountered in managing inputs into the computer. Poorly trained staff contributed to classification errors, and final outputs were far from recognizable to those needing to use them. Where successfully implemented, however, EDP systems have demonstrated a capability for handling a greater volume of work, quickness of compilation, ready retrieval procedures, and lower cost of operations.

Evaluation of Results

Traditionally, ex post evaluation of a budget has been undertaken in the form of financial audits by a government agency. These audits have been confined largely to ascertaining whether expenditures were made in accordance with the appropriations in the budget and whether the tenets of financial propriety were observed. Although some advances have been made by government agencies in examining the substantive implementation of development programs and projects, their work generally leaves much to be desired, especially with regard to audits of performance or efficiency. An encouraging sign, as noted earlier, is the increasing importance being given to evaluating results in order to determine the efficiency with which budget resources are being utilized— as opposed to merely ensuring that financial regulations are observed.

The concept of program budgeting (the "Program and Performance Budgeting System"), applied in the mid-1960s in some developed countries and subsequently tried in several developing countries, seeks to make evaluation of results an integral part of the budgeting process. Distinctive features of this approach are a clearer definition of the outputs expected from budget allocations, a multiyear framework showing costs and outputs, and evaluation of outputs for feedback into subsequent budgeting. Implementation has proved very difficult, however, and the system was abandoned by several of the developed countries in the early 1970s.

The development of program budgeting systems in the developing countries exhibits a diverse pattern. Ten or twelve countries are in various stages of implementing such systems, ranging from tentative pilot studies to full implementation; important among these are India, Indonesia, Lesotho, Malaysia, Nigeria, Peru, and the Philippines. Installation and operation of a full program budgeting and evaluation system has proved to be a lengthy and administratively complex undertaking. It requires extensive restructuring of accounting systems and is expensive in terms of time and training of manpower. A more fundamental problem is that many outputs of government services are not clearly definable or measurable. Nor is it easy to evaluate individual agency performance in programs that involve several agencies. In addition, comprehensive evaluation takes so long that it is often impractical to wait for evaluation results before determining current budget allocations.

Consequently, the search is still under way for an effective method of analyzing and evaluating the results of government expenditures using a program and output format. One promising approach is to be selective and evaluate only the outputs of major programs that have a clear potential for significantly influencing future budgets. As elsewhere, focusing on getting a few things done well may be more important than the premature establishment of comprehensive programs which there is no capability to administer. The way to more effective financial management in a developing country is more likely to be found through careful identification of problem areas specific to the country, followed by adaptive and evolutionary change, than through the wholesale import and installation of new systems such as program and performance budgeting.

The experience of the past thirty years shows that there are no simple theoretical principles for efficient management of national investment. Above all, it is important to have the right "vision" of the development process; in a growing number of developing countries, this vision now encompasses the importance of prices, markets, and private initiative within a framework of incentives and infrastructure provided by the government. Given this vision, the crucial element is the pragmatism of decisionmakers, who must steer a middle course between the extremes of the laissez-faire and the structuralist varieties. They need not seek perfection nor look for answers only from models and sophisticated analytical techniques. Common sense is an essential ingredient in the process, and it consists largely of asking the right questions and focusing on the right issues. In virtually all countries, much can be done to improve the effectiveness of the public investment program simply by systematically questioning the principal choices it embodies, remedying the more obvious shortcomings, and remaining flexible in adjusting to new information and changed circumstances. Supporting the investment program with a policy framework that avoids price distortions and provides incentives for efficient performance in both the public and private sectors is also an area in which practicality and realism yield high returns.

The foregoing discussion, concentrating as it does on an economic calculus, is not meant to underplay the political aspects of development. In the end, the allocation of resources has to be guided by the political aspirations of the country. What the economic planners can do is to clarify the choices involved and emphasize the economic costs of alternative courses of action. But they can be effective only to the extent that governments do accord priority to economic development.

PART II
Sector Analysis and Management

Indian child attending school, Mexico

5

Sector Analysis

As WE NOTED in chapter 1, if a country wishes to ensure that its project investments yield the greatest benefit, it will carry out planning and analysis at national, at sector, and at project levels, each of these interacting with and supporting the others. Among the three, sector analysis is still a relatively neglected area in many countries—even though it furnishes essential information both for formulating a sound national investment program and for selecting and designing projects that respond to the most pressing needs of the sector.

WHAT IS A SECTOR?

The inadequate attention to sector analysis may reflect the absence of widely accepted guidelines for carrying out such work. In fact, even defining what constitutes a sector is problematic. Is energy a sector, or is power? Are railways and highways sectors, or subsectors of transport? Analytically, a sector is a matter of aggregation, and it can, in principle, be fixed at any intermediate point between the individual project and the national investment program. Thus, the definition of a sector is largely a matter of convention and convenience.

In practice, there is considerable agreement as to what a sector is. Most governments are organized into sectoral ministries whose areas of responsibility and whose policy and analytical functions are broadly similar from one country to another. A sector comprises, for the most part, the producing or operating units in the economy that share a common function or output. The agriculture sector includes all the farms in the country, the industry sector all the manufacturing firms, the education sector all the schools and colleges, and so on. Each sector, in turn, can be broken down into subsectors—for example, agriculture into food grains, livestock, tree crops, cotton, and sugar subsectors; education into primary, general secondary, and vocational training subsectors. Sectors can be subdivided in many ways, depending on the purpose; irrigation, credit, research, and extension can also be considered subsectors of agriculture. Sectors are usually nationwide, and each is usually assisted and regulated by a common set of government agencies and policies. But sectors have no legal existence and do not maintain consolidated accounts for themselves—these are attributes of primary entities such as farms, firms, and schools.

Reference is sometimes made to the productive sectors (agriculture, industry, mining), the infrastructure sectors (transport, energy), and the social sectors (education, health, population). Another frequently used classification is that of primary, secondary, and tertiary sectors: the primary sector includes all activities that produce food and raw materials directly from nature (agriculture, mining, fisheries, logging); the secondary sector, all activities that process the output of the primary sector into usable products (which includes the whole industrial sector); the tertiary sector, all activities whose main output is not a product but a service provided by people. But one seldom sees a study of the productive sector or the primary sector—these are too broad and heterogeneous to lend themselves to effective analysis. Sector categories, to be useful, have to cut the economy into thinner slices composed of fairly homogeneous activities that display common problems and characteristics.

Although governments tend to subdivide the economy along largely similar lines for administrative purposes, the precise demarcation of sectoral boundaries varies among countries. Irrigation may be grouped with power or assigned to some other infrastructure ministry (while extension work with farmers in irrigated areas remains in the agriculture ministry). Modes of transport may be coordinated to varying degrees within or by a transport ministry. In most countries, the components of the energy sector—hydrocarbons, electric power, coal—are only now beginning to be drawn together in a sectoral ministry or other coordinating agency. Some of these arrangements are likely to work better than others. If, for example, responsibility for highways is assigned to the ministry of public works and that for other modes to the ministry of transport, then transport planning and policy design are made more difficult. In any event, it is necessary that the boundaries among sectors be well defined; that analysis, oversight, and coordinating responsibilities within the government be clearly assigned; and that the sectors not be so small and subdivided that scarce manpower resources are scattered in a profusion of ministries, since this magnifies problems of coordination.

In this book we have opted for a broad definition of sectors—energy, transport, agriculture, industry, and so on—although we have also sought to treat as fully as space allows, or as understanding of their special problems requires, the characteristics of subsectors such as irrigation, small industry, specific transport modes, or renewable energy resources. Population, health, and nutrition, although generally considered as separate sectors, are grouped together in one chapter because of the close interrelations among them and the advantages of coordinating their programs for maximum effectiveness and mutual reinforcement. By no means do all governments, however, group these functions under one ministry. Urbanization is treated here as a single topic, even though it is multisectoral in nature, comprising transport, power, industry, and other elements bound by a common spatial dimension and by the shared characteristic of population density. (There is no corresponding "rural" chapter since agriculture coincides more or less well with it.)

Compared with the elaboration of theories and models for national investment planning or of cost-benefit and other analytical techniques for project assessment, theoretical and practical guidelines for the conduct of sector analysis are much less developed. Nevertheless, as we shall see in subsequent chapters, many sectoral issues are amenable to analysis— for example, pricing of marketable outputs, targeting of beneficiaries, acquisition of technology, intrasectoral allocation of investments—and our analytical capability is increasing with experience. In this chapter, we describe what the World Bank, working with its member countries, has learned are the most useful ways of going about the task of sector analysis.

OBJECTIVES OF SECTOR ANALYSIS

Sector analysis, broadly defined, is concerned with the examination and assessment of the resources, needs, problems, and opportunities in individual sectors of the economy, for the purposes of

- Assisting consideration of economywide policies and strategies
- Enabling judgments to be made on sector development policies and strategies that will enhance the contribution of the sector to the country's economic development
- Determining investment priorities in the sector as a crucial step toward identifying specific projects and any additional preinvestment studies required
- Evaluating the capacity of principal institutions in the sector to implement desired policies, programs, and projects.

Some countries have long carried out sector surveys, in varying degrees of detail and at varying intervals, but systematic sector analysis for the purposes described above is still comparatively new. Many countries have been introduced to this approach by the World Bank, which needed to be sure that any project it financed was of high priority in meeting the objectives for the relevant sector. There was also a growing recognition among Bank staff that project work suffered unless the sector policy framework was satisfactory and the sector institutions functioned properly. To address these concerns and to give useful advice to member governments, the Bank now undertakes much more thorough sector analysis in the course of its project work than it once did.

But why should a ministry of agriculture or education or transport, in daily contact with its sector, need to undertake an analysis of that sector? The answer is that a ministry's activities tend to relate to particular problems or to the administration of particular policies. In the normal course of its work, it seldom has an opportunity to gain an overview of the sector as a whole—with the risk that it loses sight of the forest for the trees. Many ministries do carry out studies of specific topics, but generally only when there is an important and pressing problem to be solved.

All governments collect and issue statistics about economic activities, and all have ministries and departments that assist or regulate activities in the major sectors. Thus, every country possesses at least some data on which to base sector work, as well as some people with knowledge about each sector. But officials, pressed to keep up with daily operational or administrative responsibilities, are usually too busy to provide—or to organize the provision of—the kind of analysis that lies at the heart of sector work: framing questions carefully, collecting and interpreting data, and arriving at conclusions and recommendations to promote sector development. Even if they could be detached from their daily responsibilities and assigned to sector work, they might not be trained to think in sector terms.

Even the simplest economy faces complex questions, and answers offered without the help of sector analysis can give rise to poor policies or ill-considered investments. One reason for this is that everything is related to everything else. Investment in roads, for example, will affect the ability of farmers to move crops to market and of traders to move goods into the countryside; it will also affect the demand for steel and cement, the size of the government's recurrent budget (for maintenance), the demand for trucks and buses, the tax yield from fuel, and so on. Questions will come up about the composition of the road investment program: perhaps building a different kind of road—such as a trunk highway connecting major cities instead of additional rural roads—or locating the road project in another part of the country would contribute more to development.

Sector analysis is indispensable for resolving these questions of choice and priority and of interconnections among projects. Successful planning requires translating nationwide objectives and policies into the specific requirements of individual sectors and subsectors, as well as into the still more specific details of individual projects. Too often, this process of translation is not done very well. Or it may not be done at all, in the sense that people working in the central planning agency and in the sectoral ministries may not communicate adequately with each other. No one may be paying much attention to the interconnections between projects and the relevant sector, between one sector and another, or between the sector and the economy as a whole. No one, therefore, may be answering important questions about proposed investments in the sector; indeed, the questions may not even be asked. In short, the typical development program moves forward with weak connections between "the top" and "the bottom."

A basic purpose of sector analysis is, therefore, to bridge the gap between the macroeconomics of country-level policies and investment programs and the microeconomics of individual projects. It promotes "top down" and "bottom up" activity in several ways. First, it complements macroeconomic work by analyzing the effects on the sector, and on projects within the sector, of such general policy variables as the exchange rate, tax structure, wage policies, and interest rates. (Policies and problems in important sectors of the economy—such as agriculture and industry—act, in turn, on the macroeconomic setting.) Second, sector analysis provides estimates of output and employment potential and investment requirements for the sector as a whole; these are essential inputs into the central planning agency's decisions regarding the national investment program and priorities. Third, by assessing the development potential and the relative advantages of different projects and programs within a sector, sector analysis helps to ensure that individual projects are selected and designed on the basis of a sector's needs and priorities, and that policy and institutional changes necessary for good performance at the project, or microeconomic, level are identified.

Because no sector functions in isolation from the rest of the economy, an important contribution of sector analysis is to determine the impact of a sector on the development of other sectors and to ensure consistency in policy and investment recommendations from one sector to another. Therefore, sector analysis—while obviously focused on a particular sector—should ideally be conducted in close coordination with studies and analyses being done of other sectors and of the economy as a whole. Admittedly, this will cause difficult problems of coordination for many governments. When properly done, however, sector work is highly useful to governments because it points up intersectoral relations, constraints, and opportunities that previously were either not perceived or not fully appreciated.

One thing sector analysis cannot do is furnish clear criteria for the allocation of investment funds among sectors. Indeed, as noted in chapter 4, the most sophisticated analytical techniques available can offer only limited—though useful—guidance on intersectoral priorities. Good sector work, illuminating the costs and benefits of different choices, can nonetheless provide the best technical foundation for choices that must ultimately be a matter of judgment.

GENERAL SURVEYS OR SPECIAL STUDIES?

The kind of analysis required in a particular sector will vary from year to year and from country to country, depending on the current state of knowledge about the sector, the relative importance of the sector, the complexity of its developmental problems, and current operational concerns and circumstances. Despite great variation in specifics, however, most sector analysis falls into one of two broad types: general surveys of an entire sector (or important subsector) and special studies of particular topics within a sector (or subsector).

For years, many governments as well as the World Bank believed that a comprehensive survey was required from time to time to provide a broad analysis of the main medium- to long-term strategy and policy options in a sector or major subsector. Such comprehensive surveys assessed existing policies and the changes in them needed to meet a sector's objectives, as well as the state of physical infrastructure, productive facilities, and institutions in the sector and improvements needed. In addition, these surveys indicated the total level of investment expenditure required to meet the objectives and, within this total, they identified high-priority projects and any preinvestment studies needed to move the projects forward.

Although such broad surveys are still sometimes prepared, experience with them has shown a relatively low return for the substantial investment of manpower and other resources. In any large and complex sector, like agriculture or transport, or in a major subsector like irrigation, such surveys tend to be carried out at such a level of generality that few specific decisions can be based on them. The survey team typically requires both generalists and specialists, many of them for six months to a year or even longer, to analyze the sector and prepare a report. In an attempt to do justice to the subject, most of these studies are heavily descriptive and institutional, their policy and project recommendations diffuse and numerous, and the survey reports themselves so bulky that busy officials are discouraged from tackling them. Such volumes, seldom opened, fill the bookcases of officials in many developing countries. In a world where resources, including the talent to do good sector analysis, are scarce and time is short, it is usually advantageous to concentrate instead on more tightly focused studies that address specific sector and subsector problems.

Special sector studies have proved indispensable as a basis for specific policy recommendations and for the design of individual projects. They are also required in most sectors for another very practical reason: over a period of time a wide range of issues must be examined in each sector, including institutional and decisionmaking structures, manpower and training needs, sector investment plans, incentives for resource allocation, technology policy, shadow prices for project evaluation, statistical requirements, and so on. No single study can adequately cover all the relevant issues; moreover, much is gained from having up-to-date analyses of specific issues based on current data, rather than a comprehensive survey report that can, at best, be done no more often than every five to ten years. Governments will accordingly find it desirable to devote most sector work to a program of special studies of priority issues, phased over several years.

Many types of questions may be addressed in special sector studies. Is it worthwhile to revive a declining sugar industry and, if so, how can this best be done? What is the role of small- and medium-scale industry, and what can be done to assist it? How can cost recovery in irrigation projects be increased? What are the priority investment needs of the road transport sector for the next ten years? How is the structure of agricultural prices, taxation, and subsidies affecting the sector's performance as well as the national budget? What can be done to minimize oil imports in the future—what policies, what investments, what new government programs should be pursued? What is the state of vocational and technical training, and what needs to be done to expand its output and improve its quality? What should the country do to achieve its objective of slowing population growth? Each such question breaks down into a number of subsidiary questions that help analysts set the boundaries for their study and that define their terms of reference. Only if analysts can frame their central questions clearly is their work likely to be fruitful.

Much painful experience indicates the importance of keeping the reports on these studies brief and concise. They should concentrate on the analysis of important issues and convey the main findings and recommendations, with just sufficient background to indicate the bases on which these rest. Otherwise, reports become too long and diffuse to be useful to busy decisionmakers. Sector work is operational in purpose, concerned with identification of high-priority investments (projects), with analysis of how government policies and institutions are functioning, and, if changes seem advisable, with what those changes should be. The reports are intended for senior government officials, people who can be assumed to be generally familiar with a sector, but who may never have looked at some of its important problems in an organized, systematic way or in enough detail to make informed judgments. Sector reports should thus be selective, focusing on specific issues; analytic rather than descriptive; issue-oriented, with specific recommendations; and brief (or at least with a brief summary).

RESPONSIBILITY FOR SECTOR ANALYSIS

The number of governments that regularly carry out sector work is increasing, and the will and capacity to produce high-quality sector analysis on which policy and investment decisions can be based are growing steadily. In many countries, however, efforts are still inadequate. Governments often undertake sector studies only when confronted with serious problems, such as recurrent power or transport shortages. Some sectors may never be analyzed; others are studied only in connection with a proposal for a large investment, and then only at the urging or with the assistance of an external lender. Some governments and ministries—even in countries which devote substantial resources to investment management and planning at the national level—are not yet convinced of the need for detailed analysis at the sector level, or they believe that a general familiarity with the problems of a sector gained from normal operational experience is adequate.

It is nevertheless widely accepted that each operating ministry, department, or agency has prime responsibility, in its sector or subsector, for analysis of investment proposals, for formulating investment projects and programs, and for carrying them out or supervising their execution. Most operating ministries or agencies establish a unit of some kind—sometimes called a programming unit—to perform these functions. The characteristics of these units vary greatly among countries and ministries, but however named or organized, each unit is essentially a microcosm of a central investment planning agency. It has the same kind of relationship to the operating units and to the head of its own agency that the central investment planning agency has to the government's operating entities and to the national political authority.

Frequently, however, such programming units are not assigned clear responsibility for sector analysis of the kind described above, and as a consequence, their functioning leaves much to be desired. Sector analysis of a high quality demands substantial manpower and other resources for long periods, as well as high-level commitment. It also demands a great deal of information; as a result, it may show up gaps—often serious—in the data needed for analysis of a particular sector problem. Sector agencies often do not have the necessary mix of technical, economic, financial, and other skilled staff for sector studies; if they do, they find it difficult to spare them from other duties. Their programming units are often understaffed, headed by junior officials, and established at too low a level in the organization. Furthermore, within many traditional ministries, a variety of organizational, procedural, and bureaucratic impediments to coordination interferes with the establishment and effective working of programming units. When, on top of all these difficulties, the intellectual and resource demands of good sector analysis are added, the hurdles may simply be too high for many old-line operating organizations to clear.

Although central planning agencies benefit from the presence of programming units in operating ministries that can provide sectoral expertise and programs, few of them are in a position to help establish or strengthen such units. Most central agencies are themselves understaffed and overworked, and they may not have the particular talents needed. A country without universities or research institutes may have to rely heavily on expatriates, lending agencies, or foreign consultants to do sector work while local staff is being trained to take over increasing responsibility. External assistance is available from many sources, including both bilateral institutions and multilateral institutions such as the World Bank, regional development banks, and various agencies of the United Nations (UNDP, FAO, Unesco, WHO, and UNIDO). Substantial resources are provided by these institutions to supplement country efforts.

In the following chapters of part II, we look at the main sectors of the economy. Each chapter, after describing the distinctive characteristics of the sector, assesses the important development issues, including government objectives, the policy and institutional changes needed to achieve such objectives, and problems that arise in designing and implementing investment programs and projects in the sector. These chapters draw on the Bank's work with many countries on policy reforms, institutional improvements, and investment projects—action on all three of which, experience has shown, is essential to enhance a sector's performance and its contribution to the national economy.

Although the sector chapters generally follow a similar format, they vary considerably in emphasis and scope depending on the characteristics of the sector and on the experience of the Bank in that sector. Decisive in the way each sector is presented are the amount of project lending that has been completed and has reached the stage of evaluation, and the aspects of that experience that can most usefully be brought to the attention of officials in developing countries.

Readers are reminded that they are not expected to read straight through part II, but are advised to focus on those chapters that cover sectors of immediate interest or concern and then to move on to the discussion of the project cycle in part III.

Choosing seeds from wheat hybrids at Punjab Agricultural University, India

6

Agriculture

Characteristics of the Sector

AGRICULTURE REMAINS the backbone of the economy of most developing countries. Typically, it is the largest source of employment; often two-thirds or more of the population are dependent for its livelihood on farming. The labor-intensive character of the sector reduces its contribution to the gross domestic product, but it nevertheless ranges between 20 and 60 percent in most developing countries. Agricultural exports are a principal earner of foreign exchange. A strong and growing agricultural sector, it is increasingly recognized, is essential to economic development, both in its own right and to stimulate and support the growth of industry.

Several characteristics of agricultural production differentiate it from other productive sectors.

- Crop and livestock production are complex biological processes interacting in ways that continually change. Despite improved knowledge about how these processes work, much is still not well understood.

- Even with advanced and sophisticated production techniques, there is an inescapable natural rhythm of events in farming. Output is influenced so greatly by climatic conditions and uncontrollable biological phenomena that a large degree of variability and therefore risk always exists.

- Production can be organized in a wide variety of ways. Different production technologies are needed for plantations and for small village plots; for nomadic herdsmen and for intensive, feed-lot cattle operations; for individual farms, collective farms, and state-owned farms; for full-time and part-time operators; and for tenants and landowners under commercial and subsistence conditions.

- Farming is frequently in the hands of millions of family units. For widespread technological change to take place, very large numbers of decisionmakers have to adopt innovations.

- The practice of agriculture has close links with the life of rural people. Many customs and traditions spring out of the cycle of the farming year, while farming fortunes and the general welfare are inextricably entwined. Any innovation that modifies farming activities has a greater effect on the fabric of society than innovation in a sector in which work and home, employment and leisure, are separate.

- Agricultural development depends on a host of complementary activities. Whether or not they are embraced in a single project, investment in agriculture—both public and private—may include settlement, improvement, or reorganization of land; development and use of irrigation; research to develop a technological package and extension services to disseminate it; supply of inputs (seeds, fertilizers, pesticides); credit for purchasing seasonal inputs or for equipment and other longer-term investments; facilities for storage, processing, and marketing; rural roads, potable water, electricity, schools, health services, and other infrastructure; and measures to strengthen the relevant institutions and to train their management and staff.

Economic Aspects

In most developing countries, agriculture is both the main traditional pursuit and the key to sustained growth of the modern economy. Economic growth has gone hand in hand with agricultural progress: stagnation in agriculture is the principal explanation for poor economic performance, while rising agricultural productivity has been the most important concomitant of successful industrialization. A thriving agricultural sector fulfills several functions:

- It absorbs considerable increases in the labor force, especially as seasonal labor.
- It provides a market for goods produced by industry and fosters the growth of secondary industries in the countryside.
- It provides food for urban workers and fiber and other raw materials for industrial processes.
- It generates investable funds for the industrial sector. This occurs when there is both a surplus of capital in agriculture and mechanisms for its transfer through private investment, taxation, or changes in the domestic terms of trade.
- It furnishes labor to industry. This is also a transfer of capital when the cost of educating and training the workers has been borne in the countryside.

By comparison with earlier periods of history, world agricultural growth from 1950 to 1980 has been impressive, averaging 3.1 percent a year in the 1950s, 2.6 percent in the 1960s, and 2.2 percent in the 1970s. The developing countries fared even better, sustaining an agricultural growth of almost 3 percent a year during the entire period (see table 6-1).

Table 6-1. *Growth Rates of Agriculture and Food Output by Region, 1960–80*

	Agricultural output				Food output			
	Total		Per capita		Total		Per capita	
Region	1960–70	1970–80	1960–70	1970–80	1960–70	1970–80	1960–70	1970–80
Developing countries	2.8	2.7	0.3	0.3	2.9	2.8	0.4	0.4
Africa	2.7	1.3	0.2	−1.4	2.6	1.6	0.1	−1.1
Middle East	2.5	2.7	0.0	0.0	2.6	2.9	0.1	0.2
Latin America	2.9	3.0	0.1	0.6	3.6	3.3	0.1	0.6
Southeast Asia	2.9	3.8	0.3	1.4	2.8	3.8	0.3	1.4
South Asia	2.5	2.2	0.1	0.0	2.6	2.2	0.1	0.0
Southern Europe	3.1	3.5	1.8	1.9	3.2	3.5	1.8	1.9

Note: Production data are weighted by world export unit prices. Decade growth rates are based on midpoints of five-year averages, except that 1970 is the average for 1969–71. China is excluded.

Source: World Bank, *World Development Report 1982* (New York: Oxford University Press, 1982), p. 41.

Indeed, agricultural growth in the developing countries has exceeded all earlier experience and expectations. Among the notable achievements, India and the Philippines are now self-sufficient in food grain production. Much of this growth has occurred in staple food production, in contrast with earlier periods when most of the expansion took place in export crops such as coffee, cocoa, rubber, and oilseeds.

But optimism must be tempered. Because of the relatively rapid rise in population, per capita growth rates were modest for both food and agriculture during the 1960s, 1970s, and early 1980s. Africa's plight is particularly difficult; the continent as a whole has not increased its food output over the past decade, and the dependence of African countries on food imports has increased. Some 100 million people in the developing world cannot rely on having sufficient food. Perhaps ten times that number are in a precarious nutritional situation because instability of production, owing mainly to the weather, poses the threat of food shortages. The hungry can be identified as those without an income adequate to give them access to available food supplies or to the means to produce food directly.[1] The race to keep developing-country food supplies ahead of population growth will continue—and indeed its pace may accelerate. Moreover, food demand will grow with rising incomes. Continued growth of production to meet these pressures will be more difficult since much of the best land and the most accessible water resources are already being exploited. Once production problems are solved, the second generation of problems—achieving better distribution through marketing—will take on greater importance.

Land and water, the principal natural resources used in agriculture, are very unevenly distributed among developing countries. Wide differences in the quality of land, the climate, and the size and structure of landholdings add to the diversity of growing conditions. Slightly more than half (54 percent) of the earth's arable land is in the developing world, much of it divided into more than 100 million smallholdings (less than five hectares), especially in Asia and Africa.

Availability of water has been a crucial factor in agricultural growth. About 20 percent of the cultivated land in developing countries is under irrigation, but it accounts for more than 40 percent of annual crop production. China, with 49 million hectares, and India, with 40 million, contain more than half of the world's irrigated land.

Social Aspects

Contrary to the opinion once prevailing, farmers, though influenced by sociocultural traditions, are not bound by them. Throughout the developing world—whether their holdings are small, medium, or large—farmers respond positively to incentives and opportunities. The principal constraints on agricultural growth lie less in the attitudes of farmers than in the environment, both natural and man-made, in which they operate and in the technology and resources available to them.

1. See C. Peter Timmer, Walter P. Falcon, and Scott R. Pearson, *Food Policy Analysis* (Baltimore, Md.: Johns Hopkins University Press for the World Bank, 1983).

Population

The total population in developing countries grew at an average rate of 2.2 percent a year from 1955 to 1980. The population growth rate in rural areas was lower (1.7 percent), owing in part to migration to the cities, but nonetheless substantial and on a very large base. These are higher rates of growth than those experienced by developed countries during comparable stages of industrialization. The vast and growing populations in the rural areas are at the root of the serious problems of hunger, unemployment, low incomes, poor health, and inadequate education. Moreover, rural populations are often split into small, isolated communities and villages, separated by physical and cultural barriers and often by caste and religious differences as well. Severe unemployment and underemployment in one village may coexist with unfulfilled demand for labor in another. These barriers tend to break down as the economy grows and commercial links are forged. In the early stages, however, they make equitable access to basic infrastructure and social services difficult.

Access to Infrastructure and Services

The countryside in developing countries is underserved in almost all respects. Many villages lack access to larger communities or to major markets over an all-weather road. Rural electrification, safe water, and sanitation services reach much smaller proportions of the population than in urban areas. Telephones, except for official use, are largely unknown. Health facilities are widely dispersed, and health personnel assigned to rural areas gravitate to large centers where conditions of service are less onerous and better equipment is available.

Rural education, on the whole, is poor, with facilities well below urban standards. Attracting good teachers to rural areas is a perennial problem. Adult illiteracy rates are still high since the education programs launched recently concentrate on children. School attendance is frequently interrupted by the demands of farm work. Low standards of academic performance are also linked to the widespread problems of disease and malnutrition.

Poverty

Close to 1 billion people are estimated to be living in absolute poverty. A preponderant majority of these live in rural areas, principally in South and East Asia, especially in India, China, Bangladesh, and Indonesia.[2] One-sixth live in sub-Saharan Africa. The incidence of poverty is spread unevenly within the family, with the primary income earners kept physically able to work at the cost of acute deprivation for women and children (especially girls), who make up a disproportionate share of those in absolute poverty.

The majority of families in poverty are net purchasers of food. Those with the lowest incomes get too few calories to sustain healthy lives; they tend to be without assets (in particular, without land), illiterate, and with insufficient access to productive employment. Many of them live either

2. World Bank, *World Development Report 1982* (New York: Oxford University Press, 1982), p. 78.

on extremely small farms or on larger tracts that do not lend themselves to farming because of climatic or soil conditions. Poor families have few income earners relative to the number to be supported. This is why the solution to undernutrition is to increase employment and income rather than the food supply itself. The poor play a minor role in village life; they have little opportunity to participate meaningfully in society's institutions and equally little power to influence the course of their own lives.

An important feature of rural poverty is its seasonal stress. During the wet season, after crops are planted, the poor have increasing difficulty in finding paid work, and they run down their food supplies. This is also the time that diseases are at their peak because of weather conditions. Undernutrition increases the susceptibility of the poor to illness, which in turn makes it difficult for them to get the limited work that is available. Survival may sometimes depend on borrowing, which can lead to an inescapable burden of indebtedness.

Migration

The expansion of income-earning opportunities in agriculture has not been sufficient to forestall large-scale migration from the countryside to urban areas. In India, the urban population grew an average of 3.9 percent a year from 1970 to 1982; in other low-income countries (excluding China), it grew 5.2 percent. It is striking, however, that in low-income Africa, where agricultural production has grown less rapidly than in other low-income developing regions, the rate of urbanization has been greater.

Although many urban areas have handled the tremendous influx well, the need remains to employ as many people as possible in rural areas, if not actually on farms. Stimulating agricultural productivity will not only help stem migration but will also support urban employment by providing enough food to keep prices and hence wages within bounds and to encourage labor-intensive production.

Financial Aspects

Because agriculture looms so large in the economies of developing countries, it is traditional for governments to look to it as the main source of development funds for the whole economy. Governments have gained access to agricultural surpluses through various taxes, levies, and charges. The earliest and most common form of taxes—poll (head) taxes in Africa and land taxes in Asia—have tended to be regressive, weighing more heavily on low-income than on high-income families. In principle, land taxes can be fixed at higher rates for better quality land, but many countries have found it difficult to set a progressive rate structure.

Another device commonly used in developing countries is the export tax, which is simple to collect if the agricultural commodity being exported passes through the hands of a marketing agency. Export taxes have been an important source of public revenue in some countries, but have frequently acted as a disincentive to production of the commodity. Income taxes have proved to be complicated to levy and collect in rural areas. It is difficult to assess incomes and prevent tax evasion when there are few written records and many informal transactions, and such taxes are seldom effectively imposed on low-income farmers. The category of levies that is generally least satisfactory as a source of revenue is user charges. Governments frequently provide farmers with inputs such as electricity or irrigation water for charges or fees that are insufficient to cover even operation and maintenance costs, let alone repayment of the capital investment.

Public funds flow back into agriculture through subsidies on inputs or outputs or through public investments. Traditionally, governments have provided physical infrastructure, agricultural research, and activities that develop human capital such as extension, education, and health facilities. Provision of irrigation and drinking water usually involves a mixture of public and private initiatives. Construction of irrigation infrastructure often absorbs a large proportion of the public funds devoted to agriculture. Farm improvements, including equipment, buildings, livestock, wells, and minor irrigation structures, are most often the result of private investment. The credit to finance such investments frequently comes from public sector institutions, usually at subsidized interest rates. This practice, combined with poor performance in debt collection, has weakened the financial position of the credit institutions.

The net flow of funds through these various channels is away from agriculture in most developing countries. Perhaps more significant in the long run is the differential and uncertain impact of the various levies, charges, and subsidies on incentives for agricultural production.

Institutional Aspects

Once subsistence farming becomes commercialized, with technology beginning to change and cash to flow, then basic infrastructure—roads, electricity, communications, and markets—must be built and a multifarious network of institutions established. The latter is, in many respects, the lengthiest and most difficult phase of agricultural development; creating skilled cadres to manage institutions and finding means to improve planning, decisionmaking, and implementation are especially problematic.

The principal institutions needed to support a dynamic agriculture include those associated directly with the processes of production and distribution: research, extension, input supply, rural finance, diagnostic services, transportation, storage and marketing, operation and maintenance of infrastructure, processing of agricultural goods, and repair and maintenance of equipment. Intertwined with all of these are the regulatory institutions that preside over land tenure arrangements, trading practices, licensing and certification, price policies, labor and employment practices, collection of statistics, and dissemination of information, along with the welfare institutions that attempt to protect the poorest groups in society and to promote greater equity. Finally, the basic institutions that shape the conduct of community life—religious and political groupings, local government, cooperatives, farmer associations, and the like—all have important effects on farmers as producers.

There has been a notable growth in the postwar period in the role of public and parastatal organizations in developing-country agriculture. Centralized buying and selling agencies for both domestic and foreign trade of food and nonfood products have proliferated. Their performance record has been uneven, and numerous problems have arisen as a result of distorted price incentives, inefficient operations, political interference, and large deficits. Defining the proper role for government intervention and executing that role properly are now high on the agenda for public action.

DEVELOPMENT OBJECTIVES

There are five broad objectives of agricultural development to which most governments subscribe: growth, sustainability, stability, equity, and efficiency. The priority given to these objectives may vary from country to country, but poor performance with respect to any of them has commonly been grounds for government intervention. These objectives, therefore, condition the framework of agricultural policies and the scope and character of public action.

For many governments, the primary objective is *growth*, both in output and productivity. Additional output is needed to meet the growing demands of an expanding population with rising incomes, to increase exports or reduce import dependency, to create jobs and incomes for rural people, to meet the demands of other sectors for raw materials, and to generate more revenue to invest in both the rural and urban sectors. Of these, the need to make more food available to a growing population is often a government's main priority.

Sustainability means being able to maintain adequate levels of production in the future. The finiteness of some global resources is being increasingly recognized, as is the need to renew periodically the elements of scientific farming (such as seeds of high-yielding varieties) to ensure their effectiveness. To preserve the production base, fixed resources must be conserved and renewable resources (including soils and forests) managed so that they can rejuvenate. Not only investment but also innovation need to be fostered as a continuing, self-sustaining process, with profits reinvested and technology continually upgraded.

Economic policy has traditionally been concerned with *stability*, which has particular significance for agriculture. Not only must farm policy seek to ameliorate the booms and recessions of the trade cycle, it must also take account of the inherent instability of agricultural output because of weather and biological exigencies. While modern farming methods help to insulate production from some of the vagaries of nature, it remains essentially a biological process not totally subject to managerial control.

The three objectives of growth, sustainability, and stability relate closely to the goal of "food security." This concept, to which we shall return, has recently gained prominence in policy discussions.

Equity in the distribution of the benefits of agricultural activity among the participants is a prime objective of most governments. How these benefits are distributed is often determined by the marketplace; the outcome is influenced by who owns and earns what at the outset and by how different markets function. As a consequence, a policy framework that tries to foster higher production in agriculture must also address questions of equity.

The fifth objective is *efficiency*. Any waste of resources as a result of using more inputs than are necessary to generate a given output is a real loss to the economy; given the size of the agricultural sector in most developing countries, such losses can be of very large magnitude. Some inefficiency is unavoidable, especially when it stems from imperfect information, uncontrollable external influences, or other characteristics of a dynamic environment. But few countries can afford the inefficiencies associated with the distortion of resource allocation caused by inappropriate price and other policies.

POLICY ISSUES

Prices and the Economic Environment

One of the most pervasive lessons of Bank experience, already stressed in part I, is that it is difficult to do good project work in a bad policy environment. Nowhere is this more evident than in agriculture. As the largest sector and one that typically comprises many small, dispersed, and independent decisionmaking units, it is particularly exposed to the economic environment and to the effects of government policy.

Most farmers in developing countries have a small margin for survival, can ill afford to suffer losses, and display considerable skill in managing their limited resources. As a result, their production and consumption choices are very responsive to relative prices. Economic incentives help to determine how resources are allocated, which crops produced, which inputs used intensively, and which longer-term investments made.

Macroeconomic Policy

Prices play a central role in determining the direction, character, and rate of agricultural progress. Fluctuations of commodity prices in world markets can be a major destabilizing factor, and government interventions—fixed procurement prices, price guarantees, or deficiency payments of some kind—have frequently been useful in buffering the prices received by farmers so that production incentives are maintained. But too often government interventions have distorted relative prices, sending inappropriate economic signals to producers. At the macroeconomic policy level (discussed in chapter 3, Pricing Policy), a common intervention has been the imposition of price controls on farm products so that food is cheap for urban consumers—who are better educated, more vocal, and better organized to exercise political power. The effect is to transfer income from rural producers to urban consumers.

A further and frequently massive shift in the internal terms of trade against agriculture results from the extensive use of tariffs, quotas, and other trade restrictions to protect local manufactures against foreign competition. This kind of protection allows the prices of manufactured goods to rise in the domestic market relative to those of agricultural products. Similarly, by fixing an exchange rate that undervalues foreign exchange, imports (typically of industrial goods) are encouraged while exports (typically of agricultural products and other raw materials) are taxed and inhibited.

Government policies affecting the relative prices of inputs such as labor and farm machinery have a major bearing on the farmers' choice of technology. Implicit import subsidies through the exchange rate encourage the use of capital-intensive methods among the small group of farmers who can afford to import equipment. Incentives to the domestic equipment industry, often in the form of below-market interest rates, can also exacerbate the tendency toward excessive use of capital by large farmers.

An extreme case of the impact of distorted prices on the choice of technology arose in a tea project in western Uganda in the early 1980s. The country had a highly overvalued currency along with a tight exchange control regime to deal with the ensuing acute shortage of foreign exchange. Tea export prices, in local currency, were severely depressed by the official exchange rate and, by the same token, imported equipment was highly subsidized—for those who could acquire a foreign exchange allocation. Faced with these low prices for tea and for capital equipment, the tea-producing companies were nonetheless required to pay high wages inflated by labor regulations and taxes and by the scarcity—and therefore high prices—of goods on which wages could be spent. Consequently, the companies found that tea harvesting, normally a highly labor-intensive activity, could be done more cheaply by machine. For the economy as a whole, however, labor resources were relatively abundant and cheap, while foreign exchange and (imported) capital equipment were scarce and expensive; therefore, the use of tea-harvesting machinery made no sense. The distorted incentive system had sent producers an entirely wrong signal.

Specific Prices, Taxes, and Subsidies

Policy interventions within the agricultural sector have tended to reinforce the effect of macroeconomic policies, and for the same reasons. When prices of crops have been fixed not for general anti-inflationary reasons but as part of specific commodity programs, policymakers have been prone to give greater weight to the desire of urban consumers for low food prices than to the need of rural producers for adequate incentives. If pressures on producers' margins became too great, an "offsetting" subsidy for farm inputs such as fertilizer was provided. While this might seem to offer some rough justice, in fact it may compound the problem for several reasons. Input subsidies are not likely to offset the effect of low output prices, since typically the cost of agricultural inputs is a small part of the total cost of production. Also, a subsidy may induce excessive or uneconomic use of an input such as fertilizer or, more likely, divert it for sale through extralegal channels. The benefits of subsidies are most frequently garnered by the larger and more prosperous producers and may seldom reach those for whom they are presumably intended. Finally, the cost of the subsidies can be a heavy burden on the public budget, as it has been in Bangladesh and Nigeria, for example.

Overvaluing the local currency imposes an implicit tax on agricultural exports. This is sometimes accompanied by direct taxes or levies, often a favorite means of raising revenues since they are relatively easy to collect and can generate substantial funds. Their economic effect, however, is to squeeze farmers' profit margins and reduce the incentive to produce. In some countries, export taxes or levies have frustrated another important government objective, that of increasing exports and thereby earning foreign exchange. In extreme cases, the combination of implicit and explicit taxes has caused exports to decline so much that the revenue base for government has been eroded. The familiar adage not to kill the goose that lays the golden eggs makes good economic sense.

A variation on the above theme occurs when, again ostensibly in pursuit of an equity objective, uniform prices for agricultural outputs or inputs are fixed throughout a large area or even countrywide, despite wide differences in transport costs. Such official systems of panterritorial pricing inhibit the development of an efficient network of commercial trade and storage based on comparative costs. They are further contraventions of the efficiency rule that, in most cases, market prices should be allowed to reflect opportunity costs to the economy as a whole.

The links between the policy framework and the performance of individual agricultural projects can be very close. Only if new production methods are clearly seen to be more profitable than existing ones will farmers adopt them—and the profit margin must be sufficient to cover whatever premium is required to overcome the perceived risk. There are many cases of projects trying unsuccessfully to move counter to general government policies or of successful projects suddenly running aground because of a policy shift. What this calls for is flexibility in project design, along with as close ties as possible between project officials and government policymakers.

Income Distribution and Poverty

Many government interventions, through the price mechanism and otherwise, have the commendable objective of improving the distribution of income and alleviating poverty in rural areas. Unfortunately, rhetoric and reality do not always coincide. Unless carefully designed to reach specific target groups and rigorously administered for that purpose, the actual transfers of income have tended to reflect less the relative poverty than the relative political power of various groups in society.

In Malaysia, for example, land with more profitable alternative uses has been kept in high-cost rice production through subsidies designed to support the incomes of a poor but politically important group. These subsidies, which have been applied to both inputs and outputs, have gone overwhelmingly to larger, richer producers who deliver paddy to the official or licensed agencies. The system has left the poorest rural group virtually untouched. In Sudan, massive consumer subsidies for wheat have been justified on the grounds of consumer poverty. But the low wheat prices have undermined the incentives for local wheat producers. The result has been large wheat imports and consequent budgetary and foreign exchange problems. Furthermore, most wheat is consumed in urban centers, so the poorest people, located in rural areas, have generally not benefited at all from the subsidy.

Governments, of course, have an important role to play in alleviating rural poverty. But it is essential to choose methods of intervention carefully, and to recognize that when wealth and political power are unevenly distributed it is difficult to target subsidies so that they reach the intended groups.

Infrastructure and Services

Often more effective than subsidies in alleviating poverty, while at the same time stimulating economic growth, has been the provision of infrastructure—roads, electricity, water, schools, and so forth—on which farm productivity and the quality of rural life depend. (The provision of agricultural research and extension services and other forms of technical assistance to raise the productivity of poor farmers is discussed later in this chapter.)

It has long been recognized that sustained agricultural development requires striking an appropriate balance between investments that are directly productive and investments in infrastructure. The physical isolation of farmers makes them especially vulnerable to the effects of poor infrastructure services. Much of the high productivity of agriculture in the United States and other developed countries is the result of massive off-farm investments, over many years, in physical and institutional infrastructure. Conversely, the low productivity of agriculture in many developing countries reflects, among other things, limited investments in rural roads, water, and the like. This is not merely a consequence of underdevelopment; it also stems from a concentration of public investments in urban areas, where the unit cost of providing service is typically less and the logistical problems fewer.

Progress toward providing adequate rural infrastructure has inevitably been slow, but it has been more rapid and self-sustaining when local communities have been mobilized to help plan the facilities, provide part-time labor for construction, and above all assume responsibility for operating and maintaining the facilities. Planning a rural development project provides an opportunity to incorporate basic infrastructure for people currently without access to services. Indeed, because certain types of infrastructure—such as roads and markets—are essential to increased agricultural production, unless they are made available through the project or parallel investments, the project's production goals may not be attainable.

Roads

Provision of rural roads is often a first step, since access to markets must accompany the shift from subsistence to commercial agriculture. Improved all-weather roads bring traders, truckers, and officials to villages, help encourage health and education personnel to live there, and enable villagers to travel to markets and elsewhere.

It is difficult to measure the benefits of rural roads, and especially to separate these benefits from those of other investments undertaken simultaneously. Because the benefits are widely shared, responsibility for road maintenance tends to be diffuse. Maintenance is often neglected and measures to ensure its adequacy have to be built into the design of rural infrastructure projects at the outset. The two most challenging tasks in the design of rural roads are deciding their location and resisting the temptation to incorporate design standards or construction techniques that are too elaborate and costly. Labor-intensive methods may often be the most appropriate.

Livestock Services

The need to coordinate productive and infrastructure investments also applies to livestock. Improved animals are more productive but also more susceptible to disease. An adequate disease-control facility should be able to identify and monitor epidemics, acquire appropriate vaccines and drugs, and administer a disease-control program. Farmers have often learned the hard way that investing in genetically improved livestock is too risky without such services.

The livestock example also illustrates the importance of drawing the appropriate line between public and private services. Experience has shown that epidemiological veterinary services can best be provided by public entities rather than by individual producers and private clinicians because of externalities (uncontrolled infectious disease in one herd can affect other herds) and economies of scale (some diseases need to be addressed on a regional basis). Clinical veterinary services to individual animals and farms, in contrast, are usually not well handled by the public sector. Many small, specific decisions need to be made about how much to spend on an animal given its chances of recovery, its potential productivity, and its slaughter value. Such decisions do not lend themselves to across-the-board regulation by official agencies. Also, unless the costs of the intervention enter into the calculation of the user, excessive demand for services will strain the capacity of clinics. This leads, in turn, to rationing devices and, not uncommonly, to eventual bankruptcy of the sponsoring agency. In some African countries where clinical veterinary services are supposedly provided by the public sector, no money is allocated for drugs or even for the transport of professional staff. Clinical services have generally been performed by government staff acting in a private capacity, while the epidemiological services for which they are uniquely responsible have deteriorated.

Marketing

A part of the infrastructure network that assumes increasing importance as farm surpluses grow and urban populations rise is the postharvest system for collecting, storing, transporting, processing, and retailing those surpluses—referred to for brevity as "marketing." In the middle-income developing countries, the value added from marketing agricultural commodities often exceeds that from production. In the low-income countries, food marketing systems typically account for at least 10 percent of GDP and for an even greater share of employment for the poor. Yet marketing is an aspect of project work that is frequently neglected and that deserves more attention when designing projects.

The lack of marketing opportunities acts as a powerful disincentive to farmers. This has been a major problem throughout sub-Saharan Africa, where marketing accounts for a greater share of total costs of production and delivery than in densely populated, irrigated farming areas. Because producers are more dispersed, output is lower and more variable and transport costs higher. As a result, improving marketing systems can be as important as introducing farming methods that increase yields; indeed, the latter may otherwise be ineffective.

Marketing is another area where the line between private and public enterprise has not always been satisfactorily drawn in practice. The requirements for a food distribution pipeline from farmer to consumer include some activities that are clearly in the public domain: for example, organizing the flow of information on weather, crop production, and trade and providing feeder roads, rural markets, and grading services. But at the same time, efficient marketing of the surpluses of small farmers calls for rapid responses to varied and quickly changing local requirements, a task not suited to centrally administered bureaucracies. For example, when the Indian government banned all private marketing of wheat in 1973, government agencies were unable to handle the movement of food to all the places where it was needed, and the black market took over until small merchants were allowed to return. Seemingly chaotic food markets operated by traditional intermediaries have in fact been efficient and reliable in assembling supplies from thousands of small farmers, often in very small lots, and making them available to consumers hundreds of miles away.

Despite the impressive efficiency of private food markets, many developing countries have created state-owned enterprises (commonly called parastatals) to buy farmers' surpluses, manage international food trade, handle transport and wholesaling, or engage in processing food or supplying inputs. A survey by the FAO indicates that in 1981 there were more than 100 such institutions in developing countries.[3] Their annual sales turnover was probably well over $10 billion. The relative importance of such parastatals varies greatly. Their share in the marketing of food commodities, for example, depends on the commodity (largest in rice, wheat, and maize), the part of the country (largest in the principal cities), and the time of year (largest when the seasonal production cycle is at its peak).

Experience has shown that food marketing parastatals do not have to be given monopoly control, or even a major market share, to achieve legitimate government objectives with respect to food security or price stability. In some countries, the only interventions undertaken have been to control international trade; Brazil, Ivory Coast, Malaysia, and Thailand, which are among the most successful agricultural exporters in the developing world, use this approach. Elsewhere, parastatals have operated in farming districts without displacing existing distribution networks, as in Indonesia, where the great bulk of food entering commercial channels continues to be handled by merchants (who may resell to the parastatal).

When parastatals have been given a monopoly position, however, they have often become fertile breeding grounds for political interference, patronage, and corruption. In the absence of competitive pressures, operations have generally been costly and inefficient, and the ensuing large deficits have drained government revenues. When private merchants have been in competition with less efficient parastatals, subsidies given to the parastatals have sometimes driven out the private traders, with a corresponding reduction in marketing efficiency and in the access of small farmers to markets. The performance record of parastatals in food production and food processing is even more unsatisfactory: the

3. Food and Agriculture Organization, *List of Marketing Boards, 1981* (Rome, 1982).

almost universal inefficiency of rice mills operated by the public sector is a case in point. Experience with the use of parastatals for input supply is no better, again with small farmers usually those least well served.

Food Security

Few things have so pervasive an effect on the lives of people throughout the world as uncertainties associated with the food system. These begin with the element of risk faced by every farmer in deciding how much of what kinds of food to grow, and they extend to decisions by each household about how much can be spent on food, and even about how the food will be shared. The food system, it should be remembered, comprises not only a great diversity of farmers, consumers, and markets; it also includes—or, more correctly, "excludes"—millions of chronically undernourished people whose access to food is constantly threatened.

Enough food is available worldwide to satisfy the nutritional requirements of everyone; in the past decade, the global capacity to produce food has outstripped the growth of population and kept pace with global demand. With over 200 million tons of grain in reserves, the world's overall supply of food in 1984 was greater than it had been for decades. These reserves were sufficient to meet 20 percent of current worldwide consumption needs.[4] But the purchasing power with which to acquire food is very unevenly distributed both among and within countries. Moreover, fluctuations in domestic production and in the supplies and prices of imported cereals can substantially alter the amount of food available for domestic consumption, as can changes in the availability of foreign exchange with which to purchase food imports. Countries in sub-Saharan Africa have been the hardest hit by prolonged droughts, and per capita production has declined in recent years.

The major challenge for governments in developing countries is to pursue the economic policies that will ultimately enable every household to produce or purchase sufficient food. Moreover, governments need to promote more efficient marketing and trading of food along with greater food production. Governments must, in other words, address both the demand for and the supply of food.

Enabling poorer households to purchase an adequate supply of food means increasing their incomes. This occurs in part through the normal process of economic development and the generation of employment. More specific steps to be taken in the rural areas, among the many discussed in this and other chapters, include raising producer prices, increasing farm yields through the spread of new technologies and improved management, and providing off-farm employment opportunities.

Experience has shown that, in many countries, once demand for food—backed by purchasing power—increases, the supply side generally responds appropriately. Nevertheless, this is by no means guaranteed, and specific actions may be necessary to remove constraints on production. Similarly, food must be available in the right form and place and at the right time to meet demand, including emergency demand resulting

---

4. Montague Yudelman, "Agricultural Lending by the Bank, 1974–1984," *Finance and Development*, vol. 21, no. 4 (December 1984), p. 47.

from drought. Upgrading the infrastructure needed to move food efficiently from ports or production centers to storage points and places of consumption can make an important contribution to improving the distribution of food and reducing its cost to consumers. Efficient marketing services, as we have seen, also play a part. Furthermore, trade policies with respect to such matters as exchange rates and tariffs can be managed to influence the prices of food imports and exports and thereby the supplies and prices to consumers.

Many developing countries have a comparative advantage in the production of certain foods and other agricultural commodities that can earn foreign exchange for the import of other foods. To benefit from this advantage, governments should avoid implicit taxation of these commodities through the kinds of price policies previously discussed. Such taxation of farm output has been a deterrent to production in many countries and regions, notably in sub-Saharan Africa.

Some holding of food stocks to smooth out seasonal variations may be necessary, particularly in the face of market imperfections, but long-term storage of food reserves in large quantities has proved costly and difficult to manage. It is preferable to put in place and rely on appropriate food production, distribution, and trade policies.

Countries that cannot increase the supply of food sufficiently through production and trade or that suffer serious droughts usually seek food aid. Except in dire emergencies that mobilize the sympathy and support of people around the world—such as the Ethiopian famine of 1984—the amount of food a country receives depends on the overall availability of world food aid and on its relations with aid donors. The Compensatory Financing Facility of the International Monetary Fund provides another means through which governments can finance above-normal food import needs. It provides a country with an additional credit drawing to compensate for a loss of foreign exchange due to a decline in world prices for its commodity exports, a reduction in the quantity of those exports, or higher prices for its non-oil commodity imports.

Even if a country's overall supply of food can be made adequate to meet demand, it may be necessary to give direct subsidies to the poor or distribute food to them when minimum supplies cannot be afforded or do not reach them through customary channels.[5] Such measures must be carefully targeted and controlled if the intended beneficiaries are to be helped.

Land Management

Agriculture is distinguished from other economic activities by the unique importance of land as a means of production. The arrangements that societies establish concerning the ownership and use of land are diverse and have a major bearing on both economic growth and equity. Among the many issues involved in the use of land, we shall consider four: land rights and tenure, land consolidation, agrarian reform, and land degradation.

5. See Barbara Huddleston and others, *International Finance for Food Security* (Baltimore, Md.: Johns Hopkins University Press for the World Bank, 1984); and Timmer, Falcon, and Pearson, *Food Policy Analysis.*

Security of Tenure

How farmers use land is greatly affected by the degree of security of land tenure—with respect to such matters as duration of user rights, clarity of land rights, ability to sell these rights or to pass them on to succeeding generations, and ability to obtain compensation for investments. A farmer with unclear, insecure, or short-term tenure is more likely to "mine" the land, that is, to seek maximum short-run production gains through crop rotations and other practices that may degrade the biological and physical qualities of the soil. With reasonable security of tenure and appropriate rents, owners and tenants do not seem to differ in their willingness to adopt innovations, particularly those pertaining to annual crops (new varieties, fertilizers, plant protection chemicals, or improved husbandry practices). There may be a profound difference, however, in their attitudes toward investments that enhance land productivity in the long run or are essential for certain high-value uses whose benefits are realized only over time (irrigation and drainage structures, land terracing, buildings, fences, or investment in treecrops or livestock pastures). The expectation of reaping the income from such investments is critical to the decision to proceed. Differences in tenure arrangements also affect access to credit with which to finance the investment, since land is customarily used as collateral.

Governments everywhere have assumed responsibility for defining the legal conditions of using and owning land. Measures to provide more secure tenure and to protect tenants against exploitation need not affect the basic structure of landholdings, yet can have profound effects on farm productivity. Moreover, secure and favorable financing arrangements may make it more feasible for young farmers who have not yet accumulated much capital to buy land.

Land Consolidation

Under certain inheritance systems, it is common for one farmer to own a dozen or more small plots of land, sometimes scattered over a considerable area. Production problems may arise because of the small size of individual plots and the distance between them. Some irrigation projects have encountered serious difficulties when land consolidation was not identified as a need at an early stage and given high priority. Consolidation is, however, a time-consuming process; farmers are attached to their parcels of land, and it is hard to persuade them that another parcel received in exchange is of at least equivalent value. (In some circumstances, the fragmentation of landholdings can be advantageous to a farmer—for example, by spreading the risks if plots are of different soil types or affected by different weather conditions.)

Agrarian Reform

A more drastic redistribution of landholdings and rural wealth than that which results from programs to provide security of tenure or to consolidate land has sometimes been undertaken by governments through programs of agrarian reform. Ownership of land is usually skewed, with a relatively small proportion of the owners (perhaps 20 percent) holding a high proportion of the total land (perhaps 80 percent).

The distribution of farm income is likely to be even more skewed. Governments may mandate the maximum amount of land any individual or family can own or otherwise provide greater opportunities for small farmers or landless peasants to acquire land.

Experience with land reform suggests that careful preparation is essential for success. Detailed cadastral surveys have to be carried out and appropriate schemes for compensation devised. Frequently overlooked is the need for training new owners and assisting them in their initial production efforts by supplying inputs and services. A thoroughgoing land reform, even one judged to be successful in the long run, has typically been characterized by upheaval and significant declines in production in the early years. The biggest problem with most agrarian reform, however, is that governments lack the political will to implement the laws fully once they are placed on the statute books. Access and rights to land are so important to the balance of power and influence in all rural societies that, without sustained and forceful action over many years, reform laws remain mere expressions of equitable sentiment. Governments with short political horizons seldom have the staying power for this purpose. When agrarian reform is implemented successfully, however, it can bring about profound long-term changes in a society, stimulating and shaping economic development in significant ways, as in Japan, Taiwan, Egypt, and Korea.

Land Degradation

The inexorable growth of rural population has brought greater pressure to bear on fragile land ecosystems in many parts of the world. Manifestations of this pressure are soil erosion, deforestation, and overgrazing. In some places these have been proceeding at an alarming rate.

Soil erosion is most often the result of denuding areas of vegetation and leaving their soils exposed to the ravages of wind and water. The practices of shifting cultivation, extension of farming onto soils that are structurally unsuitable, multiplication of grazing animals, and cutting down forests to make room for crops or to provide fuelwood or commercial timber have all contributed. The results are not only a loss of production from affected lands, but also floods, silting up of lakes behind dams, pollution of drinking water, decreased efficiency of river navigation, and adverse changes in the habitats of wildlife and fish. Since the environmental damage caused by soil erosion transcends the responsibility or influence of individual farmers, a strong case can be made for government initiatives. Measures that can be employed range from incentives to farmers— to plant trees, construct contour bunds, or carry out other control measures—to government investments in flood control structures, compensation to farmers who abandon their land, or the establishment of institutional arrangements to control grazing of livestock.

An estimated 10 million hectares of forests are removed each year in developing countries. About three-quarters of the population of these countries rely primarily on organic materials, principally fuelwood, for cooking. Fuelwood supplies are dwindling rapidly and the costs of obtaining them increasing. One result has been greater use of dung and agricultural residues as fuel, which deprives soils of nutrients and organic conditioning materials. An FAO study identified twenty-five countries with an acute fuelwood deficit.[6] Eighteen of these countries are in Africa, stretching in a broad belt from Somalia and Sudan to Tanzania and across the continent through the Sahel region to Mauritania. The others are Bangladesh, Nepal, and Afghanistan in Asia, the two Yemens in the Middle East, and Haiti and Peru in Latin America.

A potentially important measure for dealing with this problem is the introduction of more efficient cooking stoves in rural areas. These stoves may be able to save large amounts of fuelwood, although design and distribution problems have not yet been fully solved. Another emerging response, used in India, is to grow fuelwood species as an alternate and commercially viable crop on farms or in village woodlots. Sometimes food crops can also be used to produce fuels, the most striking example being sugarcane for ethanol production in Brazil.

Overgrazing has occurred where grazing land is under various forms of communal ownership or use. A classic problem is that individuals using communal land cannot reap the full benefits of any improvements they undertake, nor do they bear the full costs of any exploitative action in which they engage. As a result, livestock owners have tended to increase the size of their flocks and herds grazing on common land, and the overall carrying capacity of the land has declined as it has become denuded of vegetation. Severe water or wind erosion may follow. The problem is exacerbated when social status is proportional to the number of animals owned.

Overgrazing is particularly acute in nomadic pastoral areas of Africa's Sahel and on communal lands in India, Nepal, and the Middle East. In China, it is confined to areas in the north, and in Latin America to higher altitudes. Although this problem clearly calls for government action in the collective interest, finding a solution has proved virtually impossible under communal forms of ownership and use. Drastic changes—which are politically difficult and socially disruptive—are required. With different tenure arrangements, it would be possible to make investments in pasture improvements and to implement management measures that would raise the land's carrying capacity and sustain it at a higher level.

Water Management

Water is a scarce resource throughout most of the developing world, and farmers must compete for it with other users. Most agricultural production depends on rainfall. Irrigation investments enable farmers to supplement rainfall and to gain some control over climatic conditions. More important, irrigation water makes it possible both to expand the area farmed and to intensify land use through double- or even triple-cropping.

Irrigation systems vary with the nature of the water source (surface water or groundwater), the scope of the irrigation program (storage, distribution, on-farm, or drainage), the stage at which management interventions are applied (new projects or rehabilitation projects), and the

6. Food and Agriculture Organization, *Map of the Fuelwood Situation in the Developing Countries* (Rome, 1981).

agent under whose control each part of the irrigation system lies (public or private sector). The complexity, cost, and profitability of irrigation systems vary greatly. Tubewells for groundwater are cheaper when this source of water is available, but they have less capacity than surface water systems with dams and canals. Grandiose schemes to develop large river basins often are politically attractive, but construction costs have tended to be very high and economic justification questionable unless high-value crops can be grown. Smaller irrigation works, in the Bank's experience, are likely to yield higher economic returns.

An important and frequently neglected irrigation problem is that of drainage. All irrigation systems need drainage either through natural means or through installations specifically for this purpose. Nevertheless, the great majority of the world's irrigation schemes were constructed without deliberate provision for drainage. Sometimes it takes many years for the problem to become apparent, as it now has in many areas. Unless the irrigation water is removed, soils eventually become waterlogged or salts toxic to plants accumulate. If soils are allowed to reach this state before something is done, restoration may be very costly and require leaching or the use of ameliorative chemicals. In some cases, the damage may be irreversible.

Proper management of irrigated water in all parts of the system is essential to obtain the full benefit of the investment made. Management approaches depend upon the nature and complexity of the system. Among the many issues relating to water management, those that the Bank has found most important include operation and maintenance of irrigation infrastructure, cost recovery, farmers' participation, and completion of ongoing projects. We shall discuss each of these in turn.

Operation and Maintenance

After irrigation projects are completed, their potential benefits will be realized only if operation and maintenance are satisfactory. These activities are complicated to organize and implement since they require skilled professionals at all levels, adequate guidelines and standards, specialized machinery and equipment, proper information and monitoring, and comprehensive system management. In many developing countries, these components are not in place. Consequently, irrigation systems do not perform efficiently, and investments deteriorate to such an extent that water supplies are not reliable and major rehabilitation efforts are needed prematurely.

Sedimentation of major dams owing to inadequate maintenance has been a common occurrence. With the actual rate of sedimentation many times higher than that assumed, expensive investments intended to yield benefits for several decades have in fact had much shorter lives. Inadequate operation and maintenance of water distribution networks, as in India and Indonesia, has limited the system's ability to allocate water to areas where its marginal productivity is highest and has deprived farmers of the full benefit of irrigation when water arrived late, if at all.

While managerial capacity to implement operation and maintenance programs is often a serious constraint, at the heart of the problem lies a failure to provide the sizable financial resources required. These resources come typically from the government, whose efforts to raise revenue for irrigation, from whatever source, are often very weak. Irrigation investments in many countries are being jeopardized because the entities responsible for the projects are unable to obtain sufficient resources in a timely fashion to manage existing systems (let alone to provide for their replacement in due course). Project justification assumes that operation and maintenance will be carried out at standards which ensure an uninterrupted flow of benefits, but Bank experience shows that without adequate resources devoted to that purpose, the basic assumption does not hold true.

Cost Recovery

To finance the operation and maintenance of irrigation systems, as well as to cover the capital cost of investment projects so that they can be expanded or replicated in other areas, the government can use not only general revenues but also—and often preferably—some form of levy on the beneficiaries. The latter is usually referred to as cost recovery. Recovery of a reasonable share of the costs from beneficiaries, whose incomes typically rise substantially, is justified on the grounds of equity. User fees also promote the more efficient use of water (especially when it is possible to charge an efficiency price) and provide additional funds to the government. (These points are discussed more fully in chapter 21, Financial Analysis.) For a variety of political and administrative reasons, it is rare for irrigation levies to be fixed at a level high enough to finance operation and maintenance, and rarer still for actual collections to match official levies. But, despite the difficulties, most countries will have to give greater attention to cost recovery if they want adequate funds for operation and maintenance. As a matter of fiscal principle, funds recovered from the beneficiaries need not be earmarked for these activities, but there are practical advantages in linking farmers' payments to tangible evidence of improved service.

Farmers' Participation

Successful management of water as it is distributed and applied below the water outlet depends largely on how efficiently farmers are organized to participate in the system. Allocation of water rights, regulation of access to water, and the timing of water supply during the cropping cycle are among the issues that need to be addressed. One reason for low cost recovery is that these issues are not considered well in advance of construction or in close consultation with the potential beneficiaries. This leaves the door open to ad hoc distribution schemes in which individual farmers cannot be sure they will receive water in the right quantities and at the right times for them to engage in intensive cropping. A water users' association can play an important role. In most developing countries, however, farmers are not well organized or do not actively participate in water management decisions. Establishment of water users' associations has now become a component of water management schemes in many Bank-assisted irrigation projects.

Completion of Ongoing Projects

In numerous instances, authorities responsible for irrigation projects have focused only on the construction of components for storing water (primarily dams) and distributing it through the main canals; they have erroneously assumed that the complementary investments would be undertaken by other authorities or by the farmers themselves. Many irrigation systems, therefore, lack a well-designed network of secondary and tertiary canals and on-farm outlets. The economic returns associated with the completion of such a network are high; the cost of the main system has already been incurred while few, if any, benefits can be realized in the absence of complementary investments in the rest of the system. Expanding the distribution network and lining canals to decrease seepage losses have also helped to provide the more reliable and secure water supplies needed for efficient management.

Technological Change

Technological change has been an important generator of agricultural growth throughout the ages. As the supply of unused arable land diminishes, technological change plays an ever larger role in increasing farm production.

The process of change from traditional to modern scientific agriculture involves a complex web of biological and socioeconomic interactions: modifying the biological processes themselves through, for example, improved seed varieties and livestock breeds; reorganizing labor operations such as weeding, pruning, or row planting; applying new chemicals such as fertilizers, veterinary medicines, and disease, pest, and weed controls; and using tools and mechanical aids such as tractors, pumps, ploughs, and threshers that supply additional power and increase the speed of operations. The distinctive features of the rural scene must be taken into account in designing strategies for introducing innovation. New technology may not be adopted in the absence of far-reaching changes in the infrastructure, institutions, distribution of gains, power structure in rural communities, organization of family and social affairs, and even in the values that guide people's lives.

Farmers generally are rational decisionmakers. They select the most productive technology they can use, given the resources available to them, their own state of knowledge, and their concern about risk. Why, then, do they often not take advantage of the best technology available? First, the inputs that embody the new technology, or are complementary to it, may not be available where and when needed because of deficiencies in the marketing and distribution system. Second, the technology may be available at the research station, but farmers may not have been made aware of it through the extension service. Third, its cost may make the new technology unaffordable, or financial disincentives may make the return on the farmers' investment in the new technology unacceptably low. Fourth, the new technology may not be suitable to their particular circumstances, in which case farmers must wait for results to emerge from the ongoing process of research and development.

Research

Research is the principal source of new agricultural technologies in the modern world. During the 1950s and 1960s, agricultural research in or for the benefit of developing countries focused on improving irrigated crops. The scientific discoveries resulting in the high-yielding varieties of rice and wheat that sparked the Green Revolution constitute one of the most significant research events of modern times. Today, farmers raising rain-fed crops in areas with poor natural resources are receiving increasing attention from national and international researchers, and their technical problems are spurring research on farming systems. With multicrop and often mixed farming systems, recommendations for each type of crop or livestock must take into account its place in the farming system, the relative importance the farmer places on it, and the fact that, under the high-risk conditions of rain-fed agriculture, farmers are concerned with greater yield stability as well as with higher yields. No spectacular breakthroughs have taken place or are within sight to improve the more intractable conditions of rain-fed agriculture, but the prospects for steady if slow progress are good.

Agricultural research has long been underfunded in many developing countries. These countries spend, on the average, only one-third as much of their agricultural GDP on research as do developed countries, although agriculture constitutes more than six times as large a share of their GDP. Well-conducted agricultural research has proved to be a highly profitable investment, and it should receive a larger commitment of public funds, even in the constrained circumstances of developing-country budgets. However, the management of research to ensure that it is well conducted is not an easy task. A balance needs to be struck, especially in small developing countries, between funding national research on problems specific to the country—including adaptation of new varieties to local growing conditions—and relying on research coming from regional or international agricultural research centers.

International assistance has played a key role in augmenting the flow of resources to this neglected field. National agricultural research has been supported by both bilateral and multilateral agencies. In addition, international agricultural research is conducted through international centers and funded by more than forty donors under the aegis of the Consultative Group on International Agricultural Research, of which the World Bank, the FAO, and the UNDP are cosponsors.

External funding cannot do the task by itself, however, and continued government support over the long haul is essential. This means generating resources internally for research on a sustained and increasing scale. If such support is not forthcoming, the long-term benefits from external assistance will be reduced.

A shortage of human resources is as serious a constraint in national agricultural research programs as the lack of funds. Even in some countries where the funds allocated to agricultural research have been adequate, research programs have had limited impact for lack of qualified staff. Moreover, staff are often dispersed among a large number of separate and uncoordinated activities. Persuading staff to work and live in remote rural areas is an additional problem, especially in Africa. It is important, therefore, that any program to strengthen national research capability give attention to staff training, pay and incentives, and an integrated organizational and managerial structure that brings researchers together to work on common problems.

Extension Services

While the first link in the chain of technological progress is improved knowledge through research, the second is an effective system for transmitting that knowledge to farmers through the extension service. A major weakness of national research programs has been inadequate coordination with extension services. Effective coordination is essential not only to communicate research results but also to obtain feedback from farmers, which in turn puts pressure on researchers to be more responsive to farmers' needs. The two functions—research and extension—are frequently administered by separate organizations, each jealous of its own authority, and satisfactory communication between them is not easily established.

The design and implementation of an extension service is one of the most complex and problem-prone aspects of agricultural projects. Some factors that determine the effectiveness of extension systems are:

- The level of schooling and literacy of the farm population
- The degree of mutual trust between government and farmers
- The nature and scope of the responsibilities assigned to the extension service (Extension agents are frequently too absorbed in policing government regulations or collecting statistics to develop the necessary ties to farmers.)
- The extent and effectiveness of grass-roots organizations
- Links with research and the amount of unused technical information available
- The operation of commercial organizations, including the suppliers of inputs and machinery
- The efficacy of various forms of mass media as well as informal channels of communication
- The performance of extension workers, which is affected by the pay and incentives they receive, by their living arrangements and other aspects of job satisfaction, and by their level of training.

The Bank has now accumulated considerable experience with the training and visit system of extension service.[7] This system emphasizes close ties with research and a systematic approach to the routines of field staff. Extension agents attend monthly or semimonthly training programs at research centers on specific subjects; they then transmit the information to farmers on a regular schedule of frequent visits. Responsibility for adaptive research is shared by extension workers and researchers, and rapid feedback from farmers is integral to the system. A limited number of improved inputs and farming practices form the core of the extension

7. Daniel Benor, James Q. Harrison, and Michael Baxter, *Agricultural Extension: The Training and Visit System* (Washington, D.C.: World Bank, 1984).

message at any one time. Agents are recruited as much as possible from among local farmers so that they have a practical understanding of local conditions, and "contact farmers" are used to help disseminate the message to many more farmers than could otherwise be reached.

Lessons from implementing the training and visit system suggest that effective leadership from higher-level staff in introducing and managing the system is a necessary ingredient of success. When their participation and support have faltered, the system has lapsed into just another set of bureaucratic procedures. Close supervision of all levels of staff is also important. Finally, effective monitoring and evaluation are essential if the system is to remain dynamic.

Input Supply

The third link in the technology chain is a system to ensure a regular and timely supply of the inputs called for by the new technology (improved seeds, fertilizers, crop and animal protection services). Credit to finance their purchase may also be necessary; this is the subject of the next section.

In most instances, as we have suggested earlier, supplying inputs can reliably be left to private traders and merchants, provided that there are no infrastructure bottlenecks, such as poor roads, or financial disincentives. Sometimes agribusinesses have successfully diffused technology, as in the case of dairy improvements by Indian cooperatives, cotton promotion by the "Compagnies des Textiles" in several Sahelian countries, and development of treecrops, especially oil palm, by large plantations. In such cases, the commercial entity usually provides all three components—technology, inputs, and credit.

Truly profitable innovations tend to spread quickly as long as the economic environment permits. If it does not, a technical innovation may be halted in its tracks even though the government has made sure that extension, marketing, and credit are available. Government agents may then blame farmers for their resistance to change, but close analysis usually shows that the technical innovation is not financially attractive to farmers.

In the early years of the Green Revolution, one concern was that the new technical packages might be inherently biased in favor of the larger, wealthier farmers. Many studies done since then have indicated that the technologies themselves are, in fact, neutral with respect to both size of farm and type of land tenure. When supplies of inputs are insufficient, however, they tend to be appropriated by the more influential farmers. Rapid technological change is most likely to have adverse effects on small farmers and the landless where landownership is markedly skewed, where institutions and market organizations favor large farmers, and where public policy in support of small farmers is weak. An important aspect of public policy in this regard is to ensure that labor-displacing technologies are not given an advantage through subsidies.

Overall, there is little doubt that the average prices of major food grains have fallen in real terms as a result of technological change and agricultural growth. Urban consumers have been the prime beneficiaries. The benefit of low food prices has also spread to other sectors: there is less pressure to raise wages (since food is a large share of a wage earner's budget), which in turn means more jobs, especially in labor-intensive activities.

FINANCIAL ISSUES

As agriculture advances beyond subsistence to the production of marketable surpluses, it becomes increasingly commercial and monetized. Payment for marketed produce puts cash into the hands of farmers, which is used for the purchase of inputs and for increased consumption of goods and services.

Seasonality and Savings Capacity

The most striking feature of the flow of farmers' funds is its seasonal character. Seasonality is especially marked in areas with monsoon rainfall or with only one crop a year, and it creates substantial short-run savings capacity. The agricultural community has to save from each harvest to survive until the next, and virtually all producers save. Managing these savings is the largest financial challenge facing farmers. In more traditional agricultural societies, savings are frequently held in nonfinancial forms, such as livestock and stores of grain. Or some of the resources may be provided by merchants or moneylenders who extend credit to farmers short of cash or staple foods prior to the harvest.

Debt and Risk

The extent of rural indebtedness is frequently exaggerated. A few farmers are perpetually in debt and have little prospect of ever being able to repay their creditors without surrendering their land. But some rural households never borrow, and many borrow only from time to time. Overall, agriculture is characterized by low levels of debt. Debt-to-asset ratios for the agricultural sector of developed countries rarely reach 20 percent, and those for developing countries are usually much lower.

Low indebtedness reflects a general reluctance of farmers to borrow; agriculture is inherently risky because of conditions beyond the individual farmer's control, such as weather, prices, and uncertainty about the timely supply of purchased inputs. In less developed areas, these problems may be exacerbated by weak physical and institutional infrastructure. Not only is small-scale agriculture inherently risky, it is often subject to low financial returns, which reflect the competitive nature of most agricultural markets and the generally low levels of productivity. In many countries, as noted earlier, returns to farmers are reduced by price controls on food crops, taxation, and public sector marketing arrangements, especially for export crops.

Rural Financial Intermediaries

Conditions in rural areas have not been propitious for financial intermediaries such as commercial banks to arise or flourish. The costs of serving rural populations are high because of the riskiness of agricultural lending, the large number of widely dispersed rural households, the underdeveloped state of commercial practice, and the cultural distance between farmers and bankers. The small size of average savings deposits and loans makes it difficult to spread overhead costs. Furthermore, government regulations often do not allow banks to charge interest rates that fully cover the costs of rural lending. Thus, government policy, while sometimes forcing commercial banks into rural areas, has not included parallel measures to make the fundamental conditions for such branch operations more attractive.

The financial difficulties of commercial banks have sometimes led to the establishment of government-owned agricultural banks or credit institutions. These agencies are typically required to lend at rates of interest similar to, or lower than, those of the (regulated) commercial banks. This restriction, combined with the inability to capture economies of scale because of the specialization imposed on their activities, frequently leads to poor financial performance by these lenders as well. Difficulties in administering loans cause arrears to build up, and financial losses ensue. The institutions continue to be financially dependent on government or external aid because they do not have the creditworthiness to obtain funds in the financial markets.

Toward More Effective Financial Markets

A different approach is called for if the majority of rural farmers are to have some access to formal credit. One of the first requirements is to raise interest rates enough that financial institutions can recover the costs of operating in rural areas. This may imply higher interest rates in rural areas than in the cities—which is difficult politically, as Bank experience in lending to many rural credit agencies has demonstrated. But in practice, farmers without access to public credit are paying higher rates to moneylenders than those needed to make public credit institutions self-sustaining.

Other ways of strengthening the performance of rural credit institutions include:

- Emphasizing savings in conjunction with credit. More people normally save than borrow in rural areas, and savings could be mobilized to supply significant amounts of capital for investment.

- Lending on the basis of the soundness of the proposed investment and the debt-servicing capacity of the borrower. The traditional use of land as collateral is biased toward large landowners. Smallholders often lack clear title to their land, and tenants have none. Moreover, enforcement of repayment is ineffective since lenders cannot afford the political costs associated with alienating the land used as collateral.

- Supervising loans more closely to ensure that they are used effectively and enforcing loan conditions more strictly. The latter implies several measures, including the use of penalty interest rates on amounts overdue and the restriction of credit in cases of delayed repayment.

SOCIAL, CULTURAL, AND POLITICAL ISSUES

A farm family must make decisions about employment, production, marketing, consumption, saving, and investment. Intrafamily relationships as well as cultural traditions define who makes decisions in each of these areas. Projects may fail to produce their anticipated results because of ignorance, misconceptions, or oversights by project planners on these points. Problems have arisen in projects to promote credit when men are the borrowers but the crops being planted are traditionally grown by women, and in projects to expand cash crops when men control the proceeds but husbandry tasks such as transplanting or weeding are performed by women. The land tenure arrangements of an extended family may prevent individuals from borrowing (if there are no titles) or lead to abuse of credit regulations (if family members obtain credit separately and bypass credit ceilings). Conservative elders may discourage innovation by younger family or group members. Attempts to introduce a more fuel-efficient cooking stove may founder on religious beliefs about the cooking process and methods used.

Production problems may also arise from relationships among families, clans, villages, or ethnic groups in the wider rural milieu. These problems are often related to access to natural resources such as arable land, pasture, water, firewood, and fishing grounds. Traditional schemes for allocating these resources may break down or cause conflicts under the changed circumstances wrought by a project. An activity such as irrigation, which significantly alters the value of land, may engender disputes where boundaries were formerly vague but nothing much depended on them. Communal grazing lands or water holes may deteriorate when additional livestock are financed under a project and traditional access rules break down. Powerful families or clans, seizing project opportunities, may enclose land previously held in common or restrict access to a communal fishing area, while feeder roads or long-range fishing boats may expand access to public lands or waters formerly used only by the local populace. Traditional associations of certain tribes or castes with particular activities may undercut plans to expand these activities as part of a project.

Some of the issues having to do with the way benefits and costs are spread among various groups may bring different political jurisdictions into opposition. Tensions may arise between federal and state governments over relative shares of power and decisionmaking responsibility, as well as over the physical location of project activities. Local authorities may support subprojects in their own jurisdictions while opposing them in others. Issues such as the introduction of labor-displacing technologies—favored by landowners and opposed by wage earners—or the regulation of access to scarce job opportunities or subsidized credit may also have political overtones.

These social and political issues are present—either in the foreground or, less visibly, in the background—in many agricultural projects. There are no standard answers to how to deal with these issues, but recognizing their existence, appreciating their complexity, and seeking to enlist the participation and support of the interested parties are the first essential steps. Some of the solutions that have been found to be effective in particular kinds of projects are discussed elsewhere in this chapter.

INSTITUTIONAL ISSUES

Institutional issues figure prominently in agricultural development for several reasons. First, it is characteristic of most developing countries that agricultural institutions of all kinds—government ministries, public sector enterprises, cooperative movements, and private sector entities—are weak and perform poorly. The sheer magnitude of the agricultural sector imposes a heavy burden on the institutions charged with formulating policies, establishing priorities, administering controls, and planning and implementing investments. Second, the transition from subsistence to commercial farming calls for the development of a wide variety of new or expanded institutions, ranging from those that formulate and implement a commercial code (weights and measures, grades, and standards) to those that undertake the various elements of marketing commodities (including storage, transport, and processing). Third, the emergence of a science-based agriculture also necessitates the development of new institutions and services—or the expansion of existing ones—for research and extension, seed production, quality control, input distribution, and animal health.

We have seen that certain agricultural activities, particularly those relating to regulation, must be undertaken by public agencies. In other areas, public involvement may be desirable or traditional; the provision of infrastructure, research, and extension and welfare services falls in this category. Most input supply, finance, transport, processing, trading, repair, and maintenance activities are usually carried out more effectively by the private sector. In some situations, however, a private sector does not exist; until it does, public agencies must fill the gap.

Building up effective institutions is a long and difficult process, in agriculture as elsewhere. Public organizations need a planning and budgeting capability, good management and accounting systems, a sufficient flow of funds, and, above all, a system of pay and incentives that motivates staff and management to work efficiently and that reduces the likelihood of corruption. Large numbers of people have to be trained in various technical and management skills. Institution building also involves the establishment of organizational structures that are self-renewing: key people must stay long enough to achieve continuity and a measure of stability, and they must provide for a smooth transition when they leave. A public organization that is service-oriented and does not earn revenue, such as an agricultural extension service, is vulnerable to chronic underfunding. Such organizations often lack political power but are open to government interference in ways that may be haphazard and arbitrary. Managers must cope with these strains and pressures, as well as with gaps between their own goals and values and the generally more traditional goals and values held by the people they are serving.

At the project level, the ultimate objective is to create or strengthen institutions that are capable of implementing new investments and of operating and maintaining existing ones, and to arm them with an adequate and reliable flow of funds for these purposes. These agencies must also be capable of growth and change. The emphasis in institution-building efforts, therefore, should be on planning, on systems to monitor and evaluate the progress of projects, and on research.

Reviews of Bank experience suggest that institution building in the agriculture sector is especially difficult. By its nature, agricultural development demands the provision and integration of many physical inputs and services; this frequently results in complex projects that are difficult to manage. Many of these inputs and services are provided by different institutions, whose activities must be coordinated. When a large number of dispersed communities and households are involved, coordination must be achieved at the central, regional, and local levels. Further, since the participation of farmers is largely voluntary, institutions need to be aligned with the farmers' own goals and forms of social organization.

Not only is institution building a feature of most agricultural projects—figuring in 80 percent of Bank-assisted projects in recent years—but deficiencies in institutional performance are a common source of problems during project implementation. Roughly half of the Bank-assisted agricultural projects completed in the past decade encountered management problems, and a similar proportion encountered difficulties arising from inappropriate institutional arrangements. When agricultural projects supported by the Bank have proved unsuccessful, problems associated with institutional design have been a strong contributing factor in over 80 percent of the cases. Two important issues in this regard are the use of special project units and interagency coordination. Both are discussed briefly here and also in chapter 17, Project Implementation, and chapter 23, Institutional Analysis.

With responsibilities for project implementation often divided among several agencies, there has been a tendency, fostered by external lenders, to create independent project units to direct project activities. Inherent in this practice is a conflict between what works best to reach short-run production targets and what is best to meet long-run development needs. New units or agencies have been able to employ more expatriate staff, especially in managerial positions; they have sometimes adopted higher salary scales than elsewhere in the government; and they have been able to circumvent some of the bureaucratic procedures encountered in government departments. However, the short-term advantages of these units have also tended to reduce their long-term viability and the possibility of integrating them into the regular agencies; in the meantime, the regular agencies are likely to have suffered the loss of their best personnel to the units.

Whether or not a special project unit is established, problems of interagency coordination are likely to arise in agricultural projects in an acute form because of their complex and multidimensional nature. This may call for interagency planning or clearance procedures, or it may entail substantial changes in the formal structure of the agencies to accommodate implementation needs. Decisions must be made about the scope of coordination (requiring too much can create an intolerable bureaucratic burden), the level at which it takes place (ministers and other high officials cannot pay sufficient attention to details, although their authority may be needed), and the form it assumes (one agency may take the lead, or several may share responsibility). In addition, incentives for better coordination among agencies must be set up or those that already exist fully exploited.

INVESTMENT ISSUES

Three special characteristics of agriculture, noted earlier, lend distinctive features to agricultural projects. First, these projects entail a substantial degree of risk and uncertainty because farming depends on unpredictable weather conditions, which interact with biological processes that are imperfectly understood. Second, agricultural projects are directed for the most part toward creating the environment for production rather than production itself. In contrast with building and operating a steel mill, for example, an agricultural project typically makes available the means of production to many thousands of small producers who may or may not take them up. Third, agricultural projects directly affect the lives of large numbers of rural people, the day-to-day rhythm of family activities, and their ultimate consumption patterns. Therefore, the project outcome is often conditioned by the age, education, health, and value systems of farm families.

Overall Project Performance

For these and other reasons, projects in agriculture are more difficult to design and implement successfully than those in any other sector, as Bank experience has shown. Nevertheless, the results of Bank lending for agriculture have, on the whole, been very positive. Some 212 agricultural projects were completed and subjected to an ex post evaluation by the Bank during the five-year period 1978–83.[8] Individual project costs ranged from a low of $1.3 million (Mauritania Gorgol Engineering Project) to a high of $596 million (Mexico Sixth Agricultural Credit). Projects were deemed to have been successful if they had an economic rate of return, reestimated at the time of evaluation, of at least 10 percent, except in a few cases where projects with slightly lower reestimated returns were considered to have succeeded in their main objectives—or were well on the way to doing so—and had other important, nonquantifiable benefits, such as significant policy reform or institution building.

On this basis, 75 percent of the agricultural projects by number, and 85 percent by the value of total investment, were classified as successful. These results are below the average for all Bank-assisted projects (see chapter 17, Project Implementation) but may be considered a favorable outcome in a sector that is fraught with difficulties. The reestimated economic rate of return on all agricultural projects was 20 percent, slightly above the Bank-wide average (18 percent). On a geographical basis, projects in Africa, and notably East Africa, fared less well than those in other regions. Projects designed to reach large numbers of rural poor generally achieved this objective and had about the same performance record as other agricultural projects.

---

8. World Bank, Operations Evaluation Department, *Tenth Annual Review of Project Performance Audit Results* (Washington, D.C., 1985), and other World Bank materials.

Subsector Variations

Perhaps more significant than the overall results are the wide differences in performance among subsectors. The performance of *irrigation
projects* was about average in terms of the proportion of successful
projects (84 percent) and the reestimated economic rates of return (18
percent). The engineering aspects of these projects have usually been
straightforward, but the establishment of viable crop production systems
has caused more problems. Several projects have not been able to achieve
the intensity of cropping expected at appraisal. It has also proved difficult
in many projects to arrange efficient and equitable systems for water
distribution. Cost overruns and completion delays have been greater than
with projects in other subsectors, mainly because the design of an
irrigation system tends to be inflexible and projects cannot readily be
scaled down to reduce cost overruns or speed up construction.

Credit projects had the best results, with a reestimated rate of return
of 31 percent and an overall success rate of 97 percent. This rosy picture
is clouded, however, by the poor record of loan repayment by farmers in
many projects, which prejudices the long-term outlook for some credit
agencies. The provision of credit has undoubtedly helped to promote the
use of improved farming practices, although this use was less than
optimal when government policies affecting farmers' incentives (notably
prices of outputs and inputs) were inappropriate.

Treecrop and estate projects have generally performed well, in large
part because they were based on well-tested technologies and managed
by established institutions. Large cost overruns have been experienced,
but cost increases were often offset by real increases in the price of the
output. The performance of *crop and area development projects* has been
uneven; overall, only 62 percent of them satisfactorily achieved their
objectives, with an average rate of return projected at 12 percent. The
majority of these projects were located in Africa, where environmental
conditions were generally harsher than elsewhere. Many of the projects
were designed on the assumption that farmers would make significant
changes in their production systems, which were largely subsistence-
oriented, but farmers proved to be more concerned with risk aversion
than profit maximization.

Bringing up the rear are *livestock projects*, whose performance can
only be characterized as dismal. Less than half—48 percent—were
satisfactorily completed. The failure rate was particularly high in Africa,
where only one out of twelve livestock projects turned in a good performance. Several of these projects established large-scale ranches, which
did not fit well into the African environment. Others assumed that
pastoral families would make significant changes in their traditional
lifestyles and husbandry practices, but these were not sufficiently understood by the project designers. In one project, for example, imported,
purebred Brahman bulls were loaned to villagers to upgrade their livestock. However, the bulls were not hardy enough to breed well under the
indifferent management found in the villages, while fodder supplies were
inadequate to allow farmers to derive the full benefits from more productive crossbred stock. The Bank is now engaged in a fundamental rethink-
ing of its approach to livestock projects.

Table 6-2. *Reasons for Unsatisfactory Performance*
in Fifty-Three Agriculture Projects, 1979–83

Contributory factor	Number of projects affected	Number of projects where problem was		
		Most important	Second most important	Third most important
Design problems				
Inappropriate project content (too complex, insufficient local resources, or unsuitable technology)	51	24	9	9
Inappropriate institutional arrangements	46	8	16	7
Insufficient borrower support (for project goals, policy changes, finances, or staffing)	42	12	3	8
Problems with procurement	21	0	3	5
Difficulty in executing civil works	16	0	1	0
Poor institutional performance	32	1	4	9
Poor performance by consultants or poor technical assistance	16	0	3	1
Adverse economic conditions	34	3	5	8
Political difficulties	17	4	2	1
Natural calamities	9	0	2	1
Adverse effect of pricing and other government policies	31	1	6	2

Source: Data from the World Bank, Operations Evaluation Department.

Factors Influencing Project Outcome

Some interesting conclusions emerge when the fifty-three unsatisfactory projects in the group are isolated. As shown in table 6-2, two factors—inappropriate project design and lack of borrower support—occurred with greatest frequency. The latter, of course, does not apply as such to projects financed entirely by the country itself, but its equivalent—lack of sustained political commitment—can also undermine the success of projects. Aside from the institutional issues already discussed, cases of unsatisfactory design included projects in which the number of components was excessive, the scale of development attempted was too ambitious, the technology was unsuitable, or the traditions of farmers were inadequately understood. A common shortcoming was to overestimate the rate at which the improved technology would be adopted by farmers. As a result, these projects have not attained the yield targets or production increases forecast at appraisal.

On the other side of the coin, we can identify some of the principal factors accounting for the success of the majority of agricultural projects; most of these apply to other sectors as well.

• Projects must be based on the use of a technology that is both technically sound and appropriate given the socioeconomic environment of the intended beneficiaries. When a project has introduced production technologies used successfully in similar areas, and especially if some members of the target community have already adopted the new method, a high degree of success has ensued. When this favorable combination of circumstances has not occurred, pilot projects have been useful in testing the new technology before it is introduced on a large scale. In either case, flexibility to adapt to changing circumstances during implementation should be built into the project.

- Good project design must include careful attention to the institutional arrangements, a point we have already stressed.

- Strong and continued support for the project's objectives is required on the part of all levels of government as well as of the intended beneficiaries. For projects supported by external lenders, a full meeting of the minds on project objectives and on the policy and other measures to attain them must be reached at an early stage.

- Appropriate sector policies are of overriding importance in determining the outcome of a project. This applies, in particular, to policies on the pricing of farm inputs and outputs, which affect virtually all projects. But how taxation, credit, land use, marketing, and other policies are designed and administered also has an impact.

- Special care is called for to ensure the long-run viability of a project. Training staff, strengthening institutions, and securing adequate financial resources for the recurrent costs of operation and maintenance are of particular importance.

- More attention should be given to the monitoring and evaluation of ongoing projects. Complex and sophisticated monitoring and evaluation systems have frequently failed to produce worthwhile results, but well-designed, simple systems have been an indispensable tool of project management.

Secondary school student, Nairobi, Kenya

7

Education

CHARACTERISTICS OF THE SECTOR

THE PERSPECTIVE from which the contribution of education to development is viewed has undergone considerable change over the past few decades, in keeping with changes in the perception of the development process itself. Education was once regarded primarily as a means of raising political and social consciousness and of supplying the trained manpower needed for the production processes of a modern economy. Vocational and technical skills were considered the key to modernization, and secondary and higher education geared to its manpower requirements were emphasized.

By the early 1970s, the prevailing view of development had widened; to the concern for greater production was added a concern for human welfare and the alleviation of poverty. Education came to be seen as a basic human need, as a means of meeting other basic needs, and as an activity that sustains and accelerates overall development. It is now generally recognized that development of a country's human resources is essential to its prosperity and growth and to the effective use of its physical capital. Education—investment in human capital—is an integral component of all development effort. It follows that education must cover a wide spectrum in content and in form, and that general education is as essential for the achievement of development objectives as training in specific skills.

Developing countries are educating more of their population than ever before. All governments have pledged to provide basic education to their citizens, and universal primary education has, in fact, been achieved in thirty-five developing countries. Enrollment ratios at all levels have risen at an unprecedented rate in the past two decades, during which time public spending in the sector has steadily increased. Earnest efforts have been made to improve the efficiency and quality of educational systems and to increase the relevance of education to national needs. Nevertheless, vast numbers of people—an estimated 250 million children and 600 million adults—have had little or no access to education. Educational opportunities within countries are inequitably distributed, dropout and repeater rates are high, the quality of education is often poor, and graduates frequently find that what they have to offer is not what employers want. Many governments, in the rush to expand education, have overlooked or underestimated the recurrent cost requirements arising from capital investment, thereby both limiting the funds available for additional investment and wasting investment already made. Although these problems vary in seriousness from country to country, they are faced to some degree by all.

Economic Aspects

The conclusion that education contributes to economic growth, and that spending on education should therefore be considered productive investment and not merely the satisfaction of consumer demand, is now widely accepted. A variety of relationships have been examined in the course of reaching that conclusion. For example, a recent World Bank study of eighty-three developing countries showed that, in the ten countries that had the highest growth rate of real per capita GNP between 1960 and 1977, the literacy level in 1960 averaged 16 percent higher than it did for other countries at the same income level.

It has also been demonstrated that investment in education has a direct effect on individual productivity and earnings. Most of the evidence comes from agriculture. Studies comparing the productivity and innovativeness of schooled and unschooled farmers in low-income countries show that, when inputs such as fertilizers and high-yielding seed varieties were available for improved farming techniques, the annual output of a farmer who had four years of schooling averaged 13 percent higher than that of a farmer with no schooling. Even when these inputs were lacking, the schooled farmer's output was 8 percent higher.[1]

The economic effects of education extend beyond improvements in the skills and productivity of labor. Parents with a primary education are more likely to learn about, and to use, improved health, hygiene, and nutrition practices, and their children are more likely to be healthy and well nourished. Educated people, moreover, tend to have a lower fertility rate. They more readily perceive the disadvantages of having too many children to feed and educate; they have a greater number of alternative sources of family interest and satisfaction that compete with child care for time and money; and they are generally more willing to accept new ideas, such as the use of modern contraceptives, and to seek family planning advice. The woman's role in bearing and raising children makes the education of girls particularly significant. Studies show a positive correlation between a mother's educational level and her children's nutritional status and life expectancy. Further, the benefits of better health and nutrition and of lowered fertility that result from investment in education enhance the productivity of subsequent investments in the sector.

A study undertaken for the World Bank and presented in the *World Development Report 1980* examined estimates of the economic rate of return on investments in education for forty-four developing countries. It concluded that all the rates were well above the 10 percent figure that the Bank normally considers the acceptable minimum, that the returns to primary education were the highest of all educational levels, and that returns at all levels were highest in the poorest countries. The average rate of return on investment in primary education was found to be 27 percent in the low-income countries and 22 percent in the middle-income countries. For secondary education, the corresponding figures were 17 percent and 14 percent, and for higher education they were 13 percent and 12 percent. These rates of return measure costs and benefits to the country's economy; the "private" returns to the individuals receiving schooling, which exclude public costs and taxes, are normally higher.

Social Aspects

The percentage of children of primary and secondary school age enrolled in school in the developing countries has risen strikingly since 1960: from 47 to 62 percent for the 6–11 age group, and from 14 to 26

---

1. World Bank, *World Development Report 1980* (New York: Oxford University Press, 1980) p. 38.

percent for the 12–17 age group. Since the school-age population has been rising, these enrollment rate increases imply very large numerical increases. The other side of the coin, however, is equally striking. About a third of all children of primary school age are not enrolled, while only about a third of those aged 12–17 and less than 10 percent of those aged 18–23 are in school. These ratios are well below the corresponding figures for developed countries. Moreover, only about half of the primary school pupils reach the fourth grade; in the poorest countries, only about a third stay in school long enough to have any chance of achieving literacy. Of those who do remain in school, an average of about 15 to 20 percent are repeaters. In many developing countries, a third or even a half of all pupils repeat the first grade, and a fourth or more repeat later grades. Dropouts and repeaters are most common among students from a poor socioeco-nomic background, and are more prevalent in rural than in urban areas and among females than among males.

In education, as in other social sectors such as health, the bias in providing facilities has been toward urban areas and more prosperous regions. Children in rural or impoverished areas often find the nearest school far from home. Classrooms are likely to be overcrowded and teaching materials scanty. In Brazil in 1979, 74 percent of the urban children but only 26 percent of the rural children were enrolled in school. Enrollment in 1980 in the impoverished northeastern state of Ceara was 25 percent, a fraction of the 80 percent enrollment rate in the more urbanized and affluent southeastern state of São Paulo. Similar disparities exist in the Sudan between the northern Nile province (with 100 percent enrollment) and the southern Lakes province (with 7.4 percent enroll-ment); and in Indonesia between Jogjakarta Province (with 58 percent in junior secondary school) and Kalimantan Province (with 29 percent). Such differences in enrollment are exacerbated by differences in the amount spent on each student. Expenditure per pupil in 1980 was four times higher in the Southeast of Brazil than in the Northeast; and within the Northeast it was three times higher in urban than in rural areas.

In some instances, low enrollments may reflect not so much inequality of opportunity as social or cultural considerations that keep parents from taking advantage of the facilities that are available. Household demand on girls is one such reason; opposition to the language of instruction—if it is the national, rather than the local, language—is another. Parents may also feel that the quality of the education available is so poor that it does not justify the monetary outlay or the sacrifice of a child's labor or earnings that schooling would entail. Yet, despite these considerations, the demand for education for both boys and girls is growing because it is no longer taken for granted, as a social principle, that children will follow in the occupational footsteps of their parents.

Some of the ways in which education helps to relieve poverty—by improving health and nutrition practices or reducing fertility—are as important for their social consequences and their effects on family behavior as for their economic impact. Education has further functions: to transmit cultural, religious, and sometimes political values and to preserve national identity. How to balance and harmonize sociocultural and economic objectives is a difficult question for governments or other school sponsors, one that has implications for such aspects of educational policy as curriculum content and language of instruction.

Financial Aspects

Public spending on education by developing countries (excluding China and centrally planned economies) rose in real terms from a total of about $9 billion (in 1976 dollars) in 1960 to $38 billion in 1977. As a percentage of GNP, it rose over the same period from 2.3 to 4.1 percent. In 1960, developing countries were spending an average of 11.7 percent of their national budgets on education; by 1977, the average share reached 16.3 percent. For some countries, the proportion was much higher, well over 25 percent. Impressive though these figures are, they are below the corresponding ones for the developed countries: in 1977, the average was 21.3 percent of national budgets, up from 11.3 percent in 1960 (see table 7-1).

Thus, by the mid-1970s, the largest share of many national budgets was going to education; where education was not first, it was usually exceeded only by military spending. In the past decade, however, the growth in educational expenditure has leveled off in several regions of the developing world, and in some—South Asia, Latin America, North Africa, and the Middle East—the proportion of public funds directed to education has been falling. For a variety of reasons, including general economic conditions in the developing countries and competing claims from recently emergent social sectors, education has lost its budgetary primacy. It seems evident that financial constraints on the sector, far from easing, will become more severe, with implications for the ability of governments to expand educational systems and improve educational quality.

In developing countries, a very high proportion of total spending on education—often more than 90 percent—goes to recurrent costs. Within this category, teachers' salaries predominate, usually accounting for 85 percent or more of the total: at the primary school level, the average for Asia is 91 percent and for Africa, 96 percent. Nonsalary expenditures, for items such as teaching materials and classroom equipment, are typically only about 5 percent of recurrent costs at the primary level.

The bulk of expenditures for public education is financed from public funds, principally revenues from general taxation. Customs duties or excise or other specific taxes may be earmarked for education or training. In some countries, funds are raised through national lotteries. A few countries have imposed fees for public schooling at the primary level, but such fees are modest and rarely cover more than about 10 to 15 percent

Table 7-1. *Public Education Expenditure as a Percentage of GNP and National Budget, 1960–77*

Item	1960	1965	1970	1974	1977
Percentage of GNP					
Industrial countries	4.0	5.2	5.7	5.7	6.4
Developing countries	2.3	3.0	3.4	3.9	4.1
Percentage of national budget					
Industrial countries	11.3	15.2	16.1	15.6	21.3
Developing countries	11.7	13.1	13.8	15.1	16.3

Source: Based on data compiled by Unesco and the World Bank.

of recurrent costs. Fees meet a larger proportion at the secondary level (20 percent in Sierra Leone and as much as 44 percent in Lesotho). Fees are rarely charged for higher education, and university students in many countries receive a stipend. Where fees have been imposed, they have generally been falling in real terms, especially in Africa. Hence, the educational equivalent of user charges has tended to supply a declining proportion of finance for education.

The level of expenditure per student in the developing countries is well below that of the developed countries, with the greatest gap at the primary level. In 1960, OECD countries were spending an average of 14 times as much per primary school pupil for salaries and classroom materials as the low-income developing countries; by 1970 the ratio was 22:1, and by 1980 it was 50:1. Part of this, of course, reflects differences in the level of teachers' salaries. But Bolivia spends the equivalent of $0.80 per primary school pupil for classroom materials, Malawi spends $1.24, and Indonesia $2.24; in contrast, Italy spends $75, the Netherlands and the United States $220, and Sweden more than $300. Whatever is taken as the measure or standard—access to textbooks, to technology, even to desks and chairs—developing-country pupils are seriously handicapped, and the differences in investments in school quality are translated into wide differences in learning achievements.

Data on private spending for education are limited and difficult to isolate in national accounts, where statistics identify the type of goods purchased (such as food or clothing) but not their purpose. Only school fees, directly paid, can be identified in national accounts as linked to an educational purpose. (There are also indirect private costs for both public and private schooling as earnings are forgone during the period of schooling.) To a growing extent, employers meet the cost of training their workers either directly or through the payment of taxes earmarked for this purpose. In much of Asia, endowments from individuals and religious or other organized groups are a significant source of funds for private education. In some parts of the developing world, particularly in Latin America and Asia, private schools are common. The proportion of students attending private schools in 1980 was 38 percent in the Philippines, 45 percent in Korea, and 60 percent in Indonesia. In other regions, private schools are rare. The share of private spending on education thus varies widely among developing countries, so that its quantitative and qualitative contribution to the formation of human capital is difficult to assess.

Institutional Aspects

The task of managing the sector is formidable. The educational system is generally a country's most sizable public activity. It not only commands the largest, or next to largest, share of the national budget, but typically accounts for 25 percent or more of public employees. In India, for example, there are 1.3 million teachers at the primary level alone. Each must be trained, supervised, evaluated, and paid on time. Apart from financial and human resources to be managed, there are supplies and equipment to be purchased, stored, accounted for, and replaced. In Mexico, 82 million textbooks must be distributed each year to 57,000 schools. Hundreds of reports—on attendance, achievement, expenditures, facilities—must (or should) be made, reviewed, acted upon, and filed. Decisions must be taken on educational policy issues: the language of instruction, criteria for admission, mix of subjects in curricula, and what services should be provided at what level and by what type of school and method of instruction.

Most educational systems urgently need to improve administration and management. Their rapid expansion and increased complexity, both in subject matter and in the technology of teaching, have strained developing countries' administrative, managerial, and analytical capacities. Much of the expansion has been undertaken without an appreciation of what is required to run the enlarged system efficiently. Moreover, senior level managers are usually drawn from the teaching profession and have no managerial training. Responsibility is typically fragmented and its division unclear, both at the center and down the line. The ministry of education is likely to share responsibility for school construction with the ministry of public works and for technical and vocational training with the ministries of labor and agriculture. The relationships between the education ministry and local authorities, community groups, and the schools themselves are often not well defined.

Planning is difficult because information is usually inadequate. At the national level, planning has tended to emphasize quantitative expansion and the setting of goals, with insufficient attention to quality. In developed countries, education ministries collect and analyze many kinds of data: on learning levels, costs, effectiveness of curricula and skill specializations, and use of facilities. In the developing countries, little more than enrollment data are available. Typically, public authorities have little reliable information on the availability, use, and condition of physical facilities and classroom materials or on unit costs, sources of finance, learning achievement, and the occupational destination of school-leavers. Consequently, decisions are taken without due regard to cost implications. Curriculum changes are made without assurance that teaching materials to implement the changes are available. There is little or no monitoring of educational quality and comparison of output on a national or regional basis, and no monitoring of the external efficiency of the system.

Finally, even if the requisite data were available, many of the questions to which planners need answers if they are to assess alternatives properly—questions on cost-effectiveness, cost-benefit relationships, and labor market needs—depend on a capacity to employ a variety of analytical techniques. This capacity is lacking or in short supply in many developing countries.

DEVELOPMENT OBJECTIVES

From the foregoing description of the characteristics of the education sector, it will be apparent that governments should have five principal objectives:

- As a first priority, provision of basic education to all children as quickly as resources, both financial and human, permit; and ultimately, development of a comprehensive system of education at all levels and for all age groups

- More equitable distribution of educational opportunities and reduction of existing inequalities based on sex, economic status, and geography
- Greater internal efficiency of the educational system, through a reduction of the waste of resources caused by students dropping out or repeating grades, and improved quality of education
- Greater external efficiency of the educational system, through an increase in the relevance of schooling to the job market, so that students are equipped with the knowledge and skills needed to find employment
- Development and maintenance of an institutional capacity to formulate and carry out educational policy and to plan, analyze, manage, and evaluate education and training programs and projects at all levels.

These objectives are broadly accepted by developing countries. But how to allocate resources to achieve them is open to substantial debate. How many years of school are necessary for primary (also called basic) education? What should be the mix between general and vocational education and between formal and nonformal education? Is it more important to improve the quality of primary education for those already in school, or to expand primary (or secondary) enrollments, or to teach adults to read and write? What is the role of curriculum reform? Each country needs to formulate its own answers to these and similar questions in the light of its circumstances and development priorities.

POLICY ISSUES

Private Financing

The level of funding necessary to move with reasonable speed toward the objectives of expanding the educational system and improving the quality of education (as well as preventing any deterioration in quality) is likely to be beyond the financial capability of many governments through increases in budgetary allocations alone. One way or another, governments must explore and develop strategies for generating other financial resources and for improving the efficiency of the system. The first of these courses of action is considered here; ways to increase efficiency are discussed in a later section.

Education is heavily subsidized in developing countries. It is difficult to define an optimum mix of public and private finance in the sector, but some scope for readjusting the balance between the two generally exists. Recent research done for the World Bank suggests that upper-income families are likely to benefit from education subsidies to a greater extent than poorer families, especially at secondary and higher levels of education, so that a larger share of education costs could be borne by private individuals without prejudice to equity objectives. One approach with considerable potential is the introduction or development of cost recovery mechanisms through a system of fees or charges for services; another is a program of student loans. Other approaches include incentives to increase the number of private schools, a larger role for employers in the provision of vocational training or in meeting the costs of training in public facilities, and community contributions. These are not novel methods of financing; some countries have already successfully adopted one or more of them. But introducing or raising fees may be impracticable for political reasons, and collecting fees and loan repayments imposes an administrative burden, so that the feasibility of each approach must be evaluated in the light of the particular circumstances.

Fees

The tendency to charge no fees, or very modest ones, for public schooling is attributable largely to governments' commitment to "free" public education. It is also believed that a charge would be both inefficient, because it might discourage enrollment with a consequent loss to society of the benefits of education, and inequitable, because it might limit access to those who could afford to pay. However, studies conducted for the World Bank suggest that in some circumstances both efficiency and equity objectives may be served by imposing or increasing fees. When there are minimal or no charges to the individual, demand for education is likely to be encouraged to a point unjustified by the economic returns to society. If demand exceeds available school places, experience indicates that the poor are most likely to be excluded. When excess demand is substantial, charges could be instituted or raised, with the additional revenue being devoted to expanding the system. This could produce greater social benefits than would very low or no fees.

It is essential that the revenue from fees actually go to improve educational quality or to expand the system, and that it not be diverted to other purposes or used merely to replace other funds that were intended for investment in the sector. It is also important that fees not be set so high that poor families cannot afford them on top of the other direct and indirect costs they pay to educate their children. The fact that schools run by religious organizations and private volunteer groups typically charge fees confirms that there is an ability and willingness to pay for schooling that in some countries is still largely untapped.

Raising or imposing fees, with the caveats noted, may increase demand for education among poor rural households if the revenue is used to expand education by bringing schools closer to villages or to improve the quality of education, for instance by financing educational materials. In Lesotho, fees cover all textbook costs at the primary level and over 60 percent at the secondary level. It may be easier to raise fees if the administration of education is centralized. Malawi is such a country. It had an open-door admissions policy and low fees. Faced with a combination of budgetary constraints, overcrowding in primary schools, a shortage of secondary school places, and low-quality schooling, Malawi raised school fees by 50 percent in secondary and in rural primary schools in 1982.

The argument for introducing or raising fees at the university level is even stronger. In many developing countries, postsecondary education is more heavily subsidized than primary education, both in relation to unit costs and in absolute terms. In Malawi, university students receive not only free tuition, board and lodging, and books, but pocket money as well. This is the pattern in many countries, especially in Africa and Latin

America, even though the economic returns to society are higher for primary education than for other levels of study. It seems reasonable to assume that fees for higher education, and perhaps even for secondary education, could be raised, since students at these levels are likely to come from families with relatively high incomes. Such a move might have little effect on enrollment, but to the extent that reducing the subsidy were to affect demand, it could be a useful rationing device. Nevertheless, resistance or political opposition may influence or dictate the pace at which progress can be made.

Student Loans

Programs providing loans to university students have been introduced in some Latin American, African, and Asian countries. Typically, the loans cover not only tuition, where it is not free, but also living expenses. They are repayable after graduation or when the student leaves the university, and are either interest-free or carry a very low rate of interest. The programs have helped to satisfy the demand for higher education while lightening the burden on the national budget. Moreover, in some countries, including Colombia, Brazil, Sri Lanka, and Pakistan, it has proved possible to interest commercial banks, private enterprises, and trade unions in helping to finance the program; the government usually guarantees the loan but does not advance the funds. Loan programs are obviously less costly to the government than grant programs; moreover, it can be argued that they are more equitable than a system in which public funds meet all the costs of higher education, since the graduates are likely to have higher-than-average future earnings precisely because of that education. However, no student loan scheme has succeeded in becoming self-financing, and the long repayment periods and low rates of interest make regular injections of capital necessary. These programs cannot, therefore, be looked to as an immediate means of easing the burden on public funds. Over the longer term, however, they can provide a significant source of finance for higher education.

The capacity of loan programs to shift the financing burden can be enhanced by associating them with the introduction of tuition fees (or an increase in fees where they have been only nominal) and with charges for room and board. While experience shows that loan programs do work, it has also revealed formidable administrative problems and costs, primarily in late repayments and defaults. These difficulties are by no means unique to programs in developing countries. They can, however, be overcome, or at least minimized, if anticipated. Often banks have proved the most effective collection agents. As in so many other undertakings, a principal ingredient of success for a loan program is management of good quality.

Private Schools

In Pakistan, the Philippines, Korea, and some other countries, the number of private schools has increased as a growing demand for education has coincided with a slower rise in the availability of public funds. But elsewhere, notably in Latin America, where there has for some time been an active and extensive private schooling system, private schools are facing financial difficulties. The proportion of private school enrollment to total enrollment at the primary school level fell in eleven out of twenty-three Latin American countries between 1965 and 1975, and at the secondary level in nineteen out of the twenty-three. This may, however, have been a reaction to the substantial increase in public spending for education during the decade. Now that public expenditures have stabilized or are declining, it may be necessary to assign a greater role to private schools.

Vocational Training

Employers are becoming more involved in providing training for their employees on the job or in helping to finance training in vocational schools or similar institutions. Governments have a dual motive in encouraging the development of such programs. One, discussed below, is to relate vocational education as closely as possible to the needs of the labor market. The other is to share the costs of training with both the student and the private sector. Singapore and many Latin American countries use a system that combines on-the-job, workshop experience with classroom instruction in specialized facilities; employers make a compulsory contribution to the training costs through a payroll tax. Other countries have adopted an incentive system to encourage business enterprises voluntarily to provide in-plant training for their workers, not only to teach basic skills at the entry level but also to upgrade skills. For example, the enterprise may be allowed to deduct the expenses incurred (or sometimes more) from its taxable income, up to a specified percentage of that income. Incentive systems of this kind can mean a loss of potential tax revenue in the short term, but this may be more than offset by improvements in the quantity and quality of vocational training. When the private sector pays for the training, it takes an active interest in seeing that the content is appropriate. Combining private sector involvement with a larger share financed by the trainee himself helps to keep vocational training from being expanded to the point where it becomes uneconomic.

Community Involvement

In some countries, local communities have contributed to the costs of school construction through self-help efforts and donations in kind. In Nepal, local communities have built and maintained almost all primary and many secondary schools. In Tanzania, the government supplies materials for construction of primary schools and teachers' accommodations; villagers do the building. Some direct financial contribution, such as meeting a portion of teachers' salaries, is common. Community contributions have represented only a small part of the total costs of education, but in addition to easing the financial strain on the central budget, such participation helps to ensure that the type of education and training offered is relevant to local needs. It should therefore be encouraged.

Improving Educational Opportunities

In the education sector, certainly at the primary level, opportunities would be improved by making it easier for all prospective students in an area, especially a rural one, to attend school and by equalizing enrollment ratios between rural and urban children, poor and well-to-do children, and boys and girls. Efforts at both are hampered not only by limitations on financial and human resources but also by geographic and demographic conditions that make it difficult and costly to construct schools, supply learning materials, and provide qualified teachers. Ways to increase access and equity include improving mechanisms to meet basic education needs, drawing on local resources, and building schools in areas where they are most needed.

Local communities can mobilize financial resources and self-help labor; some can also provide teaching talent, albeit of unequal quality. These additional resources may be important in countries where the educational system is not highly centralized, but precisely because there will be little if any coordination, qualified teachers and teaching materials will be unevenly distributed in different parts of the country. Particularly in regions where incomes are low, community efforts will require support from the central government. If educational activities that are locally initiated and managed do not receive central support, enthusiasm is likely to evaporate rapidly and the quality of education remain low.

In the early 1970s, there were many experiments, especially in Africa, with nonformal alternatives to formal schooling. Ways were sought through a variety of organizations, usually rural, to confer literacy and numeracy on children and youths without regular access to the school system. The efforts have not been rewarding, and it has become apparent that those so educated have little chance of eventually transferring or being promoted to primary or secondary facilities within the formal system. In the absence of that opportunity, nonformal arrangements, notwithstanding their worthy intent, generally have lacked institutional support and have had limited results.

School Location Planning

An obvious means of increasing enrollment is to bring schools closer to communities that lack facilities. Just as obvious, however, are the resource constraints on the number of schools that can be built, so it makes sense to determine where they are most needed. School location planning can be an efficient technique for determining the distribution, size, and spacing of schools and the kind of educational and related facilities to be provided. It requires, first, an inventory of present facilities and, next, an analysis of a variety of data—demographic, geographic, social, and economic. Preconditions for the effective use of school location planning for expanding an education system are, therefore, the development of a country's data base—for instance, through more frequent sample surveys of population movement and distribution than are provided by a national census, typically conducted only once a decade—and development of its analytical capacity.

Increasing Utilization

It cannot be assumed that a service will be used simply because it exists. Girls are particularly vulnerable to sociocultural constraints on school attendance, and special arrangements, such as sex-segregated schools, may be necessary to address the problem of low female enrollment. Low utilization may also reflect views concerning the quality or type of education: where quality is perceived to be low, parents may feel that the benefits of education are outweighed by the cost of forgoing the help of children at home. Moreover, some types of underutilization arise from a misunderstanding of felt needs. In Lesotho, parents preferred formal secondary schools to the rural-oriented curriculum offered in nonformal education centers. Girls attending secondary school in Somalia were not happy with domestic science workshops, preferring to be identified with professional rather than household tasks.

If it is certain that the new spaces to be provided at a given level of education or in a certain geographic area will be matched by a proportional increase in enrollment, both equity and efficiency objectives can usually be met. There are circumstances, however, when a tradeoff between the objectives of equity and efficiency cannot be avoided, as when deciding between investments that will reduce the unit costs of education (or improve its quality) and those that will extend its benefits—even at higher unit costs—to underserved populations. A government may decide, for reasons of equity, to invest more in new schools than can be justified on efficiency grounds, but it should do so only after making an informed choice. This requires mechanisms to identify both the needs and the probable reactions of the consumers of educational services, and the feeding of that information into the analytic and planning process.

Improving Efficiency

Investment decisions have to take into account both external and internal efficiency. The external efficiency of a school system is judged by the extent to which it improves students' employment prospects and productivity. Internal efficiency is concerned with the extent to which particular educational goals are achieved with a given input of resources; the goal is for students to flow through the system with a minimum of waste. This section considers first the quantitative aspects of efficiency, both external and internal, and then the qualitative aspects.

Quantitative External Efficiency

The external efficiency of an educational system depends on relationships between general and vocational education, and between school and work opportunities. In other chapters, the point is repeatedly made that most developing countries suffer from a shortage of the technical and managerial skills necessary to sustain economic growth. This is a major challenge for the educational system, as well as for enterprises that could provide some of the requisite training.

What mix of education or training is best suited to meet the highly diverse needs of the labor market? There are various possible modes of delivery from which to choose, and various possible combinations: general education, diversified schools, technical and vocational schools, on-the-job training, and nonformal educational programs. In many countries, most or all of these types of training will be needed at the same time. In allocating resources it is necessary to decide on the balance between general and specialized education, between various levels of schooling, and between alternative delivery vehicles or methods of teaching, all of which may differ with respect to both cost and effectiveness. For example, should a particular skill be taught by a specialized institution in the public system, or by the private sector through on-the-job training, or in a proprietary school? Should an engineering college be set up or, for an equivalent investment of funds, should the number of primary school places be very substantially increased, if available resources do not permit both? Such policy decisions require analyzing the economic and institutional circumstances and comparing alternative mixes of educational output to determine what will best meet the skill requirements of the labor market.

Primary schools. Earlier in this chapter, we referred to the evidence that education, especially at the primary level, increases the productivity of workers. Both economic efficiency and equity argue for continued investment at the entry level of formal education. Moreover, the core curriculum of general education supplies the discipline, communication skills, and foundation in mathematics and science that are the basis for further training. Educated workers are more concerned with achievement, more self-reliant, more readily adaptable to new situations, and more trainable than workers with little or no education. This may call for the further expansion of education, at least at the primary level, in many developing countries.

Diversified schools. During the 1960s and 1970s, many developing countries introduced into the curricula of their secondary schools a number of prevocational subjects, such as agriculture and industrial arts, alongside the academic program. Many of the education projects supported by the Bank during that period included provision for these "diversified" schools. No definitive conclusions about the effects of these programs on learning and on how students fared in the labor market have emerged as yet. First indications suggest, however, that in Tanzania the addition of prevocational subjects slightly reduced learning achievements in academic subjects, and that in both Tanzania and Colombia the employment experience of students who attended diversified schools is no different from the experience of those who went to purely academic schools.

At the same time, there is considerable evidence that diversified schools are complex and costly: they require special training for teachers and special curriculum design, and because of their specialized equipment they make heavy demands on maintenance. Unit costs of diversified schools are estimated to be 20 to 40 percent higher than those of traditional secondary schools. Somalia's secondary schools were equipped to teach metalworking, woodworking, and farming, until it was realized that this added 20 percent to the cost for each student attending secondary school and that, because of budgetary constraints, places could be provided for only 3 percent of the relevant age group. The government then decided to narrow the secondary school curriculum and increase the number of places. Another risk is that the prevocational curriculum will not be attuned to the needs of the local economy or adequate to develop entry-level skills, or that students will prefer a wholly academic curriculum, with the result that the expensive facilities will be underutilized. For all these reasons, the diversified schools do not appear to be a good vehicle for training or recruiting large numbers of students for the labor force. In countries in which secondary enrollments are low and graduates readily find employment, the economic returns are likely to be greater if resources are invested in general secondary education instead.

Technical and vocational schools. The long-standing difference of opinion over what kind of technical skills to develop within the formal educational system, and how best to develop them, remains unresolved. Part of the problem lies in the difficulty, discussed below, of forecasting accurately the economy's requirements for specific skills. Accordingly, full-time, preemployment vocational training should be flexible and impart occupational skills that can be applied in a variety of work situations. It should transmit vocational and technical knowledge that will serve as a preparation and foundation for later on-the-job training, together with the theoretical knowledge that is appropriate to the vocation and that can best be presented in a classroom. There is a risk that students will not gravitate to a facility that emphasizes vocational training; on the average, enrollments at vocational and technical schools assisted by the Bank have been found to be 7 to 10 percent below capacity at the time of project completion.

Vocational and technical school instructors should, therefore, have an academic as well as a technical background. In addition, involvement of employers in planning the curriculum will increase the likelihood that the school will produce employable graduates. Finally, it should be appreciated that economic growth, especially the pace of industrialization, plays a greater role in creating employment opportunities than training does.

At the postsecondary level, the introduction of nonuniversity institutions such as polytechnic and community colleges into the educational system has had both advantages and disadvantages. Unlike universities, they can concentrate on specialized, industry-related fields, provide short programs, and relate more directly to the requirements of the economy and of the local community. The capital cost being lower than for a general university, such schools can more readily be extended to different parts of the country; but their unit cost of operation is one and a half times as high. Furthermore, the economic benefits of a full-scale university program are perceived to be greater than those of a nonuniversity program, so the demand for a university education is stronger. Since the short, ad hoc courses of the polytechnic colleges are difficult to manage, underutilization is also more common than with general university facilities. Nonetheless, if properly managed, polytechnic and community colleges have their place in countries that cannot afford to provide a full university education to all those desiring it.

Other training. Whereas technical and vocational schools train for the labor market generally, individual enterprises may run programs to train new employees and to upgrade existing staff. The skills taught are specific to the enterprise, and there is no problem of relating supply to demand. An example of this type of program is the project-related training frequently incorporated into Bank-assisted projects. It is designed to ensure the availability of the skills necessary to make efficient use of capital investments, and it encompasses skills at all levels and in all sectors of the economy. Such training can take a variety of forms.

As a general rule, the closer such training is to the workplace in which it will be needed, or to equivalent conditions, the more effective it is likely to be. On-the-job training is often the preferred choice, if it is feasible in the particular project circumstances and if it is planned, organized, and supervised specifically as a training activity. It is also the least expensive method, since the training is conducted by the supervisor. A variant is in-house training conducted away from the workplace and the pressures of an actual production process ("off-the-job" training). An effective supplement to on-the-job training is institutional training, provided in a local vocational or technical training institution, and sandwiched between work periods during which the training can be put into practice. Although the costs of these apprentice programs can be high, they are successful in training skilled workers to accepted standards of proficiency. Still another approach is to set up a twinning arrangement with a similar, well-established entity abroad, which allows hands-on learning through association with those who have more experience.

Study tours are of more limited value since they normally provide training by observing rather than by doing. They are most effective when preceded by on-the-job training. They are useful especially for senior project staff, if the work objectives are well defined and the host institution clearly understands the purpose of the visit. When formal education is called for as part of the training program, or when an opportunity to observe the actual functioning of new techniques is desirable, personnel are sometimes sent abroad for training through fellowship programs.

Foreign fellowships do involve certain risks. Study in developed countries may offer little that is relevant to the needs of the trainee's country; this puts a premium on the careful selection of programs. It may be difficult to adapt what has been learned to local circumstances. Trained personnel may not return from abroad. Or they may look for other, more lucrative or advantageous ways of applying their new or improved skills; for an employee of a public agency, this usually means leaving for a job in the private sector. If lengthy overseas training is part of a specific project, the project may have progressed so far by the time the trainee returns that it may no longer need what he can contribute. In view of the cost of overseas training, these considerations have to be carefully weighed and safeguards built into the program. For example, trainees may be required to post a bond that would be forfeited by failure to return to the country or to the project entity. Bonding has proved of limited success in individual projects, but a loss to the project may still be a gain to the economy as a whole because of the training acquired. The possibility of a brain drain from the public to the private sector should be recognized and anticipated by training more staff than are likely to be required by the particular institution. Even a brain drain to foreign countries may be thought of as an export of skilled manpower that brings economic benefits in the form of remittances from abroad.

"Counterpart" training of local staff involved in the project by expatriate consultants is a common arrangement. Although it enables new, usually imported techniques and technologies to be quickly introduced, the results often fall short of expectations. When, as often happens, the consultant has other responsibilities as well, the training task tends to become subordinate to them. The consultant's terms of reference should define the training role precisely, make clear its relative priority, and specify the level of proficiency that counterparts are to achieve within an indicated period. In a number of Bank-assisted projects in which an effective expert-counterpart relationship did not develop, the failure occurred largely because the expert's terms of reference were deficient in these respects. Another problem to be anticipated arises when the educational (as distinguished from the skills and experience) levels of the consultant and the counterparts are very different: effective communication for training purposes may then be impossible.

Demand forecasting. Since one objective of the educational system is to turn out graduates and school-leavers who are readily employable, it is necessary, as noted earlier, to take account of labor market needs. The efficiency and success of the system will depend on how well it satisfies those needs by producing a broadly appropriate pool of people with the required skills and professional and technical knowledge. Over the past twenty years, many developing countries have based their educational plans on forecasts of manpower requirements. However, forecasting the manpower demands of an economy is a difficult task, hampered by a lack of accepted theoretical and analytical techniques. Such forecasts have not proved reliable even in developed countries that have considerable data available as well as analysts trained to interpret the data. For developing countries with limited information and analytical capacities, the likelihood of inaccuracy and unreliability is magnified. When, as is typical, manpower forecasting is the single or predominant technique used to plan for labor demands and thus to justify expansion of education facilities, mistaken judgments about investment priorities may well be the result.[2]

While manpower forecasts need not be discarded, they should play a less dominant role. It is still desirable to collect accurate and comprehensive information about the labor market—including data on hiring, promotion, and termination practices, wage rates, international labor markets, and private sector earnings. Tracer studies can yield information about the employment and careers of small samples of labor force entrants or school-leavers and university graduates; the scope of such studies needs to be carefully defined, however, since they are complex and costly to mount and need a strong institutional mechanism to collect and evaluate the data. Planners also need evaluations of educational institutions—agricultural colleges, for example—to determine how successful they have been in preparing students for employment, and what effect particular curricula have had on employability. All of this implies a continuous process of analyzing the demand for manpower on the basis of current labor market information, assessing alternative ways of producing skills (through formal or informal education and training, or a combination of the two) and alternative ways of financing the acquisition of skills (through a mix of individual, private, and public contributions), and establishing their relative costs. To achieve the requisite breadth of data and diversity of analytical techniques will require substantial efforts to improve planning and research capacity, a topic dealt with below.

2. For further details, see Manuel Zymelman, *Occupational Structures of Industries* (Washington, D.C.: World Bank, 1980). This study presents data on productivity and occupational distribution for fifty-eight industries in twenty-six countries. See also Manuel Zymelman, "Forecasting Manpower Demand" (Washington, D.C.: Education Department, World Bank, 1980).

Quantitative Internal Efficiency

The efficiency with which a school system produces graduates can be improved in a number of ways. Some of these do not require significant investments of capital but are achievable through administrative action. They relate to the flow of students, class size, and the use of space and facilities.

Student flow. As noted earlier, a high proportion of primary school places in developing countries is occupied by repeaters. A Unesco study in 1977 estimated that about 15 to 20 percent more children of primary school age could have been admitted to school, without any increase in costs, had there been no grade repetition. Dropout rates are likewise high. Together, repeaters and dropouts consume scarce resources with low returns to the individual or society. One of the most effective ways to reduce both is to improve the quality of education by providing better trained teachers who use pedagogical methods of a higher standard, by providing more and better teaching materials, and so on. But the dropout rate, like the rate of failure to enroll children in school, is affected not only by the quality of education but also by the importance attached to children's contribution to the family economy, by their health and nutrition, by the level of education attained by their parents, and by the kind of preschool stimulus given at home. Suggestions for addressing some of these problems have been made above or are the subject of other chapters.

Overly rigid or poorly designed promotion policies, especially as applied in the lowest grades, may be keeping children in a grade too long. In some countries of Latin America, pupils must take a literacy test before they can advance to the second grade. The tests are designed, administered, and graded by individual teachers without any central control of the quality of either the tests or their interpretation. In Morocco, restrictions on entry into the secondary level cause pupils to repeat the last grade of primary school so that their scores on the entrance examinations for secondary school will be higher. In countries such as Tanzania and Zambia, where promotion is virtually automatic at primary levels, repeater rates are comparatively low. Studies done for the Bank suggest that repetition does not improve academic standards or class homogeneity, while it clearly has an adverse effect on a pupil's morale and self-esteem.

Class size. Many developing countries associate low student-teacher ratios with higher-quality education. Accordingly, they have given high priority to reducing the average size of classes. Research on the relationship between class size and learning achievement, however, has demonstrated that, if physical facilities remain unchanged, smaller classes do not necessarily improve educational quality (unless the class is very small, say, less than sixteen pupils). Conversely, research shows that achievement does not necessarily drop if the size of a class is increased up to a point short of overcrowding (say, forty pupils at the primary level). In West Africa, primary classrooms are generally crowded; in eight of twenty-two countries, the average size is over fifty. Repeaters contribute to this problem. Another relevant consideration is cost: a reduction in class size means an increase in the number of classes. Although it may be possible to accommodate the larger number by increasing the teaching load without sacrificing the quality of instruction, sooner or later more teachers will be needed. Hiring more teachers adds substantially to the costs of running a school system, however, since teachers' salaries are by far the largest element in those costs. Therefore, rather than assuming that reductions in class size are desirable, governments should consider which is more cost-effective: to provide more teachers so that class size can be reduced or to put the funds that would otherwise be used to pay the additional salaries into alternative improvements, such as training or teaching materials, to make teachers more effective.

Use of space and facilities. More intensive use of facilities allows an increase in enrollment without an increase in capital costs (which, in turn, has implications for recurrent expenditure). Space utilization surveys may well reveal excess capacity in classrooms and science laboratories, as they did in Morocco and Ghana, and point to opportunities for increasing class size. Greater use may also be made of classrooms, laboratories, and workshops through rotation and staggered scheduling of classes.

Where population density is high, double shifts may be introduced; this can mean two sessions a day, or attendance on alternate days, or staggering and overlapping terms to allow three groups to use facilities designed for two. The double-shift system has been incorporated into a number of Bank-assisted projects, as has the system of rotating class-rooms for use by several grades; both have encountered managerial problems, and the second session, in the afternoon, may be regarded by pupils and their families as inferior to the morning session. Some loss in learning achievement or in the diversity of curricula may result if there is a ceiling on available classroom time per student, but this may be offset by the greater accessibility of education. Whether or not more teachers will be needed for double shifts depends on how teaching loads are organized and on how teachers are compensated. In Malaysia, the same teachers are used for both shifts, and they are paid for a full day's work. Nearby, in Indonesia, teachers receive low salaries and work short hours, but they hold down two or even three teaching jobs, often at widely scattered locations.

Where population density is low, so that there are insufficient pupils to fill individual classes, the use of facilities and the student-teacher ratio has been improved through such techniques as biennial intake (admission into the first grade every other year), multigrade teaching (grouping of different ages and adjacent grades under one teacher), and nuclear-satellite networks (in which a group of schools with a limited number of grades feeds into a complete school in the same area). Not all of these techniques are free of difficulty. The nuclear-satellite system requires considerable administrative control to be effective and implies expenditures (whether from public or private sources) for board or transport of pupils. Effective multigrade teaching depends on the availability of specially trained teachers. Biennial intake is accordingly the most widely applicable approach, since it does not make heavy administrative demands nor call for specialized teaching qualifications.

School design can contribute to the optimum use of the facilities. Planners can seek to maximize the usable space within the overall campus area. Economies can be realized in planning student (or teacher or boarder) space standards. Most important, specialized facilities such as laboratories and workshops can be utilized more efficiently if they are provided only in the quantities required for their specific intended uses; care should then be taken that they are not diverted to general classroom use, as often occurs.

Qualitative Efficiency

What is ultimately achieved through technical and professional training depends in good part on what students have absorbed at lower levels. It is many times more expensive to teach mathematics and science at specialized and higher-level education and training institutions than at primary or secondary schools, yet it has been found that these institutions may have to allocate as much as one-third of class time to compensating for gaps and deficiencies in instruction at lower levels. Thus, improvements in the quality of education at lower levels not only are significant for students who proceed no further with their education, but also have beneficial consequences for the efficiency of any later professional or technical training. Improving the qualitative output of education implies improving the quality of school inputs—curriculum, teachers, and teaching materials (books, maps, references, and the like). The effects of changes in class size have already been discussed. Nonschool factors such as health, nutrition, and home environment—also referred to above— likewise have consequences for learning achievement.

Curriculum development. The educational systems in many developing countries, inherited from colonial days, were found upon independence to be following curricula inappropriate to the new situation. The principal efforts at curriculum change were designed to place less emphasis on general education by introducing job-related subjects, on the premise that this would help school-leavers to find employment. Reference has already been made to the introduction of diversified schools at the secondary level, and to the doubts entertained by the Bank, on the basis of its project experience, concerning the usefulness of that approach. Efforts were also made, at the primary level, to distinguish the curriculum in rural schools from that of city schools. Several African countries, in particular, experimented with the introduction of manual work into rural schools. In part because rural schools tend to have less qualified teachers and inferior teaching materials, however, it is difficult to make rural pupils literate and numerate, and any dilution of teaching efforts can reduce learning achievements. Moreover, as noted earlier, the introduction of a rural curriculum has not always been welcomed by parents. The mixed success and popularity of such schemes has muted enthusiasm for a rural curriculum.

In many instances, curriculum changes that appear promising on paper have in the end proved ineffective. Some were not supported by the requisite teaching materials. In other instances, the new content or objective was not regarded by students and their families as likely to lead to the kind of employment sought. In still others, the curriculum changes were unrealistically expected to bring about wider social change, for example by discouraging migration to urban areas or instilling greater appreciation of low-skilled employment.

Still, steady advances have taken place in adapting educational curricula to the needs of developing countries, and the process should continue. No longer are biological examples drawn from temperate zones or historical lessons from the former colonial powers. Local history, art, and geography are normal components in all national curricula. Theories of learning are being adapted to local cultural, familial, and linguistic groups and are helping to guide the development of new curricula. Most countries have now established local institutions that are responsible for continuous review and improvement of curricula in the light of new knowledge and new educational purposes.

Finally, the Bank's project experience abundantly demonstrates that curriculum reform should not be undertaken lightly. It is a complex and time-consuming process, often requiring more than a decade for full implementation. Aspirations and the time frame for achieving them must be realistic. Development of new curricula, training or retraining of teachers, and elaboration of suitable testing materials take longer than the typical cycle of a single project, and have to be supported over a series of projects.

Teacher training. Research commissioned by the Bank shows that a teacher's qualifications, experience, education level, and knowledge have significant consequences for what students achieve. In most developing countries, the percentage of unqualified or insufficiently qualified teachers is high. In the public system, teachers are classified by their educational attainment and the duration of the training they have received; this may not accurately reflect their teaching ability. Increases in compensation are based on seniority rather than merit, and compensation rarely reflects the market value of the subject expertise. Science and math instructors are in short supply because educational systems cannot offer the salaries necessary to attract and retain those competent to teach the subjects. Teacher-training programs and in-service training programs are poorly designed and equipped. Ways to deal with these shortcomings include expanding training facilities, systematizing in-service training, improving the quality of training programs, and providing teachers with resources and incentives that will help them to improve the quality of their instruction. Which, or what combination, of these approaches to adopt should be determined in the light of country conditions and the cost-effectiveness of the alternatives. Upgrading is likely to be particularly important as an adjunct to the introduction of a new curriculum or new teaching materials. At the same time, experience suggests that providing teachers with a general education beyond a certain minimum level will not have a significant effect on pupils' learning; it is more important to develop knowledge and skills in specific subject areas, such as science and mathematics, than to add a university or professional degree.

Teaching materials. Research indicates that one of the more cost-effective determinants of learning achievement, particularly in the lower grades, is the availability of textbooks. A recent study in the Philippines found that after enough textbooks were provided so that only two pupils, instead of ten, had to share a book, first grade learning in science, mathematics, and language improved significantly. The Philippine experience suggests that the learning gains will frequently be greatest among the poorest pupils. Yet the supply of textbooks in low-income countries has been inadequate, and in many rural areas no textbooks at all are provided. As we mentioned at the beginning of this chapter, the proportion of education expenditures devoted to teaching materials by developing countries is very small; the average is less than, and in Africa much less than, the 10 percent of public recurrent expenditure that experience indicates should be the minimum allocated for the purpose.

Whether the production of textbooks should be a private sector activity or whether, as in Mexico, textbooks should be published by the government, and whether textbooks should be free or sold at low prices, are matters for each country to decide, although some measure of cost recovery may often be justified. In Mexico, for example, primary school books are provided free by the government, while secondary school books are sold by the private sector. Whatever the specific arrangements, greater attention to the production and distribution of reading materials is needed. The reading comprehension skills of students in developing countries fall far below those of students in developed countries; better textbooks can be expected to contribute directly to building such skills. Between 1969 and 1973, only eight of the education projects assisted by the Bank made provision for reading materials; in the next five years, nineteen did, and in the past five years, thirty-two. Currently, four out of every ten education projects include a reading material component. The first textbook projects assisted by the Bank, in the Philippines and Indonesia, were designed to fill a gap in the education cycle—namely, the production and distribution of teaching materials. Subsequent projects were designed to carry this objective further by creating the institutional capacity to ensure a continuing process of design and supply from local sources.

Designing textbooks is a highly refined skill. Appropriately designed textbooks require a lengthy period of pretesting among representative samples of a nation's ethnic and social groups. Such an effort is expensive and demanding. Moreover, its importance is commonly underestimated, with the result that textbooks in developing countries are frequently lengthy, complicated, badly illustrated, and inappropriately bound. Problems of supply and delivery must also be mastered if the quantity—as well as the quality—of textbooks is to meet acceptable standards.

INSTITUTIONAL ISSUES

Management

The inadequacies of managerial capacity in the education sector are part and parcel of the much wider problems of limited national administrative, managerial, and analytical capacity, the limited scope and reliability of data, and the inadequacies of public administration generally, from which developing countries typically suffer. Their deficiencies in this area contrast with the progress made in the industrial countries, where educators have acquired the management skills needed to deliver a complex array of services through the schools, including programs tailored to individual needs. In view of the constraints on financial, physical, and human resources in the sector in developing countries, the need to make most effective use of whatever resources are available is urgent—and this requires good management. Competence in managing an educational system cannot be achieved in isolation from other improvements. Nevertheless, there are some measures specifically applicable to the sector that may help to improve the situation.

Whether schools will be centrally or locally governed usually depends upon a country's political system. The tendency has been to centralize responsibility for decisionmaking. In the interests of preserving the national character of education, governments have been disinclined to delegate to local community or school authorities responsibility for such matters as curricula and textbooks. Resistance to decentralization has also come from, among others, teachers, who prefer employment by national authorities both for the more advantageous terms of employment and for the freedom from local pressures and from accountability to local communities. But with the growing complexity of educational systems, the increase in the number of students at all levels, the broadening of curricula, and the diversity of teaching materials, managerial challenges have increased. Education ministries have become overburdened with administrative concerns, sometimes to the detriment of their policymaking role, and they find it increasingly difficult to respond to, or even to determine, the needs of local communities. Although a greater degree of decentralization is indicated, it will not result in lasting improvement in the management of the system unless the administrative units down the line can supply qualified administrators; often they cannot. One approach is to establish specialized management institutes for education; another is to provide managerial training for educators at general management institutes or universities. National and regional institutions offer the advantage of ready access and the possibility of suiting training methods and aims to national needs, as well as the possibility of mixing formal training and on-the-job experience. But the extent to which managerial capacity will be improved obviously depends on the quality of the institutes that are set up to provide this training. Many of the existing institutes suffer from a shortage of good staff and effective training materials.

Planning and Research

Planning for the education sector encompasses such varied subjects as student selection criteria, teacher training, salary scales, classroom size, and curriculum development. It requires personnel in the field who can supply requisite data to the central planners and can monitor and report on results of policy implementation. Special qualifications are required for both the planners and the data gatherers and monitors.

In many developing countries, planning suffers from the common practice of making decisions ad hoc, without adequate consideration or appreciation of their impact on other issues of educational policy. Moreover, where plans have not worked as expected, it has often been because innovations were imported or undertaken without first establishing their appropriateness or likely effectiveness in the local socioeconomic environment. Expansion has been given priority over quality improvement, and in some cases the level of learning in the new facilities has proved so low as to call into question the economic justification of the investment. Furthermore, uncoordinated funding of disparate activities has too often

led to a disjointed approach to a country's education needs. The inadequacies of data noted earlier mean that the typical education planner in
a developing country lacks the information essential for making sound
decisions and for monitoring progress. The basic issue for governments
is how to plan for the sector as a whole, by addressing both short-term
and long-term needs, and then to translate the plan into individual
projects that are integrated through the plan and that take into account
the links between education and other sectors.

The components of a research capacity for the education sector are no
different from those of other sectors: trained personnel, documentation,
procedures for collecting and handling data, arrangements for disseminating results, and funding. The expansion of research capacity through
training is perhaps the most urgently needed of these, together with
arrangements to ensure that the problems worked on are relevant to
making decisions and shaping policy. Examples of relevant topics are the
determinants of educational performance and alternative sources of
educational finance. Because many of the issues to be investigated are of
concern to several countries, and because of financial constraints, some
training and research efforts and experience have been shared on a
regional basis. These cooperative efforts might usefully be intensified.

Investment Issues

The foregoing discussion has drawn heavily on the Bank's experience
in lending for educational development, including its findings on such
matters as diversified schools, nonformal education, curriculum reform,
and project-related training. We conclude this chapter with some general
observations on the Bank's investment experience, followed by more
detailed comments on several specific issues.

Performance

Time and Cost Overruns

Bank-assisted education projects have characteristically taken longer
to implement than expected at the time of appraisal. Projects have taken
an average of eight years to complete, more than two years over the
average original estimate. Cost overruns have also been pervasive, but
are difficult to measure since they are often concealed by reductions in
the scope of the project during implementation.

Reaching Targets

Projects have nonetheless generally achieved their physical objectives
with respect to the number of student places provided, and enrollments
have equaled or even exceeded the targets—for example, through double
shifts or night classes, as in Korea. General primary and secondary
schools have rapidly been fully enrolled, or even overenrolled. Technical,
vocational, and agricultural schools have had much more difficulty, partly
because they are considered less desirable by students and partly because
of problems in recruiting teachers for the specialties offered.

Project Complexity

As we have observed, educational reform is a complex and time-consuming process. Elaborate projects that try to accomplish many things at once have been less successful than those with more modest objectives that leave other types of reform or change to subsequent projects. Projects can also be too simple, however. The addition of "software" (such as teacher training, textbooks, and curriculum revision) to the traditional brick-and-mortar investment in school buildings has greatly enhanced the latter's development impact.

Recurrent Costs and Maintenance

One factor whose importance to successful project performance cannot be stressed too often is that of financing recurrent costs. As we have seen, investments in educational facilities have typically led to high recurrent costs for teachers' salaries and for operating and maintaining the facilities. When these costs have not been anticipated and suitable arrangements made both for budgetary support and for the requisite institutional mechanisms, project-induced improvements and reforms have often not been sustained once the facilities came into operation. This is a responsibility that most governments must shoulder themselves, since external lenders are not often willing to help finance the recurrent costs of education.

Design

Construction Standards

Construction policies have affected the speed with which countries have been able to expand their educational facilities. Some governments, intent on a rapid increase in the number of school places, have adopted designs that, while meeting minimum standards, are relatively cheap; others have been prepared to hold back the rate of expansion in order to permit adoption of higher, and therefore more costly, design standards. There may also be tradeoffs between high initial capital costs and subsequent maintenance costs, or between improvement of existing facilities and their replacement. High initial costs may sometimes imply high recurrent costs as well; for example, the recurrent costs of specialized laboratories and workshops, as well as the capital costs, are high in comparison with those of traditional schools without such facilities. A cost-benefit analysis can help to elucidate these choices. In general, however, school buildings—at least at the primary level—are simple structures, and standardized designs have helped to provide better space utilization, more rapid construction, and lower cost.

Local Materials and Building Techniques

Similar issues are involved in the choice of construction materials and building techniques. Maximum reliance on local materials and community participation may be the preferred approach in many, but not necessarily all, cases. On the one hand, locally constructed facilities may be more replicable, require less foreign exchange, and be easier for local communities to maintain. On the other hand, they may have a shorter life and require more frequent maintenance. Self-help construction, too, has its pluses and minuses. A community may identify more closely with a school it has helped build and therefore take more responsibility for it. But by its nature, communal construction is more difficult to organize, the project implementation period can be longer and therefore more costly, the standard of construction may be lower, and self-help labor may be exploited. Self-help construction has been most effective when it was the traditional practice rather than something first introduced through a project. Even then, minimum design standards must be set and the construction adequately supervised. Locally designed school buildings with so little light that children cannot read inside them are not unknown.

Appropriate Technology

Another issue of project design concerns the choice of technology. A decade or two ago, the expectation was high that transmitting lessons to students in schools by radio or TV would increase access to schooling, while maintaining quality, at no extra cost. Teachers would be able to teach larger groups of students since the media would transmit much of the instruction; or less qualified teachers (usually "monitors" without formal qualifications) would be able to run classrooms in which students were taught by the media. During the 1970s, many experiments were conducted to test this concept. The results have taught us that

- Instructional programs delivered through media can teach children effectively. Some subjects can be taught this way better than others. Radio and TV each impose their own constraints on the types of instruction that can be transmitted, but children do learn.
- Developing effective instructional materials is far more difficult than anyone had anticipated. It is time-consuming and expensive because it must be based on an analysis of the curriculum, careful specification of learning goals, program evaluation, and the development of instructional strategies specifically suited to the medium.
- The expected savings on teachers' salaries have not materialized. In those projects that have tried to use higher student-teacher ratios or underqualified teachers, the instructors have forced the authorities, through strikes and other means, to raise salaries or lower class sizes. In fact, since the production of software has turned out to be expensive, programs using media almost always cost more than comparable programs without media. At the same time, some media experiments have improved achievement levels, rather than simply substituting for teachers. Whether the improvement in quality is worth the added cost must be judged in the specific context.
- Some of the experience gained in one country can be transferred to others. The Radio Math lessons developed in Nicaragua have been translated into Thai and are teaching Thai children as effectively as they taught Nicaraguan children.

The appropriate use of electronic media can extend well beyond formal education. Media-based instructional programs have proved their effectiveness in improving correspondence education, in upgrading the skills of teachers, nurses, and agricultural agents, and in building community support for social change. Moreover, the term "technology" covers more than use of the electronic media. It applies equally to reference materials, background reading, library loan programs, maps, charts, models, and experimental equipment of many kinds. No longer perceived simply as a means of reducing costs, appropriate technology offers many opportunities for improving educational quality.

Project Management and Implementation

Project Implementation Units

An important issue in education as in other sectors is whether to assign the responsibility for managing a large project to the established ministry or to a specially created project implementation unit. The principal argument for selecting the line ministry as manager is that this contributes to the desirable objective of institution building. In many countries, however, the managerial capacity of the education ministry is weak. As noted earlier, its high-level managers are usually former teachers without managerial training. Its staff of civil servants does not usually include economists and sociologists with competence in sector and project evaluation, and its auditors and financial personnel often have less experience than their counterparts in other ministries. Moreover, all these individuals have other responsibilities to discharge.

Whenever an existing department of the ministry of education—or another ministry or a university—is properly organized and capable of handling the managerial responsibilities for a particular project, or can be made so with technical assistance provided as part of the project, this is the preferred course of action. Of the Bank-assisted education projects now under implementation, 70 percent are being managed in this fashion. When this is not possible, a special project implementation unit should be established, but with the explicit intention of eventually integrating the unit into the ministry as a permanent body.

A special project implementation unit has only one central function to perform; it devotes all of its time to the full scope of project activities— school design, administration of bids, hiring of consultants, and so on. Typically, it is located outside the ministry's line of authority. Its staff, sometimes including expatriates, receive compensation higher than is permitted by civil service scales, and its personnel and operating policies are not subject to civil service constraints. For these reasons, the institution-building potential of such a unit is limited. Nevertheless, some of the project implementation units have made important contributions to that objective. They have been a valuable training ground for local staff who may, as in the Philippines and Korea, become the nucleus for a larger group charged with responsibility for implementing all government-financed or externally financed projects in the sector. The project implementation unit in Sierra Leone designed and administered an education sector study that helped the education ministry to analyze alternatives, determine priorities, and plan investments. More than half of the units established in Bank-assisted education projects have by now "graduated"; that is, they have been made a part of the parent ministry, where they are exercising wider managerial responsibilities.

Monitoring and Evaluation

Project design must address the important information needs of those who manage and implement the project. Most education projects, particularly those with innovative or experimental features, should include some procedure for ongoing monitoring or evaluation. This might cover special studies to assess the impact of a particular intervention, such as measuring the gains in student achievement from instructional radio programs, as in the Philippines; or tracking the course of implementation of educational reform, as in Haiti; or monitoring the delivery of educational supplies and materials, as in Ethiopia; or assessing improvements in the content of textbooks, as in Guatemala. These activities provide information to help managers and policymakers guide the course of project implementation and modify it as necessary. They also build and institutionalize the capacity to collect and evaluate information.

Like other aspects of project design, however, a monitoring and evaluation system must be planned from the outset rather than added as an afterthought. The staff needed to perform these functions should generally be on board, and base-level data collected, by the time project implementation begins. The monitoring and evaluation unit must be closely integrated with the project management unit, the staff of which may have to be trained in the use of the information system if it is to serve effectively its intended purpose.

Constructing a spillway at the Victoria dam, Sri Lanka

8

Energy

CHARACTERISTICS OF THE SECTOR

THE NEED TO DEAL with energy problems in developing countries (and in developed ones) on a sectorwide basis has been recognized only recently. This is hardly surprising in view of the great diversity in the origins, operations, and products of the major components of the sector—hydrocarbons, electric power, and coal. The disparities in structure and institutions between, for example, the oil industry—which, until recently, was dominated in most countries by foreign private firms—and the electric power industry—which generally consists of local government-owned companies—also made it appear that the components of the sector had little in common. The events of the 1970s, however, clearly signaled the developing countries and the world not only that profound shifts in energy supply and use patterns were needed, but also that the necessary transition could be effectively managed only if it was realized that the oil crisis was, in fact, an energy crisis.

The 1970s also saw a growing recognition that developing countries face critical problems in another, very different part of the energy sector. The great majority of people in developing countries do not use oil, electricity, or other forms of commercial energy in their daily lives, but depend on traditional, noncommercial fuels such as animal and crop wastes and wood to meet their basic energy need, which is for cooking fuel. This is true not only of rural populations but also of the urban poor. Noncommercial fuels account for some 20 to 25 percent of total energy consumption in the developing world, and for as much as 70 to 90 percent in the poorer Asian and African countries. Many developing countries now face a severe fuelwood shortage, caused by the growing pressures on the natural forests from rising population and expanding land clearance. This so-called second energy crisis not only has serious economic, social, and environmental consequences of its own, it also has important links to the commercial energy situation. In some places, growing shortages of fuelwood have led to increased use of commercial fuels (especially kerosene) for household purposes—particularly in urban and semiurban areas—while in other places rising prices for commercial fuels have shifted some semiurban demand back to traditional fuels, with adverse consequences for supplies in rural areas.

Economic Aspects

The oil crisis of the 1970s underscored the pervasive influence of the energy sector on the domestic economies of the developing countries, on their international financial position, and on their growth prospects. Energy is an input or output in almost all productive activity; consequently, the links between energy and the rest of the economy are strong and intimate. Not only do energy investments compete with those in other sectors for scarce investable resources, but decisions on them cannot be taken without considering how they interrelate with policies and trends elsewhere in the economy. These relationships have many dimensions. In all countries, industrial strategy is closely linked to energy demand, and energy costs have a strong bearing on industrial structure and efficiency. As a rule of thumb, an investment in industrial capacity of $100 requires a complementary investment of $30 in electric power. The investment costs of providing power to one job in industry range from about $3,000 in labor-intensive industries (textiles, food processing) to as much as $200,000 in heavy industry (petrochemicals, steel, cement). Energy policies and prices can also profoundly affect the pattern of urbanization, the relative demand for different modes of transport, and agricultural development.

Increased energy consumption is an intrinsic part of the process of modernization, industrialization, and urbanization through which the developing countries are passing. There is a strong positive correlation between income and the consumption of commercial energy: consumption in the poorest developing countries averages about 73 kilograms of oil equivalent of commercial energy per person, while consumption in the middle-income developing countries averages about 800 kilograms per person (still less than 20 percent of the energy consumed per person in the industrialized countries). There is an inverse correlation, however, between income and the consumption of noncommercial energy since rising income levels and growing urbanization lead to greater use of commercial fuels for domestic purposes.

In the past, consumption of commercial energy has risen more rapidly than income. As table 8-1 shows, consumption in developing countries grew at the rate of nearly 6 percent a year in the 1970s, while the rate of increase in GDP was about 5 percent a year. Most of the increase went to meet the needs of the industrial and transport sectors, which together account for more than 50 percent of commercial energy consumption in the developing countries.

Energy also plays a critical role in the development process because it is a major determinant of the external viability of virtually all developing countries. Among the developing countries that import oil, the share of export earnings absorbed by oil imports is a good indication of the direct impact of oil quantities and prices on the balance of payments. This ratio

Table 8-1. *Consumption of Commercial Primary Energy in Developing Countries, 1970–95*

Energy source	Million tons of oil equivalent			Annual growth rate (percent)	
	1970	1980	1995	1970–80	1980–95
Oil	355	626	934	5.8	2.7
Coal	298	494	940	5.2	4.4
Natural gas	47	95	324	7.3	8.5
Primary electricity	56	130	396	8.8	7.7
Total	756	1,345	2,594	5.9	4.5
Gross domestic product (GDP)				5.1	4.8

Source: Data and projections are taken from World Bank, *The Energy Transition in Developing Countries* (Washington, D.C., 1983).

varies a great deal, depending on the importance of trade in the economy, the level of industrial and transport activity, and the availability of alternative energy sources. For a sample of thirty-nine oil-importing developing countries in 1980, payments for net oil imports took over half of merchandise export earnings in seven countries, between one-fourth and one-half in seventeen countries, and less than one-fourth in the remaining fifteen countries. Another measure of dependence on imported oil is the share of oil imports in a country's total commercial energy consumption. About half of the oil importers, including many of the poorest countries, rely on imported oil for more than 75 percent of their commercial energy requirements.

Looking ahead to 1995, World Bank projections prepared country by country indicate that the energy requirements of the developing countries will continue to rise, although consumption will grow significantly less rapidly than in the recent past and at a somewhat slower pace than GDP. During the same period, energy production in these countries is expected to grow more rapidly than in the past. Consequently, the gap between consumption and domestic production should be much narrower than in the 1970s. Nevertheless, as table 8-2 shows, the oil import requirements of the oil-importing developing countries are still expected to grow substantially. Development prospects in these countries will remain highly dependent on world oil markets, and reducing this dependence will continue to be a matter of the highest priority for them.

Social Aspects

The social consequences of developments in the energy sector, no less important than the economic aspects, are related mainly to noncommercial rather than commercial energy. Some 2 billion people in the developing world are almost wholly dependent on traditional fuels, particularly

Table 8-2. *Production and Consumption of Commercial Primary Energy and of Oil Imports in Oil-Importing Developing Countries, 1970–95*

Activity	Million tons of oil equivalent			Annual growth rate (percent)	
	1970	*1980*	*1995*	*1970–80*	*1980–95*
Production					
Oil	63	65	145	0.3	5.5
Coal	118	192	384	5.0	4.7
Natural gas	14	27	115	6.8	10.1
Primary electricity	41	98	306	9.1	7.9
Total	236	382	950	4.9	6.3
Consumption					
Oil	223	360	531	4.9	2.6
Coal	121	186	442	4.4	5.9
Natural gas	12	26	120	8.0	10.7
Primary electricity	41	98	306	9.1	7.9
Total	397	670	1,399	5.4	5.0
Oil imports	160	295	386	6.3	1.8

Sources: United Nations and World Bank estimates.

fuelwood, to meet their domestic energy needs. It is estimated that fuelwood supplies are at present, or may soon be, inadequate to meet these needs in some sixty-five developing countries. The human cost of the fuelwood crisis has been high, both through its immediate impact on the lives of the poor and through its long-term effect on the prospects for alleviating poverty. Many villagers, mainly women and children, who could previously collect fuelwood in the immediate vicinity of their homes, now find they must search for it a half-day's walk, or more, away. For example, families in the upland areas of Nepal are spending the equivalent of 60 to 230 days a year on fuelwood collection, while in some parts of Tanzania it takes 250 to 300 days a year to meet a family's needs. The impact is not limited to rural areas. A World Bank survey found that poor families in the capital of Burundi are spending as much as 30 percent of their income for cooking fuel.

While the fuelwood shortage poses a clear and present danger to the welfare of many of the poorest people in developing countries, it is only part of the more general lack of rural energy that is a serious obstacle to long-term efforts to alleviate poverty. Raising the productivity and incomes of small farmers, who are now almost wholly dependent on their own energy and that of their animals, requires that they be provided with power for productive purposes such as pumping irrigation water, drying crops, and grinding grain. Providing energy for such purposes as village water supply, health, and education is also an essential part of the rural development process. The relatively small amount of energy required for these purposes is not likely to have an appreciable impact on the energy balance in any country, but can contribute importantly to welfare and development. The classic approach of providing rural energy through electrification has made little progress in most countries because of the high cost of delivering centrally generated power to isolated, often sparsely populated areas. Greater attention is now being focused, therefore, on the possibilities of providing power from small-scale, decentralized sources, particularly where locally available renewable resources can be used for this purpose; wind pumping and solar crop drying are examples of this approach.

Financial Aspects

The energy sector has been making increasingly heavy claims on the internal and external financial resources of the developing countries. In the late 1970s, energy sector investment in the developing countries rose to about 2 to 3 percent of GDP, equivalent to some 10 percent of total investment. Capital spending by the energy sector is expected to continue to grow rapidly because of the need in most countries to invest heavily in the development of indigenous resources (and in conservation) and because of the high capital cost of the investments called for by the energy transition. For example, whereas a large oil-fired plant requires an investment of about $800 (in 1982 prices) for each kilowatt of installed capacity, a large coal-fired plant requires a comparable investment of $1,100 ($2,000 for a small one). Hydroelectric projects generally cost from $1,500 to $2,500 per installed kilowatt, and nuclear plants about $2,000. World Bank projections indicate that over the next decade energy investment in the developing countries will have to rise to about 4 percent of GDP and average about $130 billion a year. As table 8-3 shows, about

$110 billion of the required annual investment is for electric power and oil, with the balance split fairly evenly between gas and coal.

The financing of energy investments has important implications for the balance of payments of developing countries, particularly in view of the high foreign exchange component of the sector's capital spending. Dur-

Table 8-3. *Commercial Energy Investment Requirements in Developing Countries, 1982–92*
(billions of 1982 U.S. dollars)

Activity	Low-income countries	Middle-income countries		All developing countries	Annual average 1982–92
		Oil importers	Oil exporters		
Electric power					
Hydro	74.4	132.2	31.8	238.4	21.7
Nuclear	6.3	40.8	6.1	53.2	4.8
Geothermal	0.1	4.3	2.1	6.5	0.6
Thermal	43.2	75.8	39.7	158.7	14.4
Transmission and distribution	49.9	101.8	49.9	201.6	18.3
Total	173.9	354.9	129.6	658.4	59.8
Oil					
Exploration	21.2	48.9	99.1	169.2	15.4
Development	43.2	32.4	195.9	271.5	24.7
Other[a]	2.5	6.0	16.7	25.2	2.3
Total	66.9	87.3	311.7	465.9	42.4
Refineries[b]	30.8	52.8	39.7	123.3	11.2
Natural gas					
Exploration, development, transmission, and maintenance	17.5	16.8	30.2	64.5	5.9
Domestic distribution[c]	4.3	4.7	7.4	16.4	1.5
Exports	0.0	3.0	6.2	9.2	0.8
Total	21.8	24.5	43.8	90.1	8.2
Coal	55.2	27.2	6.3	88.7	8.1
Total	348.6	546.7	531.1	1,426.4	129.7

Note: These estimates are for the investments required during 1982–92 to achieve the projected levels of energy production. Some additional investments amounting to $13 billion a year will be required in the 1993–95 period to complete the projects for 1995 production. Expenditures shown in this table do not include investments for fuel storage and retail distribution (except for pipeline investments for domestic distribution of natural gas) or for infrastructure associated with energy imports.

a. Estimates include maintenance of old fields, enhanced and secondary oil recovery, pipelines, and infrastructure.

b. Estimates include investments in refinery modifications necessary to achieve a balance between the supply of and demand for petroleum products within developing countries, as well as investments in refinery rehabilitation, replacement of old plant, and energy conservation. These estimates could vary by as much as 20 percent, depending on assumptions about the refinery mix in China and the extent to which product imbalances in the developing countries are met through direct trade in refined products. Estimates exclude investments in infrastructure development, which amount to about $10 billion.

c. Distribution of gas is from major transmission pipelines to residential and commercial users.

Source: World Bank estimates.

ing the 1970s, developing countries began to increase rapidly their external borrowing for energy investment. The $16 billion borrowed by them in 1980 was more than 60 percent higher in real terms than the amount borrowed in 1975, and the total debt outstanding for energy purposes in 1980—nearly $100 billion—was some 19 percent of their total external debt. More than 70 percent of this debt was incurred to finance power sector investments, with the remainder going almost entirely to oil and gas projects. The need for external financing of energy investments is likely to grow even more rapidly in the coming decade. About half of the energy investments projected for developing countries, or about $65 billion a year, is estimated to represent foreign exchange costs. Since external capital inflows to the energy sector probably do not exceed $25 billion a year currently, foreign borrowing for this purpose will have to grow by some 15 percent a year in real terms to cover the projected requirements. The energy sector already accounts for a major share of developing countries' foreign borrowing, and it seems unlikely that the sector's investment requirements can be met without a significant expansion of external capital flows.

Increased effectiveness in mobilizing domestic resources will be at least as important as greater foreign borrowing in enabling the developing countries to meet their energy investment needs. Since in most developing countries the energy sector is largely, if not entirely, in the hands of the public sector, this will require a decisive improvement in the finances of the public sector generally and of public enterprises. Most energy enterprises suffer from the same basic financial weaknesses as other public companies—inadequate revenues along with overstaffing and other excessive costs. The financial position of most power utilities has deteriorated badly since the early 1970s; tariffs have not risen sufficiently to meet sharply escalating fuel and borrowing costs, while the cost and the gestation period of their investments have increased. The resulting inability of the utilities to generate their own financing, as they once did, has imposed a heavy burden on the budgets of many countries, while making their investment programs more vulnerable to the pressures on those budgets. Domestic finance is, if anything, an even more critical issue in the coal industry, in which prices have often been insufficient to cover even operating costs and companies have long had to rely almost wholly on budgetary transfers. National oil and gas companies, in contrast, are frequently important sources of public revenue, although they, too, sometimes encounter financial difficulties as the result of government controls on consumer prices and delays in payments from government agencies.

Institutional Aspects

As already noted, the energy sector in most developing countries is dominated by large, state-owned public enterprises, although the international oil companies play an important role in some places. While the power utilities and national oil and gas companies frequently rank among the most modern and advanced elements in the public sector, they have generally been afflicted by the usual panoply of state-enterprise problems. These include, most importantly, wage and salary scales too low to enable the companies to attract and retain qualified personnel, bureaucratic encumbrances affecting internal operations and personnel practices, and slow decisionmaking and political interference by the executive and legislative bodies on which they depend. Needless to say, the problems of energy enterprises do not stem wholly from their being public companies, and the character and effectiveness of energy institutions vary widely from country to country as well as within a country. In some countries, particularly the poorest ones, institutional problems may reflect mainly the general scarcity of experienced technical and managerial personnel; in others, long-established organizations, such as power companies, may be well managed while newer institutions, such as national oil companies, may lack the legal framework, policy guidance, and personnel to function effectively.

In addition to the problems of individual enterprises, the fragmentation of responsibility for energy policy and operations is a critical institutional weakness in most developing countries. The need to approach energy problems on a sectorwide basis, as noted earlier, is a relatively new concept that has yet to be effectively institutionalized in most developing countries. Energy enterprises are frequently responsible to different government ministries, with little policy guidance or coordination coming from the prime minister's office or planning department. Since the 1970s, however, efforts have been under way in many countries to consolidate responsibilities and eliminate overlapping jurisdictions by setting up central sector institutions and strengthening the policy and planning process. Nevertheless, with energy ministries and sector planning units struggling to establish themselves in many countries, and still absent in others, institutional concerns continue to rank high among the sector's problems.

DEVELOPMENT OBJECTIVES

The objectives that developing countries must pursue in the energy sector are defined by the two main problems they face. First, they must make the transition to an era of higher commercial energy costs as rapidly and as painlessly as possible, and second, they must ensure that rural energy needs for both domestic and productive purposes are adequately met. To achieve these objectives they will need to

- Increase the efficiency with which both commercial and noncommercial energy is used so that demand reflects the true needs of the economy
- Ensure that the amounts of energy required are supplied in a least-cost manner
- Develop domestic energy resources, nonconventional as well as conventional, wherever economically feasible.

Increasing Energy Efficiency

Although the developing countries will continue to increase their energy consumption substantially, the rate of growth of demand and the size of their total energy bill will be determined to an important extent by the efficiency with which they use energy. Developing countries should, therefore, give high priority to ensuring that they use only as much energy as is needed to support the processes of growth and structural change. Whether pursued under the banner of "energy efficiency," "demand management," or "conservation," programs that seek to minimize the amount of energy used to produce a given output can yield high returns quickly by reducing fuel costs and by making it possible to avoid or postpone investment in increasing energy supplies. Indeed, a calorie saved is often worth a good deal more than a calorie produced. For example, the World Bank estimates that the cost of saving a kilowatt of electricity by improving the distribution system may be only a third as much as the cost of producing an additional kilowatt from new generating equipment.

The level and pattern of energy consumption, and hence the scope for improving energy efficiency, vary widely from country to country. A rough idea of the potential for greater efficiency can be obtained by comparing national levels of commercial energy intensity (energy used per unit of GDP). Most low-income countries are less energy-intensive than the industrial countries, but middle-income developing countries are generally at least as energy-intensive. Some developing countries, including India, Korea, and Yugoslavia, are close to the levels of the most energy-intensive industrial countries, while others, notably China, are above these levels. There is also substantial potential for improving the efficiency with which noncommercial energy is utilized. Most wood is burned on open cooking fires in which only about 5 to 10 percent of the wood's energy potential is used, and most charcoal is produced in primitive kilns in which energy losses may amount to 60 percent or more. The introduction of simple, enclosed cooking stoves and improved kilns can make an important contribution to alleviating the fuelwood problem. Unfortunately, it has proved more difficult than envisaged to design cooking stoves that are efficient, affordable, readily constructed from available materials, and socially acceptable. More rapid progress should be possible, however, as a result of the systematic effort now under way to design and distribute better stoves. This effort is focused on urban and semiurban households facing rising fuelwood costs, and on fabricated metal or ceramic stoves that can be marketed commercially.

Industries may be the most promising target for energy efficiency programs in developing countries since they account for a large share of commercial energy consumption and often use more energy than do similar industries in developed countries. Substantial savings can be realized by concentrating on a limited number of large, energy-intensive industries, including iron and steel, petroleum refining, cement, and chemicals. Many plants in these industries in developing countries have been found to consume 10 to 30 percent more energy per unit of output than is the best international practice, and some plants consume over twice as much. The recent experience of the developed countries has shown that energy costs per unit of output in these industries can be significantly reduced through a variety of measures ranging from better housekeeping (including improvements in insulation, combustion, and steam system efficiency) and better monitoring and control systems to more capital-intensive investments in retrofitting existing equipment and greater use of energy-efficient processes. Even with small investments, mainly of a housekeeping nature, energy savings of up to 10 percent are possible, and with larger investments—including the replacement of inefficient equipment—savings of 10 to 30 percent can be realized.

Smaller, less energy-intensive industries are a secondary target for conservation efforts since, although the potential for savings is large, results are likely to be achieved more slowly and with greater effort because of the need to reach out to many medium-size and small firms. Getting energy prices right, so that they provide the correct signals to producers and consumers, is an important element of this process, and is discussed below in the section "Mobilizing Finance."

Although transport may consume as much energy as industry, or even more, the scope for savings and the means to achieve them are less well known. It is clear, however, that the primary focus should be on trucks and other road vehicles, which typically account for 65 to 80 percent of energy consumption in the transport sector and some 13 to 32 percent of national petroleum consumption. Experience suggests that better driver performance can cut fuel consumption by some 20 percent, and that even larger savings can be achieved by maintaining vehicles better, using them more efficiently (for example, by reducing empty backhauls), and choosing the type of vehicle best adapted to particular loads. As in industry, efforts should be concentrated, at least initially, on large users such as bus companies, trucking firms, and taxi fleets. Significant improvements in fuel consumption by private as well as by commercial vehicles can also be achieved by improvements in urban traffic management (see chapter 11, Transport).

Further significant opportunities for energy savings are to be found in the electric power industry, particularly by reducing power losses in transmission and distribution. Such losses amount to about 15 percent of power generated in half of the developing countries for which data are available, and take on added significance as energy costs rise. Since research indicates that, under normal circumstances, transmission and distribution losses could be reduced—in a way that is economically justified—to between 4 and 8 percent of the total power generated, many developing countries should try to cut present losses by a third to a half. A reduction of distribution losses from 10 to 5 percent would be equivalent to one year's growth in demand. There may also be considerable scope for reducing generation losses, particularly where, as in China and India, electric power systems depend heavily on thermal plants. Finally, important savings in electric power (and other forms of energy) may be achieved by reducing consumption in commercial and institutional buildings. The commercial sector is becoming an increasingly important user of energy in the middle-income developing countries, especially in countries where air-conditioning accounts for a significant portion of the demand for electricity. In existing buildings, better energy management, improved control and monitoring systems, and minor retrofitting investments can result in savings of up to 25 percent. In new buildings, improved design standards and regulations can reduce heating and cooling requirements to 50 percent of those of buildings designed as recently as ten years ago.

Reducing Energy Supply Costs

If developing countries are to hold down energy costs, they need to ensure not only that they are using no more energy than necessary, but also that they are obtaining their energy at the least possible cost. The increased price of oil has made several alternative energy sources attractive—mainly coal and gas, but also hydro and geothermal power, as well as biomass and other renewables. The scope for savings through fuel switching that is economically justified varies widely among developing countries, depending on their resource base, transport and distribution costs, and technical and institutional capabilities. Some countries have already begun to make good progress in shifting toward cheaper fuels, and the potential is there for many other countries to do the same. Developing countries will generally find that their most promising prospects for reducing energy supply costs are in industry and power, but the replacement of gasoline and diesel fuel in the transport sector by alcohol, compressed natural gas, or liquified petroleum gas may be worth considering in countries with substantial biomass or gas resources.

Converting industrial plants to coal or gas can cut fuel costs by 50 to 80 percent, a fact already reflected in extensive fuel switching in manufacturing in the industrialized countries. For example, the share of petroleum fuels in industrial energy consumption declined between 1973 and 1980 from 60 to 57 percent in Japan, from 52 to 43 percent in Germany, and from 54 to 41 percent in the United Kingdom. Substitution efforts already under way in developing countries include the replacement of oil by gas in Pakistan and Bangladesh (where gas now accounts for about 50 percent of industrial energy consumption), by coal in Zambia, and by biomass (charcoal) in Brazil. While substantial investments in new burners and boilers and in fuel transport and handling equipment may be necessary to permit substitution, the resulting savings usually provide a high rate of return on such investments. An industry may also be able to reduce its costs by using waste heat from nearby utilities to help meet its processing needs, and by the "cogeneration" of electricity in excess of its own needs for sale to the public grid. Cogeneration is likely to be most economic when an industry requires both heat and electricity, but less of the latter than the former; it may be particularly attractive to energy users with sizable amounts of waste fuels, such as sugarcane bagasse.

For many countries, changing the energy sources from which electric power is generated can be a powerful instrument for achieving a least-cost national fuel mix, and this should be a major objective of policy over the coming years. While some countries with limited domestic resources and high import costs may have little scope for fuel substitution, most countries should be able to phase out a large portion of their oil-based power generation, keeping some installed capacity for peaking and cycling. Indeed, World Bank projections indicate a dramatic decline in oil usage by developing countries, from 26 percent of total power generated in 1980 to 7 percent in 1995, mainly as a result of increased reliance on coal. These projections do not allow for the conversion of existing oil-fired plants to coal, since this generally seems to be less economic than accelerating the construction of new coal-burning units which, depending on their size and the cost of coal, can offer substantial cost savings. For example, at current prices, large coal-based plants located at the mine, using coal at $40 a ton, generate electricity at about 4¢ a kilowatt hour, compared with 7¢ a kilowatt hour from oil-based plants; the same units using imported coal at $80 a ton generate electricity at about 5.5¢ a kilowatt hour. Hydroelectric power can be more economical than coal or oil when capital costs remain in the range of $2,000 to $3,000 per kilowatt of generating capacity, and its development should be given priority in countries with suitable sites. Gas can also play an important role in reducing power generation costs in countries well endowed with this resource, while biomass-fueled plants and small hydroelectric stations may be an economical alternative to diesel generators for small-scale power generation in rural areas.

Nuclear power may also be an economically feasible means of generating power in countries without sufficient domestic fossil fuel or hydroelectric or other natural energy resources, and with power systems large enough to accommodate economically viable nuclear plants. At the present cost of constructing a nuclear plant, it is unlikely that units smaller than about 600 megawatts can compete with alternative fuels, so that only relatively large power systems (about 5,000 megawatts) can be considered eligible to have a portion of their needs supplied by nuclear power. Only fifteen developing countries appear to fall into this category today, but power systems have not stopped growing, and it is reasonable to expect that more power development programs will contain economically justified nuclear projects. The start-up costs of a nuclear program—establishing institutions, training staff, putting control mechanisms into place—can be substantial. As countries approach nuclear eligibility, they will need not only to consider carefully whether and when nuclear plants may form part of a least-cost power program but also to assess such noneconomic factors as the safety and reliability of nuclear power, the environmental hazards, and the general public concern about nuclear power.

Developing Domestic Resources

Domestic energy sources are frequently the cheapest ones, and their development is both an intrinsic part of every country's efforts to reduce energy supply costs and a potentially important means of achieving greater energy independence. The events of the 1970s brought home powerfully to many countries how vulnerable to external shocks their dependence on imported oil makes them, and led them to place a premium on obtaining greater control over the supply and cost of energy as a matter of national security. In addition, developing domestic energy sources can help generate employment and income, and it offers high returns; this makes it especially attractive to developing countries.

The potential for increasing domestic energy supplies varies with a country's resource endowments. Some countries have only limited potential for meeting their full energy needs themselves because of a lack of resources, their high cost, or a mismatch between resources and needs. Other countries either have modest amounts of one or more important resources or, in the most fortunate cases, are blessed with substantial and varied reserves of primary energy. Of 80 oil-importing developing countries classified by the World Bank, 51 were deemed to have moderate or substantial resource potential—including 31 of the 59 countries which depend on oil imports for more than 50 percent of their commercial energy consumption (see table 8-4 on page 162).

Nonrenewable Resources

Although estimates of the potential for oil production in developing countries vary greatly, there is general agreement that widespread opportunities for the economic expansion of domestic output do exist, including opportunities in countries that are not now oil producers. The World Bank has projected that domestic oil production in the oil-importing developing countries will increase by about 125 percent between 1980 and 1995 (see table 8-2). This is an estimate of what can be accomplished using known resource potential since it assumes that the present low level of exploration in these countries will persist and that any increase in production will come from already known reserves or from new discoveries in known basins.

While the growth of oil production in developing countries is constrained on the supply side, large known reserves of natural gas have remained unexploited, primarily because of doubts about the demand side of the market and the cost of serving this demand. It is becoming apparent, however, that the cost of gas development is lower, and the potential domestic demand higher and more diverse, than previously believed. Recent World Bank studies demonstrate that the cost of producing and transporting gas is well below the c.i.f. price (that is, the cost including insurance and freight) of imported petroleum fuels. The use of gas to generate electricity and as a boiler fuel can provide large economic benefits; in many countries, this will constitute a major part of total gas use. Since these markets already exist and can be tapped speedily and with relative certainty, the World Bank is projecting that gas production will more than quadruple in the 1985–95 period.

Coal is produced in some thirty-five developing countries. Reserves in these and other countries that are not yet producers are large, and coal remains as much as 30 to 40 percent cheaper than oil for electricity generation and for many industrial uses. Despite the apparent lack of fundamental resource or market constraints, however, there is probably more uncertainty about the future of coal production in developing countries than about oil and gas. This reflects the existence of serious organizational and management problems, which have impeded the development of coal resources in almost all countries (see below, "Institutional Issues").

Geothermal energy is different from coal in that it is a "new" energy source. So far, only a fraction of the resource potential in the developing world has been explored, and only nine countries are exploiting this form of energy. The situation is similar to that of coal in that the principal obstacles to further exploration and development appear to lie on the institutional side. Electric utilities are frequently not interested in geothermal energy because they are unfamiliar with geological exploration and feel it poses unwonted risks, while oil and gas companies consider it a poor alternative to their normal operations, especially because their only market would be the utilities.

Renewable Resources

In the area of noncommercial and renewable energy, developing countries face both serious problems and challenging opportunities. The fuelwood shortage is, as already noted, the principal problem. To bring projected demand and supply into better balance by the year 2000, it is estimated that at least 50 million hectares of trees would need to be planted; this would necessitate a fivefold increase over present planting levels worldwide and a fifteenfold increase in Africa, the most severely affected region. The physical resource base—land—and the technical know-how for stepped-up afforestation programs are generally sufficient (except in the most ecologically difficult regions, such as the Sahel), but progress to date has been slow in many countries owing to problems inherent in mobilizing rural people for "social" forestry (that is, small-scale and noncommercial tree growing).

Few countries have the infrastructure and institutional capability to support fuelwood planting on a large scale. Strong local participation in planning and implementation is vital to the success of such planting programs; however, fuelwood is usually most scarce where there is high population pressure on land and where people are consequently most reluctant to devote land and effort to purposes other than food production. Establishing nurseries and other facilities, and training foresters or special extension agents in rural afforestation, is a slow process. Development of appropriate technical packages for a specific area also takes time and requires extensive local trials and research to identify the proper species and provenances and the best combination of planting, fertilizing, and pest control techniques.

Quick action to deal with these problems is often impossible, since many national forestry services lack the expertise for the nontraditional tasks required in social forestry, and forestry training programs are weak. In addition, some governments are still unaware of or unmoved by the fuelwood problem, or are unwilling to review the price and incentive structure essential to a sustainable fuelwood program. National programs, where they exist, are often poorly designed to meet the objectives. Even when donors have provided support, it has not always been easy to mobilize domestic counterpart funding: long-term fuelwood programs are vulnerable to budgetary cuts during times of economic difficulty.

The principal renewable energy opportunities for developing countries stem from the ample potential to be found in their biomass, solar, wind, and small hydro resources. Unlike fossil fuel deposits, which yield energy in the relatively concentrated and portable forms suitable for large-scale industrial and urban use, many renewable energy technologies are best exploited on a small scale and are thus easily matched to the needs of dispersed rural populations. This relative advantage is heightened by several facts. First, conventional energy sources are frequently not available, or available only at high cost, in rural and remote areas of developing countries. Second, although some technologies for harnessing these resources have long been in use—hydroelectric plants and windmills, for example—recent technological advances have broadened their applicability and improved the efficiency with which they capture useful energy. Third, much of the equipment needed

Table 8-4. *Commercial Energy Typology of Developing Economies*

Oil exporters		Oil importers — Net oil imports as a percentage of primary commercial energy consumption in 1980			
Large	Small or medium	0–25	26–50	51–75	76–100
		LIMITED ENERGY RESOURCES AND OPTIONS[a]			
		Middle income		Low income	Low income
		Lesotho		Burundi	Bhutan
		Namibia		Kampuchea	**Burkina**
				Lao PDR	**Ethiopia**
				Nepal	Guinea Bissau
				Rwanda	Haiti
					Niger
					Somalia
					Sri Lanka
					Togo
					Middle income
					Barbados
					Cuba
					Dominican Republic
					Hong Kong
					Israel
					Jamaica
					Jordan
					Lebanon
					Liberia
					Mauritania
					Singapore
					Uruguay
					Yemen, AR
					Yemen, PDR
		MODERATE ENERGY RESOURCES AND OPTIONS[a]			
	Middle income	Low income	Low income	Low income	Low income
	Syrian Arab Rep.	Zaire	Ghana	**Bangladesh***	**Benin**
		Middle income	**Pakistan***	Central Afr. Rep.	Guinea, Rep. of
		Botswana	Middle income	Chad	Madagascar
		Korea, Dem. Rep. of†	*Brazil*†*	Equatorial Guinea	Mali
		Vietnam†	Chile*	Malawi	Sierra Leone
		Zambia	Guatemala	Mozambique	**Sudan**
		Zimbabwe†	Ivory Coast	**Uganda**	**Tanzania**
			Mongolia	Middle income	Middle income
				Costa Rica	**Greece†**
				El Salvador	**Kenya**
				Honduras	**Morocco**
				Korea, Rep. of†	**Nicaragua**
				Paraguay	**Panama**
				Portugal	Papua New Guinea
				Turkey†	**Philippines**
					Senegal
					Thailand

Oil exporters		Oil importers			
		Net oil imports as a percentage of primary commercial energy consumption in 1980			
Large	Small or medium	0–25	26–50	51–75	76–100
SUBSTANTIAL ENERGY RESOURCES AND OPTIONS[a]					
Low income China*†	Middle income Algeria* Angola Congo, PR Ecuador Egypt* Gabon Malaysia* Peru* Trinidad & Tobago* Tunisia	Low income Burma **India***† Middle income Argentina* Cameroon Colombia*†	Low income Afghanistan* Middle income **Yugoslavia***†	Middle income Bolivia*	
Middle income Indonesia* Iran* Iraq* Mexico*† Nigeria Venezuela					

Note: Not shown are economies with less than 1 million population and without production (or prospects of future production) of oil, gas, or coal. The economies included in this table are classified according to their energy resource potential (oil, gas, coal, and primary electricity) that could be economically developed during the next decade. Oil exporters are countries whose official earnings from net oil exports exceeded 10 percent of their total export earnings in 1980–81. Large oil exporters are countries that produced more than 70 million tons of oil equivalent during 1980.

*Produced 1 million or more tons of oil equivalent of gas in 1980.

†Produced 2 million or more tons of oil equivalent of coal in 1980.

Economies shown in *italics* produced more than 5 million tons of oil in 1980.

Economies shown in **bold print** had net energy imports amounting to 30 percent or more of their merchandise exports in 1980. (Information is not available for all countries.)

a. Relative to country size.

Source: World Bank, *The Energy Transition in Developing Countries* (Washington, D.C., 1983), p. 12.

for many renewable energy technologies is suitable for production in even the less industrially advanced developing countries.

Nevertheless, developing renewable resources is a long-term process. Although awareness of the potential of renewable resources has increased, and although some technologies for exploiting that potential are now ready for commercialization and several others soon will be, there are only a few areas and a few countries in which the utilization of renewable energy technology on a significant scale has already begun. There are two principal reasons for this. First, certain technologies are proving more difficult to develop, adapt, and apply, and have remained more expensive, than was foreseen. For example, while photovoltaic array costs have continued to decline, they have not fallen as much as forecast, partly because the expected volume of production has not been reached. Biogas digestors have proved to be more complex and demanding to maintain and operate than many early investigators had assumed, and conditions allowing the economic production of alcohol for vehicle fuel are less common than was anticipated. Second, and perhaps more important, renewable energy development has been slowed by weak institutions and policies. National programs are often made more difficult to coordinate by the multiplicity of interested agencies—both local and international. In addition to strengthening their institutional structure for renewable energy development, most developing countries urgently need to begin formulating strategies to evaluate the potential of the various technologies, and their probable importance, in the light of the country's specific energy needs and circumstances.

POLICY ISSUES

Achievement of the three broad sector objectives discussed above will require three types of government action:

- Mobilizing additional domestic and external financing to meet the sector's investment needs
- Restructuring energy prices both to improve sector finances and to provide the correct economic signals to producers and consumers
- Directly encouraging conservation, fuel switching, and the development of indigenous resources through financial incentives, regulatory measures, and promotional programs.

Mobilizing Finance

Bridging the gap between the energy sector's burgeoning investment needs and the limited domestic and external financial resources must be a paramount concern of national policy. Mobilization of adequate domestic financing for the sector is not only as important a policy goal as seeking external resources, but one that is more amenable to government action. Given the need to husband creditworthiness and the limited availability of external finance, a prime objective should be to ensure the mobilization of sufficient financing from within the sector and from other domestic sources to cover at least the local cost of sector investments. This is an especially onerous, but especially important, task in the electric power and coal industries. Domestic costs account for about one-half and about one-third of total investment, respectively, in these industries, and the finances of the operating enterprises have been very weak. Mobilization of adequate domestic financing is also important as a means of enhancing the attractiveness of the sector (and of the country) to external lenders.

Pricing policy is the principal tool for generating the maximum resources possible in the sector, and it is the policy area most in need of improvement. As indicated earlier, prices have failed to keep up with costs in many parts of the sector. In the electric power industry, tariff-setting mechanisms effectively broke down in many countries during the period of rapid inflation in the 1970s. Recent tariff increases have been granted on an occasional and haphazard basis to overcome immediate difficulties faced by the utilities, rather than to ensure their long-term financial equilibrium and provide the basis for financing expansion. What is needed is to bring the tariffs of power companies into line with the marginal costs of supply and to maintain them at this level by using frequent, systematic adjustments to compensate for inflation and fuel cost increases. But price increases are only part of the answer. Cutting costs by reducing swollen wage bills and improving technical operating efficiency (for example, by better load management or fewer system losses) can also help to achieve revenues that exceed operating costs.

As a result of the dramatic changes that occurred in the 1970s, it is not unusual to find that increases of 60 to 80 percent are needed to restore the tariffs of many power companies to appropriate levels. The increases in coal prices called for in many countries are also very large. Such prospects tend to reinforce the doubts of many governments about the appropriateness of applying commercial pricing criteria to public services, and to aggravate their fears about the inflationary impact of tariff increases and the political repercussions of such unpopular measures. But if forced to accept low prices, energy companies must either cut back on the investments needed to increase supply in pace with demand, or else undertake borrowing, which will increase their debt burden in future years. Moreover, inflationary fears are often exaggerated, given the modest share of energy in total production costs in all but the most energy-intensive industries. In addition, insufficient attention is often paid to the possibilities of reducing political fallout by a gradual phasing of tariff increases and by protecting the great mass of small consumers from the full brunt of these increases through cross-subsidies.

Mobilizing external finance is a major problem for virtually all oil-importing developing countries and for every part of the energy sector. The problem is most acute, however, for low-income countries, which must depend on concessional financing, and for the hydrocarbon subsector, which has especially high foreign exchange requirements. Most publicly owned companies in this subsector have done relatively little borrowing abroad in the past. Economic policies that enhance the country's credit-worthiness, and measures that strengthen the financial standing of energy enterprises, are essential to deal with these problems. In addition, governments can do much to encourage the flow of foreign funds into the sector by pursuing borrowing policies that seek to exploit all available sources of financing, public as well as private, bilateral as well as multilateral; that pay special attention to those parts of the sector having the greatest external financing difficulties; that try to match up the diverse needs within the energy sector with the special requirements of different lenders; and that take advantage of the full range of financing mechanisms and packaging techniques developed in the energy and other sectors.

For example, many developing countries need to reorient external capital flows toward hydrocarbons from the existing heavy emphasis on power, the foreign exchange costs of which weigh less heavily in total investment requirements, and which has long been attractive to official lenders and especially to export credit agencies. Efforts to raise funds for oil or gas production for domestic consumption should focus on official agencies, while requests for funds for export-oriented investments may be directed toward commercial lenders. National oil companies should be encouraged to formulate their borrowing requirements in terms of projects rather than to depend on general purpose, balance sheet borrowing, and to make maximum use of cofinancing in order to obtain the widest possible participation of official and commercial lenders. Efforts should also be made to develop the use of nonrecourse financing techniques, whereby loans needed for oil development programs can be secured by the anticipated earnings of the project rather than by government guarantees, thus making it possible to obtain funds for projects in countries where creditworthiness is lacking or should not be further encumbered. Finally, if oil-importing countries can attract even a small share of international oil companies' investments, their financing problems will be significantly alleviated.

Efficiency Pricing

Setting energy prices at levels that fully reflect economic costs is critical not only to mobilizing financial resources, but also to accomplishing the three basic objectives of improving demand management, selecting the least-cost sources of supply, and spurring the development of domestic resources. To achieve these objectives, governments will have to follow policies ensuring that the prices of different energy sources correctly reflect their relative cost, as well as that the general level of energy prices is appropriate. In recent years, many developing countries have recognized the importance of efficiency pricing in their strategies to manage the energy sector and have begun to raise prices to reflect increased costs. However, many countries still tend to keep some energy prices considerably below their real economic (or opportunity) cost (see chapter 20, Economic Analysis). Although, as already noted, underpricing of electric power and coal remains a common phenomenon, in the oil-importing developing countries increases in the cost of imported oil have generally been passed on fully and promptly to final users; the weighted average of retail petroleum product prices is higher than import parity in nearly all of them. Many countries, however, still need to adjust the relative prices of petroleum products, particularly when kerosene and diesel fuel prices have been kept uneconomically low by governments seeking to protect domestic consumers and the agriculture and transport sectors from the full force of rising energy costs. In the oil-exporting countries, domestic retail prices are generally still well below international levels, and relative price distortions are more pronounced than in the oil importers.

Efficiency pricing is an essential instrument of energy demand management since, with prices artificially low, consumers will not have sufficient financial incentive to use energy more efficiently. Investments in improved boilers, systems to recover waste heat, heat exchangers, or process changes are not likely to be profitable if the equipment has to be purchased at commercial prices but the fuel oil saved is subsidized. Moreover, pricing policy can have an important long-term effect on the level and distribution of energy consumption through its influence on the pattern of development and on the choice of technology in the sectors using energy. If energy prices are set below the economic cost of supply, the wrong priorities may be assigned to investments that will consume energy, and technologies may be chosen whose use is not in the nation's economic interest. Some countries, such as Egypt, might not have developed such energy-intensive industries as aluminum smelting had their power prices reflected economic cost. Many others, such as Brazil, might have given greater emphasis to rail transport if diesel fuel had not been subsidized.

The relative prices of different energy sources strongly influence the substitution of one fuel for another. In an economy where fuel oil prices are subsidized, commercial development of indigenous coal and biomass resources may require that these fuels also be subsidized, as an interim measure, until fuel oil prices are adjusted to an economic level. In rural areas, subsidized prices for kerosene and diesel oil frequently impede the introduction of renewable fuels and technologies such as solar and wind-powered systems for irrigation and other water-pumping applications. Changes in the relative prices of fuels can have a marked effect on consumers' choices. The price of diesel oil in the oil-importing developing countries for which data are available rose from 38 percent of gasoline prices in 1975 to 61 percent in 1979 as diesel subsidies were reduced. The pattern of consumption changed in response: for example, Pakistan's diesel oil consumption decreased from about 550 percent to about 300 percent of its gasoline consumption in five years. In contrast, Brazil's decrease in the price of diesel oil relative to that of gasoline contributed to an increase in diesel oil use from about 90 percent to about 150 percent of gasoline use during the same period.

Although the need for price adjustments and the general direction of change are often painfully apparent, detailed technical and economic studies may be required to determine the most appropriate price levels and to establish the processes and procedures needed to ensure that prices are maintained at these levels in the future. For example, although the extensive international trade in oil products provides ready benchmarks for establishing domestic prices, natural gas is rarely traded internationally and its pricing can pose difficult problems. The economic value of gas should be determined by assessing likely supply and demand trends over time in order to estimate the marginal value of gas in alternative uses as development proceeds. In addition, gas pricing policy will need to take into account such criteria as the value of gas as a depletable resource, the impact of prices on the financial viability of the entities that produce and transport gas, and the ability to pay of different consumer groups. Similarly, the pricing of electric power may require extensive studies of the marginal costs of supply that take into account the various options for developing a power system. Still, the better should not be allowed to become the enemy of the good. Pending the development and implementation of tariff structures for power based on marginal cost, adjustments based on conventional rates of return (see chapter 21, Financial Analysis) can be implemented; in most cases, they will provide reasonable short-term guidance, at least for the overall level of tariffs. It may also be necessary to make appropriate tradeoffs between efficiency and financial objectives as, for example, when prices have to be set above marginal cost levels to generate financial resources for investment.

Action Programs

Important as it is, pricing policy cannot do the job alone. Normally, it must be supplemented by a variety of direct measures for accomplishing sector objectives. The need for such interventions arises, as in other sectors, because it will not always be possible to get prices right or to get them right soon enough, and because of the inevitable imperfections of the marketplace. In the energy sector, these market imperfections include both the lack of technical and economic information about energy efficiency improvements and skepticism about new fuels and technologies that may prevent producers and consumers from reacting to price signals. Furthermore, in many developing countries, input and output prices are regulated in many sectors that use energy, and they are thus effectively insulated from market forces. To address these problems, energy policy will generally have to make use of a mix of activities, including

- Education, promotion, and technical assistance
- Research, development, and demonstration programs
- Financial assistance and incentives
- Regulatory measures.

Education, promotion, and technical assistance have been found to play an important role in national conservation programs. They are needed to increase awareness of the potential for energy efficiency improvements, to highlight the cost savings that can be achieved, and to provide technical assistance in designing and implementing such improvements. These efforts are most effective when shaped to meet the needs of different target groups. Programs for large, energy-intensive industries are normally based on audits sponsored or supported by the government and frequently conducted by foreign consultants. These audits are designed to analyze the patterns of energy use, to identify opportunities for substantial energy savings and the specific investments needed to bring them about, and to estimate the economic returns on such investments. Programs for smaller industries concentrate on less direct measures like improving the flow of information on energy savings, promoting the growth of local energy audit capabilities, and stimulating the production of energy conservation equipment.

Research, development, and demonstration programs can play an important role in supporting fuel switching and the development of domestic energy resources, particularly when new and renewable energy resources and technologies are being explored. Most developing countries have such programs for renewables, but few of these are well adapted to the country's major resources and needs or to the pursuit of specific commercial objectives. Such programs are probably most effective when organized to meet particular user needs and conducted in close collaboration with users, as in Brazil's program to develop alcohol and other biomass fuels for use in industry, transport, and agriculture.

Financial assistance and incentives in many forms are being deployed in support of energy policy objectives in almost all developing countries. Measures to ensure that adequate credit is available on suitable terms for financing high-priority investments can play an especially important role. These measures may include such familiar devices as earmarked lines of credit or more innovative types of financing suited to a particular sector, such as leasing arrangements for energy conservation equipment. The financial measures commonly used also include subsidies in the form of low-cost credit, as well as tax deductions and exemptions. Subsidies are rarely the preferred solution, but they can be justified as short-term measures to promote new technologies and energy alternatives, as countervailing measures to offset other subsidies, or as necessary measures in situations with external economies, when investments are more attractive in the national interest than they are to individual investors. For example, credit or tax subsidies may be used to stimulate and encourage manufacturers to begin investing in energy conservation. The production of biomass fuels may be subsidized to put them on an equal basis with fuel oil or diesel when the latter are underpriced. Seedling trees or improved stoves may be distributed free of charge when there is a strong national interest in stemming deforestation but little or no market incentive for rural people to participate in this effort. Except when the need is a long-term one, subsidy programs should incorporate plans for phasing them out over a reasonable period.

Regulatory measures can also take many different forms and serve a variety of purposes. Regulation is most likely to be effective as an instrument of energy policy and least likely to be disruptive when the purpose is to direct investors and consumers to economically rewarding activities, and when the method is to establish general standards. Building codes can, for example, be used to establish design and construction standards that will reduce heating and cooling loads in new buildings. They can also be used to force the adoption of new technologies, as in Israel, where all residential buildings of a certain height must employ solar water heaters. Similarly, regulation may require more energy-efficient standards for industrial and transport equipment and for domestic appliances. More direct and extensive forms of regulation may also be employed to support national goals, as in Brazil, where efforts to reduce oil imports and encourage the use of biomass fuels have included requiring that all gasoline be mixed with a minimum amount of alcohol, that all service stations sell pure alcohol as well as gasohol, and that industries that use large amounts of fuel oil reduce their consumption.

INSTITUTIONAL ISSUES

Strengthening of energy sector institutions is crucial to the process of improving the selection, implementation, and finance of development projects. Institutional issues are complex in the energy sector because of its diversity, because the different parts of the sector are highly interdependent but usually independently managed, and because the sector needs to be closely linked with the rest of the economy. In most developing countries, there is a need both to strengthen central institutions responsible for sector planning, policymaking, and coordination, and to improve the efficiency of the operating agencies responsible for project formulation and execution in different parts of the sector. In addition, the petroleum industry raises special concerns about the roles of the public and private sectors.

Strengthening Sector Management

Considering energy problems from a sector and economywide vantage point and seeking to solve them in an integrated manner are essential if costly planning and investment errors are to be avoided. To cite one important example, planning for fuel switching in electricity generation must be based not only on the investment needs and alternatives of the power industry, but also on a realistic appreciation of the potential for expanding domestic production of coal or gas and of the cost and time involved. The latter will, in turn, often be highly dependent on development prospects and investment plans in other sectors, particularly industry and transport. Thus, effective management of the energy sector requires the institutionalization of responsibility for planning and policymaking for the sector as a whole, for ensuring that all investment options (including conservation) are considered, for coordinating project financing and execution, and for serving as a focal point for integrating sector plans and projects with the rest of the economy. These functions may be performed by an energy ministry, by an energy planning and coordination staff in a planning ministry, or by some other central office, depending on a country's needs and preferences.

The location of the planning function is less important than that the staff have clear authority for planning, project review, and coordination and that it be fully incorporated into the national decisionmaking process. It is also important that the planning staff have close institutional links and working relationships with national economic planners and with planners in energy sector enterprises. The planning staff should be responsible for coordinating enterprise plans (for example, by making sure that all assumptions about the growth of energy demand are consistent), for evaluating the effects of exogenous changes (for example, in economic activity or international energy prices) on the demand and supply prospects for individual fuels, and for ensuring that subsector investment programs and price policies are altered quickly to take account of these changes. The planning staff might also see to it that each of the subsector operating agencies is devoting adequate financial and managerial resources to improving the efficiency of existing plants and operations.

Other main tasks of the planning staff should be to promote the preinvestment work essential to sound planning and project selection and to ensure that the preparatory steps are taken and that the administrative arrangements necessary to carry it out are made. Such preinvestment work includes resource surveys, assessments of new technologies, feasibility and market studies, and design and engineering efforts. Planning power systems requires systematic surveys of hydro potential, while petroleum exploration must be guided by geological and geophysical studies. Preliminary studies of the market potential of natural gas are needed so that discoveries can be speedily exploited. Site-specific data on wind speeds and solar energy are a prerequisite for assessing the potential of these renewable resources. Such preinvestment work can be costly, but the cost is likely to be only a small proportion of the total investment cost and well justified in terms of potential savings.

Increasing Enterprise Efficiency

At the enterprise level, the most important issue is to improve efficiency. Experience in the sector, as well as generally accepted management principles, teach that the best guarantee of efficiency lies in responsible and autonomous institutions. In the public sector, however, the principle of operational autonomy often conflicts in practice with the workings of the political system. Even when enterprises are formally autonomous, vital decisions on matters such as pricing may be delayed, supervision by government ministries can sometimes extend to interference in routine decisions by civil servants who lack operating knowledge, and time-consuming procedures for procuring and allocating funds may be imposed. It is entirely appropriate that long-term objectives and strategic issues be determined by a high political authority, but once clear national guidelines are set, the operating enterprises should be given the autonomy as well as the responsibility to achieve the output targets agreed upon at acceptable costs. It is no coincidence that government intervention in the operation of coal and power enterprises, where this problem is most acute, has grown in step with their increasing dependence on budgetary funding. Improving the financial health of energy enterprises can do much to shore up their operating autonomy.

Another important way to increase the operating autonomy and efficiency of energy enterprises is to strengthen their management and staff. Governments can help enterprises to recruit and retain qualified managerial and technical personnel by freeing them from civil service restraints on hiring and firing, on salaries and wages, and on working conditions. For their own part, most enterprises need to pay much more attention to upgrading the skills of their staff at all levels through systematic training programs. They also need to develop specific programs to increase technical operating efficiency and to raise labor productivity to levels closer to good international practice by improving equipment, processes, and procedures. While the focus of such programs will differ from enterprise to enterprise, planning, equipment maintenance, and financial controls are likely to be the areas in which most can be done to improve efficiency.

Managing the Petroleum Industry

The principal actors on the institutional scene in the petroleum industry are governments, national oil (or oil and gas) companies, and international oil companies. The roles of these three differ widely depending on the circumstances of each country, but working out an effective division of labor among them is crucial to the efficient development and utilization of a country's petroleum resources. In the oil-importing developing countries, the basic role of government is to articulate and oversee the implementation of a strategy for the petroleum industry. To do this, they often need to strengthen their capabilities in three areas:

- *Promotion.* Governments need to establish appropriate legislative and contractual frameworks for exploration. They must also be able to identify areas to be promoted for exploration and development, to package and relay technical data, to conduct informational campaigns, and to negotiate with international oil companies where appropriate.
- *Oversight.* Governments need technical skills to review the exploration proposals of international oil companies, to monitor and evaluate the work of national and international companies, and to identify

specific opportunities to be followed up as the work of international companies progresses.

- *Management.* Governments must be able to prepare and retrieve reports and information, deal expeditiously with requests for a wide range of approvals, and maintain and audit financial accounts.

State-owned oil companies can range from small organizations that distribute petroleum products to large, fully integrated companies that cover all activities from exploration through distribution. (Given the very large capital requirements and special technology of the petroleum industry, practically no oil-importing developing country has developed even a fledgling capability in the private sector.) These national companies can serve two important functions. First, they can assist the government in developing a petroleum strategy and in managing the activities of foreign companies in petroleum exploration and development. Second, they can carry out exploration and development programs, either alone or in association with foreign companies, when direct public sector operation of such programs is an appropriate part of the country's petroleum strategy. National companies have been playing a growing role in petroleum development, especially in the larger developing countries where the industry is well established. It is important, however, not to let the companies' policies become, de facto, the country's petroleum development policies, since their concerns can be parochial and do not necessarily coincide with the national interest.

The role of the international oil companies is a subject that carries much historical, ideological, and political baggage. The fact remains, however, that the international companies are the main sources of risk capital, that they bring a wealth of management experience and up-to-date technological expertise to any project in which they are involved, and that they are making an important contribution to the process of exploration and development in many countries. Each country will of course decide for itself what role it wishes the international oil companies to play, taking into account, among other things, what technical and financial resources may otherwise be available and what delays and cost increases may be incurred by restricting their role.

An open-door policy toward the international companies is often the best way to give a much-needed impetus to national petroleum programs. But merely unlocking the door is not the same as actually opening it. The international companies are, by and large, no longer eagerly seeking opportunities in developing countries; they have to be attracted by positive inducements to participate in the development of national resources. To attract the interest of the international companies, governments will want to take four steps. The first is to establish a legal framework that addresses the companies' concerns about such matters as the division and repatriation of profits, the control of operations, and procedures for settling disputes. Second, they need to facilitate access to existing geological information, and must sometimes generate new information; this entails low-risk and low-cost investments in the orderly compilation of existing data and in the limited acquisition of new data. A third critical step in the door-opening process is to ensure that sufficient attractive acreage is available to the international companies and that it is available on competitive terms. Fourth, promotional efforts are usually needed to acquaint the industry with the opportunities being offered, especially when small countries are seeking to attract the smaller, independent oil companies.

INVESTMENT ISSUES

The importance of energy and the high cost of investment in the sector underline the need to choose projects wisely and execute them efficiently. Since energy investments tend to be lumpy (indivisible), and projects costing hundreds of millions of dollars are more the rule than the exception, misjudgments can result in financial as well as economic calamities. Unfortunately, making wise energy investment decisions is as difficult as it is important. The extent of the underlying resource base, whether it be oil or gas reserves or hydropower potential, is often uncertain at the time decisions must be made; moreover, the technology being considered may be new, rapidly changing, and risky. The economic appraisal of energy investments requires a long time perspective. The rate of economic growth and direction of structural change and, hence, the domestic demand for energy must be forecast for many years ahead, as must price and supply trends in world energy markets. The uncertainties attending such forecasts may tempt decisionmakers to keep their options open as long as possible, which may be wise, but delay can also be costly, especially given the lengthy gestation period of most energy projects.

Considering Alternatives

To guard against costly errors, those making investment decisions need to make it a cardinal rule to consider all the options. This means scrutinizing the full range of potential energy sources; for example, domestic natural gas and coal should be evaluated as possible fuels for electric power generation along with the usual hydro and oil options. It also means considering unconventional options, such as the use of biomass instead of fuel oil and gasoline in industrial boilers and vehicles when this seems technically and economically feasible. Also to be considered is the option of *not* investing in the expansion of energy production, to the extent that this can be avoided by conservation, by better pricing, or by opting for a higher level of imports if that is cheaper than developing domestic resources. Weighing all the options requires not only a sound sector planning mechanism and thorough preinvestment work, as already emphasized, but also a continuing effort to overcome institutional rigidities, such as the reluctance of power companies to become involved with agricultural or industrial suppliers of energy (from bagasse or cogeneration).

A related set of issues concerns the need to maintain an appropriate balance of investments among the different energy subsectors, as well as within each subsector. Maintaining a well-balanced investment program across the entire sector is likely to receive more attention from central planning institutions than the no less important task of ensuring the most efficient allocation of resources within a subsector, a task that is normally the responsibility of the enterprises concerned. Establishing an appropriate mix among investments in generation, transmission, and distribution in the electric power system, for example, is important both to ensure optimum utilization of capacity and to maximize efficiency by reducing system loss and improving load management capability. Nevertheless, power companies frequently give undue priority to the expansion of generating capacity while underinvesting in transmission and distribution, despite the fact that the expansion or improvement of system interconnections and the strengthening of distribution networks may offer higher rates of return. Another frequently underfunded area is maintenance. Decrepit diesel generating plants and overloaded distribution networks are all too common results of the financial straits in which many power companies recently have found themselves. Moreover, because of poor maintenance, many countries have been forced to build excessive reserves of generating capacity, at considerable cost. The high returns to be obtained from restoring system efficiency through increased spending on maintenance are a vital but often absent consideration in system planning, not only in electric power, but also in other parts of the sector.

Technical Choices

Technical choices frequently weigh heavily in decisions about broad investment strategy, as well as in the selection of projects. This is especially true when new or unfamiliar technologies are involved. In determining the viability of the nuclear option, for example, decisionmakers must consider such factors as the size and structure of the country's power system, the way the design, fuel requirements, and operating characteristics of different types of reactors mesh with the country's resources and needs, actual construction and operating experience with similar systems elsewhere, the environmental impact (including the disposal of radioactive wastes), and their own present and potential technical capabilities and the quality and quantity of technical assistance they can expect to receive. Proposals to start constructing nuclear plants for training purposes before such critical technical and economic questions have been answered should be closely examined since training in research facilities and in plants overseas is generally both cheaper and quicker.

With regard to the further development of an already well-established energy industry, the technical issues faced are likely to be very different, but often equally complex and difficult. Countries that are producing oil may face a choice between undertaking further investment in exploration drilling to discover additional reserves or seeking to increase yields from known fields through "enhanced recovery" projects that introduce sophisticated pressure-maintenance and field-rehabilitation technology. The latter may often be the less risky option, but it is usually one that can be properly evaluated only through intensive technical studies. Moreover, its choice requires a commitment to expensive new technology that should be made only if there are good grounds for confidence that the country can acquire or develop the necessary expertise.

The careful phasing of projects can, in some cases, alleviate the problems stemming from the lumpiness and riskiness of energy investments. Gas development projects can be risky because of uncertainty about the extent of reserves (which are usually less clearly identified than oil reserves) and because of the need to invest heavily in infrastructure to carry the gas to consumers who may represent a large potential, but not actual, market. Bank experience has shown, however, that initial estimates of both reserves and markets are usually conservative. In order to avoid costly delays, it is customary in the industry to develop projects in stages and to allow for a reasonable amount of excess capacity in the design of gas processing and transmission facilities. The phasing of projects may also be dictated by the lack of experience and of technical or institutional support for large-scale investments. Despite the magnitude of the fuelwood shortage in many countries, it has often been found necessary to begin tree planting programs on a small scale in order to allow time for training forestry department staff, building up networks of nurseries, and testing popular response to these programs.

The design of petroleum projects may be heavily influenced by technical issues such as the need to provide for flexibility during implementation, the cost-effectiveness of state-of-the-art technology, and tradeoffs between contracting out for specialized services and developing local technical capabilities. In the case of exploration drilling projects, it is rarely possible to specify fully in advance the scope of exploration activities to be supported, since any exploration program has to be reevaluated and revised as it yields new data. Therefore, the project design should focus on the need to establish and maintain an adequate inventory of drilling prospects, to use a ranking system for evaluating these prospects geologically and economically, and to reevaluate priorities periodically as new data become available. Since exploration technology is advancing very rapidly, emphasis should be placed on obtaining the latest technology by contracting out services requiring investment in a large inventory of equipment that may quickly become obsolete. When a national petroleum company is responsible for drilling for oil and gas, however, the project should be designed to provide the technical assistance and equipment necessary to strengthen the company's ability to carry out this central function.

Power Demand Forecasting

Because so many factors must be taken into account, load forecasts for power projects are a complex exercise. Demand forecasting has been complicated in recent years by the downturn in economic activity following the 1973 oil crisis, which affected the growth in demand for power. Energy sales of most electric power utilities associated with the World Bank have been lower than those forecast when the projects were appraised. Load forecasts underlying the Bank's decisions to support power projects have differed fairly widely from actual loads, and some systematic tendency to overestimate future peak load can be observed. Attempts to improve the accuracy of these forecasts have not proved very successful. Nevertheless, in some Bank-assisted projects, overestimates of future peak load tended to be offset by underestimates of the time required to complete the power plants. As a result, most of the investment programs ultimately proved reasonably well balanced, in the sense that new capacity came on line at about the time it was required to meet the growth of demand. Reserve generating capacity has, in fact, generally fallen a little short of expectations.[1]

Cost-Benefit Analysis

The economic appraisal of energy projects raises some issues that have special importance because of the characteristics of the sector. On the one hand, relatively small cost differences can be critical when several options exist, as is often the case in the choice of fuels for power generation. On the other hand, how much confidence to put in small cost differences is a difficult question, especially if projects have very long gestation periods (hydropower) or if they depend on the development or expansion of domestic energy supplies (coal and gas). Cost estimates can be especially problematic for projects using new technologies with which international experience is limited, as several countries have discovered to their dismay when the capital cost of biomass alcohol plants turned out to be substantially higher than expected on the basis of Brazilian experience. Environmental costs may be substantial but are usually difficult to quantify, especially since the direct cost of damage control measures (such as the cost of resettling people displaced by the construction of a dam) may tell only part of the story.

The calculation of economic benefits can pose even greater difficulty for certain types of projects. This is true not only of exploration and promotion projects—which can be judged a success to the extent that they attract capital for oil drilling, but lead to tangible benefits only when and if oil is found—but also of traditional investment projects such as power plants, the benefits of which can be measured, in practice, only by taking expected revenues from the sale of power as a proxy for true economic benefits. The calculation of benefits also poses a difficult problem in fuelwood projects, since the product is sometimes a noncommercial one whose value cannot readily be established and since such projects are also designed, in part, to produce important but unquantifiable environmental benefits. Another type of problem arises when a government wishes to take into account the national security benefits of a project that enhances energy independence by developing indigenous resources. Although such benefits cannot be meaningfully quantified, it is important that the project be evaluated in such a way that policymakers are made aware of the amount of the implied national security subsidy (that is, the excess cost over the most economical project) so that they can make a more informed judgment.

Because of these difficulties, cost-benefit analyses and rate of return calculations should be applied with caution to certain types of energy projects, and not at all to others for which sensible estimates of benefits cannot be made. Since electric power projects yield the same benefits

1. See Dennis Anderson and Vilma Villaflores, "Ex-Post Evaluation of Electricity Demand Forecasts," World Bank Economics Department Working Paper no. 79 (Washington, D.C., 1970); and Hugh Collier, *Developing Electric Power: Thirty Years of World Bank Experience* (Baltimore, Md.: Johns Hopkins University Press for the World Bank, 1984).

whatever the energy source, the choice among alternatives can be made by determining the least-cost option (assuming all the options have been considered). Rates of return are calculated for such projects, but since the benefits are based on revenues, they are more akin to financial than to economic rates of return. This is an important distinction since, with power tariffs frequently set at less than economic levels, the returns calculated are likely to be substantially lower than the true economic returns. They will, therefore, give a misleading impression of the economic worth of power projects compared with projects in other parts of the sector showing higher returns. Revenues form only the directly observable part of total economic benefits, which also include consumer surplus. This is very difficult to measure, but studies of consumer willingness to pay indicate that the value of power to consumers substantially exceeds the average tariff in developing countries. This surplus is most evident in the case of industrial users who, when not connected to a reliable power grid, have had to invest in costly generating units (such as diesel) of their own.

In oil exploration projects, no attempt is made to estimate an expected rate of return because benefits can be negligible, or they can be many hundred times the exploration cost. Instead, a quantitative comparative analysis is carried out, which involves a ranking of the potential benefits and risks of alternative exploration strategies and drilling programs. This ranking draws attention to the minimum size discovery that would be needed to yield an acceptable rate of return on the total capital requirement for the exploration and subsequent development programs, and to the degree of probability that this volume of oil or gas would be found.

Links with Other Sectors

The close links between the various parts of the energy sector and between energy and the rest of the economy make the availability of complementary investments in energy resource development, infrastructure, and markets an important issue. The lack of coordination among investments in coal, transport, and power is, for example, the main reason that coal development has fallen behind schedule in many countries. To develop their coal resources more efficiently, developing countries will need to coordinate better the planning of coal, power, and transport investments—which are usually the responsibility of separate entities that depend on different ministries—and to take more fully into account the differences in the implementation techniques, construction practices, and start-up times of coal, power, rail, and port projects. The viability of energy projects may also depend on investments in user facilities, as in the case of a gas pipeline whose location and timing are bound up with those of a fertilizer project. Moreover, some investments in fuels or in equipment to use them may depend on the adequacy of efforts to develop markets; examples are improved wood stoves, liquified petroleum gas for household or vehicular use, and solar or other renewable energy sources.

As obvious and as crucial as such links are, the lack of coordination has undermined many otherwise promising projects. This underscores again the importance of sectorwide planning for energy development and of integrating energy sector planning with national economic planning.

Project Performance

Although World Bank lending for petroleum and for renewable energy (other than hydro) is of relatively recent origin, so that few of these projects have yet been completed and subjected to an ex post evaluation, power has been a staple in the Bank's project portfolio from the outset. Various aspects of the Bank's experience in lending for power have been incorporated throughout this chapter.

A recent review of fifty-six completed power projects that were evaluated during the five-year period 1979–83 indicates that, on the whole, power projects have fared well, both absolutely and relative to performance in other sectors. Physical objectives have generally been reached, albeit with some delays in completion time (averaging twenty months) and with sizable cost overruns (averaging 39 percent). At the time of the review, most of the power companies were operating efficiently, and the evaluations confirmed that the investment options chosen were the least-cost approach to meeting power demand.[2]

The record in reaching institutional objectives—which were generally to strengthen the management of power utilities and to rationalize and coordinate sector development and operations—is more mixed and difficult to summarize. One of the factors that appears to have influenced the success of power companies (and other public utilities in water and telecommunications) is the degree of autonomy that the company has had in planning and conducting its affairs within the broad policy objectives and guidelines established by the government. In the area of management and staffing, this applies to personnel policies, recruitment, training, and conditions of service. In financial matters, while some public regulation of tariffs is necessary, the impact of government tariff regulations on orderly financial management often depends on how the regulations are administered. When approval of new tariffs has been delayed, or granted for amounts substantially less than the utility requested, performance has been adversely affected, not only in reaching financial objectives but also in many other aspects of the utility's operations, including the implementation of the power investment program. Even in some matters within a utility's control, however, progress has often been slow—notably in efforts to reduce energy losses in transmission and distribution and to install or improve accounting systems and procedures.

2. World Bank, Operations Evaluation Department, *Tenth Annual Review of Project Performance Audit Results* (Washington, D.C., 1985), and other World Bank materials.

Manufacturing clocks, Bombay, India

9

Industry

CHARACTERISTICS OF THE SECTOR

FOR MOST DEVELOPING COUNTRIES, expansion of industry offers prospects of increased employment, an improved balance of payments, and more efficient use of resources. Because the demand for manufactured goods is highly elastic (that is, very responsive to changes in prices and incomes), industry does not face the same market constraints that agriculture does and can therefore stimulate faster growth. In addition, industrialization makes intangible contributions toward raising productivity by encouraging technological innovation, discovering and reinforcing entrepreneurial and managerial talent, promoting the acquisition of technical skills, and creating a more hospitable climate for modernization throughout the society.

How successful a country is in reaping the benefits of industrialization depends on such factors as its location, its resource endowment, the size of its internal market, and—where relevant—its colonial experience. These affect a country's access to markets, capital, and technology. Probably of greatest importance, however, are its strategies and policies for industrial development. Without a stable policy environment that encourages efficient industrialization—mainly by ensuring that prices of productive factors such as capital and labor reflect their real value, and by providing incentives for exports as favorable as those for import substitution—a country's industrialization efforts will yield disappointing results.[1]

Economic Aspects

The development process typically involves the transformation of rural, agricultural societies into more urban, industrialized societies. The share of industrial production in the economy is thus an important indicator of the stage a country has reached in this process of structural transformation. Although the nature and tempo of such change differ substantially from one country to another, some general patterns have become apparent.[2] Increases in per capita income have been associated, in a fairly regular way, with a rise in the share of industry and a fall in the share of agriculture in total output. In the early stages of industrialization, when per capita income is very low, primary production is paramount. As capital and skills accumulate, both productivity and per capita income rise, and the composition of aggregate demand shifts, with resultant

1. This chapter draws heavily on the analysis in Keith Marsden, *Trade and Employment Policies for Industrial Development* (Washington, D.C.: World Bank, 1982). Useful background is contained also in John Cody, Helen Hughes, and David Wall, eds., *Policies for Industrial Progress in Developing Countries* (New York: Oxford University Press for the World Bank, 1980).

2. See the discussion in World Bank, *World Development Report 1979* (New York: Oxford University Press, 1979), pp. 44–45, which utilizes data from Hollis Chenery and Moises Syrquin, *Patterns of Development 1950–1970* (Oxford, Eng.: Oxford University Press for the World Bank, 1975).

changes in the sectoral composition of output. (Consumption of food, for example, accounts for two-fifths of aggregate demand in an economy with a per capita income of $150, but for less than a fifth of aggregate demand in an economy with a per capita income of $3,000.) Data on the developing countries confirm this transformation: in the low-income countries, the share of manufacturing industry in gross domestic product (GDP) is less than 10 percent (excluding India, with 16 percent, and China, for which the figure is not available), while in the lower middle-income countries it is 17 percent and in the upper middle-income countries it is 22 percent. The corresponding figure in the industrialized countries is only slightly higher, 24 percent, mainly because of the high proportion of GDP arising from the services sector.[3]

Manufacturing industry has been the most vigorously growing sector in the developing countries, its growth rate substantially surpassing that of agriculture and of services. Exports of manufactures grew by some 13 percent a year in real terms during the 1970s; by 1981, they accounted for 50 percent of total merchandise exports in the low-income group and for 43 percent in the middle-income group.[4] This shows conclusively that the developing countries are not limited to exporting primary products, but can compete internationally in exporting manufactured goods.

Although most countries and regions of the world have experienced this industrial boom, performance has varied considerably. Latin America, where manufactures account for only 16 percent of total exports, is still suffering from the legacy of the inward-looking, import substitution policies of the 1950s and 1960s. In sub-Saharan Africa, the change in export composition has been dominated by the increasing share of minerals, which are exhaustible; diversification into manufacturing activities is essential to provide a firmer foundation for sustained economic growth. The middle-income developing countries have achieved the highest rate of industrial growth, averaging roughly 7 percent a year in the two decades 1960–80. East Asian countries have been particularly successful in diversifying their exports into manufactured goods, and South Asia has also made substantial progress in reducing its dependence on agricultural exports.

These trends over the past three decades amount to a second industrial revolution. Indeed, the transformation of the world economy occurring now is even more radical than that of the British economy in the nineteenth century. At the end of World War II, the developing countries had almost no manufacturing industry and were greatly handicapped by

3. World Bank, *World Development Report 1984* (New York: Oxford University Press, 1984), annex tables 2 and 3. Low-income developing countries are those with GNP per capita of less than $410 (in 1982 dollars); lower middle-income developing countries, $410–$1,650; and upper middle-income developing countries, $1,650–$6,840. Industry is often defined to include manufacturing, mining, construction, and utilities—as, for example, in the World Bank's annual *World Development Report*, which divides economic activities into "agriculture," "industry," and "services." We are concerned in this chapter with manufacturing industry, which is the most dynamic element of the industrial sector; references to industry in the text, unless otherwise noted, relate specifically to manufacturing.

4. *World Development Report 1984*, annex table 10.

inexperience in economic management, deficiencies in physical and social infrastructure, and a lack of capital as well as of technical and entrepreneurial skills. Nevertheless, in less than two generations, some of these countries have built up a fully industrialized structure, several of the larger ones are now partly industrialized, and most are definitely in an industrializing stage. Some countries, especially in sub-Saharan Africa, are just beginning the process, while only a few—mostly those with a very small population—are still completely nonindustrial. Industrialization, once restricted to Europe, North America, and Japan, has thus become a worldwide phenomenon.

Social Aspects

Although manufacturing has been the largest single source of new urban employment in most developing countries, increases in the proportion of the labor force employed in industry have lagged behind increases in the share of industry in total output. One reason for this is that in most countries industry has been relatively capital-intensive, so that labor productivity in that sector is higher than in agriculture. A second and more important reason is that the growth of the labor force in the developing countries in recent decades has been far beyond industry's capacity to absorb labor.

Earlier hopes that industrialization could solve the unemployment problems of the developing countries have proved unrealistic. This fact must, however, be seen in historical perspective. Between 1950 and 1970, the rates of growth of the population and of the labor force in developing countries were roughly three times as great as those experienced in the nineteenth century by the now developed countries. Consequently, industry in the developing countries absorbed only about a fifth of the increment in the total labor force during the 1960s, whereas industry in the now developed countries absorbed two-fifths during the 1880s. In contrast, the growth rate of industrial output in the developing countries in recent decades has been almost twice what it was a century ago in the now developed countries. The developing countries today are, in fact, compressing the development process: the growth rates of industrial employment, of industrial output, and also of productivity are all well in excess of those achieved historically.[5]

The creation of adequate employment opportunities is likely to be more difficult in the future. Whereas it took ninety years for the labor force to double in the now industrialized countries, it takes only thirty years in today's developing countries; and recent annual rates of growth of the labor force in most of the developing world will be exceeded in the remainder of this century. This prospect makes even more urgent the task facing developing countries of finding a labor-demanding path to development. Some measures that can help to foster industry's absorption of

5. In this and the preceding paragraph, industry is defined to include manufacturing, mining, construction, and utilities. A summary and analysis of the available evidence is presented in Lyn Squire, *Employment Policy in Developing Countries: A Survey of Issues and Evidence* (New York: Oxford University Press for the World Bank, 1981).

a greater share of the labor force are discussed below in the section on "Promoting Employment."

Financial and Institutional Aspects

In most developing countries, industry is predominantly in private hands. Private entrepreneurs, especially in the middle-income developing countries, can be expected to make an appreciable contribution to industrial ventures from their own resources. Given the pervasive scarcity of private capital in most developing countries, however, governments commonly undertake to supplement private efforts through provision of medium- or long-term finance for industrial ventures, usually through local development finance companies (discussed below) and sometimes through the establishment of special funds.

Such measures reflect the fact that, among the institutional shortcomings hindering industrial development, the lack of a properly functioning financial system may be the most crippling in many countries. The financial system plays a crucial role in market-oriented economies in stimulating broadly based industrial development—by fostering indigenous entrepreneurship and enabling small firms in urban or rural areas to function efficiently, to grow and to invest, and to take risks with new technologies. The financial system needs to be encouraged and assisted, but the emphasis instead is too often on regulation.

In most developing countries, formal credit markets are distorted and their growth and functioning limited by public policies that keep interest rates artificially low to benefit certain target groups, and that impose rigidities in banking procedures to protect depositors and, in some cases, borrowers. The combined effect of these policies is to hinder the establishment of new instruments and forms of financial intermediation, with the common result that industrial development is dominated by a few wealthy families, by public enterprises with privileged access to subsidized bank credit, or by multinational firms with access to capital from abroad. Small enterprises, in particular, may be financially isolated, without access to term finance or equity capital apart from their own limited savings or family resources.

Probably most crucial is the need for governments to recognize the fundamental importance of allowing interest rates to be set by the market, so that they reflect accurately the scarcity of capital in the economy. We noted in chapter 3 various adverse effects of artificially low interest rates. The fundamental problem is that they repress the growth and development of the financial system so that it is prevented from meeting the changing needs of the economy. We return to the role of interest rates, and of the development of the financial system generally, in succeeding sections.

DEVELOPMENT OBJECTIVES

Although the drive for industrialization has many motives, in most countries the central concern is to increase productive employment and generate higher income. When developing countries began formulating strategies for economic growth in the 1940s and 1950s, industrialization was seen as the key to catching up to the higher per capita incomes enjoyed by the wealthier nations of the world. Manufacturing industry in particular, incorporating modern technology, held out prospects of a rapid rise in productivity and capital accumulation and thus of accelerated investment and growth throughout the economy. The depression of the 1930s had brought home to countries that relied on the export of primary products the need to diversify their economies. For all these reasons, industrialization came to be looked upon as synonymous with development.

Industrialization programs in the developing countries also reflect noneconomic considerations: national independence, modernization, defense, and prestige. For many countries, development of industry has been seen as an essential aspect of their escape from colonial and neocolonial dependence. The drive for independence, however, may run counter to the goals of economic efficiency—as often happens, for example, when a country follows policies of self-sufficiency in basic metals, chemicals, or defense industries.

The initial strategy of most countries seeking to industrialize is to create industries that will replace imports with domestic production. Import substitution is the logical first step in industrialization. It is a way of encouraging local entrepreneurs to go into industrial production where a market already exists, where the characteristics of the goods demanded are known, and where nascent domestic industries can be protected in a straightforward way from import competition—though preferably only for an initial period of growth and of learning-by-doing.[6]

Few countries, however, have found a proper level of tariff protection. Giving too little protection runs the risk of not encouraging any new industrial activity at all, so governments have often given too much. This has unduly limited competition, which has lessened the pressure to increase productivity and has led to demands for indefinite continuance of favored treatment. Tariff protection is not the only inducement offered. Others are quantitative restrictions on imports and administrative controls over the establishment of new firms, the effect of which is to protect existing firms from both foreign and domestic competition. Many governments also offer subsidized rates of interest, tax exemptions, and sometimes subsidized infrastructure and utilities. Such a package of incentives has often been provided to investors without determining whether the industry being assisted accorded with a country's comparative advantage and was likely to be viable in the long run. The results have often been disastrous; an inefficient and unduly capital-intensive industrial sector has been created, with low utilization of capacity, high cost of production, little generation of employment, and little saving of foreign exchange.

6. For a discussion of the benefits of properly administered protection for import industries, see Larry E. Westphal, "Fostering Technological Mastery by Means of Selective Infant-Industry Protection," in Moises Syrquin and Simon Teitel, eds., *Trade, Stability, Technology, and Equity in Latin America* (New York: Academic Press, 1982); also available as World Bank Reprint Series no. 253 (Washington, D.C., 1982).

POLICY ISSUES

Outward-Looking Strategies

The orientation of a country's industrial and trade policies is crucial to the pace and direction of its industrial growth and to the benefits to be derived from that growth. Over the past twenty-five years, the countries that have had the best record of growth and of withstanding external shocks have been those that have adopted "outward-looking strategies." This phrase is a shorthand term for a policy framework that, instead of concentrating on replacing imports or expanding exports, is in fact neutral in that it seeks to provide equal incentives to producers for export or for import substitution. As suggested above, there is nothing wrong with import substituting activities if they are planned and administered in a way that is economically justified. In many countries, opportunities for beneficial import substitution are numerous, far exceeding the limited export capacity. But the policy framework should give equal encouragement to manufacturing for export; in virtually every case where this has been done, it has not only contributed to increased employment and income but also led to more efficient allocation of resources, permitted exploitation of economies of scale, and generated technological improvements in response to competition from abroad. In contrast, once the "easy" stage of import substitution has been passed (that is, turning out products in which local producers have advantages over foreign producers in the domestic market), further substitution of domestic production for imports has entailed rising costs because of the absence of economies of scale in small national markets. In short, for countries seeking to bring about structural change and efficient growth in their economies, using trade to exploit resources more fully has been a more effective instrument than efforts toward self-sufficiency.

The economic "success stories" of the post–World War II era have decisively proved the efficacy of outward-looking strategies in bringing about industrial growth, labor absorption, and higher income. Which specific policy elements have been found to work best? The diversity of national endowments and situations means that no one policy prescription is universally applicable; policies must be adapted to the circumstances of each country. Nevertheless, it would be wrong to conclude that no general lessons can be drawn from past experience. The strategies of developing countries that have been the most successful in promoting exports share most of these elements:

- Realistic foreign exchange rates
- Easy, duty-free access to imported inputs for exporters
- Competitive wage and labor policies
- Incentives to encourage foreign investment and other forms of cooperation with foreign companies
- Moderate and relatively uniform protection for domestic import substituting industries
- Perceptive political leadership and constructive government intervention in the development process.

On the last point, the nature of government intervention in this process has varied greatly from country to country. In some, it has been quite effective in assisting exporters. The abundant evidence now available indicates, however, that even the most adept and imaginative intervention by government is not a sufficient condition; a policy mix that gives appropriate signals and rewards, and is reasonably stable, is indispensable.

Replicability of Successful Performance

The evidence also shows that it is not only the original spectacular performers—the "four little tigers," Hong Kong, Korea, Taiwan, and Singapore—that have been able to succeed in export production. Initially, it is true, a large percentage of manufactured exports came from a handful of developing economies, and the principal East Asian exporters still account for nearly two-fifths of the total. This has created the impression that the characteristics of these economies—relatively poor in resources but with energetic entrepreneurs, a disciplined, hard-working labor force, and special ties to major importing countries—were the main factors behind their export performance. But suppliers of the balance of manufactured exports include a wide range of countries. Thirty-seven developing countries realized more than $200 million each in exports of manufactures in 1981; eighteen of these had exports of more than $1 billion.[7] While the most successful exporters among them fall mainly in the middle-income group, some began their export drive at low income levels and with few natural resources. Per capita income in Korea in 1950, for example, was well below the average for Africa at the time.

The successful exporters differ in size, resource endowment, geographical location, extent of industrialization, and other factors. A World Bank study examined the characteristics of twenty-eight countries that achieved an average annual growth of manufactured exports of between 8 and 36 percent from 1965 to 1975.[8] They can be grouped into four broad categories:

- Economies that specialized relatively early in export of manufactures and have followed generally outward-looking policies: for example, Hong Kong, Singapore, Korea, Israel, Portugal, and Greece. They are all characterized by limited natural resources and a relatively educated labor force. With some exceptions, their exports initially were built around labor-intensive products, whereas in recent years they have begun to diversify into more knowledge-intensive products.

- Large semi-industrial countries that have achieved a considerable degree of industrialization based on a substantial home market, and in recent years have sought to promote the export of manufactures: for example, Brazil, Mexico, and Turkey.

- Countries now shifting away from specializing in primary exports to diversifying their exports: for example, Malaysia, Colombia, Ivory Coast, Morocco, Tunisia, Philippines, Thailand, and Chile.

- Large, poor countries that have achieved a significant volume of manufactured exports: for example, Egypt and Pakistan.

7. *World Development Report 1984*, annex table 12.

8. See Hollis Chenery and Donald Keesing, *The Changing Composition of Developing Country Exports*, World Bank Staff Working Paper no. 314 (Washington, D.C., 1979); and *World Development Report 1981*, annex table 12.

The wide variety of economies with successful export performance shows that entrepreneurship, organization, and hard work are not unique to East Asia. The key to good performance is to avoid policies that suppress these characteristics and to make full use of whatever comparative advantages a country possesses.

Penetration of Developed-Country Markets

Are there, however, other limits to how much new exporters can benefit from outward-oriented strategies? It has been suggested that penetration of the markets of industrial countries has reached or will soon reach a limit and that developing countries will face increasing barriers to their exports to industrial countries.

In fact, such penetration has been greatly exaggerated. Although products from developing countries doubled their share of industrial-country markets between 1970 and 1980, they still accounted in 1980 for less than 3.5 percent of consumption (production plus imports minus exports) in the industrial countries. Even in the clothing, textile, and leather industries, which claimed the largest share, penetration of the markets in industrial countries reached only 10.5 percent of total consumption. If market penetration by developing countries were to continue to rise in the 1980s at the rate it did in the 1970s, developing countries' share of total consumption of manufactured goods in industrial countries would rise only to about 5 percent. In the most successful industries, such as clothing and textiles, that share might grow to 15 percent. Even so, the production of these goods in the industrial countries would continue to increase at an average annual rate of 2 percent.[9]

Similarly, the effect of imports from developing countries on job displacement in the industrial countries is generally exaggerated. In fact, the industrial countries' exports of manufactures to the developing countries have increased by much more than the counterflow.[10] When both the direct and the indirect impact of the expansion of trade between industrial and developing countries is taken into account, the evidence is that there are net employment gains for the industrial countries. The problem, however, is that employment dislocations in the industrial countries tend to be specific to industries or localities; thus they attract considerable attention and generate political pressure for relief from imports.

With recession and high unemployment in the early 1980s, strong political pressures have led industrial countries to shore up weak industries by protecting them with tariffs, subsidies, or quantitative restric-

9. See Bela Balassa, *The Process of Industrial Development and Alternative Development Strategies* (The Frank D. Graham Memorial Lecture, Princeton University, April 17, 1980), Essays in International Finance no. 141 (Princeton, N.J.: Princeton University, Department of Economics, 1980); also available as World Bank Staff Working Paper no. 438 (Washington, D.C., 1980).

10. Between 1960 and 1978, for example, the value of industrial countries' exports of manufactures to developing countries increased by almost three times as much as did their imports from those countries. Trade with the developing world, far from retarding growth in the industrial world, made a significant contribution to the vitality of its manufacturing sector. See J. M. Finger, *Industrial Country Policy and Adjustment to Imports from Developing Countries*, World Bank Staff Working Paper no. 470 (Washington, D.C., 1981).

tions, including so-called voluntary quotas. The new protectionism is highly discriminatory against the fast-growing exporters of manufactures. Continued moves by the developed countries to block further penetration of their markets would have profoundly deleterious effects on the developing countries' efforts to achieve more rapid growth through trade.

Promoting Employment

Outward-oriented strategies not only raise output and income but also provide more jobs. Countries that have followed such strategies—for example, Korea, Singapore, Malaysia, Thailand, and Mauritius—have achieved higher rates and levels of labor absorption in industry than most other middle-income developing countries. Exports contributed heavily to increasing employment, in part because the products exported were mostly labor-intensive: textiles, clothing, electronic components, footwear, and other light consumer goods. In addition, by raising the levels of savings and investment in the economy generally, outward-oriented policies have helped to increase employment in industries producing primarily for the domestic market.[11]

Although manufacturing has been the largest single source of new urban employment in most developing countries, it has, as noted earlier, failed to fulfill hopes that it could resolve unemployment problems resulting from the population explosion. The International Labour Organisation (ILO) has estimated that between 1980 and the end of the century the labor force in the developing countries will increase by some 650 million people. Finding productive employment for them, as well as for the large numbers of those currently unemployed or underemployed, will be a formidable task. Data for many developing countries indicate that the unemployed (those actively seeking work) account for only about 5 percent of the labor force—but this is a very misleading figure. The poor take any job available, no matter how low paying, since they are unable to finance a prolonged job search. Visible unemployment is therefore only the tip of the iceberg; the real problem is the disguised unemployment or underemployment resulting from jobs that are so irregular or so unproductive that they provide inadequate income to cover the basic requirements of workers and their dependents. A large proportion of those living in absolute poverty are the working poor, who fall in the category of underemployed.

What are feasible policy approaches to improve the very serious employment situation in most developing countries? In those countries that have adopted a comprehensive approach to increasing employment, the strategy has included at least three elements, which are discussed below.

11. Export growth accounted for about 38 percent of the increase in Korea's manufacturing employment and 33 percent of its total employment growth between 1960 and 1970; in the latter year, exports were estimated to account for more than a fourth of all employment in manufacturing industry. Exports were responsible for 45 percent of industrial expansion in Malaysia in 1970–75 as well as a substantial proportion of the additional jobs created in manufacturing. Export promotion has also been shown to have a favorable impact on employment and income in a large country such as India. See Marsden, *Trade and Employment Policies*, pp. 31–32, and references cited there.

Correct Pricing of Capital and Labor

A common mistake made by developing countries with surplus labor seeking to encourage the growth of industry has been to introduce measures that make capital relatively cheap and labor relatively expensive. Such measures, and their adverse impact on growth, resource mobilization, and efficiency of investment, were described in chapter 3, Pricing Policy. In industry as in other sectors, these distortions have provided an incentive to firms to adopt more capital-intensive techniques, which were privately profitable but socially inefficient. Most countries that have increased employment rapidly have either avoided undue wage-capital price distortions or were able to remove those already in place. Correct pricing policies alone are not sufficient to alter significantly the employment situation in developing countries with high population growth—but they do help.

Selecting Labor-Intensive Technologies

The number of jobs generated in particular industries is largely determined by the technology used. Too often in making investment decisions, the technology has been taken as a given and alternatives have not been adequately examined. There has been a widespread assumption that most modern industrial technology must be capital-intensive and that little scope exists for varying the proportions of capital and labor. Evidence is accumulating, however, from studies of particular industries and processes that considerable technological flexibility does exist for a wide range of products, and that a more careful selection of technologies can offer substantial benefits.[12]

As would be expected, countries in which industry absorbs labor at a high rate are generally those that have adopted more labor-intensive technology. Capital stock per worker in Korea, for example, is substantially lower than in the United States in all industries—including fertilizers and paper, often considered to be inherently capital-intensive. Unit costs of production of metal cans have been lower for the relatively labor-intensive techniques in Thailand than for the automated techniques in Kenya and Tanzania. Even in those countries achieving rapid growth of industrial employment, however, the policies guiding choices of technology have seldom been optimal. A number of countries have, for example, subsidized imported industrial machinery, thereby discriminating against the use of indigenous—usually less automatic—machinery (see case study 1 in chapter 19, Technical Analysis).

But it is not only government policies subsidizing the use of capital that have encouraged adoption of capital-intensive methods in developing countries. Many other factors, unfortunately, have contributed to this result: the prestige of developed-country technologies and their promotion by contractors and suppliers, by consultants, and in many cases by aid agencies; lack of information on alternatives; a preference for goods

---

12. See, for example, Howard Pack, *Macroeconomic Implications of Factor Substitution in Industrial Processes*, World Bank Staff Working Paper no. 377 (Washington, D.C., 1980). See also A. S. Bhalla, ed., *Technology and Employment in Industry* (Geneva: International Labour Office, 1975).

that closely match the quality of imported products; and the difficulties of dealing with large numbers of inexperienced workers. What has worked best is, on the one hand, a systematic review of design alternatives to ensure that possibilities of more labor-intensive technologies have been fully assessed before projects are approved; and, on the other hand, a combination of institutional and policy measures to encourage the growth of an indigenous capacity to adopt and develop technology suited to local requirements.

Encouraging Small-Scale Industries

Small enterprises (conventionally defined as firms with up to 100 workers) employ more than half the industrial labor force in developing countries and account for a large proportion of total output. Their contribution is greatest in countries at the initial stages of industrialization but remains significant even in the most advanced economies. For example, 87 percent of manufacturing employment in Indonesia in 1975 was provided by small enterprises; in Colombia that year it was 70 percent; and in Japan it was still as high as 55 percent in 1978.

The potential advantages of small-scale enterprise are numerous. First, small firms tend to use less capital per worker than large firms do—not only because of differences in the type of products made but also because of differences in the technology used to make the same product. By combining more labor with capital, small enterprises can also use capital more productively: small firms have significantly higher ratios of value added to fixed assets than do large firms in Colombia, Ghana, and Malaysia, for example. Second, small firms make use of resources that otherwise might not be drawn into the development process—for example, workers with little formal training who learn skills on the job, or the small savings of proprietors who will not use the banking system but who will invest in their own firms. Owners of small firms—even those whose incomes are quite low—often have a surprisingly high propensity to save and to reinvest. Third, in addition to serving as a seedbed of entrepreneurship, small firms occupy a highly useful niche in the industrial structure, subcontracting with larger firms and engaging in small batch production, made-to-order work, or finishing operations complementary to large-scale industry.

When these potential advantages have not been realized, it has often been because small firms have operated in an unfavorable climate:

> Starved of capital, cold-shouldered by the development finance companies, overlooked in development plans, and, until recently, ignored by most foreign-capital aid programs, small-scale firms have had to rely on internally generated funds for expansion and modernization. To compound the problem, their profitability and incentive to invest is often undermined by both overt and hidden subsidies to large-scale industry.[13]

Owing to procedures too complex for them, small firms often have limited access to foreign exchange and to institutional credit; but they can

13. Marsden, *Trade and Employment Policies*, p. 42.

usually draw upon ample supplies of cheap labor. Consequently, they tend toward an even lower capital-labor ratio than would be appropriate. The opposite may be true for large firms, which can often obtain funds at subsidized interest rates or at artificially low exchange rates but may have to pay relatively high wages because of trade unions and labor legislation. As a result, they tend toward an excessive substitution of capital for labor. The economy gets the worst of both worlds: technically backward production methods and very low incomes in small firms, which employ the majority of the labor force; and excessive use of capital in the modern sector, which obtains most of the investment funds but creates few jobs.

INSTITUTIONAL ISSUES

Financing Industry

We noted earlier that, in many developing countries, government actions relating to capital markets, instead of fostering their growth, have discouraged or prevented them from serving the needs of the industrial sector effectively. The financial system has been looked on as a means of mobilizing savings and lending them to government or to modern industries at low interest rates. Controls to keep rates low—even if this meant credit rationing—have generally been favored.

In the past decade, the role of the financial system in development has come to be better understood. It is now widely accepted that low real interest rates have discouraged people from holding money (beyond minimum working cash balances) or other financial assets. This has made it difficult to create or operate a financial system that integrates financial markets (that is, that tends to equalize returns to investment throughout the economy, one of the primary goals of any financial system). In all economies except those that are centrally directed, financial markets that function reasonably well are essential for the efficient investment of savings. They may also be essential for the increase of savings, but this point is less clear. For our purposes, it is sufficient to note the fairly general consensus that "financial repression" resulting from low interest rates reduces the efficiency of investment.

The long-term goal should be to create an active and flexible financial system that will mobilize savings and allocate them to their most productive uses and in their most useful forms—be it short-, medium-, or long-term loan finance, equity, or various specialized financial instruments. An economy accomplishes this by moving from the growth of monetary deposits with commercial banks to the growth of nonmonetary assets of various types of financial intermediaries and then to the development of a securities market. To help bring about this so-called financial deepening, governments should limit their role to ensuring that financial institutions are allowed to come into existence in response to market forces and to operate on a competitive basis.

Because the financial system is not functioning adequately in many countries, governments have taken direct action to create the institutions needed. One of the most common actions has been the establishment of development banks or development finance companies (DFCs) to provide term finance to industry. These institutions offer some highly useful services: they channel funds to small and medium-size industrial borrowers, provide a professional approach to allocating funds among projects in accord with broad economic priorities, absorb and transfer technical advice, and act as a main conduit for domestic distribution of large-scale foreign loans or grants for industrial development. The World Bank has assisted in establishing, reorganizing, or strengthening more than a hundred DFCs in member countries and is currently providing financial assistance to about seventy of them. Most of them have become viable, enduring, and respected institutions that play a significant role in industrial development in their countries.[14]

Industrial development requires not only term finance but also working capital and equity finance. Many governments have established mechanisms for providing the first, but not the second. There may be a need for government measures, including legislation in some cases, to make it easier for commercial banks to provide a greater share of the needs of industry—particularly small industry—for working capital, and to facilitate establishment of institutional channels such as venture capital companies through which entrepreneurs can obtain some portion of their equity capital requirements.

Before any new institutions are established, however, existing institutions should be surveyed to determine if any of them—suitably strengthened or reorganized, if necessary—can be used to carry out some of the proposed functions. The working relationships of existing and proposed institutions, and the possibilities of mutually reinforcing roles, need to be assessed. An unplanned proliferation of new institutions has often led to the fragmentation rather than to the desired integration of financial markets. Special caution is called for in establishing new credit agencies in an economy where the regular commercial and savings banks have been repressed by low interest ceilings, high reserve requirements, or other controls. It is better to correct the underlying repression than to create new institutions needlessly.[15]

While formal credit markets have been distorted by government policies, informal credit markets—typified by the traditional moneylender—have been either ignored or discouraged. These informal credit markets, nevertheless, tend to expand in the vacuum created by financial repression. They have a comparative advantage in lending to small, scattered, and first-time borrowers not able to provide collateral: their transaction costs are often lower than those of banks, and they can more cheaply and reliably assess the risks. They can form a useful part of a country's financial system, at least until the country can afford a greatly expanded formal system. Accordingly, rather than attempting to suppress informal credit markets, governments should encourage commercial banks both to compete with the informal sector and to supply it with credit—which would reduce the monopoly power that the informal sector has in many areas and, in effect, use it as an agent where it has a comparative advantage.

14. World Bank experience with development finance companies is summarized in World Bank, *Development Finance Companies*, Sector Policy Paper (Washington, D.C., 1976).

15. See Ronald McKinnon, "Financial Policies," in Cody, Hughes, and Wall, eds., *Policies for Industrial Progress in Developing Countries*.

Managing Public Industrial Enterprises

Both public and private enterprises have functioned best when government intervention in their operations has been minimized. Those governments have been most successful that have concentrated on creating the proper external environment and on ensuring that management has sufficient autonomy as well as motivation, including price incentives, to produce efficiently.

With public sector enterprises, however, governments have additional concerns. Many state industrial enterprises enjoy monopolistic conditions; without the pressure to maximize profits, it is difficult to create a management environment that encourages a sustained search for efficiency. Measures found useful in some countries to overcome this situation include:

- Setting clear objectives for state enterprises. Such enterprises are often intended to serve several, sometimes conflicting purposes related to social (to increase employment) or political (to benefit particular groups or regions) as well as financial and production objectives. The government needs to agree with an enterprise as to which objectives are paramount and how the enterprise is to pursue them. The merits of using negotiated contracts (like the *contrat plan* developed in France; see chapter 23, Institutional Analysis) to establish agreement on objectives and targets and to set the framework for monitoring performance should be examined for each enterprise.

- Developing mechanisms, in the absence of market forces, to expose state enterprises to market surrogates. The establishment of shadow prices (see chapter 20, Economic Analysis) for efficient decisionmaking on prices, sales, distribution, and operations is of fundamental importance, since appropriate prices—actual or surrogate—are needed for firms to evaluate any proposed course of action.

- Encouraging private competition by removing barriers (such as restrictive licensing) to entry into the market, and by allowing product prices to be set at market levels to encourage private investment. Competition among state enterprises producing the same products should also be encouraged.

- Avoiding policies, such as unrealistic minimum wages, that raise salaries and wages appreciably above market levels.

- Seeing to it that state enterprises obtain their loan funds at market interest rates that reflect the true scarcity of capital.

If these enterprises are to be allowed to operate autonomously, governments may find it necessary to review their internal organization and procedures to make sure they are conducive to efficient management and operation. One aspect of this review is to assess the adequacy of the enterprise's management information system for planning, budgeting, internal control, and monitoring; another is to evaluate its policies and procedures for managing financial flows, plant operations, marketing activities, and project selection and evaluation.

An important problem area in many countries has been the provision of adequate compensation and incentives to top staff. Assuring managers of some security of tenure (for example, through renewable appointments for three to five years) has often been a way to avoid too frequent personnel changes. It has been difficult, however, for most governments to cut the link between the (usually inadequate) salaries of civil servants and those of the management and technical staff of state enterprises. Some have managed to do so, since the alternative to providing adequate compensation and incentives has been continued inefficiency of operations and loss of staff to the private sector. Although such movements of staff may provide benefits to the economy as a whole, they are nevertheless highly disruptive to running a state enterprise.

It has sometimes been found useful in the *contrat plan* to link compensation to performance indicators that have been agreed on. Managers as well as workers in a state enterprise can then feel confident that advancement and promotion in their careers are based on performance.

INVESTMENT ISSUES

Large and Complex Projects

Large industrial undertakings are the classic project prototype. They face virtually all the problems discussed in parts III and IV of this book: the need for detailed design, for careful demand forecasts, for painstaking financial and economic analysis, for efficient procurement, for choosing appropriate technology, for close monitoring of implementation, for building effective institutions with sound management, for avoiding cost overruns, and for including environmental damage in their costs. In this section, we shall discuss some of these issues as they relate specifically to industrial projects.

Investing in large industrial plants nearly always carries substantial risk because of their technical complexity, their large investment requirements, and their demands for skilled management and trained manpower. Moreover, markets, especially for exports, have been unstable. The market difficulties faced by many branches of industry in recent years reflect not only the economic recession of the early 1980s but also longer-term problems arising out of shifts in demand, changes in technology, and the emergence of substitutes. For all these reasons, large industrial projects have to be scrutinized closely to ensure that they are technically, economically, and commercially feasible and that their management and organization are sound.

The Bank recently reviewed results obtained under fifteen Bank-assisted industrial projects that were completed and evaluated between 1979 and 1983.[16] Eight of these produce fertilizers, six steel, and one cement. The experience gained during the preparation, implementation, and operation stages of the projects is summarized in the following paragraphs. Probably the most important lesson is that the best guarantee of a project's success is from the very outset to devote adequate attention and planning effort to all the major elements likely to affect its outcome.

- To avoid delays in the start-up phase and to ensure that the people who will operate the project participate adequately in its preparation and design, a full-time project implementation team should be ap-

16. World Bank, Operations Evaluation Department, *Tenth Annual Review of Project Performance Audit Results* (Washington, D.C., 1985), and other World Bank materials.

pointed early in the project cycle. Responsibility for implementation, including procurement, should be entrusted to a project manager on the site (independent from the management of the existing operating firm, if there is one); and project management arrangements should be designed to ensure efficient decisionmaking authority on the site and adequate monitoring of contractors' performance.

- The need for technical assistance should be carefully assessed well in advance of any major decisions. The investor's appreciation of the need for consultancy services and his openness to consultants' recommendations can be of crucial importance. The division of engineering responsibilities between the company and its engineering consultants should be clearly defined from the beginning. When there are cofinanciers, close cooperation among them and between them and the engineering firm or firms should be ensured to avoid scheduling and budgetary problems, particularly in complex projects where cofinanciers may be financing separate engineering contracts.

- If the project entails expansion of existing capacity, needed modifications in existing facilities and plant layout should be identified at an early stage and the possible disruptive effects of the expansion on existing operations carefully assessed. Operating companies, even those with experience in constructing their own plants, may still need technical assistance to implement a major expansion because of the complexity of handling both ongoing operations and new construction simultaneously.

- Realistic estimates of costs and implementation schedules are essential to a project's success. Detailed capital cost estimates should be prepared prior to commitment of any funds and continuously monitored during construction. Project implementation schedules, to be realistic, should take into account physical and other constraints and the amount of experience of the investors.

- Procurement arrangements should also be worked out well in advance. Tradeoffs with respect to possible delays, higher costs, and any losses in operating efficiency when introducing innovative technologies should be carefully considered. When locally produced equipment is to be procured, there may also be a tradeoff between the expected benefits of encouraging local technological capacity and the potentially longer delivery periods and higher costs of supplying such equipment indigenously.

- Since construction contracts on a cost-plus basis tend to encourage inefficiency and cost overruns, contracts should be based on a schedule of rates for different kinds of work. The capabilities of both local and foreign construction and engineering firms should be evaluated realistically before the award of contracts. When delivery times are long and price inflation is occurring, provision should be made for appropriate price escalation in contracts.

- Provision should also be made for building adequate social infrastructure when projects are to be located in relatively small towns or remote areas; these expenditures will have to be included as a project cost if they serve primarily the interests of the project.

- Major sector policies relating, for example, to price controls, marketing, or foreign exchange allocations can have a great impact on the success of a project. The relevant policy considerations should therefore be identified early in the project cycle and taken fully into account during project preparation and execution.
- Quality of management and staff is also decisive. Throughout the implementation of the project and its subsequent operation, management should have sufficient autonomy in setting pay scales to attract and retain qualified supervisory and technical staff. Training needs should be identified early and appropriate programs devised and implemented.

Parts III and IV of this book discuss at length many of the issues and lessons touched on above, including project preparation, project implementation, technical analysis, and procurement. Here we focus on five issues: use of consultants, choice of technology, marketing, role of a foreign partner, and training.

Use of Consultants

Many of the foregoing lessons reflect the fact that reducing risks to acceptable levels in complex industrial projects requires sound planning and timely execution. If the project investor lacks capability or experience to do this, qualified local or expatriate consultants will be required, usually for three main tasks: feasibility studies, project design, and project implementation or construction supervision. The investor or the consultant must look closely at all facets of a proposed project, including market demand, availability of raw materials and of infrastructure, choice of equipment and process, capacity and product mix, capital and operating costs, procurement procedures, marketing and distribution, financing plan, training, project management, and organization of the company or project entity. Such a widely ranging assessment is required both for choosing the optimum design for a project and for determining that it is financially and economically justified.

Guidelines for selection and use of consultants are given in chapter 26. As noted there, it is essential that consultants be not only capable but also impartial; special care has to be taken in industrial projects to ensure objectivity if the consulting firm is an arm of an operating company or equipment supplier. In no aspects of a project are the impartiality and competence of consultants more important than in the choice and adaptation of technology and in market analysis. The first of these is crucial to the project investor's ability to operate the project efficiently, while the second helps determine whether the project should be undertaken at all and on what scale.

Technology and Capital-Labor Ratios

A major contribution of consultants in large and complex industrial projects should be to increase the scope for successful technology transfer. This process is affected by government technology policies and by the level of industrial development already achieved. An important factor at the project level in such transfer is the investor's ability to manage the adoption or adaptation of new technology. This may depend heavily on the choice of a technology that is proven as well as appropriate—that is, so adjusted to the relative scarcities of capital and labor in the country that returns to the investment are maximized.

The scarcity of capital in developing countries means that a relatively low *average* capital-labor ratio (usually achieved by using labor-intensive techniques) is necessary to meet industrial employment objectives. We examine below one of the most effective ways of encouraging labor-intensity in industry: assistance to the development of small and medium-size enterprises, which tend to use less capital per worker and per unit of output. It must be recognized, however, that the total industrial investment program of a developing country may properly cover a wide spectrum from very labor-intensive to highly capital-intensive projects. Several examples of the latter may be cited:

- Resource-based industries such as petrochemicals and fertilizer are among the most capital-intensive, yet they often yield very high economic returns.

- Projects in many high-technology areas may also offer limited employment opportunities because of the nature of the product or process, yet yield high economic returns.

- Rehabilitation or plant replacement projects have a high incremental capital-labor ratio for the new jobs created. The principal effect, however, is to save existing jobs.

- Projects aimed at raising the income levels of those engaged in cottage industries or handicrafts may result in more capital-intensive investment than previously. The goal is not more jobs but more *productive* jobs, usually through adoption of improved technology. In such cases, the incremental capital-labor ratio is very high even though the activities remain relatively labor-intensive.

Even in large industrial projects such as those in the first two categories described above, developing countries should actively seek ways to increase efficient labor absorption. It should not be assumed that particular industries have fixed technical coefficients that rule out greater substitution of labor for capital. As noted earlier, a number of studies have indicated that efficient substitution of labor for capital is possible in a broad spectrum of activities even in heavy industry (for example, by performing peripheral and material-handling operations manually) without affecting product quality or unit costs adversely. When consultants are employed, their terms of reference should direct them specifically to explore design alternatives to increase labor absorption in individual projects.

Market Studies and Marketing Organization

Weaknesses in preparing the marketing aspects of industrial projects are common. Adequate priority has not always been given to the market study needed to determine the demand for a project's output, or to the arrangements for actually marketing the output during the life of the project.

In doing market studies, it has been found advisable to use not one but several scenarios, reflecting both optimistic and pessimistic forecasts. Given the variability—even, at times, volatility—of markets for many industrial products, investors have had to assess not only the most likely outcome but also the downside risks—possible cost increases, reductions in demand and prices, and so on—and to make certain that the size and likelihood of such risks are acceptable. To estimate the various possibilities, it has often been necessary to look at the market and the industry in a context that extends beyond the country or the region; this, in turn, has required contact with operating companies and market information sources worldwide. Sometimes the engineering consultant on a project has subcontracted the market study to a qualified firm specializing in the product under consideration. Despite the difficulties, good market studies can be obtained if a concerted effort is made—and if the project investor makes clear from the beginning that he wants an objective study rather than a justification for proceeding with a project.

In marketing the product, problems often arise if sufficient time and effort are not invested in building an effective marketing arm. Project investors who are relatively sophisticated in engineering and operations are frequently less strong in marketing and may not recognize that marketing is just as important as production. Marketing is difficult enough when the output goes entirely to the domestic market; marketing for export usually presents even more problems, since it requires a detailed knowledge of the exacting conditions that must be met to penetrate what are usually very competitive markets. Local investors have often found it beneficial to enter into agreements with foreign companies who will market the product or to seek an equity partner whose strengths may lie not only in engineering and production but also—perhaps mainly—in marketing know-how and access to world markets. It must be recognized that even take-or-pay agreements with export marketing companies are not entirely reliable; companies can and do back out of these arrangements to protect their own interest. An equity partner's interest, however, tends to be of a more enduring nature, as discussed below.

In a number of cases, governments have established separate organizations to market the output of public sector manufacturing or mining companies. Such organizations frequently pursue objectives not strictly related to efficient marketing. Featherbedding has sometimes occurred because governments have treated the marketing agencies as providers of jobs. The costs of this form of government intervention are added to the price of the product, which hampers the competitiveness of the operation. In a tight market, such additional costs cannot be afforded.

Role of a Foreign Partner

For major industrial investments in countries where domestic experience is lacking, efficient management and operation has often best been achieved through the full participation of an experienced foreign producer. The foreign company, to be effective, should serve as more than a project engineer or backup to the equipment supplier. Usually, the best results have been achieved when it becomes a cosponsor of the project by making a substantial investment in the equity of the company. Large equity investments, however, are often difficult to obtain. A way should be sought to give at least quasi-partner status to the foreign company; even a small portion—say, 10 percent—of the equity investment would give the foreign company some financial stake in the project and thus encourage its full corporate commitment. As a partner, a foreign company does not restrict its input to the technical aspects of the project but helps to establish the equally important functions of finance, marketing, administration, training, and long-range planning that assist the local company in starting up and operating the project successfully.

It has been found that the slope of the learning curve of a new company has a crucial impact on the profitability of the project. Financial and economic rates of return are sensitive to revenues in the early years of operation. An experienced foreign partner can often make a significant contribution in this regard. For example, the appraisal of a Bank-supported steel mill project in Mexico revealed so pronounced a difference in cash flow between two projected learning curves—one with and one without substantial participation by expatriate experts—that the government decided to make maximum use of expatriates during the start-up and initial operation of the project.

Foreign private investors have often been more successful than local management in fending off government interventions that make for inefficiency. The foreign investor is usually in a position to bargain for a degree of autonomy that may not be available to a local investor (though the former may be more vulnerable in some respects—for example, to public and press attacks). When the foreign investor takes an equity share and also undertakes a management contract for a specified period, it has usually proved a good idea to put expatriates in important line positions (that is, in operating rather than in advisory positions) for some initial period, even though the long-term objective is to train local staff to take over. The presence of a foreign private manager is not, however, an assurance of success. Adequate planning, proper project design, and a good local management team are still needed.

Even though foreign investors have the advantage of access to export markets and to experienced management, some countries may attach greater importance to the perceived disadvantages of foreign control over national assets and of payments abroad for dividends and for salaries of expatriates. Each country must weigh for itself the advantages and disadvantages of foreign investment in particular fields. For many technologies and branches of industry, the tradeoff is fairly clear: greater self-reliance and independence on the one hand, more rapid development with foreign investment on the other. The costs of the tradeoff can be much reduced and greater self-reliance achieved without slowing development if indigenous efforts are made to master the technology in a systematic and determined way.[17]

If the choice is made in favor of foreign investors, officials must still face up to the problem that these investors usually have to be attracted to, not merely allowed into, their country. Manufacturing for export carries its own risks in any situation, but these are compounded for a foreign investor when policies on taxation, labor remuneration, repatriation of profits, and so on are not clear, not stable, not embodied in

17. See the discussion on Korea in Carl Dahlman and Larry E. Westphal, "Technological Effort in Industrial Development: An Interpretative Survey of Recent Research," in Frances Stewart and Jeffrey James, eds., *The Economics of New Technology in Developing Countries* (Boulder, Colo.: Westview Press, 1982); also available as World Bank Reprint Series no. 263 (Washington, D.C., 1982).

legislation, or do not automatically cover all foreign investors and must be negotiated in each case. At the same time, developing countries, particularly those relatively unsophisticated in the branch of industry in question or in negotiating with foreign investors, may need to take special measures to protect their interests. Experienced foreign advisors—lawyers, engineers, geologists—may be retained to sit on the developing country's side of the table. The outcome of negotiations must be beneficial for both sides if the relationship is to endure.

Training Programs

Many industrial projects have experienced difficulties because of a failure to take account of training needs and to set about meeting them far enough in advance. The start of training should usually coincide with that of construction of a new plant or facility and should be considered an integral part of the project. For plants employing a technology new to the country or to the project investor, the investor is well advised to work out training arrangements with a firm that has access to a plant with similar characteristics. The training program must be of sufficient size to allow for losses of staff from a public enterprise to the private sector or from a private firm to other firms at home or abroad.

Training abroad in another developing country has often proved useful, as well as more appropriate than training in developed countries. A particularly successful example was the training of Bangladeshi staff at a fertilizer plant in Indonesia. Training abroad is always more costly, however, and some of it is irrelevant; it can become a luxury trip, especially for management trainees. Consequently, the emphasis is shifting to on-the-job training within the country. Foreign operators brought in to run a complex new facility for the first few years should be responsible for training. In general, experience indicates that a foreign contractor or equipment supplier can provide adequate operational training in a relatively short period. Adequate management training, however, presents greater difficulties and requires more planning and effort.

Small and Medium-Size Enterprise Projects

We examined earlier the advantages, especially in labor intensity, of small and medium-size enterprises, along with some of the factors hindering them—including a policy environment that, often unwittingly, discriminates in favor of large and against small industry. In this section we examine the kind of projects and programs found helpful, and some found unhelpful, in expanding the role of small and medium-size enterprises (generally referred to here for the sake of brevity as small enterprises). We also review recent experience with World Bank–assisted development finance companies set up to assist such enterprises.

Need for a Market-Oriented Approach

In general, governments have found it most useful to adopt a market-oriented approach to fostering small-scale industry. Small enterprises have flourished where governments have allowed markets to operate relatively freely. In addition, some steps may be necessary to ensure that small and large firms are put on a more nearly equal footing. Inputs commonly needed by small firms may be made more readily available (for example, by issuing import licenses if necessary) and the range of marketing opportunities may be increased (for example, by encouraging subcontracting from large firms to small). Evidence in many countries indicates that if small enterprises are economically efficient, they will thrive without special subsidies—provided they are not handicapped by measures favoring large firms. The provision of more nearly equal incentives and access to scarce resources is likely to produce more beneficial and lasting results than special programs tailored exclusively for small-scale enterprises. Specific measures found useful include:

- Providing information and advice to make it easier for small firms to compete in procurement by government departments
- Aiding the establishment of subcontracting clearinghouses
- Developing industrial estates, especially those that promote links between large and small firms, and making available common services and technical assistance
- Providing working capital, often needed as much as or more than fixed-asset finance
- Reducing collateral requirements or devising alternative means of securing loans that are acceptable to lenders and feasible for borrowers
- Designing simpler lending criteria and procedures for allocation of funds and loan supervision to reduce red tape and delays.

When not properly designed and market-oriented, however, government programs to aid small enterprises have failed to promote, or have even discouraged, growth and efficient operation. Several examples can be cited. First, selective controls to protect small firms from competition have sometimes had unexpected adverse effects. Such devices as reserving government procurement of various items for small firms may discourage technological development and adaptation among the protected firms; consumer demand may then switch to more attractive products coming from the modern or large-scale sector. Sometimes protection has been combined with subsidies, but this carries a cost to the rest of the economy. Using tariffs or other means to protect small enterprises from foreign competition has had deleterious effects similar to those discussed above and in chapter 3 for industry generally.

Second, small-industry institutes to provide various centralized services to small enterprises, unless carefully designed, have had disappointing results. The great diversity of small enterprises makes it impossible to include the range of expertise they need in a single institution—although assistance in management practices has often been found not to require industry-specific expertise. Salaries have usually been too low to attract and retain qualified staff, and relations of mutual confidence between civil service staff and entrepreneurs or clients have frequently been difficult to establish. Small-industry institutes limited to specific subsectors of industry or to a relatively small geographical area appear to have been most effective.

Third, subsidized interest rates on funds provided through specialized institutions—probably the most common form of assistance to small enterprise—often lead to high credit demand, credit rationing, and abuses in the allocation process. Since interest rate ceilings are generally applied to all financial institutions lending to small industry, institutions such as commercial banks that do not receive subsidized funds are deterred from lending to small firms. The result may be a contraction rather than an expansion in the total supply of credit to small firms.

Role of Development Finance Companies

Development finance companies, one of the most useful institutional innovations of the postwar era in this field, have proved invaluable in most developing countries in assisting the growth of small and medium-size enterprises. We mentioned earlier their extensive growth in the past two decades, the increasing competence and sophistication of most of them, and the heavy reliance by the World Bank on loans to DFCs for relending to small and medium-size enterprises. Experience with these loans affords some useful lessons.

First, more study of a country's financial system is frequently needed before a project is prepared, in order to understand better the workings of the system, to identify gaps in the financial structure, and to clarify the DFC's role in relation to other institutions.

Second, institution building is a long-term process. The quality of management is the driving force behind development of a viable and competent DFC. Also, the more autonomy the institution has, the greater its ability to maintain sound operating policies and a strong portfolio of investments. This includes the ability to make investment, staffing, and other decisions free from outside influence; to establish salary scales and benefit packages appropriate to attract and retain high-caliber staff; to raise resources (domestic and foreign) on its own; and to set lending rates in line with its costs and risks.

Third, development of financial independence by building up a diversified resource base should become an important objective of financial intermediaries as they mature. When there is easy access to official funds, the incentive to mobilize other resources is reduced. The more mature DFCs can also take the initiative to promote new institutions (such as venture capital companies) and financial instruments (such as industrial bonds) conducive to the deepening of the financial system. Active involvement of a DFC in arranging term financing in local currency beyond what it can itself provide can be crucial for effective and timely implementation of its subproject lending proposals. In addition, the ability of a DFC to finance working capital requirements itself can be especially helpful and can enhance its competitive position.

Fourth, when appraising subprojects, DFCs need to review technical designs more carefully and to assess project costs, financing plans, implementation schedules, and cash flow projections more realistically so that time and cost overruns and financial difficulties for the subborrowers are reduced. Early action to identify clients' problems and to seek solutions should be undertaken on a continuing basis. DFCs also need to monitor the performance of subprojects after the construction phase ends. In countries where publicly owned DFCs finance public sector enterprises, there is often a need to develop an effective bank-client relationship between the DFC and its parastatal subborrowers so the DFC can provide guidance, help instill financial discipline, and have an impact on operations and performance when circumstances warrant such intervention.

Fifth, it must be recognized that there are practical limits on the extent of review of technical designs and on cost-benefit analysis when lending to medium-size and especially to small enterprises. Not only are the projects simpler, but the investor is less able to afford the necessary technical expertise for detailed project design. In dealing with large numbers of small loans, regular cost-benefit analysis would require an inordinate amount of time and effort by the lending agency, and in many cases the cost would represent an undue proportion of the loan amount. Some countries have found it useful to lend to small enterprises through the commercial banking system—with its network of branches and its relatively quick and simple loan approval procedures—as well as through DFCs, which typically have more limited outreach (usually only one or a few offices) and more complicated appraisal and loan procedures. An approach found useful in many countries is to equip commercial banks as well as DFCs and other specialized lending institutions to provide technical assistance to small borrowers, not only on technical matters but also in accounting and marketing, tasks which in a large firm are turned over to specialists but which in a small firm are often handled by the owner-manager. Access by small enterprises to such technical assistance is often just as important for their success as the availability of term financing.

Sixth, DFCs should be encouraged to broaden their lending to small firms in construction, transportation, trade, maintenance and repair, personal services, tourism, handicrafts, and other activities. Although DFCs in some countries are doing this to an increasing extent, many still tend to concentrate on their traditional borrowers, manufacturing enterprises. But small firms in these other areas also have considerable employment potential; the service sector, in particular, can be expected to grow rapidly in developing countries. Many firms of this type obtain working capital from the commercial banks, but they also need the term finance that DFCs can provide.

Restructuring of Industry

Many developing countries are currently engaged in intensive efforts to adjust their economies to higher energy prices, reduced growth of markets in the industrialized countries, and associated changes in the international environment. Among the essential elements in these long-run adjustment efforts are steps to restructure industry to increase its efficiency, to make better use of existing capacity, and to reorient manufacturing toward products and processes in which the country has a comparative advantage.

Restructuring typically concerns the firms in a specific industry, such as textiles, rather than a single firm or the manufacturing sector as a whole. By their nature, restructuring programs relate to existing rather than new industries; nevertheless, investment in new product lines or industry branches may be an essential component. The World Bank has assisted a number of restructuring programs, which normally have encompassed both rehabilitation and expansion of capacity. While working through individual companies, these programs have been directed toward improving the efficiency, productivity, and capacity utilization of the industry as a whole. Such programs may entail closings, mergers, and the reorganizing of individual companies—including, where appropriate, forward or backward integration as well as increased specialization. The important elements of a restructuring program are:

- Making the use of machinery more efficient (higher capacity utilization) through multiple shifts, improved maintenance, and other changes in operating practices
- Improving production technology, changing the composition of output, or changing the organization of the industry by increasing plant size to a more economic scale, by combining (integrating) smaller plants into larger units where necessary, or by phasing out uneconomic smaller plants
- Relocating plants (and workers) to more advantageous sites
- Above all, examining and making needed changes in policies affecting the industry—such as pricing of inputs and outputs or investment incentives—to increase efficiency.

In most successful programs for restructuring an industry, the choice of specific units to be modernized, expanded, or otherwise assisted has been made not by government officials but by the two parties most directly involved—the entrepreneurs or managers of the enterprises and the financial institutions providing funds—on the basis of their assessment of market prospects. Also, the funds have been lent at or near market rates of interest. Otherwise, restructuring programs can end up subsidizing firms or products that ought to be abandoned. A rehabilitation project can have a high rate of return and yet bring the firm or the operation from losses of, say, 20 percent to losses of 5 percent. Although this may be a valuable contribution, the real answer may be to scrap the firm or operation rather than to rehabilitate it, so that losses are halted, not merely minimized. Finally, it is no less important in a restructuring project than in a new project to look at all the alternatives, including that of importing the product rather than producing it domestically, with a view to ensuring that the country's resources are invested in activities in which it has a comparative advantage.

Family planning and nutrition information program, Kenya

10

Population, Health, and Nutrition

CHARACTERISTICS OF THE SECTORS

POPULATION, HEALTH, AND NUTRITION activities are closely intertwined, and, although the objectives of their policies and programs are distinct, it is useful to consider the three sectors together. Impressive changes have occurred since midcentury in these sectors' basic indicators. Life expectancy in the developing world has increased by more than a third since 1950, from 43 years to 59 years by 1982. The crude death rate has declined by 58 percent, and the infant mortality rate by more than 40 percent. Although population is still growing rapidly, the rate of increase has slowed appreciably. Annual growth, having risen from about 0.5 percent in 1900 to a peak of 2.4 percent in the mid-1960s, has leveled off and dropped slightly to about 2.0 percent. Given the decline in mortality that has taken place, this implies a significant reduction in fertility: the crude birth rate fell by 27 percent between 1950 and 1982.[1]

Nevertheless, the need for further progress is great. Nearly one out of ten children in developing countries dies in the first year of life, and in parts of very low-income countries this figure is one out of five. Children in developing countries are nine to twelve times as likely to die before their fifth birthday as those in developed countries. Malnutrition is a contributing factor in the deaths of at least 10 million children annually. Population growth rates in nearly two-thirds of the developing countries are still at levels that imply a doubling of their populations within three decades.

Furthermore, continued rapid growth in the future promises to magnify the problems. World population took thousands of years to reach its current 4.8 billion; if present trends persist, it will climb to more than twice that number in the next century. The population of developing countries will double or triple by the year 2050, that is, within the lifetime of children now being born. This unprecedented growth can be expected even if current fertility rates in developing countries (ranging from four to eight births per woman) were to decline to replacement level (just over two children per couple when minimal mortality levels are attained) at a somewhat faster pace than appears likely.[2] Future increases will be fueled not only by falling mortality but also by the momentum of past high fertility, manifested in the large and still growing proportion of young people who have yet to pass through their childbearing years.

Researchers seeking to understand population trends have hypothe-

---

1. The crude death rate is the number of deaths per thousand population in a given year. The infant mortality rate is the number of deaths that occur between the ages of 0 and 1 per thousand live births in a given year. The crude birth rate is the number of births per thousand population in a given year. World Bank, *Health*, Sector Policy Paper (Washington, D.C., 1980); World Bank, *World Development Report 1983* and *World Development Report 1984* (New York: Oxford University Press, 1983, 1984).

2. The World Bank's *World Development Report 1984* contains an extended discussion of the population problem, on which parts of this chapter are based. See also the article by Nancy Birdsall, "Population Growth: Its Magnitude and Implications for Development," *Finance and Development*, vol. 21, no. 3 (September 1984).

sized that countries evolve through two transitions—one demographic and the other epidemiological. The developed countries have reached the final stage of each transition, whereas the developing countries are at an earlier stage.

As countries proceed through the demographic transition, they pass from an initial stage of high mortality, high fertility, and slow population growth—a stage from which developing countries have only recently emerged—through a period of declining and then low mortality but continued high fertility, during which population grows more rapidly, to a third stage of low mortality and low fertility, when population growth slows again. The progress of today's developed countries through the first and second stages to the third stage is well documented, and some Asian countries increasingly show signs of following suit. Whether countries still in the earlier stages of the transition, especially in Africa, will also follow this pattern remains to be seen. The reduction in mortality that leads from the first to the second stage is associated causally with many facets of economic and sociocultural development, including public health improvements, rising incomes, better education, better housing, and an increased food supply. The decline in fertility that comes later is a behavioral change correlated with a lessening of the economic advantages of having large families. (For example, children are no longer needed in household production or for support in parents' old age.)

The epidemiological transition traces changes in the leading causes of illness and death. In an initial stage, which endured at least into the last century in today's developed countries and which still persists in many parts of the developing world, health profiles are dominated by widespread infectious diseases linked to poverty, malnutrition, unsanitary environments, and poor hygiene. This stage is marked by high infant and child mortality and low life expectancy. The principal causes of death are influenza, pneumonia, tuberculosis, diarrheal infections, and familiar childhood diseases (such as measles), with undernourishment a major contributing factor. As these diseases are brought under control and more individuals live to maturity, a second stage is reached, during which other problems—present but overshadowed earlier—become salient, including diseases of advancing age (cardiac and cerebrovascular afflictions, cancer, and arthritis) and other chronic disorders (diabetes and mental illness). Infant and childhood mortality rates drop and stay at low levels, and life expectancy rises to seventy years and more. Some observers define a third stage, in which conventional views of disease are supplemented by a concern with the health hazards stemming from environmental exposure and from changes in the social conditions of the family, community, and workplace. This stage is associated with absenteeism, violence, and alcohol and drug abuse, sometimes of epidemic proportions.[3]

Developing countries proceeding through these demographic and epidemiological transitions today face obstacles that did not exist in the past. With the help of modern medicine (such as vaccines), mortality rates have fallen much faster than formerly, and life expectancy has risen more quickly. Consequently, in countries where fertility decline has not been

3. John R. Evans and others, "Health Care in the Developing World: Problems of Scarcity and Choice," *New England Journal of Medicine*, vol. 305 (1981).

correspondingly rapid, population growth in the second stage will be faster and more prolonged than it was in today's developed countries. And, whereas the epidemiological transition evolved over the course of more than a century in today's developed countries, many developing countries must now cope with all stages at once, as the rural and semiurban poor struggle to escape the first stage while urban groups are deep in the second or third. Finally, with the epidemiological transition now running further ahead of the demographic transition than heretofore, unprecedentedly large demands are being placed on health budgets and delivery systems. Resources already inadequate to deal with first-stage problems are being pressed to support the expensive requirements of second-stage chronic diseases as well, using sophisticated technologies undreamed of a century ago.

Economic Aspects

The impact of changes in population, health, and nutrition on economic growth, and vice versa, has been the subject of considerable research and debate. Continuing rapid population growth on an ever larger base is increasingly seen as a development problem that leads to a lower quality of life for millions of people. The main cost of such growth, borne principally in developing countries by the poor, is lost opportunities for improving people's lives.

Rapid population growth slows development for three reasons. First, it exacerbates the difficult choice between higher consumption now and the investment needed to bring higher consumption in the future. As population grows more rapidly, a larger investment is needed just to maintain the current amount of capital per person; this applies not only to physical but also to human capital—that is, a person's education, health, and productive skills. Otherwise, each worker will have less equipment and fewer skills to work with, and productivity and income will stagnate or even fall. Ultimately, the key to development is more people with better education and skills, yet every effort is required simply to maintain the status quo. And where it is hard to raise the level of physical and human capital per worker, it is even harder to raise incomes and living standards. For example, the high fertility and falling infant mortality of the mid-1960s mean that in most developing countries today about 40 percent of the population is aged fifteen or younger. Many of these countries face a doubling or tripling of their school-age population by the end of the century, which will vastly increase the demand for educational services. In Malawi, which is one such country, rapid fertility decline could bring about savings in education of more than 50 percent by the year 2015 by slowing the rise in the number of children entering school.

Second, in many economies that are still highly dependent on agriculture, population growth threatens what is already a precarious balance between people and scarce natural resources. In part, the problem arises because rapid population growth results in more rural laborers remaining in low-productivity agriculture, since the possibilities of transfer into modern agriculture or other modern jobs are limited. Much of the huge projected increase in the labor force will have to be absorbed in agriculture, a difficulty that most of today's developed countries never faced. In Kenya, 70 percent of the labor force will probably still be working in agriculture as late as 2025, and the number of agricultural workers will be twice what it is today. The result is likely to be continuing low incomes for many families and, in some cases, continuing stress on traditional agricultural systems, with consequent environmental damage that threatens the economic well-being of the poor. In the lowland areas surrounding the Ganges River in South Asia, for example, population growth and competition for land have forced many people to live too close to the water, in the path of annual floods.

Third, rapid increases in population make it difficult to manage the adjustments necessary to promote economic and social change. High fertility is a major contributor to rapid urban growth. Cities in developing countries are growing to unprecedented sizes. Such growth poses enormous new problems of management even to maintain—let alone improve—living conditions for city dwellers (see chapter 12, Urbanization).

Illness and malnutrition also restrict economic development. They impair the productivity of workers, constrain learning and mental development in school and at work, divert public and private resources to expenditures on health care, impede efficient utilization of other resources, such as land (for example, where onchocerciasis has inhibited settlement in fertile areas) and domestic animals (where human and animal diseases interact), and cause scarce food supplies to be used inefficiently, since the capacity to absorb nutrients is reduced by disease.[4] (In Indonesia, iron deficiency anemia resulting from hookworm infestation has been found to reduce the productivity of construction and rubber plantation workers by nearly 20 percent, relative to levels observed after treatment with iron supplementation.) In addition to lowering the output for each hour worked, disease can also curtail working time through absenteeism and premature death. (The purely economic significance of work time losses may, however, be limited where there is a labor surplus.)

Although economic development generally contributes to progress toward population, health, and nutrition objectives through its role in the demographic and epidemiological transitions, it can also have a negative impact. Shifts in agricultural production stimulated by economic change can reduce the availability of nutritious foods to disadvantaged groups. Construction of dams and irrigation canals can increase the incidence of water-borne and vector-borne diseases. After completion of a dam in Ghana, the prevalence of schistosomiasis among schoolchildren in some localities soared from 5 to 90 percent. Malaria cases more than doubled in the area surrounding a new dam in Sudan.

Social Aspects

In few other sectors are the social aspects—especially traditions, habits, values, and beliefs—so central. Cultural and religious customs still contribute powerfully to high fertility. Even when it is recognized that rapid population growth can have far-reaching adverse consequences,

4. World Bank, *Health.*

government leaders are often reluctant to contravene such customs. Unhygienic practices at home and in the community are among the leading causes of the spread of illness, while traditional beliefs about the treatment of children contribute to their undernourishment.

Three social aspects that have implications for policymaking and program design should be noted. First, there are gaps between the private and public gains to be realized from the necessary behavioral changes. The greater part of the costs of rapid population expansion, and of the benefits from slowing growth, accrue to society. From the perspective of the individual, large families may make economic sense long after they cease to do so from the perspective of society, or they may have offsetting cultural advantages. Failure to prevent or treat an illness can have consequences for society of which the individual may be only dimly aware (such as spreading infectious diseases that otherwise could be controlled). These gaps between private and social gains are a principal reason for stressing public action rather than relying exclusively on market mechanisms.

Second, both the incidence of disease and access to health services are very unevenly distributed among income groups and between urban and rural areas. The poor need more services but receive less. They need more health and nutrition care because they live in more disease-ridden environments and have less adequate diets; and they need more family planning help because, being less educated, they are less aware of their choices and less able to exercise them without help. Yet service delivery systems usually favor economically advantaged groups. Moreover, urban populations are much better served than rural ones. In some countries, less than half the rural population has access to modern health services, except at prohibitively long distances. Migrants fare worst of all.

Third, the roles of women and children, who are the primary recipients of many population, health, and nutrition services, must be understood and taken fully into account. The knowledge, attitudes, practices, control over resources, and decisionmaking authority that shape the lives of women and children, as well as their willingness to seek appropriate services and to comply with recommended procedures, are determined through the dynamics of the household. Programs and policies must also take into account how customs differ across each distinguishable subgroup (ethnic, religious, regional) in the target population.

Financial Aspects

Developing countries spend between 2 and 5 percent of GNP annually in these sectors, counting both public and private, and both capital and recurrent expenditures on family planning, preventive and curative health care services, nutrition monitoring and rehabilitation, and supplementary feeding programs. Family planning accounts for relatively little of this total—frequently no more than one-tenth of that spent on health care. Spending on health care is strongly correlated with income level, ranging from under 3 percent of GNP in low-income countries, to 2 to 6 percent in middle-income developing countries, up to 6 to 10 percent in industrial countries. Outlays for nutrition activities vary by country, but usually are very low. On a per capita basis, spending on family planning is generally less than $1; on health care it is $1 to $3 in low-income countries, $10 to $30 in middle-income developing countries, and $300 to $900 in industrial countries.[5]

Contrary to common perception, private sector activity is not inconsequential. In health, private expenditure is a larger proportion of total expenditure in developing than in developed countries, if use of traditional practitioners is included. In a recent survey of 39 developing countries, the private share of health costs was more than 25 percent in 35 countries, more than 50 percent in 19 countries, and more than 75 percent in 6 countries. In contrast, of 13 industrial countries, in only 4 did the private share exceed 25 percent. In family planning, private suppliers provided more than 20 percent of all services in 10 out of 15 developing countries studied in recent surveys. In two—Mexico and Korea—they provided over 35 percent.

Private services are financed mainly from fees for services (including "gifts" in kind) and payment for medicines. Public services are financed predominantly from general government revenue; user charges for public services are minimal in many countries. In 16 out of 17 developing countries for which data were available, less than 15 percent of the annual cost of public health services was recovered through user charges; 14 countries recovered less than 8 percent. Government family planning and nutrition programs typically recover even less. In all three sectors, the public services depend heavily on annual government budget allocations, which significantly colors their substantive and institutional character.

Despite the reliance on budgetary outlays to finance public services, the share of government funding allocated to population, health, and nutrition is small. In 32 out of 37 developing countries, according to 1981 data, health received less than 8 percent of total government spending, and in 19 of these, less than 5 percent. By contrast, education accounted for more than 10 percent of government spending in 30 of these countries. The share of family planning is usually less than 1 percent.

Institutional Aspects

A bewildering array of institutions exists in these sectors, forming a complex and usually fragmented network not well structured for the task of shaping change. In the public sphere are central agencies (health ministries and population commissions), regional and district counterparts, and local government and community groups. On the private side are voluntary organizations (religious or secular), commercial ventures (clinics, hospitals, pharmacies, street vendors), facilities affiliated with industrial and agricultural enterprises, and large numbers of individual practitioners. Quasi-public entities range from social security systems to medical schools, food subsidy outlets, and pharmaceutical suppliers.

In some countries, publicly supplied services for all three sectors are delivered by the government health system; other countries maintain separate staffs and facilities for each sector. Health infrastructure tends to be organized as a hierarchical referral pyramid, with community-level

---

5. David de Ferranti, *Paying for Health Services in Developing Countries: An Overview,* World Bank Staff Working Paper no. 721 (Washington, D.C., 1985).

workers and small clinical units (health posts and subcenters) at the base, large units (health centers) in the middle, and hospitals at the top.

Developing strong institutional arrangements for the delivery of services is made more difficult by the nature of the services themselves. Family planning, health, and nutrition services require one-on-one contact and depend on staff judgment and discretion in assessing individual client needs. A large number of widely dispersed delivery points is necessary, especially for primary health care services. Many of these are very small units, remotely located and thinly staffed by personnel with minimal training, who may be answerable to various overseers simultaneously (for example, to village leaders, to several sector-specific public agencies, and to local and district government entities). Critical supplies may require special handling, such as the preservation of "cold chains" for certain medicines and sterile packaging for contraceptives. Supplies must be skillfully procured (often on international markets, where the penalty paid for ill-timed or ill-chosen purchases can run to several hundred percent or more) and then safely stored and distributed at timely intervals. Large support systems must be kept going for needs ranging from maintenance of an extensive vehicle pool to in-service training of many types of staff as well as education of future physicians and paramedical staff.

Close cooperation—inherently hard to secure—is required among different sectors: family planning with health, and both (plus nutrition) with water supply and sanitation, agriculture, and education. Often it is necessary to accommodate the competing demands of several separate programs, each with its own staff and support systems (for example, "vertical" programs for disease control and "horizontal" programs for other services), and to harmonize the divergent views and interests of numerous professional cadres and specialists. Few developing countries have established the institutional capacity to deal with these complex requirements.

DEVELOPMENT OBJECTIVES

For population, the principal objective of most developing countries should be to slow the rate of growth. For health and nutrition, it should be to avert premature (that is, preventable) death and reduce the extent and severity of illness and malnutrition. Reasonable targets for progress toward these goals will vary with country characteristics and circumstances, as will feasible time frames for achieving them. Countries in the final stages of the demographic and epidemiological transitions typically have population growth rates below 1 percent, crude birth and death rates below 15 per thousand population, infant mortality rates below 50 per thousand, and prevalence rates for malaria below 10 percent. These levels will not be suitable benchmarks for all countries, but can be useful points of reference. Similarly, goals such as reducing fertility rates to replacement level or eradicating selected diseases, even if not attainable in the short term, should be kept in mind for the long run.

The apparent simplicity of these aims belies an underlying complexity. Reasonable targets and feasible time frames are not easily determined.

The pace of progress must be reconciled with the demands of other sectors competing for scarce resources. Choices must be made within the sectors as well. In health, for example, it may be necessary to choose between controlling childhood diseases and improving adult health. Such decisions raise difficult questions of equity and efficiency. Priorities must be established before broad sectoral objectives can be translated into concrete policies and programs. We consider in the next section what those priorities should be.

First, though, the rationale for slowing population growth merits further comment. The rationale for the health and nutrition goals is straightforward: lengthening life and minimizing disability, pain, and retarded physical development are universal human desires in their own right, and contribute to raising living standards by improving productivity. But what is the basis for advocating slower population growth?

We have already noted the principal argument, that continued rapid increases in population portend potentially disastrous setbacks for future generations in the effort to raise living standards and alleviate poverty. Some developing countries will experience more widespread and severe poverty, malnutrition, and social unrest if present trends persist.

This argument is compelling by itself, but there are others. High fertility endangers the health of mothers and infants when pregnancies occur in rapid succession, at a very young or advanced maternal age, or after many prior pregnancies. Health complications associated with frequent childbearing are a principal factor in high infant and maternal mortality. Furthermore, it is argued that couples, and women in particular, should have freedom of choice in shaping their own future.

Neither economic nor health reasons compel a preference for smaller over larger populations; nor is fertility decline a desirable end in itself. A few developing countries, with high education levels, adequate physical infrastructure, and a relatively stable political and economic environment are relatively well able to cope with rapid population growth. But these are the countries that have already reduced the rate of population growth. Most developing countries are not so favored, and for them—for the reasons given earlier—rapid population growth will seriously retard economic development.

Nevertheless, some people contend that population increases stimulate the innovation and technological change that raise living standards. It is true that both population and living standards have risen dramatically in the past. However, the future will differ from the past in many respects, not the least of which is that population size for the next hundred years will be increasing much faster than ever before. For living standards to keep pace, the rate of technological change and its diffusion and application would have to be far more rapid than can plausibly be expected. Moreover, many developing countries whose economies are largely dependent on agriculture can no longer draw on large tracts of unused land. Nor can population pressure be relieved by large-scale emigration, as it was in nineteenth-century Europe. Finally, compared with Europe, Japan, and North America in their periods of fastest population growth, income in today's developing countries is still low, human and physical capital are less developed, and in some countries political and social institutions are less well established.

POLICY ISSUES

In setting priorities for policies to further the broad objectives we have outlined, three problems, familiar in other sectors as well, deserve mention. They are, first, the pervasive misallocation of resources (for example, in health, overemphasis on hospital-based curative services concentrated in urban areas, at the expense of preventive and primary health care services that also reach rural areas); second, deficiencies in the performance of the operating institutions (such as management or organizational weaknesses that reinforce the misallocations); and third, inadequate efforts at mobilizing resources and financing services (for example, lack of a clear policy for cost recovery). These and other problems affect the setting of priorities in each of the three sectors in different ways.

Population

Priorities within the population sector should be consistent with the stage the country has reached in dealing with population issues. Where policies have been pronatalist, as in parts of Africa, emphasis may need to be placed first on changing opinions. Where commitment to slowing population growth is strong and family planning programs are working well, attention can be devoted to other initiatives, such as disseminating information to previously unserved segments of the population or reducing tax incentives or family allowances that favor large families. Progress toward fully developed policies requires governments to take certain crucial steps:

- Develop greater awareness and understanding at all policymaking levels of broad population issues (such as the adverse consequences of rapid growth) and of the need to approach these issues more comprehensively than through family planning alone. The rate and pattern of socioeconomic and cultural development affect population growth through the impact on fertility behavior of changes in income levels, educational attainment, women's status, employment opportunities for the poor, and other circumstances. Population strategy should therefore be an integral part of national planning and span several sectors, rather than solely the concern of family planning agencies.

- Adopt a clear statement of population policy, backed by support at the highest levels, by action to assure that the policy is well understood and accepted as a national priority, and by effective implementation mechanisms. In 1982, 62 out of 134 countries surveyed did not have an official policy favoring slower population growth.[6] Among those that did, some have yet to take any concrete action.

- Eliminate governmental restrictions on private sources of family planning services, such as charitable organizations and commercial distributors of contraceptives. Private programs can usefully complement public activities and help economize on public funds.

6. Dorothy L. Nortman, *Population and Family Planning Programs: A Compendium of Data through 1981* (New York: Population Council, 1982).

- Provide adequate funding and institutional support for public family planning programs that foster the spacing of children and that benefit the health of mothers and children.

- Develop and implement policies and services that go beyond child spacing to broad family planning programs designed to assist parents to appreciate the advantages of smaller families and to achieve their desired family size. This will normally entail the full range of family planning services, including contraceptive distribution and counseling through public health facilities and other outlets, as well as outreach efforts to inform, educate, and communicate with potential users.

- Reduce existing incentives that favor large families (such as family allowances or preferential access to housing) and provide incentives to encourage smaller families. The first type of incentive may be politically easier to implement, but the second, if properly designed and fairly applied, can be a logical way of extending conventional family planning approaches while still allowing people ample opportunity for free personal choice. In addition, legal reform may be called for (for example, regarding inheritance laws that affect women's status or the minimum age at marriage).

- Increase public spending for family planning programs significantly. There is currently a large unmet need for family planning services in developing countries: millions of women want no more children yet risk pregnancy because they are not using any contraceptive method.[7] (In the chapters of part II, we have generally refrained from advocating increased public spending for particular sectors, since the circumstances and needs vary so widely among countries. But the provision of adequate programs to control fertility is an overriding priority in many countries, and the additional funds required to carry out the measures mentioned above will in most cases not require a significant increase in total public outlays.)

Health

The main need in health is to rechannel existing support in order to progress toward accepted objectives more rapidly and efficiently and at affordable cost. Policy measures should include:

- Expanding preventive services relative to curative services. Prevention generally offers more cost-effective possibilities for saving lives and minimizing illness. Given limited resources, consideration should be given to cutting back, or at least curtailing growth in, curative services (such as urban hospitals) to permit expansion of preventive programs. In all countries, but especially in those still in the early stages of the epidemiological transition, prevention should stress immunization against the most prevalent communicable diseases of childhood, monitoring of infant growth, promotion of breastfeeding and better prenatal and perinatal care, as well as improved water

7. *World Development Report 1984*, pp. 130–34.

supply and sanitation. Oral rehydration therapy, although not strictly a preventive measure, should be given priority as well.

- Strengthening simple, safe, low-cost medical procedures that can be delivered at the primary health care level (for example, by a community-based worker or a small health post or subcenter). Particularly in rural areas, better access to rudimentary curative services for minor injuries and common infections, if these services are effectively administered, is a more cost-effective means of improving health status than specialized care at the secondary and tertiary levels (health centers and hospitals), which reach only a small proportion of the population.

- Containing costs at the secondary and tertiary levels, since rising hospital expenditures reduce funds available for preventive and primary care services. More efficient hospital procedures should be adopted to reduce unwarranted admissions or unnecessarily long in-patient stays. Acquisition of the most advanced technology (for example, the latest generation of CAT scanner) is a luxury few developing countries can afford.

- Extending programs to control the main parasitic diseases (such as malaria, schistosomiasis, intestinal worms, trypanosomiasis, Chagas' disease, and onchocerciasis) when such programs are cost-effective. It should be recognized, however, that current treatment and control technologies are of limited effect, and eradication is not feasible in most instances. Also, a long-term commitment is required; ambitious short-term efforts have little lasting effect if followed by periods of relative neglect. (A resurgence of malaria has occurred in countries, such as Peru, that have cut back on formerly intensive control projects.)

- Ultimately, giving greater attention to nondisease health hazards, especially those associated with the use of toxic substances, unsafe workplace practices, and road accidents.

Although there are still large unmet needs for health services in many developing countries, increasing the allocation of funds to health must be weighed against other priority claims in a resource-constrained environment. This underlines the importance both of freeing up resources within the health sector by curtailing activities of lower priority and of ensuring that programs are carried out in an efficient and cost-effective manner.

Nutrition

In nutrition, as in health, the objective—to reduce malnourishment, particularly when it impairs health, growth, or productive activity—is not in dispute. But progress toward that objective requires coordinating the efforts of several distinct agencies: agriculture and rural development ministries, health and sometimes education ministries, and central planning bureaus. Initiative and action tend to be lost in uncertainty as to who is supposed to do what. The first priority for many countries is, therefore, to clarify responsibilities and achieve better coordination. Assignment of a lead role to a cross-sectoral agency (a central planning bureau or special commission) has proved effective in some countries but not in others. A common difficulty with this arrangement is that program and policy implementation, usually performed by sectoral agencies (agriculture and health), is weakened when the lead role is assigned elsewhere.

Improvements in nutrition require simultaneous progress on at least three fronts. First, national economic and social development policies that promote sustained economic growth and the equitable distribution of its benefits will help to increase food production and to raise the purchasing power of the poor. These are essential steps toward reducing overall deficiencies in their intake of protein and calories.

Second, nutrition concerns must be adequately addressed in the formulation of policies in agricultural development, and in any other sectors or activities that can have a substantial impact, positive or negative, on nutritional status. Careful consideration must be given to the long-term effects of agriculture and rural development investments on the food consumption patterns of the poor, for whom the risk of undernourishment is greatest. (For example, substituting refined cereals for more nutritious unrefined products as the main staple of the diet of the poor may unintentionally make them worse off than before.) Experience suggests that explicit recognition of nutrition issues need not interfere with production goals or add unduly to project cost.

Third, special programs focused on nutrition may be needed. Some program options are:

- Fortifying food staples with micronutrients. This should be a high priority in countries in which population groups suffer from deficiencies of vitamin A (a cause of blindness and skin infections) or iodine (a cause of goiter and mental retardation). Iron fortification to combat anemia should also be considered. The requisite technologies are cheap, safe, effective, and easily administered.

- Providing nutrition education. Programs for mothers and young children that can be incorporated into health-related services are relatively inexpensive and have had promising results (as in Indonesia). Programs that work through schools, community groups, or the media have proved more difficult to sustain at an acceptable level of effectiveness.

- Targeting food distribution (for example, to children under the age of five). Four Bank-supported, largely experimental projects in Brazil, Colombia, India, and Indonesia have tested alternative approaches to food distribution and subsidy programs. They demonstrate that targeting those most in need is feasible, cost-effective, and a promising way of making an impact without becoming enmeshed in the problems of broad programs. The program in India, for example, provides food supplements to infants and young children, one of the population groups most vulnerable to nutrition deficiencies. Program costs are kept low by intensive screening to identify those whose physical development is subnormal. Screening costs are more than offset by savings in food purchases (compared with mass coverage) and, because comparatively little food is required, food prices are not affected. A similar program has been effective in Chile.

- Broadening food distribution or food stamp programs, or providing subsidies. Experience with such programs has been mixed. In some countries, costs rose out of control, producers' incentives were undermined when prices were kept low, subsidies benefited the wrong groups, or administrative problems proved overwhelming. A carefully designed program can avoid a negative impact; by and large, however, food distribution and subsidy programs, unless narrowly and precisely targeted, should be used with caution.

Financing

Who should pay for population, health, and nutrition services, and through what mechanisms? Decisions about payment and the design of policies to implement these decisions deserve far more attention than they usually receive from country planners and administrators. Poorly conceived and weakly administered policies contribute significantly to the perpetual financial crises in these sectors. A broader understanding of the full range of issues must be encouraged. Alternative funding mechanisms (taxation, fees, insurance schemes, and so on) should be explored together with the closely linked organizational issues, such as what the respective roles of public and private providers of services should be.

Often these organizational questions should be addressed first, since the assignment of responsibility affects how services can—and should— be financed. Many governments have tended to concentrate on publicly administered facilities and programs, without a comprehensive view of the sectors that recognizes the substantial role already played by private entities, and the larger role they might assume. Too few governments have considered the full scope of policy options: not only direct administration of services, but also guidance and oversight of mixed systems in which private and quasi-public entities are permitted or encouraged to provide a larger proportion of the services in demand. Public funds could then be channeled primarily to those services for which government intervention is needed. The potential of mixed systems to reduce the financial burden on government and to increase overall efficiency should be explored more actively, particularly in the many countries in which progress under a wholly government-administered system is likely to remain painfully slow because of budgetary constraints.

Many governments have placed excessive reliance on direct public outlays, largely from tax revenues, to fund population, health, and nutrition services. Alternative approaches that would require users to share the cost have been viewed with disfavor, even though fees for public services are not uncommon in the health sector and are a regular feature of private services. These attitudes should be reconsidered. While user charges are not appropriate or advisable for all types of public services, they are for some. Planners should start, as in other sectors, from the dual propositions that concerns about equity and income distribution require that most beneficiaries of a service contribute to its cost, and that efficiency is best served when prices (that is, user fees) cover marginal costs (see the discussion of cost recovery in chapter 21, Financial Analysis). They may then consider whether circumstances justify a lower charge or none at all—for example, to provide a minimum level of service to poverty groups. Departure from full marginal cost pricing may also be warranted when the public benefits of a service exceed the private benefits (as in immunization programs); when consumers have little knowledge or understanding of the need for or the purpose of the service (such as the monitoring of disease patterns to anticipate an epidemic); when the service is a "public good" whose benefits are enjoyed equally by all (such as black fly control for onchocerciasis); or when the administrative costs for collecting fees would be very high.

Examples of services that might be provided at little or no charge to users on one or more of these grounds include disease control programs (vector control, mass immunization campaigns, and environmental intervention); education and promotion of health and hygiene through schools and other institutions and the media; control of pests and zoonotic diseases; monitoring (such as for outbreaks of communicable diseases); out-patient services for maternal and child health care; family planning; nutrition rehabilitation and supplementation programs; and curative village health services.

Services such as these usually account for only a small portion—perhaps 25 percent—of total public spending on population, health, and nutrition programs. Of the remainder, the two largest items by far are out-patient and in-patient care at hospitals and other health facilities. These services raise difficult questions: for example, since in-patient care is a referral service, should a fee be charged when decisions are made primarily by the service supplier? By and large, however, the extent of cost recovery should be greater than it is for many public institutions.

User charges can also, as we have noted, help improve resource allocation by discouraging the wasteful use of services that may occur when fees are too low. The additional revenue to government from increased user charges for public services over the next ten years is likely to be modest, given the probable pace of change. But the benefits from better resource allocation may be considerable, as pricing encourages the more efficient use of services.

Another mechanism for cost recovery, particularly in the health sector, is risk-sharing, through which participating households make regular contributions to a common fund which covers their medical costs. Examples of this approach are health insurance, community-based prepayment schemes, cooperative-based schemes, and employer-run services for employees. So far, private third-party insurance is rare in the developing world, though risk-sharing is common in quasi-public services, such as semiautonomous social security systems with their own health facility network (widespread in South America) and parastatal enterprises with employee health plans. Although existing risk-sharing schemes have their practical shortcomings, the concept has considerable appeal. Schemes can be designed that mobilize more revenue more equitably than user charges do. More widespread risk-sharing ought therefore to be encouraged.

INSTITUTIONAL ISSUES

Progress toward the objectives and priorities just discussed is hampered by institutional weaknesses. What can be done to strengthen the delivery system infrastructure? There are possibilities for improvement at every level, from community-level workers at the base of the pyramid, through primary-level facilities, to higher-level facilities and support systems. Initiatives relating to management and planning are needed at all these levels.

Community-Based Workers

Under various labels, from "promoter" to "barefoot doctor," community-based workers are increasingly being used to extend services into the community and the home. Such workers reach out beyond the formal delivery system but are supervised by staff from that system. Some community-based workers have only promotional functions, such as urging communities to adopt recommended practices. Others may also engage in monitoring (for example, checking children for immunization) or perform such simple services as administering malaria medicines. They usually work part-time and are not always compensated, although they may be given some kind of "badge of office." They typically have little education but receive a few weeks of instruction in how to carry out specific tasks.

Despite the difficulties (including high dropout rates) of setting up and maintaining successful schemes using community-based workers, such networks are now widely accepted as necessary for the effective delivery of many population, health, and nutrition services. Several important lessons about using health workers effectively have been learned from project experience.

- The tasks to be performed should be clearly and precisely defined: not, for example, "encourage better family hygiene," but "visit each home and demonstrate the specific do's and don't's of hand washing, using the poster provided by the district health officer."
- The number of tasks should be limited to no more than, say, six. If an excessive number of tasks is assigned, there is a risk that none will be done well.
- Adequate supervision through frequent visits by supervisors from the formal delivery system is essential. The number of workers supervised by each staff person should be kept low, in many cases not more than seven or eight. Supervisors must be well trained and should offer constructive advice, in-service instruction, and moral support.
- Basic supplies (contraceptives and simple medicines) should reach the community-based workers in sufficient quantities and on a reliable, timely basis if the workers are to establish and retain credibility in the community.
- Staff in the formal system must be adequately informed of the activities of the community-based workers and convinced of their merit. Otherwise, the effectiveness of the workers may be undermined by lack of backup support.
- The characteristics of the workers (sex, age, socioeconomic status, and ethnic, religious, or familial affiliations) should be matched with the tasks to be performed and with the social norms and customs of the community. Common mistakes have been to assign males to tasks for which only females were acceptable, and to select as workers community leaders who considered certain tasks to be beneath them.

- Involvement of the community in the selection process is important, but may call for compromise between giving the community a sense of responsibility for the outcome and avoiding poor choices which might result, for example, from power struggles within the community.

- The workers must have an incentive, whether through income or some other benefit (such as status), to sustain participation after the initial enthusiasm has passed. Experience suggests that, if this is not the case, the program rarely survives long.

- At least one service should provide immediately visible benefits to the community, preferably to meet a felt need. For example, a curative activity might be added to the preventive or promotional tasks assigned to workers.

It is not always easy to reconcile these concerns with other planning considerations. For example, keeping the tasks of each worker to a minimum requires either appointing many specialized workers to a community or else rigorously setting priorities, which means that many worthwhile activities will have to be postponed. When, as often happens, a choice must be made between a few things done well or many done poorly, the courageous decision—to do a few things well—is likely to be the better one in the long run.

Primary-Level Facilities

The clinics, centers, subcenters, posts, mobile units, and other small, widely dispersed local facilities that are most families' first and sometimes only contact with the formal system fill a gap between community-based workers and higher-level facilities such as hospitals. Investment in extending and upgrading this primary-level network has accounted for the largest share of capital expenditure on population, health, and nutrition in the past quarter century.

Designing the facility network raises a number of issues. Should limited resources be devoted to adding new facilities or to improving existing units at important focal points? Which is preferable, a few large facilities or more smaller ones? The wisest course will usually lie somewhere between the extremes, but, in the past, many countries have tended to build new facilities without regard to the human and financial resources required to staff and operate them. Also, very small units have often not lived up to expectations. Hundreds, perhaps thousands, of health posts are now closed or empty; others see only four or five patients a day. Without more dependable drug supplies and more and better trained personnel, these posts have little to offer. People continue to rely on trusted traditional practitioners, and to travel to the nearest larger facility despite the hardship or inconvenience. This suggests caution in locating new, small facilities near existing, larger ones.

A related issue concerns the use of mobile units, in lieu of additional fixed facilities. Such units can range from an individual on a bicycle to a team of four in a van. Despite some disadvantages, such as the high cost of gasoline and the lack of continuing contact with the communities, they can be cost-effective in certain situations, especially when the staff of the health system is limited.

Another problem is that of attracting and retaining suitable staff for primary-level facilities, particularly in rural areas. In many countries, more liberal compensation policies as well as rewards and incentives, such as the provision of adequate housing, would help compensate staff for the lost advantages of working in modern, urban facilities.

To be effective, staff of primary-level facilities, no less than community-based workers, need dependable sources of supply. They also require close, constructive supervision and good training, with continuous in-service instruction.

Higher-Level Facilities

District and regional institutions (such as hospitals other than large central ones and family planning offices overseeing several primary units) manage the managers of lower-level facilities, keep those facilities supplied and staffed, handle clients referred to them, and provide primary-level services for nearby communities and other clients who come in directly. Large city hospitals deal with the most complicated referral cases and provide specialist training. National institutions (ministries, population planning boards, and so on) set policy from the capital. Finally, the network includes support agencies (such as training centers and pharmaceutical procurement and distribution departments). The national institutions risk losing touch with the field, while the support agencies have a degree of independence that may make them less responsive than they should be to the needs of the facilities they are intended to backstop.

Misallocation of resources and operational inefficiencies result in part from deficiencies in staffing and managerial training. Administrators and other top staff of facilities and programs are typically technical specialists, often physicians or other medical personnel. Yet their responsibilities call for effective management in the broadest sense. While some may be good at this instinctively, they receive little training in management skills or in related areas, such as financial control procedures. Moreover, advancement to higher positions depends largely on seniority or personal contacts, rather than on demonstrated managerial skills. Recent Bank-assisted projects have therefore included funds to upgrade these skills through training fellowships.

Compensation is as difficult a problem at higher levels as at the primary level. Physicians and other professionals are loath to move to semiurban or rural areas and thereby relinquish the earning opportunities available in larger cities.

A question related to compensation—and one that is very controversial—concerns joint service. Should medical personnel in public service be permitted to engage in private practice as well? Many medical authorities answer no, concerned that joint service would lead to duplication, inappropriate incentives to the medical profession, deterioration in the quality of public care, and underutilization of government facilities. Proponents maintain that none of these problems need arise if the public-private relationship is properly planned and managed. They argue that without the possibility of additional income from private practice, it will be even more difficult to attract well-qualified staff at public service salaries. Other arguments in favor of joint service are that it enables greater benefits to be obtained from the limited public funds allocated to health, through what amounts to cost-sharing between the public and private systems; and that it is, in any event, impracticable to enforce a prohibition against joint service, so that there will be fewer abuses if the practice is openly regulated. Experience under Bank-assisted projects has been too limited to point to a general conclusion.

Support Systems

Pharmaceutical supply, maintenance of buildings and equipment (especially vehicles), financial management (billing, collecting, and record-keeping), and medical education are among the many aspects of support systems in need of strengthening.

Pharmaceuticals

Most drugs are imported at considerable expense. Brand name products are often selected over much cheaper generic preparations. Cumbersome procurement procedures cause delay in acquiring needed supplies. Storage facilities and transportation are inadequate to ensure efficient distribution. Poor inventory management leads to excessive supplies of some items and shortages of others. The importance of drugs to the quality of care and the credibility of service makes it essential to develop better mechanisms for assessing requirements, reviewing procurement procedures, and improving inventory and quality control, storage, and distribution. Better training in the prescribing and use of drugs is also essential. Evidence suggests that for technical and economic reasons, few countries will be able to overcome supply problems simply by establishing local production. Other approaches must be tried as well, such as bulk purchasing of generic drugs or imposition of controls to prevent excessive prescribing of drugs. Experience in Tanzania and Ghana indicates that up to 70 percent of what is spent on drugs could be saved by improving procedures. These are significant savings inasmuch as expenditures on drugs in developing countries account for an average of 25 to 30 percent of health budgets.

Maintenance

As in most sectors, expenditure on maintenance of facilities, equipment, and vehicles is seriously inadequate. Consequently, vehicles break down and buildings deteriorate, which interrupts service delivery. Capital items often need to be replaced in half the expected time because of inadequate maintenance. Even within a fixed overall health budget, greater allocation of funds for maintenance is called for in many countries.

Financial Systems

Financial management in these sectors is particularly weak and in need of upgrading. Recordkeeping and reporting systems fail to capture and adequately summarize the details needed for budgeting and for the equally important task of monitoring progress toward program objectives. Accounts fall behind and bills remain unpaid. When fees are charged, it is often difficult to collect them. Cost accounting is virtually unknown. Facilities at most levels tend to be understaffed, and the staff they do have are not well trained in recordkeeping.

Medical Education

Governments have invested heavily in medical schools and teaching hospitals to provide the skilled manpower and technical expertise for the health care system. Priority has been given to expensive, conventional training of doctors and nurses. This training typically follows an international curriculum; it is heavily biased toward Western-oriented curative care, neglects diseases that are common locally, and assumes the availability of sophisticated equipment and facilities. Such an educational system produces an abundance of highly skilled personnel in the cities, but does little to increase the supply of less skilled personnel willing to work at the community level and prepared to cope with the health problems of rural areas.

Countries need to develop manpower plans that address both short- and long-term needs. To increase the outreach capacity of the delivery system effectively, larger numbers of less skilled personnel need to be trained and made part of a health system that provides them with adequate supervision, supplies, and support. For the short term, continued in-service training for primary-level workers is especially important to reinforce skills. A clearer definition of responsibilities is needed to avoid costly duplication of training activities among the many groups involved in providing them.

Management

Underlying many of the current weaknesses in these sectors is a generalized need for better management. Improvements may entail changes in many areas, including incentive structures, program design, personnel mix, promotion criteria, and organizational relationships.

The precise nature of the management challenge depends on the division of responsibilities among public, private, and quasi-public entities. When public authorities have a large role in the direct administration of services, the central need is to increase the efficiency of government-run facilities and programs. When the public role is smaller or more indirect (as when government institutions act as intermediaries in cooperation with private or quasi-public agencies), greater attention must be devoted to designing, monitoring, and enforcing suitable regulatory frameworks and subsidy schemes.

One pervasive problem is overcentralization of responsibility. Most managers below the highest levels have very little autonomy, and even less incentive to use what limited authority they do have. Decisions about hiring, firing, and reassignment of staff, about budget requests and resource allocation, and about changes in procedures that might improve efficiency remain highly centralized, either by fiat or because lower-level staff believe that there are no rewards (but possibly heavy penalties) for risking independent action. The result is a system which dilutes any sense of ultimate accountability. Amelioration of this problem will not be easy. Top officials must be willing to take risks in introducing fundamental changes that will push decisionmaking power downward and outward into the field, while at the same time strengthening the incentives and controls that encourage the best performers and weed out laggards.

Planning

Most countries now recognize the desirability of more systematic planning for population, health, and nutrition activities to encourage more rational decisionmaking. Actual practice, though, remains weak. A widespread tendency to equate planning with the preparation of a lengthy document that covers a long period, is often outdated by the time it is released, and is not read fully by most of the intended audience is self-defeating. (Not infrequently, donors and visiting expatriates are partly to blame for fostering such volumes.) Shorter, more frequently revised plans are preferable. More important than such documents is the assurance that the main options on important issues have been adequately examined and that clear-cut choices have been reached, with input and evidence of real commitment from both top officials and line managers.

INVESTMENT ISSUES

Sound investment strategies are needed to improve resource allocation, not only for individual projects but also for broader program choices affecting the overall composition of expenditure, recurrent as well as capital, in these sectors. In developing strategies and reviewing allocation patterns, the same questions must be addressed as in other sectors, and the same general approach to analyzing options can be used, even though some of the detailed techniques may differ. Attention must be devoted, in particular, to selecting appropriate technologies, matching the technologies with the cultural setting, providing for coordination, ensuring complementarity among different investments, and assessing the affordability of projects and programs.

Analyzing the Options

Although these sectors have made less headway than most others in introducing the systematic appraisal of options or alternatives, there is nothing inherent in population, health, and nutrition projects that warrants exempting them from careful and at least partially quantitative assessment. As in other social sectors, cost-benefit analysis is difficult, the more so since the obstacles to quantifying benefits are even greater. Alternative methods, however, are feasible and useful. At the least, an effort should be made to select the least-cost way of providing the services needed to reach the objectives agreed on, given the technical, institutional, and other considerations. To do this, the net effectiveness of alternative approaches must be analyzed.

In population, health, and nutrition, the first step for planners is to forecast the various determinants of demand for the services to be offered—which means forecasting the use of facilities and programs. These forecasts must try to allow for the impact over the life of the project of changes in knowledge, attitudes, and practices—changes that the project may be intended to help foster. In addition, the forecasts may need to take into account that what the target group wants, even if it is well-informed, may not be optimal from the perspective of society as a whole. (For example, the level of immunization that a government believes is necessary to protect society may be higher than recipient households themselves would choose without encouragement.) These complications may explain, in part, why demand forecasting has yet to develop very far in these sectors, compared with others. Nevertheless, reasonable planning figures can be prepared within the context of sectoral studies and project design. Assessments should take account of the nature and causes of prevailing population trends and health and nutrition indicators, the strengths and weaknesses of existing delivery systems in relation to current needs, and the general and detailed objectives of the country in these and other sectors.

To proceed to the next step of identifying least-cost strategies requires a means of relating a strategy's cost to its effectiveness. Ideally, the measure of effectiveness would include both the direct effects on fertility, mortality, or morbidity (births, deaths, or disability days averted) and the welfare consequences of these effects, valued in monetary terms (both production-related and consumption-related benefits, including special benefits such as opening up new lands and improving school performance). Attempts to measure these effects within the framework of cost-benefit analysis have generally pointed to high rates of return, but fundamental questions about the assumptions are still the subject of debate.

When the information required to estimate the welfare consequences is limited, it may be necessary to concentrate primarily on the direct effects on fertility, mortality, or morbidity. This analysis, when combined with cost data, leads to unit-cost estimates such as cost per birth averted or death averted, cost per healthy day gained (which can be a composite of mortality and morbidity effects), or, at a more elementary level, cost per unit of service delivered (that is, cost per contraceptive user, acceptor, fully immunized child, recipient of nutritional supplementation, outpatient visit, or in-patient day). By way of illustration, a sampling of figures on cost per death averted for different programs in different countries is shown in table 10-1.

Although unit-cost estimates are less desirable for appraising options than estimates taking into account the full benefits to be derived, they can nonetheless provide a much better basis for decisionmaking than can the largely qualitative analysis that has generally been used. Despite the inherent limitations of the data—which are averages and are usually not calculated annually—such data can provide useful insights for analyzing cost-effectiveness and for identifying least-cost solutions for given objectives. This type of analysis can establish the relative cost-effectiveness of alternative immunization strategies or of immunization compared with other interventions.

Unfortunately, analysis of this sort is seriously hampered by the paucity and poor quality of relevant data, particularly on costs, routinely collected by government agencies. Many agencies, relying on standard government accounting, are unaware of individual program costs. Even the simplest breakdowns of aggregate expenditures—by type of service, geographic

Table 10-1. *Cost per Death Prevented in Selected Countries*

Method	Country	Cost per death prevented (U.S. dollars)
Measles immunization (includes all costs of a program of polio, DPT, BCG, and tetanus)	Ivory Coast	490
Total immunization program	Indonesia	130
BCG program only		455
DPTT program only		135
BCG, marginal[a]		101
DPTT, marginal[a]		77
Mass vaccination	Morocco	
BCG		24
DPTT		38
Polio		1,100
Total immunization program	Kenya	85
DPT, TT, and BCG only		274
Measles only		50
Polio only		6,357
DPT, TT, and BCG		69
Measles, marginal[a]		26
Polio, marginal[a]		568
New births only		70
All immunizations, marginal[a]		113
DPT, BCG, and polio, marginal[a]		1,375
Separate health program	Nepal	508
Health program integrated with family planning		271
Prenatal nutrition program	India	8
Health care for infants	Narangwal	25
Health care for children		31
Hospital care	Morocco	
Large hospitals		2,640
Medium hospitals		2,820
Small hospitals		2,360
Hospital treatment for diarrhea	Bangladesh	
	Sotaki	187
	Matlab	1,262–1,352
Malaria eradication (spraying and drugs)	Bangladesh	809–25,090
Mosquito control for malaria (infants and children)	Cross-country	600
Selective primary health care	Cross-country	200–250

Note: DPT = Diphtheria-pertussis-tetanus vaccine; DPTT = Diphtheria-pertussis-teta-nus-tetanus toxoid vaccine; and BCG = Bacille-Calmette-Guérin vaccine for tuberculosis.

a. "Marginal" is a program added to one designed for another purpose.

Source: Specific sources are cited in Susan H. Cochrane and K. C. Zachariah, *Infant and Child Mortality as a Determinant of Fertility: The Policy Implications,* World Bank Staff Working Paper no. 556 (Washington, D.C., 1983), p. 24.

area, or disease group—are often impossible to obtain. What is worse, agencies in some countries are years behind in completing their annual accounts, the most rudimentary type of expenditure information. In some countries in Africa, the sum total of all cost information routinely tabulated consists of the few pages of planned expenditures used in preparing the national budgets; actual expenditure accounts, if they exist in usable form, are often out of date, highly aggregated, and marred by inconsistencies. In other countries, as in Latin America, detailed cost categories have been defined, but the numbers are so poor they are universally regarded as without much meaning.

High priority should be assigned to improving data collection procedures. First must come recognition by the relevant ministry officials that a problem exists, followed by a sustained effort to improve matters. Guidance on appropriate procedures, including upgrading of financial management systems in general, is available from the World Bank and other sources.

Appropriate Technologies

In the past four decades, remarkable advances in the discovery and development of simple, safe, reliable, lower-cost technologies have opened up dramatic possibilities to meet population, health, and nutrition needs. At the same time, the misallocation of resources to older or inappropriate technologies has restricted the adoption of these new methods in some developing countries.

In population, new contraceptive methods, new knowledge about what to recommend to clients, and enhanced understanding of how to promote acceptance have emerged. Until the 1950s, the only real alternative to age-old methods—abstinence, abortion, prolonged breastfeeding, and withdrawal—was the condom. Since then, more effective and convenient methods have come into regular use, including oral contraceptives (the pill), several types of intrauterine devices (IUDs), injectables, and new sterilization and abortion techniques. Early family planning programs tended to promote a single method. Although concentrating on one or two methods may still be easier for administrative reasons or because of supply constraints, it is now recognized that providing a couple with the widest possible range of options helps achieve higher initial protection rates and increases the likelihood that the couple will continue to practice contraception. Indonesia, which relied almost exclusively on the pill for many years, has begun to emphasize IUDs more. Experience has also underscored the importance of informing clients of the characteristics of different methods and of following up with acceptors to reinforce their commitment. Because the Indian and Pakistani IUD programs, in their early stages, failed to explain fully the side effects or to examine patients medically, the use of IUDs remained low for years afterward.

In health, revolutionary advances have occurred in vaccines (first polio and then measles), treatment of diarrheal illness (oral rehydration therapy), new medicines (especially antibiotics) as well as more affordable medicines (generic drugs in place of brand names), and equipment suited to primary care requirements (such as better small refrigerators for heat-sensitive vaccines and supplies in field units). Better methods are available for controlling specific diseases (schistosomiasis and malaria) and for reducing health risks by making environments safer. In addition, health care staff have become more aware of the value of breastfeeding and of monitoring children's growth, and they understand better how to motivate desirable behavior in these respects. In nutrition, techniques for fortifying foods to compensate for dietary deficiencies have been improved. If full advantage were taken of the enormous potential of these advances, significant reductions in preventable deaths, estimated by some to account for over 75 percent of total deaths, could be realized.

Yet adoption and effective use of these new technologies are impeded by the slow pace at which the allocation of resources is adjusted to the new possibilities. The health systems in most developing countries were patterned after those in the industrial countries, and efforts to shift away from that pattern have not been vigorous enough. Too much is still spent on older technologies oriented around curative hospital-based services; too little is left for family planning, primary health care, and preventive health and nutrition activities.

Examples of continued misallocation are common everywhere. In Malawi, three hospitals together received over half of the total recurrent public health expenditure in 1981, while all field services combined were allocated less than 30 percent. In Peru, per capita public health expenditure in the major urban area is more than twice the corresponding per capita level in some remote regions. In Thailand, there are three times as many physicians in the capital city as in the rest of the nation.

Not only are some existing resources being misused, but also the total resources available for population, health, and nutrition have not been rising significantly in real terms. Progress in bringing cost-effective technologies to underserved groups has, therefore, proceeded very slowly. Prospects for a faster increase in total resources in the next ten years are no brighter. In low-income countries, under optimistic assumptions, it is unlikely that the total recurrent funding available to these sectors will rise by more than $3 to $6 per capita in real terms. Although this would amount to a doubling or tripling of present levels of spending in these countries, funding would still be low in relation to the needs as well as to the levels of spending in middle- or high-income countries.

Technology Choice and the Cultural Setting

In population, health, and nutrition, the task of ensuring that the technologies are appropriate to the cultural setting is especially complex because long-standing traditions and religious beliefs often run counter to the behavioral changes sought. To succeed, investments in these sectors must have two attributes. First, they must be designed to fit the target group's characteristics and circumstances, with account taken of attitudes, values, customs, and habitual practices. Second, because some alteration in these preexisting conditions inevitably will be required, they must be designed to include adequate measures to convince prospective beneficiaries that change is warranted.

Designing investments to fit prevailing conditions must start with an awareness of precisely what those conditions are. Simple as this sounds, it does not always happen. Early population projects supported by the World Bank in Jamaica, Tunisia, Trinidad and Tobago, and India focused on hospitals and maternity centers for the delivery of family planning services; the purpose was to reach women during the postpartum period. While this approach is useful in areas where a majority of births take place in institutions, it is ill-suited to areas where births at home are common. It also ignores the need to reinforce a couple's commitment to family planning and to ensure dependable supplies of contraceptives at other times during a woman's childbearing years. Furthermore, it overlooks the importance of the male's role in the couple's decisions. Later projects have relied more on an outreach effort that brings services directly to the community and to the home.

Political commitment is essential but cannot of itself guarantee success. Investment planners must be armed with information on the family's decisionmaking process: when, where, and by whom decisions to seek health care or family planning assistance are taken; what is expected regarding the quantity and quality of care; who is responsible for child care. In Indonesia, prominent political support for family planning, coupled with well-conceived and well-executed delivery systems, has been remarkably successful. In contrast, where high-level commitment has been linked to weak planning and follow-through, efforts to improve access to primary health care facilities have been singularly ineffective.

Planners must consider the impact of factors such as the hours during which health and family planning clinics are open, the distance to be traveled, and the waiting time. They must allow for the fact that villagers who have traditionally sought health care from, say, local healers or pharmacists may not place much faith initially in community health workers, particularly if those workers' drug supplies are not dependable. Planners must anticipate the skepticism with which preventive services are likely to be regarded if no visible changes are evident immediately. And they must be ready for reluctance to accept unfamiliar medicines (such as generic rather than more expensive brand name drugs) and for suspicion of government programs.

Investment projects must also provide sufficient funds and mechanisms for fostering acceptance by the target groups. The initial population projects supported by the Bank, like many others begun prior to the late 1970s, assumed that a large unmet demand existed and that acceptance would evolve of its own accord as users discovered for themselves the availability of new or better services. Activities to change attitudes and practices and to enhance understanding were relatively modest, experimental, and unstructured. Since then, vigorous promotional and educational efforts that reach out to potential users have been emphasized, rather than simply building, equipping, and staffing more facilities. Experience has been acquired, in particular, with information, education, and communication activities and with initiatives in community participation.

Information, Education, and Communication

Besides simply informing potential clients of what services are available, information, education, and communication activities have been used to change attitudes (for example, toward hygiene in the home), promote better practices (breastfeeding and weaning), dispel ignorance (about vaccination for childhood diseases), break down opposition (to using the formal health system rather than relying solely on traditional practitioners), and reinforce existing demand or create new demand (for family planning).

There are many ways to accomplish these goals. The contacts of delivery system staff with patients provide excellent opportunities for an implicit form of outreach; health facility patients and family planning clients may pass along their own experiences to others by word of mouth. Community-based workers can be another vehicle for facilitating change. Beyond these are methods ranging from large-scale mass media campaigns to home visits, community meetings, and folk theater.

To succeed in using information, education, and communication, the strategy must be carefully prepared. Preliminary research is necessary to assess factors such as determinants of usage, social organization, and literacy levels of the population. Proper identification of the audience to be reached is critical: it may comprise numerous distinct linguistic or socioeconomic subgroups, and it may extend beyond the immediate target population of the program. Selection of the communication media must take into account availability, cost, and expected effectiveness in achieving the objectives. Small-scale field testing should be conducted before a strategy is widely applied to see if messages get to the right people, are understood, and elicit intended responses. Without careful preparation, the results can be disastrous. In one country, the picture of a woman taking an oral contraceptive failed utterly to convey its message because the intended audience, noting the braided hair and youthful clothing, took it to be a girl eating candy.

Strategies that use mass media tend to be less expensive but also less effective, in terms of knowledge retention and behavioral change, than strategies that rely on face-to-face contacts over extended periods. A combination of the two, with media messages reinforcing direct contacts, is often best.

It is also necessary to ensure the ready availability of the services or supplies being promoted. Campaigns to increase attendance at facilities do more harm than good if the facilities fail to respond adequately.

Community Participation

Growing attention to primary care (and to related aspects such as the use of community-based workers and of information, education, and communication activities) has been accompanied by extensive literature on how to involve communities more effectively in the planning and decisionmaking processes. Initiatives in community participation have generally concentrated on organization (providing volunteers, forming and supporting village health committees), finance (raising funds to pay for drugs or to compensate community-based workers), construction (contributing local labor and supplies to build health posts), and planning (identifying needs and seeking solutions).

While the idea of community participation is sound, success can be elusive. Communities tend to support activities but not initiate them. Activities directly related to service delivery stimulate community involvement, whereas "self-diagnosis" by a community of its health problems and possible solutions takes much longer. Activities (such as constructing a health post) demanding a one-time effort and limited follow-up have been more successful than those requiring long-term commitment (such as tending communal gardens). Recruitment of volunteer workers has generally been satisfactory, but sustaining their involvement is a problem. Communities have been more receptive to paying for tangible products such as drugs than to compensating workers, whose contribution may be less visible to community members.

Future efforts to nurture community participation need to be more realistic about what is possible and at what pace. Government planners must deal with preexisting constraints that may hinder participatory schemes, as when the target groups lack historical or cultural precedents for communal enterprises. What works in China or Thailand may fail in Africa or Latin America. Planners should anticipate that the usefulness of proposed ventures may not be perceived. And governments must be ready to commit considerable time and resources to helping local schemes get started and to providing follow-up support.

Nevertheless, where adequate preparation and support have been assured, the outcome has been encouraging. In a village family planning program in Indonesia, each family planning group is led by a woman responsible for seeing to it that the group members are kept supplied with contraceptives; she also acts as a resource for women with questions or complaints, and she may refer women to the local clinic. In addition, family planning field workers, who are temporary government employees, provide limited and specific services. Consistent and regular contact with village family planning groups has been the most important feature in developing and maintaining well-organized, motivated community organizations. Community leaders, when motivated, have been influential in promoting a receptive attitude toward family planning.

Coordination, Complementarities, and Integration

Better coordination among projects and programs is critical to reduce duplication and inconsistency. In parts of India, population, health, and nutrition functions are divided among three separate systems of field staff all working in the same communities. While separation of responsibilities is not necessarily bad (a single worker might be overburdened with too many tasks), poor communication among the three systems has resulted in considerable overlap. Indonesia at one time duplicated supply infrastructures at a far greater cost than that of a combined network. Peru is implementing several separate and distinct approaches to community health worker schemes, with inconsistent policies on payment of workers. Proponents of each scheme insist the others must conform to theirs, and unpaid workers resent the preference shown to paid counterparts elsewhere.

The inherent complementarities among population, health, and nutrition interventions, and between them and investments in other sectors, are a further reason for improving coordination of investments. Expansion of family planning services that depend on health facilities may need to be synchronized with investments to strengthen those facilities, and these investments, in turn, may depend on upgrading pharmaceutical supply and other support systems. Health education and hygiene promotion must proceed in step with the completion of water supply and sanitation projects. Construction of power dams and of irrigation works must be planned in cooperation with health authorities wherever health risks (such as schistosomiasis or malaria) might be exacerbated.

Coordination and complementarity issues, along with considerations of efficiency, have spurred debate about the merits of integrating services, and particularly about whether family planning programs should be integrated closely with the health delivery system or administered independently. This integration can take many different forms, ranging from having one set of institutions responsible for both family planning and health care services, to maintaining separate chains of command that simply share certain resources.

Experience with integration has been both positive and negative.In one of the best-known and best-documented experiments in health care and family planning, carried out in the village of Narangwal, India, integration proved more effective in recruiting family planning acceptors, more cost-effective, and more equitable in delivering family planning services than separate units, without sacrificing any health benefits. But this is not invariably the case. Integration places a heavy burden on the health delivery network, and unless that network is reasonably competent and effective, supervision of staff and provision of specialized assistance is difficult.[8] Moreover, as long as health services are concentrated in urban areas, the integrated approach necessarily gives an urban bias to the delivery of family planning. Integration underscores the need to expand health system coverage in rural areas.

Bank experience with projects that have sought to integrate family planning and health delivery systems indicates that they are likely to encounter a host of problems and cannot automatically be advocated as the preferred approach for every country. There are good reasons to regard family planning as part of health services in general, and so best administered by the health ministry. The danger is that after integration, family planning may be subordinated to other activities because the health ministry assigns it a low priority. At the least, a firm organizational base for family planning within the health ministry should be ensured. Clear lines of responsibility and authority, strong commitment from the top, agreement on funding priorities for programs and projects, equitable personnel policies, and additional training and compensation for health personnel who take on added functions are all necessary ingredients for successful integration.

Affordability

For any project or program to be viable, those expected to commit resources to it must be able and willing to do so. This must be true for each institution or group that participates in or is affected by the activity and for each phase of construction, implementation, and operation. Consideration must, therefore, be given to ensuring that central government agencies receive sufficient budget allocations to cover their share of both capital and recurrent costs; that local government authorities and village committees are able to supply whatever resources—monetary, human, material—are expected of them; and that the ultimate users of

8. Ministries of education also have a role to play with respect to the population, health, and nutrition sectors. Some World Bank–assisted projects in rural development, for example, have included a family planning component through the education system. Such arrangements pose the issue of the extent to which ministries with primary responsibility in other fields will promote or effectively supervise family planning services, and present difficult practical problems of intersectoral coordination both at the center and in the field.

the services are able and willing to meet the fees and other costs (travel and forgone earnings) they will have to incur to use the services. Failure to appreciate and provide for the typically large recurrent costs of new investments is a principal reason for slow progress and continuing resource misallocation in these sectors.

Two aspects of financial feasibility must be considered. First, the project or program itself, covering a particular geographic area and having a given implementation schedule, must be affordable from government revenues and whatever fees are to be collected. Second, insofar as the project is intended to be replicable in other areas, the proposed expanded program must also be affordable over a reasonable period. If a project is not replicable in this sense, then a case can be made that it should not be undertaken: it would establish a precedent that the country cannot sustain, and absorb resources that might be used more beneficially, from the standpoint of the society as a whole, in some other way.

Analysis of financial feasibility involves large elements of judgment. There are no fixed rules for determining when an activity can be afforded and when it cannot be. Nevertheless, assembling the relevant data on both costs and the likely availability of funds permits better decisionmaking. Few countries do enough in this respect at present.

Train passengers, Dacca, Bangladesh

11

Transport

Characteristics of the Sector

ECONOMIC GROWTH and social development are impossible without adequate transport. Rural roads connecting isolated areas to markets and sources of supply are essential for converting agriculture from a subsistence to a commercial activity. Rail lines and roads are often prerequisites for the extraction of mineral and forest resources, and port facilities must be adequate for exporting these and agricultural products and for importing the goods needed in a developing economy. In small and otherwise isolated markets, better transport may introduce competition and weaken monopolistic practices. More reliable transport of fuel, spare parts, and other inputs to factories, and of finished goods to markets, reduces inventory costs and avoids shutdowns. In addition, reduced transport costs permit efficient regional specialization and adoption of new productive activities and techniques.

In the early and middle stages of development, demand for transport, especially on the passenger side, tends to grow faster than GNP. Table 11-1 confirms this trend for the mid-1970s. For the 1980s—despite national, modal, and route differences—the general outlook in developing countries is for a growing demand for transport services. This will put pressure on existing systems and require that they be both more efficiently used and expanded by carefully selected investments.

Economic Aspects

The transport sector accounts for an average of about 5 to 6 percent of GDP in developing countries and, usually, for the largest share—15 to 25 percent—of total annual investment. Wide variations around these averages reflect differing country situations. The contribution of transport to GDP is roughly the same in developing as in developed countries, but the share of transport in total investment is higher by 50 percent or more in developing than in developed countries, where transport systems are largely in place.

Table 11-1. *Growth of Transport Demand in the Mid-1970s*

Country group	Rate of growth per year (percent)		
	GNP	Freight (ton-kilometer)	Passenger (passenger-kilometer)
Low-income developing countries	3.6	4.0	5.7
Middle-income developing countries	5.7	6.8	9.0
OECD countries	3.2	2.6	3.2

Source: Derived from C. R. Willoughby, "Transport and Communications Research and the Developing Countries," International Center for Transportation Studies, Proceedings Series, vol. I (1981), *Transportation Research: State of the Art, Perspectives and International Cooperation* (Rome, 1982), tables 1 and 2.

Transport has important links with other sectors of the economy. In most developing countries, transport infrastructure accounts for about half of all construction, which, in turn, makes up about half of the nation's annual fixed capital formation. The manufacture, assembly, and servicing of transport equipment is a growing activity in populous, low-income countries such as China, Egypt, and India, as is the production or assembly of automobiles in some of the middle-income developing countries of Latin America and southern Europe. Transport is one of the heaviest users of commercial energy in most developing countries, accounting for 20 to 40 percent of the total. The share of the labor force it engages is probably higher than in developed countries, where it is about 5 to 7 percent. In many developing countries, railway, port, and national airline authorities are among the largest economic enterprises and employers. Railways are often the largest single employer: they employ 1.5 million people in India and some 2.5 million in China. The size of transport enterprises poses managerial challenges because of the shortage of skilled, experienced managers and the prevalence of government intervention in determining staff and employment practices and in setting wages.

The demand for transport is a derived demand; it depends on the volume and location of industrial and agricultural production and on where people live and work. (Leisure travel, which is of increasing importance in some developing countries, and which is a function primarily of income and income distribution, is an exception.) Total demand is not very sensitive to changes in the general level of transport rates, but demand for a particular transport mode, when alternatives exist, may be influenced by a change in the relative rates.

Transport infrastructure and equipment have several distinctive features. First, new infrastructure or increased capacity may take years to plan, design, build, and put into service and may be very costly. When increased capacity is required, therefore, supply response to growing demand is often inelastic in the short run. As a result, congestion may develop and the quality of transport service decline until new capacity is put into operation or until prices are introduced that restrain demand. Second, transport infrastructure must often be provided in large, indivisible ("lumpy") units—such as a road, a port berth, or a runway—so that excess capacity may exist for some time after a new facility is brought into service. Third, fixed facilities (roads and airports) are usually provided by the public sector, whereas the vehicle fleets using them (cars, buses, trucks, and aircraft) are usually under separate management, private or public. Decisions about fleets may not be consistent with those about infrastructure. Railways are exceptional in that locomotives and rolling stock, as well as tracks and other infrastructure, are under one ownership and management, usually an agency of the national government. Fourth, transport is a mixture of monopolistic and competitive modes and services, so that transport pricing is particularly complex. Fifth, large expenditures on maintenance are necessary to keep the facilities in serviceable condition.

Transport problems often need to be addressed in an intercountry, and sometimes a regional, context—as, for example, in sub-Saharan Africa, with its many landlocked countries, underdeveloped institutions, and acute shortages of skilled manpower and materials. Border crossing difficulties, differences in insurance and driving rules, and lack of coordination of common railway facilities are hindering the growth of transport systems in countries where service is already inadequate.

Transport Modes

The transport sector is made up of a variety of modes differing so widely in function, facilities, and operating characteristics that some analysts consider transport as several sectors rather than one. Railways, roads, seaports, and air transport are discussed in this chapter; pipelines, which serve only the energy sector and have little in common with other modes, are not included, while inland and coastal shipping is only touched on briefly, for lack of space.

Railways

Extensive rail networks are to be found in many developing countries. At the time they were built, many railways were the only economical mode of transport for long-haul freight and passenger movement along their main routes. They were essentially monopolies and were organized and operated accordingly. Governments, concerned that railway managements would abuse their monopoly power, typically have regulated freight and passenger rates, while strong labor unions have negotiated work rules requiring the employment of redundant labor.

The major problem confronting most railways today, however, is competition from a very dynamic road transport industry, which is a more recent entry into the sector. Much of the additional demand arising out of economic growth has gone to roads, which—compared with railways—offer shippers greater frequency and reliability of service, usually substantial savings in time, the convenience and economy of door-to-door service without the risks and extra costs of transshipment, less breakage and loss, quicker settlement of claims, and other advantages.

Railways can move bulk freight over long distances more cheaply than trucks, especially at the fuel prices of the 1970s and 1980s, and should, therefore, have a competitive advantage in this area. It is argued, however, that road freight transport does not pay enough in user charges to cover maintenance and amortization of the roads and other infrastructure that it uses, and that this reduces the railways' competitive advantage. It is true that in some countries road transport operators, especially of large trucks, do not pay the full costs of using the roads. But the railways' tariff revenues do not cover their costs either. The difference is that railways can and do incur operating losses—something that private road transport operators cannot afford. More to the point is that, even where road transport is assessed charges that are economically appropriate, it continues to gain over the railways, apparently because the services are more attractive. (In recent years some railways, assisted by higher fuel prices, have been able to slow their relative decline through such technological innovations as container transport and piggyback operations, and through better organization of transshipment and other services.)

Many railways throughout the world operate with large deficits, some of staggering dimensions. Railway subsidies in Argentina, for example, accounted for 50 percent of the budget deficit in 1979. Railways are subsidized by governments because of their political and social importance, often with little expectation that they will ever become profitable. Such subsidies may be compensating for, or encouraging, redundant facilities and inefficient operations as well as uneconomic fares and freight rates. To cure these inefficiencies and adapt to present conditions, most railways need to undergo extensive structural reform, with changes both in government policies and in the performance of the railways themselves. Because of their traditional monopoly position, most railway managements have been little concerned with service to customers or with promoting their business. This lack of commercial orientation has been a factor in the railways' loss not only of freight traffic to trucks but also of passenger traffic to airlines and buses. Yet railways continue to have an important function in nearly every country, mainly in long-distance hauling of bulk commodities and in carrying passengers on (even short) dense-traffic lines.

Railways now face difficult choices. Which services should they abandon and which ones should they develop? Should they concentrate on freight or passengers? Should they promote intermodal services, commuter services, high-speed trains? These choices have important consequences for investment, especially when long-lived, expensive assets have to be overhauled or renewed. Crucial decisions about technology and equipment have to be made. These questions may be answerable only after management has been improved, especially in the areas of marketing, planning, and costing. We return to this subject in the section below, "A Railway Plan of Action."

Roads

In sharp contrast to the continuing decline of rail transport is the aggressive growth of road transport, which is steadily taking over an increasing share of freight and passenger traffic in virtually every country. The divorce of ownership of infrastructure from that of vehicles and the competition among large numbers of truck and bus owners are other striking differences between road transport and the railways. Construction and maintenance of roads (including bridges, traffic signals, and so on) are usually the responsibility of a ministry or bureau of public works. Main routes may come under a toll road authority with its own budget and contracting power. The pattern varies, but even in centrally planned economies responsibility for infrastructure and for vehicles is usually kept separate, and a variety of agencies are involved.

Some trucks and buses are owned and operated by private firms, some by government agencies, and some by individuals. In many countries, especially where trucking is extensively regulated by the government or where large public companies exist, vehicles are also owned by firms that have their primary activities outside the transport sector but that feel a need to control the transport service they require. Passenger cars are mostly owned by individuals.

The trucking business, except in centrally planned economies, is usually characterized by competition among many operators. Some governments intervene to set rates and restrict competition; others confine their role to setting and enforcing safety requirements and weight limits. The passenger bus business is similar, except that it is more common, especially in urban areas, for the central government (or municipality) to restrict entry, set fares, and even operate the system. When fares are regulated, they are often set too low, so that either subsidies are required or service standards are depressed below the level for which users are prepared to pay.

Problems of roads and road transport include inadequate financial and institutional provision for road maintenance, lack of rational planning of road investment, and excessive government interference in the business of carrying freight and passengers. Few countries have been able to establish a practical and economically efficient scheme of user charges. Uneconomic charges have adverse effects on the way the roads are used, on the choice of vehicles, and on the resources generated for financing maintenance and new construction.

Ports

In addition to serving as transshipment points, ports sometimes have facilities for packaging or even processing certain products, they usually provide visiting ships with water and fuel, and they often offer repair services. Like other types of transport infrastructure, they require large, lumpy investments in fixed facilities and equipment, such as breakwaters, berths, wharves, and cranes. The cost of using ports can be high. Shipping costs for exports vary from about 7 percent of the c.i.f. price (cost including insurance and freight) for simple manufactures to 10 to 15 percent for the average bulk commodity, and up to 30 percent or higher for certain goods such as timber. Of these shipping costs, about 40 to 50 percent are port-related charges. Port congestion can have a strangling effect on economic activity, as events in several African countries—Sudan (Port Sudan), Tanzania (Dar es Salaam), and Nigeria (Lagos)—demonstrated in the 1970s.

General cargo ports—as distinct from ports handling specific bulk cargoes—are usually owned by governments and operated by semiautonomous port authorities, while special-purpose terminals are often privately owned and operated. In most public ports, archaic accounting systems make it difficult to know what the operating costs are, and the relative pricing of different berths, services, and types of storage does not give shippers and shipowners an incentive to use the port efficiently. (A few developing-country ports, such as Singapore, do handle accounting and pricing with great efficiency.) Large and well-organized labor forces have sometimes been an obstacle to the introduction of modern cargo-handling equipment or other operating improvements, such as using double or triple shifts. Yet almost all ports, regardless of these problems, take in more than enough revenue to cover their costs since they have a substantial degree of monopoly.

Faced with the prospect of rapidly growing trade, new technological developments, and a long gestation period for building new facilities, port authorities must decide whether to install container-handling equipment and make room to store the containers, how to handle bulk cargo, whether to provide for "roll-on-roll-off" operations, and how to finance such major investments. Whatever they decide about new construction and equipment, however, they can benefit from improved management and operating procedures, better maintenance, and other ways of making more effective use of existing facilities.

Air Transport

Both international and domestic air transport can play important roles in a country's development. International air service is essential for a thriving tourist business—an important source of foreign exchange for many developing countries—while international travel by business and professional people helps link the country with its trading partners and with external sources of capital and technology. Air freight service has enabled some developing countries to market exports that have high value per unit of weight or are extremely perishable, and that are produced advantageously because of climate, natural resources, or low labor costs. A national airline is not necessary for these purposes, and some developing-country airlines have incurred substantial losses on their international routes.

International airports are usually owned by governments and operated by semiautonomous authorities. Providing service to foreign airlines, they are mostly profitable and bring in considerable foreign exchange.

Domestic air transport makes an important contribution to development in some countries and could do so in others. It is the principal mode for business travel where distances are great and air service is adequate. In countries with vast, sparsely settled areas or difficult terrain, air service to remote locations makes it possible to avoid or postpone large investments in roads or railways. In some countries of Asia and Latin America, domestic air transport is well developed; but in many countries, especially in Africa, it has been hampered by government regulation of fares and restriction of competition. Airport construction has had insufficient priority, and maintenance of runways (like maintenance of infrastructure in other transport modes) has often been neglected. Scheduled domestic air services are sometimes monopolized by a government-owned airline or a government-regulated private line, while charter services are more likely to be open to competition.

Institutional Aspects

Where governments control the operation of transport facilities, they have usually set up semiautonomous agencies or parastatal corporations to manage them. Thus a country may have a port authority, an airport authority, sometimes an airline, often a railway company, and, in large cities, a municipal bus company. A ministry or bureau of public works is almost always responsible for building and maintaining roads.

The extent to which port authorities operate the sundry activities of a port—warehousing, packaging, repair of ships and containers, and so on—varies greatly from country to country. Many of these activities can be carried out by private firms. Similarly, the extent to which ministries of public works contract out road construction and maintenance or do this work themselves also varies. Passenger bus services, whether inter-city or local, are run by government agencies in some countries, by licensed private monopolies in others, and by competing private firms in yet others. Railways are almost always run by a monolithic parastatal organization, whereas road freight transport usually operates as a competitive private industry, albeit often hedged in or protected by government regulation.

Some countries have tried to harmonize the disparate operations of these numerous actors on the transport scene and to coordinate their investment planning or operations by means of a ministry of transport. This has worked well in a few countries, but in most the ministry has not been given enough power, staff, or funds to carry out the role nominally assigned to it, and the problem of coordination persists.

Weaknesses in the institutional machinery include the lack of well-organized programs for collecting and analyzing data and conducting studies as a basis for effective planning. To design and carry out such programs requires larger and better-qualified staff than are usually on hand in government departments, so that measures to strengthen staff skills are also needed.

DEVELOPMENT OBJECTIVES

The primary goal of a national transport policy should be to provide transport services of a level, quality, and geographical pattern that will meet the needs of the economy at least cost and at acceptable rates of return. Three subsidiary objectives follow from this goal. First, existing infrastructure and equipment should be used more efficiently; this means obtaining maximum output from existing facilities at a given cost, or minimizing the cost of using these facilities to meet specific transport demands. Second, new investments should be distributed efficiently among the transport modes on the basis of demands for different types of service and their relative costs and benefits. Third, within each mode, projects must make efficient use of available investment funds.

Attaining these objectives is not simply a technical planning task. In most developing countries, important changes are needed in general macro-economic policies—such as those relating to exchange rates at which imported equipment can be bought, interest rates on loan capital, and wage rates—that affect transport as well as other sectors. Also needed are changes in policies specific to each of the transport modes, improvements in the institutional setting, better coordination of the agencies concerned with transport planning and development, and more effective project selection, design, and execution. Finally, governments must refrain from imposing extraneous burdens on the transport system—by requiring them, for example, to create jobs or favor certain locations, industries, or groups—the costs of which discourage efforts toward efficient operations. Such changes are discussed in the following sections.

POLICY ISSUES

Regulation and Competition

Government regulation of the transport sector is common, but the reasons for it are not always well defined and they may, at times, be contradictory. Regulatory measures may be intended to achieve a wide range of objectives:

- To contain monopoly power, such as that of railways not faced with any effective truck competition
- To control "excessive" competition, particularly in road transport
- To ensure the financial viability of public or parastatal transport enterprises
- To assist groups considered to be meritorious or needy
- To integrate transport more closely with broader policies such as land use or industrial development
- To reflect real economic costs in transport when the market mechanism fails to do so
- To improve transport coordination among a multiplicity of independent investors or suppliers
- To protect highways, bridges, and other public infrastructure from overloading or abuse
- To ensure safety in transport
- To protect the environment.

The regulatory instruments used in support of these multiple ends include restricting certain activities to a limited number of enfranchised operators, fixing passenger fares and freight rates, requiring certain services to be provided even though they are not financially viable, and establishing standards for safety, noise levels, and exhaust emissions. There is no realistic alternative to regulation for purposes of safety, health, protection of the environment, and protection of public facilities. But attention must be given to how cost-effective, how practical, and how enforceable the regulations are. Given the difficulties of devising regulations that will have the desired effects, and of implementing and enforcing them, they should be used sparingly and with great care.

Regulating the conditions of doing business in the private sector is, however, a different matter. In general, where competitive markets exist, or would exist in the absence of regulation, efficient operations and sound investment decisions have been achieved best by allowing the supply of transport services to be matched to demand through the price mechanism. When governments restrict entry of competitors into an activity and set prices for services, they interfere with the normal adjustment mechanism, usually without having a valid economic or statistical basis for ensuring a better result. These arguments apply with particular force to the regulation of road transport. It is sometimes contended that because entry into the industry is easy (enterprises owning one or a few trucks, buses, or taxis are common) free competition would be ruinous to operators and make service less reliable; the industry, therefore, needs to be controlled as protection against itself. Experience does not support this contention. When road transport operations have been left to the marketplace, consumers have benefited from the lower prices induced by competition, capacity has adapted to demand, and the industry has generally thrived.

Prices and Subsidies

When competitive markets do not exist—as for railways, ports, and airports—public agencies must set prices. Pricing issues in transport are complicated by the existence of several modes that have fundamentally different characteristics and cost structures, but that are interdependent or competitive. The basic principle for economically efficient pricing, as noted in chapter 3, is to try to emulate the working of a competitive market by keeping prices in line with marginal costs. The application of this principle, however, varies among the transport modes, as does the need to depart from it because of objectives other than the efficient allocation of resources.

In the years when they enjoyed a monopoly, railways generally followed a policy of charging not what the transport of goods cost but what the traffic would bear, roughly in accordance with the value of the goods transported. As road competition developed, this policy resulted in the diversion of high-value goods to road transport. Today intense competition with trucking and busing limits the railways' freedom in setting tariffs. The starting point for efficient pricing of railway services is, nonetheless, the marginal (that is, the variable or out-of-pocket) costs of shipping the goods in question. When, as often happens, average costs are declining or excess capacity exists, marginal cost will be below average cost. Marginal cost pricing would, therefore, result in operating losses to many railways if followed for all traffic. But it would also result, most often, in an increase in demand, and the railway would soon encounter capacity constraints—of track, or wagons, or whatever. Efficiency pricing would then require an added charge to reflect the very real costs of congestion or to reduce that congestion. If demand permits, the charge could be high enough to enable the railway to cover both marginal costs and some or all of the fixed cost of the congested facility or equipment. The additional revenue would give a signal that investment to expand capacity is appropriate.

In addition to these considerations, financial viability (that is, the ability to cover costs and generate a surplus to finance new investment; see chapter 21, Financial Analysis) is also an important objective and a useful discipline for efficient operation. Accordingly, achieving the financial targets of an enterprise may sometimes, when demand permits, justify prices above the efficiency price; this entails the sacrifice of some degree of efficiency in the interests of financial viability. For some goods and some hauls, a convenient way to raise higher revenues without distorting demand is a two-part tariff: one part varies with the marginal cost of the output supplied, while the other is a fixed or overhead charge that does not vary with output.

Also a carryover from the earlier days of railway monopoly is the insistence of many governments on approving all changes in railway tariffs. This is now largely an anachronism since railways have little or no monopoly power to be controlled. The pricing strategy advocated above calls for a commercially oriented marketing approach, with flexible adjustments in prices as costs change or market conditions warrant. The typically slow bureaucratic process of government approval is incompatible with this need.

For ports, marginal cost pricing is also recommended.[1] Tariffs based on this principle are under consideration in several countries. Even where the elasticity of demand for a port's service as a whole is low, users can and will vary the way in which they use different components of that service (berths, port labor, crane service, storage area, or water depth), so that pricing on a cost basis helps ensure good use of resources. Experience with certain ports, such as Singapore and Hong Kong, suggests that tariffs based on marginal cost, provided they include congestion charges, not only are feasible but also can be profitable under competitive conditions. Higher charges can be levied, if necessary, again through a two-part tariff, to achieve financial viability, which is no less important an objective for port operations than for railways. The situation of airports is similar in many respects.

The trucking industry is normally a highly competitive one. Given freedom of entry, the market will function to bring prices in line with costs. As previously mentioned, there is no need for government regulation of trucking rates, as distinct from some other aspects of the trucking business. This could also apply to passenger transport by bus, but some governments have given monopolies over bus traffic to publicly owned bus companies, whose rates then need to be reviewed by a public authority.

Another question arises with respect to pricing of road transport. If the cost of truck and bus operations is to reflect the value of all the resources used in them, the costs arising out of their use of the road infrastructure must also be included. Recovery of these costs requires an appropriate system of user charges. The marginal cost of using a highway includes the damage that vehicles cause to the road, and this is measured by the cost of maintaining the road or of restoring it to its earlier condition. It also includes the costs that vehicles impose on each other by traveling the road—both the increased operating cost because of damage to the road and the cost of congestion.

User charges in the form of taxes on fuel and tires have the desirable feature of varying in accordance with the extent that vehicle operators use the roads, but they differentiate little if at all according to the degree of congestion. Attention needs to be paid to the structure of such charges: gasoline taxes are often higher, and diesel fuel taxes lower, than is justified by the damage that their respective users—passenger cars and trucks— inflict on the highway system. Congestion should and can be priced, as evidenced by schemes in operation in Singapore and several cities in the United States. Such charges discourage peak-hour use and raise funds for the road authorities. Bridge and road tolls are another way of charging users for the costs of particular parts of a road system; but toll collection

1. See Esra Bennathan and A. A. Walters, *Port Pricing and Investment Policy for Developing Countries* (New York: Oxford University Press for the World Bank, 1979).

costs may be high, and, if there are alternative toll-free routes, traffic may be diverted to them.

In some developing countries, revenues collected from highway users are insufficient to cover the full costs of adequately maintaining the roads. There may be sound fiscal as well as economic reasons for raising highway user charges to cover these costs rather than imposing them on the general taxpayer. Charges that do not vary with road use, such as those for vehicle registration, can contribute a portion of the needed revenues. Some governments, for reasons of fiscal convenience and on the grounds that services should be paid for by the beneficiaries, have used highway charges to cover part of the cost of new road construction.

The fact that railway and road transport are in close competition underlines the need for proper and consistent pricing of both modes. In some instances, truckers can charge low rates because the user charges they pay—such as taxes on diesel fuel—do not reflect the full impact of their operations on highways. (When public expenditures are not adequate to maintain the roads properly, however, the operating costs of trucks are higher than they would otherwise be.) Railways, for their part, often require large subsidies because governments, for reasons of public interest or on other grounds, not only keep tariffs below efficiency prices (and considerably below prices that would ensure financial viability for the railways) but also require the railways to operate uneconomical services or to retain redundant staff. These subsidies distort decisionmaking and the efficient use of resources. Although it may be impossible to determine the final economic outcome of these subsidies because of their complexity, there is no reason to assume it will be optimal. The economically rational solution to the problem involves deregulation and appropriate pricing, both of which are easier to prescribe than to achieve.

The thought of deregulation and competition without subsidies is shocking to some railway managers. But the combination can be made to work, as has been demonstrated in several countries. In Canada, for example, since 1967 private and state-owned railways of similar size, in open competition and under progressive management, have had a healthy financial performance. In Chile, the large railway subsidies were withdrawn in 1975, and the railway, after closing some lines, streamlining its work force, and competing actively for business, became self-supporting in 1980.

Adjustment to External Price Changes

A major issue of transport pricing in many countries is the necessary adjustment to higher energy costs following the oil-price shocks of the 1970s. The long-term goal is to minimize the effects of higher energy prices on the total economic cost of producing the nation's output. Up to certain limits, reducing energy consumption is an essential move in that direction. Since transport in most developing countries uses from 20 to 40 percent of total commercial energy (compared with 15 percent in the EEC countries and 25 percent in the United States), it is appropriate to look for ways to conserve energy in that sector and hence reduce oil imports.

A 1982 World Bank study made some concrete suggestions about how to save energy in the transport sector:[2]

- Since road transport uses twice as much energy per ton-kilometer as rail for the same haul, some savings could be realized by shifting appropriate road freight traffic to the railways. Shifts to river transport could save even more. The energy advantage of railways is less obvious, however, in passenger traffic, where the unit consumption of energy is similar to that of buses. All in all, the scope for energy savings through intermodal shifts appears limited.[3] Savings are likely to be achieved mainly through better management within each mode. Achieving savings through either intermodal shifts or improved management requires sending out correct signals in the form of energy prices that reflect true costs to the economy.

- Car, bus, and truck drivers, under the stimulus of higher fuel prices, could save about 20 percent of the fuel they use by driving more slowly and smoothly, shutting off engines whenever possible, and following proper maintenance programs.

- Car and van pooling significantly cuts down on the number of vehicles used to carry a given number of commuters to and from cities. Encouraging the shipment of goods by common carrier trucks instead of company-owned vehicles—again, through relative price changes—usually increases load factors. Since transport regulations often segment the market for trucking, their removal would encourage a rational, cost-minimizing (and energy-efficient) allocation of traffic among vehicles.

- Measures to control congestion promise good returns in terms of energy savings. As the speed of cars rises from, say, 10 to 30 miles per hour, energy requirements drop by over one-third. Appropriate policies include congestion pricing, use of parking meters, and a variety of traffic management techniques.

- Updating vehicle fleets can also save fuel. Recent models of automobiles are some 30 percent more energy-efficient than the ones they replace in developed countries. The difference in trucks is 10 to 20 percent, with further progress expected. The average age of vehicles in most developing countries is greater than in developed countries. To induce the right economic choice by operators, fuels should not be priced below their opportunity cost; in addition, import duties on vehicles should take into account not only the foreign exchange costs of such vehicles but also the foreign exchange savings (in the form of reduced fuel imports) resulting from the import of vehicles that are more energy-efficient.

In the United States, truck mileage per gallon of diesel fuel increased 12 percent between 1978 and 1980, presumably as a result of changes in

2. World Bank, Transportation and Water Department, "Energy and Transport in Developing Countries: Towards Achieving Greater Energy Efficiency" (Washington, D.C., 1982).

3. See Liviu L. Alston, *Railways and Energy*, World Bank Staff Working Paper no. 634 (Washington, D.C., 1984).

driving techniques and the replacement of old vehicles with new ones. In developing countries, even larger savings can be expected from such improvements. An improvement of energy efficiency in road transport of some 30 percent over a five-year period is both technically and economically feasible in many developing countries.

Energy efficiency is only part of the total efficiency of transport operations, however, and there are offsetting costs. The goal should be to minimize total costs, not just energy costs. Buying new vehicles is expensive. And while slower operating speeds save fuel, they result in more driving time and higher wage costs. Energy savings in recent years have sometimes been bought at an unduly high price, but this need not be so if policies are properly designed and if time is allowed for effects to materialize.

Labor Policy

Railways almost everywhere have been persuaded by labor unions, often with the help of politicians, into featherbedding, that is, hiring or retaining on the payroll more people than needed for efficient operations. The policy has also commended itself to some governments as a convenient way to reduce unemployment. If a railway is seeking to become viable through commercialization and increased efficiency, as suggested below in "A Railway Plan of Action," surplus staff may constitute a serious obstacle. At the same time, it is unlikely that staff can simply be dismissed without touching off acute labor problems.

Retraining may make it possible to find other employment for some staff. Beyond this, the best alternative is to effect reductions through attrition by not replacing most of those who leave, retire, or die. While it may take a long time to reduce the staff to an efficient size, and many railways have failed to sustain the effort over a long enough period, several railways (including those in Brazil, Argentina, Spain, Hungary, and Yugoslavia) have greatly improved efficiency in this way.

An excess of personnel on the railway's payroll is often accompanied, as in many other public sector enterprises, by a shortage of well-trained skilled workers and qualified managers. Part of the problem is the practice of underpaying such people in public sector jobs. Moreover, in times of inflation, pay raises in the public sector typically lag behind those in the private sector, and this creates a strong inducement for the best people to leave. Besides raising pay rates to a more adequate level, training is essential to upgrade staff qualifications and enable staff to move into higher-paying jobs. In addition, if jobs incorporate more substantive content, more authority, and more opportunity to innovate, they will be more attractive to creative technicians and managers.

Ports, like railways, tend to be overburdened with excess workers, and for similar reasons. Improving efficiency by mechanizing cargo-handling processes or by substituting containers or bulk cargo for general cargo can create large numbers of surplus workers. Sometimes alternative work opportunities can be found right in the port, processing or packaging goods to be exported. Retraining and attrition must also be relied on to deal with the problem.

INSTITUTIONAL ISSUES

Operation of Systems

Many developing countries face the question, noted earlier, of who should own and operate the various transport modes. To what degree should the national or local government be involved in managing a trucking business or a bus service? In these services, a multiplicity of private operators can compete, and that has proved to be the most efficient approach. If there is no private company to provide service, the government can contract with one to do so, rather than set up its own company. Direct involvement of the central government in road transport operations (or of the municipal government in local bus service) has more often than not led to inefficient and unsatisfactory service. In contrast, there are compelling technical reasons for the railways, seaports, and airports in a country to be operated as single enterprises—and, therefore, in most countries, to be publicly owned. It is usually appropriate that each of these modes be under a separate public organization or authority.

Although examples of completely unregulated urban transport service are uncommon, there are different degrees of competition and of public or private operation. In many cities (Manila, San Juan, Istanbul, and Nairobi among others), a multitude of private small-scale operators of relatively small vehicles (five to twenty passengers) provide passenger service in competition with a municipally owned or regulated bus company. These small-scale operators typically make a profit, or at least cover costs, while the public system requires a subsidy. (Public companies often have to be subsidized even where there is no competition.) Usually the small operators also provide better service.

In the city of Calcutta, privately owned, full-size buses operate on assigned routes under conditions comparable to those under which the state-owned bus system operates. About 1,500 privately owned buses, organized into route associations, carry about two-thirds of all passengers and make a profit, while the Calcutta State Transport Company, operating on similar routes and charging the same fares, has to be subsidized to the extent of about $1 million a month. The viability of the private operations seems attributable to the profit motive, which stimulates efficiency and responsiveness to demand. The state company payroll is overloaded (thirty employees per bus, one of the highest ratios in the world). In addition, a much lower proportion of privately owned than state-owned vehicles is out of service for maintenance or repairs at any time, and fare collection on the private buses is almost 100 percent compared with about 75 percent on the state buses.

The situation is the same in the trucking business, which seldom offers a rational justification for government operation. Competition among many private operators yields service responsive to demand and minimizes shipping costs. Although the government provides the infrastructure and must set and enforce safety standards and weight limits, it should not try to manage trucking operations. The unimpressive record of publicly owned trucking companies fully supports this conclusion.

In general, transport activities should be operated whenever possible on a competitive basis. Competition within the rail mode, however, is seldom practical. Nevertheless, the railway is in active competition with trucks and buses, and its management—if given a chance and the incentives to do so—can act competitively.

Planning and Coordination

Investment plans for building new or upgrading old facilities are naturally formulated by the managers of each mode, yet the relationships among such plans may be important. Expansion of an existing port or construction of a new one may imply a need to increase the capacities of the railways or highways that serve it. If a new area is to be opened for mining, a decision may be needed as to whether the ore is to be brought out over a new highway or a new rail line. Thus, investment in one mode may be an alternative, or a necessary supplement, to investment in another, so the infrastructure plans for the various modes need to be coordinated.

If the coordinating role is not handled ad hoc, it is logical to assign it to the ministry of transport—when there is one—if the ministry has adequate means to carry it out. As noted earlier, however, too often the ministry lacks both the expertise and the control of other agencies' resources that would empower it to do the job. Operating and investment funds are often allocated directly to the ministry of public works, the port authority, and other executing agencies, without even consulting the ministry of transport. If it is to be an effective coordinator, the ministry of transport will usually need to upgrade its planning capabilities by adding qualified staff, and to strengthen its hand in coordinating the investment (and maintenance) plans of different modes by exercising more influence over the allocation of funds. This can be done by requiring the ministry's approval of the budget requests of the various transport agencies, for example, or of all investment proposals above a certain amount.

Bringing all transport activities fully under one ministry's authority is not likely to work well, however, because of the complexity of each mode and the large number of staff. The ministry need not be directly involved with actual management of transport operations; that can be left to the various operating entities, public or private. Several countries, including Korea, Nigeria, and Turkey, have tried the alternative of a separate transport coordinating agency, which has the purely technical role of analyzing and coordinating plans for each mode. Such agencies appear to be effective only when they have direct input to a powerful ministry with control over financial resources—such as the ministry of finance or planning—or direct access to the president's office.

Coordinating plans for the transport sector requires not only adequate institutional links, but also some criteria for choosing among proposed investment projects. As a minimum, the coordinating agency should insist that all projects be subjected to as thorough a cost-benefit analysis as the available data permit. Such analysis can help ensure that only economically sound projects are approved; and, when closely related projects in a particular subsector are proposed, it can help determine which ones should be preferred. But just as cost-benefit analysis gives limited (though useful) guidance to intersectoral investment priorities (see chapter 20, Economic Analysis), so it gives only limited (though useful) guidance to intermodal transport priorities. Choosing between two transport projects that would serve widely different purposes—say, between improving the freight-handling facilities of a port and providing better passenger service on a rail line—calls, above all, for the exercise of judgment. In contrast, when there are alternative ways of achieving a specific transport objective, the respective costs should be analyzed to arrive at the least-cost solution. While some costs and benefits may be intangible, those that can be quantified should be; the coordinating agency must evaluate the others qualitatively in making its decision.

Policy Formulation, Analysis, and Research

Another important aspect of transport coordination is that of policy coordination among the various transport modes. This function obviously must be exercised by an intermodal unit, logically one located in the ministry of transport. This unit must be competent to analyze alternative policies on such matters as tariffs, standards of service, and levels and methods of cost recovery to ensure economically sound and consistent treatment of the various modes. It can either make recommendations to a higher authority or, as permitted, set policies to be carried out by the separate modal agencies.

Both the planning and policymaking functions need to be based on a technical and economic analysis of alternatives. This analysis, in turn, has to be grounded in adequate statistical information about current conditions and operations. Most of the data must be collected, and some analysis performed, by the various modal agencies. The overall analysis, however, should be done by whatever unit is responsible for planning and coordination. Since the analysts will be most aware of what data are needed, the same unit should set the requirements for data collection and probably collect some of the data as well.

Training

Institutional improvements should also include increased staff training in technical and managerial matters. Although much depends on the scale and quality of the national education system, most large transport agencies can increase the quantity and improve the quality of their own training programs, especially in the use of modern management and financial information and control systems. Training in project and policy analysis and management is also critical. Each developing country should either have or seek association with a qualified center for managerial training in general transport and in the specific modes. If a country is too small to sustain an institution of its own, it should join with others in the region to establish a regional institute—such as the Eastern and Southern Africa Management Institute at Arusha (Tanzania), which is financed by seven nations and open to the officials of eleven others. Compared with the common practice of sending middle- and high-level management to developed countries, training in regional institutes is less expensive and better adapted to local conditions.

The need for more and better training of road construction supervisors, mechanics, and other technically skilled personnel has been met more successfully through structured on-the-job training than through class-room teaching alone. A particularly effective approach is to set up a special unit to give training in road maintenance. In several World Bank–assisted highway projects in Latin America, Africa, and elsewhere, the loans include funds for training equipment, other training costs, and road maintenance equipment. After several weeks of instruction, usually in a classroom, the whole unit—instructors and trainees—moves to the field for practical training, which includes maintenance operations on paved and unpaved sections within the government's annual mainte-nance program.

Organizing for Maintenance

A major continuing problem in transport is the overemphasis on new construction and the inadequate attention to maintenance. In the course of greatly expanding transport systems over the past twenty years, the difficult job of building up capacity to maintain them was neglected. As a result, the deterioration of roads, bridges, port machinery, locomotives, and railway roadbeds, and of the maintenance machinery itself, is becom-ing an urgent problem—especially since the scarcity of new capital means that existing facilities must be made to last longer. Regular preventive maintenance and timely repairs are essential. To accomplish this at reasonable cost, the inefficiencies of existing maintenance practices need to be overcome. Public sector maintenance organizations for railways, roads, and ports need to cut back on surplus unqualified workers and increase their training of managers, supervisors, machinists, and other skilled staff. For all transport modes, inventory control, adequate work-shops, and foreign exchange for spare parts are necessary for efficient maintenance.

Many middle-income countries have found it possible to increase the efficiency and quality of road maintenance work (as well as of new road construction) by relying more on competitive contracting with private firms and less on the forces of the ministry of public works. In poorer countries that do not yet have a strong private sector, regular mainte-nance work offers an excellent base for the development of small con-tracting firms and mechanical workshops. To make this shift requires, among other things, modernization of the public sector's contracting procedures, increased training of both technicians and managers, and explicit recognition of the contracting industry as an important activity with its own problems and potential.

Particularly interesting is the growing use of private contractors for routine as well as periodic (less frequent) maintenance of highways. In both developed and developing countries, such work as cleaning roadside drains and patching bituminous pavements has traditionally been done by labor forces employed by the government. Recently, however, Argen-tina, Brazil, Colombia, Kenya, Nigeria, and other countries have turned over more of this work to private contractors. Significant economies have resulted. Yugoslavia has had a similar system in effect since the mid-1950s with very good results; in the province of Slovenia, as few as five road officials manage a high-standard, well-maintained network of 4,700 kilo-meters. Private contractors operate more efficiently and cost the government less because competitive bidding is a strong incentive to lower costs. In addition, private enterprises have greater flexibility in hiring, paying, and dismissing personnel according to their performance and the actual work load. In Ponta Grossa, Brazil, where data on fully comparable costs under similar conditions were available, the force account (or government-hired labor) operation, commonly viewed as very efficient, was 60 percent more costly than unit-price contracts with private firms.

In Argentina, the majority of road maintenance work is submitted to competitive bidding, but a residual force account operation, reorganized along commercial lines, is retained to provide the government with flexibility and to counter possible collusion among contractors. The government was able to reduce its force of road employees from approximately 20,000 to 8,300 between 1979 and 1981, when maintenance of approximately 70 percent of the federal network was contracted out.

For rural roads in inhabited areas, a quite different form of road maintenance contracting is being used successfully by several countries. It is the "lengthman" system. The lengthman, a local resident, is responsible for a short stretch of road on which he spends about half of his working day. He is paid a half-time wage at the end of each month provided the supervisor finds the road in satisfactory condition. Kenya now maintains some 2,000 kilometers of rural roads in this manner and is planning to extend its application.

Maintenance needs more emphasis in ports and railways also. Railway roadbed and track maintenance is a specialized function that must be carried out by the railway's own work force if train service is not to be interrupted. Maintenance of equipment, in contrast, can sometimes be done by private contractors. Cargo-handling equipment in ports can also be maintained through competitive contracting, as can repairs to bulkheads, berthside pavements, and so on.

INVESTMENT ISSUES

More Efficient Use of Facilities

Given the inevitable scarcity of investment funds, it is especially important for policymakers and managers to find ways of using existing facilities more effectively. Often this can eliminate, or at least postpone or reduce, the need for expensive new construction.

When a single-track rail line has reached its capacity under existing procedures and techniques, it is desirable, before a decision is made to construct a second track, to analyze the possibility of increasing capacity by running longer trains, installing automatic traffic controls, or scheduling service more efficiently. Instead of widening a road that carries commuter traffic into a city, its capacity may be increased by better traffic engineering, by incentives for car- and van-pooling and, in some cases, by special bus lanes. The capacity of a berth in a port can be effectively increased by faster cargo-handling methods, use of multiple shifts, and judicious pricing of berth space per unit of time.

In some instances, excess demand during a peak period can be diverted to other times by adding congestion charges that price services differently at different times of the day or seasons of the year. Airports in Saudi

Arabia charge higher fees during the pilgrimage season. The economy air fare across the North Atlantic in the summer (the peak season) of 1983 was 18 percent higher than it was during the rest of the year. The port of Singapore charges a steeply increasing rate for berth occupancy after completion of cargo handling to encourage faster turnaround.

Scope of Projects

Many officials in developing countries and many external lenders have come to realize that simply creating new physical facilities may have little impact on the performance of the transport sector in the absence of reforms of institutions, policies, and operating procedures. They are learning that, to be effective, the scope of projects must be more comprehensive and include measures to improve capacity utilization, better organization and methods for maintenance, training for management and technical staff, and policy changes to enhance competition and put decisionmaking on an economically sound basis. These requirements add to project complexity and, therefore, to the difficulty of designing and executing a project to acceptable standards.

A Railway Plan of Action

The kind of project typically needed to improve a railway is broad in scope and complex in design. Many railways in developing countries are in serious trouble. Projects to modernize individual parts of their systems will have limited success unless accompanied by reforms both of railway management and of government policies affecting railways. Both railway management and government must be committed to a comprehensive, phased plan of action based on a thorough study and diagnosis of the railway's problems. The plan of action should identify the need for changes in management policies, organization, pricing formulas, operating and maintenance procedures, staff training, and labor policies, as well as the need for investing in new equipment, for rehabilitating existing equipment and infrastructure, and for discontinuing unprofitable operations. Railways are a complex system of interlocking operations, all of which may need to be addressed lest bottlenecks in one part of the system (such as maintenance and repair of locomotives) impede progress in another part of the system (such as expansion of the rail network).

A plan of action, now a standard concomitant of World Bank lending for railways, focuses attention on important areas that need improvement. Targets for better performance are agreed upon, together with concrete measures to achieve them within a designated time. In the course of project implementation, progress toward these targets is closely monitored. Although some governments and railways have not stayed the course, this approach has been a crucial element in improving the performance of railways in Yugoslavia, Korea, Bolivia, and Zaire. Even when no external loans are sought, it is appropriate for developing countries to follow a plan of action, though some outside help may be useful.

A central element of any plan of action is to give railway management a commercial orientation and put competition with trucks on a businesslike basis. This entails a change in attitude on the part of most railway managers, who must learn to think of marketing their more profitable services, closing down unprofitable operations, reducing costs, and setting rates and fares competitively. The government will have to allow managers the freedom to take these steps, and it will also have to address related issues in other transport modes that affect railway performance. With regard to highways, as noted, users will have to be charged in relation to their use of the roads and at a rate high enough to cover the cost of maintaining them.

Getting fares and freight rates on a sound basis in both modes is important, but other factors, often ignored in the past by railway managers, also affect the user's choice of a transport mode. Time savings, comfort, and convenience matter to passengers, while access and transshipment costs, as well as the convenience of door-to-door service, matter to shippers. In some countries, goods requiring transshipment are, unless containerized, subject to theft or damage to such an extent that some shippers refuse to use the railway. To overcome these problems, railway management must make its services more attractive to customers. By upgrading passenger services, the railways of Malaysia, Spain, Taiwan, and Korea and the railway linking the Ivory Coast with Burkina (formerly Upper Volta) have all stimulated sustained growth of intercity passenger traffic. On Korea's Seoul-Pusan route, the number of passengers increased from 540,000 in 1971 to 4 million in 1978 because of improved service. For freight shipments, railways can provide door-to-door service, operating the access service themselves (or on subcontract) and guaranteeing security. Railways that serve seaports equipped to handle containers can organize an attractive service by making provision for loading, hauling, and delivering containers, if necessary by several modes, between the port and points of origin or destination.

Technical design of railway projects must be based on sound economic and financial analysis. In track rehabilitation, some railways have adopted standards of engineering excellence and national uniformity with little regard to cost. Expensive investments such as high-speed passenger trains have been proposed on the grounds that they are modern and prestigious and are being adopted in other countries; in practice, however, it takes a very large volume of passengers to justify such investments. This applies also to system electrification, which involves a large investment as well as a long gestation time. Each proposal must be evaluated in terms of the particular circumstances—the opportunity cost of capital, the cost of locomotives and fixed installations, the cost to the economy of generating additional electricity, the price of diesel fuel, the nature of the terrain, and the expected volumes of passenger and freight traffic.

Improving the viability of railways often necessitates disinvestment by closing down existing lines, stations, workshops, or other services or facilities. A number of factors should be considered before a decision is made to close a railway line. It is advisable, for example, to look beyond the immediate financial question of whether the line generates enough revenue to cover its costs, and analyze its overall economic benefits and costs. Could service of equivalent quality be provided at lower cost by, say, road transport? Would shippers and passengers have alternate transport available? If not, tariffs might be increased; or, if there is a valid public interest to be served and if the line still provides the least-cost service, a subsidy to the railway to continue operating for a time may be justified. If the closing entails a reduction in the railway's work force, is severance pay adequate and alternative employment available for those displaced?

The Railway Transport Organization, Sarajevo, serving the Republic of Bosnia-Herzegovina in Yugoslavia, successfully reduced its staff by about 8,000 people (approximately 33 percent) in conjunction with closing about 430 kilometers of uneconomic lines and modernizing the remaining lines. The staff reduction was carried out over two years, during which the government of the republic provided funds to keep redundant staff on the payroll until they could be employed elsewhere, either within or outside the railway organization. Measures to ease the transition included:

- Retraining of workers, chiefly for jobs outside the railway
- Government grants and bank loans to attract new industries to areas of high labor redundancy
- Government assistance in transferring workers to jobs on expanding railways elsewhere in Yugoslavia as well as in West Germany.[4]

If, in the end, a government decides to maintain some uneconomic services for public interest, national defense, or other reasons, the railway should be compensated for the services, and their cost should appear in the budget as a charge against the relevant agency (such as the ministry of defense). The latter must then bear the public responsibility for justifying the expenditure, while the railway retains the incentive to operate efficiently those services over which it has control.

Road Projects

Planning

The main task confronting highway planners is to determine economic priorities among competing demands. In the 1960s and 1970s, highway networks were greatly expanded in many countries. These assets are now aging and increasingly in need of maintenance and renewal. The economics of scale of larger trucks add to the need for strengthening the pavement, which makes substantial demands on capital. Failure to act in good time raises the costs of rehabilitation and upgrading. As traffic resumes its growth after the dampening effect of the worldwide recession of the early 1980s, road capacity will have to be expanded in many countries. Fortunately, planning methodology is contributing new analytical techniques to deal with these problems.[5]

In any development planning, the transport implications of the pattern of development must be taken into account. This is especially true of

4. An interesting manifestation of entrepreneurial spirit came from a group of former railway workers who established what is now a thriving export business, growing mushrooms in a tunnel on one of the abandoned railway lines.

5. See, for example, Thawat Watanatada and Clell Harral, "Determination of Economically Balanced Highway Expenditure Programs under Budget Constraints: A Practical Approach," in J. S. Yerrell, ed., *Transport Research for Social and Economic Progress*, Proceedings of the World Conference on Transport Research (London, 1980), also available as World Bank Reprint Series no. 224; Thawat Watanatada and others, "Highway Design and Maintenance Standards Study," vol. 4: "HDM III Model Description and User's Manual" (World Bank draft final report, March 1984); and G. Gynnerstedt, L. R. Kadiyali, and others, *Indo-Swedish Road Traffic Simulation Study* (New Delhi: Swedish National Institute for Road and Traffic Research and Central Road Research Laboratory, 1984).

programs to open up new areas for agriculture, logging, or mining; constructing the necessary roads must be an integral part of the program and their costs and benefits included in the analysis.[6] Moreover, it may be fallacious to assume that economic development—and hence traffic— will automatically follow when rural roads are built, even in the absence of concrete measures to promote the growth of the region. Planning of rural roads and of agricultural development must go hand in hand.

When rural roads are being planned, arrangements should be made for local people to participate; they can help planners to ascertain needs, adjust designs to local circumstances, and improve the chances of local participation in construction and future maintenance. The most promising solution to the difficult problem of maintaining minor rural roads appears to lie in cooperation and cost-sharing between local communities and the government's technical agency. Communities can, for example, be required to contribute local materials and labor.

Technical Design

Limited investment funds can be conserved by paying more attention to organizing and carrying out maintenance and rehabilitation and by finding ways to use infrastructure more effectively. When new construction is undertaken, overdesign and consequent overinvestment as well as underdesign and consequent operating and maintenance problems are both to be avoided.

Many main roads with medium and low traffic are designed with too high standards of vertical grade, horizontal curvature, and especially width. The decrease in vehicle operating costs and accidents obtained by avoiding tight curves or steep grades may not justify the more generous alignment. Many excesses have occurred in pavement and shoulder widths where design standards have been copied from Europe and North America. Instead of the common international standards of six to seven meters, a pavement width of five meters may be adequate for roads carrying not more than 500 to 1,000 vehicles a day, unless there is a high proportion of unusually wide, heavy vehicles (such as logging trucks). Road width is very costly (particularly in terrain requiring large cuts and fills), and extra width normally yields little additional benefits for any but high-traffic roads.

When traffic on roads is low but nevertheless sufficient to warrant some pavement, and especially when forecasts of future traffic growth are uncertain, one way of conserving capital and hedging against uncertainty is to construct the road in stages. A relatively light pavement is built initially, good maintenance provided, and a stronger pavement added only after the volume of traffic justifies it. Although this is the theoretically optimal approach in many situations, it has proved a costly failure when maintenance has not been good enough or when the pavement has not been strengthened in time, often for lack of funds. Then the damage has

6. See Curt Carnemark and others, *The Economic Analysis of Rural Road Projects*, World Bank Staff Working Paper no. 241 (Washington, D.C., 1976), and H. L. Beenhakker and Abderraouf Chammari, *Identification and Appraisal of Rural Roads Projects*, World Bank Staff Working Paper no. 362 (Washington, D.C., 1979).

required extensive rehabilitation. A better strategy when these conditions are likely to be present is to build stronger pavement in the first place.

Pavements have also suffered from overloading when enforcement of axle weight limits has been inadequate, as it often is. Recent studies have shown that the most cost-effective strategy to deal with this problem is to build stronger pavements at the outset, and to permit heavier loads—which are often the road transport industry's (appropriate) response to the need to use vehicle capacity efficiently.

Maintenance Projects

Road maintenance can be "projectized," and the World Bank has made many loans for such projects. Building institutional capacity for road maintenance has proved far more difficult than building roads. Establishing a successful maintenance program requires a comprehensive approach, often through a series of projects over a number of years. Among the issues to be addressed through such projects are:

- Securing an adequate and timely flow of maintenance funds in the annual public budget
- Designing and implementing an appropriate and efficient organization of maintenance services at the various levels of government administration
- Ensuring an adequate supply of fuel and spare parts (with regular allocation of scarce foreign exchange for this purpose)
- Properly maintaining the maintenance equipment and renewing it periodically
- Establishing a system of accounts and of charges for equipment use
- Preventing the diversion of equipment and staff to other uses (frequently new construction)
- Training and motivating mechanics, operators, and other staff through suitable institutional programs and incentives.

Despite the numerous problems encountered in implementing comprehensive maintenance projects, the importance of highway maintenance is evidenced by the fact that completed maintenance projects show rates of return often several times greater than the opportunity cost of capital. Economic rates of return on road maintenance are typically higher than on road construction. These high returns reflect the profitability of relatively small expenditures to preserve the value of the much larger investments made earlier in new construction. The amount required for efficient maintenance operations is not very large; funds amounting to some 1 or 2 percent of the value of the road capital stock are generally sufficient to cover routine and periodic operations for a year, as well as upkeep and renewal of the maintenance equipment itself. This sum seldom represents more than a fraction of annual government revenues from road users and, provided it is efficiently spent, it almost immediately pays for itself severalfold.[7]

7. World Bank, *The Road Maintenance Problem and International Assistance* (Washington, D.C., 1981).

Substitution of Labor for Capital

Countries with high unemployment and underemployment have strong reasons for using labor-intensive techniques in road construction and maintenance. Whether this approach is economically advantageous requires careful analysis in each case. This subject is treated in greater detail in chapter 19, Technical Analysis, case study 2.

Rural Access

Farmers need access to a local market or collection point on a road, railway, or waterway, as well as to centers where schools, medical care, and other social services are available. It is, of course, not realistic to envisage that a feeder road accommodating trucks can reach every farm gate, nor is that required; access can be greatly improved by primitive tracks and paths that can be used by pack animals, handcarts, and oxcarts, as well as by motorcycles and small farm tractors pulling trailers. Tracks and paths can be built largely by local labor through community self-help programs, perhaps with some technical assistance and mechanized work for difficult spots.

Ports and Inland Shipping

Although the foreign trade of developing countries can be expected to continue its rapid growth, construction of new ports or of additional berths in existing ports is likely to be justified in relatively few countries in the near future. Instead, ports typically need to be provided with modern container-handling equipment and, in some instances, with loading facilities for bulk cargo. These can reduce the time required for loading or unloading from more than a week to one or two days, thereby multiplying the effective capacity of a berth by a factor of four to eight. (When container-handling facilities are planned for a port, complementary plans must be made for trucks or trains to carry incoming containers to their inland destinations and outgoing containers to the port.)

In many developing countries, coastal and river shipping should be seriously studied as an alternative or supplement to land transport. It may be that building wharves, dredging a few channels, and installing some aids to navigation would enable a country to use water transport for a substantial part of its freight. Coastal and inland shipping can serve some transport needs, especially for bulk commodities and those not requiring rapid delivery, with less capital investment and lower operating costs than railways or roads.

Airports and Aviation

Once traffic forecasts have indicated that an international airport is justified, the requirements for runways, ground equipment, radar, communications, customs arrangements, passenger facilities, and so on are largely dictated by the types of aircraft to be accommodated and the operating procedures of international airlines. For domestic air service, the planning of airports needs to be coordinated with the decisions of airline and charter operators about routes and destinations to be served and the types of aircraft to be used.

Planning a pattern of airports and air service should also be related to the planning of ground and water transport. If traffic volume in the next five to ten years is uncertain or likely to be low, building a few low-cost airports and landing strips, along with wharves for river craft, could postpone the need for much larger capital expenditures for roads or railways.

Priority should be given to rehabilitating existing runways or other facilities that have become dilapidated for lack of maintenance, and to establishing the appropriate organization and procedures for regular maintenance. Next in importance is constructing ground facilities for servicing planes, handling baggage, and accommodating passengers. Dependable communication links with other locations and with aircraft in the vicinity, as well as aids to navigation, are essential components of any aviation system, and ground staff must be trained to use such equipment. The airline and charter service operations are likely to be handled most efficiently by private companies competing with a minimum of regulation, except for traffic control and safety.

Evaluation of Projects

Evaluation of the economic soundness of projects in the transport sector, as in other sectors, requires a careful forecast of demand and a detailed analysis of costs and benefits.

Forecasting Demand

Since traffic volumes need to be forecast over long periods, errors in forecasts can lead to serious discrepancies between calculated benefits and those actually realized. Forecasting transport demand faces many uncertainties, including those arising from competition among transport modes. Shifts in the relative shares of traffic carried by each mode are constantly taking place as circumstances change, and these shifts are difficult to predict. Forecasting also requires that estimates be made not only for *normal traffic* (that is, traffic without the project), but also for *generated traffic* (that is, traffic arising from the reduced costs of transport as a result of the project or from new development stimulated by improved transport) and for *diverted traffic* (that is, traffic diverted to or from other modes or other parts of the same network).

Fortunately, a number of practical considerations make long-term traffic forecasting more manageable than it might appear at first sight. First, a large part of the traffic of many railways and ports consists of a few bulk commodities, to which the analysis can mostly be limited. Second, many transport investments are relatively lumpy. A port berth might be justified for 80,000 tons of general cargo a year, but might also handle 150,000 tons efficiently, so that refinement of forecasts within that range may not be needed. (This lumpiness may, however, present difficulties if the traffic forecast is at the margin of, say, no berth or one, or a two- or four-lane road.) Third, traffic that already exists and can be expected to continue will make up much of the future traffic, since basic patterns in the location of industry, agriculture, and population do not change drastically in the short or medium term. Fourth, the forecast need be made only until the time when traffic reaches the project's capacity, provided it can be assumed, as it frequently can, that traffic will not decline thereafter. Fifth, because road transport is very dynamic, an overestimate of road traffic might be made up a short time later. Forecasting the need for investments in railways tends to be riskier because traffic for most railways has been declining or, at best, growing slowly.[8]

Indeed, experience shows that freight forecasts in conjunction with railway projects almost always prove too optimistic, largely because they fail to take adequate account of competition from road transport. Between 1965 and 1975, 60 percent of freight traffic forecasts in World Bank–assisted railway projects were overoptimistic.[9] Specific traffic categories that faced intermodal competition were insufficiently analyzed, and some long-term trends, such as a decline in the railways' share of a particular type of traffic, were taken to be transient and reversible when for the most part they were not. A lack of commercial and marketing awareness in the railway itself often resulted in a lack of proper information on which to base traffic forecasts.

In contrast, prior to the big jump in fuel prices in the 1970s, buoyant growth of traffic on new or improved main highways often exceeded forecasts by large margins. This was due in part to a greater diversion of traffic from railways than had been forecast and in part to a greater volume of generated traffic. On rural and feeder roads, actual traffic has typically been widely dispersed above and below the levels forecast, with no consistent bias; this reflects the greater difficulties of forecasting what amount to quantum rather than marginal changes.

Predicting port traffic is made difficult by the dependence of exports and imports on economic conditions throughout the world as well as on those within the country. Traffic can also be affected by local circumstances in individual ports—including congestion in the ports of neighboring countries. Anticipating changes in the nature and composition of port traffic has also proved difficult; the demand for container-handling facilities in developing countries, for example, has grown much faster than was predicted a decade ago, and rapid technological change continues. In many projects, traffic forecasts have been affected by unforeseen developments relating to particular commodities: cotton in Burkina, groundnuts in Senegal, coal in Korea. In this as well as other transport modes, a more disaggregated analysis, separating out each of the important segments of traffic, might produce better results.

Because forecasting is inherently uncertain, the benefits of a project should be analyzed for a range of future traffic levels, not just for one "best estimate," and sensitivity tests applied (see chapter 20, Economic Analysis). To the extent possible, projects should be designed flexibly to accommodate faster or slower traffic growth (but see the earlier comments on staged construction of roads). Determining the optimum time to initiate a project, and its proper phasing, can have a profound influence on the returns from the investment. The benefits of reduced congestion must be weighed against the costs of undertaking the investment rather

8. See Hans A. Adler, *Economic Appraisal of Transport Projects: A Manual with Case Studies*, 2nd ed., revised (forthcoming).

9. World Bank, Transportation and Water Department, "The Economic Role of Railways: Determinants of Railway Traffic—Final Report" (Washington, D.C., 1979).

than postponing it. If the proposed investment is lumpy, traffic may have to increase substantially beyond existing capacity before further expansion is justified.

Valuation of Costs and Benefits

The transport sector has been an early and important user of cost-benefit analysis. Much effort has gone into the quantification of costs and benefits, which raises both conceptual and practical problems. Journeys for whatever purpose entail costs—direct operating costs (for fuel, labor, and maintenance of vehicles and infrastructure) as well as intangible costs of travel time and accident hazard, noise, pollution, and so on. Savings in these costs apply to normal, generated, and diverted traffic and constitute the chief benefit of transport projects.

To the extent that the main purpose of a new transport facility is to open up a new area for development, reductions in transport costs on generated traffic are not an adequate measure of the benefits, which consist instead of the value of the new production. Often, however, the developmental impact of a transport investment may be difficult or impossible to measure. It is not easy to estimate the likely increase in output from the new development, and it may not be clear whether any portion of the development would have taken place without the transport investment, or whether any portion of the resources used in the new development would otherwise have been used less productively or not at all. A further problem is that other investments are usually required to obtain the increased production, and the transport investment may be a relatively small part of the total. Allocating the benefit of any increased production among all the investments is often so difficult that the transport and other investments may have to be treated as joint costs, and not amenable to calculation of separate rates of return. When it can be established, however, that a transport facility is responsible for an increase in output, the net value of this additional output is the proper measure of the economic benefit.[10]

As explained more fully in the chapter on economic analysis, the proper basis for measuring costs and benefits is the "with and without" test: what will the costs and benefits be with the new facility, and what would they have been without it? Sometimes, however, a quite different standard is mistakenly applied—the "before and after" test: what were the costs and benefits before the new facility was constructed, and what will they be afterward? This latter test usually leads to a serious underestimate of the economic benefits of transport investments. It does not take account of the fact that, without the investment, congestion would increase as traffic grows and the existing facilities would deteriorate; these factors would result in higher vehicle operating costs or increased expenditures on maintenance and repairs. For example, in one case in which a new expressway was evaluated, the comparison of costs on the existing highway with those on the new expressway failed to take into account the important fact that increasing congestion on the existing highway would

10. For a fuller discussion of the foregoing points, see Adler, *Economic Appraisal of Transport Projects*.

raise operating expenses considerably by the time the expressway was built. Moreover, operating costs on the existing highway would continue to increase thereafter, while those on the new expressway were likely to remain relatively stable for several years. The "with and without" test showed the expressway to be justified; the "before and after" test indicated the opposite. Similar situations can occur in rail and port investments if operating costs are expected to rise sharply in the absence of the project.

In addition to the problems of measuring the benefits of transport projects, it is necessary to consider how such benefits are distributed among the beneficiaries. Decisions on transport projects often have a significant impact on the distribution of income and wealth. The location of roads or rail lines affects the economic position of people and enterprises on or near the route selected, as well as of those in areas bypassed. The placement of rural roads can be of profound significance in benefiting targeted groups or areas. A different kind of question arises in connection with transport facilities that serve only a very few beneficiaries. When, for example, a new road is essential for marketing the output of a private industrial company, which will account for virtually all the traffic, the costs of building the road should be considered an integral part of the industrial project and recovered fully from the project investor.

A similar issue arises in the distribution of benefits between domestic and foreign users. For example, if improvement of a port reduces the turnaround time of ships, much of the benefit may go initially to foreign shipowners; how much of this benefit is returned to the country paying for the investment depends largely on the degree of competition in shipping. In contrast, improvement in storage facilities at the port can be directly recovered through storage charges paid by shippers and consignees. The distribution of benefits is, therefore, important both in determining the economic justification of an investment and in selecting an appropriate policy of user charges.

In evaluating a transport project that consists of a number of distinct subprojects, a separate economic analysis should be made of each subproject. Otherwise it is possible that the large benefits of one subproject may hide the insufficient benefits of another. For example, in the case of one port expansion project, the engineers recommended the construction of two new wharves. The cost-benefit analysis indicated a satisfactory economic rate of return of about 12 percent. When separate analyses were made for each wharf, however, the rate of return on one was found to be 20 percent, while that on the other was only about 4 percent, even after allowance was made for the extra costs that would be incurred later were it built separately. The second wharf was clearly not justified.

The same principle applies to various degrees of highway upgrading and frequently also to different sections of a highway between two urban centers. Traffic densities and construction conditions on different sections of the highway may vary widely, as may the economic returns even though different design standards are used. (It is possible, however, that an improvement of one section of the road, by stimulating new traffic, could affect other sections; this interrelationship must also be taken into account.) The proper division of a proposed investment into meaningful subprojects must rely heavily on practical experience and judgment since obviously not every possibility can be analyzed.

Valuing savings in journey times can assume considerable importance in aviation and urban transport projects, in which time savings constitute a large part of quantified benefits. Sophisticated, often ingenious methods have been devised to infer time values from the choices travelers make among alternatives that involve tradeoffs between time and cost. But interpreting these choices is not entirely straightforward, and the values to use in the analysis are still subject to debate.[11]

In valuing differences in accident costs, the first problem lies in estimating the difference in frequency and severity of accidents with and without the proposed project. This is primarily an empirical problem, as is estimating the costs of property damage, hospital and medical care, and so on. These empirical problems are made especially difficult by lack of data, particularly for developing countries. Evaluating personal injuries and deaths, while relevant, is very difficult; there is little agreement among experts on how to go about it. Fortunately, this factor is usually not significant in the decision about whether to proceed with a project, unless the investment is directly intended to increase safety.

11. Nail Cengiz Yucel, *A Survey of the Theories and Empirical Investigations of the Value of Travel Time Savings*, World Bank Staff Working Paper no. 199 (Washington, D.C., 1975).

Before and after a slum upgrading program, Manila, Philippines

12

Urbanization

A COMMON CHARACTERISTIC of developing countries is their increasing urbanization. Despite differences in geography, in political systems, and in the level of development, all countries have seen the population and area of their cities and towns expand rapidly during the past twenty-five years. The transfer of population and economic activities from countryside to city has been an important feature of recent economic growth.

The trend toward urbanization appears virtually certain to continue. Globally, the urban share of total population increased from 29 percent in 1950 to 41 percent in 1980, as shown in table 12-1 on the following page. In developing countries, it grew from 17 percent to 31 percent during the same period. While urban growth has slowed considerably in developed countries, the developing countries as a whole continue to experience a substantial rise in their urban population. As a result, although the large majority of the people in developing countries still live in rural areas, more people are being added each year to the urban than to the rural population. This process is accelerating: it has been estimated that more than 1 billion persons will be added to urban areas between 1980 and the year 2000, twice as many as were added between 1960 and 1980. Thus the developing world will be predominantly urban by the end of the century. This is already true in East Asia (except for China) and in Latin America, where in Brazil, Mexico, and Argentina the urban share of the population has reached 65, 67, and 82 percent, respectively. Moreover, the cities have become their own source of growth. Except in parts of Africa, natural population increase has replaced migration as the main engine of population growth in urban areas, although migration continues to contribute significantly.

Even where growth rates have been relatively low, the numbers can be enormous. In absolute terms, South Asia leads. In India, which had 150 million urban residents in 1981 and an annual urban growth rate of 3.8 percent in 1971–81, about two-thirds of its population increase from 1980 to 2000 is expected to occur in urban areas; this means adding about 175 million people. Large increases have also taken place in East Asia, where such metropolitan areas as Manila, Bangkok, and Jakarta have grown to more than 5 million each over the past decade. Shanghai and Beijing demonstrate that, even when strong efforts are made to reduce the number of births, large existing agglomerations with important economic and administrative functions are likely to continue to grow. The 1982 census figures for these cities were 12 million and 9 million, respectively; by the year 2000, populations of 23 million and 20 million, respectively, are forecast.[1]

Very rapid rates of growth, although not the large absolute increases of

1. Figures for 1982 are from the Chinese census; projections for 2000 are from United Nations, *Patterns of Urban and Rural Population Growth* (New York, 1980), table 23; see also *World Development Report 1984*, p. 68.

Table 12-1. *Proportions of Population Living in Urban Areas*

Region	Urban population percentage			
	1950	*1960*	*1970*	*1980*
World	29.0	33.9	37.5	41.3
Developed regions	52.5	58.2	64.7	70.2
Developing regions	16.7	21.9	25.8	30.5
Developing regions without China	19.6	23.4	27.7	32.6
Developing regions without China and India	21.0	26.0	31.3	37.1
Africa	14.5	18.2	22.9	28.9
Latin America	41.2	49.5	57.4	64.7
South Asia without India	14.4	17.7	21.3	25.7
India	16.8	17.9	19.7	22.3
East Asia without Japan and China	28.6	36.3	47.5	58.9
China	11.0	18.6	21.6	25.4

Note: All 1980 data are projections.
Source: United Nations, *Patterns of Urban and Rural Population Growth* (New York, 1980), annex 2, tables 48–50.

Asia and Latin America, are being experienced by cities in other regions—notably in Africa, still the world's least urbanized region. In some African metropolitan areas, growth has been as high as 10 percent a year. The urban populations of African countries, including North Africa, are expected to increase by some 250 percent from 1975 to 2000.[2] This would raise the total urban population in Africa from 104 million in 1975 to 350 million in 2000, an increase equal to about 60 cities the size of Lagos or 250 cities the size of Nairobi. This is a startling conclusion, yet urban demographic projections have, in fact, consistently underestimated the pace of growth. For example, in 1960 French demographers forecast that Abidjan would have a population of 500,000 by 1980, but that number was reached by 1967, and the city had swelled to about 1.8 million by 1980. Similar underestimates have been made for Kinshasa, Dakar, and the large Nigerian cities. Growth of capital cities since independence has been followed by rapid growth of secondary towns, such as Kano, Bouaké, and Mombasa. This explosive growth means that countries that are among the world's poorest are faced with the greatest pressure to adapt their urban institutions to change and to accelerate the provision of urban services.

2. United Nations, Department of International Economic and Social Affairs, *Estimates and Projections of Urban, Rural and City Populations, 1950–2025: The 1980 Assessment* (New York, 1982), table 2.

Economic Aspects

The rapid urbanization described above—accompanied by the growth of primarily urban-based industry and services—has dramatically increased the urban contribution to GDP in the developing countries. It is probably more than 50 percent in virtually every developing country. A rough indication of the urban share of GDP is the contribution of the industry and services sectors, as distinct from that of agriculture, to national output. So defined, the urban share of GDP in 1982 was 67 percent in Kenya, 84 percent in Korea, 93 percent in Mexico, 78 percent in Nigeria, and 79 percent in Turkey.[3] For the low-income developing countries as a group, the share rose from 51 percent in 1960 to 63 percent in 1982. Urban-based activities, including manufacturing, processing, construction, banking, commerce, and other services, will probably continue to grow in importance as economic development progresses. Most significant, the cities have become sources of productive employment for large numbers of people.

If cities perform their functions inefficiently, the entire national economy suffers. The speed of urban expansion has created mounting problems of too few dwellings and services. In neither major cities nor secondary towns has infrastructure kept pace with growth—not in utilities (with the exception, in some cases, of water supply), or transport, or ancillary services. Lagos and Cairo are dramatic illustrations of the consequences of failure to provide adequate urban infrastructure services or to make them work properly. Congestion and service deficiencies hamper the efficiency of production. Along with the inadequacy of urban housing and of health facilities, these circumstances raise the real costs of urban residence and employment, lower productivity or the rate at which it grows, and reduce possible surplus income or profit available for other productive purposes.

The prospect of megacities of historically unprecedented size, such as a Mexico City of more than 20 million people, has focused attention on the question of optimal size from the standpoint of economic efficiency and of physical manageability. Both theoretical and empirical research over the past decade has concluded that there is no optimal city size. The advantages of agglomeration—accessibility to markets, economies of scale, availability of skilled labor—evolve over time in relation to a city's economic base, the availability of services, the city's role within the national economy, and the pace of growth itself. Negative externalities that lower productivity, such as congestion and pollution, may develop at various points in the growth process. But it is misleading to assert that a city has become too big, because there is no reasonable set of criteria on which to base such a judgment. It is more pertinent to observe that a city has become more or less efficient (in terms of the features noted above) as new economic activities develop, as infrastructure is added, and as population grows.

Some policymakers have suggested creating new or satellite towns to serve as alternative destinations for migrants and as sites for growth, to help limit the size of primary cities. This view seems to assume, mistak-

3. *World Development Report 1984*, annex table 3.

enly, that "bigness" is inherently bad. Moreover, the evidence is that the up-front costs of infrastructure and other expenditures required to create a new city are very high. New towns have consumed large amounts of scarce capital, often without providing commensurate economic benefits. Even when capital is available for initial investments, the fact that the revenue base to finance recurrent costs remains very small for many years creates serious problems. Experience in more than a few countries confirms that the justification for such investments can seldom be solely economic. Accordingly, the decision to create new towns should be made only after very careful study.

The pace and scale of urban growth raise the question why rural people have moved to towns in such large numbers. The primary motivation has been the difference in income-earning opportunities. Rural-urban income differentials have exerted a powerful pull toward cities in almost all developing countries. Per capita incomes in urban areas are typically two or three times those in rural areas (though living costs are higher, too), and the disparity can be even greater in the largest city, usually the capital. Labor market studies in many countries suggest that migrants, who tend to be young and relatively highly motivated, often find jobs more easily than locally born residents. In addition, elaborate social systems based on the extended family or on associations of people of shared ethnic or regional origins facilitate the entry of migrants into the urban labor market. Thus, experience generally confirms the migrants' view that the city offers jobs and the hope of a better life.

Migrants leave their villages for secondary towns as well as for metropolitan centers. In some countries, a pattern of stepwise migration can be discerned, with people eventually arriving in the large cities after living for a time in secondary urban centers. The latter may offer better job and income opportunities than can be found in villages, yet not as good as those available in the large cities. Studies of regional development also indicate that secondary towns in productive agricultural regions are able to develop commercial and other tertiary employment that can hold migrants and delay, if not arrest, their move to big cities. This has led to the "market town" thesis: that these towns offer a significant opportunity for deflecting migrants' trajectories toward primary cities. Although this view loses some of its significance as the proportion of urban population growth attributable to natural increase rather than migration rises, it does point to the important role that a healthy agricultural sector plays. Thus the poor performance of much of African agriculture is an important explanation of why men, and subsequently whole households, have left the land for the cities.

This process of urbanization needs to be viewed from a long-term perspective. All developed countries have undergone the change from a predominantly rural to a predominantly urban society; the developing countries are experiencing this change more rapidly, however, and it is superimposed on a faster overall population growth. Historically, for both developed and developing countries, increased GDP and higher levels of economic development have accompanied urbanization. Urbanization is therefore a process to be managed, not an outcome to be deplored. Cities should be regarded not merely as centers of congestion and claimants for heavy budgetary expenditures, but as massive generators of employment and income.

Social Aspects

Inefficient cities tend to be inequitable also. Urban services have all too often benefited only a minority of the population; high standards, and therefore high unit costs, have frequently made these services too expensive for the urban poor. Urban water supply and sanitation services, described in the following chapter, are a good case in point. Politically powerful groups, usually already provided with services, have often obtained government subsidies for higher-standard facilities—utilizing resources that could have been stretched to serve a larger number of people at lower standards. Moreover, upper-income groups can afford alternative solutions to inadequate urban infrastructure; the poor cannot. As a result, the poor pay high prices to private water vendors, their health is impaired by unsanitary living conditions, and they waste long hours traveling on inadequate transport to their place of employment.

Similarly, low-cost housing has often meant units that, even though subsidized, were not affordable by the poor; costs have been low only to the relatively few beneficiaries, who have come from the middle- and upper-income groups. Poorer households that are willing and able to invest in new housing or in the improvement of existing housing are frequently prevented from doing so by the scarcity of serviced land or by public policies—on land acquisition and tenure, building codes, zoning regulations, access to credit, and so on—that do not address their needs.

This situation adds to the number of urban households living in poverty. The physical evidence is found in all regions of the developing world: the major cities are characterized by many thousands of people crowded together in poorly serviced slum areas and in largely unserviced squatter areas. In South Asia, the absolute numbers of urban poor are greatest, while in Latin America and Africa, the proportions are highest. In 75 percent of African cities, for example, more than half the total population lives in squatter settlements.

The linkages and complementarities among infrastructure, shelter, transportation, and social services mean that all of these should be planned together. Households and neighborhoods for which any one of these elements is lacking remain poor. The physical location of housing may determine who will live in it: if services must be brought in from a distance, the cost of delivering them may rise above what the poor can afford. Residences must also be within a reasonable distance of employment. When they are not, the demand for urban transport increases dramatically and consumes a significant share of a household's time and money; it also contributes to already growing national energy costs.

Financial Aspects

Despite the demonstrable importance of the urban contribution to the national economy and the undoubted potential for greatly increasing urban efficiency and productivity, the long-standing urban-rural controversy over the allocation of resources persists. The increasing awareness of urban needs among those in the development community coincided with an emerging consensus among international donors that high priority needed to be given to the rural sector. Advocates of investment in urban infrastructure often met with the response that this would divert scarce resources from rural areas. For their part, rural development advocates have complained of an urban bias in resource allocation, charging that cities are bottomless pits into which scarce national resources disappear. They have pointed not only to the vast amounts of capital invested in subsidized urban infrastructure but also to pricing policies that subsidize food for urban consumers and so discriminate against rural producers. The urban sector has often been perceived, with some justification, as a privileged enclave within the economy.

Population pressures in urban areas have exacerbated the need for large-scale provision of urban services such as water supply, drainage, roads, electricity, and public transportation. Yet public agencies, hampered by insufficient financial resources, have been unable to supply those services—as the spread of poorly serviced residential areas, which are often squatter communities, demonstrates. Competing claims on limited public funds keep the scale of projects too small to cope with the backlog of current needs, let alone to satisfy any significant portion of future requirements.

Given the high level of demand for urban services and housing, it is not surprising that, in most cases, the budgetary resources provided by the central government do not cover more than a fraction of the needs. Individual cities are attempting to become more nearly self-sufficient financially and to meet a larger portion of both capital and recurrent expenditures from local resources. There is considerable scope in most cities for increasing user charges for urban public services and for raising more local taxes without increasing the relative tax burden on the poor. The available data indicate that the urban poor pay somewhere between 8 and 12 percent of their income in the form of taxes—a greater proportion than the rural poor pay, and not much less than what middle-income groups in urban areas pay.[4] The urban poor are generally not reached by direct taxation such as income and wealth taxes, but they contribute considerably through indirect taxes such as import duties, sales taxes, sumptuary taxes (on such items as tobacco, alcoholic beverages, and gambling), and other excise taxes. Since municipalities are often forced to rely on indirect taxes—the only major exception being the real property tax—local government levies add heavily to the taxes paid by the poor.

The problem of resource mobilization is often complicated by an intricate web of fiscal relations between the national government and municipalities. On the one hand, many national governments claim for their use some of the taxes collected in cities. This is the pattern in many countries with French or Spanish traditions, where local governments are closely tied to the administrative and political authority of ministries of the interior. In Burkina or Senegal, for example, municipal governments are required to turn over to the national government most of the revenue they collect, including proceeds of sales and fuel taxes; they retain only income from property taxes and certain license fees. Moreover, most property of the national government is tax exempt, which severely reduces potential sources of local revenue. On the other hand, many national governments allocate a part of their revenues to local governments for various purposes and to varying extents.

---

4. Johannes F. Linn, *Cities in the Developing World: Policies for Their Equitable and Efficient Growth* (New York: Oxford University Press for the World Bank, 1983), p. 74.

Institutional Aspects

Institutions operating within urban areas or concerned with one or another aspect of the urban sector—roads, water supply, electricity, education, health, municipal markets, public transportation—have proliferated. They are found at a variety of levels, from the municipal through the regional or provincial to the national, and typically there is little overall coordination. Municipal governments, usually the only institutions with jurisdiction over many of the subsectors within a city, have historically been poorly staffed and underfinanced. Where the financial and technical responsibilities for operating and maintaining facilities and services lie, and what the scope of those responsibilities is, have been unclear. Fragmentation of responsibility among many public institutions, often at different levels of government, has impeded integrated planning and coordinated action. Citywide investments have been made without due consideration of how one relates to another or what future needs might be. When a multiplicity of agencies share responsibility, with each playing a small, albeit significant, role, achieving effective coordination is an uphill task.

The institutional problems may be illustrated by reference to urban transport, and specifically to traffic management. It is now widely recognized that many of the serious traffic problems plaguing cities can be alleviated without large-scale investment in infrastructure by introducing simple measures to reduce congestion and improve traffic flows. Project planners may find, however, that several ministries or municipal agencies have full or partial responsibility for various aspects of traffic management. The assignment of responsibility may sometimes be clear, but more often responsibilities overlap, with the result that there is inadequate coordination both in planning and in resource allocation and the traffic problems are slow to be resolved.

In the urban sector, as in any other, the effectiveness of efforts toward improvement depends on the existence and capacity of appropriate institutions. The variety of urban investment needs, the differences in extent of urbanization and of institutional development, and the diversity of urban conditions mean that prescriptions must be designed to suit individual situations. The appropriate solutions will vary from country to country—perhaps from city to city—but strengthening and improving coordination among the several agencies responsible for urban development must be common ingredients.

DEVELOPMENT OBJECTIVES

The primary objectives in the sector can be succinctly stated: to increase the productivity of cities and to meet or more nearly meet, at an affordable cost, the needs of a growing urban population, particularly of the urban poor. These twin objectives of greater efficiency and greater equity imply a need for improved mobilization, allocation, and management of resources, and for improved coordination among the agencies responsible for citywide investments in shelter, transport, and infrastructure. To accomplish this, many governments may have to adopt a broader perspective, reorienting their thinking toward integrated solutions to urban problems rather than approaching each subsector separately. Such integrated solutions will require policy changes to achieve more appropriate pricing and better cost recovery. Revisions in laws and regulations will be needed to encourage greater participation by the private sector and to ease land acquisition and the granting of secure tenure to private households. Improving and strengthening the institutional framework are also imperative for effective program and project implementation, as well as for adequate cost recovery and maintenance, particularly if programs are to be replicated on a scale that comports with the pace of urban growth. In planning investments, emphasis needs to be placed on ending demolition of squatter settlements and upgrading them instead, on curtailing overly ambitious infrastructure programs—especially in urban transport—and on encouraging the use of appropriate technology and design standards to keep unit costs low and services affordable to the urban poor.

POLICY ISSUES

We have often noted in preceding chapters that a project, no matter how well designed, cannot be successfully implemented if prevailing policies tend to frustrate its objectives. In the urban sector, there have been many such policies—for example, zoning laws, building codes, and credit policies—that overregulate the use of urban resources and discriminate against the poor. Programs or projects that are permitted to bypass such policy constraints, but are not accompanied by broader policy reform, result in enclave activities that are not easily replicable. (They also frequently provide windfall gains to the beneficiaries; in such cases, the poor are often under pressure to sell their newly acquired land or housing—at a profit to them, but contrary to the purpose of the project.) The following sections examine some of the more urgently needed policy changes.

Public versus Private Resources

Limited public resources for the sector would obviously go further if more of the financial burden were shifted to private sources. Many services—such as electricity, water supply, urban road and rail infrastructure, and telecommunications—cannot readily be provided by private sources; but others can. Shelter is a prime example of the latter. In most countries, public institutions are unable to make housing available on a scale commensurate with the demand arising from rapid urban population growth. Some countries have active public shelter programs, but these rarely meet more than 10 percent of the annual demand. Indeed, urban governments can generally act only in an indirect and limited way to increase the supply of housing—by acquiring urban land, for example, or arranging for clear land titles. Consequently, most housing in developing countries is provided by a variety of private means. Governments can most usefully concentrate on supplying those services that the private sector cannot provide—such as neighborhood roads, drains, water supply and sanitation systems, and off-site services like markets or schools—as well as on adopting regulations that permit and encourage private

initiatives. Actual housing construction should be left to private enterprises, cooperatives, or households themselves.

Some interesting programs have been undertaken in the Philippines
and Morocco, where public agencies extend guaranteed credit to private
construction firms as a way of encouraging them to build low-cost shelter.
The Ministry of Human Settlements in the Philippines has promoted a
system of "private sites and services," under which private firms agree
to build specified numbers of shelter units at specified costs for lower-
income groups. A similar scheme is being carried out in Morocco, where
a public hotel construction agency administers lines of credit to small
firms building housing according to publicly approved design standards
and costs. Both schemes reflect increasing government interest in developing a public-private partnership in the housing sector.

Financial Policies

Pricing

Governments, as we have noted in earlier chapters, should normally
seek to set prices of public services in accordance with marginal cost to
achieve the most efficient use of resources. The constrained financial
position of most municipalities and the need to serve ever larger demands
from growing populations lead governments at times to pursue, though
not often to achieve, pricing policies under which users are charged the
average total cost of services, comprising fixed capital costs as well as
operating costs.

Much more common, however, is the tendency of municipalities deliberately to set charges far below either the marginal or the average cost of
the services provided. This is often defended on the grounds that it benefits
the poor. On balance, however, the subsidies involved—for public housing,
public utilities, urban roads, secondary and tertiary education, and modern
hospital care—favor the wealthier income groups. These groups have the
political or economic influence to draw services into their neighborhoods.
They can also preempt public housing, benefit disproportionately from
their ownership of urban land that increases in value owing to the
subsidized services, or utilize services the poor cannot easily afford even
when subsidized (higher education, hospitals, use of streets by a private
automobile). The elimination of subsidies for urban public services would
in many cases provide additional revenues mainly from the more affluent;
in addition, cost-related pricing would curtail demand for services and help
increase efficiency in resource allocation.

An exception to the rule of pricing public services at marginal cost can
be to set lifeline rates for a minimum level of consumption. This usually
involves cross-subsidization, the higher income groups paying more while
the poor pay less. (In principle, a similar differential pricing tactic could
be followed between two or more different service accounts: for example,
bus fare collections could be used to meet deficits in the water accounts.
But because separate agencies are usually responsible for the different
services and each has its own problems in collecting charges from users,
this is rarely possible or desirable.)

As unit costs of urban services fall—with economies of scale, better
organization, or a different choice of technology—governments are in a

better position to recover costs, but only if they have the political will and administrative capacity to do so. Whether cost recovery for urban services is desirable is no longer an issue in many countries; the question is how to do it. We shall return to this question in connection with the issue of project replicability (see the section on "Investment Issues" below).

Taxation

Since municipalities will probably continue to have difficulty in collecting sufficient revenues from charges for public services to cover costs and to finance steady expansion, they should look for other ways to strengthen their revenue base. We noted earlier that the urban poor already pay a relatively high proportion of their income in the form of taxes. Tax measures can be designed to shift more of the burden from lower-income groups to those who can better afford it. Governments can exempt basic necessities, such as unprocessed foodstuffs, from general sales taxes, import duties, and other indirect taxes; these items absorb a large share of the budget of the poor. Ensuring that sumptuary taxes are restricted to items of luxury consumption and reducing or eliminating local excise and nuisance taxes, which frequently have a regressive impact, will also help alleviate the tax burden on the poor.

To raise more public revenues, reliance on taxes whose impact can be progressive—such as property taxes, taxes on automobile ownership and use, and various types of benefit taxes—is desirable. These taxes constitute excellent but often neglected possibilities for augmenting the resources of municipalities. Real estate taxation, especially urban land taxation, has the advantage of being hard to evade if properly administered. Yet average property tax rates tend to be extremely low in cities in developing countries compared with those in developed countries.

As for automobile ownership and operation, this is an urban phenomenon in all developing countries; use is heavily concentrated in the largest cities and has grown much faster than city populations. Automobiles constitute the overwhelming proportion of the urban motor vehicle fleet, and typically are owned by people in the upper-income class. Urban traffic congestion and pollution are often as bad in developing as in developed countries. Special attention to automotive taxation—through fuel taxes, automobile licensing and ownership transfer taxes, and other taxes related to automobile use—can yield substantial revenues. In addition, congestion charges, along with area licensing fees and parking fees, can add both to revenues and to urban efficiency. Improvement of neighborhood streets and even major arterial roads may best be financed from betterment levies—that is, taxes based on the increase in the value of property as a result of public investment—as is widely done, for example, in cities in Colombia. National authorities would have to agree that cities could retain enough of the revenues from such taxes to cover the costs incurred by the cities as a result of automobile traffic.

Public Expenditure

Although taxes are important, the main potential for improving the equity and efficiency of urban growth lies on the expenditure side of the public budget and in related regulatory and pricing policies for urban services, especially for transport, housing, and social services. Careful policy analysis is required to ensure that public expenditures made ostensibly on behalf of the poor will actually reach them and that the welfare of as many of the poor as possible will be improved. In the past, urban policies have frequently dictated bulldozing slums, banning street vendors and traditional modes of transport, and building high-cost housing, subways, and limited-access highways—all measures that have primarily served the interests of the wealthier residents. In place of these approaches, urban investment, along with pricing and regulatory policies, can and should be designed to assist those forms of transport, housing, sanitation, and other services that meet the needs of a majority of the urban population at costs they can afford.[5] (Some examples of investment programs to meet the needs of the urban poor are discussed below under "Investment Issues.") Such measures always encounter opposition from groups with substantial political clout, but most municipalities have little choice but to move, slowly but surely, in this direction.

Housing Finance

Housing finance presents many difficult problems in developing countries. In publicly financed projects to provide urban shelter, funds typically flow from central or municipal budgets, or both, and in some cases from external lenders, to a public agency for on-lending to individuals for housing construction, frequently through an intermediary such as a housing bank or a housing corporation. More attention needs to be paid, however, to how housing is financed in the country as a whole. Such issues as the availability of credit for housing construction, especially to the poor, the way in which the housing finance system relates to the national financial system, and the macroeconomic effects of housing finance need to be better understood. Conventional lending institutions frequently lend for housing at low interest rates and for long periods— for example, 7 or 8 percent annual interest for twenty-five years—in sharp contrast to the informal housing finance market, whose interest rates are frequently much higher and maturities much shorter. Given the difficulties that conventional lending institutions face in attracting savings at rates compatible with their low on-lending terms, it is not surprising that they do not have sufficient resources to reach a large part of the housing market. The rates in the informal housing finance market indicate that low-income households have a high demand for credit and some ability to pay. Accordingly, an objective of government policy should be to integrate special project-related housing finance mechanisms into the general housing finance market, to the extent possible. Governments should also seek to supplement and strengthen—not supplant—the informal finance market, even supplying it with funds to enable it to do more.

Some countries have sought to mobilize private savings through mechanisms such as savings and loan associations, which, among other things, enable the poor to demonstrate their dependability by making regular payments to their accounts. This performance serves as a criterion for

---

5. Linn, *Cities in the Developing World*, p. xv.

construction loans from financial institutions, which traditionally have been wary about lending to the poor without collateral. While high rates of inflation have created difficulties for these mechanisms in Latin America, they have nevertheless served to mobilize private savings elsewhere (as in Nigeria and the Ivory Coast). Such efforts need to be supported by laws permitting housing construction in stages, to allow households to make maximum use of their savings.

Land Acquisition and Tenure

In urban housing projects, land acquisition and subsequent granting of secure tenure to households have proved to be encumbered with legal and traditional constraints that, unless resolved, can effectively block construction. Clouded title, absence of official maps and registration, legal challenges to expropriation, disputes over compensation, traditional customs such as communal ownership or occupancy rights, and local complexities concerning sanctioned forms of land tenure have all served to thwart the start-up of urban housing construction in countries as diverse as India, Burkina, and Ecuador. Experience suggests the importance of resolving land issues before projects are initiated. In many countries, this will require extensive changes in public policy regarding land.

It has often been difficult for the urban poor to acquire security of land tenure in any form, even an occupancy permit or a long-term lease, much less a freehold right. In addition, building codes that prohibit use of low-cost materials and set high standards for construction have often forced the poor to build "illegal" units. Zoning regulations have contributed to this pattern by establishing residential districts far from where jobs are located. The poor, who cannot afford high daily transportation costs, have settled on empty or only partially occupied sites, likewise illegal but closer to job opportunities. They have had limited access to credit for housing construction not only because of their poverty but also for reasons related to their illegal status.

Regularization of tenure rights on land that is publicly owned but occupied by squatters is often a way to improve the housing conditions of the squatters. Tenure security and ownership rights act as incentives for making improvements and permit better access to capital markets since the new owner-occupants are able to offer their land as collateral. World Bank–assisted urban development projects in Cairo, Manila, Rabat, and Lázaro Cárdenas in Mexico, to mention just a few, provide numerous examples of this approach. To ensure that the effect is not to encourage more squatting on public land, it has been found useful to require some payment in exchange for conferring the land title. This is made more palatable when combined with measures to upgrade living conditions, such as improving public services. The urban development project in Cairo is particularly interesting: payments for regularization of land titles in squatter areas on public land are expected to bring a sizable surplus to the executing agency within a relatively short period, which can be used to finance upgrading programs for squatter areas elsewhere.

Where privately owned land is occupied by squatters, the regularization of tenure also requires negotiation with and compensation of the owners. The Rabat urban development project is a case in point. Although government acquisition of private land generally takes a long time, in Morocco legal instruments permit "provisional public acquisition," a procedure similar to expropriation that gives the government considerable strength in bargaining over acquisition prices and timing. The existence of a legal framework permitting such public action is obviously important, but is often absent in developing countries.

Finally, complementary action to strengthen the cadastral services in urban areas is often an essential component of public land policy. The absence of valid land registration, property surveys, and land assessment records not only creates uncertainty about tenure rights and reduces the usefulness of land as collateral in borrowing, it also impedes the functioning of the land market (by interfering with real estate transactions) and hinders property taxation.[6] Improvements in urban real estate registers, however, are often useful only when combined with efforts to regularize tenure rights. Concerted action is therefore needed. Fragmentation of responsibility among various public agencies has often hampered a coordinated approach in this as in other areas of urban policy action.

Creating Jobs

As noted earlier, cities function as massive generators of employment. The migration they have stimulated has contributed historically to alleviating what would be even worse poverty than now exists in the countryside in most developing countries. Nevertheless, unemployment and underemployment (the latter reflected in swollen numbers working in the informal sector at very low levels of productivity) are pervasive problems in most cities in the developing world.

Efforts made under urban projects to create jobs through measures to support small businesses, as described below, have generally been disappointing. It is just as important to understand what cannot be accomplished through measures specific to a particular city or project as to understand what can. There has been a growing recognition that the objective of increasing urban employment is best subsumed within the broader goal of improving urban productivity; indeed, it should be tied in with national efforts in this regard. Solving the problem of urban unemployment calls for coordinated action at both the municipal and the national levels to address the issues of labor demand, labor supply, and labor market imperfections.

Many of the constraints on private sector development in fact originate from inefficiencies in the public sector, including technical inadequacies in the output and distribution of services and economic distortions associated with incorrect pricing policies. These inefficiencies increase the costs of engaging in productive activity in urban areas and reduce opportunities for employment and income generation. In some cases, improvements in telephone service, in traffic management, or in the availability of electricity and water may be a more effective way to promote industrial and commercial growth, and hence employment, than direct support to the private sector. The extent to which this is possible must be based on an analysis of local conditions.

6. See Harold Dunkerly, ed., *Urban Land Policy: Issues and Opportunities* (New York: Oxford University Press for the World Bank, 1983).

INSTITUTIONAL ISSUES

Special Project Units

The question whether projects should be executed by existing agencies or by special project units is not unique to the urban sector, but is complicated by the existence of citywide institutions with separate responsibility for various components of an urban project. Many urban projects (including several with which the World Bank has been associated and which are described below) have been given special status within national and municipal institutional structures. Emphasis on construction and engineering capability has frequently led governments to assign a project to an agency that can take responsibility for project construction but not for subsequent operation and maintenance or cost recovery—functions that must be performed by established institutions designated for the purpose. National ministries or development agencies have frequently been designated to execute projects because municipal institutions were considered technically and financially weak as well as more susceptible to local political pressures. As a result, even when project implementation has been efficient, the necessary follow-up activities have not always materialized owing to a failure to strengthen the municipal units responsible for them. What is required is a long-term effort to strengthen municipal agencies through technical assistance and training in operations, maintenance, and financial management.

Management and Coordination

Experience cited in this chapter demonstrates the need for a broad perspective in undertaking improvements in the urban sector in developing countries. Progress toward the multiple objectives of an urban strategy requires the coordinated management of many interdependent policies, actors, and resources. Many factors outside the control of municipal authorities play a large role in determining the rate of growth, the increase in employment opportunities, and the improved functioning and productivity of cities; among these are regional economic endowments, public and private investment patterns, and changes in the transport network.[7] The national government controls some of the most relevant policy instruments: trade protection, capital market policies, national public investment and taxation, education and health policies, and so on. Other important determinants of urban efficiency are within the purview of the city: management of central city congestion; improvement of public utility services and road infrastructure financed by appropriate, cost-related charges; administration of local taxes, regulations, and pricing policies so that all residents of the city are benefited; and encouragement or provision of housing, marketing, and other facilities. These matters do not in general require intervention by higher levels of government unless, as is too often the case, constraints on local revenue and expenditure authority limit local freedom of action.

The quality of management by urban authorities has a crucial effect on

---

7. See Bertrand M. Renaud, *National Urbanization Policy in Developing Countries* (New York: Oxford University Press for the World Bank, 1982).

how these tasks are carried out, and therefore on how a city grows. There can be little doubt that the past failure of urban management in such cities as Calcutta or Barranquilla, for example, has contributed heavily to the poor performance of these cities compared with that of, say, Bombay or Medellín, where urban management has been of higher quality. A comprehensive approach to improving urban management across the board is required in many cities. Social objectives must be translated into an institutional, policy, and investment framework. This is the essence of urban management; improving this process remains the central goal of efforts in this sector.

Urban investments often include the construction of a variety of facilities such as roads, water supply systems, electric power generation and distribution, schools, clinics, and municipal markets, each of which, as we have noted, is the responsibility of a different public agency. This creates a continuing and difficult problem of coordination both during and after the construction phase. Locating urban investments on appropriate sites and executing them in an efficient sequence are critical to improving the productivity of the investments. Examples of poorly coordinated investments abound: industrial areas without access to roads or water, residential areas without transport facilities or schools, and so on. Agencies responsible for installing water mains frequently ignore their sister agencies responsible for building and maintaining the streets under which the mains will run.

Although interagency coordination can present formidable political and bureaucratic problems in urban areas, its absence results in delayed and inefficient use of investments and constitutes one of the most frequent failures of urban management. Few municipalities have, for example, an effective approach to resolving such questions as how the supplies of urban transport, housing, and social services can be rationed efficiently and equitably at the city level, while at the same time extending the delivery of these services more rapidly to those areas and groups least adequately served. Similarly, accessible and well-serviced land for industrial, commercial, and residential use is essential to the efficient and equitable growth of urban areas—yet few cities are in a position to manage urban land in its manifold dimensions: land transfer and tenure regulation, public investment decisions, taxes and user charges, and so on.

Some national governments and municipalities have created coordinating bodies to assist in improving urban management. Usually, this takes the form of a planning agency with well-defined statutory functions and its own resource base, which permits it to collect and disseminate information throughout the metropolis, to develop plans for action and financing, and to enforce interagency agreements. The metropolitan authorities recently created in Calcutta, Manila, and Tunis show that such measures are feasible and can help to improve urban administration and management.

Finally, there is a continuing need to increase coordination and cooperation between municipal and national authorities for finance, planning, and other functions germane to urban resource management. The extent and importance of the issues facing urban management call for commensurate attention from the highest decisionmaking bodies of the central

government. All too often, the national ministries with oversight responsibility for local governments enter into an adversary relationship with
their local counterparts, confining themselves to supervision and control,
rather than establishing a spirit of cooperation, support, and assistance.
Municipal governments badly need technical assistance for financial and
personnel management, land use planning, infrastructure investment and
operation, and manpower training. One successful model for this type of
assistance has been the Venezuelan Municipal Development Agency, an
autonomous public agency that has provided technical assistance and
training in accounting and budgeting, in cadastral and property tax
systems, and in local regulatory and planning procedures.

Training

Although a consensus has evolved that training in disciplines relevant
to the urban sector should be a priority activity, relatively little action has
been taken. Efforts sponsored by the United Nations, the World Bank's
Economic Development Institute, and national training institutions are
not nearly on the scale required to increase significantly the number of
trained personnel. In some cases, training has been offered in classical
disciplines such as architecture or engineering with little attention to the
more operational aspects of providing shelter and urban services, such as
land packaging and surveying, construction financing, community organization, or traffic engineering and management skills. Moreover, in
many countries (Nigeria and Kenya are examples), personnel trained in
urban-related disciplines have left public sector jobs to work in private
firms where compensation is higher. It is unlikely that public sector
salaries will be able to match those in the private sector for some time to
come, if ever. As a result, competence in requisite skills is increasing
much faster in the private sector. While some loss of trained personnel to
the private sector is inevitable, and not without benefit, it means both that
the training effort needs to be expanded and that more emphasis needs
to be put on incentives—and perhaps also on penalties, although it is
difficult to make them effective—to encourage trained personnel to
remain in public service.

INVESTMENT ISSUES

Planning Urban Investments

Experience in countries as diverse as Turkey, Ivory Coast, Malaysia,
and Kenya has demonstrated that comprehensive master planning of
urban investments is a slow, complex process that cannot keep pace with
the rapid changes in growing cities. Furthermore, urban planning traditionally has tended to emphasize the physical aspects; this has often
diverted attention from the more important policy, institutional, and
financial problems that ultimately set limits on the amount that can be
effectively invested. A Bank review of sophisticated urban economic
models devised during the 1960s led to the conclusion that they had little
relevance for developing countries. Governments may more usefully
focus on the need to plan and coordinate specific, complementary

investments for specific periods in shelter, infrastructure, transport, business support, and social services. Doing this calls for

- Relating the scale of planned investments to resource availability
- Emphasizing short- and medium-term priorities consistent with several long-term options rather than devising a single, optimum long-term plan
- Paying attention to complementarities and other interrelationships among different types of investment
- Setting pricing and other policies that encourage private activity in desired directions.

If a municipality follows this course, it can develop an approach to urban management in which decisions on the location and timing of new investments are taken with a practical view to making the city work better—for its residents and for the economic and other activities centered there. Improved efficiency of production in the urban sector, for example, is linked to the location of productive facilities. Private decisions on investing in housing take account of the location of employment opportunities, while public decisions concerning such matters as neighborhood density, space, and utilities affect people's need for transportation to jobs as well as access to schools, food markets, health facilities, and so on. Most urban employment creation—whether in Bogotá, Seoul, or Abidjan—occurs on the periphery of cities, where land costs are lower, rather than in the central districts. That being so, residential developments should likewise be sited on the periphery, with transport networks designed not radially but circumferentially, establishing links around the periphery instead of primarily to the downtown areas.

Project Design Features

Replicability

Experience has shown the importance of a coordinated approach to urban management that takes account of the many distinctive features of urban areas and pulls them together within a sound financial framework. It has also underscored the need to expand dramatically the size of programs and projects that provide services and shelter; these now satisfy only a fraction of the demand and are failing to keep pace with its rise. Without greatly expanded efforts, urban growth will overwhelm the capacity of cities to meet the needs of their populations.

Two essential and complementary elements in replicating urban investment programs and projects on a substantially enlarged scale are, first, the use of appropriate technology and designs to reduce costs to the minimum required to provide low-standard but adequate service that the intended beneficiaries can afford; and, second, a determined effort to recover, through taxes and user charges, the costs incurred. Only in this way can developing countries afford to extend urban services to a significantly larger proportion of the vast numbers of people requiring them. These elements are examined below; a third element needed for large-scale expansion of efforts—training of staff—has already been discussed.

Technology and Design Standards

It is fair to say that the design standards used today in the towns and cities of most developing countries are unnecessarily high, that they result in costs which are not affordable—since they do not allow replication on the large scale required—and that few developing countries are devoting adequate attention to adopting technologies that will enable services to be provided more cheaply.

The use of criteria such as minimum levels of per capita water consumption or living space, generally adopted from industrialized countries, may appear sound, yet technical design standards based on them could lead to financial disaster for municipal or other government agencies unable to recover their costs and for households unable to pay their bills. What is "appropriate" technically must also encompass what is financially appropriate given the income of the users. How appropriate technology has been applied to urban shelter and transport investments is discussed below under "Lessons of Project Experience"; its application to urban water and sanitation investments is discussed in the next chapter.

Experimentation in housing construction, particularly in ways to reduce costs, should be promoted. In many countries, the high cost of materials such as cement, wood, and nails makes construction prohibitively expensive for the poor, especially since, as noted earlier, building codes have traditionally required the use of such high-cost materials. Other, cheaper materials need to be developed. As to new construction methods, progress has been made, for example, with prefabricated housing in developed countries—but almost nowhere in the developing countries has such housing been made affordable by the poor. Designers and builders of shelter must become increasingly committed to the search for new and more appropriate solutions.

The exchange of information and of technology among and within countries can do much to further the search for new design solutions. Experience gained by various countries during the 1970s needs to be communicated to the agencies, neighborhoods, and individuals concerned with providing shelter and services to large numbers of low-income households. Many projects have devised new approaches that can be applied elsewhere. Demonstration shelter projects in Senegal and Mali have attracted wide attention in francophone West Africa; shelter projects in Kenya, Zambia, and Botswana have demonstrated new possibilities in East Africa; projects in Madras have drawn observers from elsewhere in India and in South Asia interested in learning how effective solutions can be applied on a large scale. At the global level, the 1976 United Nations Conference on Human Settlements at Vancouver, and its follow-up, have disseminated useful information. It is nonetheless clear that sharing experience and establishing networks of concerned groups and individuals must be a priority in the 1980s.

Cost Recovery

Even projects that are designed to be affordable by the intended beneficiaries are unlikely to result in cost recovery if the requisite administrative organization and mechanisms for collection are not in place and functioning effectively. The capacity and willingness of participating households to pay are necessary but not sufficient conditions for effective cost recovery. This is confirmed by comparing the record on cost recovery in sites and services projects—which provide basic infrastructure and serviced sites on which private individuals can build their own housing—with that in slum upgrading projects. (These two types of projects are described more fully below.) In sites and services projects, households are self-selected and have a high degree of interest in investing to improve their residences. Their payment record on the whole has been good, although if the new communities have not been maintained, or if promised social services have not been provided, households have tended to be less regular in their payments. In upgraded slum neighborhoods, some households have inevitably objected to paying for improvements they had not requested or did not consider necessary. And even among the majority of households that agreed to pay, there were some laggards. Yet little can be done to compel payment short of eviction, which is impractical politically. It will, therefore, often be found preferable in such projects to charge for specific services—such as water and sewerage—rather than for the upgrading investment generally.

Community Participation

Active community involvement at all stages of project design and implementation is probably the most effective (although not a guaranteed) way to develop and maintain commitment for cost recovery. This was demonstrated by a sites and services project in El Salvador, in which households were committed to the project from its outset and understood the need for cost recovery; community organizations played a major role in various aspects of the project including collections (see also chapter 22, Social Analysis). Other community organizations have played similar roles in Senegal, the Philippines, and elsewhere. Mutual-help construction (several families working together as a team) has contributed to a sense of community at the same time as it has promoted other objectives. In addition, specific measures to strengthen community institutions have helped foster a high rate of debt repayment.

In the rush to prepare and initiate urban projects, however, too little attention has generally been directed to encouraging household and community participation, especially when it comes to the design of improvement programs. This absence of community involvement, frequently reflected in a "top down" public works program, has resulted in a relatively low level of neighborhood commitment in some projects. As a consequence, these projects have encountered problems not only in cost recovery, but also in maintenance and, in some cases, in a lack of social cohesion in the neighborhoods.

In contrast, when projects have incorporated community participation, most of them have proved highly effective and have led to other kinds of improvements. Recent studies of credit unions in some African cities, as well as the effective use of neighborhood groups in recent projects in Lahore and Addis Ababa, suggest that there is a large untapped potential in this field. Community participation helps to create an organizational structure and a momentum that continue after project activities are concluded. It can facilitate completion of public facilities such as community buildings, and it can make an important difference in obtaining or providing through community resources such services as garbage collection and street lighting. It can promote a community's capacity for self-management and provide the basis for a sense of mutual responsibility that makes the community a more vital place in which to live. The number of people participating in the process of improving urban living conditions needs to be increased, and this can be achieved only through direct involvement of neighborhoods at the design, construction, and implementation stages.

Employment

More than half the urban projects that the World Bank has assisted have had as one of their objectives to support small businesses as a way of increasing employment opportunities in urban areas. Direct measures have included provision of services to land used for business purposes, construction of markets and sheds, and greater access to credit, as well as technical assistance and training. Other efforts to promote employment as part of urban development projects have taken a variety of forms, such as location of project sites near business districts, integration of residential with commercial or industrial development, and promotion of the construction industry. These efforts were experimental and have had only limited success; in most instances, the employment objectives have not been achieved, and there is growing recognition that the problem of creating new jobs in urban areas can most effectively be addressed through the macroeconomic and industrial policy approaches discussed earlier.

One reason for the lack of success is that these business-support components have been relatively small and therefore without enough leverage to initiate needed changes in the policy or institutional framework. The provision of credit illustrates the problem. The limited amount of credit made available under a typical project has not given participating lending institutions sufficient incentive to modify their procedures to facilitate lending to small entrepreneurs, nor has it induced project authorities to make sufficient effort to ensure that the funds would be efficiently used, that goods and services would be produced and marketed, or that financial returns would be accounted for properly. Yet when business-support components have sought to deal with all the steps in the process, they have turned out to be cumbersome and have added substantially to the organizational problems faced by already overburdened municipal institutions. In recent projects, accordingly, the use of such components has generally been limited to the construction of market sites for small businesses.

Complexity

Experience demonstrates the importance of keeping projects manageable by striving for realistic design and prompt implementation. The difficulty of doing so is that frequently several components must be included if the project is to succeed. Shelter projects, for example, must address such concerns as appropriate location, secure tenure, effective credit mechanisms, provision of roads, water, and sanitation, and availability of schools, markets, and so on. But planners must be selective, resisting the temptation to include components that, while worthwhile, are not clearly needed to achieve the central objectives of the project. It is also useful to view a project as one in a series of interventions; then certain elements or services can appropriately be excluded from an initial project and taken up in subsequent ones.

Lessons of Project Experience

In response to the diversity of concerns in the urban sector, four principal types of projects were developed and implemented by governments with Bank assistance during the 1970s: projects for urban shelter, projects for urban transport, integrated urban projects, and regional development projects. Although these projects received external assistance, they have the merit that the foreign exchange content of their cost is relatively low. These projects have proved to be within the capacity of national governments to organize and implement, and experience with them has provided valuable lessons. One clear lesson is that such projects, no matter how well designed, depend for their long-run success on simultaneously improving the ability of institutions in the sector to staff their operations with qualified personnel, to plan and budget effectively, and to carry out their implementation responsibilities. In the following paragraphs we examine some of the more specific lessons learned in each of the four types of projects.

Shelter Projects

The shelter projects address a twofold need: to improve existing substandard units and to create new units. The first of these has been addressed by slum upgrading projects, which not only provide residents with tenure and better access to credit for remodeling or improving their housing but also upgrade infrastructure—water supply, sewerage, electricity, roads, and sidewalks. The conventional attitude that slum areas are a blight and should be torn down is extremely wasteful and anti-economic. The advantage of upgrading projects, besides their lower unit costs, is that—since demolition is minimal—they allow households to remain in place while infrastructure is being extended. Representative unit costs amounted to about $38 per person for improving infrastructure and to about $1,000 per unit for improving housing in the late 1970s.

The second need, to create new housing stock, has been addressed by sites and services projects, which provide both necessary infrastructure and serviced sites on which families are encouraged to construct their own homes. Under some projects, a core housing unit, consisting, for example, of one room with toilet and shower for $1,000–$2,000, is also provided. Representative costs for core units of this type contrast sharply with costs of $10,000 or more for conventional low-cost houses of several rooms.

Both types of shelter project help to provide affordable housing and infrastructure to low-income residents by mobilizing their own savings together with institutional credit. Construction is done by artisans or firms hired by the residents, supplemented by their own efforts and those of their extended families and neighbors. Both approaches require that households be given security of tenure as an incentive for investing their time and their savings; and both require that households pay for publicly provided infrastructure and for the core unit, if there is one, and that they finance the remainder of the housing construction or improvement. The evidence is that if land tenure is ensured and if building codes or zoning regulations are revised to eliminate unaffordable standards, households will respond by investing in shelter, often to an extent well beyond what the income of the principal wage earners would suggest. Indeed, many also build extra rooms for rental purposes.

The design of a project varies with the income level of the beneficiary households. In sites and services projects, estimated household incomes are taken as an indicator of capacity to pay; project designers are given cost parameters within which choices are made among standards of water supply, sanitation, plot size, and room size—all of which add up to shelter costs and monthly mortgage and utility payments. Tradeoffs between, for example, private water connections and larger plots are common, with some households preferring the convenience of a private connection while others desire land for future development. Multiple tradeoffs are possible within projects; each alternative can be priced according to service standards and location. Differential pricing permits charging more to higher-income families, thereby generating surpluses that can be used to subsidize services for the poorer residents. Commercial plots, as noted, can also be included in projects to generate such surpluses.

Between mid-1972 and mid-1980, the World Bank helped twenty-nine developing countries to provide approximately 310,000 lots through the sites and services approach and to improve some 780,000 lots through urban upgrading efforts. Given ten people per lot, which is probably a conservative figure, more than 10 million people were expected to benefit from these projects at a total project cost of about $2.5 billion. Despite many implementation problems, both types of project have met with reasonable success. They have proved to be feasible alternatives to the spread of uncontrolled, unserviced settlements on the one hand and traditional, so-called low-cost housing on the other. The approaches are complementary: adding new housing reduces the incidence of squatter settlements and thus the need for upgrading, while improving existing housing reduces the need for new units. Governments are coming to recognize the merits of dealing with the shelter problem in both ways.

The available data indicate that, in all the countries concerned, the projects were able to reach considerably poorer groups than did conventional housing programs. Slum upgrading projects have had a somewhat better record than sites and services projects in reaching the very poor—although the major difference is that upgrading projects, with a lower cost per household benefited, generally reach a larger total number of beneficiaries.[8]

Both types of project have experienced some leakage of their benefits to households with incomes in the upper half of the income range. (It is estimated that, on the average, about 20 percent of the plots in sites and services projects have gone to such households.) To the extent that the projects were designed to improve overall conditions in the urban housing markets, this is not a serious concern. But most of the projects were

8. The discussion in this and the following paragraphs is taken largely from Linn, *Cities in the Developing World*, pp. 169–81.

designed mainly to alleviate poverty among the poorer half of the population, so further improvements in project design are needed to limit the extent to which higher-income groups preempt benefits. Lower standards, amended cost recovery schemes, and, for sites and services projects, improved procedures for selecting applicants, can help reduce the leakage; these are being incorporated into current projects. Realistically, however, some leakage must be expected to continue even with the most careful control measures—particularly in upgrading projects, where the preexisting distribution of residents in a project site, not project design and allocation criteria, largely determines who the beneficiaries will be.

Significantly, low-income groups were reached in these projects without extensive subsidization. In fact, virtually all the projects have sought substantial, if not full, recovery of shelter costs from plot holders. Interest rates charged in these projects were frequently above those in conventional housing programs, which have relied on large subsidies.

The key to providing shelter that the poor could afford under these projects lay in the drastic reduction of the cost per plot compared with those of conventional public housing programs. This was made possible by using reduced housing standards (in sites and services projects) along with lower service standards for water and sewerage (for example, standpipes and sewer systems that are not water-borne), smaller lot sizes, and low-cost standards for road circulation (for example, heavier reliance on footpaths than on streets). Standards and costs were generally lower in projects carried out in low-income countries (that is, in most of sub-Saharan Africa and in parts of Asia).

Experience in both types of shelter projects also makes clear that the dual objectives of efficiency and equity (or poverty alleviation) can be met. In most cases, the rates of return are above reasonable estimates of the opportunity cost of capital, which are generally between 10 and 15 percent. The estimation procedures for these rates of return are necessarily rough, relying as they do on estimated increases in rental or capital values of the improved lots as a measure of the benefits. If anything, they tend to underestimate the benefits derived from the projects since they cannot measure the external benefits generated, particularly improvements in public health.

The shelter program in Indonesia is particularly interesting for several reasons. The Kampong Improvement Program began in 1969 in Jakarta as an attempt by authorities to deal with the overwhelming slum problems of that city. The scale of the program was indeed impressive. Improved infrastructure for more than 60 percent of all kampongs (slum areas) in Jakarta was provided over a ten-year period. More than 200,000 plots were affected and some 3.7 million people benefited. Standards and costs of services provided were very low but nevertheless included paved footpaths, roads, drainage, water supply, sanitation, primary schools, and health clinics. Project costs were not directly recovered from project beneficiaries but were borne by the local government in Jakarta, which initiated a major effort to increase its fiscal resources, especially through significant improvements in property taxation. Property tax revenues increased more than fourteenfold between 1971 and 1975 (admittedly from a very low base), and revenues raised locally from all sources increased more than fourfold during the same period. The Kampong Improvement Program provides an encouraging example of the potential for improving housing conditions even where average incomes are quite low.

The replicability of shelter projects, and thus the prospect for eventually reaching most of the world's urban poor, depends only partly on how low the standards (and therefore the costs) are kept and on how much of the costs are recovered from project beneficiaries. There are also other constraints on replicability, as some of the Bank-assisted projects have shown. For sites and services projects, one problem is the scarcity of land in reasonable proximity to employment opportunities. As the program expands, project sites may entail higher land costs; or they may be farther from employment opportunities, in which case the attractiveness of the project to low-income groups is reduced unless additional investments are made to improve transportation to the project site or to generate employment opportunities nearby. A different kind of land problem affects the replicability of slum upgrading projects. Tenure regularization tends to be easiest when slums are located on public land. Upgrading programs usually tackle these areas first. When follow-up projects then turn to squatter settlements on private land, tenure regularization becomes a more difficult issue and will generally run into greater political obstacles, longer delays, and higher costs.

The government's overall housing strategy is important in this regard. As long as scarce capital is devoted to large, high-cost housing programs, the availability of funds for low-cost housing programs is limited, and the pace and scale of replication of such programs are considerably impeded. In any event, housing agencies and related governmental units need to explore ways to raise more revenue if they are to provide additional housing for the poor as well as the complementary components (such as community facilities or technical assistance, the costs of which are not usually recouped directly from the beneficiaries). A strengthening of the fiscal base of local governments along the lines discussed earlier in this chapter has, therefore, been of concern in various Bank-assisted urban shelter projects (for example, in Kenya, India, the Philippines, and Indonesia).

Urban Transport Projects

Many cities have devoted sizable amounts of capital to the construction or improvement of major road and rail systems in urban areas, but few of them have had a coherent view of the urban transport sector as a whole or of the long-term financial implications of a heavy reliance on new investment. In the past, the tendency was to solve problems and ease bottlenecks through new, usually costly, investment. More recently, urban transport projects have focused on better use of existing facilities, with the result that additional major investment is avoided or postponed. In addition, the principles of affordable, low-cost solutions and cost recovery are now being applied with some success.

Included in this newer approach are efforts to improve urban traffic management, to upgrade public transport services, and to improve roads and pedestrian walkways. Traffic management has been improved by the use of one-way streets, parking regulations, synchronized traffic lights, bus and bicycle lanes, and by widening roads where necessary. Existing

transport services have been upgraded by helping bus companies purchase buses and by providing technical assistance for transport planning
and financial management. Cost recovery has been enhanced by raising
the tariffs charged by urban bus companies. Abidjan, Tunis, Manila, and
Lima are among the cities that have benefited.

While the institutions responsible for urban transport are relatively well
developed in some countries, in most they require strengthening if they
are to manage all the varied components effectively. Urban transport
projects have therefore emphasized institutional development. Traffic
management units have been created under the above-mentioned
projects in Abidjan, Tunis, and Manila, as well as in many Brazilian cities.
The Brazilian example is noteworthy because the national urban transport agency has developed the capacity to provide technical assistance to
municipal transport authorities and thereby to plan and supervise a
national program.

A brief account of Singapore's experience may be instructive. The
scheme here described was not financed by the Bank, although it was
carefully monitored by Bank staff. For numerous organizational and
political reasons, it has not been replicated elsewhere; nevertheless, the
experiment has added a new dimension to discussions of financing and
managing urban transport.

Singapore is a city with relatively high levels of income and of motor
vehicle use. The government has pursued a comprehensive, efficient, and
remarkably effective urban transport policy. The principal elements are:

- A scheme to relieve central city congestion by a combination of area
  licensing for private automobiles and graduated parking fees
- Control of motor vehicle ownership and use through various tax
  measures
- An improved mass transit system largely based on buses
- Various improvements in traffic management
- A long-term policy of locating employment opportunities close to new
  housing developments, and vice versa.

The effects of the program include a dramatic reduction in congestion,
increased travel speeds for passengers and goods in the center of the city,
a significant shift from the use of single-occupant cars to the use of buses
and car pools, and lower pollution levels. Singapore is, of course,
exceptional in a number of respects: it is a city-state with a strong and
dynamic metropolitan government, a highly qualified staff, and a strong
political commitment to and popular support for dealing with rising
congestion and environmental deterioration. Nevertheless, the example
is worth careful study and replication to the extent feasible. The various
practical aspects that helped to make the scheme work are worth
emphasizing: adequate study and preparation, including an extensive
publicity campaign; simplicity of regulation and flexibility in implementation; preexistence of an effective vehicle registration system.[9]

9. A detailed description of the Singapore experience is contained in Peter Watson and
Edward Holland, *Relieving Traffic Congestion: The Singapore Area License Scheme*,
World Bank Staff Working Paper no. 281 (Washington, D.C., 1978).

Integrated Urban Projects

Integrated urban projects comprise various combinations of components dealing with shelter, infrastructure, transport, solid waste disposal, business support, health, nutrition, and education. They are intended to achieve broad improvements throughout a city, although not all components may be citywide in scope. The rationale for a citywide approach is that, as we have already observed, complementary investments are likely to have a greater impact on urban development than narrower subsectoral efforts. A precondition for such projects is that priorities across subsectors be identified through a systematic planning effort.

Integrated urban projects differ from shelter projects, as might be expected, in the larger scale and greater number of components, the larger number of agencies involved within a citywide framework, and the deliberate integration of investments into a single project. Individual components may be prepared as part of the sector plan of a national or local agency (schools by educational authorities, roads by transportation authorities, and so on). But what is essential is that each activity be viewed by national and city authorities as part of a coordinated project whose components are mutually reinforcing and whose policy goals are consistent. The projects thus represent an effort to manage urban resource allocation efficiently. Projects in Recife, Bamako, and Cairo are examples of efforts to develop this type of strategic approach to the city as a whole.

As suggested earlier, this approach confronts the problem of institutional coordination endemic to urban areas. Special efforts have been required to overcome the tendency of individual agencies to insist on their jurisdictional prerogatives. These efforts have succeeded only when strong political support has been forthcoming. A further problem arises from the fact that these projects are, almost by definition, complex to prepare and even more complex to implement. Although the comments made earlier about project complexity apply, projects in cities such as Calcutta and Madras have demonstrated both the advantages of an integrated approach and its administrative feasibility when there is a strong coordinating agency.

Regional Development Projects

Regional development projects extend the multisectoral approach of integrated urban projects beyond individual cities to a region as a whole. A regional project usually covers several secondary cities located in a common agricultural hinterland or industrial region, and is intended to have a broad multisectoral impact on regional development. Thus, two Korean projects were located in a relatively remote area that had not benefited from national economic growth. The first included shelter and infrastructure in three towns, a fishery harbor complex, a city market, a road, and technical assistance in planning; the second included industrial development zones, water supply and transportation, and fishery development. A Mexican project involved ten towns, and its components included credit facilities for artisans and small-scale enterprises. The design of each project took account of the need to strengthen the regional perspective within existing institutions, while at the same time improving individual sector agencies. The programming of investments, operations, and maintenance in such projects is complicated, but many of the activities are not new and would be carried out in the absence of the project, although at lower levels of investment and uncoordinated with related activities.

Such projects have a place in efforts to improve efficiency and stimulate growth in an area regarded as having a long-term economic potential. The objective is to make the most of a region's comparative advantage, rather than to achieve a theoretical balance among regions. These projects can have a significant impact on regional development. Since efforts in agriculture, industry, and transportation may also have a regional impact, urban projects should be closely linked to them, as part of a comprehensive approach to regional development.

Well on a smallholder's farm, Kenya

13

Water and Sanitation

SAFE DRINKING WATER and sanitary disposal of wastes have long been recognized as basic needs of society, helping to safeguard human health and to make possible a more productive life. Health and environmental problems caused by inadequate water supply and waste disposal are made more serious by the growth of population and its concentration in urban areas.

Satisfying basic needs for water and waste disposal means providing everyone with twenty to fifty liters daily of safe and convenient water for drinking, food preparation, and personal hygiene, and providing ways to dispose of excreta that do not contaminate humans or the environment. Most of the people in developing countries are not receiving services that meet these minimum standards. The World Health Organization has estimated that in 1980 about 73 percent of the urban population but only about 32 percent of the much larger rural population in developing countries had access to safe water. In the same year, facilities for the sanitary disposal of wastes were available to about 48 percent of the urban and 12 percent of the rural population. These proportions would be still lower if allowance were made for systems and facilities providing inferior service or making water available for only a few hours a day. At present the coverage of services varies greatly among countries. At least two-thirds of those without adequate water supplies live in South and Southeast Asia, although the share of population unserved is even greater in Africa.[1]

Progress in extending coverage has been slow. The number of people with access to public water supply and sanitation systems has been rising, but only rural water supply has increased faster than overall population growth. Furthermore, the quality and safety of the service provided by many existing systems have been deteriorating because of inadequate maintenance.

Deficiencies in water supply and waste disposal are principal reasons for the high mortality and morbidity rates of developing countries. In many areas, diseases related to these deficiencies are contributory causes of most infant deaths and account for a large proportion of adult sickness. Water and excreta are prominent factors in the transmission of many of the more serious diseases of the developing world. A United Nations–sponsored study suggests that control of water-related diseases—such as diarrhea, malaria, schistosomiasis, and filariasis—would add an average of about ten years to the low life expectancy in the developing world. Inadequate water supplies also force people to spend excessive amounts of time collecting water—more than six hours a day per family in rural East Africa. Even in urban areas, waiting in line to fill containers at public standpipes can take several hours.

In addition to meeting personal requirements for drinking, cooking, and washing, clean water is essential for manufacturing and commercial

---

1. The figures are from unpublished World Health Organization sources and exclude China, for which information is not available.

activities, which can account for up to 40 percent of water consumption in the urban areas of developing countries. Removal or management of industrial wastes—whether solid, liquid, or airborne—is another important need, which is often inadequately served.

Economic Aspects

Few countries have given high priority to water investments in their development programs. Most developing countries appear to have devoted some 4 to 6 percent of public investment to water supply and waste disposal in recent years. The proportion is significantly higher in a few countries with large arid regions.

This past neglect may reflect in part the incorrect perception that investment in water is not a productive use of resources. This misperception has been reinforced by the practical difficulties of measuring the economic returns on investment in safe water and sanitary waste disposal. The health benefits are difficult to quantify and are attributable to other improvements, including hygiene training and nutrition, as well. The use of a proxy for these benefits, such as the observed willingness of consumers to pay for clean water, usually substantially understates the benefits.

The importance of improving water supply and waste disposal has been gaining recognition, however, as evidenced by the declarations of various international conferences in recent years, culminating in the designation of the 1980s by the United Nations General Assembly as the International Drinking Water Supply and Sanitation Decade. The original objective fixed for the decade—to eliminate the vast service backlog by 1990—was soon understood to be unrealistic. The revised goal, therefore, calls for each country to set its own target, in the light of competing priorities and local constraints, for substantially increasing the proportion of its population with adequate access to water and sanitation. So far, eighty-one of the less developed countries, with a total population of 1,750 million in 1980, have initiated or completed decade plans, and fifty-one have established national action committees to implement them.

Given the magnitude of the service gap to be filled and the resource constraints facing most developing countries, significant improvements in the supply of water and sanitation will require both that existing facilities be utilized more efficiently and that new investments be as economical and cost-effective as possible. The choice of technology has a critical effect on the rate at which progress can be made. Too often, technologies are selected to duplicate the standards of industrialized countries rather than to suit local conditions. The convenience of modern systems has led to their widespread acceptance, especially in urban areas, but at unit costs that severely limit the possibilities of expansion. Fortunately, thanks to recent research and development, there now exists a wide range of alternative technologies, providing a lower but still acceptable standard of service at substantially reduced unit cost. Even with maximum efforts to use less expensive technologies, to mobilize community and self-help initiatives, and to raise more funds externally, governments will still be confronted by difficult choices in seeking to mobilize and use effectively the resources necessary for improved water and sanitation services.

Social Aspects

Since water supply and sanitation are basic needs, expanding coverage to the urban and rural poor, who characteristically are the least adequately served, can be an important means of advancing a country's social objectives. Among the poor, women and children, who lack information on the effects of unsanitary conditions, suffer most from present deficiencies. In addition, the productive potential of women in low-income households and the amount of care they can give their families are reduced by the time and energy women must spend to obtain water from distant sources.

Safe water in adequate quantity and sanitary waste disposal, while important, are not enough to ensure better health. They must be used properly. The past record of efforts to control diseases in rural areas through improved water and sanitation is, at best, a mixed one. Failures, which have been all too frequent, have been owing not only to poor initial design and inadequate maintenance, but also to lack of consumer acceptance of the new facilities, which is reflected in continuing low standards of personal and household hygiene.

Improvements in public health are, therefore, dependent on better knowledge both of the interrelations among water, sanitation, and health, and of cultural and religious beliefs, personal hygiene habits, and nutritional status. The planning, implementation, and operation of water and sanitation projects must involve the user community at all stages and give full consideration to the sociocultural setting. Above all, personal hygiene education must convince the consumer that it is important to use the water from the new source and to do it in a way that keeps it safe. Waste disposal is even more beset by ritualized practices and taboos, which make behavior difficult to change.

Pricing policy has been used to ensure that all those with access to safe water consume at least the minimum amount considered essential to good health. Many countries have adopted a rate structure for water comprising a low, subsidized rate for "lifeline" consumption and higher rates for residential consumption above the minimum and for industrial and commercial use.

Financial Aspects

Although a shortage of resources is a universal characteristic of underdevelopment—indeed, a way of defining it—in few sectors of the economy is the gap between identified needs and available resources as large as in water and sanitation. This gap can be narrowed only by working simultaneously on mobilizing more resources and on reducing investment costs. The need to reduce costs highlights the issue of service standards and technological choice, which will be discussed below under "Investment Issues." To mobilize resources, countries should look to water and sanitation agencies to finance a substantial part of their investment needs from internally generated funds, raised through an appropriate level of water charges.

Reality, unfortunately, is often otherwise. Urban water and waste disposal agencies are relatively well-off, at least compared with their rural counterparts, and most are able to cover their operating and maintenance costs and to service their debt, which typically is not large. Industry and commerce may provide a stable source of revenue. Few urban water companies, however, earn a rate of return on their revalued assets of more than 4 to 6 percent, and many earn less. Financial performance is generally less satisfactory than is the case with other utilities, such as telecommunications and power companies, and it has worsened appreciably as a result of the worldwide economic recession of the late 1970s and early 1980s. As a result, few urban agencies can provide a significant part of their investment needs from internally generated financial surpluses.

The situation is worse in rural areas. Investment costs per capita are lower than in urban areas, for a lower standard of service, but few rural systems can even cover their costs of operation and maintenance. Raising revenues from low-income villagers has proved difficult, although more could be done in association with improved service. Construction is usually financed by public grants or low-interest loans, and subsidies are frequently required for operation and maintenance costs as well. Reliance on the public exchequer has led to variable and uncertain levels of funding and hence to declining standards of maintenance, so that an increasing number of systems no longer functions properly.

The tariffs charged by water and sanitation utilities play an important role in their financial performance. Since these utilities generally enjoy a monopoly position—at least in urban areas—tariff changes need the approval of a public authority, an approval too often delayed or granted at a level below that requested or necessary to cover increases in costs. While cross-subsidy of low household consumption by larger consumers is often built into urban tariff structures, the possibility of cross-subsidy among rural users is limited by the generally low level of income and the absence of sizable local industrial and commercial users. The attachment of villagers to their traditional sources of supply makes it difficult to collect funds for new systems. Low levels of cost recovery, therefore, remain the rule in rural areas.

Nontariff issues also have a significant impact on the financial situation of water and sanitation entities. A common feature of many urban water utilities is the excessive amount of water unaccounted for. Losses can be caused by physical leaks, mainly in the distribution system, but about half of them are attributable to administrative deficiencies such as lack of metering and unauthorized connections. The effect of these losses is reinforced by the many bills long in arrears because of inadequate accounting and lax enforcement. The financial stringency resulting from inefficient administration together with low tariffs is a prime reason that many water entities cannot provide adequate facilities and service to fill the backlog of unsatisfied demand and meet the needs of a growing population.

Institutional Aspects

Sources of water for drinking and sanitation can usually be found in many parts of the country, and water is costly to transport over long distances. These two facts have shaped the distinctive character of the institutions in the sector. Unlike the situation in the power and telecommunications sectors, national water and sewerage companies that operate throughout the country, and nationally or regionally interconnected systems, are the exception rather than the rule. Because the sector is fragmented into numerous entities, each typically serving a single municipality, the burden on human resources is too heavy for most developing countries to sustain. A shortage of skilled staff, excessive numbers of untrained staff, management without sufficient autonomy and frequently subject to political appointment and removal, and weak or nonexistent commercial accounting and financial systems are common features of local water and sanitation entities. Water and waste disposal are frequently combined in a single organization; when separately administered, institutions charged with sanitation are especially likely to be problem-ridden, in part because of their weak financial position.

Organizing water and sanitation services in rural areas poses even greater problems than in urban areas, and only rudimentary structures are in place in most countries. Responsibility for rural water supply and sanitation is most often given to a national ministry of health, less often to another ministry or agency such as public works, and least often to a central or regional organization solely responsible for rural water supply and sanitation. The primary interests of the ministries and agencies lie elsewhere, and given the difficulties of creating and maintaining a support organization to service many small communities, it is not surprising that rural water supply and sanitation suffer from neglect. Construction of new facilities and their maintenance when completed may call for separate institutional arrangements that are difficult to put in place.

The operational links among water supply, waste disposal, and instruction in personal hygiene have already been stressed. They need to be planned together, a point we return to below. Health services, housing development, and urban planning also have important links to water supply and sanitation. Coordinating and facilitating all these activities, which customarily are the responsibility of separate and independent organizations and agencies, present another set of organizational challenges, which many countries are still struggling to meet.

DEVELOPMENT OBJECTIVES

The basic objective of public policy in the water and sanitation sector can be put simply: to provide a minimum supply of safe drinking water—twenty to fifty liters per person daily—and sanitary waste disposal to all members of society, at a price they can afford, at the earliest feasible date. So stated, the issue becomes one of determining what is "feasible." Clearly the answer will vary from country to country, depending on circumstances, but for most of the developing world the gap between basic needs and existing levels of service is very large.

Of the 3 billion people living in the developing world in 1980, some 400 million to 500 million in urban areas and 1.7 billion in rural areas—together about two-thirds of the total population—were without adequate service. The proportions are roughly the same if China's population of 1 billion is excluded. Progress in extending service was made during the 1970s, but most of it has been absorbed by population growth, so that the absolute number of people unserved remains roughly the same. In addition, substantial rehabilitation of services now being provided is needed where systems have broken down or are no longer functioning adequately owing to insufficient maintenance and repair. When service is interrupted, the ensuing inconvenience, while serious, may be less significant than the impairment of the water's safety.

To meet the objective originally set for the International Drinking Water Supply and Sanitation Decade—to eliminate the vast service backlog by 1990—would require, according to World Bank estimates, at least $30 billion a year (in 1983 prices). UNDP estimates suggest that the 1983 level of investment was actually about $10 billion, or a third of that required, of which about 20 percent came from external sources. Even if it were possible to attain the 1990 objective of closing the existing gap—and clearly it is not—population growth in the intervening years would leave many people without access to adequate service.

The issue, then, is how to set priorities and establish targets that are within the range of public budgets, given that the allocations to water supply and sanitation are not likely to increase much in real terms in the foreseeable future. Investment costs can vary widely, depending principally on the standard of service to be provided and on site-specific conditions such as the type of water source, climate, and topography.

For many governments with large unserved or underserved populations, the most attractive strategy is likely to be to give first priority to providing as many people as possible with a basic level of service through an appropriate low-cost technology. The second priority would be to upgrade or improve facilities for those receiving service that is inadequate in quantity or quality, and the third priority would be to achieve higher standards of convenience. Usually a project area will include some customers in each category, and as a matter of policy it may be desirable to provide some benefit to all. Provided that appropriate tariffs are charged, increasing the convenience level (that is, offering a higher standard of service) to the more affluent users will generate surpluses that can be used for the extension of basic services, while also enhancing overall support for the project.

Particular attention should be given to rural areas, where most of the people without access to service live and where the incidence of waterborne diseases is generally greater. The choice of an appropriate technology is usually simpler, since piped systems of water supply or waste disposal are not likely, in any event, to be a practical alternative. More difficult problems arise from the need to strengthen institutions, train staff in adequate numbers, and enlist the support of local communities in financing, operating, and maintaining new facilities. Education in personal hygiene and proper water use is also essential.

If significant progress is to be made toward the extension of basic services, simultaneous action on many fronts will be required. Realistic sector plans and strategies have to be devised and implemented, appropriate technologies promoted and disseminated, institutions and organizational relations created or strengthened, large numbers of workers trained, financial performance and disciplines improved, and complementary actions in health and hygiene undertaken. We shall revert to most of these points in the discussion that follows.

POLICY ISSUES

Mobilizing Financial Resources

Raising the funds necessary to cover operating and maintenance expenditures, to service debt, and to make a significant contribution to the expansion of facilities calls for sound financial institutions with tariffs of an appropriate level and structure. This goal should be well within the reach of water and sanitation utilities in urban areas serving large residential groups and industrial and commercial users; since the supply of water is usually a monopoly and the demand for it relatively inelastic, the utility has broad latitude to set tariffs without the risk of losing customers. The wide spectrum of consumers served provides opportunities for cross-subsidization within a satisfactory overall level of tariffs. The economies of scale inherent in the treatment and distribution of water reinforce the monopoly position of the water and sanitation companies.

There are water companies that have lived up to these expectations. The Tunisian national water company, with responsibility for urban water supply throughout the country, has steadily increased both the level of its annual investment and the share financed internally, so that the sector now pays more in taxes to the government than it receives in contributions from it, and it finances investments entirely from internal cash generation, customer contributions, and borrowings. World Bank borrowers in cities such as Nicosia, Managua, and Singapore have turned in a strong financial performance. Unfortunately, such performances are more the exception than the rule. Relatively few water and sanitation entities, even those serving urban centers exclusively, have been able to earn sufficient revenues to finance a substantial portion of their investment needs internally. This disappointing record is due principally to inadequacies in the level and structure of tariffs.

In view of their monopoly position, it is appropriate that water and sanitation companies be subject to public scrutiny. Preferably, regulation should take the form of establishing standards for financial performance, such as a prescribed rate of return on net fixed assets or a prescribed contribution to expansion (see chapter 21, Financial Analysis). Within these guidelines, the enterprise should be left to manage its own affairs. If tariffs must be approved by a public body, then approval should be related to objective criteria such as identified increases in costs (as measured, for example, by an appropriate index of the rate of inflation) or the need to attain the prescribed rate of return. A time limit should be set, after which approval would be automatic if no objection has been raised. In practice, however, approval by municipal or national authorities has often been either purposely delayed—as a means of controlling inflation or for social, political, or other reasons—or else subjected to lengthy bureaucratic procedures. It has happened that a water company was not granted any price increase for ten or even twenty years. When the government finally faced up to the need to deal with the parlous financial condition in which the company found itself, the increases needed to restore viability may well have created more serious political reactions than those avoided by the deferral of increases.

An appropriate tariff structure for pricing water consists of at least two blocks. Minimum or lifeline consumption is set at somewhere between twenty and fifty liters a day per person, an amount reflecting not only basic needs (for drinking, food preparation, and personal hygiene) but also climatic conditions. The price of this minimum block of water is commonly set at 3 to 5 percent of household income (based on the official minimum wage), which experience suggests is affordable. For water consumption above this minimum, charges can be at a higher but flat rate approximating the marginal cost of additional water supplies—which is the customary economic criterion—or they can be progressive, rising with the amount used in additional blocks in order to gain more revenue. Industrial and commercial clients are usually charged the rate applicable to the highest level of domestic consumption. These charges are easiest to apply when water can be metered. Where metering is not practical—either because water pressures are too low or because the costs of metering are prohibitive—the same basic principles of lifeline rates and incremental cost can be applied, with rates generally based on less precise measures of water use such as the size of the service connection, the number of fixtures in the house, or the size or value of the property being served.

Such a price structure can be entirely compatible with a financially strong water supply company. Since average costs tend to rise as cheaper water sources are fully exploited and more costly alternatives must be developed, pricing in accordance with marginal costs can generate substantial revenue surpluses. Once the minimum consumption is assured, there is no economic argument in favor of charging less than the full cost of water. This gives ample scope for a high level of cost recovery, and the financial surpluses can be used to extend services to low-income users, both urban and rural. In some countries, seasonal differences in the level of water charges may be appropriate, with higher tariffs in the summer when demand is high and water supply low. The historical evidence is that expansion of coverage has generally lagged most when the water supply or sewerage enterprise has had to depend on government subsidies—either because the consequent loss of financial discipline has encouraged inefficiency or because the subsidies have often been cut in the face of government budget constraints, or both.

House Connections

In addition to regular tariffs for the amount of water consumed, a new user often has to pay an initial house connection fee as well as the cost of putting in the connection (laying pipes on the lot, providing meters, and installing household plumbing). The cost of putting in the household connection can be large in relation to the cost of water used, and it is often necessary for the utility to make loan financing available for this purpose. In general, such financing should be on commercial or market terms, although a case can be made for low-interest financing or direct subsidies for low-income residents to ensure lifeline consumption or to take advantage of economies of scale and bring the newly installed distribution network to full utilization. Levying a separate, one-time fee for households to join the system has been found to discourage participation. A compromise approach that has worked well in some cases is to charge only for connection sizes larger than the minimum or to base the fee on the value of the property.

Standpipes

Urban residents who receive water from communal standpipes or from courtyard connections that serve a number of households do not generally pay charges related to use. Although charging for each pail of water drawn would clearly have advantages in controlling water use, it has encountered administrative difficulties, and the cost of having an attendant permanently present at each standpipe is high. The concessional system under which a licensed private operator collects a fee for each bucket filled is still used in a few countries, among them Indonesia and the Ivory Coast, but the fees charged by the licensees are generally high and make water relatively expensive to the users. There is no easy answer to the problem of cost recovery from standpipes, but many municipalities are relying increasingly on property taxes or general municipal revenues rather than direct charges. Normally, the quantities of water delivered through standpipes for residential consumption are relatively small (less than 10 percent of total supplies) so that standpipe revenues, however low and by whatever means collected, do not have a major impact on the financial situation of the water entity.

Urban Sewerage

The costs of urban sewerage are frequently collected as a supplement to the water bill, at a flat or progressive rate, set as a percentage of the water tariff. This has the advantage, from the viewpoint of public health, of discouraging attempts to dispose of wastes other than through the connected system. A less satisfactory alternative is a tax on local property, since it will not be seen by the consumer as being related to the use of water.

There is little justification for subsidizing the use of water-borne sewerage. If a subsidy is provided, it should be for the lowest-cost technology that is practicable in the area, limited as much as possible to the lowest income groups, and financed out of revenues from services of higher quality and quantity. Loan financing for the capital cost of installing a water-borne sewerage connection has sometimes proved necessary when public regulations have required that all houses be connected once the water mains were in. Direct subsidies or financing at lower than market rates have been extended to low-income groups since some of the public health benefits of sewerage are external to the individual household and therefore not appropriately charged to it. Subsidized interest rates are also justified for low-income households located in areas where no alternative to water-borne sewerage is permitted.

Rural Water and Sanitation

Financial self-sufficiency remains a distant goal for rural water and sanitation systems. Rural needs can generally be met at lower per capita costs, corresponding to lower standards of service; but low incomes, the absence of industrial and commercial users, and the attachment of villagers to their traditional, free sources of supply lessen the prospects for recovery of any significant part of capital costs. Higher charges could discourage rural users from switching to the new facilities. They should thus be deferred until the new system has demonstrated the benefits of convenience and better quality of water.

Substantial capital contributions, usually from the central government, have therefore been a necessary feature of any program to extend service to rural areas. Nevertheless, governments are increasingly calling for a minimum local contribution toward construction costs, usually in the range of 10 to 15 percent, which is generally made in kind through use of local labor to dig wells and trenches or through the provision of land and materials. Care must be taken to ensure that local labor is properly organized and directed, and that contributions are provided in an equitable manner from within the community. There is also a growing trend to make rural communities responsible for continuing operation and maintenance of the facilities once completed, or at least for providing the funds for these purposes. Experience in several countries indicates that this level of cost recovery is possible once safe water has been made available and its advantages demonstrated, particularly if the new water source is more convenient than the traditional one. This is important both to ease the fiscal burden on the central government—and thereby make it possible to expand rural service more rapidly—and also to secure the community support and active participation that may be essential if maintenance and repairs are to be done effectively and promptly.

Rural sanitation usually depends on relatively simple technologies such as latrines for on-site disposal of wastes. These facilities are likely to be privately owned and provided from the users' own resources, although a subsidy or incentive has sometimes been necessary to encourage their construction in the interest of public health.

Measuring Benefits

The low financial returns earned by most water and sanitation enterprises, if not properly interpreted, could lead to the conclusion that investments in these services are of low economic value and consequently of low priority in national investment programs. Part of the problem arises from the fact that the real benefits of water and sanitation investments lie in better health and the avoidance of disabling diseases and epidemics. But little is known specifically about the responsiveness of diseases to improvements in sanitation and in the quantity and quality of the water supply, accompanied by education in hygiene. The ways in which the time saved from fetching and carrying water is used are also little understood.

Accurate methods of carrying out a full-scale cost-benefit or rate of return analysis (see chapter 20, Economic Analysis) are still evolving; in their absence, economic returns on water and sanitation projects are customarily measured by the consumer's willingness to pay, as reflected by the prices charged for the services. But this proxy tends to understate the benefits substantially since, as has been seen, these prices are often kept low for various reasons. Moreover, some of the public health benefits, such as the avoidance of epidemics, are external to the individual consumer and so not necessarily included in the price he is prepared to pay. That water is highly valued is evidenced by the fact that rural users, mostly women and children, often walk long distances and spend many hours to acquire a minimal supply. Urban poor, if without access to piped water or convenient standpipes, often pay local vendors twenty to fifty times the equivalent metered rate of the water system—albeit for very small quantities (a few liters a day).

INSTITUTIONAL ISSUES

Any lasting improvement in financial performance will demand a strengthening of the institutions involved in the water and sanitation sector at all levels. Institutional change is slow under the best of circumstances; the particular challenges in this sector arise from the multiplicity of urban systems and the rudimentary character of rural ones.

Although provision of water and sewerage is everywhere accepted as a public function, individual countries have devised a wide variety of organizational forms to handle this responsibility. Most countries have a national water agency with some role, although a varying one, in approving tariffs, planning investments, and assisting with finance. Urban systems are most commonly organized on a municipal basis, with operating departments or semiautonomous or autonomous authorities responsible for all or some part of water, sewerage, and solid waste disposal. Municipal entities, enjoying different degrees of independence, may be grouped under a regional or national authority, while the largest urban centers may have completely independent systems.

Regional groupings have made possible economies of scale in staffing, procurement, and administrative overhead to overcome some of the inherent deficiencies of small municipal entities, and such groupings should be encouraged. The relationship between the areawide (state or regional) and municipal units can be adapted to particular needs, ranging from complete management and operation by an area institution to the provision of only technical assistance and special services. Integrating a municipal water system with other municipal entities to make possible the planning of services on a citywide basis is still not widely practiced (see chapter 12, Urbanization). So far, no developing country has followed the lead of the United Kingdom in reorganizing the sector into regional authorities responsible for all water resource development in specific drainage areas or river basins. This reorganization has greatly reduced the number of water and sewerage authorities, cut the number of senior staff, and streamlined planning and operations.

The World Bank has had experience in lending to water and sewerage enterprises in all their organizational forms. A variety of institutions in Kenya, Morocco, Nicaragua, Singapore, and Tunisia—ranging from government departments to autonomous public companies—have been substantially strengthened through such projects. But similar types of borrowers in other countries have failed to make significant progress. Management of water services by private sector concessionaires has proved very effective in Gabon and the Ivory Coast. The use of central government units as intermediaries to on-lend external funds to state and municipal utilities has been developed in some countries, such as Brazil and Mexico.

This diverse experience suggests that the specific nature of the institutional problems facing a country, region, or municipality, and the way in which they are addressed, count more than organizational forms in determining the success or failure of water and sanitation enterprises. Among the institutional problems most frequently encountered are:

- Inadequate sectoral planning on a medium- or long-term basis, which results in piecemeal planning of investments and stop-and-go implementation of investment plans
- Excessive government interference (at various levels of government) in the policies and operations of the utilities, including the setting of tariffs, appointment of managerial staff, and fixing of salaries and conditions of employment
- A serious shortage of trained staff, especially technical and commercial staff, often coupled with an excessive number of unskilled workers hired for political reasons
- A lack of financial and commercial accounting systems, and more broadly of management information systems, resulting in large losses through water not accounted for and unpaid bills
- Inadequate coordination between water and sanitation organizations (when they are administered separately) and with other agencies operating in related fields.

Planning

How best to deal with these pressing problems depends on the particular conditions, but certain broad generalizations can be made. First, each country needs an overall strategy for the sector. This means drawing up plans covering an adequate time span, but with sufficient flexibility to handle changing circumstances, and setting realistic targets in terms of numbers of people to be reached, standards of service to be provided, and standards of operation and maintenance to be met. Planning objectives must be matched against financial resources—federal, state, and local—including those obtained from the maximum feasible level of cost recovery and self-financing.

Ideally, water resources should be planned for an entire river basin or watershed and for all competing uses (including power generation, irrigation, flood control, industry, drinking water, and sanitation) to obtain the most efficient allocation of resources among as well as within these activities. Environmental effects must also be considered. Unfortunately, few developing countries have the political, institutional, and technical capacity to deal adequately with these issues.

Autonomy

Stability has proven to be a prerequisite for institutions to improve their operations. When agency heads and senior staff shift with each change in political leadership, continuity of management and operations obviously suffers. Chief executives and senior staff should be appointed on merit and for fixed terms, subject to removal only for demonstrated cause. Autonomy in day-to-day management is crucial and should be secured within an overall framework of objectives, policies to meet them, and targets of operational performance established in agreement with a higher authority, to which the entity is accountable for the results actually achieved. This is particularly important with respect to tariff policies, as has already been mentioned.

Staffing

Staffing problems are endemic in the sector. They are rooted in the large number of relatively small enterprises to be staffed and in the political interference that arises because the enterprises are often viewed by governments as social rather than commercial undertakings. Grouping into large organizations covering several municipalities will help to economize on staff, but granting greater responsibility to management in hiring and firing staff, in fixing salaries and conditions of employment, and in selecting consultants and contractors is also necessary. Although salaries cannot realistically match those in the private sector, there is ample scope to reward merit and provide incentives for better staff performance.

Training

Training deserves special mention because it is so frequently neglected. Water supply and waste disposal services have to function twenty-four hours a day for the entire life of the facilities. Few enterprises can satisfy the requirements for trained manpower that this entails. Poor maintenance practices and periodic breakdowns are more frequently due to inadequately trained staff than to shortage of funds, although the latter is certainly a problem. For many years, the World Bank gave inadequate attention in its water and sanitation projects to training staff other than senior management. Many early borrowers have now built up effective and comprehensive staff training programs, largely through their own efforts. But it is striking that most of the entities with the largest training programs—covering about 20 percent of their total staff each year, as in the Bangkok Metropolitan Water Works Authority and the São Paulo State Company—are among those already best provided with qualified staff, which demonstrates the need for continued training efforts. Much larger training programs for operators, accountants, and supervisors are needed, especially in Africa.

Some governments prefer to reserve foreign exchange loans provided by external agencies for the procurement of hardware, but unless local finance or ample grant assistance from other external sources is available for training, this is a shortsighted policy. Given the magnitude of the task, project-by-project training programs will not be sufficient. National training programs, which can yield significant economies of scale and promote cross-fertilization of experience within the country, must be more widely developed.

Billing and Collecting

A commercial, as distinct from an accounting, department is still a rarity in the sector. The absence of a commercial orientation toward building up markets and generating profits with which to finance future expansion helps to explain the poor financial performance of many entities. Billing and collecting procedures are deficient, and cost control is ineffective if it exists at all. Many companies have receivables of unpaid bills equal to six months or more of billings. The government itself and public sector agencies are often among the most delinquent customers.

Another common feature of many urban water utilities, as noted earlier, is the excessive amount of water unaccounted for. It is customary to find that 30 to 40 percent of the available water is not being sold to consumers, and the figure frequently reaches 50 percent. (In developed countries, well-managed utilities keep total losses to 15 to 20 percent.) Typically, half of the water loss is due to administrative failures, such as illegal connections, faulty meters, and lack of meter reading and billing, and to the provision of unmetered water to a variety of public or other institutions. The other half is attributable to physical leaks in the distribution system.

Better detection and repair of physical leaks can help to improve financial performance, but this is a difficult and time-consuming process. It should be pursued diligently as part of a program of rehabilitation of facilities but without expecting much short-term improvement. More can be accomplished immediately through efforts to decrease administrative losses as well as losses that result from arrears in billing. A crucial element is better accounting for arrears—including the segregation of old arrears that have become virtually uncollectible—and more rigorous enforcement of collection from both public and residential users (industrial users are usually not a problem). Disconnection of nonpaying customers is a potent weapon; so much so, that legal obstacles to disconnection have sometimes been imposed and may need to be modified or removed. The repair and replacement of meters and the short-term training of staff in meter repair and calibration should also be part of the program.

Coordination

Arguments can be advanced on both sides of the question whether water supply and sewerage should be administered by the same or separate entities. As observed earlier, there are examples of both successes and failures with each type of organization, which suggests that the form of the organization may be less important in determining the outcome than other considerations, such as quality of management and soundness of policies. Other things being equal, however, the advantage probably lies in combining these two complementary activities into a single organizational structure. As will be discussed further below, it is important to plan water supply and sewerage investments together, even though there may often be a substantial time lag in carrying out the sewerage program. Billing to common customers also favors consolidation. The collection and disposal of solid wastes, less elegantly known as garbage, is usually a separate undertaking. Administrative convenience is likely to be the principal consideration in determining its organizational home, although it shows important links with water supply and especially sewerage.

Easier to map out, but more difficult to accomplish in practice, is coordination with the various other agencies administratively separate from water and sewerage but essential to realizing the broad objectives of the sector. These include such disparate activities as urban housing (in conjunction with which water and sewerage facilities need to be planned), health services (including education in health and personal hygiene), and urban streets (for surface drainage). No universal formula for effective and timely coordination exists. But the need must be recognized, and coordination machinery put in place that can be tested and modified as local experience dictates (see chapter 17, Project Implementation).

Rural Service

New or improved institutional structures are perhaps the greatest need in rural areas, where a smaller proportion of the population is served, service levels are typically much lower, and service breakdowns from inadequate maintenance much higher, than in urban areas. A strong and continued government commitment to improving rural institutions is perhaps the single most important ingredient for success. For best results, this commitment should be embodied in a senior government official charged with continuing responsibility for carrying out the rural program and overseeing the allocation of resources to it.

Rural populations are either located in small towns and villages that cannot independently sustain a service institution or dispersed on many small farms. Responsibility for rural service has most frequently been given to a national (or in some instances regional) multipurpose entity, the main interest of which is not water and sanitation, and which in practice has little contact with the intended beneficiaries.

New institutional structures will therefore have to be built up, from very skeletal beginnings in most countries. In India, a three-tier system stimulated by UNICEF has been established. It consists of caretakers at the village level, mobile maintenance teams working out of district centers, and a regional support center providing technical assistance, training, and other backup services. Substantial improvements of rural water supply have been realized in the areas covered (sanitation has not been part of the program). Some doubt exists, however, about the long-term viability of this system in view of the high cost of transporting the mobile maintenance teams. Newly designed hand pumps are being developed and tested in rural areas in many countries participating in a joint UNDP and World Bank program, and the prospects are good that these hand pumps can be maintained by a village caretaker with only minimal outside support.

Whatever new institutional arrangements may evolve, they are likely to contain two elements: strong community participation and extensive backup services from a regional or central organization. Private voluntary organizations have been quite successful at the community level, in part because they have been sensitive to the local culture and have involved the community closely in project development and execution. (Examples include the Sarvodaya Shramadana in Sri Lanka, Agua del Pueblo in Guatemala, and the Population and Community Development Association in Thailand.) They can be an effective instrument in mobilizing community support, although their geographical scope has usually been severely restricted by lack of funds. If there is no voluntary organization, a local zation, a local cooperative can be used for the purpose or a special community water committee formed; it is usually preferable, however, to work with existing organizations that have a known performance record and to reinforce them if necessary. In Korea, rice cooperatives at harvesttime withhold a predetermined percentage of the harvest to pay for the operation and maintenance of the members' water supply.

Local committees can assume broad responsibilities when they are given proper authority and guidance. These responsibilities may include liaising with higher-echelon public agencies; organizing the voluntary labor force, local material, and land contributions and helping to ensure that work is scheduled in harmony with agricultural seasons; selecting community members to be trained to maintain facilities; determining the method of raising funds for maintenance and collecting maintenance fees; and keeping accounts and making periodic reports.

An alternative to community participation and self-help is for the government to contract with a private organization to take responsibility for operation and maintenance; this has been used successfully in India and the Ivory Coast, among other places. Routine maintenance of hand pumps, for example—the critical element in preventing a breakdown of rural water systems—can be contracted to a caretaker in the village or to a local entrepreneur serving several villages or towns. This approach may be preferable when ethnic, cultural, or other differences make it difficult for a community to form or to operate a viable association.

However institutions are organized at the community level, they need support from a district, regional, or national agency; at the same time, a large degree of decentralization through a network of field offices is necessary to reach and service the many local communities adequately. The principal services to be provided include technical assistance for designing rural systems and for major maintenance and repair, planning and implementation of community health and education programs in conjunction with the other authorities involved, and greatly expanded training programs for community workers.

For rural sanitation, adequate standards can be provided inexpensively by the use of any one of a number of on-site disposal methods. The principal need is for hygiene education to convince people to use the facility, to maintain it in clean condition, and to practice adequate personal hygiene. Initially, assistance in construction and possibly in financing the purchase of some materials may be required. Where interest in sanitation lags behind that in water supply, attendance at hygiene education sessions and the construction of a latrine have sometimes been made a condition for providing assistance in the construction of a water supply system.

If external agencies are to finance rural services on a large scale, intermediary organizations such as those just described, or a suitable alternative, are needed to channel funds to the many local communities that cannot be reached directly without excessive administrative cost. What is required is that the organization have the capacity to appraise, directly or by subcontract, many small-scale projects on the basis of agreed criteria and to allocate funds among projects within the framework of an agreed plan.

INVESTMENT ISSUES

Rapid expansion of urban areas, combined with the continuing needs of rural populations, is placing increasing strains on the financial and administrative capacity of institutions in the water and sanitation sector. Investments need to be made within a framework of improved efficiency in operations and maintenance as well as a more careful examination of factors governing supply and demand. The incomes and other socio-economic characteristics of consumers (industrial, commercial, and residential) need to play a more critical role in determining the size, timing, distribution, and technology of investment.

The design of investments in the sector presents a classic case of the need for appropriate technology. "Appropriateness" in this regard has several dimensions, among them the extent of demand for the service, the affordability of different technical solutions, the prevalence of diseases and health problems, sociocultural habits and practices, the need for complementary investments, and the capacity of institutions to implement investment programs and to operate and maintain the facilities once built. The issues involved are not inherently complex, but they offer ample scope for judgment, and thus for error. Bank lending for water and sanitation projects has experienced its share of failures as well as successes.

The design of individual projects requires, first, determining what the demand for the services will be—given the size of the market (including industrial and commercial uses), the income status of the proposed residential beneficiaries and their social customs and constraints, and the expected tariff levels. The second step is to decide what is the most appropriate way of providing the requisite services in the light of technical, institutional, and other considerations.

Demand Forecasting

Since in many areas the unsatisfied demand for clean water is greater than can be met by available investment resources, water supply projects, more than those of some other public services, are sized according to the funds available rather than to actual need. Experience in water supply projects indicates, nevertheless, that demand is often overestimated because forecasts are based on sophisticated methodologies that are valid only for the patterns of consumption found in the cities of industrialized countries. This results in overinvestment and insufficient revenue when consumption fails to grow as forecast. Some projects in Africa have had connection rates several years after completion that were less than 50 percent of those expected at the time of appraisal because the intended beneficiaries did not have the financial means to pay for house connections or in-house plumbing. Financial assistance for these purposes was not part of the project since the need for it had not been anticipated.

Demand forecasts should, therefore, be based on specific market surveys to identify the potential beneficiaries. This should preferably be done by income group, since water consumption varies closely with income, at least up to a point. Account needs to be taken of current levels and types of consumption; sanitary conditions and prevalence of various diseases, which may call for different responses; expected rates of population increase (again by income group); ability to pay for improved services at various levels of convenience through tariffs that cover costs; and social customs that influence the way water is used and therefore the amount consumed. Daily consumption per person from house connections to a water system is usually at least three times that of consumption from standpipes. Forecasting the future is inevitably risky, but more careful market analysis can reduce substantially the margin of error.

Appropriate Technologies

In arriving at the best approach to meeting the expected demand, a wide variety of technologies are now available from which to choose. Given the basic objective of providing a minimal standard of service to as many people as possible, it is important to resist the temptation, to which local engineers may be as prone as expatriate experts, to adopt the sophisticated technologies now in use in industrialized countries. These technologies involve a centrally controlled and treated source of water, wide-ranging transmission lines, and metered, multiple-tap connections in every dwelling. They were designed not to improve health—that goal was reached at an earlier stage—but to provide a high standard of convenience, to which most developing countries cannot at present aspire. In planning water and sewerage systems for the urban areas of developing countries, much greater use has to be made of standpipes, courtyard connections, and staged development of water distribution systems.

The potential for cost savings through the use of simpler technologies is dramatic. Construction costs for water distribution systems can range from $10 per person for standpipe service to over $100 per person for service through house connections (in 1980 prices). Unit costs of providing sanitary services are higher, and the spread even larger: from $20 per person for a dry on-site system to $400 or more per person for a waterborne system. The range of alternative sanitation technologies is very wide (see table 13-1), but all provide the same benefit—removal of excreta from human contact—albeit at different levels of convenience. In view of the very high costs of water-based sewerage systems, they are likely to be economically justified only when population densities, levels of water consumption, or geological considerations make on-site disposal of wastes costly or impossible. In urban areas, this occurs when water consumption reaches about 100 liters a day per person. Otherwise, new construction should be mainly of simple sanitation systems, of which a wide variety reaches fully acceptable hygienic standards.

World Bank lending experience confirms the wide range of costs for different technological options. In 1981 dollars, the average capital costs of supplying water by house connection in a large number of Bank-assisted projects was $130 per person newly served, compared with half as much where courtyard connections were used, and a quarter as much for standpipes providing fifty liters a day per person. Similarly, waterborne sewerage costs $250 or more per person, in contrast to latrines installed at $20 per person and to intermediate systems relying on larger quantities of water and providing higher levels of service (pour-flush toilets or small-bore sewers) that typically cost $30 to $60 per person.

Table 13-1. *Alternative Sanitation Technologies and Costs*
(1978 U.S. dollars)

Technology	Total invest-ment cost[a]	Monthly invest-ment cost[b]	Monthly recurrent cost	Monthly water cost	Hypo-thetical total monthly cost[b]	Percentage of income of average low-income household[c]
Low-cost						
Pour-flush toilet	70	1.5	0.2	0.3	2.0	2
Pit latrine	125	2.6	...	...	2.6	3
Communal toilet[d]	355	7.4	0.3	0.6	8.3	9
Vacuum-truck cartage	105	2.2	1.6	...	3.8	4
Low-cost septic tank	205	4.3	0.4	0.5	5.2	6
Composting toilet	400	8.3	0.4	...	8.7	10
Bucket cartage[d]	190	4.0	2.3	...	6.3	7
Medium-cost						
Sewered aquaprivy	570	7.1	2.0	0.9	10.0	11
Aquaprivy	1,100	13.7	0.3	0.2	14.2	16
Japanese vacuum-truck cartage	710	8.8	5.0	...	13.8	15
High-cost						
Septic tanks	1,645	14.0	5.9	5.9	25.8	29
Sewerage	1,480	12.6	5.1	5.7	23.4	26

... Zero or negligible.

a. Includes household plumbing as well as all other on-site and off-site system costs.

b. Assumes that investment cost is financed by loans at 8 percent over five years for the low-cost systems, ten years for the medium-cost systems, and twenty years for the high-cost systems.

c. Assumes average annual income per capita of $180 and six people per household.

d. Based on costs per capita scaled up to household costs to account for multiple-household use in some of the case studies.

Source: World Bank, "Water Supply and Waste Disposal," Poverty and Basic Needs Series (Washington, D.C., 1980), p. 20.

Some of the low- or intermediate-cost technologies are the fruit of World Bank–sponsored research and demonstration projects undertaken with the participation of the UNDP and bilateral agencies. While some of these are still in progress, the basic technologies are by now fully field-tested and in operational use in several developing countries.

Examples of the use of innovative, simple technologies in Bank-assisted projects include the Manila water treatment plant, the Jakarta and Dar es Salaam sewerage and sanitation projects combining water-borne sewerage and on-site sanitation technologies, the low-cost sanitation component of a project in Gujarat, India, and the simplified treatment technologies tested at the Pan-American Sanitary Engineering Center in Lima and employed in a number of Bank-assisted projects in Latin America. Manila was also the recipient of the first major comprehensive waste disposal project to use mainly drains and simple sanitation technologies, while the Jakarta and Dar es Salaam projects are noteworthy because they were designed by multidisciplinary teams including engineers, behavioral scientists, and health educators in close consultation with the user community.

The potential for upgrading standards of service over time should also be considered in the process of project selection and technical design, so as to avoid initial overdesign and consequent underutilization of capacity. Water systems can be expanded by stages as the economy develops, incomes rise, and the level of affordable service increases. The spacing of hydrants or standpipes can be narrowed over time and the number of courtyard or house connections increased, and a single project can provide for a mix of services that can be progressively upgraded. In this manner, per capita water consumption can rise from 20 liters to 200 liters or more a day, with incremental investments made as consumption increases. The technical analysis should be closely linked to the evaluation of potential demand, so that the initial service standard selected and the sequence of future improvements result in the least-cost solution over time.

Water conservation is another important consideration in project design, especially in water-scarce areas or where the availability of water from the source (rain or streams) varies greatly during the year. The choice of service standards and of technology can be used to manage water demand, since the amount of water consumed is directly related to these two decisions. Similarly, sanitation technologies determine the amount of water required for excreta disposal. Water conservation, therefore, has to start with the selection of standards, complemented when necessary by the modification of housing codes and with incentives to motivate existing users to retrofit their facilities with water-saving appliances. The tariff structure can also encourage conservation by charging higher prices for higher levels of consumption.

In rural areas where population concentrations and consequently present levels of service are much lower, the technical problems are generally less complex. An exception is the identification and testing of groundwater aquifers, which often require sophisticated techniques. For most small towns and villages, however, shallow wells with hand pumps and simple latrines can provide acceptable service. To keep the water safe, such wells must be protected from contaminated surface water and seepage and from foreign matter by means of a lining of concrete or brick, a cover, and adequate drainage around the wellhead. Notable progress has been made in the design and testing of improved but simple hand pumps (which in the past suffered from frequent breakdowns) to reduce the maintenance problems that have plagued so many rural water systems.

Operation and maintenance requirements should also figure in the choice of technology. Improper operation of water supply systems may compromise the intended benefits or introduce new threats to health through contamination of the water. The scarcity of qualified technicians to maintain the facilities, along with the ubiquitous problems of ensuring a reliable supply of fuel, lubricants, and spare parts, argue against complex or sophisticated equipment. A system consisting of many independent, discrete parts (latrines, hand pumps, and so on) is inherently more stable than a single, large, centralized system—especially when maintenance capacity is low—and a breakdown or failure will have less damaging effects on health and the environment.

Finally, inappropriate legal restrictions have sometimes been major obstacles to the adoption of affordable technologies. At the time they achieved political independence, many countries adopted the housing and sanitation codes, zoning restrictions, and professional licensing standards of the former colonial power, which may have little relevance to local conditions and needs. International standards of plumbing and sanitation, for example, may be excessively conservative and bar the use of otherwise suitable technologies, such as pit latrines and septic tanks, in established neighborhoods. Removal or modification of legal constraints may be a necessary part of the introduction of appropriate technology.

A country's ability to exploit the wide differences in the cost of various technologies will bear directly on the speed with which it can reach the objectives of the Water and Sanitation Decade. To cover the existing backlog of unserved people throughout the world (except in China), at the service standards of most earlier Bank-assisted projects, would cost the impossible sum of nearly $600 billion (in 1981 prices). Providing only the simplest standard described above would cost $60 billion. These figures are only illustrative, since technical and political factors require that a mix of standards be provided. But it is clear that average costs can be drastically reduced; a reasonable estimate for a technically and politically realistic mix would be $200 billion.

Technology Choice and the Cultural Setting

An appropriate technology must also take into account the sociocultural setting. In many societies, how water is used and excreta disposed of involves a complex web of social obligations, cultural practices, family traditions, and religious beliefs. These have a particular bearing on the acceptability of the lower-cost technologies, which have the disadvantage of being less convenient than in-house plumbing and water-borne sewerage. Numerous water and sanitation programs have not succeeded in bringing about the expected improvements in health, especially in rural areas and urban slums, due to a combination of lack of consumer acceptance, continuing low standards of personal and household sanitation, and transmission of diseases at food stalls, workplaces, schools, and markets.

Traditional water sources have sometimes been kept in use, even when improved water facilities were provided, because their location was more convenient. Water from new sources may be perceived as inferior in taste, odor, or appearance to the water previously used. In some parts of West Africa, households bound by tradition have refused to use an improved water supply because local religious teachings—probably rooted in an ancient discovery that contaminated water was dangerous to health— prohibited drinking water that has a strange taste.[2]

Changing sanitary habits is even more difficult. Many societies have ritualized waste disposal practices and have erected taboos around defecation. Sharing of defecation sites, for example, is thought by some societies to cause infertility. Convincing consumers of the benefits of improved waste disposal may be particularly hard when the solution being advocated is confined, malodorous, or shared with others. Keeping

2. For a useful discussion of this subject, see Frederick L. Golladay, *Appropriate Technology for Water Supply and Sanitation: Meeting the Needs of the Poor for Water Supply and Waste Disposal*, World Bank Technical Paper no. 9 (Washington, D.C., 1983).

community sanitation facilities clean is generally difficult, and failure to maintain water seals or vents or to relocate privies as pits are filled may discourage use or render a given facility unsafe.

Some of these problems are complex or have deep roots in the culture, and no formula or approach to solving them is universally applicable. It is axiomatic, however, that consumers must understand and be convinced of the importance of using safe water and sanitation methods and of keeping them safe. This means that the local community has to be involved closely from the earliest stages of project design through to project implementation and the maintenance and operation of the facilities. Within the household, which is the critical point at which decisions are made, women are especially important as both providers of health care and carriers of water. They also suffer most when facilities are inadequate. Getting women to participate requires special sensitivity by project designers in some cultures, lest traditions be offended and the project therefore rejected.

The impact of new or improved facilities on people's health can be enhanced if other health measures, such as immunization programs (which are not expensive and make a significant contribution to controlling disease) can be undertaken simultaneously. Complementary information and education programs to improve general health and nutrition as well as personal hygiene are important; an effective way to set them up is to combine the use of classroom teaching and public media, especially radio, with group and individual discussions. Water utilities generally are not in a good position to conduct such programs themselves, but it is in their interest to collaborate with educational and other authorities to make sure that the message reaches the right people at the right time. Much remains to be learned, however, about how the requisite information required to change attitudes and behavior can best be disseminated. Overcoming deep-seated reluctance to abandon traditional customs may be especially difficult when the health improvements that are the rationale for the new facilities will not be apparent for months or even years.

The results of information programs have often been disappointing. Excessive reliance on the medium itself rather than the message has sometimes compromised the effectiveness of the communication. Professionals at times have provided the new information in ways that were intellectually satisfying to themselves but unconvincing to low-income people. Efforts to improve hygiene through education and communication have typically been based on the germ theory of disease, which may not correspond to the perceptions and beliefs of the society. Messages must be targeted to the members of the household who decide what is done, and to those in the community whose approval or example is needed for widespread adoption of improved practices. The messages themselves must stress the positive elements of the new technology in terms relevant to the prospective users, and they must fit in with the traditional customs and beliefs of the locality.

The health and nutrition campaigns conducted by the government of Tanzania are sometimes cited as a successful approach. With the aid of the local organizations of the national political party, an estimated 90 percent of the country's population was informed about latrine construction, improvement of water supply, basic hygiene, food preparation, and child care. A formal evaluation of the campaigns revealed that a large percentage of those who received information were able to recall the main messages, and that about half of them initiated construction of latrines. Later follow-up revealed, however, that only a small number of latrines were completed and used. The success of the campaigns in promoting latrine construction appears to have reflected the influence of the political party rather than a commitment to newly acquired ideas. In the absence of individual commitment to the new technology and a sustained effort by local organizations, longer-term use was disappointing.[3]

Coordination and Complementarities

Improvements to water supply and to sanitation should ideally be carried out concurrently, both to provide the maximum benefits to health and to take account of complementarities between the two services. The water supply system adopted has important implications for the standard of waste disposal required. For example, the level of water consumption associated with standpipes is compatible with the use of latrines, whereas disposal of the much larger volumes of water supplied through house connections—70 to 90 percent of which emerges as waste water—requires a water-borne system.

The interdependence of the two systems can also be expressed in negative terms. If a community does not have the means to finance a waste water collection system, water supply projects should not introduce greater quantities of water than can be disposed of on-site. Otherwise, the waste water will form ponds on the surface or run off into streets and alleys, creating more of a health hazard, especially to children attracted to play in the water, than the clean water has eliminated.

The high cost of sanitation, especially of water-borne sewerage, makes it impractical for many communities or countries to expand both services concurrently on a large scale. Whenever possible, water supply projects should include at least those minimal sanitation improvements that will increase the health impact of the investment. More important, the analysis of water supply alternatives should from the outset include the phased introduction and expected cost of the complementary investments in waste disposal, even if they cannot be initiated at the same time.

Other complementarities affecting environmental health exist between surface water drainage and solid waste disposal. In the absence of better alternatives, drainage ditches are often used as disposal sites for garbage; when drains and sewers are blocked by the accumulation of garbage, ponds are formed which become breeding grounds for mosquitos and a habitat for rodents. Solid waste disposal projects, in turn, must reflect not only sociocultural conditions but also existing informal recycling activities that may be an important source of income for the poor.

3. Golladay, *Appropriate Technology for Water Supply and Sanitation*, p. 8.

PART III
The Project Cycle

World Bank staff discussing a project with the Office of Posts and Telecommunications, Burkina

14

Introduction

WHAT IS A PROJECT?

IT IS FORTUNATE that successful project work does not demand a universally accepted definition of what constitutes a project, since none exists. This reflects the great variety of activities subsumed under the term "project." Some sense of this variety should have been conveyed by the many different types of projects referred to in the sector chapters in part II.

In chapter 1 we gave our own definition of a project and listed its essential features. A project, we said, can be defined as a discrete package of investments, policies, and institutional and other actions designed to achieve a specific development objective (or set of objectives) within a designated period.[1] We also noted that a project is likely to comprise several or all of these five elements:

- Capital investment in civil works, equipment, or both (the so-called bricks and mortar of the project)
- Provision of services for design and engineering, supervision of construction, and improvement of operations and maintenance
- Strengthening of local institutions concerned with implementing and operating the project, including the training of local managers and staff
- Improvements in policies—such as those on pricing, subsidies, and cost recovery—that affect project performance and the relationship of the project both to the sector in which it falls and to broader national development objectives
- A plan for implementing the above activities to achieve the project's objectives within a given time.

For many external lenders, the packaging of investment into distinct projects is an important feature of their lending operations. Regardless of the source of finance, however, it is desirable for national planners to organize into a project such major investments as a large dam, a fertilizer plant, a mining complex, or a program to settle and develop a region of the country. The case is perhaps less clear for the ongoing investment program of an operating agency such as a ministry of education, with its large, continuing program of rehabilitating old schools and building new ones, or a ministry of public works, with its responsibility for the maintenance, rehabilitation, and expansion of a national highway system. But for reasons that should become apparent in the discussion which follows, the discipline of the project approach can still be very useful

---

1. Another World Bank author, also noting the absence of an "academic definition" of a project, calls it "an investment activity in which financial resources are expended to create capital assets that produce benefits over an extended period of time" and "an activity for which money will be spent in expectation of returns and which logically seems to lend itself to planning, financing, and implementing as a unit." J. Price Gittinger, *Economic Analysis of Agricultural Projects*, 2d ed. (Baltimore, Md.: Johns Hopkins University Press for the Economic Development Institute of the World Bank, 1982).

when dealing with a large number of relatively small investments of this kind.

Strengthening the relevant institutions is no less a concern of government officials charged with planning and implementing projects financed with the country's own resources than it is of external lenders. Inclusion of policy issues in the project approach, however, may appear to local officials in a different light. The close association that exists between economic policies and project performance is one of the principal themes of this book; nevertheless, linking the two may be easier for the staff of external agencies than for officials in developing countries, where there is a greater diffusion of responsibility. Thus, constructing an irrigation project may be the responsibility of the ministry of irrigation or of public works, while achieving the proper level of cost recovery and fixing the appropriate prices for the irrigated crops—both important elements of project success—may be the concern of the ministry of agriculture or of finance.

THE PROJECT CYCLE

It is convenient to think of project work as taking place in several distinct stages. These stages are commonly referred to as the "project cycle" to make the point that they are closely linked to each other and follow a logical progression, with the later stages helping to provide the basis for renewal of the cycle through subsequent project work.

Different terms can be used to describe the various stages of the project cycle. The World Bank uses these:

- *Identification.* The first phase of the cycle is concerned with identifying project ideas that appear to represent a high-priority use of the country's resources to achieve an important development objective. Such project ideas should meet an initial test of feasibility; that is, there should be some assurance that technical and institutional solutions—at costs commensurate with the expected benefits—will be found and suitable policies adopted.

- *Preparation.* Once a project idea has passed the identification "test," it must be advanced to the point at which a firm decision can be made whether or not to proceed with it. This requires a progressive refinement of the design of the project in all its dimensions—technical, economic, financial, social, institutional, and so on.

- *Appraisal.* Before approving a loan, external agencies normally require a formal process of appraisal to assess the overall soundness of the project and its readiness for implementation. For an internally generated and financed investment, the extent of formal appraisal varies widely in accordance with government practice. Some explicit appraisal, however, is a necessary, or at least a desirable, part of the decisionmaking process before funds are committed.

- *Implementation.* The implementation stage covers the actual development or construction of the project, up to the point at which it becomes fully operational. It includes monitoring of all aspects of the work or activity as it proceeds and supervision by "oversight" agencies within the country or by external lenders.

- *Evaluation.* The ex post evaluation of a completed project seeks to determine whether the objectives have been achieved and to draw lessons from experience with the project that can be applied to similar projects in the future. Although some lending agencies such as the World Bank routinely require an ex post evaluation of all projects that they finance, few developing countries have established a comprehensive system for evaluating the results of their project investment portfolio.

The distinctions among the various stages of the project cycle, especially the earlier ones of identification and preparation, are often blurred in practice, and their relative importance can vary greatly, depending on the character and history of each project. The process is an iterative one; the same issues may be addressed, with varying degrees of detail and refinement, as the project advances through the cycle. This should be borne in mind in the discussion that follows since, for ease of presentation, the principal substantive aspects of project analysis (technical, economic, financial, social, and so forth) are discussed separately in the individual chapters of part IV.

The project approach has proved a potent instrument for rationalizing and improving the investment process. Its principal advantage lies in providing a logical framework and sequence within which data can be compiled and analyzed, investment priorities established, project alternatives considered, and sector policy issues addressed. It imposes a discipline on planners and decisionmakers, and ensures that relevant problems and issues are taken into account and subjected to systematic analysis before decisions are reached and implemented. Correctly applied, it can greatly increase the development impact of a country's scarce investment resources.

The project approach also has its limitations. It depends on quantitative inputs of data and can be no more reliable than those data. It also depends on estimates and forecasts, which are subject to human error. Value judgments must be made, but the project approach should at least force them to be made explicitly. Risks can be assessed but not avoided, and projects must be designed and implemented against a constantly shifting background of political, social, and economic change. In the last analysis, the effectiveness of the project approach depends on the skill and judgment of those who use it. How to take advantage of this approach, while avoiding some of its pitfalls, is the theme of the remainder of this book.[2]

2. Some of these points are elaborated more fully in Gittinger, *Economic Analysis of Agricultural Projects*, pp. 9–12.

Surveying the construction site of the Tarbela dam, Pakistan

15

Project Identification

VIEWED IN STATIC TERMS, project identification can be described as the beginning of the process through which the national investment plans and sector strategies discussed in parts I and II are translated into specific investments and action programs. As we have stressed earlier, however, the process is typically dynamic and iterative, moving backward and forward across the principal stages, at any of which new project ideas may be generated.

Projects originate from a multiplicity of sources. In the course of developing a sector strategy, potential projects will have been identified and ranked in some rough order of priority. In sectors or subsectors with large, discrete capital investments, such as power, a more elaborate investment program is often prepared with the use of a systems analysis approach. This provides a coherent framework for the timing of specific projects that together constitute the least-cost solution to meeting the anticipated demand for power.

In practice, project ideas often result from the identification of

- Unsatisfied demands or needs and possible means to meet them
- Problems or constraints in the development process caused by shortages of essential facilities, services, and material or human resources and by institutional or other obstacles
- Unused or underused material or human resources and opportunities for their conversion to more productive purposes; or, conversely, overused natural resources that need to be conserved or restored
- The need to complement other investments (such as providing railway and port links to a mining project)

Project ideas may also emanate from

- Initiatives by local private or public entrepreneurs who wish to take advantage of opportunities they perceive or who are responding to government incentives
- A government response to local political or social pressures originating, for example, from economic, social, or regional inequalities
- The pursuit of national objectives, such as self-sufficiency in food production
- The occurrence of natural events (drought, floods, or earthquakes)
- A desire to create a permanent local capability to carry out development activities by building up local institutions.

Finally, project ideas originate not only from within a country but also from abroad as a result of

- Investment proposals of multinational firms
- Programming activities of bilateral or multilateral aid agencies and their ongoing projects in the country
- Influence of investment strategies adopted by other developing countries as well as opportunities created by international agreements (for example, on the use of offshore resources)

- Prevailing professional opinion or public consensus within the international community in such fields as population, environment, and the alleviation of poverty.

DEFINING PROJECT OBJECTIVES

Initial identification and preliminary screening of project ideas constitute a critical stage of the project process. Decisions made implicitly or explicitly at this stage can have far-reaching consequences for the project: some decisions are likely to be irreversible no matter how thorough the subsequent preparation and appraisal, while others may largely determine the quality of the project and its impact on development. As in other fields of endeavor, there is no substitute for being right in the first place.

Obvious as it may seem, it is worth emphasizing that it is important to begin by identifying explicitly the objectives that the project is intended to achieve. In doing so, it may become apparent that not all of the objectives are mutually compatible. Thus, the objective of maximizing production or exports may have to be weighed against the objective of increasing domestic employment or of improving the distribution of income. It may also become apparent that the proposed project is not equally suited to reach all of the possible objectives; the project may have to be broadened or some of the objectives pursued through other channels. To cite one example: the objective of an agricultural project could be functional (to provide a national service), regional (to develop a particular area of the country), or subsectoral (to expand the production of a particular crop)—but probably not all of these at once. Selection of a simple and clear objective, such as strengthening a national agricultural extension service, may enhance the prospects of success. It may also, however, limit the contribution to development unless other, complementary investments (such as in agricultural research or credit) are also undertaken. This raises the issue of project complexity, already mentioned in some of the sector chapters and to which we shall return in the next chapter.

Explicit attention to a project's objectives at the earliest stage should include efforts to ensure that all of the parties who will be engaged in its implementation and operation share a common view of the objectives and of the strategy for meeting them. Among those who should be consulted from the outset are the relevant political authorities as well as the ultimate beneficiaries, whose active participation is often necessary for the success of a project—as, for example, in rural and urban development. The same applies to the external agency or agencies that may be expected to help finance the project. Failure to reach a mutual understanding of a project's objectives and to secure a firm commitment from all the parties concerned has often generated friction between lenders and borrowers and resulted in poor project implementation.

Identification of projects and their subsequent preparation can be viewed as a process that moves in two complementary directions. On the one hand, the number of project ideas under consideration needs to be narrowed down; on the other hand, the surviving project ideas need to be defined in increasing detail.

- *Elimination of alternatives.* It is important at the outset to consider a wide range of possible design alternatives. All too often, project ideas are put forward and processed through appraisal without adequate consideration of alternative, and possibly cheaper or more effective, ways of achieving the same objectives. Whether the result of vested interest, of political pressure, or simply of lack of information on feasible alternatives, the consequences are the same: opportunities lost or forgone, which can seldom be recaptured. As identification and preparation advance, the initially wide range of alternative approaches is narrowed down to a few and then to one that is well enough defined in its physical and institutional components, costs, benefits, and risks to be ready for appraisal and implementation.
- *Elaboration of details.* As alternatives are eliminated, the detail and precision of the design of each aspect of the project are sharpened. This avoids unnecessarily detailed preparatory work on alternatives that are eventually discarded. The difference between identification and preparation work is often one of degree rather than of kind.

Screening Project Ideas

Criteria for screening or modifying project ideas—and their design alternatives—will be very broad initially and become more refined as the work proceeds. To view the process from another perspective, some of the reasons for rejection of a project are:

- Inappropriate technology in relation to the project's objectives or to local capabilities
- Excessive risk
- Inadequate demand for the proposed output or lack of comparative advantage
- Inadequate supply of raw materials or skills
- Overambitious design in relation to institutional and managerial capabilities
- Excessive recurrent costs of operation in relation to available financial resources
- Excessive economic, social, or environmental costs relative to the expected benefits
- Lack of commitment of the intended beneficiaries or lack of political support from key authorities.

Many of the screening criteria are inevitably vague, and it is important that staff who share in the decisionmaking try to arrive at a common understanding of the criteria to be used and how they will be consistently applied.

A review or evaluation of actual experience with similar projects under way or already completed can provide valuable insights to aid the screening process. If there is no project design under consideration that meets the screening criteria, research may be called for to develop new approaches.

PREFEASIBILITY STUDY

For large investments, a prefeasibility—also called a preinvestment—study may be desirable. It should be carried out in just enough detail to determine the broad justification of the project idea and the possible design alternatives to be considered further, together with reasons for the choices made or proposed. More elaborate technical, economic, financial, social, institutional, and other analyses should be postponed, although any aspects that will deserve special attention should be flagged. To permit a decision on the merits of the project idea, the study should briefly examine

- The size and nature of the demand or market for the product or service, and the intended or expected beneficiary groups or target areas
- The alternative technical solutions or packages available, with corresponding estimates of outputs, including identification of technologies already in local use and their potential for improvement
- The availability of the principal physical and human resources and skills that will be required
- The order of magnitude of the costs, for both the initial investment and for continued operation
- The order of magnitude of the financial and economic rates of return (where applicable)
- Any institutional constraints or policy issues likely to have an important impact on the proposed project.

If a project idea shows merit, the additional information that will be needed during project preparation should be specified. This may include, for example, detailed market studies, geological or environmental surveys, investigation of potential local sources of raw materials, details of pertinent government regulations and policies, and the economic, social, or cultural characteristics of the people in the project area. The availability of technical and managerial skills and, more generally, of existing or potential sources of local capacity for project preparation and implementation are other issues which may call for more information.

PROJECT BRIEF

The World Bank has established a procedure under which a Project Brief is usually prepared for each project being considered for financing. This procedure can also be useful to developing countries. The Project Brief is designed to identify and reach early agreement within the Bank and with the prospective borrower on

- The development objectives of the project
- Basic features of the project and alternatives to be considered further in project design
- Institutional, policy, and other issues that need to be addressed during preparation, appraisal, or implementation
- The steps necessary to prepare the project and the human and other resources to be employed.

The Project Brief, which is periodically updated as identification and preparation progress and decisions are made, has proved to be a valuable tool for these purposes, as it may be to a national development agency in planning its project work and seeking approval from its authorities before scarce resources are committed to further preparation. Care must be taken to ensure that it does not become just another piece of bureaucratic paperwork—as it has in some countries—but serves to focus the attention of busy policymakers and decisionmakers on the specific questions that need answers at the successive stages of project identification and preparation.

The Identification Test

Whatever mechanism for internal review or reporting is employed, a project may be deemed to have passed the identification "test" and be ready for detailed preparation when

- Major options and alternatives have been identified and some initial choices made
- The principal institutional and policy issues affecting project outcome have been identified and appear amenable to solution
- The project options selected are likely to be justified, given rough estimates of the expected costs and benefits
- It appears that the project will have adequate support both from the political authorities and from the intended beneficiaries
- The prospects are reasonable that adequate funding will be available from domestic and, if needed, external sources
- A specific preparation program has been established.

Sources of Assistance for Project Identification

As we commented earlier, projects are identified in a multiplicity of ways. Many arise as part of the normal process of investment planning by line agencies of the government. Some develop out of ongoing projects in the same sector and the continuing relationship with external lenders funding these projects. Others arise from general discussion with such lenders on national or sector development strategies. Some bilateral and multilateral aid agencies, including the World Bank, have regional or local resident missions, one of whose purposes is to help identify and prepare projects, or they may send specific identification missions from headquarters. Specialized United Nations agencies such as the FAO and Unesco— either on their own or through cooperative programs with other aid agencies—provide services for project identification and preparation in their special fields. The United Nations Development Programme is a major source of financial and technical assistance for resource surveys and prefeasibility studies undertaken as part of project identification, as well as for work at later stages of project preparation. Sources of assistance are also discussed in the next chapter on project preparation.

Unit supervisor describing boundaries of family plots in Lilongwe Land Development project, Malawi

16

Project Preparation

THE PROCESS that is launched when a project is identified continues through the stages of preparation and appraisal and leads ultimately to the decision whether to commit funds for its implementation. As noted, this is not a neat, consecutive process, but an iterative one involving retracing steps, reformulating ideas, measuring tradeoffs among options by weighing their respective costs and benefits, and analyzing technical, economic, financial, social, and institutional matters in varying degrees of detail.

Refining project objectives and the means of achieving them is an important part of project preparation. This refinement takes various forms. Production objectives need to be spelled out in terms of specific, phased increases in output of a particular mix of products. Project beneficiaries need to be targeted more precisely as to geographic regions, production or consumption units, income groups, or social and behavioral characteristics. The level of service to be provided should be clearly specified. Technical constraints, such as adverse soil conditions affecting a construction project, need to be examined in detail. The institutional reforms to be achieved must be translated into action programs, as must the various policy changes that impinge on the execution of the project. As the objectives are refined and the options or alternatives for achieving them narrowed to a manageable number, the project takes shape and more detailed preparation is done on those options that remain.

FEASIBILITY STUDY

Whether or not a prefeasibility study has been made, a feasibility study should form the central core of the preparation process. (Some agencies use the term "preparation report" instead of "feasibility study," but the underlying concept is the same.) While the need is perhaps most obvious for large infrastructure projects, the discipline and systematic approach of such a study is desirable for all save the most routine and repetitive investments.

Purpose and Scope

The purpose of the feasibility study is to provide decisionmakers—national or foreign—with the basis for deciding whether or not to proceed with the project and for choosing the most desirable option or alternative among the few remaining. As its name implies, this study is undertaken to establish the feasibility or justification of the project as a whole in all of its relevant dimensions (technical, financial, and so forth). Each of these dimensions is analyzed, not only separately but also in relation to all the others, through a process of successive approximations. Thus, the "right" technical package will depend on the scope of the commercial market or demand for the product, the administrative capacity of the implementing agency, and the cultural attitudes and social behavior of the ultimate producers or consumers. The economic benefits to be derived from different technological approaches or project sizes will have to be weighed against their respective costs. Above all—and this is a crucial point to remember—the objective of the analysis is not to determine whether a particular project idea is *good* enough to be financed, but to arrive at the *best* solution possible under prevailing conditions, as they may be modified by the project.

Beyond these common characteristics, feasibility studies can vary as widely as the projects themselves. The scope and duration of the study will depend on such considerations as the inherent complexity of the project, how much is already known about it, and whether it is innovative or repetitive. The study can take as little time as three months or as much as two years or more. Costs can range from several thousand dollars to tens of millions; for industrial or infrastructure projects involving substantial technical work, a rough rule of thumb is that the feasibility study represents about 5 percent of the overall project cost.

Since the feasibility study is likely to constitute the first substantial investment of public funds in project preparation, the question is bound to arise whether this expenditure is justified. While those designing the study should be cost-conscious, this is not the place to skimp; if done well, the study is bound to pay for itself several times over through cost savings or increased benefits.

It will be evident from the foregoing that there can be no standard model for the design of a feasibility study. Essentially, whatever the degree of complexity or detail, the study must provide answers to the basic questions that we have referred to earlier:

- Does the project conform with the country's development objectives and priorities?
- Is the relevant policy framework compatible with achievement of the project's objectives?
- Is the project technically sound, and is it the best of the available technical alternatives?
- Is the project administratively workable?
- Is there adequate demand for the project's output?
- Is the project economically justified and financially viable?
- Is the project compatible with the customs and traditions of the beneficiaries?
- Is the project environmentally sound?

Issues to be Covered

The geological, hydrological, and other surveys and the engineering studies required for the technical design of an infrastructure project are usually carried only as far as "preliminary" engineering in the feasibility study. This should provide cost estimates that are accurate within a margin of error of 15 to 20 percent. Detailed engineering, which is both more time-consuming and more expensive and produces estimates generally within the range of accuracy of 5 to 10 percent, should be done later in the preparation process and only after a decision has been made, on the basis of the feasibility study, to proceed with a particular project option. The information needed to establish the basic parameters for the technical design of other than infrastructure projects (for example, data on rainfall, landholdings, population densities, and income distribution for an agricultural settlement project) should also be gathered at this stage.

The economic analysis of costs and benefits should be carried to the point at which an economic rate of return can be calculated with a reasonable degree of accuracy for the project design that is recommended. The analysis should ascertain whether the demand for the project will enable the output to be sold at prices that are remunerative. For projects that do not produce any output to be sold, forecasting demand is nevertheless essential—to establish, for example, proper design standards for a highway or the number and size of vocational training institutions. Financial analysis should ascertain the financial attractiveness of the investment to the entity undertaking it and to the intended participants and beneficiaries (such as farmers), and provide the general outline of a financial plan to ensure the availability of funds to implement the project. As with the technical design, the economic, financial, and other analyses may be pursued in greater detail, as necessary, after the feasibility study has served its purpose. The study may identify the need for further action in other areas to help ensure that the project can be successfully implemented and achieve its intended objectives; such actions might include strengthening the management and staff of the project entity or of other institutions, modifying macroeconomic or sectoral policies, or securing the support of the intended beneficiaries.

Partly because the practice of conducting feasibility studies was first applied to large, capital-intensive projects such as dams, power plants, and major highways, and partly because the consulting firms that frequently were charged with these studies usually began as engineering firms, the technical aspects of feasibility studies have traditionally been given most attention and been done most expertly. For revenue-earning enterprises, the need for financial analysis has also long been recognized—although its scope has broadened considerably with time—as has the need for market analysis. Cost-benefit analysis of alternatives and measurement of economic rates of return are more recent additions to feasibiliity studies; the techniques for doing this analysis have subsequently undergone considerable refinement. Institutional, managerial, environmental, and sociocultural dimensions have been the last to receive the attention they deserve, both because their importance to project success was not properly understood and because the state of the art with respect to them is the least advanced (which may be an effect as well as a cause of their relative neglect). The larger international consulting firms can now put together the interdisciplinary teams that most complex feasibility studies require. The scarcest—and most valuable—member of such a team is a skilled and experienced project leader.

Checklists

The major bilateral aid agencies, and some of the specialized agencies of the United Nations, among them the World Bank, the FAO, and UNIDO, have prepared checklists of subjects that should be covered in feasibility studies or similar types of project preparation reports. Such checklists exist, often in voluminous detail, for most of the principal types of projects and can normally be obtained on request from the originating agencies.

These checklists can be useful guides for ensuring that the relevant issues are taken into account in the feasibility study. Their very comprehensiveness, however, can be a danger if it induces excessive reliance on them. No two projects are alike, and no checklist can cover or give suitable emphasis to all the possible considerations. The checklist should not become a substitute for creative thinking in tailoring the feasibility study to the particular characteristics of the project.

Consultants

Designing and conducting a feasibility study is an exacting professional task. The use of local staff for this purpose, if they are qualified, offers several advantages. They bring to the project superior knowledge of the local environment, institutions, legal requirements, and social customs. For some activities, such as contacts with local farmers, experience indicates that local staff are essential. Moreover, building up a national capacity to design and implement feasibility studies and to carry out project work in general is also an important development objective in its own right. Technical assistance is available from external agencies to train local staff and develop their capabilities. Some of the more advanced developing countries, such as Brazil, India, Korea, and Mexico, now have strong technical departments in their national agencies that are competent to prepare all but the most complex or sophisticated feasibility studies, although like their foreign counterparts they have tended to be stronger in engineering than in economic and social analysis. In addition, private or quasi-public consulting firms have grown up in these countries and some others and have successfully completed assignments in other developing countries as well as in their own.

Local staff, however, are not likely to be able to take on highly specialized studies, such as the design of a cost-based tariff system. Experienced and qualified foreign consultants, available in virtually every field, will then have to be employed. Such consulting services can be expensive, both absolutely and relative to the salaries of local staff with comparable responsibilities. This, together with other, often nationalistic concerns, has led to a reluctance on the part of some countries to employ expatriate consultants. This attitude is understandable, but it can be costly to development. We discuss the selection and use of consultants in chapter 26; suffice it to say here that there are various ways to mitigate the cost and other drawbacks of foreign consultants, including the use of joint ventures with local firms, the employment of local staff by the consultant to the maximum extent feasible, or the use of qualified firms from other developing countries. But quality of service should be the overriding consideration.

TRADEOFF BETWEEN PROJECT PREPARATION AND IMPLEMENTATION

The importance of adequate preparatory work has been borne out again and again by experience. There is no doubt that better project preparation reduces the likelihood of implementation problems. This lesson has led the World Bank to adopt the policy of lending late in the cycle of project preparation, after detailed engineering has been completed, cost estimates are relatively firm, any land needed has been acquired, and the organizational and institutional framework has been designed. Completion of the detailed economic and financial analyses will also enable sounder judgments to be made about a project's justification and viability before investment funds are committed. However, the question still remains: how much preparatory work, and in what detail, is enough? Behind this question lies the recognition that there is, at least beyond a certain point, a tradeoff between the investment of additional resources in project preparation and the use of those resources to help implement the project.

As usual, there is no simple answer. But the terms of the tradeoff can usefully be analyzed in relation to a spectrum ranging from "hard" items (such as large infrastructure components, including civil works and major items of equipment) to "soft" items (such as institution building, school curriculum reform, and the design of mechanisms for beneficiary participation). Completing the detailed engineering or design of the "hard" components before funds are committed substantially reduces the risk of construction cost overruns and implementation delays owing to imprecise estimates of the physical quantities of work to be performed. At the other end of the spectrum, it can be unproductive beyond a point to devote detailed preparation effort to a project's "soft" components, the success of which is largely determined by behavioral patterns about which less can be known in advance. After the project is begun, the design of such components may require considerable adaptation to fit various user requirements or a rapidly changing environment.

Even when there is much that cannot be known in advance, it is essential that project preparation make the fullest possible use of the information that is available. Such preparation should specify clearly the project objectives, ensure the commitment of all parties (including the proposed beneficiaries) to those objectives, and outline in some detail the essential inputs and arrangements with respect to organizations, institutions, and procedures. For example, a common shortcoming of Bank-assisted training programs when included as components in projects has been that they have not been adequately prepared in advance, with consequent delays, misunderstandings, and mistakes during the course of their implementation. But there may be a point beyond which more elaborate analysis is not justified by the state of knowledge. When important uncertainties exist, sufficient flexibility should be built into the project design so that elements can be reappraised, and arrangements and procedures modified, in the light of experience. The need for flexible implementation should be anticipated during preparation and staff resources budgeted accordingly. If uncertainties with respect to project design are very large, it may be preferable to begin with a small pilot project that is deliberately experimental in nature and to monitor its implementation closely.

SIMPLE OR COMPLEX PROJECT DESIGN?

One of the fundamental questions that must be addressed in preparing a project, and one that cuts across technical, economic, social, and other issues, is how simple or complex the project design should be. For every objective, there are a number of design alternatives, some of which are more difficult to implement than others. Given the scarcity of skilled staff and managerial resources in developing countries, projects with relatively simple, well-defined objectives that make use of proven technologies or institutional approaches have the best chance of being implemented successfully. Consequently, efforts to simplify and redefine objectives and to select technologies and administrative approaches that are known to work in a particular environment have paid off very well.

Although a simple design should always be sought, there may at times be a delicate and difficult balance to strike in this regard. A project that is too complex for the administrative capacity of the agencies responsible for implementation will almost certainly encounter problems. Yet the administrative capacity of an agency may be capable of expansion under the project through well-planned technical assistance. More important, there are numerous examples of projects that did not yield their full benefits, or even failed, because the need for complementary investments and activities had not been recognized and taken into account. This is true of many kinds of agricultural projects, of urban and regional development programs, and of highway maintenance projects, among others. Projects can be too simple as well as too complex. But even when a multicomponent approach, with its inherent complexity, is necessary, it is desirable to streamline the project as much as possible by concentrating on those elements essential to achieving the primary objective or objectives and to leave desirable but secondary objectives to subsequent stages or to operations carried out parallel to but outside the framework of the project. Both the scale of a project and its phasing offer other ways of dealing with the need to match design with implementation capacity.

EXTERNAL SOURCES OF ASSISTANCE

Technical and financial assistance in preparation work is available from a variety of external sources. When it is intended that a project be externally financed, it is highly desirable that the prospective lenders be closely involved in the design and implementation of the feasibility study and other preparatory work. If the preparatory work is done by the country in isolation, with the intention of then "shopping around" to find lenders for the finished product, much of the work may have to be redone, at considerable cost in time and money, to meet lenders' standards or requirements.

Mention has already been made of assistance available from the UNDP, which is an important source of finance for feasibility studies and other preparatory work, and of the cooperative programs between the World Bank and both the FAO and Unesco, which are primarily concerned with preparation of projects on behalf of developing countries. The Bank has resident missions in East and West Africa and in Indonesia that also perform this function.

In addition to its role as executing agent for some UNDP studies and as cosponsor of the cooperative programs, the World Bank finances project preparation work on its own account in several ways. One important technique is called "piggybacking." As its name implies, preparatory studies for the design of future projects are included in the loan for a project, normally in the same sector, that is ready for financing. This helps ensure that the Bank is closely involved with the borrower in the preparatory work through review and approval of the terms of reference of the study, selection of consultants (if any), and review of interim and final reports. Detailed engineering may also be financed in a second phase of the piggybacking, usually after Bank approval of the results of the feasibility study. When an appropriate vehicle for piggybacking is not available, funds for studies can be provided in the form of technical assistance loans and engineering loans. Borrowers in a position to prefinance the cost of preparatory studies may be eligible for retroactive financing under a loan for the project in question.

In addition to this panoply of instruments, the Bank has established a Project Preparation Facility to finance, in the form of advances, two specific types of activity related to preparation of projects for subsequent Bank financing: small, discrete tasks, often but not always in engineering, related to gaps that arise in the preparation of a project and that need to be filled before its appraisal can be completed; and additional support to activate or strengthen the entity in the borrowing country responsible for preparing or implementing the project in order to speed up its work and get the project off to an early start.

A Note on Appraisal

The Bank does its own appraisal of each project that it expects to help finance, relying primarily on its regular staff and sending one or more appraisal missions to the field. This is followed by an elaborate procedure of internal review of the appraisal report and related documents before negotiations with the borrower and presentation of the proposed loan to the Board of Executive Directors for approval. The larger multilateral and bilateral aid agencies follow similar procedures, while some of the smaller ones, when cofinancing projects with the Bank, rely on the Bank's appraisal documents.

Such formal appraisal and approval procedures are obviously not called for in the case of some of the more routine projects financed by developing countries themselves as part of the ongoing investment programs of operating agencies. But it is desirable that feasibility and other related studies of major projects be carefully reviewed by the appropriate authorities within the operating agency, and perhaps by a separate agency (such as the ministry of planning) as well, and that their approval be explicitly granted before funds are committed to the project. Internal or external review committees established for this purpose can help to give structure and status to the process and underline the importance of ensuring that preparatory work meets an acceptable standard. Most developing countries do have some approval machinery of this kind, but often the staff needs to be strengthened if they are to evaluate critically the results of feasibility studies or to exercise independent judgment on investment proposals submitted to them.

Molding tiles at kiln in construction area of Rajasthan Canal, India

17

Project Implementation

BY NOW THE READER will have observed that each stage of the project cycle is important, indeed critical. This is no less true of the stage concerned with project implementation, where the earlier preparations and designs, plans and analyses are tested in the harsh light of reality. Since it is self-evident that a project's development objectives are realized only when it is successfully implemented, it is surprising that project implementation has received relatively little attention, not only from the academic community but also from those directly engaged in the development process. Breaking ground for a new project or signing a loan with an international agency attracts much official and press attention. But the long, slow process of tackling the myriad of problems that arise during the implementation of a project is seldom in the limelight—unless, of course, things go particularly badly.

In a sense, most of the work done in the earlier stages of the project cycle—identification, preparation, appraisal—is directed toward ensuring successful implementation. Much of the counsel given in the previous chapters derives from the lessons learned in implementing projects. If the project cycle functions as intended, the difficulties of project implementation will have been anticipated, to the extent that it is possible to do so, during project design and preparation. But in the real world, few things are done as well as they should be. Events seldom go strictly according to plan; both external circumstances and some of the principal actors change; and consequently, project implementation takes on a life of its own.

Since many of the issues have already been discussed, the main purpose of this chapter is to recapitulate, from the World Bank's experience, those factors that lead to successful implementation, the main problems likely to be encountered, and some approaches that have been effective in dealing with them. We begin, however, with a discussion of how to plan, organize, and manage project implementation and how to expedite its start-up.

PLANNING AND MANAGING IMPLEMENTATION

In a broad sense, implementation begins when resources are committed to a particular investment. The point at which a project really gets under way is more obvious for certain types of projects—such as construction of a specific road or factory—than for others. Integrated rural development, for example, comprises a variety of activities (construction of feeder roads and drainage systems, provision of extension and marketing services, credit to farmers, training programs, and so forth) that are of more or less importance and that begin and end at different times.

Until recently, planning the implementation stage of a project tended to be neglected. The emphasis was on the decisionmaking process: on defining alternatives, studying their feasibility, deciding on and then preparing a particular set of investments and action programs—often without taking adequate account of the capacity of institutions to execute and operate them. The resulting shortcomings, difficulties, and failures have helped to direct attention to the need to plan explicitly for implementation.

In this section we take up three main planning and organizational issues: the selection of an implementation unit from among different organizational alternatives, along with the related issues of coordination and supervision; the organizational implications of different technologies and types of projects; and techniques for planning and managing implementation.

Selecting the Implementation Unit

The resources needed to organize and manage projects are among the scarcest in developing countries, and if project design makes excessive demands on them, implementation will suffer. A mismatch between project design and objectives on the one hand and the implementation capacity of an agency on the other has often been the most important reason for poor performance. Many of the early integrated urban and rural development projects in Africa and elsewhere were affected by this problem. In other cases, projects financed by the Bank or other multilateral institutions represented a quantum jump in the overall investment program of an agency, straining its capacity. This has happened especially in smaller countries or with first loans to an agency.

Many projects are part of the investment program of a particular agency and will be implemented by it: roads by a highway department, agricultural credit by an agricultural development bank, small or medium-size industrial projects by a development finance corporation, and so on. If individual projects constitute a relatively small proportion of the total investment program, they can routinely be implemented as part of it. But if projects are larger or require an integrated effort by several parts of an organization, a special project unit has sometimes been established for the duration of the project. Such units, which can be an integral part of the agency and operate under its general rules, have generally functioned well, although jurisdictional problems have sometimes arisen.

A different approach, sometimes promoted by international lenders— including the World Bank—has been to establish a separate project unit, independent from the line agency and operating under special rules, particularly with regard to administrative procedures, use of funds, and staffing regulations. These "enclave" units have been used for complex projects involving several agencies or for projects considered of top priority but beyond the implementation capacity of the line agency. On balance, experience with such separate project implementation units has not been very favorable, as we have pointed out in some of the sector chapters under "Institutional Issues." They have indeed helped implementation in many cases, but without long-term institutional benefits, since they operated under conditions that could not be replicated either by the line agency or elsewhere in the government. Moreover, they have adversely affected the line agencies by attracting some of their best staff and diverting attention from the need to build up their own implementation capacity. This experience suggests that separate project units should be confined to those cases where the expected benefits of a better managed investment clearly outweigh the potential institutional damage. Even in these cases, arrangements should be made to incorporate the unit into the normal activities of the line agency as soon as possible.

Coordinating Mechanisms

Another difficult organizational issue arises in the case of multicomponent projects, such as those for urban or rural development, that have to be implemented by several agencies. Some coordinating mechanism has to be established among these agencies. There are several possibilities, but experience suggests that any coordinating mechanism can be effective only if it satisfies two conditions: a clear definition of responsibilities for each of the participating agencies, and adequate incentive for each of them to work constructively to achieve the project objectives.

One solution to the need for coordination has been, again, to establish a special project unit through which funds are channeled from the central budget to the implementing agencies. Another is for one implementing agency to take the leading role, acting as a de facto project unit to coordinate the activities of other participating entities and sometimes to allocate funds. A third alternative, frequently adopted, is to appoint some type of coordinating committee. Such committees must be given the requisite authority, and the participants should be as close as possible to actual operations. Committees composed of ministers or other high-level officials with many other responsibilities have seldom performed well.

Supervision

Another issue that arises in organizing for project implementation is who will supervise the work being carried out by the implementing agency. This depends in part on how the government itself is organized. Sometimes the supervisory function is performed by another unit in the same agency or by outside consultants working on behalf of the agency, and sometimes by another agency. Any of these solutions is appropriate provided that the supervision is done by a unit administratively independent from the one doing the implementation itself. Supervision performed by an external agency (such as the World Bank) does not substitute for the country's responsibility to oversee the implementation of its projects.

Technical Design

The technical design of a project has implications for how it is implemented. The implementation of a project that uses an advanced and capital-intensive technology may be relatively simple to organize since it requires a small number of highly skilled staff and can be structured along a well-established pattern applicable in many countries. In contrast, projects using intermediate or labor-intensive technologies—such as rural road construction—may require a more elaborate organization and management since they usually rely on a larger number of workers performing several different tasks over a wide geographical area. A road maintenance project will, for the same reasons, be even more difficult to implement, and therefore call for even closer attention to the implementation process itself.

Another way of looking at how a project's design influences the way its implementation should be managed is to distinguish between projects that can and cannot be "blueprinted." For a standard infrastructure project, detailed engineering and careful physical planning will help ensure relatively smooth execution. We emphasize "relatively" because anyone who has worked with construction knows that it is full of daily surprises. But compared with other types of projects, implementation can be planned more accurately on the basis of a blueprint that in most instances will remain essentially unchanged.

The projects for which it is most difficult to have a blueprint are those that are people-oriented and require that a large number of participants to change their behavior. For these, the state of the art and the knowledge generally available during preparation and appraisal do not allow a precise definition of the tasks required during implementation and of their sequence. Such projects include agricultural credit and extension, provision of primary or nonformal education, provision of health care or family planning services, and sites and services projects in urban areas. An extreme example would be a resettlement project intended to move several thousand people from one region to another. Short of totalitarian solutions, it is not possible to predict accurately how many people will resettle over a given period, the specific characteristics of the settlers, or the activities to which they will finally devote themselves. It is not that these projections cannot be or are not made; but the likelihood that reality will turn out to be different from the projections is much greater than it is in traditional infrastructure projects.

Projects of this type still require careful preparation, as emphasized in the preceding chapter. But, in addition, mechanisms should be put in place for regular review during implementation to incorporate the experience that is being acquired and to change or redesign the project as necessary. There are few systematic approaches to improving the effectiveness of this process. The World Bank and other international lending institutions have promoted the use of monitoring and evaluation techniques, including major midcourse evaluations, as discussed below. A prerequisite of this type of project, which we also have stressed in earlier chapters, is to ensure that the intended beneficiaries participate in the initial process of defining approaches and even objectives, and that this participation be organized so that it continues throughout implementation.

Techniques for Managing Implementation

A variety of techniques have been devised to assist in planning and managing implementation. We shall discuss three of them: critical path analysis, monitoring and evaluation, and management information systems.

Critical Path Analysis

Implementing even the simplest project requires completing a number of tasks that have to be undertaken in a particular sequence and with a particular set of interrelations. The complexity of the process increases with projects that have several components or are geographically scattered. Most of the techniques developed to deal with this problem employ critical path analysis. The analysis entails, first, establishing the sequence of activities that minimizes the cost and time of implementation and, second, identifying those activities whose timing is critical to each stage of implementation. The necessary steps can then be taken to ensure that these tasks get done on time. Critical path methods have been extended and developed in different ways, of which the program evaluation and review technique (PERT)—including PERT/time and PERT/cost—and the graphical evaluation and review technique (GERT) are the most common. These are based on the preparation of more or less complex networks representing the events and activities that lead to project completion.[1] Although these techniques are widely applicable and can make an important contribution to better implementation, they are not without problems and must be used with care.

The kind of "dynamic blueprint" provided by these techniques is particularly appropriate for standard construction projects, for which it was originally developed. In such projects, it is possible to specify clearly all the tasks to be done, and the basic features of the investment usually remain unchanged. With existing computer capabilities, critical paths can be easily adjusted in light of any technical modifications or delays in supplies. Less precise versions can be applied to projects in the social sectors—the basic features of which are more likely to change as the project evolves—and to projects under the direction of several implementing agencies. For example, if the objective of a project is to improve agricultural marketing facilities, it is more difficult (but not impossible) to specify precisely the timing of the activities, such as building access roads and upgrading infrastructure, required to achieve that objective. The analytical method is still valid for such projects, but the critical path may be subject to significant and more frequent modifications.

One of the main shortcomings in the practical application of the critical path method to complex projects has been to assume that each of the agencies or actors involved will perform efficiently. What is required is a realistic estimate of the time needed that takes into account the different strengths of the implementing agencies and actors, and a flexible critical path that allows for variations in performance without compromising the results. Not taking these factors into account often leads to disjointed implementation in which those components that are the responsibility of the more efficient institutions or that are intrinsically easier to implement get completed earlier, whether or not they are on the critical path. Conversely, components executed by weak institutions or intrinsically

1. A PERT network is summarized as follows: "The events represent the beginning and/or ending of activities. An event is a specific accomplishment, or milestone. The activities represent things that must be done in going from one event to the other. The activity is the time-consuming task. The activities are related to their order of precedence in accomplishing the events. The end result is a network depicting a well-thought-out plan. After the flow of activities and events is mapped, schedule timing can be superimposed. When completion times are included on the activities, the critical path can be determined." D. T. DeCoster, "PERT/Cost: The Challenge," *Management Services* (May–June 1964). A good compilation of articles on these techniques, and about project management more broadly, is included in E. W. Davis, ed., *Project Management: Techniques, Applications and Managerial Issues* (Norcross, Ga.: Industrial Engineering and Management Press, 1983).

more difficult are completed later, even though they may appear early on the critical path. For example, in integrated rural development projects, the equipment is likely to be acquired early and the infrastructure completed next, although possibly with delays, while the reorganization of services such as extension or marketing takes much longer. As a consequence, the benefits expected from the roads or the equipment are not fully realized, resources are wasted because equipment and facilities lie idle, and the increases in agricultural production take longer to materialize. A realistic critical path analysis would have revealed the need to begin work on the reorganization of services at a much earlier date. Railway rehabilitation projects have faced similar problems: high-performance equipment has been acquired promptly but could not be used to full capacity because of delays in track rehabilitation or signaling works; new investments have remained underutilized because of delays in reorganizing the railway's commercial operations, with lower than expected traffic the result.

Project implementation schedules are a modified and simpler form of critical path analysis used by many project authorities and advocated by some international agencies. They are designed to identify at the earliest possible stage the actions required to implement different project components and to specify the sequence in which components should be implemented, the time required to implement them, and the agency responsible for implementation. These schedules deal not only with construction or other investment components, but also with actions such as appointment of staff and consultants, adoption of legislative or administrative measures, or changes of policy.

Monitoring and Evaluation

Monitoring can be a relatively straightforward and inexpensive system that provides an early warning to project management about potential or actual problems. Or a monitoring system can be so elaborate and time-consuming as to be counterproductive, as the Bank learned from some of its initial efforts. Monitoring should be based on a set of simple indicators that can be collected and processed in time for management to take necessary action. Examples of such indicators are traffic counts and costs per kilometer in highway projects; fertilizer amounts consumed, yields, and number of farmers affected in agriculture projects; and construction costs and enrollments in education projects. Monitoring, is, in effect, a streamlined management information system, with the design of appropriate indicators an essential element. It can also be used to inform higher officials in the planning bureau or the ministry of finance of implementation progress and problems.[2]

Evaluation, in this context, is an ongoing activity, as distinct from ex post evaluation (described in the next chapter), which is undertaken when implementation has been completed and is used for accountability, planning of future projects, and research. The purpose of ongoing

2. For more details, see Dennis J. Casley and Denis A. Lury, *Monitoring and Evaluation of Agriculture and Rural Development Projects* (Baltimore, Md.: Johns Hopkins University Press for the World Bank, 1981).

evaluation is to reassess project objectives and the means of achieving them in the light of experience and of new developments as implementation proceeds. It goes hand in hand with project monitoring, drawing on the information supplied through monitoring as well as special studies to reconsider project objectives and modify them accordingly. Evaluation must be done on a timely basis if it is to serve its purpose—an obvious point, but one that is often missed.

Monitoring and evaluation are normal functions of project management, to be performed and then used directly by it. Generally, a monitoring and evaluation unit is established under the project director. It needs to be well integrated with the rest of the organizational structure. Neither in appearance nor in reality should its function be to manage or control.

Practice has not always been consistent with theory. There are many instances in which monitoring and evaluation systems have made a substantial contribution to improved project implementation. But too often monitoring has become just another data-gathering effort, seldom influencing management's decisions. Large amounts of data are collected but not processed; if processed, they are not used. This experience suggests several prerequisites for a successful monitoring and evaluation system:

- Managers have to want the system and be committed to its use.
- Decisions on the data to be collected should be based on the problems that will need to be solved during implementation.
- Requirements for data collection have to be adapted to realistic standards of accuracy, timeliness, and cost.
- The system has to be designed at an early stage of project preparation and baseline data collected well in advance.

Too often monitoring and evaluation systems are added as an afterthought, late in the cycle of project processing and without consideration of the above prerequisites.

Management Information

The unsatisfactory state of management information systems has been identified in several of the sector chapters. In fact, their endemic inadequacy in developing countries gave rise to monitoring and evaluation as a simplified and more feasible technique for managing implementation. Still, minimum information systems covering financial transactions as well as technical and staffing issues are necessary for project implementation and later for project operation. For example, projects cannot function without an adequate accounting system, including one that records the flow of funds while the project is being constructed. Experience has shown that, as with monitoring, this information system has to be adapted to the local conditions and customs and made compatible with the information system of the parent agency.

Different types of projects need different information systems. At one extreme, traditional infrastructure or industrial projects, which use standard technologies, can adapt well-established systems designed for similar projects in other countries. At the other extreme, people-oriented projects that include the provision of services by many agents in geographically scattered areas need an information system sensitive to the local circumstances and to the near impossibility of keeping accurate records at the local level. The training and visit extension system (see chapter 6, Agriculture) has adopted an extreme solution: to reduce report writing to a minimum, the extension agent's only obligation is to keep a diary to record visits to farmers, the type of advice given, and the problems raised by the farmers. This is an incentive to keep the agent in the field and out of the office, since one of the main risks of a cumbersome management information system has been the wrong signal it gives to concentrate on reports instead of field work. However, this degree of simplicity cannot be maintained for all activities of this type. The initial application of training and visit principles to health delivery systems already suggests that minimal information requirements will be more elaborate than those for extension because of the wider range of services provided. The requirements for activities that entail financial transfers, such as agricultural marketing or provision of inputs, will inevitably have to be still more complex.

THE START-UP PERIOD

The start-up period, when implementation has begun but has not yet reached its full stride, is probably the most difficult and troublesome phase. How well the project has been prepared and its implementation planned become crucial, as does timing; the prerequisite for a smooth start-up is not to begin implementation until these phases have been completed. Too often implementing agencies, with commendable zeal, go ahead with projects before they are in fact ready. The shortfalls in preparation quickly become apparent. The time originally "saved" is lost in a protracted start-up phase, with adverse consequences such as cost overruns for which there is no financial provision. The developing world is replete with examples of projects that suffered long delays at the outset because the engineering studies had not been completed, legal arrangements for the acquisition of land finalized, or financial arrangements for project funding determined. Adequate preparation—as far as possible— is no less important for projects in the social sectors than for the more traditional infrastructure projects, particularly with regard to institutional arrangements. (The concept of an adequate level of preparation was discussed in the preceding chapter. It is worth reiterating that preparation can be extended ad infinitum and that a tradeoff has to be made between the cost of further preparatory work and the risks likely to be encountered during implementation, including start-up difficulties.)

A variety of problems arise during the start-up period. First and perhaps foremost are delays in selecting and appointing staff, especially the project manager and other senior officials. For best results, the project manager and other key staff should be appointed prior to the start of implementation and should participate in its planning. This, of course, is easier to do when a project is one of a series or when it fits into the regular program of a line agency. Recruitment of consultants, particularly expatriates, has also frequently been subject to procedural delays.

Second, delays in budgetary allocations and in establishing the legislative or administrative channels for the flow of funds have often left the implementing agency without adequate resources to begin project implementation. This is particularly troublesome if funds have to be allocated from a central source to local districts or provinces. In World Bank–assisted projects, revolving funds are being used increasingly to ensure an adequate flow of funds from the outset. The revolving fund receives a deposit from the Bank and preferably also from the government to cover payments for an initial period. As the name implies, periodic replenishments are made as funds are spent. This is a useful procedure for large projects, particularly those with external financing, but for a country's investment program as a whole it obviously is no substitute for adequate budgetary procedures that make funds available on time.

Third, delays are common in completing legal or administrative arrangements, especially in projects in which more than one implementing agency is involved. The establishment of a workable mechanism for interagency coordination has proved to be one of the most difficult and time-consuming steps in many projects. A similar difficulty has been encountered in projects that seek to incorporate activities (such as agricultural credit or extension programs, health or educational services) that are already under way under separate administration. Fourth, arranging for the initial procurement of goods and services often takes much longer than anticipated. This is especially true when procedures must comply with the procurement requirements of aid agencies.

Special arrangements to bring together the many officials from various agencies who are to participate in the initial stages of implementation and who may have had no prior experience of working together—and indeed, may never have met before—have proved useful in clarifying the expected role of each participant. The Bank is fostering the use of project-launching seminars and meetings for this purpose. These seminars gather together the representatives of the agencies responsible for implementation to discuss the common objectives of the project, the implementation schedule and strategy, procedures for handling the relationships among agencies, and, in the case of Bank-supported projects, the relationships between the agencies and the Bank and the expected role of the Bank during implementation. The seminars were begun for urban projects, which involve a multiplicity of agencies, but could as well be used for other types of projects, even when only one implementing agency is involved.

SUCCESS IN PROJECT IMPLEMENTATION

Experience in implementing Bank-assisted projects, as has been observed throughout this book, has varied widely. Some projects have been highly successful; they have been completed on time, at or reasonably close to the original cost estimates, and with the expected benefits realized or even exceeded. Others have experienced shortcomings in one or more of these respects, and sometimes in all of them. The mixed experience applies not only across countries and sectors; within a given country, sector, or even implementing agency can be found examples of both successes and failures. How, then, to account for the differences?

Or, to put it another way, what are the essential ingredients of a successful project?

Before addressing this question, two points should be made. One is that, despite the wide range of experience noted, the project record of the Bank has, on the whole, been very favorable. This is not to say that the projects have been problem-free. Many have experienced cost over-runs, which have averaged 35 percent, and delays in completion time, which have averaged about 60 percent, relative to the estimates made at the time of appraisal. In about two-thirds of the cases, the scope of the project changed significantly during the course of implementation. A very large number of completed projects (1,014 projects representing about $22 billion in Bank loans or credits and about $67 billion in total investment) were subject to an ex post evaluation by the Operations Evaluation Department (see chapter 18) during the ten-year period through 1983. Of this total, 86 percent of the projects by number, and more than 90 percent by value of Bank lending and of total investment, appeared to have achieved their major objectives, or were well on the way to doing so, and were adjudged to have been worthwhile. For those projects for which an economic rate of return was calculated, the reestimated rate of return averaged about 18 percent.

The second point, however, refers to how relevant this experience is to developing countries. Bank-supported projects are able to command financial and technical assistance, spanning all phases of the project cycle, that may not be available to the same extent when a country undertakes a project entirely from its own resources. Nevertheless, Bank-supported projects are implemented by the countries themselves, who can claim the lion's share of credit for the successes—and of blame for the failures. Moreover, the very diversity of results achieved and of problems encountered suggests that a great deal can profitably be learned from this experience.

We shall consider first the principal factors that account for successful projects, and then those that lead to problems and difficulties during implementation. This twofold discussion is necessary because, as will be seen, the reasons for success are not always symmetrical with those for failure.[3]

Political Commitment

The first and probably most important reason for success is strong and sustained commitment by the government to the project's objectives. This is a complex matter, not always readily discernible, that applies not only to projects supported by international development agencies but also to those financed from the country's own resources.

What is political or government commitment? It is the continuing interest and active support of those agencies and individuals who are in

3. The analysis of reasons for success is based in part on a special study of the composite profile of fifty "successful" projects, which was carried out by the Operations Evaluation Department in 1984. A successful project is defined as one that achieves a moderate to high rate of return, helps to strengthen borrower institutions and policies, and lays a solid foundation for sustainability.

a position to influence attainment of the project's objectives, whether through the allocation of human and financial resources or through the workings of the administrative and political apparatus. The "government," of course, is not a monolithic entity. Several agencies, each with a number of key individuals, are usually involved. It may be that the director of the executing agency is the original sponsor and proponent of the idea. The minister may also be in favor, although less so. However, the ministry of finance or of planning may be neutral or even against the project if, for example, it has been included in the investment program through the pressures of special interest groups and over the objections of these ministries. In this event, the "commitment" is probably weak, since lack of support by such agencies can have adverse consequences, particularly for the availability of funds. It can also happen that the director of an agency is interested in a project but his staff is not, in which event they will give it less than enthusiastic support. What one finds in the truly successful cases is a coalition in which all or virtually all the relevant actors have compatible interests and strongly favor the project.

Commitment is a dynamic concept. The coalition can change, at times drastically, during the several or more years of project implementation. The main supporter may retire or resign, or the political makeup of the administration shift. Thus, a coalition has to be not only powerful but enduring. This does not mean that a project for which there is a full commitment will not face problems owing, for example, to exogenous factors. But if everyone is pulling in the right direction, most such problems can be overcome, and others will be avoided.

Commitment is difficult to achieve and sustain. It is particularly important in ensuring that the overall policy framework (prices, taxes, subsidies, incentives, foreign trade regulations) is supportive of the project objectives. The various instances cited in part II when prices charged for services were not increased on time or prices paid to farmers not raised to give them adequate incentives to produce are examples of a lack of support from one or more critical elements. Commitment, or the absence of it, will have more effect on some kinds of projects than on others. At one extreme, if the project is to construct a large dam or power station, changes in commitment may slow down implementation, but seldom will they result in cancellation or major modification of it. At the other extreme, numerous education projects have had to be modified in midcourse because a new government brought a new orientation to educational policies; railway projects have been stalled because a new minister of transport would not accept the exigencies of the plan of action adopted by his predecessor; rural road projects have received an unexpected boost when a highway department director with a farming background was appointed. Many changes in the scope of projects can be traced to these vagaries of commitment.

Projects financed by multilateral or bilateral development agencies introduce another dimension of commitment. Differences in objectives and purposes between the country and the lending agency often arise. The latter might seek to promote a project or to set certain conditions about project design or implementation with which the country's authorities do not agree, but which they feel obliged to accept in order to obtain the funds. This virtually guarantees that the project will be implemented reluctantly, if at all. Time and effort must be expended by both parties to ensure a reasonable meeting of the minds before the loan is signed, and both must show flexibility—and receptivity—in the negotiating process. Even then, a change of government during implementation can lead to the reopening of issues that had previously been agreed on.

How can commitment be ensured? As usual, no one solution fits all projects, but the first step is to make sure that sufficient attention is given to the question. An informal appraisal carried out at an early stage to identify the gainers and losers in the political arena might help to focus on those whose support is critical to project success. The process of internal project appraisal or review and of budgetary approval can give strong signals as to where support does (or does not) lie. A careful monitoring of the political environment is one of the duties of a good project manager. Changes in the nature and intensity of commitment may call for modification of the project as its implementation progresses; in some extreme cases of loss of commitment, projects may have to be dropped or postponed. Another way of ensuring commitment is to incorporate the main agencies and actors in the preparation and appraisal process and thereby to engage their interest and anticipate and deal with their objections. In short, to ensure commitment, an internal consensus should be built as early as possible and a mechanism established to maintain it during implementation.

Simplicity of Design

The second reason for successful implementation has to do with design. As noted in the preceding chapter, projects with relatively simple and well-defined objectives and based on proven and appropriate technologies or approaches have a better chance of being implemented successfully. Extending an irrigation network by means of a construction technology that has been used before in the country is likely to proceed more smoothly than a complex project in one of the social sectors. This is not to say that the choice among projects in different sectors should depend on this distinction. The point, rather, is that for each objective, no matter how complex, there are at least several technological and design alternatives, some of which are more difficult to implement than others. It is important, therefore, to simplify and redefine objectives and to select technologies that have the best chance of working in the particular circumstances of the project. But, as we have also pointed out, projects can be too simple—as well as too complex—to make a significant impact on development. Without repeating the discussion in the preceding chapter, we wish to emphasize that selection of the proper project design is central to successful project implementation.

Careful Preparation

As we have already stressed, thorough preparation pays handsome dividends. This appears obvious, but it cannot be said too often. There is a widespread tendency to start projects before they have been sufficiently prepared. Although the extent of preparation that is feasible or desirable varies according to the type of project, certain actions should always be undertaken during preparation; if they are ignored or short-circuited, the likelihood of implementation difficulties mounts. For example, the preparation of an education project is sometimes considered to be completed when the sites of some of the schools have been selected and a preliminary design for them prepared. During implementation, there may be difficulties in acquiring sites, problems with soil foundations, or large increases in cost because of changes in design. A clear plan for land acquisition and detailed engineering studies would reduce or eliminate such problems. The Bank observed many years ago, beginning with road construction projects, that insisting on the completion of detailed engineering before making a loan substantially reduced the probability of cost overruns and consequent implementation delays. Standard guidelines have been developed for each type of project, which require that project design be well advanced prior to loan commitment.

Adequate preparation includes not only such traditional matters as detailed engineering and land acquisition but also, for example, testing technical packages for agriculture projects, verifying the availability of support services, and ascertaining beneficiaries' responses to the proposed approaches. One point that we have often made in the sector chapters is the need to adapt project objectives and approaches to local conditions. Lack of such adaptation has been cited as an important cause of failure of many projects, just as proper attention to it has been a principal reason for success. A large number of livestock projects in Africa have not succeeded because they were based on a technical and organizational approach emulating ranch operations in other parts of the world but ill-adapted to local culture, traditional practices, and patterns of land tenure. A pilot project to test the proposed approach under local conditions would have saved both time and money.

Among the aspects of preparation most likely to be neglected are the organizational and institutional arrangements. Projects with a clear and well-defined institutional setup and with the right managerial arrangements have greatly enhanced prospects for success. This rule of thumb applies across the board, but in particular to projects that encompass the provision of services, where the central issues are institutional ones. Reliance on well-established and time-tested institutions has often been the key to project success; when they are not available, strengthening the institutions that are responsible for implementation becomes an important feature of project design.

Good Management

It is almost a tautology that good projects are associated with good managers. The influence of the quality of management on project performance is usually very visible. Many projects in serious difficulty during implementation have been turned around by the appointment of a competent manager, just as performance in others has noticeably declined when a good manager has departed.

What can be done to ensure the availability of good project managers? This is a vexing question, particularly for projects in the public sector. Good managers are not likely to be attracted if the package of remuneration and incentives is significantly inferior to what they can obtain elsewhere in the country or, in some cases, abroad. Political commitment makes a difference; projects characterized by strong commitment have attracted good managers. A problem for many developing countries is that they do not have enough qualified managers to run all the projects or activities under way, so that attracting a manager to a particular project is at the expense of another one. We have already discussed the need to adapt projects to the managerial capabilities that are available. Aside from this, the only alternative in the short run may be to import the managerial talent of expatriates and consultants. If this is done, care should be taken that it does not delay the development of local managerial capacity but rather fosters it through counterpart and on-the-job training arrangements.

The best long-term solution lies in the education and training of more managers, which can take several forms, from special short courses to the establishment of management institutes. The latter has proved to be an extremely slow process; numerous management institutes have been created in developing countries, but few have thrived and succeeded in developing a substantial pool of fresh and well-trained talent.

It is tempting to attribute the success or failure of a project to factors exogenous to it—such as a financial crisis, a shift in world demand, a shortage of foreign exchange, or a government policy or intervention—over which a manager has no control. While this may often be true, skillful and dynamic managers have been able to accomplish much even under the most trying of circumstances. In some countries, they have created an aura of efficiency around a project which has been an effective form of protection against outside interference and has enlisted a political commitment that did not exist before their arrival. Numerous examples could be cited of well-run agencies that have been able to maintain high staff morale and thereby to withstand major political upheavals: power companies in Ghana, Tanzania, and several other African countries; telecommunications in Ethiopia and Burkina; development finance companies in Iran and Turkey.

Success, like most other things, is relative. To say that good managers make good projects is not to imply that they have achieved flawless performance in an unfavorable policy environment or to gainsay the importance of that environment. But experience shows that good managers have brought about a better performance than would otherwise have been possible.

Good managers attract good staff and are alert to the importance of doing so. The need to strengthen staff performance, particularly in the senior cadres, has been a recurrent theme of this book; it is taken up, along with some further points on management development, in chapter 23, Institutional Analysis. Improved pay and incentives, greater opportunities for promotion, and more and better training are among the ways to deal with this endemic problem.

In summary, there is no simple formula for success. Each project faces a unique set of circumstances, many of which can be foreseen and controlled but some of which cannot. Fortuitous factors may play a part; an element of chance intervenes in projects as it does in other aspects of life. But effective project planning, design, and implementation lie at the heart of successful projects. If their presence cannot always guarantee success, their absence is almost certain to lead to failure.

PROBLEMS IN PROJECT IMPLEMENTATION

Trying to establish a comprehensive typology of the problems encountered in project implementation is tantamount to describing the problems inherent in the development process itself. Furthermore, it is necessary to distinguish between problems that are symptoms and those that are underlying causes. Thus, lack of funds could be the result of a shortage of resources on the part of the government, an administrative mixup or inefficient procedure that delayed the allocation of those funds, or a lack of political commitment. A lack of political commitment, in turn, could be caused by bureaucratic infighting or by the clash among pressure groups, while these clashes could stem from cultural factors, and so forth.

The following discussion of implementation problems is derived from reports of World Bank project officers and of project staff in developing countries. This identification of the factors leading to unsatisfactory performance gains from being based on operational experience, but it suffers from mixing proximate and deeper causes. We shall discuss project implementation problems under four of the categories used in Bank reporting: financial, managerial and institutional, technical, and political.

One aspect of implementation has to be kept in mind throughout the discussion. Projects change, sometimes drastically, during implementation. As previously mentioned, two-thirds of Bank-assisted projects have changed significantly while they were under way. The reasons are many, but the most common are delays and cost overruns that force a reduction in the scale of the project; design changes, made necessary sometimes by insufficient preparation or inadequate technical solutions; changes in priorities that materialized during implementation; or external factors, such as a sudden decline in the world price of the project's output. To illustrate from just one sector in one region:

- In an education project in Algeria, most of the original components were deleted but the scope of one of them was increased sixfold when the government changed its priorities.
- In an education project in Nigeria, the size was increased greatly when extra resources unexpectedly became available during the oil boom.
- In an education project in Chad, the physical location of the principal education facility was changed because a new government did not want to have it in the capital city.

Financial Problems

Financial difficulties occur frequently during implementation. For projects supporting revenue-earning activities, the most common financial problems are pressures on the cost side because of general salary and price increases; difficulties in raising prices, tariffs, or interest rates; and losses due to fluctuations in foreign exchange rates. These circumstances result in operating losses or in a financial rate of return so low that the agency is not able to meet its debt obligations or finance its expansion. For other types of projects, inadequate allocations of budgetary funds and, to a somewhat lesser extent, of foreign exchange are the most common problems; cost increases also frequently occur.

The effect of financial difficulties on implementation is clear: the project is delayed, its cost increased, and in some cases its scope reduced. Lack of funds has often meant that contractors or consultants could not be paid, spare parts obtained, or services provided. Initiatives to strengthen project institutions are also likely to founder when financial problems persist.

Financial problems have been exacerbated in recent years by world-wide inflation. Public and private agencies have been affected not only because of the resulting increase in costs but also because governments have resisted granting the tariff and interest rate increases necessary to cover them. For example, many governments struggling against inflation have set limits on the tariffs and fares charged by public utilities and transportation companies. Similarly, development banks have suffered financial difficulties owing to governments' reluctance to allow increases in the interest rates charged to their borrowers. As we have argued elsewhere, this is often a shortsighted policy. The budget deficits resulting from the increased subsidy payments, together with the general decline in the efficiency of the enterprise in question, can have greater inflationary consequences, and distribute the inflationary burden more inequitably, than would the tariff or interest rate increases had they been allowed.

The structural or long-term reasons for financial difficulties are numerous. A few are outside the control of the project or the agency, such as a reduction in world prices of a commodity or a countrywide or worldwide economic crisis. Others may be inherent in the structure of the sector, such as the perennial difficulties faced by railways in meeting competition from the trucking industry. Still other reasons are a reflection of political decisions—for example, obligating a public utility or a transportation company to provide uneconomic services without adequate compensation. In some countries, government-owned enterprises are considered public services that do not have to cover their costs; nor are governments always convinced of the need for financial discipline.

To revert to a theme of chapter 4, financial problems may also derive from a basic mismatch between the national investment program of a government and the financial resources available to implement it. When this happens, the flow of public funds for project finance will frequently be interrupted. The shortage of funds may also make itself felt in such mundane but serious matters as chronic delays by government agencies in paying their bills. This mismatch can be exacerbated by a general economic recession, as it was in the early 1980s. Countries have often been unable or unwilling to face up to the need to cut back on their investment programs, with the result that many projects have run into financial difficulties.

Cost overruns are both a cause and an effect of financial difficulties. It is important to distinguish between cost overruns that reflect changes in the scope of the project, those that derive from a change in the technical design or specifications, and those that are the result of price variations or currency realignments. Some of these overruns may reflect real changes in costs or benefits while others do not, and this may have different implications for the outcome of the project. One essential factor explaining overruns is implementation delays, which, given inflation, result in higher financial outlays. A vicious circle is then set in motion: delays induce higher costs, which—in view of budgetary constraints—means funds are inadequate for project implementation. This, in turn, causes more delays and further cost increases.

Other causes of overruns stem from implementation problems described elsewhere. Inadequate management, insufficient project preparation, deficient technical design, political interference, and procurement problems will all result in higher than expected costs. Underestimating the volume of work required or the time to do it is one of the most common problems, especially when adequate physical and price contingencies have not been provided. Thus, the measures that should be taken to avoid cost overruns largely coincide with those necessary for avoiding delays and ensuring successful implementation. In effect, cost overruns are a barometer of the implementation process.

Management Problems

In the Bank's experience, managerial problems are the most pervasive. The term is used very broadly to encompass what are usually considered institutional problems. Lack of managerial talent can make itself felt at three levels: in the government administration (a situation that affects all projects in a country); in the upper or middle management of the project or implementing agencies; and at the provincial, state, or local level. Other facets of this problem are a dearth of people with specific skills (accountants, technicians) and with general administrative capabilities; inadequate management, accounting, and reporting systems and procedures; an ill-defined organizational setup; low salaries and poor staffing policies; and lack of coordination among agencies. Discontinuity of management as a result of frequent changes for political reasons can be highly disruptive, quite independent of the quality of the management itself.

These managerial or institutional problems are often the root cause of implementation delays and cost overruns. They result, among other things, in inadequate planning, failure to obtain necessary legislation, delays in land acquisition, protracted bidding and contracting procedures, insufficient project supervision, slow response to changes in the policy environment, and low staff morale and productivity. Later, they may drastically reduce the effectiveness of project operation.

We have already cited good managers as a major determinant of project success. Here, the causes of success and failure are symmetrical. Projects can get into a virtuous or a vicious cycle. When an agency administering a project acquires a reputation for effective management within the government, this creates a willingness on the part of other agencies to help because they know that such support will reflect positively on them. Conversely, bad management inevitably makes other agencies suspicious and engenders in them a natural tendency to protect themselves in their dealings with the inefficiently managed entity.

Technical Problems

Many problems can and do arise in constructing civil works and in procuring or operating equipment. These include difficult or unexpected soil conditions, poor quality of materials, technical defects in design, mistakes in the installation and start-up of equipment, unsuitability of imported equipment for local conditions, or otherwise inappropriate technology. In agriculture, inadequate technical packages or disappointing results from newly introduced technologies are common problems; the lack of technical packages for rain-fed areas in Africa is a striking example. In people-oriented activities such as health delivery or education, the lack of approaches fully tested for the particular circumstances of a country or region is another technical or design problem.

Some errors in the original design of the project, and in the underlying estimates and projections, can generate "benefit underruns." It is a common failing to overestimate the rate at which beneficiaries (such as farmers) will adopt new technologies and use new services (agricultural extension or credit) by basing projections on the performance of the "best" rather than the "average" farmer. In addition, overoptimism can often mean that it takes longer than predicted to solve institutional bottlenecks and to provide services essential to the project. Similarly, the growth of demand is sometimes overestimated by not allowing for events such as recessions, policy changes, or strikes. These errors can be as important as cost overruns in explaining economic rates of return that are lower than expected.

Although in many cases technical problems stem from the difficulty of defining appropriate solutions, some are the result of a calculated risk. We have commented earlier on the tradeoff between the cost of further technical studies and the risk of encountering technical difficulties during implementation. One extreme example is tunnel construction, for which the cost of complete soil studies is so high that it is usually preferable to make less detailed studies during project preparation and deal with the risk of technical problems during implementation through such devices as special physical contingencies, as described in chapter 19, Technical Analysis. Civil works such as dams, highways, and buildings raise this tradeoff question constantly, but the issue is also relevant to projects in the social sectors, even though designs and cost estimates are necessarily less accurate.

In Bank-assisted projects, technical problems of an engineering character are not frequently cited as a major problem. This probably reflects the greater availability of engineering skills in most countries than of managerial or financial skills, or the availability of consulting services for engineering tasks and the greater willingness of borrowers to accept them (or of external lenders to require them). Although technical problems do arise continuously in the course of implementation, satisfactory solutions are generally found. We do not know how extensive these technical problems are in projects financed by the countries themselves, but their incidence is likely to be higher because preparation standards are more uneven. In any event, the experience with Bank-supported projects demonstrates that better preparation standards result in better implementation, particularly with regard to technical aspects.

Political Problems

Even in the absence of such obvious disruptions as wars and serious internal upheavals, political problems are at the heart of many of the difficulties experienced by projects. Government commitment has already been discussed; when it is absent, weak, or variable, project implementation suffers. The public administration of a country is closely linked with its political machinery, and it is almost impossible to disentangle political problems from the administrative difficulties encountered by a project entity in its relations with the rest of the public sector. For example, the rapid rotation of political appointees in managerial positions generally results from a mixture of administrative and political factors reinforcing each other.

Project managers must adapt to the level of efficiency of the public administration, with which they are linked both directly and indirectly. Bureaucracies in many developing countries are overstaffed; yet there are too few high-quality, trained staff, because of inadequate pay and incentives, inadequate commitment to training, and political interference. The organization of government agencies is often badly in need of streamlining and overhaul. Project management has to take into account the potential impact of such political and administrative factors, anticipate the problems insofar as possible, and modify the implementation path accordingly.

IMPLEMENTATION OF TECHNICAL ASSISTANCE

World Bank–supported projects generally have two major sets of components. One is a package of investments in physical assets and the other is a set of technical assistance activities intended to ensure the successful implementation and eventual operation of these investments and to strengthen the institutions in charge of implementation and operation. Some projects consist primarily or exclusively of technical assistance. Typically, a developing country will have several technical assistance programs going on simultaneously, financed by the UNDP or other multilateral and bilateral sources or entirely through its own resources.

In reviewing the implementation experience, it is important to distinguish between what may be classified as engineering and as institutional technical assistance.[4] Engineering technical assistance consists of the professional services of architects, agronomists, engineers, and similar specialists for civil works and other hardware investments. Institutional technical assistance has to do with the strengthening of institutions at different hierarchical levels and in various aspects: management and planning, policy formulation, training, public administration, finance and accounting, and so on. Of the two, engineering services are more universally applicable and more readily accepted by governments. The problems encountered most frequently are poorly drafted terms of reference and

4. For a fuller description, see Francis Lethem and Lauren Cooper, *Managing Project-Related Technical Assistance: The Lessons of Success*, World Bank Staff Working Paper no. 586 (Washington, D.C., 1983).

difficulties connected with selecting and contracting consultants. At times external donors (including the Bank) have provided technical assistance as a substitute for more complete preparation of the project—a sure recipe for creating difficulties during implementation. Institutional technical assistance, in contrast, requires behavioral changes, is more difficult to define and control, and must be thoroughly adapted to local conditions. Consequently the need for this kind of technical assistance is less clearly perceived by countries and is more often resisted.

Implementing technical assistance activities, especially institutional ones, faces problems similar to those described above, but often in a more acute form. The record of implementation of technical assistance in virtually all sectors is less favorable than that of investments. First, knowledge has been less readily available or has not been suitably adapted to local conditions. Second, how the technical assistance should be delivered and what product or benefits should be expected from it have not been specified in sufficient detail; for example, training is sometimes treated as an afterthought or is expected to occur automatically. Third, the internal administrative arrangements and responsibilities for technical assistance have not been clearly delineated. Fourth, some countries do not have the capacity to administer adequately this kind of activity without outside help. Technical assistance programs have often suffered from serious deficiencies in the selection and hiring of expatriate personnel and have not made effective use of their services.

In general, technical assistance has been more effective and more readily accepted when associated with an investment and when addressed to institutions that already have a relatively high level of performance. Here, again, a vicious circle is found: those entities that need technical assistance most have been the least willing and able to profit from it. Several factors have been identified that are prerequisites if technical assistance is to succeed:

- A strong commitment on the part of all parties concerned, based on a clear definition of objectives and the demonstrated feasibility of the program
- Careful design and preparation, with specification of the mode of delivery, the role and responsibility of the various parties, and the administrative and logistical arrangements
- Adequate provision both of the requisite budgetary resources and of the local counterpart staff to be assigned to the technical assistance project
- Administration of the technical assistance on a flexible basis and with a close partnership between the recipient organization and the technical staff
- Continuity of staffing from initial design through implementation, or at least some provision that those responsible for design and for implementation have access to each other.

Teaching the use of electric hand tools at a vocational school, Brazil

18

Ex Post Evaluation

PURPOSE OF EX POST EVALUATION

THE PROJECT CYCLE does not end when a project has been implemented. There is yet another—and final—stage, that of ex post evaluation. It takes place after a project has passed through the construction or implementation stage and has entered into operation.

Ex post evaluation needs to be distinguished from the ongoing monitoring and evaluation which, as we have seen in the preceding chapter, should be an important feature of project implementation. The purpose of ongoing evaluation is to help ensure effective project execution by identifying and dealing with problems and issues that arise while the project is being implemented. In contrast, ex post evaluation looks more broadly at the probable impact of the completed project in relation to original expectations. It takes place at a later date, when investment costs are firmly known, some benefits may already have been captured, and—although operating costs and benefits still lie mostly in the future—earlier estimates of results can be updated.

An important purpose of ex post evaluation is to ascertain the reasons for a project's apparent success or failure, in order to pinpoint the features that deserve replication in future projects and to identify the pitfalls to be avoided. Ex post evaluation also informs managers, and those to whom they are responsible, how far and how effectively individual projects are achieving the desired results. It thus has both a learning and an accountability function. Many of the lessons of experience that this book seeks to pass on to those engaged in the work of development have been derived from the Bank's own evaluation process (described below) as it has evolved since its inception in 1970.

Typically, evaluation looks for the answers to a series of questions with which the reader should by now be familiar. Were the original objectives of the project clearly defined and feasible? Were the technical choices and the procurement procedures appropriate? Was the local socioeconomic environment adequately understood? Was the project's target group the correct one, and was it effectively served? Was reasonable progress made toward strengthening project institutions? Were there sizable cost overruns and, if so, why? And finally, notwithstanding all the difficulties encountered and any expected shortfall in results, was the project nevertheless worth doing? By synthesizing the results of the evaluation of a number of projects, first within a sector and then for all projects, valuable clues and lessons for the future may be obtained.

Ex post evaluation has the benefit of hindsight. From that vantage point, it will almost certainly disclose ways in which things could have been done better. But if the process is to function well and serve its intended purpose, it must be made clear to all concerned that mistakes are not being uncovered to point the finger of blame. Some mistakes are bound to occur. The objective should be to learn from them so that they are not repeated.

ELEMENTS OF THE PROCESS

There is no single pattern for an evaluation system, and the few national systems that have so far been adopted differ in detail. The Bank's experience suggests that certain features are essential for maximum effectiveness: operational staff should be involved in the process, evaluation should be objective and seen to be so, evaluation results should be fully disclosed, and the largest feasible number of projects should be subject to evaluation. In addition, the process should be timed to heighten its usefulness.

Participation of Operational Staff and Objectivity

Feedback and follow-up are not automatic processes. The evaluation system must be built into the operational procedures of the organization to ensure that the lessons of experience are taken into account in the design and implementation of new projects. Evaluation would be an exercise in futility if the information gathered were to remain on file. At the same time, it would be wasteful to collect more information and generate more reports than can usefully be assimilated and acted upon. For developing countries, typically short of staff qualified to collect as well as to use data, this is an important consideration in designing an evaluation system.

Evaluation results are most likely to reach managers promptly, and the lessons of experience most likely to be absorbed and applied, if operational staff participate in evaluation. Their involvement will also help to achieve accountability to management. However, a wholly self-evaluative process is open to the suspicion—justified or not—that difficulties are being ignored or minimized or benefits exaggerated. Objectivity can be achieved by carrying out the evaluation process in two stages: first, an evaluation by the operational staff, using insofar as possible the same people who were responsible for the project's design and implementation; and second, a review by evaluators who are independent from the operational managers and report to a higher authority.

Disclosure of Results

Wide dissemination of the evaluation results will promote the objectives both of learning from experience and of achieving accountability. The first objective is served by reviewing the results with all operational staff in the relevant organization, whether or not they have worked on the project that has been evaluated. This will enable judgments to be formed not only about the adequacy and cost-effectiveness of the evaluation process itself (whether the right questions have been asked, whether the evaluation methodology employed was appropriate) but also, and more important, about the extent to which the findings and recommendations are being reflected in the design and implementation of new projects. The second objective of evaluation, accountability for expenditure of public funds, will be served by making the results widely known.

Comprehensiveness

Ideally, to derive maximum advantage from experience, all projects should be evaluated. But this may not be practicable, in which case evaluation should extend at least to all projects that are large or otherwise especially noteworthy, along with a random sample of other projects. Inevitably, some projects will fall short of expectations; the risk is that they may loom out of proportion to their numerical and substantive significance unless they are seen in the context of all projects. Moreover, without a reasonable degree of comprehensiveness, overview questions about project effectiveness cannot readily be addressed, nor will it be easy to determine how adequate has been the response to the lessons of success and failure. Comprehensiveness, like disclosure, is thus important for the sake both of learning from experience and of accountability.

Timing

The timing of an evaluation has much to do with what can be learned from it. Once a project has been completed, the actual cost to construct or implement it—which is an important element of the economic rate of return—is known. Much can also be learned about what went well, or badly, during implementation. But, as already noted, the cost of operating and maintaining the project and the benefits to be derived from it still lie mostly in the future. It is possible, and desirable for purposes of the evaluation, to update these estimates using the most recent data available and to recalculate the economic rate of return where applicable. Nevertheless, the evaluation may still have to rest largely on informed judgments about the future. The implications of this are more serious for projects that evolve during their operation, such as those in agriculture and rural development, than for infrastructure projects, such as a hydroelectric plant. For projects in the first category, definitive conclusions about long-term impact may have to await a later assessment, and it is possible that this assessment will reverse the earlier conclusions.

WORLD BANK PROCEDURE

The Bank is the first of the multilateral aid organizations to have instituted a comprehensive evaluation procedure and to publish the results. Its evaluation system has been a model for those adopted by some other aid organizations. Although the procedure the Bank has worked out is designed to fit its particular needs and organization, it can be adapted to suit those of others. It may, therefore, be useful to depart from the practice that we have generally followed in this book of discussing country rather than Bank practices and to sketch out in some detail the way the Bank evaluates projects.

One to two years after completion of disbursements, every Bank-assisted project is reviewed by the operational staff, who prepare a project completion report. Whenever possible, this is done by those who were directly involved in the preparation and implementation of the project. This first stage of the process ensures both comprehensiveness and the participation of operational staff. To ensure objectivity as well, the evaluation process moves on to a second stage, which is carried out by staff outside the operational complex and assigned to the Operations Evaluation Department (OED). The Director General, Operations Evaluation, is nominated by the President of the World Bank and appointed by the Bank's Executive Directors. He reports separately to both the President and the Directors. The evaluation system is subject to continuing oversight by a committee of the Executive Directors that reviews its adequacy and considers in detail some of the principal reports.

The number of Bank-assisted projects completed each year, after climbing steadily, has leveled off at about 250. Although all of the projects are the subject of a project completion report, only about half of them are selected for a detailed performance audit by the OED staff; the rest of the reports are issued to the Executive Directors without audit. About 10 percent of the approximately 125 projects to be audited are chosen at random to ensure that authors of completion reports have no way of knowing which projects will be selected for audit. Also audited are all projects that are the first of their type in the country, projects to be grouped for eventual comparative analysis of experience, projects that invite further inquiry because of the significance of their experience or their poor performance, and additional projects chosen to round out the geographical and functional mix. The evaluation staff's independent assessment of a project is based on a reading of the files and the project completion report, on interviews with operational staff, and often on visits to the project site. It is recorded in a detailed project performance audit memorandum.

Disagreements of analysis or interpretation arise, not infrequently, between the operating staff who prepare the project completion report and the OED staff who prepare the audit memorandum on the same project. Most of these disagreements are resolved in the course of discussion; any remaining differences must be noted. Responsibility for the content of the final audit memorandum, however, resides solely with the Operations Evaluation Department.

Bank borrowers participate in the evaluation process. Under the terms of Bank loan agreements, they prepare completion reports as the culmination of their other reporting obligations to the Bank. This provision was introduced rather recently, and the number of such reports actually prepared by borrowers is quite small, but it is growing. In addition, governments can contribute substantially to the evaluation process by working with the Bank staff sent to prepare project completion reports and audit memoranda and by commenting on their drafts.

OED staff also prepare an annual overview of all the evaluated projects, intended to highlight trends and recurrent problems. The review contains comments on each sector that identify areas of continuing concern and indicate what the Bank has done or proposes to do about them. This review is published, with country and project identification omitted to respect the confidentiality of the information provided by borrowers, as the *Annual Review of Project Performance Audit Results*. In addition, each year OED conducts several special studies—for example, on groups of projects (such as irrigation projects in a particular country) or on particular aspects of the Bank's operational experience (such as delays in project execution across a broad sample of countries, sectors, and types of project).

Much is learned by operational staff in the course of preparing or commenting on evaluation reports, but the process of internalizing the lessons of experience does not stop there. Drawing on the vast amount of evaluation material now available, operational staff prepare special analyses and reviews suited to their particular needs and interests. For example, managers in the operations complex typically prepare periodic reviews in which the findings from evaluation reports are combined with those from supervision reports on projects still being implemented; these reviews focus on the status of the Bank's loan portfolio and on the issues and problems arising within it.

Finally, to deal with the timing problem noted earlier, the OED takes a second look at selected projects five years or more after completion and prepares impact evaluation reports on them. Initially, impact evaluation was confined to projects in agriculture and education; it is gradually being extended to other sectors. A project may be selected for a second look if, for example, its economic and institutional impact was uncertain at the time of audit, if it was the first project designed to achieve a particular objective in the country, if it was the first project in a particular sector, or if it embodied an innovative or controversial approach. We have noted in the preceding chapter that projects are frequently modified in scope in the course of implementation. Similarly, projects frequently undergo a metamorphosis of their economic, institutional, and social features in the years following completion as they adjust to the local environment and to local capabilities, often in ways that were not foreseen even at the time of audit. In some cases, the second look has confirmed that a project has been a success; in others, it has favorably resolved earlier doubts about a successful outcome; in still other cases, it has revealed that a project that was doing well at the time of audit has become an economic and social failure. By establishing the reasons for the failure, the impact evaluation report helps to ensure that, when the relevant factors are within the control of planners, subsequent projects in the sector will profit from the experience.

RESULTS OF THE SECOND LOOK

In 1983, the OED surveyed a large sample of its impact evaluation reports on agricultural projects—prepared an average of five years after project completion—to determine what factors contributed to the long-run sustainability of project benefits.[1] The findings, which are a mirror image of the lessons of success (or failure) of projects during their implementation that we discussed in chapter 17, are briefly recapitulated here.

- The institution—its nature, strengths, autonomy, and flexibility—was a dominant factor in determining project sustainability. The projects that maintained their success were those that enhanced institutional

1. World Bank, *Tenth Annual Review of Project Performance Audit Results* (Washington, D.C., 1985) and other World Bank materials.

capacity, often through a grass-roots organization of the project beneficiaries that gradually assumed increasing responsibility for project activities during implementation and particularly during the operational stage following completion.

• Adoption of improved and appropriate technology (and provision for its renewal) was a strong factor in achieving sustainability; conversely, failure to use an appropriate technology was a major factor leading to loss of project benefits.

• Sociocultural factors had implications for both institutional development and successful technology transfer. Attempts to accomplish either in ways alien to local traditions or values ran a high risk of failure once the project was in operation. Social forces also affected long-term sustainability when the project worsened—or failed to improve—income distribution among the beneficiaries.

• When government policies were incompatible with project objectives or worked at cross purposes with project-initiated activities, they undermined long-run sustainability.

• The adequacy of recurrent cost financing also had an important bearing on long-run sustainability. In irrigation, for example, the extent of cost recovery was correlated with the standards achieved in operating and maintaining the system. Inadequately maintained irrigation facilities deteriorated rapidly.

ISSUES FOR GOVERNMENTS

The Bank's ex post evaluation process, as we have described it, may seem to be elaborate and staff-intensive, and it is. The cost to the Bank of the evaluation process is estimated to be about fifty-nine staff years for fiscal year 1985, of which thirty-nine is for operational staff to prepare project completion reports and twenty for the work of OED. But the process has proved its value many times over as a vital source of experience and insight that continually enhances the effectiveness of the Bank's project assistance.

A well-designed evaluation system can make no less valuable a contribution to a developing country's investment program. Evaluation lends itself to many variations in design. Resource and other constraints may preclude immediate adoption of a full-blown system, but a limited system is much to be preferred to none at all. Although lip service has been paid to the usefulness of such systems, and government officials have repeatedly professed an intention to establish national machinery, progress has been slow and uneven. More active government participation in the Bank's evaluation process can be a first step in this direction.

The obstacles to progress are many. Governments traditionally have been more concerned with inputs than with outputs; they attach more importance to project starts and the flow of expenditures than to the effectiveness of results. The consequence is that managers consider themselves accountable for controlling expenditures rather than for achieving stated objectives. In many countries, agencies are not obliged to account to their own governments for project performance—although in a period of financial constraint, a greater interest in obtaining maximum value for money might well be expected. The primary difficulty, however, is the lack of political will to have a fully functioning and independent central evaluation process. This difficulty is compounded by a general shortage of trained investment planners and project managers and leads to a widespread and not unnatural feeling that, in such a situation, greater priority attaches to efficient planning and execution than to ex post evaluation. The normal divisions within the political system and the territorial imperatives of political power make centralized evaluation even more difficult.

All of these are real difficulties. A few developing countries have overcome them, however, and have gone beyond participating in the evaluation of Bank-assisted projects to reviewing the results of their other development projects and programs as well. They include India, Korea, Pakistan, Philippines, Tanzania, and Yugoslavia. There is some movement in this direction in several other countries, including Mexico, Colombia, and China.

A government that does intend to put in place an evaluation system of its own must resolve a number of practical problems. These include the location of the evaluation function, the selection of projects for evaluation, and the timing of evaluation.

Location

The evaluation function may be performed from any of several bases within the government. It may be located within the project executing agency or ministry, provided that the responsible staff do not report to or take direction from the operational managers. Or the planning agency may carry out evaluation. Or a central evaluation agency at the national level may be established. Evaluation may even be performed by nongovernmental personnel, although this is less likely to be satisfactory. Multisector projects may create problems for the evaluation process by confronting governments with the question of how to organize and manage relationships among a number of agencies. A central evaluation agency would seem to be the answer, but that may be resisted by line agencies, which are more prepared to evaluate their own performance than to have another agency do so.

Governments that have established national systems have gone about it in different ways. The Philippines has opted for a two-tier arrangement like that of the Bank. All implementing agencies must prepare and submit project completion reports to the National Economic and Development Authority. This central agency is the Philippines' highest policymaking body on economic and social development matters. It is responsible for reviewing project proposals and recommending their inclusion in the national budget and the external borrowing program. The agency then prepares its version of a project performance audit for consideration and appropriate action by the agency's board, a cabinet subcommittee. A different approach is being developed by Mexico, where a national evaluation system has been established in the office of the president that includes representatives of evaluation units in several ministries, executing agencies, financial agencies, and the auditing department. Guidelines have been issued for self-evaluation procedures, and evaluation units have been organized in the major institutions that borrow externally to assist them in ex post evaluation. The system is still evolving and is under review. Korea, taking yet another approach, has set up a Bureau of Post Evaluation and Coordination in its Economic Planning Board.

Selection for Evaluation

As noted earlier, the ideal would be to evaluate all projects, if only for purposes of accountability. But as a practical matter, it is not feasible for most developing countries to do so, and a judiciously selected sample—which, however, includes all major projects—may suffice to yield useful lessons. In the Philippines, the National Economic and Development Authority identifies the major projects in each category by applying criteria that include the comprehensiveness of the feasibility study and the size of the investment cost in relation to the size of the sector. Other countries have begun by tracking and thoroughly evaluating the results of those programs that significantly influence the budget. Another approach is to begin by addressing selected issues or focusing on projects in a single sector. It is much better to start with a limited system than not to begin at all—provided that the intention is to institutionalize evaluation activity on a long-term and comprehensive basis, and that early and visible steps are taken to work toward that goal.

Timing

The limitations of an evaluation carried out soon after project completion and the need for a second look some years later have already been commented on. The Philippines' system calls for a report six months to a year after completion, with another report after at least five years of operation. If resource limitations dictate only one look, then a choice must be made. On the one hand, a project's impact and effectiveness may more accurately be assessed after some years of operation. On the other hand, too long a delay means that the operational staff most familiar with the project may no longer be available and that the opportunity to learn from the lessons that emerge is postponed. Each government must reach a practical compromise on the best way to evaluate completed projects in light of its own institutional and human constraints.

PART IV
Project Analysis

Using laser technology for tunneling at the Kotmale project site, Sri Lanka

19

Technical Analysis

As WE HAVE NOTED in part III, throughout the several stages of the project cycle various dimensions of project work need to be addressed, both separately and in relation to each other and in varying degrees of detail. These dimensions—which include technical, economic, financial, social, institutional, and environmental analysis—as well as procurement and the use of consultants are the subject of part IV.

Technical analysis is an appropriate place to begin a consideration of these specific dimensions of project work since it is usually the first to be addressed. As we have already stressed, however, and shall elaborate further here, technical issues are interwoven with economic, financial, institutional, and other issues and cannot logically be examined in isolation.

ISSUES OF TECHNICAL DESIGN

Wide as is the range of types of projects, the range of technological alternatives is wider still, so much so that little can usefully be said by way of generalization. Many issues of technical design are specific to a project and must be addressed in that context. Nevertheless, certain broad issues relevant to many, if not all, projects can be identified. These can be grouped into four categories: size, location, timing, and the technology package.

Size

The size, scale, or scope of a project is almost always a variable that must be determined in the course of its preparation. For a project concerned with industrial or agricultural production, size may depend on the market demand—local or foreign—for its output. Or size may depend primarily on the administrative capacity of the implementing agency (for example, a local water company) or of the producing units (for example, farmers). In some projects, physical limitations of the site or of the natural resources to be exploited may be decisive. In others, economies (or diseconomies) of scale in the technological process may impose minimum (or maximum) limits on the size of the operation. Whatever the particular situation, a bias in favor of "bigness" as such on the part of planners may have to be guarded against. Absence of a proven technology package may dictate a phased approach, starting with research or adaptive work and continuing with a pilot project that is scaled up subsequently as experience warrants. Finally, financial considerations, such as the burden of recurrent costs to operate the project once it is completed, may determine project size (for example, the cost of teachers' salaries may limit the number of schools to be constructed and teachers trained).

Location

Issues affecting the choice of location can be as diverse as those affecting size. Sometimes the nature of the project dictates a unique solution, as for example the siting of a port. But in most instances, site selection, like project size, entails a tradeoff among various considerations. An industrial plant may be located in proximity to needed raw materials, to a primary source of energy, to its principal markets, or to suitable infrastructure (public utilities, roads, and other transport modes). Choosing a labor-intensive technology—for example, for carpet weaving—would logically lead to locating the facility in an area where labor is relatively abundant and inexpensive. The quality of soils, pattern of rainfall, structure of landholdings, and availability of ground or surface water may all enter into selecting an area for an agricultural development project. Population densities and service areas will determine the number and location of school buildings or of health and family planning clinics. In some cases, a project's location may reflect a deliberate government policy to decentralize industrial investment away from the nation's capital, to open up an underdeveloped region, or to protect a fragile environment from further encroachment.

Timing

The timing of the project investment should also be a matter of separate consideration during the preparation stage. Timing issues may be less obvious than those of scale and location and therefore more likely to be neglected. A project is sometimes put forward because it is "ready"—in the sense that some sponsoring agency in the country or an external lender has worked out the project idea—rather than because the appropriateness of its timing has been explicitly determined. A project may be premature because the demand for its output, the state of the technology, or some complementary investment is not yet sufficiently advanced to make it economically justified or financially viable. Or a project may be too late, in the sense that its overall contribution or benefit to the economy would have been greater had it been undertaken sooner. For example, a high rate of economic return on a port expansion or road improvement project may reflect heavy traffic congestion or high operating costs resulting from underinvestment or inadequate maintenance in the past. The first year's rate of return, rather than the overall return on the investment, may be a better guide to decisionmaking in such cases.

Technology Package

Among the four broad issues we have mentioned, the choice of a technology package is the one that lends itself most to generalization. By now it is a commonplace that the technology selected for a project should be "appropriate." Appropriateness is a relative concept. It is generally taken to mean that the technology chosen should be suited to the development objectives of the project, to the intended users, and to local conditions—including the availability and cost of local capital, raw materials, and labor, as well as the size of markets and the actual and potential capacity for local planning and implementation. This implies that the technology chosen need not be the most modern that is available internationally, nor the traditional one widely used in the country; it can be selected, and perhaps designed, specifically to meet the objectives of the project.

In most developing countries, capital is relatively scarce and expensive and labor is relatively plentiful and cheap—and largely unskilled. An appropriate technology would therefore tend to be one that made full use of labor while minimizing the use of capital and advanced technical skills. Particularly if the project objective is to provide services to a large segment of the population at a price it can afford, appropriate technology implies acceptance, at least in the short run, of standards and levels of service lower than might be found in most developed countries. Although this is useful as an initial guideline, the situation is often more complicated, as this chapter makes clear.

Before exploring in more detail the question of the choice of an appropriate technology, it is worth noting briefly some of the factors that may lead to the choice of an *inappropriate* technology. These can include the kind of government policies referred to in chapter 3 that overprice labor (through minimum wages), underprice capital (through subsidized interest rates), or undervalue foreign exchange (through unrealistic exchange rates). Such price distortions can lead to adoption of technologies that are financially profitable but economically inefficient. Engineers and planners from developing countries who have been trained in the developed world may be more at home with sophisticated industrial technologies, or they may simply equate the most modern with the best. Engineers and consultants from developed countries naturally tend to promote technologies with which they are most familiar, and they may find allies among special interest groups in developing countries. Moreover, if foreign aid is tied to payments for imports from the donor country, it may favor the use of advanced machinery. (There are also cases where obsolete machinery not suited to the recipient country's needs has been sent abroad under the guise of foreign aid.) Choosing a technology specially designed to be appropriate to developing countries places increased demands on local managers and technicians and may call for institutional innovations as well as changes in public attitudes and in government regulations and policies. Finding an appropriate technology is not an easy task.

While the search may often lead to a choice that occupies an intermediate position on the scale of technical complexity, there are situations in which the advantages of the most sophisticated, modern, or "high" technology are so great, even in the least developed countries, as to override all other factors. Thus, remote sensing by earth satellites may be an indispensable tool for national resource surveys. Long-distance telecommunications will justify the installation of modern electronic equipment—whether it be a microwave radio system or coaxial cable—once minimum levels of traffic have been reached. Generating electric power calls for advanced technology, as does large-scale development of mineral deposits. Offshore oil exploration, deep well drilling, and enhanced oil recovery also use sophisticated and rapidly changing technologies that are difficult even for international oil companies to handle without specialized contractors. Somewhat paradoxically, a more capital-intensive and highly mechanized technology often places less of a burden on the implementing capacity of a developing country than does a more labor-intensive technology (see chapter 17, Project Implementation). At the other end of the scale of complexity, projects for maintenance of rural roads, construction of rural schools, or provision of tertiary irrigation ditches are very likely to call for a highly labor-intensive approach that entails difficult managerial and logistical problems in handling large numbers of workers.

Most decisions about an appropriate technology are less straightforward, however, than the examples cited above. Some situations require very careful analysis; in others (as in deciding between hydro and thermal power generation or among steam, diesel, or electric railway locomotion) the underlying factors have by now been widely studied. The following abbreviated case studies, drawn for the most part from the operational and research experience of the World Bank, are intended to suggest the range of considerations that may enter into the choice of a technology package, not to set forth definitive guidelines applicable in all circumstances. The cases are chosen to illustrate

- The tradeoffs between imported and domestically produced technology, between capital- and labor-intensive technology, and between new investment, maintenance, and operating costs
- The interdependence between choice of technology and administrative and institutional feasibility
- The way the choice of users, as well as environmental concerns, influence technical design
- The impact, intended and otherwise, of the policies of governments and of aid agencies on technical design
- The role of economic and financial analysis in elucidating the choice of technology
- The opportunities that the choice of technology provides for developing local resources and capabilities
- The need for better information to guide the decisionmaking process.

Case Study 1: Cotton Textile Weaving

At issue in this first case was the choice between imported looms and locally made looms for cotton textile weaving in a middle-income developing country, Korea. During the late 1960s and early 1970s, indigenous looms sold for less than one-third the price of imported looms, yet looms were imported in large numbers. To understand why, a study of the government's incentive policies that produced this result was carried out.[1]

In essence, Korea's cotton textile weaving industry at the time of the study had a dualistic structure, with large firms using the more expensive, automatic looms and smaller firms—organized under single proprietors or partnerships—using less expensive, semiautomatic looms. (The distinction between the two types of loom depends on whether the shuttle is changed automatically or manually when yarn is exhausted.) The large firms paid higher wages (85 percent more) to a relatively small work force

1. This case study is based on Yung Whee Rhee and Larry E. Westphal, "A Micro-Econometric Investigation of Choice of Technology," *Journal of Development Economics*, vol. 4 (1977), pp. 205–37.

(one-third the size) and produced superior varieties of cloth, largely for export. The small firms had a large work force with a different occupational mix and substantially lower wages, and they tended to produce inferior varieties of cloth, mostly for the domestic market. The imported, automatic technology allowed a small saving in raw materials but entailed eight times the outlay for loom maintenance, required more than fifteen times as much electric power to run, and had a shorter economic life (sixteen years compared with twenty-five years for the locally produced, simpler looms).

Imported looms could be obtained in widths up to 103 inches, while indigenous looms were available only up to 60 inches. Within their loom widths, however, the indigenous looms were capable of producing export-grade cloth of the same specifications and quality as that produced on the imported looms.

Government policies, which were designed to provide strong inducements for companies to export, had an important impact on the industry. Nearly all imports of automatic looms were financed by foreign suppliers' credits, on which the real interest rate was less than 2 percent. Most purchases of semiautomatic looms were financed by rolling over short-term domestic credit, on which the real interest rate was 14 percent. In addition, there were important differences in tax treatment that depended on the share of output exported. For example, no indirect tax was imposed on yarn used to produce cloth for export, but a minimum tax of 10 percent was imposed on yarn used to produce cloth for the domestic market. The business turnover tax was not levied on exports or on imports used to produce exports. Income derived from export sales was taxed at half the rate otherwise applicable. Also, exporters were allowed to use a somewhat higher rate of depreciation.

Benefit-cost ratios were calculated for the two technologies. Based on actual prices that producers paid or received, the ratios were virtually the same for the imported and for the domestic looms (see table 19-1 on the following page). Given the government policies that determined those prices, as well as the varieties of cloth to be produced, the choice by producers of one technology or the other was consistent with their desire for maximum profit.

The situation would become very different, however, were the distortions caused by government price policies removed. To arrive at the social (or economic) benefit-cost ratio, adjustments were made to the private (or financial) benefit-cost ratio by using shadow prices to allow for the differences in interest rates and tax treatment as well as for the effects of preferential tariff policies and of an overvalued exchange rate. (For a discussion of these concepts, see chapter 20, Economic Analysis.) The social benefit-cost ratios were almost four times higher for the indigenous than for the imported technology. It therefore appears that few, if any, imported automatic looms would have been purchased in the absence of the government's preferential policy, except for the relatively few cases where it was necessary to produce fabrics for export wider than could be produced on domestic looms. For the same initial investment, use of the domestic, semiautomatic technology would have generated more than five times the number of jobs.

Recognizing that these incentives were leading to economically inap-

Table 19-1. *Benefit-Cost Evaluation of Alternative Weaving Technologies*

Measure	Domestic semiautomatic looms	Imported automatic looms
Size of sample		
Loom models	26	32
Loom-fabric combinations	65	73
Average benefit-cost ratio		
Private (financial)	4.14	4.39
Social (economic)	5.48	1.49
Average subsidy rates		
Percentage increase in benefit due to policies affecting		
Interest rates	-67.8	76.8
Direct and indirect taxes	-36.5	19.4
Input and output prices	128.8	53.7
Percentage decrease in cost due to policies affecting		
Loom purchase price	0.0	21.3

Note: Averages are simple averages over all the loom-fabric combinations for which estimates were made under each technology.

Source: Data from Yung Whee Rhee and Larry E. Westphal, "A Micro, Econometric Investigation of Choice of Technology," *Journal of Development Economics*, vol. 4 (1977), p. 224.

propriate choices and were discriminating against domestic loom manufacturers, the Korean government changed its policies shortly after the study was made. Imports of capital goods were no longer favored by tariff exemptions or access to credit on softer terms; in some cases, there were even restrictions on imports that competed with domestically produced equipment. Income from exports was no longer taxed at a preferential rate, and other export incentives were substantially reduced. In addition, with the increasing maturity of the engineering industry, wider looms were produced domestically, so that the imported technology no longer had an advantage on this score. As a result, more than two-thirds of the new looms purchased by cotton textile producers in 1973 and 1974 were locally manufactured.

Case Study 2: Civil Works Construction

The use of manual methods in constructing civil works is sometimes motivated by sociopolitical factors, such as the need to provide jobs for low-income people who would otherwise be unemployed. Public works officials are often skeptical about the quality of work achieved through manual methods and about their cost-effectiveness. This skepticism is not unfounded, for many labor-intensive public works programs have accomplished little more than income transfers to the work force.

The World Bank began a major research and demonstration project in 1971 to help resolve the controversy both within and outside the Bank over the feasible scope for efficient substitution between labor and machinery in the construction of civil works. The purpose of this study was to determine whether, to what extent, and under what circumstances more labor-intensive methods could provide an efficient means for converting abundant labor into sound capital assets.[2]

Carried out with support from nine bilateral agencies, the study initially examined the productivity of traditional technologies. Subsequently, it experimented with a number of modifications to labor-intensive technologies and to methods of work organization; this ultimately led to a series of pilot projects to demonstrate the cost-effective use of labor-intensive methods. In several countries, including Kenya, Malawi, and Honduras, these pilot demonstrations have since grown into substantial national civil works programs providing productive employment for many thousands of people who would otherwise be unemployed.

In the research phase, detailed investigations were made of a wide range of technologies used in construction activities such as stone crushing, stonemasonry, and the excavation, hauling, and compaction of different types of soil. The outputs of different factor combinations were derived from observations of construction work in progress. These observations led to the determination of optimal working conditions for the various hand tools and haulage methods used in building civil works.

When hauling earth over distances of less than 100 meters, for example, wheelbarrows were found to be more efficient than the head baskets traditionally used in parts of Asia, except on steep terrain (gradients in excess of 15 percent) and poor rolling surfaces, where people with head baskets or animals with panniers performed better. For distances on level ground of 100 to 1,000 meters, animal-drawn carts proved to be economically and technically efficient, with camel carts outperforming mule and donkey carts by factors of two and three respectively; the use of large numbers of draft animals, however, introduced problems of logistics and work organization. For distances between 500 meters and 2 kilometers, the combination of one agricultural tractor and two five-ton trailers (working in teams, one being loaded while the other was in transit), with low beds to enable easier loading and unloading by hand, performed better than tip trucks.

The study found that for certain types of construction, particularly those related to rural civil works, labor-intensive methods can meet the technical requirements as well as methods that depend on machines. In practice, the choice of a particular technology for one task (for example, using large-scale excavators to dig a canal) tends to dictate the use of a similar type of technology for most of the other tasks, partly because machines work faster than gangs of laborers and it is costly to keep them idle, and partly because each type of technology calls for the work to be organized in a particular way. This need for technological standardization can also extend to maintenance work; if a road, for example, has been built with labor-intensive methods, it may be most easily maintained with such methods. But many routine maintenance functions even on machine-built roads can be done as effectively by labor-intensive methods.

What is technically feasible is not necessarily economically justified. Traditional labor-intensive civil construction work, as observed in the

2. For a general summary of the study, see Basil Coukis and others, *Labor-Based Construction Programs: A Practical Guide for Planning and Management* (New Delhi: Oxford University Press for the World Bank, 1984).

course of the study, was often economically inferior to more capital-intensive work except at extremely low wages. Labor productivity was improved dramatically, however, by introducing certain organizational, management, and mechanical improvements.

Organizational and managerial factors were critical. The most important of these was the structuring of incentives so that all levels of staff, from management to the casual laborer, were motivated to work efficiently. Indeed, the study showed that the productivity increases that could be fostered by an effective system of wage incentives (based on piece or task rates instead of daily wages) were exceptionally high; in the case of earthworks, for instance, output per worker could be increased by a factor of two or even three. However, the development and administration of an effective incentive system is in itself a difficult and complex task. Detailed job analyses have to be carried out and a schedule of productivity norms established. Furthermore, the payment basis must be fully understood by the workers and regarded by them as fair. It is also important that wages be paid regularly and promptly.

By their nature, labor-intensive construction projects require more supervisory staff than equipment-intensive ones. While a small bulldozer manned by one or two skilled workers could easily move 1,000 cubic meters of noncohesive soil in a day, 300 to 500 unskilled laborers—organized in labor gangs of twenty to thirty people and often dispersed over a fairly wide area—were needed to do the same amount of work. To motivate the laborers, organize their work, and control its quality required a dozen or more competent supervisors.

In many countries, the scarcity of skilled supervisors is a constraint on the feasibility of labor-intensive projects. Training fairly large numbers of people to assume supervisory tasks can add significantly to the cost and implementation time of the first such projects undertaken in areas where labor-intensive methods are not traditional. At the same time, it must be recognized that this training also creates valuable human resources and provides higher-level employment opportunities for otherwise unskilled laborers. Experience in Africa and Latin America shows that, after a learning period of four to six years, permanent cadres of competent field staff can be formed and labor-intensive methods established as the accepted practice for constructing rural infrastructure.

A more serious bottleneck in many cases has been the shortage of engineers and other high-level technical personnel with the ability and inclination to organize and supervise projects of this type. Many local professionals feel that the work offers them too little opportunity to apply more sophisticated engineering skills, as well as too little prestige compared with work on larger, capital-intensive projects. These problems have been overcome in demonstration projects when experience with labor-intensive programs has been integrated into a ministry's career development programs, as it was in Kenya and Honduras.

Concern that the rural population would be unwilling to work on labor-intensive projects because manual work was considered undignified has been shown to be misplaced. The demonstration projects, carried out across a broad range of cultures in Africa, Latin America, and Asia, revealed few problems in recruiting local people for manual tasks. In fact, in most cases the supply of laborers has been greater than the demand,

and sometimes the competition among workers has stimulated higher productivity. In areas with pronounced seasonality in agriculture, however, construction programs must be timed to avoid conflicts with peak agricultural demand for labor.

Although wages and incentives are important elements in the success of labor-intensive civil works construction, they are but a part of the broader problem of financing. The study showed that many such projects sponsored by public authorities suffered from an irregular flow of funds to pay the workers and contractors, which had a negative effect on worker morale and on productivity. The problem can be particularly acute when the work is carried out by small contractors. They usually do not have the financial strength to overcome the difficulties caused by delays in payments, nor do they have the resources to make the initial investments for mobilizing manpower (advances to prospective workers, purchase of tools, site and logistics costs, and so on).

The productivity of workers is also influenced by their health and nutrition. Many workers engaged in construction projects are undernourished and in poor health, and one of the most productive investments that can be made is to provide them with an adequate diet and good health care. It was observed in Indonesia, for example, that a simple and inexpensive iron supplementation program resulted in productivity increases of up to 25 percent.[3] Another study, this one in India, indicated a close correlation between output and the body weight of workers. It was also found to be important to provide clean drinking water and sanitary waste disposal facilities on the work sites and within the camps where the laborers were housed.

In summary, with proper planning, good supervision, improved equipment or tools that can often be made locally, incentive payment systems, proper organization of the work, and interventions to upgrade the health and nutrition of the workers, the productivity of labor can be increased severalfold. Moreover, most of the production increases can be achieved without any significant increase in capital investments, although a substantial investment in technical assistance and training may be needed when these methods are first introduced. Under these conditions, labor-intensive methods of constructing civil works can be economically competitive with the use of modern equipment in many labor-abundant economies—generally, whenever labor is readily available at daily wage rates of about $4 or less (in 1984 prices)—and can provide productive employment opportunities for some of the most disadvantaged members of society.

Case Study 3: Waste Disposal

Water-borne sewerage, the conventional method of human waste disposal in most developed countries, requires heavy capital investment. When such sewerage systems have been built in developing countries, they have often resulted in charges that were beyond the ability of many consumers to pay. To address this problem, the World Bank in 1976

3. See Samir S. Basta and Anthony Churchill, *Iron Deficiency Anaemia and the Productivity of Adult Male Workers in Indonesia*, World Bank Staff Working Paper no. 175 (Washington, D.C., 1974).

launched a research project on appropriate technology for water supply and waste disposal in developing countries. The emphasis was on identifying and evaluating sanitation technologies, particularly as they were affected by the level of water supply service and the needs and resources of project beneficiaries.[4]

The study covered twenty-nine countries in various stages of development. Its first and most important finding was that there are many technologies between the extremes of the unimproved pit privy and of water-borne sewerage that can be recommended for widespread use. In all, five types of household (on-site) systems and four types of community systems were identified, with many variations of each type. Improved designs were prepared for several of these; for only one (bucket latrines) was it concluded that introduction into new sites should be avoided. Two of the other technologies—aquaprivies and communal toilets—were found to be limited in their applicability by social factors. All of the remaining technologies (improved pit latrines, pour-flush toilets, composting toilets, and modified septic tanks, vacuum cartage, small-bore sewerage, and conventional sewerage) can be recommended for adoption subject to the physical conditions of the site and the social preferences and economic resources of the beneficiaries. Except in unusual circumstances, both sparsely populated rural communities and densely populated urban ones should find themselves with two or more technically feasible options, each with a range of design alternatives.

The nine technologies studied can be classified by cost into three groups. Five of them cost less than $100 a year per household (in 1978 prices; the range was from $19 to $65) when all input costs are assigned shadow prices and both capital and recurrent costs are included. Two technologies, aquaprivies and Japanese-type vacuum cartage, cost between $150 and $200 a year per household. Septic tanks and sewerage costs averaged $370 and $400 a year per household, respectively. Thus the ratio of the lowest- to highest-cost system was 1:20.

The two most important components of total household cost have often been ignored in engineering analysis: the cost for on-site improvements such as internal plumbing and the cost of flushing water for water-borne systems. The first was important for all technologies and never accounted for less than 45 percent of a household's costs, calculated on an annual basis. The second was most important for sewerage and septic tank systems. Because the ratio of sanitation costs to water supply costs ranges from about 1:1 for village wells and household latrines to 9:1 for sewerage of a high service level, there is a large payoff from designing systems with low requirements for flushing water.

One of the most important technical contributions of this research study is the design of "sanitation sequences," step-by-step improvements leading from one option to another and planned from the beginning to minimize costs over the long run. Thus, a community can begin by selecting one of the low-cost technologies; then, as its socioeconomic

4. The findings of this research project and other parallel research activities in the field of low-cost water supply and sanitation are presented in a series of publications entitled "Appropriate Technology for Water Supply and Sanitation" by the Water Supply and Urban Development Department of the World Bank.

status improves, it can upgrade its system in a predetermined series of improvements to a sophisticated "final" solution. This is something that is not possible with conventional sewerage; for it to function properly, large investments and large volumes of water are needed from the outset.

Social customs have an impact on the types of technology that are acceptable. There are countries where reuse of human waste on the soil is against local custom, where communal facilities are frowned upon, or where human waste is deposited only into running or stagnant water. In contrast, there appear to be no social constraints in any country on the use of water-borne sewerage—possibly because the system remains largely invisible.

This research has demonstrated that methods exist for the disposal of excreta that can meet every public health test at only a fraction of the cost of conventional sewerage. Since technological alternatives to sewerage do exist and can provide full health benefits at a substantial cost saving, why have they not been adopted in the past? What are the obstacles to their selection that need to be overcome, and what new incentives need to be provided? One important obstacle has been the information gap. The results of these studies need to be disseminated as widely and as quickly as possible. A second obstacle is the need to retrain most professionals in the field so they can cope with the nonconventional solutions being proposed. An even bigger change is needed in the way project feasibility studies are carried out; interaction with the eventual users in the community must be greatly increased. This probably means that multidisciplinary teams, including sociologists, should be included from the first phase of planning through the later phases of technology selection and detailed design. Involvement of the users is essential since many of the technologies will be partially built and then maintained by them.

In addition to increased community participation, the successful implementation of many of the nonconventional technologies calls for institutional arrangements different from those appropriate for conventional sewerage. A more decentralized administration and better coordination with health, housing, and other agencies are the main requirements.

New types of financial incentives are also needed to promote the adoption of appropriate sanitation technologies. In many developing (and developed) countries, the government provides large subsidies for the construction of interceptors and sewage treatment plants. This makes it very difficult for a community to choose any other waste disposal system since it would have to bear the full financial burden. In general, sewerage systems are not the least-cost way of achieving either better health or environmental protection except in areas where population density and water consumption are high. To subsidize such systems exclusively may preempt the appropriate solution.

International and bilateral lending agencies have sometimes exerted a financial bias in favor of sewerage. Loans which cover only the foreign exchange cost of projects have tended to favor technologies based on imported equipment and foreign consultants, to the detriment of technologies using mostly local materials and self-help construction. Fortunately, most aid organizations have now changed their policies to permit some financing of local costs. They are also increasingly interested in projects that directly benefit the poorer groups in society. These two shifts in approach should make aid organizations more willing than previously to finance low-cost sanitation packages.[5]

Case Study 4: Use of Tractors in Agriculture in South Asia

The extent to which agriculture should be mechanized—specifically, by the use of tractors—in low-wage countries has been the subject of a virulent and emotional debate over the past twenty years. A careful analytical review of the extensive literature to which this debate has given rise has been undertaken with respect to one of the principal areas involved, the Indian subcontinent. While the results are specific to the agronomic and economic environment of South Asia, they nevertheless illuminate the issues involved in the choice of an appropriate technology.[6]

The evidence fails to demonstrate that tractor use has resulted in substantial increases in cropping intensity, timeliness of work, yields, or gross returns on farms in India, Pakistan, and Nepal. Although large farms utilizing tractors sometimes displayed higher output per hectare than small farms, this was usually associated with substantially greater use of fertilizers and with greater access to or use of irrigation water; the part attributable directly to mechanization is difficult to isolate. At best, the benefits from using tractors were so small that they could not be detected and statistically measured, even with massive survey research efforts. The surveys largely support the view that tractors served primarily as substitutes for manpower and bullocks; the financial rates of return to farmers on the use of tractors for agricultural operations under existing wage rates and bullock costs and prevailing farmgate prices were close to zero.

That extensive investment in tractors took place in areas such as the Punjab was partly due to the opportunities for larger farmers to expand their farms and to practice self-cultivation methods instead of having to rely on hired labor. A large public subsidy on tractors in Pakistan, based on the proposition that they were necessary to modernize agriculture, also was undoubtedly a factor. Tractors shifted the cost advantage in farming toward larger farms and led to increased concentration of landholdings in fewer hands, contrary to the avowed objectives of policymakers.

Nonagricultural benefits of tractors must also be taken into account. Tractors reduce the drudgery of farm work, but where wages are low and underemployment of landless labor widespread, less drudgery, if translated into fewer jobs, is clearly not a benefit. In contrast, the use of tractors for transport has some clear-cut benefits. It also appears that large-scale farmers sometimes invest in tractors and other machines to avoid what they perceive as potential problems of labor management and discipline. This can sometimes be an important consideration, particularly in view of the fact that high-yielding varieties of wheat and rice have

5. John M. Kalbermatten, DeAnne S. Julius, and Charles G. Gunnerson, *Appropriate Sanitation Alternatives: A Technical and Economic Appraisal* (Baltimore, Md.: Johns Hopkins University Press for the World Bank, 1982).

6. This case study is based on Hans P. Binswanger, *The Economics of Tractors in South Asia: An Analytical Review* (New York: Agricultural Development Council and Hyderabad, India: International Center Research Institute for the Semi-Arid Tropics, 1978).

led to an increased demand for labor and hence have enhanced the bargaining power of farm laborers in the areas where most tractor investment has occurred.

Given the nonagricultural benefits of tractors, investment in them can occur even if the purely agricultural net benefits to farmers are low. But the rationale for public support or subsidy of the investment disappears.

The other main conclusion of the survey relates to the labor-saving nature of the tractor investments. While farms using tractors do not generally show much less use of labor per hectare than farms using bullocks, this does not imply that tractors are not labor-displacing. The higher levels of output frequently obtained with tractors are generally achieved with no increase in the amount of labor, that is, with less labor per unit of output. Moreover, it is necessary to count as an "employment" cost of tractors the forgone employment that would have resulted from putting the same capital into other, employment-creating farm investments, such as irrigation, or into nonfarm investments.

It is not suggested that the economics of the substitution of tractors for labor will work out the same in all situations or in all countries. Tractors may be highly productive, for example, in areas where additional land can be brought under cultivation (as in some parts of Latin America) or where wages are rising rapidly. We emphasize again that the purpose of these case studies is to illustrate issues involved in technological choice, not to set forth solutions of universal application.

Case Study 5: Highway Design and Maintenance Standards

Another major World Bank research effort illustrates how an appropriate strategy can be designed for dealing with a technological tradeoff: in this case, between initial highway construction costs, future maintenance costs, and the operating costs experienced by road users. In 1969 the Bank, in conjunction with research institutions in the United States, the United Kingdom, and France, initiated a long-term program of research to evaluate alternative design and maintenance strategies for asphalt, gravel, and earth roads in developing countries.

Studies in this program have examined the tradeoffs between the volume of earthwork to improve vertical and horizontal alignment, on the one hand, and vehicle costs in terms of travel time, fuel consumption, and vehicle wear on the other; between the quality of initial pavement construction and the cost and frequency of subsequent road maintenance; and between the quality of road maintenance and vehicle wear, operating speed, and fuel consumption.

On the basis of primary research into both the physical and economic relationships in Kenya, Brazil, and India, a computer model—known as the Highway Design and Standards Model—has been developed to predict the costs of different highway design and maintenance options. The model can be used to estimate quickly the total costs for large numbers and combinations of alternative designs and maintenance practices year by year. Decisionmakers are thereby provided with an information system for arriving at the strategy that will minimize the total costs of highway construction, maintenance, and vehicle operation.

Among the preliminary and tentative results to date are these:

- The economic returns to road maintenance that have been quantified demonstrate the high priority of maintenance outlays.

- Doubt has been cast on the conventional strategy of phasing road construction over time, with a progressive upgrading of pavement design as traffic grows. Because of large economies of scale both in construction of high-quality pavements and in truck sizes and weights, it may sometimes be economical to build very strong pavements from the outset even in countries where the opportunity cost of capital is high and traffic relatively light. Difficulties of funding several construction stages in a timely manner and of ensuring adequate outlays for routine maintenance on a regular basis reinforce this tentative conclusion.

- Equally surprising is the finding that, under noncongested traffic conditions in an African country, most improvements in geometric road standards (that is, vertical and horizontal alignments) beyond the bare minimum provide only limited benefits. If this result proves to be generally valid, the potential for reducing costly earthworks and pavement width would be substantial.

- There may be major distortions in highway resource allocation in many developing countries, reflected in overinvestment in new road construction and underinvestment in maintaining existing roads and in strengthening their pavements.

More empirical data are being collected so that the model can be tested under a wider variety of climatic, geological, and traffic conditions. Even on the basis of the limited empirical validation available until recently, however, the model has been used in more than thirty countries worldwide in planning programs to maintain and strengthen highways. This suggests that planners find it a useful adjunct to the engineering rules of thumb and policy judgments hitherto employed. With the completion of major studies in Brazil and India in 1983, validation of the model has been extended to a much wider range of environments.[7]

COST ESTIMATES

Once the appropriate technology for a project has been selected, detailed engineering and design work can proceed to the point that a realistic cost estimate and implementation schedule can be prepared. One of the most pervasive shortcomings of project work is the underestimation of the cost and of the time required to implement a project. Many project planners share an occupational bias toward viewing their world through rose-colored glasses; this can apply to all projects—large and small, complex and simple—in virtually all countries, developing and developed alike. World Bank staff have not been immune, as the data on the incidence of cost overruns and time delays in Bank-assisted projects (presented in chapter 17, Project Implementation) abundantly demonstrate. Underestimation of costs is not just a statistical phenomenon; it

7. Thawat Watanatada and others, *The Highway Design and Maintenance Standards Model: Model Description and Users' Manual* (Washington, D.C.: World Bank, 1985).

can have very adverse consequences for the project. Since the cost estimates are used in determining the economic and financial viability of the project, underestimation can lead to the acceptance of projects that would not otherwise be justified. Furthermore, the financing requirements of the project, both local and foreign, will be understated, which can lead to a shortage of funds that impedes project execution.

It is axiomatic, therefore, that the cost estimate should be as accurate as the nature of the project and the state of the art reasonably permit, and that the estimate should be available by the time funds are to be committed for the project. How much engineering and design work is necessary to arrive at this stage depends on the type of project. Thus, reliable cost estimates for roads in hilly terrain require more detailed cross-sections and borings than for roads in flat terrain. Similarly, the number of test borings to be taken in the engineering of a port project varies according to the subsoil conditions encountered. Relatively accurate cost estimates, with less engineering and design work, are possible for repetitive, standard equipment purchases and for precisely definable civil works such as paving a road, lining a canal, or building a primary school.

A separate cost estimate should be prepared for each distinct component of the project. Estimates of equipment costs are based on the number and type of items and their prices; those of civil works on the physical quantities of work to be performed and their unit prices. Recent experience in executing similar projects in the country is the principal guide to prices. When projects are large and complex or when there is little record of recent bidding in the country, it may be advisable to secure the services of a specialized cost estimating firm or of a quantity surveyor, or to solicit the advice of potential contractors or equipment manufacturers.

Since the availability of foreign exchange may often present a problem, the estimates should be broken down into local and foreign costs, the latter to include both direct imports and the (indirect) foreign exchange content of goods purchased and works executed in the country. Interest during construction and incremental working capital requirements should be included when applicable. Costs are prepared in financial (not economic) terms and related to cash expenditures. Local taxes and import duties should be included but shown separately, since they are a cost to the project entity but not to the country.

An important way of improving the accuracy of cost estimates is to provide for physical and price contingencies. Cost estimates should normally consist of two parts: a base estimate, and physical and price contingencies added to it. The base estimate, which is prepared initially as part of the feasibility study and updated as the detailed engineering is completed, represents the best judgment as of the date specified of what the project will cost. It assumes that the project will be implemented as planned and that the quantities of works, goods, and services and their prices are known with reasonable accuracy and will not change during implementation. The base estimate, in other words, is not intended to reflect changes in quantities and prices that may occur after the date of the estimate; this is the purpose of the physical and price contingency allowances. They reflect the physical and price changes that can reasonably be expected to occur between the time of the base estimate and the completion of the project. The total cost estimate—base cost plus contingencies—

represents the best judgment of what the final cost of the completed project will be. Contingency allowances vary with the nature of the project and are calculated separately for each of its main components.

Physical Contingencies

Allowances for physical contingencies reflect how much costs are expected to rise above the base estimates as the project progresses, owing to changes in the quantity of work performed, in the amount or type of equipment purchased, or in the method of implementation. Although the exact amount and precise nature of such changes cannot be predicted in advance, it is highly probable that they will occur and that they are more likely to increase than to decrease the cost of the project. Some of the main uncertainties for which provision should be made are unpredictable landslides or earthquakes in geologically unstable terrain, climatic conditions such as frequent cyclones or unusual patterns of rain and wind, and difficulties of access to the site of work or to quarries and other sources of construction materials.

Acceptable ranges of physical contingencies will vary from sector to sector as well as for the various components of a project. Normally, the allowances for civil engineering works are higher than those for the supply of materials or equipment, which can more readily be specified in advance. Some typical levels are:

- 5 percent for repetitive, standard equipment items and for precisely definable civil works such as road surfacing and canal lining
- 10 percent for general civil works with routine and predictable uncertainties, such as buildings, pipelines, transmission lines, and earthwork for roads in simple terrain
- Up to 15 percent for processing plants, buildings, and civil works in more difficult terrain, major and minor irrigation and drainage facilities, and dams.

These figures assume that detailed engineering is either substantially completed or that the work is so repetitive and routine that costly surprises are highly improbable. When the appropriate physical contingencies are greater than, say, 15 to 20 percent overall, further refinement of the basic design and additional site investigation may be advisable to reduce the margin of uncertainty before inviting bids.

Certain types of work may require a higher contingency provision to reflect their inherent uncertainties when it is too costly or impractical to refine the quantity and cost estimates before work begins. Examples include structural foundations in difficult soils, pile driving, dam foundations, or rehabilitation of existing irrigation works. Thus, a 50 percent allowance for tunnel excavation in fractured rock or in mountainous country under deep overburden may be justifiable if it is not possible to sink exploratory holes into the tunnel zone.

Price Contingencies

Allowances for price contingencies reflect expected increases in project costs due to changes in unit prices for the various components after the date of the base cost estimate. Price contingencies are applied to the base costs plus physical contingencies and calculated separately for local and foreign expenditures.

In determining the appropriate level of price contingencies, two of the factors to be considered are the extent of expected local and international inflation during project execution, and the extent to which local or foreign prices for particular types of works, goods, or services are expected to diverge from general inflationary trends (for example, because of supply and demand conditions in the local construction industry or because of the potential impact of a very large project on the cost of local resources). If the contract documents for the project specify that a price escalation formula will apply to the works or equipment, this should be taken into account. The price contingencies should be calculated annually and accumulated over the period of project implementation.

There are circumstances in which, because of problematic physical conditions such as difficult access to the site or poor transportation or because of political and economic uncertainties, contractors will offer bids for work only at prices that include a premium for unusual risk. If these conditions are expected to make the estimation of costs for bid preparation particularly uncertain, a special "risk allowance" can be added to the contingencies. Any part of the risk allowance not needed after bids are received and evaluated can be deleted. In lieu of including a separate risk allowance, it may be preferable to complete the bidding process as far as bid evaluation to have more reliable cost estimates before committing funds for the project; some external lenders may make this a requirement.

Certain types of projects—such as industrial finance and agricultural credit—are essentially a line of credit to help finance a program defined in financial terms, without specific physical content. Contingency allowances need not be provided in these cases. In other projects, physical targets may have been only roughly defined, the exact scope not being essential to the success of the project (examples include installation of 1,000 tubewells or maintenance of 1,500 kilometers of roads). In these cases, no physical contingencies are necessary; however, to safeguard the scope of the project against the effects of inflation, price contingencies should be included. When projects that are part of the investment program of a public agency—say, a highway department or an education department—are financed entirely through public budgetary funds, no price contingencies may be necessary unless they are provided routinely as part of the regular budgeting process.

IMPLEMENTATION SCHEDULES

The technical preparation of a project should include at least a preliminary plan for its implementation, showing who does what and when. This is sometimes referred to as network or critical path analysis, a term that includes such sophisticated systems as the program evaluation and review technique (PERT; see the discussion in chapter 17, Project Implementation). These systems are designed to highlight particular activities that must be completed before others can commence or that would delay the project as a whole if not finished on time. Although these systems are an essential planning tool for projects that include large civil works or equipment purchases, simple bar charts showing the sequence of events, accompanied by a commentary, may suffice for other types of projects. In either case, the purpose is to identify and to provide sufficient lead time for completing those activities whose scheduling is critical to project implementation. Failure to anticipate and plan adequately for such activities has often resulted in lengthy and costly delays.

Implementation schedules should be realistic, assuming no more than due diligence and efficiency on the part of the various agencies and individuals responsible for the project. Although this advice may appear obvious, there is a widespread tendency to use the schedules as targets to expedite performance. Experience shows that the use of overoptimistic schedules as targets frequently proves counterproductive. It can distort operational planning and lead to unnecessary friction among the various parties when performance falls short of the target. Moreover, since the expected time schedule for carrying out the project enters into the economic and financial analyses, it can mislead judgments in these areas. Among the activities for which scheduling tends to be least realistic are those during the initial or start-up phase of the project—including acquisition of land, recruitment of consultants, organization and staffing of the project entity, and initiation of procurement—as discussed in chapter 17.

SCIENTIFIC AND TECHNOLOGICAL DEVELOPMENT

In addition to the issues concerning the technical analysis of projects, including choice of an appropriate technology, there is another important technical dimension of project work: how can a country take advantage of its investment plan and projects, together with its policy framework, to build up a capacity to use science and technology effectively throughout the economy? Both trained people and institutions deploying their professional skills are required in order to import technology from abroad knowledgeably, to adapt it to domestic conditions, to develop local technology and integrate it with imported technology, and to do research and encourage innovation. Skills are needed not only in engineering and natural sciences but also in economics, other social sciences, and management. Some development of the capacity to use science and technology takes place more or less automatically as an economy grows, but the process will be more effective if it is planned as a regular part of project work.

Stages of Development

In the earlier stages of their scientific and technological development, countries are likely to benefit from—and to be dependent on—the transfer of technology from abroad, even as they seek to expand their own competence in this area. Government strategy should concentrate on several primary objectives:

- To overcome the most critical shortages of human and institutional resources

- To build the local capacity to select and use imported technology effectively in a few key sectors of the economy, with an emphasis on the special needs of smaller producers
- To start building the local capacity for research and innovation in key sectors, such as agriculture, when imported technology and knowledge do not meet local needs
- To ensure attention to the scientific and technological aspects of important social and environmental problems that may not otherwise be adequately addressed
- To enhance the awareness and raise the status of science and technology among students and the public at large.

In later stages of scientific and technological development, the task is to build on the activities selected during the earlier stages and thereby move toward a modern, technologically oriented economy. Policymakers should then set more ambitious objectives:

- To ensure systematic attention to developing an appropriate degree of technological capacity in all sectors of the economy
- To extend this capacity to include adaptation, innovation, research, and evaluation of results
- To create a climate that encourages industry to devote enough resources to technological effort to reach international standards of efficiency and competitiveness
- To ensure adequate technological effort in social sectors, which tend to be neglected.

At each stage, the means used to accomplish these objectives are essentially the same: attention to the scientific and technological aspects of investment projects; creation or strengthening of an infrastructure of local scientific and technological institutions and services; and policies, regulations, and other interventions by government, including those concerned with risk taking and venture capital. These are discussed in turn below.

Investment Projects

Investment projects whose primary purpose is to increase the production of goods and services may also provide an opportunity to build technological capacity. Their emphasis on operations tends to keep practical objectives in focus—something a purely technological institution like a laboratory finds difficult. A major investment project provides an opportunity to plan the training of manpower for the sector and to consult with local institutions of higher learning on relevant training programs and curricula. It also stimulates reexamination of the research and technological services available to the project and sector.

For example, agricultural investment projects may include support to local research and extension services that will provide technological packages and advice for farmers. A project to promote investment in small industries may occasion the establishment of a center or institute to provide them with common services, do troubleshooting, and extend technical assistance. A mining or petroleum project may be used to prompt local universities to revamp their curricula in geology or to strengthen the local geological survey and research institutes to deal with problems of mining and beneficiating local ores.

In large infrastructure and industrial projects, productive units must be staffed by trained technicians with direct access to modern equipment and technology. Building capacity for using technology through such projects requires both commitment by the enterprise and translation of that commitment into an explicit plan and specific investments of resources and personnel.

An investment project in infrastructure or industry can also be a useful vehicle for building local capacity through a focused training program. For example, if consultants are used for project design and preparation, they should also be asked to train the personnel who will have to manage, operate, and maintain the project. Since a foreign partner, if there is one, will always find it easier to do the job itself with only minor contributions from local staff, an explicit training program should be built into the terms of reference of the consultant or else additional resources allocated specifically for this purpose.

Projects in the social sectors such as health, nutrition, population, and education face related but different problems. Public sector service organizations typically are poorly managed and deficient in technological capacity, including the capacity to develop technologies specific to local needs. Investments in these sectors lack market-induced quality control and hence the stimulus to innovate. They need, therefore, to include special attention to monitoring and evaluation, together with research on improved methods for delivering services—which are, in the broad sense, technologies.

The design of people-oriented projects must take into account that rural villages and urban slums are often poorly organized to identify their needs for technology. Decentralized, nongovernmental organizations devoted to community development, such as the Sarvodaya Shramadana in Sri Lanka, can organize and motivate local populations and help them to identify their technical needs and to acquire basic skills. Such organizations are often more effective than official agencies in assisting communities to take advantage of low-cost technologies.

In all the projects referred to above, the objective is not only to encourage the development of technology locally but also to "unwrap" the technological packages offered by foreign suppliers. This unwrapping process may be undertaken by stages in successive projects. Even at the outset, it is rarely if ever necessary to accept a totally wrapped package—as, for example, a turnkey plant, all aspects of which are proprietary and about which the local investor is told only enough to enable him to operate the plant. At a minimum, the purchaser should demand a list of the components of a turnkey project, so that he may judge whether the package offered is suited to his conditions. Moreover, his own personnel should be associated with the design and planning of the project, so that they may be better equipped to manage, operate, and maintain it afterward. The critical step in the process of unwrapping the package is reached when the customer becomes his own prime contractor and purchases various parts of the overall project from different suppliers, taking on himself the responsibility for the interfaces between them and for the soundness of the overall design.

Technological Infrastructure Projects

Some projects have as their primary objective the building of technological capacity, either in the productive sector, in government, or in universities. According to the stage of a country's scientific and technological development, these may include:

- Establishing universities and basic research programs, along with administrative mechanisms for their funding, coordination, and control
- Promoting the local engineering and consulting industry
- Providing service institutes for testing, standards, quality control, and troubleshooting
- Establishing multidisciplinary technological research institutes and services related to natural resources—such as meteorology services, oceanographic and geological surveys, and mapping and remote sensing agencies.

Such projects require a sustained political commitment at a high level of government, coupled with constant vigilance to ensure that the quality of performance is not undermined by the problems that typically beset government bureaucracy: low salaries, stop-and-go funding, and inflexible administrative procedures, especially on staffing and procurement. This usually calls for a substantial measure of autonomy for the public institutions involved and a commitment to quality in staff and performance.

Perhaps the most difficult task in building an effective public institution concerned with science and technology is to ensure that it maintains close contact with its clientele in the productive sectors and that its services meet their needs and are, in fact, put to work. This is a problem even in developed countries, but is more serious in developing countries because of the historic isolation of the local scientific and technological community from the productive sectors. One of the most effective means of promoting close contact is to require that a substantial portion of the income of such service institutions be derived from fees paid by users. Another is to put members of the user community on the board of directors, and to press for close contact with users at all levels of the organization.

Government Intervention

The investments of personnel, money, and other resources that a manager makes to select and use technology and to develop technological capacity depend on his assessment of market conditions and incentives. These, in turn, are influenced by a variety of government policies, including those pertaining to interest, exchange, and wage rates, profits, and the prices of basic commodities. For this reason, government policies in areas apparently distant from science and technology inevitably affect the process of technological change and the building of technological capacity.

One of the most important elements of technological strategy is to avoid discouraging private investment in improved technology. Specifically, the government should refrain from those policies (unfortunately very common) that discriminate against small-scale production, distort prices in ways that result in misuse of scarce factors of production, or provide excessive protection against foreign or domestic competition (see chapter 9, Industry).

Many governments have attempted to improve the terms and conditions of technology transfer from abroad by regulation and sometimes by direct intervention in negotiations between local and foreign firms regarding technology transfer. The effectiveness of such intervention depends on the way it is done. Skillfully handled, it may help to equalize the negotiating position of the parties, improve the terms and conditions of technology transfer, and increase the care and effort with which local firms choose and absorb technology. But a rigid and excessively bureaucratic or nationalistic approach may simply obstruct the transfer of needed technology.

A critical issue is the ability of local managers to determine when it is cost-effective to import technology from abroad and when to build indigenous capacity. In general, governments would be well advised to put their efforts into enhancing this ability by correcting or compensating for distorted price signals and market imperfections. Governments can help the managers of small and medium-size enterprises to benefit from improved technology by disseminating information about alternative technologies and their market availability—information not otherwise accessible—while leaving it to entrepreneurs and managers to screen and adapt the technology for their purposes. Especially in fields like microelectronics, which have wide ramifications throughout the economy, it is more important to adopt and master uses appropriate to local conditions than to achieve local manufacture, since current technology will become obsolete in a short time.

Risk Taking and Venture Capital

The selection, development, and use of technology and the building up of local technological capacity inevitably entail risks. In principle, technological risks should be accepted by developing countries on the same terms as the financial, social, commercial, and other risks presented by projects. That is to say, they should be accepted when there is no more advantageous alternative and when the benefits of doing so are expected to exceed their costs, even with allowance for the probability and consequences of partial or total failure.

Certain technological risks are avoidable and unnecessary. Unless there are strong reasons for doing so, developing countries should not be the proving ground for advanced technologies being developed elsewhere and with the needs of other countries in mind. It is preferable that such testing be carried out in a developed country, where the necessary support services, infrastructure, and technical skills are readily at hand. In particular, a developing country should guard against being sold equipment that is described as proven, but which is in fact in need of testing, lest it unwittingly pay for research, development, and demonstration costs that are the rightful responsibility of the promoter.

Other technological risks may be both unavoidable and necessary. Technologies available from developed countries may be unsuited to local conditions, so that a developing country has no choice but to accept some degree of risk if it is to find a sustainable or replicable solution to a development problem. Such a situation may arise because of a unique local resource (such as an ore of unusual composition), a specific environmental problem, or an uncommon disease. Often, the need is for a low-cost technology to meet particular local economic or social conditions. The best approach to such problems is through local research and development, preferably followed by pilot projects and demonstrations to test the new technology before full-scale commercial application.

Governments should also ensure that adequate sources of risk capital are available for commercial investments in research and development, either through specialized institutions or through appropriately staffed and managed subdivisions of existing institutions. As a rule of thumb, research should generally be supported by grant money, while development should be funded by a sharing of the costs, risks, and profits between the firm and the promoting agency.

Special mechanisms are often advisable for encouraging and financing research, development, and innovation in enterprises. As an example, the Financiadora de Estudos e Projetos in Brazil was responsible for planning and funding much of the huge expansion in the 1970s of Brazilian scientific and technological research infrastructure in universities, public institutes for applied research, and private industry. Another example is the Korea Technology Development Corporation, an autonomous financial institution partly financed by the World Bank, which works with local industry to identify and promote (or respond to) proposals for new lines of business based on local technology. This corporation finances research, development, and engineering in private industry through loans that are forgiven in part if the project fails. It also provides equity funds to companies that are set up to exploit new research and development results.

Commercializing innovative technology often requires still a different mechanism, namely a venture capital company that invests in innovative ventures and, when necessary, assists or participates in their management. Such venture capital organizations are needed to overcome the aversion of banks and entrepreneurs to the risks needed to launch new, technologically oriented lines of business.

Preparing the ground for rice planting in the Casamance region, Senegal

20

Economic Analysis

ALL COUNTRIES FACE the basic economic choice of how to allocate limited resources among many different uses, a choice that has figured prominently in the discussion in many of the earlier chapters. We have been concerned, among other things, about decisions affecting the size and composition of investments in individual sectors. Repeated references have been made to economic rates of return, derived from cost-benefit analysis, as a critical element in investment decisionmaking. We now turn to a fuller description of that analysis.

Cost-benefit analysis is a quantitative technique to help guide investment decisions in a systematic fashion. Based on a comparison of the costs and benefits of a particular project or program, it tries to answer the practical questions of whether, on balance, an investment is worthwhile; whether its worth could be increased by altering design parameters such as the location, timing, scale, composition, technology, or method of implementation; and whether the policy environment bearing on the project or program is, or could be made, conducive to its successful implementation and operation. Thus, cost-benefit analysis seeks to determine not only if a project can be expected to provide a satisfactory return to the economy, but also if there is an alternative way of achieving the project's objectives that would offer a higher return.

Over the past two decades, cost-benefit techniques have been applied increasingly to investment planning decisions by multilateral and bilateral aid agencies as well as by planning organizations in developing countries. Most projects financed by the World Bank, regional development banks, and bilateral aid agencies are now subjected to cost-benefit analysis in one form or another. Similarly, many developing countries, including Bangladesh, Chile, India, Korea, Pakistan, Philippines, and Turkey, have well-established units responsible for preparing a cost-benefit analysis of projects to be financed publicly.

The purpose of this chapter is to explain briefly the main features of cost-benefit analysis so that senior administrators and planners in developing countries can use the results of such analysis while understanding its limitations. As in other parts of the book, the treatment is intended to be neither exhaustive nor overly rigorous. The goal is to give readers an appreciation of the principal concepts associated with cost-benefit analysis, not to turn them into proficient practitioners. After the basic concepts are introduced, some additional concepts and issues that arise in practice are addressed, followed by a brief discussion of the main elements of social cost-benefit analysis. The chapter concludes with an overview of cost-benefit analysis as an aid to decisionmaking.

BASIC CONCEPTS OF COST-BENEFIT ANALYSIS

Central to the measurement of the costs and benefits of a project are two questions: Who are the decisionmakers? What are their objectives? The costs and benefits associated with a particular decision will often differ materially depending on whether they are viewed from the standpoint of the individuals directly concerned or of society as a whole. A project to expand an engineering school may clearly be very profitable to the students who decide to enroll in it if they do not have to pay for their education and can expect to get jobs at relatively high salaries after graduation. But from the standpoint of the national economy, the costs incurred by society in providing the engineering training must be taken into account. There may also, of course, be some benefits that accrue to the economy but not to the students who receive the training—for example, the savings that might result from training nationals to replace foreign technicians. This example illustrates the essential difference between financial and economic analysis: the former deals with costs and benefits measured from the viewpoint of an individual (or an agency or enterprise), the latter with costs and benefits from the viewpoint of the country as a whole. In practice, the time streams of financial revenues and costs are often a good starting point for identifying the economic costs and benefits of a project. The adjustments to be made to the financial streams so that they reflect economic concepts are discussed in more detail later in this chapter (see, in particular, the discussion of transfer payments, shadow prices, and externalities).

Setting Objectives

The objectives of a project determine how the project's costs and benefits are defined: anything that affects the objectives adversely is a cost while anything that promotes them is a benefit. This is not as simple as it may sound; in reality, a decisionmaker usually has in mind a multiplicity of objectives, some of which may conflict. A business firm, for example, may want to maximize net profits, minimize risks, be generous to its employees, and establish a favorable public image. Similarly, a country may want to increase its national income, reduce income inequalities, reduce unemployment, increase self-reliance, and strengthen national security. In principle, the cost-benefit analysis can accommodate (with increasing complexity) as many objectives as desired. In practice, however, difficulties in making tradeoffs among the various objectives make it almost obligatory to focus on at most two or three main objectives. Traditionally, cost-benefit analysis takes profit maximization as the sole objective for individuals and private business firms. Similarly, maximization of national income (or more precisely consumption) is generally taken to be the objective for the country as a whole. Economists usually refer to this as the "efficiency" objective. A more recent innovation is so-called social cost-benefit analysis, a subject to which we return later in the chapter. Its purpose is to include among the national objectives considerations of income distribution and of the national savings rate.

To make matters more complicated, a decisionmaker may not only have multiple objectives, but some of the objectives, and the tradeoffs among them, may intentionally be couched in ambiguity. This should not be surprising given the political context in which most resource allocations are made and the fact that attempts at clarity and mathematical precision may often endanger fragile political coalitions. By comparing different alternatives (and possibly by generating superior alternatives not considered earlier), cost-benefit analysis can, up to a point, help decisionmakers to crystallize their values and objectives. Ultimately, however, the relevance and usefulness of this analysis depend on how faithfully the decisionmakers' objectives, and the tradeoffs among them, are reflected in it. If one looks closely enough, at the heart of many controversies in public policy are disagreements on the appropriate objectives.

As we have emphasized in the preceding chapter and in part III, consideration of alternatives is an essential feature of project preparation and design. Experience in the World Bank indicates that all too often insufficient attention is paid to the identification and weighing of alternatives. Technical options (to use steam, diesel, or diesel-electric locomotives; to expand a railway line or build a parallel road) should be compared with each other and the best alternative selected. If different technologies can produce the same output (or benefit) both in quantity and quality—as is sometimes true in power projects—then the analysis should identify the least-cost alternative by comparing the investment and operating costs of each. If both benefits and costs vary among alternatives—as is more often the case—then each alternative, with its cost and benefit streams, must be assessed separately, so that the alternative with the highest net benefit can be selected.

With and Without the Project

All projects make use of some scarce input to produce an output of goods or services valued by society. In general, without the project the availability of these inputs and outputs to the rest of the economy would be different. Comparing the situation with and without the project (what we shall call the With case and the Without case) constitutes the basic method of measuring the additional benefits that can be attributed to the project. In most cases, the situation without the project is not simply a continuation of the status quo since some changes in input and output levels and prices are likely to take place anyway. In agricultural projects, for instance, cropping patterns, yields, output levels, and commodity prices may be expected to change substantially from their base levels even without the project, as a result of market conditions or other factors. Again, some projects, such as those to modernize a plant or expand a highway, may have as their primary objective to prevent future increases in costs or decreases in benefits in the form of deterioration of existing capacity, increasing congestion, or declining quality of service. The Without case must therefore include expected cost increases or benefit decreases in order to reflect fully the changes brought about by the project.

Conceivably, there are situations that may be even worse after a project is completed than before; the project may, nevertheless, be justified if without it the deterioration would have been much greater. Thus, an accurate comparison of the situations expected to prevail without and with the project may call for difficult judgments. It does not normally correspond to a comparison of the situations before and after the project, as is sometimes incorrectly assumed. Nor does it correspond to a comparison with the next-best alternative, another mistake that is sometimes made.

The appropriate definition of the Without case depends on the nature of the project. For projects intended to increase capacity—industrial plants, power generation, seaports, railways, and so forth—not undertaking the project means doing without such increments to capacity, with the consequences that this entails. Similarly, when the project's purpose is to reduce unit costs (such as plant modernization) or to improve the quality of services (such as agricultural extension or health care), not undertaking the project means forgoing these. Problems may arise, however, concerning the appropriate assumptions to be made about the operating practices and policies of the government or of the project entity in the Without case. For example:

- In a project to expand the capacity of an existing plant, it may be unclear whether to assume that operating on a single shift will continue or to assume that multiple shifts, if technically feasible, will be introduced irrespective of the project.
- In a railway modernization project, the justification may depend critically on a judgment whether the government would, in the absence of the project, be willing and able to close existing uneconomic lines.

As a general rule, the assessment of the Without case should rest on the best judgment as to the future scenario if the proposed project were not undertaken. To the extent that this scenario may include a course of action by the government (or the project entity) that is uneconomic or inefficient, this approach may seem to overstate the project's profitability. However, if the Without case does indeed reflect the analyst's best judgment as to the likely future, this is the correct approach; project analysis is intrinsically a second-best analysis that takes due account of the limitations imposed upon the decisionmaker by, for example, sociopolitical factors. Nevertheless, a word of caution is in order since there is clearly potential for abuse. Almost any project can be made to look attractive if the Without scenario is painted bleak enough. It is important that the analyst examine thoroughly the various options without the project and inform the decisionmaker of the implications of alternative assumptions (see the section below on "Sensitivity and Risk Analysis"). Even if reasonable people may disagree on what the most plausible Without case would be, however, this does not affect the (more important) choice of the most advantageous With case option.

Proper specification of the With and Without situations, including a thorough understanding of the relationships between project inputs and outputs and their phasing over time, is a prerequisite to any cost-benefit analysis—financial or economic. Technical specialists such as engineers, agronomists, architects, and social scientists play a critical role. Not only is inadequate attention often paid to defining the Without situation, but also the tendency is to underestimate the potential difficulties in project implementation and operation that often lead to implementation delays, cost overruns, lower operating efficiency, and smaller benefits than those assumed. However, undue pessimism is not called for either. To the extent possible, the With and Without situations should reflect unbiased expectations, and the decisionmaker should clearly understand the basic assumptions and judgments incorporated in the analysis of the two scenarios.

Demand Forecasts

Analyzing the demand for the output of a project is a logical point of departure for cost-benefit analysis since it helps to determine the revenues or benefits to be obtained from the project—and indeed whether the project should be undertaken at all and on what scale. This applies both to projects where the output is to be sold, as is the case in most industrial, power, and agricultural production projects, and to those where it is not, as in education or agricultural extension projects.

Even though demand analysis is basic to the assessment of a project's potential, it is often done inadequately. Project planners ought not to assume that a market for the output of a project exists; this must be investigated, along with the composition of demand and its price elasticity, where relevant. Some observations on the particular characteristics and problems of demand forecasting in individual sectors have been offered in part II.

Even when properly done, however, demand forecasts often turn out to be wide of the mark. Long-range forecasting is particularly hazardous. Predicting changes in technology, income, behavior, and other factors that alter previous patterns and affect the basic assumptions of a forecast is inherently uncertain and therefore difficult. Moreover, data required for forecasting are often not available or are of questionable quality. Data problems obviously limit the forecaster's choice of technique and the validity of the results. Ad hoc data collection for a specific project is expensive and has to be carefully considered to ensure that it is done in a cost-effective manner.

Nevertheless, decisions have to be made today that have long-term consequences. In transport, for example, or in major industrial or power projects, investments may be large, lumpy, and irreversible. Errors in size, timing, or location of projects can be very costly in terms of other investment opportunities that must be forgone. Demand forecasts are an essential part of this decisionmaking process. While the analyst must recognize the limitations of his work, it is better to attempt a rational forecast—or at least to make the best possible educated guess—than not to make a forecast at all.

The person preparing a demand forecast must take into account the cost of using various techniques. Two kinds of costs are involved: the cost of preparing the forecast (including collecting and maintaining data) and the cost that may result from an incorrect forecast. The decision about the tradeoff between these will vary from one project to another and particularly with the size of the project investment. As in other aspects of project analysis, a more sophisticated technique might offer greater accuracy but require a much larger commitment of resources. There is some level beyond which the added benefit of increased accuracy does not justify the added cost.

The forecaster should produce his best estimate of likely demand. At a later stage of the cost-benefit analysis, a sensitivity test should be applied, as it is to other elements of the cost and benefit streams (see below). This exercise not only indicates which of the assumptions are most critical, but also assists project planners to build in safeguards against some eventualities. Demand forecasts should also be updated regularly, both during preparation of the project and during the period of construction and initial operation. This allows new information to be incorporated and lowers the likelihood of a widening gap between forecasts and reality.

Time Preference and Discounting

For most projects, the benefits (and often the costs) are spread over a fairly long period. Many industrial plants have useful lives of twenty to thirty years, while the benefits from dams used for irrigation or power may continue for fifty years or more. The time streams of costs and benefits may differ greatly from one project to another. A hydropower plant, for example, entails a large initial investment per unit of generating capacity but relatively small operating and maintenance costs. A thermal power plant, in contrast, is cheaper to install but requires larger recurrent expenditures for fuel and maintenance.

How can the costs and benefits of different alternatives be compared? Clearly, a simple summation of the costs and the benefits would be inappropriate since it would ignore the almost universal preference of an individual, or of society as a whole, to gain benefits earlier rather than later (or, alternatively, to incur costs later rather than earlier). A million dollars spent today represents a greater cost or sacrifice than a million dollars spent a year from now because the money could be invested elsewhere, in the meantime, to earn a return in the form of interest or profit. The concept of *time preference* relates to the fact that values received earlier are worth more than those received later. *Time discounting* is the technique by which the values to be realized at different points in time are adjusted to a common period (usually the present) to make them comparable.

The effect of time discounting depends on how the costs and benefits are distributed over time and also on the level of the discount rate. The level of the discount rate can be regarded as a measure of the intensity of the decisionmaker's preference for late rather than early costs and early rather than late benefits; a higher discount rate means a stronger preference. The discount rate can help decisionmakers to apply their time preferences in choosing among projects in which the streams of costs and benefits are such that the preferred choices are not obvious.

How does one choose the appropriate discount rate (also referred to as the *opportunity cost of capital*; see the discussion below)? Several different approaches are possible. The most obvious is, of course, to refer to the returns available in domestic and international capital markets. An alternative approach is to use national income data over a period of years to estimate average returns on investment. In many countries, estimates of *incremental capital-output ratios* are available and used as a tool for macroeconomic planning. Yet another approach is to consider rates of return on a representative sample of projects undertaken in the recent past or those estimated for projects proposed for implementation over the next few years.

Unfortunately, none of the above approaches provides a very satisfactory solution. Market interest rates, as we have seen in earlier chapters, may not be a good indicator of the cost of capital because of distortions such as regulated interest rates, fragmentation of capital markets, and credit rationing. Estimates derived from national economic data are unreliable owing to difficulties in apportioning increases in national income to different contributing factors, particularly technical progress. Use of project-level data is problematic owing to variations in returns on different projects as well as variations in noneconomic objectives associated with those projects.

The proper discount rate, or the opportunity cost of capital, is therefore a notional concept. We may have a pretty good idea of the range of yields on alternative investments (and therefore of discount rates) in a particular country; we can be reasonably sure that certain discount rates—say, 5 percent—would be too low in most developing countries and that others—say, 20 percent—would be too high. Efforts to pin down the discount rate more precisely usually require a great deal of data and much guesswork. For operational purposes in the World Bank, the opportunity cost of capital is commonly taken to be on the order of 10 percent a year. (This is in real terms, that is, net of inflation; with inflation at, say, 6 percent a year, the nominal rate would be 16 percent.) Clearly, however, the figure can vary among countries or within a country at different stages of its development.

Opportunity Costs and Shadow Prices

Most economic resources have several potential uses. A parcel of land in an urban area may be used for houses, an office building, a factory, or a park. Similarly, a country may use its foreign exchange resources to import consumer goods, industrial raw materials, or capital equipment. Committing a resource to a specific use necessarily implies forgoing other options. The *opportunity cost* of a resource used in a particular way is defined as the value it could command if it were used for the best available alternative. Opportunity cost is a simple yet powerful concept that plays a central role in cost-benefit analysis. It is applicable in all economic systems—whether market-oriented, centrally planned, or a mixture of the two—and to all objectives such as profit maximization or promotion of national welfare.

Measuring Opportunity Costs

With profit maximization as the objective, measuring the costs and benefits of a project to an individual or enterprise is in most cases fairly straightforward. Usually the costs are the financial expenditure to acquire the goods and services that are needed to establish and operate the project. The benefits are the funds received for the goods and services produced by the project. In most cases, the expected market prices for those goods and services may be taken as the appropriate opportunity cost for estimating the costs and benefits to the enterprise.

In measuring the "profitability" of a project from the standpoint of society, however, the market prices for inputs and outputs may not be an acceptable measure of the true costs and benefits. This may happen because the market prices of the different inputs and outputs are distorted by various taxes, subsidies, quotas, regulatory measures, or monopolistic practices (see chapter 3, Pricing Policy). To deal with this problem, *shadow prices*—also referred to as *accounting prices*—are frequently employed.

These prices measure the value of a commodity or a service from the viewpoint of the economy. The use of a good or a service as a project input will mean either diverting that input from other uses, or increasing its production or import, or both. Depending on the specific situation, the shadow price of the input will be either its value in the alternative use (that is, the opportunity cost), or the cost of augmenting the supply (that is, the marginal cost of production or import), or a weighted average of the two. Similarly, the output resulting from a project may lead to higher consumption or export, to closing down less efficient production facilities, or to a combination of the two. The shadow price of the output will be measured by the benefits received from the increased supply, by the avoided cost of production, or by a combination of the two.

Although straightforward conceptually, there are practical difficulties in applying these principles for estimating shadow prices, including the need to understand thoroughly the production possibilities and also how to value the various goods and services in different applications. To keep the problem manageable, a variety of shortcuts and simplifications are used.

Traded and Nontraded Goods and Primary Production Factors

A basic step is to divide the various project inputs and outputs into three broad categories: traded goods, nontraded goods, and primary production factors such as labor and land. The difference between a traded and a nontraded good depends on whether its production or use will affect the country's export or import of the good concerned. Examples of traded goods in a project are capital equipment bought from abroad and output that is directly exported. Also categorized as traded is an input such as locally supplied petroleum that would otherwise have been exported, or an output such as wheat whose increased domestic production reduces the amount imported. Construction, electricity, and internal transport are examples of goods that by their nature are nontraded.

In deciding whether a good should be categorized as traded, it is helpful to know whether the country is currently exporting or importing it. Occasionally, imports are limited by rigid long-term quotas—for example, because of a government's desire to maintain national self-sufficiency or to protect domestic infant industries—in which case the good concerned should be treated for purposes of project analysis as nontraded. It is also necessary to look beyond the present, since trade policies may change. Judgment is thus needed; but even with adequate information and good judgment, the answer is not always obvious. When in doubt, it is generally advisable to assume that the good concerned is traded, in part because the procedures for calculating shadow prices for nontraded goods are usually more complicated.

Traded goods. As a general rule, the shadow price of a traded commodity is its world price, net of any import duties or export taxes but adjusted for international transport costs.[1] This is the so-called *border price.* To allow for the physical location of the project, the shadow price of an

---

1. Refinements to this rule are necessary if the project's output is expected to account for a significant fraction of the total world trade in the commodity, in which case the output may itself influence the world price.

export would be the f.o.b. (free on board) price at the nearest port (or, where relevant, airport) less the cost of transporting the commodity from the project site to the port. For an import, the shadow price would be the c.i.f. (cost including insurance and freight) price at the nearest port plus the cost of transporting the commodity from the port to the project site. Thus, the shadow price of a traded commodity depends on whether it is an export or an import, and it may vary from place to place in the country. The border prices for imports and exports, adjusted for the costs of transportation between the border and the project site, are commonly referred to as *import parity prices* and *export parity prices*, respectively. These prices may vary, of course, over time according to changes in the global conditions of demand and supply.

The procedure for estimating shadow prices described above is normally applied only to the main traded inputs of the project, typically comprising imported capital equipment and the principal raw materials, and to the main outputs. Once the main traded items have been valued in border prices by using the above approach, the usual practice is to group the remaining items and to multiply their value or cost at domestic prices by a *standard conversion factor*. This is an estimated average ratio of adjusted world prices (expressed in local currency at the official exchange rate) to domestic prices. Thus, for example, if the official dollar exchange rate is 10 rupees to the dollar and if the goods and services that can be obtained with one dollar of foreign exchange in the world market cost an average of 12.5 rupees in the domestic market, the standard conversion factor would be 10/12.5 or 0.8.

The concept of the standard conversion factor is closely related to the more commonly employed term *shadow exchange rate*; it is, roughly, the official exchange rate divided by the estimated shadow exchange rate. Using a *special conversion factor* for a major commodity or group of commodities has significant analytical advantages over using the standard conversion factor or shadow exchange rate, primarily because it permits greater precision: commodities whose prices may be subject to varying degrees of distortion in the domestic market are treated separately. (The ratio of the import parity or export parity price of a commodity to its price in the domestic market is the special conversion factor for that commodity.)

The main elements bearing on the estimation of conversion factors are the extent of trade distortions resulting from import tariffs, export taxes, and subsidies and the importance of quantitative trade restrictions; the higher the tariffs, taxes, subsidies, and quantitative restrictions, the lower the conversion factors. In countries where quantitative trade restrictions are unimportant, conversion factors can be estimated by using trade and tariff data. In other countries, a sensible procedure is to have recourse to a comparison of domestic and international prices for typical "baskets" of commodities. While the data requirements for estimating shadow prices and conversion factors for traded goods are by no means trivial, in most cases they are quite manageable.

Nontraded goods and primary production factors. Estimating shadow prices for nontraded goods and services and primary production factors is considerably more complicated. Take, for example, labor. In countries with heavy unemployment and underemployment, workers on, say, a road construction project may be paid wages (perhaps based on a legal minimum wage) that exaggerate the cost of their labor to the economy. Since the alternative for the workers would be unemployment or partial employment, the loss to the economy of their alternative production would be less than the wages actually paid. In calculating the economic costs of the road construction project, therefore, the wage rates applied should be less than what would actually be paid to the workers. This *shadow wage rate* is the rate that measures the opportunity cost of labor to the economy. How much lower the shadow wage rate is than the actual wage rate depends on estimates of what the workers would contribute to the economy's total production if they were not employed in the project.

In practice, determining shadow wage rates requires considerable judgment. The most extreme assumption would be a shadow wage rate of zero, which would mean that the workers would otherwise be totally unemployed and contribute nothing to the economy. But factors such as seasonal fluctuations in demand for labor and varying degrees of labor mobility should caution against hastily concluding that the opportunity cost of labor and the shadow wage rate are zero. Furthermore, the creation of one additional job in the urban sector may encourage several workers in the rural sector to migrate; the output forgone then becomes a multiple of one worker's marginal product. It will often be appropriate, therefore, to use a set of shadow wage rates for different skills, times, and locations, rather than a single rate for the whole country.

Other considerations suggest that a shadow wage rate based solely on the marginal productivity (or opportunity cost) of labor in alternative uses may be too simplistic. People may not be willing to work for low pay, depending on their income situation while unemployed, the value to them of leisure and other nonwage activities (such as fishing or fixing the roof), and the nature of the work. There is some *reservation wage* below which they will prefer being unemployed to taking a job. To ignore this reservation wage would imply the dubious value judgment that this preference for unemployment is irrelevant from society's point of view. The appropriate shadow wage rate in most developing countries is, therefore, somewhere between the actual wage rate and zero. In World Bank project analysis, the shadow wage rate for unskilled labor is typically taken to be between 50 and 100 percent of the market rate.

The shadow price of a nontraded input is usually derived from data on its cost of production. The actual cost of production is decomposed, step by step, into traded and nontraded elements. Thus, highway transportation costs can be decomposed into vehicle costs, fuel costs, repair costs, drivers' wages, and so forth. At each step, the traded items can be directly evaluated in border prices and the nontraded items further disaggregated into traded and nontraded components. The number of desirable decomposition steps depends on the importance of the nontraded residual after each step. It is rarely necessary to carry out more than two or three steps. As in the case of traded goods, a standard conversion factor is commonly used to derive shadow prices for expenditures on miscellaneous nontraded goods.

For a nontraded output the shadow price is usually obtained by assuming that increased spending on project output would divert expenditures from other related products. The appropriate conversion factor is derived from the conversion factors for those related products, weighted by the share of each product in the total expenditure diverted. Thus, increased sales revenue from project output releases real resources elsewhere. The ratio of the real resources released to the increase in domestic sales revenue is the appropriate conversion factor.

Because of the large element of judgment involved in estimating shadow prices, caution is necessary in presenting and interpreting the analysis. In particular, the tendency to ascribe spurious accuracy to the results should be strongly resisted. As a practical matter, it is necessary to focus on shadow prices for only the most important project inputs and outputs (typically, no more than three or four); shortcut approximations can be used for the others. More important, if shadow prices diverge significantly from market prices, attention should be paid to the causes of the underlying distortions and to the question whether it might be possible to attempt broader policy reforms at the sector or macroeconomic level to remove some of the distortions. In the absence of such reforms, individual decisionmaking—necessarily based on market rather than shadow prices—will remain at odds with national objectives and priorities. Even for public enterprises, for which investment decisions and operating policies can more easily be based on shadow prices, imposing such prices would reduce managerial autonomy and accountability. This underlines, of course, one of our recurrent themes: the importance of an appropriate macroeconomic and sector policy framework for efficient resource use at the project level.

Transfer Payments

An important difference between financial and economic analysis lies in the treatment of so-called *transfer payments*. These are payments that involve individuals or entities other than the buyers and sellers of the project's inputs and outputs. Transfer payments represent a shift of claims on real resources from one member or sector of society to another without any change in the national income. Four kinds of transfer payments are commonly encountered in cost-benefit analysis: taxes, subsidies, credit transactions, and depreciation.[2]

In financial analysis, a tax payment is clearly a cost. When a business enterprise pays, say, corporate taxes, its net profit is reduced. But the payment of taxes by the enterprise does not reduce the national income; it transfers income from the enterprise to the government and is therefore not a cost from the standpoint of the economy as a whole. Thus, in economic analysis the payment of taxes is not shown as a cost in project accounts. This applies to taxes in all their various forms, including direct taxes on income or indirect taxes such as sales or excise taxes. (Implicit in this treatment is the assumption that the transfer of resources from one member of society to another does not lead to any change in the efficiency with which the resources are used. This assumption can, however, be relaxed without complicating the analysis excessively.)

Subsidies are transfer payments that flow in the opposite direction from

2. Import tariffs and export taxes are usually adjusted by using shadow prices. In substance, they are also transfer payments. Care must be exercised to avoid double counting of such adjustments.

taxes. If a farmer is able to purchase fertilizer at a subsidized price, his costs will be reduced and his net benefit thereby increased, but the cost of the fertilizer in terms of the economy's use of real resources remains the same. The resources needed to produce the fertilizer (or import it from abroad) reduce the national income. Hence, the economic analysis of a project must take into account the unsubsidized cost of the fertilizer.

Credit transactions are relevant from the standpoint of the borrower: receipt of a loan increases the production resources he has available; payment of interest and repayment of principal reduce them. But from the standpoint of the economy, things look different. The loan does not reduce the national income; it transfers control over the resources represented by the loan from the lender to the borrower. Economic analysis does not, in general, need to concern itself with the financing of investment, that is, with the source of funds and how they are repaid. Similarly, the economic cost of using an asset is fully reflected in the initial investment cost less its discounted terminal value; provisions for depreciation are merely transfers from one bookkeeping account to another and not economic costs.

Measures of Project Profitability

Once the costs and benefits of a project have been identified and measured, the next step is to compare them in order to determine the profitability of the investment, that is, the excess of benefits over costs. Several techniques have been developed for expressing profitability by a single number or index. The index can be used to judge whether a project is profitable enough to be acceptable and also to compare one project with another. Three of the most commonly used indices are the net present value, the internal rate of return, and the benefit-cost ratio.

Net Present Value

The *net present value* of a project is the value of the benefits net of the costs, both discounted at the opportunity cost of capital. The benefits and costs are defined in incremental terms compared with the situation without the project. Two conditions must be satisfied if a project is to be acceptable on economic grounds. First, the present value of the net benefits of the project must be zero or positive; second, the net present value of the project must be higher than, or at least as high as, the net present value of mutually exclusive project alternatives. There are usually many projects or project alternatives which by their nature are mutually exclusive: if one is chosen, the others cannot be undertaken. This also applies to different options with respect to design, size, or time phasing of what is essentially the same project. It also applies, perhaps less obviously, to such cases as industrial plants in alternative locations serving the same limited market, surface irrigation development ruling out tubewell irrigation, and river development upstream instead of downstream. It should not be assumed too readily that such mutually exclusive alternatives do not exist. The need to compare such options is one of the principal reasons for introducing economic analysis in the early stages of the project cycle.

Although in principle all meaningful project options—including that of doing nothing—should be considered, in practice only a few can usually be examined. Nonetheless, it should be borne in mind that a high net present value may simply indicate that some of the inputs and outputs have not been properly valued in terms of their opportunity costs in the analysis of the With and Without cases. High profitability may also reflect the fact that the investment should have been made earlier, as when a delay in undertaking a highway project results in excessive traffic congestion.

The optimum time to launch a project is an important issue in its own right. As a rough guide to whether the project timing is appropriate, the so-called first-year benefit test is occasionally employed: if the ratio of first-year benefits to total project costs exceeds the discount rate, then the project should be started; otherwise it should be delayed. The test ensures a correct solution only under rather restrictive conditions, however, and should be used with caution.

Some projects are mutually exclusive in the sense that they are alternative ways of producing the same output (for example, asphalt or cement paving of a road, purchase of diesel or electric locomotives). Since benefits are the same, it is necessary in the first instance only to consider costs and to select the alternative with the lower present value of discounted investment and operating costs. This is the *least-cost* approach referred to earlier. But by itself this tells nothing about the economic merits of the project in relation to the Without case: even the least-cost project may have costs that exceed its benefits. Therefore, the analysis should not stop at a least-cost solution; wherever possible, it should also consider whether benefits are adequate. Care should be taken to ensure that benefits actually are the same under each alternative. If they are not, then the differences should be taken into account in a qualitative fashion or a separate cost-benefit analysis made of each alternative.

Internal Rate of Return

It has long been standard practice in the World Bank to express project profitability in terms of the *internal rate of return*, sometimes also referred to as the internal economic return or the economic rate of return. This is the rate of discount that results in a zero net present value for the project. (It is calculated by a process of trial and error that can be tedious if done manually. The advent of inexpensive hand calculators has, however, greatly simplified the task.) If the discount rate equals or exceeds the opportunity cost of capital, it can be concluded that the project is justified. The rate of return method should be avoided in comparing mutually exclusive project alternatives. In such comparisons, the project with the highest rate of return is not necessarily the one with the highest net present value, and is therefore not necessarily the best project. The rate of return may also be a poor basis of comparison for projects with significantly different economic lives, since the comparison implicitly assumes that the net surplus from the project with a shorter economic life can be reinvested at a similar rate of return.

With these exceptions, the internal rate of return is useful in comparing the profitability of a project with that of others in the same sector (cross-sectoral comparisons are more difficult, as indicated below). As in the case of the net present value, an unusually high rate of return may simply reflect the fact that the investment should have been made earlier or that some of the inputs and outputs have not been properly valued.

Although the rate of return technique is not fully satisfactory, it is widely understood and directly comparable with the opportunity cost of capital. Unlike the net present value, it does not require, in most cases, the precise specification of the opportunity cost of capital—a task which, as we noted earlier, poses practical problems. It is, therefore, a convenient way for presenting and using the results of the analysis.

Benefit-Cost Ratio

A variant of the net present value measure is the *benefit-cost ratio*, both benefits and costs being defined in terms of their present values. If the net present value is positive (or zero), the benefit-cost ratio will exceed (or equal) unity. This ratio—"so many dollars worth of benefits per dollar of costs incurred"—has some appeal as a way to present the results of the analysis. However, such ratios are sensitive to the way costs and benefits are classified, and there is no fixed rule in this respect. Simply by grouping cost and benefit items differently—for example, by showing operating costs separately or deducting them from gross benefits—the benefit-cost ratio for the same project can be changed substantially. Also, as in the case of the internal rate of return, the benefit-cost ratio cannot be used to choose the best among mutually exclusive project options or among projects with significantly different economic lives. In the World Bank, benefit-cost ratios are used only for projects that have relatively small investment costs and high recurrent costs and benefits (for example, road maintenance projects); in such cases, the economic rate of return can be very high—in excess of 100 percent, for example—and the benefit-cost ratio is therefore more meaningful.

Project Priorities and Investment Planning

Except when mutually exclusive projects are concerned, there is no need, in principle, to rank projects in order of priority. If the opportunity cost of capital has been properly established, projects are either acceptable or not. However, accepting all projects justified by their net present value or internal rate of return may lead to a larger investment program than the country can in fact undertake, in which case some further screening is necessary. In countries where investment decisions are decentralized to lower-level authorities or agencies that are given fixed shares of the national investment budget, the individual agencies may find themselves with more or less resources than required for all projects satisfying the selection criteria, even though the national investment budget appears to be in balance with requirements for the country as a whole.

The solution to imbalances, whether arising at the national or the agency level, is to adjust the discount rate or the size of the investment budget, or both, to bring investments into balance with available resources. Unfortunately, none of the selection criteria provides a foolproof ranking of alternative investments that does not vary with the discount rate chosen. Because of the difference in time patterns of costs and benefits for different projects, a higher discount rate may affect various projects differently; the relative attractiveness of some projects may even be reversed. Thus, shortages of budgetary funds may require reexamination of the entire project portfolio.

In practice, however, a number of factors usually make the task of trimming investment budgets less difficult than it appears at first glance. In most countries, a large part of the investment program is made up of ongoing projects. Since it is the incremental returns (ignoring all sunk costs) that are relevant to the decision whether or not to invest, as a starting point it is sound practice to protect allocations to all ongoing projects that are indivisible and whose implementation is well advanced. The availability of external financing tied to specific investments may further restrict the choices, with the decision then depending on the incremental costs to be financed locally relative to the incremental benefits.

Similar considerations apply to maintenance, rehabilitation, and output balancing projects (which change the balance of products so as to improve the use of existing capacity)—all of which may entail relatively small investments that yield high economic returns. Conversely, it is usually desirable to postpone the start of large, indivisible projects with modest returns or projects in which there are doubts about the absorptive capacity of the implementing agency. Ongoing projects that are divisible are also good candidates for phasing over longer periods. By using such commonsense approaches, it is often possible to decide on a large part of the investment program without recourse to elaborate analytical techniques. All this, however, may still leave some proposals in question; more detailed evaluations may be helpful in deciding whether to retain these investments in the plan. This approach emphasizes the need to exercise judgment rather than rely on a mechanical, across-the-board application of standardized analytical procedures. (See also the discussion in chapter 4, Public Investment Programs and Budgets.)

Sensitivity and Risk Analysis

The economic analysis of projects is necessarily based on uncertain future events and imperfect data and therefore calls for judgments about probabilities, whether made explicit or not. The basic elements in the cost and benefit streams, such as input and output prices and quantities or economywide shadow prices, are seldom represented accurately enough by single values. It is desirable, therefore, that cost-benefit analysis take into consideration the range of possible variations in the values of the basic elements, and that the extent of the uncertainties attaching to the outcome be clearly reflected in presenting the analysis.

A simple method of doing this is to use *sensitivity analysis*, that is, to determine how sensitive the net present value (or internal rate of return) is to variations in selected costs and benefits. Alternatively, one can measure how much an element must vary for the net present value to be reduced to zero (or the internal rate of return reduced to the opportunity cost of capital); the percentage change in a variable at which this takes place is called its switching or crossover value (that is, the percentage change in the variable needed to switch the project from acceptable to unacceptable). The use of switching values is preferable to the more common practice of testing sensitivity to a fixed variation (such as 10 or 15 percent) in individual project parameters because the switching values enable the decisionmaker to focus better on the likely project risks. Switching value tests are particularly helpful in identifying the critical elements on which the outcome of the project depends. They focus attention on the variables that warrant further effort to firm up the estimates and narrow the range of uncertainty. They may also aid the management of the project by indicating critical areas that require close supervision.

In an irrigation project, for example, the sensitivity analysis may indicate switching values of -25 percent for yield per acre, $+40$ percent for construction costs, and $+150$ percent for shadow wage rates. The most critical variable is clearly the yield to be attained—a reduction of 25 percent or more, if all else remains as expected, will make the project unviable. If experience suggests that the yield might well be that much lower owing to, say, the poor quality of the irrigation system, then the project would appear quite risky and some kind of preventive action would be needed. The project is also sensitive to construction costs, but a 40 percent increase may be quite unlikely if the engineering investigations and designs are well advanced and the unit prices used are reliable. The project's justification would appear to be insensitive to shadow wage rates, however, and therefore fairly crude estimates of that variable should suffice.

Sensitivity tests are not without their difficulties. Correlation among the variables (a change in one variable associated with changes in other variables) often poses serious problems; for example, falling crop yields because of pests or adverse weather are often accompanied by higher crop prices. Similarly, slippage in the implementation schedule may itself contribute to cost overruns. The usual technique of changing one variable at a time and keeping the others constant can be quite misleading in such cases.

More helpful in these circumstances is *risk analysis*, which incorporates a probability distribution of the values of the variables used in the project analysis and which takes account of the extent to which changes in different variables are correlated with one another (through computer simulation models). The resulting probability distribution of the net present value (or rate of return) gives a better picture of the degree of risk than a single-value calculation does. On the basis of such a distribution, judgments can be made as to the existence of, for instance, an x percent chance that the project will result in a negative net present value, or a y percent chance of a surplus exceeding $\$N$ million.

There is a danger, however, in reading too much into the numbers resulting from these apparently sophisticated tools; ultimately, the quality of the results can be no better than the accuracy with which the probabilities have been estimated and the correlation among different variables has been captured by the model. Also, although risk analysis provides a better basis than sensitivity analysis for judging the riskiness of an individual project or the relative riskiness of alternative projects, it does nothing to diminish the risks themselves.

For these reasons, although sensitivity analysis is a standard part of the Bank's project analysis, the more elaborate risk analysis is undertaken only in special cases. Risk analysis should be considered primarily for the largest and most complex projects, or for marginal projects having exceptional risks that cannot be adequately assessed by means of a simple sensitivity analysis. Consideration of how to cope better with future risks and uncertainties through such measures as a more detailed study of the relevant project features, larger contingency allowances, or a more flexible design should be part of the normal process of project preparation and appraisal.

Use of the expected net present value (or, alternatively, of the economic rate of return) of a project as a measure of its worth implies that the decisionmaker is indifferent to risk as measured by, say, the variance of that value. This is justifiable for public sector projects if their risks are pooled. In other cases, however, the risk may be borne by a relatively small section of the population; or the success or failure of a large project may weigh heavily on the national income. In such cases, it may be desirable to assess the cost of offsetting the risks—for example, by maintaining sufficient foreign exchange reserves to offset fluctuations in export prices.

ADDITIONAL CONCEPTS AND ISSUES

In this section, we review briefly some of the concepts and issues encountered less frequently than those already discussed. They crop up often enough that planners and administrators need to be familiar with them if they are to appreciate fully the uses and abuses of cost-benefit analysis.

Sunk Costs

Sunk costs are costs that have been incurred on a project prior to the time of the analysis and that therefore cannot be avoided even if they are considered to have been entirely wasteful. They should be excluded from the cost of the project for the purpose of deciding whether to proceed with it; bygones are bygones, and only costs that are yet to be incurred (that is, that can still be avoided) matter in this regard. The economic merit of a project designed to complete another project that was started earlier and left unfinished does not depend on the costs already incurred but only on the costs of completion. Similarly, the benefits from the new project are only those that will arise over and above those benefits, if any, that may already be flowing from the earlier, uncompleted work. This treatment of sunk costs may result in a high return on the investment to complete the project, but this reflects the nature of the decision to be made. Sunk-cost considerations also explain why the World Bank often advises its borrowers to focus on completing ongoing projects or rehabilitating old projects before launching new ones (see chapter 4, Public Investment Programs and Budgets).

Once more, however, a word of caution is in order. What is appropriate at the level of the individual project can lead to major misallocations in the national investment program. It is not uncommon to come across situations in which the sunk-cost argument has been elevated to a fine art form: an agency, while pleading for funds for incomplete projects on the basis of sunk costs, may be simultaneously starting other submarginal projects, presumably to produce candidates for future financing under the sunk-cost doctrine! To avoid such abuses, it is important that the analysis also focus on the total project, including sunk costs, to determine whether, with hindsight, the original decision to proceed with the project was well founded and, if not, what should be done to avoid the recurrence of similar mistakes. The issue of sunk costs also highlights the need for sound sector work to guide the selection of individual projects (see chapter 5, Sector Analysis).

Consumer Surplus

Consumer surplus is the difference between what consumers are prepared to pay for a product or service and what they actually pay. Such a surplus is common in public utility projects such as power, water supply and sanitation, and telecommunications. In many developing countries, the regulated prices set by governments are often below the market clearing prices, as evidenced by large unsatisfied demand and queues for access to the service. Although in some cases estimating the associated consumer surplus is straightforward (for example, the costs saved by an industrial enterprise that, because of access to the public grid, can do away with more expensive power from its own power plant), more often it poses serious problems. The usual practice is to ignore the consumer surplus and equate the benefits with the revenues received from the consumers, which can be estimated with some confidence. However, since consumer surplus can be an important part of the economic benefit from utility projects, leaving it out can lead to serious underestimation of overall project returns. To the extent feasible, an effort should be made to get at least a rough idea of its likely magnitude. When that is not possible, this omission should not be overlooked in judging the adequacy of returns on utility projects; the revenue-based indicators are more a measure of the adequacy of tariffs than of the overall benefit or soundness of the project. The partial nature of benefits estimated for utility projects should also warn against comparing returns on a utility project with those on, say, an industrial or agricultural project.

For some projects, the incremental output may be large enough to reduce the price to consumers below what it would be without the project. In this case, use of the reduced price will undervalue the benefits of the additional output to the economy, since consumers would have been willing to pay more. There is an increase in consumer surplus whenever a project lowers the price from what it otherwise would have been; this increase is part of the economic benefit of the project. Normally, this consideration is important only for very large projects that significantly change the overall supply of a product or a service.

Externalities

Externalities are effects of a project that do not impose a cost or confer a benefit within the confines of the project itself and therefore are not included in the project's financial accounts. But if these effects bear upon the achievement of the country's objectives (either positively or negatively), they should be included in the economic analysis. An example of an external cost is downstream silting caused by a land settlement project. Various forms of pollution and congestion, use of water that affects yields of wells elsewhere, and negative side effects from irrigation schemes on health or fisheries are other common examples of external costs.

As for external benefits, one of the most important of these is the knowledge that accrues through the learning process. Specifically, the importation or use of new technology in a particular project may make it easier, cheaper, or less risky to use the same technology in subsequent projects or may indirectly improve technology in other sectors. An obvious way in which this might happen is through using staff and workers with training and experience from the first project to train other people for subsequent projects. The knowledge acquired might also improve domestic research and development capability. Other examples of external benefits include reduction in fertility rates through improved educational standards, promotion of national integration and mobility through improved transport and telecommunication facilities, or lessening of urban migration and congestion through improved living standards in rural areas.

It is usually not feasible to trace and measure all such external effects. However, an attempt should always be made to identify them and, if they appear significant, to measure them. When externalities cannot be quantified, they should be discussed in qualitative terms. In some cases, it is helpful to "internalize" externalities, that is, to combine a package of closely related activities into one project. An irrigation project likely to cause waterlogging could, for example, be undertaken jointly with an appropriate drainage program. Similarly, a land settlement project with possible adverse effects on wildlife habitat could be redesigned to include appropriate remedial measures. This procedure is also convenient in cases where externalities, strictly speaking, play no role but where it is difficult, if not impossible, to estimate demand—and hence the economic value of the output from the project—without closely linking it to related activities. A common example is the analysis of irrigation projects in which benefits are measured in terms of the value of incremental agricultural output rather than of incremental water.

Inflation and Contingencies

The relevance of the physical or price contingencies used in estimating costs for the economic analysis of a project depends on whether or not they reflect an additional use of real resources. (For a discussion on the use of contingencies, see chapter 19, Technical Analysis.) Physical contingencies represent the estimated costs of the additional real resources expected to be required and therefore are always included in the economic analysis. Price contingencies, on the other hand, can arise either from expected changes in relative prices of project inputs or from expected general inflation and changes in the value of the monetary unit in which costs are measured; only in the first case are they included in the economic analysis. Thus, only if increases in the price of an input or output are expected to differ from increases in the general price level are the differences reflected in the economic analysis.

In financial analysis, the various costs and benefits are usually expressed in current (nominal) terms; accordingly, they reflect the effects of changes in monetary value due to inflation. For economic analysis, such items must be expressed in constant or real terms by the use of an appropriate price index. Failure to distinguish between current and constant prices is a frequent source of error in cost-benefit analysis.

Double Counting and Multiplier Effects

All relevant costs and benefits should be included when evaluating a project, but they should not be recorded twice, either quantitatively or qualitatively. For example, benefits are sometimes claimed for increased employment or for foreign exchange earnings, in addition to the estimated economic return of the project. Provided that labor inputs into the project and the project's foreign exchange costs and savings have been evaluated through shadow prices that represent their value to the economy, any such employment or foreign exchange effects have already been taken into account and should not be added or presented as separate benefits.

In an economy suffering from general excess capacity, project investment may give rise to a further increase in income as the additional rounds of spending following the investment reduce the excess capacity. General excess capacity, however, is not the situation in which developing countries typically find themselves. (If it were, development would be a far easier task and could be furthered simply by spending more!) Even when general excess capacity does exist, as a first approximation it may reasonably be assumed that all investments would have the same multiplier effects, which can thus be safely ignored. Multiplier effects related to general excess capacity should therefore be treated with skepticism unless there is strong evidence to support them. Where more specific backward or forward linkages are foreseen and are likely to be significant, it is usually preferable to enlarge the project boundaries to capture such effects as part of the project analysis. Thus, for example, if project-related expansion in the production of a crop would lead to better utilization of existing processing facilities that are currently underutilized, it may be preferable to analyze crop production and processing activities together.

International Effects

Some external effects of a project may extend beyond the borders of the country. For example, project-related increases in exports or reductions in imports may reduce world prices and thereby benefit some importing countries while harming some exporting countries. Or the increase in demand, and possibly in prices, for inputs into the project may affect other countries favorably or adversely. For example, a project in a rural area may draw labor from a neighboring country, thus increasing wages across the border and giving rise to a reverse flow of workers' remittances. Or a project in one country may influence the environment of a neighboring country by diverting or polluting a river common to both countries.

All such external effects on other countries are similar in nature to the externalities discussed above and raise similar problems. The central issue is whether, when making a cost-benefit analysis, to take account of the benefits accruing to, or of costs imposed on, other countries—and to what extent.

The World Bank has traditionally focused in the first instance on the gains and losses to the recipient country, since it is clearly necessary to test project acceptability from that country's point of view. This means that costs borne by foreign countries or foreign participants, as well as benefits accruing to them, are excluded from the economic analysis. In the case of a multinational project, however—such as a railway or a road that runs through several countries—the economic analysis tests the viability of the project from the point of view of the countries as a group and of each individual country. For the project to be acceptable, appropriate arrangements will be required so that all the participating countries benefit, or at least none loses, as a result of the project. The Bank is also concerned with the international effects that may result from a project. It attempts to take account of physical externalities, as in the case of projects on international rivers where the interests of one or more riparian countries may be involved. It has also considered the international effects of projects to expand production of a commodity of which there is already a world surplus, particularly when there is an international agreement covering its production or export. It may often be advisable, for political or other reasons, for decisionmakers in individual countries to proceed in the same fashion when dealing with projects that affect other countries, and in some instances they may be obligated to do so under international agreements.

Nonquantifiable Benefits

In many cases the benefits of a project cannot be fully quantified. Difficulties arise frequently in assessing how much beneficiaries would be willing to pay for the project's output on the basis of observable market data. As already noted, a typical problem in public utility projects is the lack of data for measuring the increase in consumers' surplus due to the project. Even more complicated is the valuation of benefits related to improved traffic safety or to lower morbidity and mortality because of improvements in health standards. In other cases, an individual's willingness to pay, even if quantifiable, is an incomplete measure because of external benefits to others that are not fully perceived by the individual. For example, when a project creates amenities that are used collectively, such as pollution control facilities or community centers, the benefits cannot be measured on the basis of individual willingness to pay. National self-reliance, improved regional balance, and national integration are some of the other nonquantifiable benefits that often figure prominently in a country's decisions about resource allocation.

In cases where the benefits cannot be quantified or can be quantified only partially, other approaches are often helpful. One approach is to analyze the plausibility of achieving the minimum benefits required for the project to be acceptable (for example, an increase in average paddy yield of x kilograms per hectare to justify an improved agricultural extension service). Another is reliance on predetermined physical or cost standards for the service to be provided (for example, access to primary health care facilities within y kilometers or cost of a rural road not to exceed z dollars per kilometer).

The significance of quantification problems differs among sectors. Not being able to measure increases in consumer surplus in public utility projects implies that their economic rates of return are often seriously underestimated. Even revenue-based measures of benefits may not be feasible or relevant in some cases, especially in sectors such as education, population, nutrition, and health. Although it is possible to use quantitative criteria in such sectors more often than is customary, as we have suggested in the relevant sector chapters, both conceptual and statistical difficulties limit their application. The most important thing that can be done in most cases is to apply the least-cost approach to issues of technical design (such as appropriate standards and techniques for construction of schools and clinics).

Infant Industries

The output of a project may benefit from tariff protection or quantitative restrictions. As discussed in chapter 9, Industry, such protection may not be undesirable from the viewpoint of the economy if it allows a new activity to grow and acquire technical expertise and experience so that it may eventually become competitive. If such a policy succeeds, then the losses during the period of protection will be offset by subsequent gains to the economy. The economic analysis in such cases should be carried out in the usual manner and the calculated returns should be considered satisfactory if the gains in the period after protection has ended are sufficiently large to compensate for the higher costs of domestic production initially. This also suggests that any infant industry protection should be only for a limited duration and on a declining basis in order to permit the firm or firms gradually to adjust to full competition. In addition, some learning-by-doing benefits may accrue to the economy at large and not be reflected in the project accounts. As noted, however, such externalities are difficult to quantify and should be used in the analysis sparingly.

Multiple Components

Many development projects contain components dealing with several sectors or activities. For example, a rural development project may combine irrigation and drainage, various types of farm inputs, extension services, rural roads, and social infrastructure such as community centers, water supply, schools, and health clinics. Similarly, a single project may combine irrigation with power generation, river navigation, and potable water supply. The first task is to specify carefully the relationships among the various components. Schools, community centers, and health clinics may be closely linked to agricultural productivity in one case and very loosely, if at all, in another. If the various components are significantly interrelated, neither costs nor benefits can be allocated meaningfully to individual components in the economic analysis, and separate economic rates of return for the various components should not be calculated. The appropriate procedure is to calculate the net present value or internal rate of return of the entire package, and then to test whether it can be increased by redesigning the project to alter one or more of the components. If the various components are not significantly interrelated, however, then they should be analyzed separately. Thus, for example, a single roadway consisting of several stretches with different traffic patterns and serving different markets requires a separate analysis for each distinct segment to decide what standards are appropriate.

SOCIAL COST-BENEFIT ANALYSIS

As mentioned earlier, the appropriate framework for the economic analysis of a project depends on the objectives that the project is designed to accomplish. The traditional focus has been on the objective of maximizing income (variously referred to as the "economic" or "efficiency" objective). In this approach, different uses of the additional income—that is, for consumption or investment—are weighted equally. All consumption gains and losses are also weighted equally, regardless of the income level of the groups affected.

Implicit in the traditional approach is the judgment that the rate of investment in the economy, and hence the rate of growth, are satisfactory. There is, accordingly, no reason to increase savings at the margin or to distinguish between the effects of a project on consumption and on reinvestment. But most countries are seriously concerned with generating greater savings and public revenues. This concern is reflected, for example, in the importance given to financial replicability of projects and to the financial viability and soundness of project entities. The premise is that, to the extent possible, the project should generate adequate funds for its operation and maintenance—or contribute to government revenue for other purposes.

More recently, many countries have become concerned with the alleviation of poverty as an important objective in project selection and design. Other things being equal, projects providing benefits to the poor are preferred. However, as with a project's effects on public revenues or savings, its effects on poverty and income distribution do not enter into the traditional economic analysis of the profitability of the project to the country; they are considered separately and in a qualitative manner.

In order to facilitate more consistent and systematic consideration of these concerns, a number of development agencies, including the World Bank, have experimented over the past decade with an expanded system of analysis that explicitly incorporates the objectives of redressing poverty and of increasing the rate of savings and investment. If the rate of investment in a country is judged to be inadequate, then special weight is given to the changes in that rate induced by the project; additional savings are also valued at a premium relative to consumption. The greater the difference between the actual and desired rates of savings and investment, the higher the premium. Similarly, to address the poverty issue, different weights are assigned to consumption gains accruing to beneficiaries at different income levels. The weights may be made uniformly progressive—the lower the income level the greater the weight—or some other income-weighting scheme can be employed. (The traditional practice of assigning equal weights to all income groups is thus merely a special case—it assumes that society has no preferences as regards accrual of benefits to different income groups.) Once the cost and benefit streams are appropriately adjusted to reflect the premiums or discounts for these two purposes, the remainder of the analysis is quite similar to the traditional approach; the resulting rate of return is referred to as the *social rate of return.*

Deciding on appropriate values for the poverty weights and savings premiums is inevitably a matter of judgment. If such weights are not made explicit, however, widely different values are likely to be used implicitly in decisions made from project to project. Difficulties in choosing the most appropriate definition of poverty or in fixing the "right" weights do not negate the need for consistency. Whatever weighting scheme is chosen, it is important to determine and display the effects of alternative schemes through sensitivity tests.

Experience to date in the World Bank indicates that although desirable in principle, across-the-board application of social cost-benefit analysis is neither feasible nor necessary. In some projects (such as construction of a steel plant), it may be impossible to make a reasonable estimate of the distribution of the benefits or to identify the beneficiaries, and a social analysis of the project will not be feasible. In other projects, the general effects on distribution and savings may be reasonably clear and may only serve to reinforce the acceptability (or otherwise) of the project as conventionally measured. A broad qualitative assessment of the expanded impact of the project then suffices to determine whether it is socially profitable.

For some projects or project components, it may not be sufficient to know whether the distributional impact, including the savings effect, is positive or negative; further quantification may be desirable. This may happen when the economic and social analyses of a project point in opposite directions, especially if the economic rate of return is marginal and the social acceptability is sensitive to the size of the distributional effects. Even in such cases, a rough approximation of the social rate of return may suffice to establish the social justification of the project; sensitivity analysis may provide assurance that greater precision is not required. Social analysis should thus be applied flexibly and pragmatically, with due regard to data limitations and simplifications that may be appropriate in a particular situation. But we would emphasize that if social analysis is used, it should be used consistently for all projects in which it can be applied meaningfully; it should not be seen as just a device to get approval for projects that are otherwise unacceptable because of low returns.

COST-BENEFIT ANALYSIS AND DECISIONMAKING

We have seen that cost-benefit analysis consists of the identification, measurement, and comparison of the costs and benefits associated with an investment project. The net present values and internal rates of return are indices that measure the merit of a project entirely on the basis of quantifiable costs and benefits. If all the important costs and benefits of different projects were quantifiable, the indices of investment worth could be used to judge the acceptability of individual projects and to compare the merits of projects within and among sectors. Under these conditions, public investment decisions could be based largely if not entirely on these indices. But reality is much more complex. Many of the important benefits and some of the costs of projects cannot be measured with acceptable reliability. The difficulties of measuring benefits vary a great deal among projects in different sectors, as one would expect; they range from problems in determining what the additional outputs produced by the project are worth to the economy to problems in assessing what the outputs in fact are. Although the general approach is always the same, the exact form that the analysis takes must be tailored to the circumstances of each sector.

To be more specific, in agricultural, industrial, or petroleum projects the outputs are generally internationally traded and thus provide a good basis for the economic valuation. Fairly comprehensive quantification of costs and benefits is usually possible for projects in these sectors, with the use of shadow prices when appropriate, and the net present value or internal rate of return is a good indicator of the project's overall impact on the country. In contrast, in many public utility projects such as power, water and sanitation, and telecommunications, the valuation of benefits raises significant problems. The usual practice is to derive a measure of the benefits from the revenues received from consumers, which can be estimated with some confidence. But, as noted earlier, since the benefits to consumers may substantially exceed the regulated tariffs they have to pay, the resulting rates of return represent a minimum estimate rather than a best estimate of the actual rate of return of the project to the economy.

For most highway projects, even tariff-based revenues are not available as measures of the minimum economic benefits of the transport services provided by the project, and recourse must then be had to estimation of the so-called avoided costs, such as expected increases in vehicle operating costs and in road maintenance costs if the project does not go forward. Finally, for many social infrastructure projects such as those in education, health, and family planning, no meaningful measures of the monetary benefits exist, and the analysis focuses on providing service levels, determined by macroeconomic and other considerations, in the most cost-effective manner. Even this may not be straightforward because the quantity or quality of the outputs (or service levels) may not be the same for different input packages.

Since the measurement of costs and benefits differs from sector to sector, it is usually not meaningful to compare project profitability across different sectors, and indices such as the net present value and the internal rate of return are not a sound yardstick for intersectoral resource allocation. Moreover, even within a sector, the importance of the non-economic and nonmeasurable benefits and costs will vary from project to project, so that any comparison of projects on the basis of an economic index of investment worth has to be made with considerable care.

Cost-benefit techniques may seem daunting in their demands on both data and time. But it is neither necessary nor desirable to go through each of the steps with equal thoroughness for every project. Even if unlimited time were available, the analysis should not be refined to the point where the costs of achieving greater accuracy in the estimate of economic profitability outweigh the likely benefits. Since time and manpower are limited, it is often necessary to stop well short of that point. One obvious guideline is to allocate analytical resources in proportion to the size or importance of projects. More careful analysis should also be undertaken when past experience or prior judgment suggests that proper economic evaluation is particularly important—for example, when the actual prices of major inputs and outputs are known to diverge substantially from world prices.

Similarly, within each project the attention paid to different components should be in proportion to their importance to the decision at hand. In a great majority of projects, it suffices to estimate shadow prices for a few major items; minor items can be dealt with more cursorily, since even leaving them at their actual prices introduces a relatively small error. Likewise, among items of similar magnitude, priority should be given to those whose shadow prices are believed to diverge most substantially from their actual prices. Preferably, the analyst should be provided with some of the key shadow prices and conversion factors by a local or central government agency. This not only saves a lot of time but means that projects are evaluated on a consistent basis. Periodic review and revision by the appropriate central government agencies of the procedures and assumptions used in economic evaluation of projects is also very important.

Although cost-benefit techniques try to make maximum use of objective information in a consistent and unified framework, much still depends on the common sense, judgment, and ingenuity of the person doing the work. Few of the procedures for estimating shadow prices are completely unambiguous, and the standard shadow prices and conversion factors are bound to be rough estimates. Moreover, no two projects are exactly alike. It would thus be a mistake to treat economic evaluation as a mechanical process. Instead, the analyst should emphasize the basic principles involved and the need to apply them flexibly and intelligently. In different sectors, for example, different sorts of simplifications may be appropriate. In most large industrial projects, shadow pricing of labor and land may not be crucial. In agricultural and some infrastructure projects, in contrast, labor may be an important component, so that greater care is needed in estimating the shadow wage rate; land may also be usable for alternative purposes. In infrastructure projects, it may be necessary to examine the forecasts of future demand more thoroughly, since such investments tend to be lumpy and it is not possible to correct imbalances between demand and supply by international trade.

It would be wrong to suggest that the cost-benefit techniques described above are ideal or always give correct results. The fact that project appraisal inherently relies on forecasting the future means that some mistakes are inevitable. But good project evaluation does reduce the proportion of mistakes, particularly the more serious ones. In all countries—developing or developed—there are built-in pressures for bad investment decisions because of bureaucratic empire-building, political favoritism and horse-trading, the promotion of projects as personal or organizational monuments, and misguided enthusiasm for ultramodern technology. Most projects are brought forward by sponsors who are prone to exaggerate benefits and underestimate costs. Systematic economic evaluation is a good defense against these pressures. But there is no magic formula for good investment decisions. Dispassionate appraisal can prevent many serious errors; yet judgment remains essential in weighing different criteria against one another and in assessing the appropriateness of the underlying assumptions.

In view of all the caveats, limitations, and technical weaknesses of cost-benefit analysis, how useful is it in practice? We have been looking at cost-benefit analysis as a quantitative analytical technique. But cost-benefit analysis may also be viewed as a rational approach to decisionmaking whether the costs and benefits are measurable or not. It does not entirely preclude whim, bias, and intuition from playing a role in the decision-making process—it would be unrealistic to expect that. But identifying all the costs and benefits to society, and measuring those that can be measured, is a major contribution to the task of approaching decision-making rationally.

"Barefoot" doctor with her medical supplies, Sichuan Province, China

21

Financial Analysis

FINANCIAL ISSUES ARISE in the course of project work in several ways. The first and most widespread financial concern, which applies to all types of projects—whether or not they involve revenue-earning enterprises—is to ensure that there are adequate funds to carry the project through to completion. A second concern, also of broad application, is to recover an appropriate part of the costs from the beneficiaries or users through a system of prices or charges. Such cost recovery is important to ease the burden on the government budget or to help finance further investments by the sponsoring agency. For revenue-earning enterprises, the need to recover costs merges with other concerns about the impact of the investment on the financial position of the enterprise and, more broadly, about the overall financial viability or soundness of the enterprise. This chapter will examine these issues in turn.

FUNDING THE PROJECT

An integral part of project preparation is drawing up a financing plan to ensure that there will be adequate funds not only for completing the project but also for operating it. Like many statements in this book, this may seem obvious, but the number of development projects launched without adequate attention to future availability of funds is legion. If the implementing agency will be undertaking other investments or operations during the project's life, then its ability to fund the project cannot be ascertained without appraising the financial soundness of the agency as a whole, along lines discussed later in this chapter.

The financing requirements of the project need to be broken down into foreign exchange and local currency expenditures, both because the availability of foreign exchange is often a constraint and because external lenders may provide funds only to cover foreign exchange costs.[1] Terms and conditions of external financing vary widely according to the source (aid organizations, commercial banks, or suppliers' credits), so these need to be identified separately. Most aid agencies place limits on the proportion of a project's cost they are prepared to finance, which may vary with the country and with the type of project. Even if the project is cofinanced by several external sources, there will usually be a residual of local currency costs, and sometimes of foreign costs, that must be financed internally. Also, some external agencies, among them the World Bank, are reluctant to finance cost overruns except under special circumstances; such overruns, whether in local currency or foreign exchange, may ultimately become the responsibility of the borrowing entity. This makes it all the more important to establish reliable estimates of project costs, based on detailed design and engineering and with appropriate

---

1. The foreign exchange financing requirements of a project may not be the same as the foreign exchange costs identified in the project's cost estimate (see chapter 19, Technical Analysis) since the latter includes the foreign exchange content of goods purchased and works executed in the country.

allowances for physical and price contingencies, as discussed in chapter 19, Technical Analysis.

The need to ensure adequate funds extends to the operating phase of the project as well. Recurrent cost obligations are frequently underestimated and sometimes entirely ignored, with the result that facilities, once completed, deteriorate rapidly for want of adequate operating and maintenance funds. This bias against providing adequately for recurrent expenditures presumably reflects the greater political appeal that new investments have for governments; it is exacerbated by a parallel bias on the part of many donors, who are unwilling to finance such expenditures on any appreciable scale.

How important the recurrent costs of operation and maintenance are depends on the nature of the project. Construction of new schools entails substantial recurrent costs for teachers' salaries and for operating and maintaining the facilities. Health sector expenditures follow a similar pattern. New investments in irrigation canals or highways call for substantial routine and periodic maintenance; this must be anticipated and both adequate funding and appropriate organizational arrangements provided. Decisions are also needed about how depreciation and eventual replacement of machinery and equipment will be handled.

Unfortunately, financial analysis at the project level cannot always come up with a meaningful answer to the question whether a given level of recurrent cost is affordable. In its appraisal of individual education projects, for example, the World Bank has sometimes noted that the additional recurrent expenditures that would arise would be only a small percentage of the total budget (or even of the operating budget) of the ministry of education. This has led to the reassuring, but sometimes misleading, conclusion that the government would have no difficulty in providing the additional funds—which, in fact, proved not to be the case. If resources are tight, all expenditure items, large or small, and particularly those that are incremental, may be in jeopardy. The impact of individual projects, therefore, has to be considered in the context of the overall financial situation of the ministry, and indeed of the public expenditure budget as a whole, as discussed in chapter 4, Public Investment Programs and Budgets.

All projects except those involving revenue-earning enterprises, which are discussed separately below, are dependent on domestic budgetary resources for funds not externally provided. It is essential that government decisionmakers have before them a clear picture of the long-term budgetary implications before embarking on a project. Analysis of a project's fiscal impact should take account of any inflow of resources that can be attributed directly to the project through, for example, user charges of the kind described below.

Earmarking budgetary receipts to finance particular investments (such as using gasoline taxes for public highways) is practiced in some countries and may occasionally be requested or required by an external lender. Such earmarking may help to ensure the financing of a particular project or program, but at the expense of others that may be of equal or higher priority; therefore, the practice is not generally recommended. Revolving funds, established by contributions from an external lender and the government at the outset of a project and replenished at periodic intervals, are a useful method for making sure funds are readily available for a quick start in implementing an important project. The more widely the practice is extended, however, the clearer it becomes that it is not a substitute for sound budgetary practices with respect to the public investment program as a whole.

Whatever the project, a minimum of financial information and reporting will be necessary to keep track of the progress of expenditures. Such information indicates whether the project is on schedule and whether the cost estimates are being adhered to. Individual project accounts, particularly of government ministries, often fail to meet even this minimum standard. The accounts should always be subject to an independent audit which, in the case of government ministries, can be performed by a separate public agency. Publicly owned revenue-earning enterprises can also be audited by a government agency if it is independent and has a competent and trained staff, although it is more common for the government to rely on private auditing firms for this purpose. As in many other instances, technical assistance can be secured from abroad to help in setting up financial accounts and in training financial analysts and auditors. The first requirement is to identify the need and recognize the importance of dealing with it.

The foregoing discussion has been concerned with the adequacy of funding for projects from the point of view of the public or private enterprises or agencies carrying them out. But for certain types of projects, it is also necessary to consider the financial situation of the users or beneficiaries who are expected to participate in the project. This means, for example, determining whether the consumers in a water supply or urban development project will be able to afford the charges proposed for the services to be provided. In agricultural credit and other agricultural development projects, it may be necessary to draw up model farm budgets and to make cash flow projections for representative farm households to be sure that the cash inflow (including any subsidies deemed necessary) exceeds the cash outflow (including repayment of debt) particularly in the early years of change and innovation. The net cash inflow should also be large enough to make the risks of change acceptable to the farmer and to compensate him for any incremental effort of labor and management or any additional investment of capital required.

COST RECOVERY

That the users or beneficiaries of a project should pay its costs is a widely accepted principle of equity. Failure to recoup these costs from the users—through some form of price, tax, or other charge—creates a privileged class of beneficiaries, who in effect receive a subsidy or income transfer from the rest of society, while it deprives the project entity of resources that could be used to extend the product or service to additional users.

Objectives

When the analysis is pursued further, three necessary ingredients of a sound cost recovery policy can be identified. These are the same as the basic criteria for pricing policy set forth in chapter 3; here they are considered as they apply specifically to cost recovery as part of the financial analysis of projects.

- *Economic efficiency*—that is, ensuring that the goods and services produced by the project are utilized efficiently
- *Income distribution*—that is, recovering project costs in a way that promotes a more equitable distribution of income within the society
- *Revenue generation*—that is, enabling the government to capture part or all of the increased net benefits for funding future investments in the same sector or elsewhere; and, in the case of revenue-earning enterprises, enabling them to secure the resources necessary to achieve all of their financial objectives.

Economic Efficiency

This aspect of cost recovery reflects the traditional concern of pricing policy with the efficient use of resources to maximize a project's net benefit to the economy. An efficient price for a product in this sense is generally taken to be the marginal cost of producing the last unit sold. Any significant departure from efficiency pricing entails a sacrifice of economic benefits—as manifested, for example, in underutilization of industrial or infrastructure capacity, inappropriate farm technologies, or congested urban highways.

The marginal cost rule may need to be modified to allow for various complications. These include the substantial costs that may be incurred in charging for the service, as in metering water or collecting road tolls; the instability that may result from adjusting prices frequently to reflect changes in costs; the way in which changes in current prices affect future demand and the price expectations of consumers; problems arising from "lumpiness" or indivisibilities in capital investment; the constraints that may be imposed by the prices of close substitutes; and the difficulties of adequately reflecting external diseconomies in prices. The practical implications of these problems for efficiency pricing and various related marginal cost concepts have been extensively discussed elsewhere.[2] Because of these and other problems, the extent to which efficiency pricing can be applied to recover costs varies widely from sector to sector, as will be noted below.

Income Distribution

A cost recovery policy based solely on efficiency pricing is not necessarily appropriate when another national objective is to improve income distribution; the prices or other charges levied should then take into account differences in income level and in the ability of beneficiaries to pay. It may be desirable, for example, to charge small farmers less than

---

2. See for example, Anandarup Ray, *Cost Recovery Policies for Public Sector Projects*, World Bank Staff Working Paper no. 206 (Washington, D.C., 1975); R. J. Saunders, J. J. Warford, and P. C. Mann, "The Definition and Role of Marginal Cost in Public Utility Pricing: Problems of Application in the Water Supply Sector," Public Utility Note, *RES*, vol. 6 (World Bank, July 1976); Ralph Turvey and Dennis Anderson, *Electricity Economics* (Baltimore, Md.: Johns Hopkins University Press for the World Bank, 1977); and A. A. Walters, *The Economics of Road User Charges* (Baltimore, Md.: Johns Hopkins University Press for the World Bank, 1968).

large farmers for each unit of service extended under the same project. In water supply projects, some allowance can be made—perhaps through a surcharge on larger consumers—for poorer users whose consumption of water is close to the lifeline minimum. In principle, equity is served by making user charges or taxes progressive; in practice, however, various considerations—including any negative effect on people's incentive to participate in the project, the likelihood of tax evasion, and the costs of collection—may significantly limit what can be accomplished through this approach.

Equity in the sense of a more equal distribution of income should be distinguished from equity in the sense of fairness, a concept that sometimes arises in discussions on pricing and taxation policies. The latter may refer to the general notion of uniform pricing (meaning that all consumers should pay the same price or that benefit taxes should be proportional to the benefits received). Interpreted this way, fairness tends to conflict with the criteria of both efficiency and income distribution; it makes allowances neither for disparities in the cost of supplying different consumers nor for disparities in their income level.

Revenue Generation

Design of a cost recovery policy must also recognize that most governments in developing countries are short of fiscal resources for development. Revenue collected from users through efficiency prices may be less than is necessary to recover the full investment and operating costs of a project. This may not matter in those rare instances in which the government is in a strong financial position. But when fiscal resources are at a premium, it is often desirable for the government to collect more revenue than would result from efficiency pricing alone.

There may also be tradeoffs between the objective of increasing public revenue and that of improving income distribution. A high level of cost recovery in, say, a rural or urban development project will help the government to mobilize the resources with which to replicate the project and extend its benefits to more of the needy. At the same time, when the beneficiaries are poor, constraints on their ability to pay and their willingness to participate in the project may limit cost recovery. A well-designed project, however, will often increase the income or welfare of the beneficiaries sufficiently that a substantial level of cost recovery can be justified on equity as well as on fiscal grounds.

When the project in question is the responsibility of a revenue-earning enterprise, cost recovery combines with other objectives related to the financial viability of the enterprise. These objectives are discussed in more detail later in this chapter.

In summary, then, the ideal cost recovery policy is one that secures maximum economic benefits from the project, with account taken of its impact on the distribution of benefits and on government and enterprise finances. The goal can be to recover part of the costs, all of them, or even full costs plus some additional part of the benefits. But there are difficult tradeoffs to be made among the efficiency, equity, and revenue objectives in practice, since not all of them can be achieved to an equal extent or at the same time. The poorer the country, the more painful the choices may be.

Implementation Issues

Designing Cost Recovery Instruments

Which instruments are used and how they are designed will have an important bearing on the effectiveness of cost recovery. In measuring the impact of a project on public savings, any increase in public revenue arising from the project that would not otherwise have occurred can be considered part of cost recovery, including revenue derived from general taxes such as gasoline taxes, agricultural commodity taxes, income taxes, and so on. However, capturing a larger part of the benefits through an increase in general taxation impinges also on those who do not directly benefit from the project and thus raises broader taxation issues. Hence the cost recovery instruments designed for a project should preferably be selective, falling as much as possible only on the project beneficiaries.

There are two instruments that generally meet this test. The first is the price charged for the product or service supplied by the project entity. Pricing can be used not only to promote economic efficiency but also to extract larger or smaller payments from the users or beneficiaries in the interests of equity or public and enterprise finance—as, for example, through a fixed charge unrelated to use combined with a variable charge based on the volume supplied. The second instrument is the so-called benefit tax, that is, a tax on improved land, which bears entirely or very largely on project beneficiaries.

These two principal options, while widely used, are not always available. In some projects, such as flood control schemes, output pricing may be impossible for technical reasons; land taxes or benefit levies, however, can be imposed. More commonly, as in the case of village water supply, village electricity, and rural roads, the administrative cost of installing and operating special devices that permit pricing based on the volume or extent of use may be prohibitive; simpler approaches must be followed. In some situations, benefit taxation may not be possible either for political or administrative reasons or because beneficiaries cannot be specifically identified.

Designing a sophisticated benefit tax is quite a demanding task. First, it must be possible to identify the beneficiaries and classify them into income groups. Second, the additional income received by a beneficiary from the project needs to be estimated net of all his incremental payments on existing taxes. Third, to reflect equity considerations, judgments must be made about the appropriate weights for valuing the consumption gains of each income group. Fourth, the adverse effects of benefit taxes—as, for example, on the production incentives of the beneficiaries—need to be minimized. These complexities may make it quite difficult to design benefit taxes that can discriminate among different groups of beneficiaries; a second-best approach to cost recovery would then be a uniform tax on beneficiaries (for example, a land tax).

Sectoral Differences

In view of the practical limitations to cost recovery through either prices or benefit taxes, the relative importance of the objectives of efficiency, equity, and revenue generation varies greatly among the sectors and with project circumstances.

In some sectors, such as education or public health, recovery from the beneficiaries of the costs of providing services traditionally has not played a significant role, although this approach may have to be reconsidered in the interests of mobilizing additional funds, as we have argued in the relevant chapters of part II. In many other sectors and subsectors, such as power, telecommunications, ports, railways, manufacturing industry, and industrial and farm credit, efficiency pricing should be the starting point, with the financial objectives of the enterprise given equal weight. Considerations of income distribution, to the extent that they apply, can usually be implemented through differential charges. In power, telecommunications, ports, and industry, economies of large-scale production and favorable market conditions may often make it possible through efficiency pricing to achieve full cost recovery or more. This is less true for railways, because of their adverse competitive situation. Water supply and sanitation enterprises have also had difficulty in meeting the standard of full cost recovery; as we have suggested in chapter 13, however, more could be done.

Generally, in most projects concerned with low-income target groups—such as sites and services, slum upgrading, rural development, or village water supply—there is little scope for establishing systems that would permit efficiency pricing. Charges imposed on beneficiaries will depend primarily on income distribution considerations, within limits determined by the government's fiscal situation and the financial needs of the agency. Even for the poorest groups, however, a minimal user charge helps to generate some revenue and to prevent the overuse of a free good or service. A high level of cost recovery has, in fact, been achieved in many Bank-assisted urban development projects.

For financial intermediaries such as development banks or development finance companies and agricultural credit institutions, the "price" in question is the interest rate charged on lending operations. A principal objective is to secure the financial viability of the intermediary. This can be done by an adequate spread between its lending rates and its cost of borrowed funds, complemented by measures to stimulate operating efficiency, such as improved procedures for reducing arrears on outstanding loans. An adequate spread can be as low as one or two percentage points or as high as six to eight points or more, depending on the volume and nature of the lending operations, which determine its administrative costs and the risks involved. If the on-lending rate to the ultimate borrowers is fixed by the government at too low a level, it may be necessary to reduce the cost to the intermediary of borrowed funds—one subsidy begetting another. Because of the close links among the various components of a country's interest rate structure, it is often preferable to deal with interest rate issues on an economywide basis rather than project by project.

Problems of cost recovery figure prominently in irrigation projects, which often are very expensive and bring relatively large increases in income to those farmers who benefit from them. In many parts of the world, water has traditionally been regarded by users as a God-given and, therefore, free good. Even when some form of water charge exists, the collection mechanisms are frequently deficient and resistance to paying is high. Furthermore, true efficiency pricing requires accurate measurement of supplies by metering the volume of water delivered to individual users, which—political and administrative problems aside—is technically difficult except in public tubewell and pumping schemes. Although true efficiency pricing may not be attainable, even a nominal charge for irrigation water would provide an incentive to use it more efficiently. Beyond this, benefit taxes on land improvement are the most feasible instrument for working toward income distribution and public finance objectives. To further complicate the situation, there are likely to be many other government interventions in the form of taxes, subsidies, and price controls that affect the income of farmers both positively and negatively and that should be taken into account in considering the appropriateness of a particular level of cost recovery.

These complications notwithstanding, the pervasive shortage of public funds and the large income benefits derived by participants in irrigation schemes suggest that substantial cost recovery should be the goal in many instances. Most governments, however, have not attained anything like full cost recovery from public irrigation schemes. A rule of thumb followed by some governments is to absorb the capital costs but to establish water charges and benefit taxes at a level that in the aggregate will at least recover the operation and maintenance costs, including repairs. The level of these costs may be a poor yardstick for measuring conformity to any of the three criteria of cost recovery, particularly if the project beneficiaries are well-to-do or experience large increases in income. But this approach will at least avoid an outright drain by the project on current government revenues and may help to ensure that funding to cover these costs is more readily forthcoming. Experience argues in favor of giving the implementing agency direct access to the operation and maintenance funds rather than making it dependent on periodic outlays from the public budget. Experience also suggests that, when the agency responsible for an irrigation system receives its operation and maintenance funds directly from the project beneficiaries and when the beneficiaries have a significant influence on how the system is operated, the system is more likely to be well managed and maintained.

Practical Considerations

Cost recovery is often an explosive political issue. Political considerations, together with practical administrative ones, will determine what can be accomplished and how quickly. Introduction of new charges, or a substantial increase in existing charges, is more likely to be accepted after project implementation is well advanced and some benefits have materialized. Educating the beneficiaries and having them participate in designing and implementing the cost recovery mechanisms may be important, even essential, steps. One of the least palatable approaches politically is to treat similar situations in a different manner, which leaves the government open to the charge of discrimination. The feasibility of introducing cost recovery in a particular project may thus depend on an across-the-board reform of the government's approach to cost recovery.

External donors need to bear these realities in mind in working with recipient governments to establish cost recovery policies that will both meet the underlying objectives and stand the test of time.

Measuring Cost Recovery

Consideration of pricing and taxation policies may often be facilitated by expressing their effects in some summary measure, such as a cost recovery or benefit recovery ratio or a financial rate of return. With public enterprises, such as railways or power entities, it has been customary to use rates of return or related measures for this purpose, as will be discussed more fully in the next section; with other public sector projects, such as those involving irrigation or urban housing sites and services, ratios that measure the extent to which costs or benefits have been recovered have become the practice.[3] Whatever instrument is used, the design of satisfactory cost recovery policies should not be reduced to the mechanical computation of ratios or rates of return. Even when all costs are recovered, the policy for pricing a project's output may be wrong in the sense that it reduces the project's economic benefits unduly or does not adequately take into account differences in the income position of the beneficiaries. Such deficiencies are not always signaled by some measure of cost recovery; use of such measures, therefore, should be supplemented by a full analysis of the proposed prices and charges as they bear on efficiency, equity, and public and enterprise revenue and the tradeoffs among them.

FINANCIAL PERFORMANCE

Recovering the costs of investment and operations is one of the principal financial objectives of a revenue-earning enterprise, but there are others that are also important. The financial objectives and performance of such enterprises need, therefore, to be examined in a broader context. We use the term revenue-earning enterprises to cover activities in the public sector (railways, ports, telecommunications, and electric power and water utilities) as well as those which, in most developing countries, are privately owned (manufacturing enterprises, agricultural processing industries, and so on).

Although the overriding financial concern of these enterprises must be their general financial viability, as discussed more fully below, a more immediate concern is the financial justification of the specific investments that constitute a project. It is not sufficient that an enterprise be financially sound; each of its principal investments should also meet the test of soundness, not only in economic terms as discussed in the previous chapter, but also with regard to its contribution to the financial position of the enterprise. The financial profitability of the project is important in all cases, but particularly when the project entails establishing a new

3. For details on how these indices are measured, see J. Price Gittinger, *Economic Analysis of Agricultural Projects*, 2d ed. (Baltimore, Md.: Johns Hopkins University Press for the Economic Development Institute of the World Bank, 1982).

enterprise or considerably expanding an existing one and new equity investors (government or private) will have to be attracted or substantial additional debt incurred.

Financial Rate of Return

The financial profitability of a project can be measured in several ways. The approach described here is sometimes called the *(internal) financial rate of return.*[4] This is closely related conceptually to the *(internal) economic rate of return* described in the preceding chapter and is, in fact, customarily taken as the point of departure for the project's economic analysis. It deals with the time streams of funds flowing to and from the enterprise as a result of the project; specifically, the financial rate of return is determined as the discount rate that equalizes the present value of the streams of financial costs and benefits over the life of the project.[5] All flows of funds are recorded in cash or financial terms. The economic rate of return, as we have seen, adjusts various financial costs and prices to eliminate transfer payments such as subsidies, duties, and taxes to the extent that they are a cost or benefit to the enterprise but not to the economy, and to compensate for price distortions in the valuation of traded and nontraded goods by using shadow prices that reflect their value to the economy. The arithmetic of the discounting, the interpretation of the various measures, and their limitations are the same for both financial and economic analysis. The essential difference is that financial analysis deals with costs and benefits from the viewpoint of an individual enterprise, measured in market costs and prices, while economic analysis does so from the viewpoint of the economy as a whole, measured in economic values.

The costs that enter into financial analysis include the capital outlays for the project investment and the incremental operating and administrative expenditures that are associated with it over the life of the project. Changes in the level of assets such as inventories are included, but depreciation is not, since capital expenditures are entered in the year that they are incurred. Nor is interest on funds borrowed for the project included, since the financial rate of return itself measures the return or "interest" earned on the capital invested in the project. The benefit stream covers the incremental inflow of funds arising from the project, the principal item being income or receipts from the sale of the project's output or services. Subsidies are included as inflows, just as customs duties and taxes appear as outflows.

What is an acceptable financial rate of return for a project? The answer will depend on many factors, including the sector in question, whether the enterprise is publicly or privately owned, and whether the economy is essentially market-oriented or centrally planned. For private investors, the return should at least equal what they could earn at the margin in

4. For an extensive discussion of this and related financial issues, see Jack Upper, "Finance for Project Analysis" (Washington, D.C.: World Bank, Economic Development Institute, 1983).

5. To equate the financial rate of return with other measures referred to in chapter 20, Economic Analysis, it can also be defined as the discount rate at which the net present value equals zero and the discounted benefit-cost ratio equals unity, all in financial terms.

alternative investments, after allowance is made for differences in risk. For revenue-earning enterprises that are publicly owned, the financial opportunity cost of alternative earnings forgone may also serve as a useful guide. Although this is a notional concept, some approximation of it can be made in market-oriented economies; the analysis becomes more difficult to apply and interpret in the case of centrally planned economies, in which investment decisions may be administratively determined with only limited reference to the financial opportunities forgone. Most frequently, the incremental financial return on new investments will be higher than the overall rate of return of the enterprise on its net assets in use, as described below.

The financial rate of return can be measured before or after the payment of income taxes, or both before and after. For private investors, a separate measure of the return on equity, after allowance for repayment of borrowed capital, may also be useful.

Enterprise Objectives

Important as is the financial soundness of a project, the ultimate objective is the financial viability of the enterprise itself. This objective can be translated into three subsidiary objectives, standards, or tests of performance:

- Will the enterprise have sufficient revenue to earn a reasonable return on all of its invested capital? As part of the test of "reasonableness," will it be able to generate enough funds from internal resources to make a satisfactory contribution to its future capital requirements?
- Will the capital structure of the enterprise enable it to meet all of its debt service and other capital obligations in a timely manner?
- Will there be adequate liquidity, that is, sufficient working capital to cover all current operational requirements?

External aid agencies frequently incorporate these tests of performance into financial covenants, which form part of the loan agreement with the borrower. Some developing countries have used similar tests, with various modifications and adaptations to local circumstances, in national legislation covering the regulation of public enterprises such as electric power companies. In francophone Africa, the *contrat plan* being used with increasing frequency to govern the relationship between the state and public-owned enterprises may contain such provisions (see chapter 23, Institutional Analysis). However and wherever prescribed, tests of performance are the essential means of ensuring not only an enterprise's financial viability but also the financial discipline that will encourage its efficient management and use of resources.

Revenue Standards

The revenue objectives of an enterprise are central to its satisfactory financial performance. There are, broadly speaking, two principal ways in which these objectives can be formulated: as an annual rate of return on invested capital or as the amount of cash generated annually as a proportion of invested funds. Although the two approaches are different, the objective is basically the same: to cover operating costs, to service debt, and to contribute to investment from internally generated funds. Given the necessary data, the two formulations can be made interchangeable. The focus of these approaches on the ability of an enterprise to make a significant contribution to its investment needs from internally generated funds reflects several considerations: the large requirements for new capital that many of these enterprises face in the course of their development; the inadequacy of domestic capital markets as an alternative source of finance; the limited amounts of external aid and the reluctance of most lenders to cover all the capital costs of an investment; and the difficulty of mobilizing public savings in developing countries, together with the competing demands for use of such savings by nonrevenue-earning activities.

The *rate of return on invested capital*—which should not be confused with the financial or economic rate of return on the investment under a project—requires that revenues be sufficient each year to cover operating expenses and taxes and to earn a specified rate of return on the capital invested in the enterprise as a whole. Operating expenses include maintenance and provision for depreciation but not interest and other financial charges. Invested capital is usually defined as the average for the year of the current value of the enterprise's net fixed assets in operation; it may also include an adequate level of working capital. Under inflationary conditions, a rate of return is meaningful only if based on asset values and depreciation charges adjusted periodically to reflect changes in price levels.

A critical issue is the establishment of a "reasonable" rate of return. Ideally, that rate should approximate the rate of return that the same resources could otherwise earn in the country's private sector under competitive market conditions, allowing for differences in business risks and barring overriding social or economic considerations. The prevailing level of interest rates in the country may be a useful point of departure. As noted earlier, another consideration in selecting a reasonable rate of return is how the resulting prices of the output relate to those that would be appropriate from an economic (efficiency) point of view. Also to be considered are the need for additional public revenue and the ability of various consumers to pay. The cash requirements of the enterprise, including, in particular, the need for self-financed investments, are an important factor, as noted above, and the estimated contribution to new investment deriving from a specified rate of return should be separately identified.

These considerations have generally led to the establishment of relatively high rates of return for telecommunications enterprises (10 to 12 percent or even higher), which can easily finance a large proportion of their investments from internal funds and, in some cases, augment government revenues through the transfer of surplus funds. In fact, rates of return earned in telecommunications would be even higher if prices were used as a rationing device when there is a large unsatisfied demand. Rates of return have also generally been high in the industrial sector, where payment of dividends may be an additional criterion. Electric power utilities, ports, and gas or fuel pipelines with suitable tariff policies can usually be expected to earn rates of return in the range of 8 to 10 percent. Water supply and sanitation agencies serving poorer consumers and providing a basic need have rarely been permitted to earn returns higher than 6 to 8 percent. Few railway companies in the world are able to earn a return on their invested capital, and the operating ratio is more commonly used as the financial target.

An enterprise with a very heavy debt-service obligation or a large capital expansion program may require a higher rate of return than would otherwise be considered normal. Whatever the specified return, provision should be made for a periodic reassessment in the light of changing circumstances. For enterprises in financial difficulties, a phased program for arriving at the return ultimately desired may be necessary.

The rate of return on capital is the more widely applied of the two main formulations of the revenue objective. Return on capital is a generally accepted measure used in many countries for evaluating the financial performance of revenue-earning enterprises. As an indicator of the rate at which costs are being recovered from the beneficiaries, it is an accurate and objective test based on generally accepted accounting principles, and it is easy to administer. Moreover, through the systematic revaluation of assets, the rate of return can be measured effectively in real terms, and it can be adjusted to reflect future capital and other requirements.

The *cash generation* criterion stipulates that the enterprise should provide funds from internal sources each year equivalent to a specified percentage of annual capital expenditures, after having met its operating expenses, debt service, taxes, dividends, increases in working capital, and other significant cash outlays. This formulation directly addresses the need to generate sufficient cash internally to finance an agreed proportion of investment requirements, but it does not provide a yardstick for measuring cost recovery. Because capital requirements can fluctuate widely from year to year, it may be advisable to compare the net funds generated in a given year with the average capital expenditures for three or four years, including the year just past, the present one, and one or two years to come. The uncertain nature of future investment programs makes periodic review of the designated percentage necessary. The rate of return implied by the percentage can be estimatcd and its adequacy judged on the basis of the considerations given above.

The cash generation test is useful when the government, for whatever reasons, does not wish to adopt the concept of a rate of return based on revalued assets, or when a more direct approach to addressing cash generation requirements is desired. What is an acceptable norm is not as readily apparent for cash generation as it is for the rate of return; furthermore, it is a more subjective measure since it includes forecasts for future years. The range of acceptable cash generation, which can vary widely from a low of 10 percent of capital requirements to a high of over 100 percent, generally follows the pattern described above for the rate of return for different types of enterprises. Because the test tends to be applied primarily to the financing plan for the implementation period of a particular investment program, it does not provide as suitable a basis for determining long-term financial policy as does the rate of return. Also, since it is directly related to changes in the investment program, it has proved to be least effective when investments were very lumpy (that is, large and indivisible), when substantial cost overruns have occurred, or when future capital requirements have otherwise been substantially underestimated.

Other revenue tests used less frequently are the *operating ratio* test, which measures the ratio of operating expenses to revenues and is intended to ensure that earnings are at least sufficient to cover expenses, including adequate maintenance and depreciation; and the *break-even* test, which ensures the continued solvency of the enterprise through coverage of its operating expenses and of depreciation or debt service (whichever is larger) without the further requirement of earning a reasonable rate of return or contributing to expansion from internally generated funds.

Measures to achieve objectives. Issues about prices (or tariffs or rates—the terms are used synonymously) will inevitably be in the forefront when measures to achieve the financial performance targets are considered, but it is essential to avoid a single-minded preoccupation with them. Financial performance can also be improved by raising operating efficiency and eliminating or reducing waste, sometimes at lower political cost. Such opportunities exist everywhere, and the search for them is an important part of project work. This is particularly important for enterprises that enjoy a monopoly or quasi monopoly and are not subject to competitive pressures to operate efficiently.

Some of these opportunities for improvement are specific to a sector or subsector, such as reducing the volume of water that leaks or is not accounted for, improving the turnaround time of railway locomotives, increasing the cargo-handling throughput of a port, or conserving the use of energy by retrofitting industry. Other opportunities are likely to be found in virtually every sector and enterprise. A brief illustrative list might include dealing with the dual problems of redundancy of lower-level staff and shortages of skilled staff through attrition, reassignment, and training; upgrading the quality of management and management systems; exercising better control of inventories; improving billing and collecting practices; improving sales and marketing procedures; and streamlining procurement methods.

Particular objectives can be fixed as part of an overall plan of action for the enterprise (see, for example, the discussion of railways in chapter 11, Transport). They should be as specific as possible—such as to reduce the collection period for overdue accounts receivable to a specific number of days by a precise date or to increase the number of customers served by each operating employee to a designated ratio. Progress should then be monitored closely as a regular part of the management and reporting system of the enterprise. External lenders such as the World Bank are increasingly introducing such plans of action into their loan agreements.

When all is said and done, however, attempts to attain the revenue and other financial performance objectives of the enterprise will almost certainly throw issues of tariff policy into bold relief. Unless the prices are "right," other elements of the financial plan will not have their full effect and may in the end be frustrated. A great majority of the World Bank's loans to revenue-earning enterprises have called for an increase in the current level of tariffs, often by large amounts. Negotiating this increase (or series of increases) and helping to bring it about during project implementation has often been a central feature of the Bank-borrower dialogue—and not infrequently a matter of contention.

Inflation presents particular problems. Governments are often reluctant to raise the rates of such basic services as electricity, water, and railways during an inflationary period, both because of the psychological impact and because the increases might touch off another round of the inflationary cost-price spiral. These arguments are understandable, but they ignore the fact that failure to raise prices may also have an inflationary impact. Without a price increase, the deficit of the enterprise may be larger (or the surplus smaller) and more funds will have to be raised for operating or investment purposes through public borrowing, which could have inflationary consequences of its own.

Attention must be given to the structure as well as to the overall level of prices, and this may be the best way of reconciling the efficiency and equity objectives of price strategy with the financial needs of the enterprise. These are complex matters. For example, difficult analytical questions arise when trying to design an "efficient" system of electricity charges that vary with the time of the day or season of the year—in order to shift usage from peak (high-cost) to off-peak (low-cost) periods—while at the same time providing sufficient revenues to satisfy the financial objectives. Similarly, it is not easy to apportion fairly the costs of providing a service among different classes of consumers. For some basic services such as water, a system of lifeline rates may be desirable to ensure access by the poor, with cross-subsidies from higher-income groups to ensure the financial viability of the enterprise (see chapter 13, Water and Sanitation). Specialized consultant services are often required to design an appropriate tariff structure.

Practical considerations. In practice, the most that can be asked from the hard-pressed policymaker is that he arrive not at an "ideal" price but at one which reasonably approaches the stated objectives and avoids the more serious mistakes and pitfalls. Progress may have to be gradual, and the direction and rate of change of prices may be the important points on which to concentrate, at least in the short run. To raise the price of a basic product or service that figures prominently in the cost of living of the population often takes an act of political courage. But not to raise prices is also a decision of a kind, and one that in the long run may have even more adverse economic, and therefore political, consequences (although not necessarily for the same politicians!).

Several possible ways of easing the political and bureaucratic pain of raising prices have already been referred to under the section on cost recovery. Whenever possible, price adjustments should be made in small increments and at regular intervals. History is replete with examples of governments that have failed to raise the price of, say, water for ten or fifteen years and have then sought to double or triple prices in an effort to reverse in one move the disastrous financial position of the water supply company—a move that has been known to lead to the downfall of governments. Linking price increases to tangible improvements in service is another way to reduce consumer resistance. There are also advantages to making some price increases automatic or quasi-automatic, as by passing on increases in fuel costs though proportionate increases in electricity prices without the need for government approval in each instance. Finally, consumer resistance to price increases is often more muted when the increases are made by private enterprises than when they result from government action—a point for governments to consider in deciding which activities to leave in private hands.

Capital Structure Standards

The two other financial objectives of a revenue-earning enterprise—concerning its capital structure and its liquidity—touch on less sensitive, and therefore less controversial, issues. The capital structure of the enterprise should be designed to secure financial solvency under adverse as well as normal operating conditions, including both business and financial risks. Business risk refers to the uncertainties, or the variability of expenditures and revenues, inherent in the nature and type of business activity. Financial risk is the uncertainty inherent in the obligations (interest and debt repayment) associated with borrowing. A well-managed enterprise with a low business risk can count on a fairly dependable cash flow and can therefore assume a relatively high financial risk in the form of a large ratio of debt to equity in its capital structure. This could apply, for example, to a public utility with a relatively stable and predictable demand for its services, little competition from other sources of supply, and fairly reliable production facilities. In contrast, an enterprise subject to wide fluctuations in demand and prices, such as a steel company or a rubber estate, is likely to experience substantial swings in its cash flow from year to year. It should, therefore, have a conservative capital structure with low fixed financial obligations.

The risk of inflation is another factor affecting the cost of capital and, consequently, the design of a prudent capital structure. Although inflation may lower the burden of servicing outstanding debt at fixed terms, it may also increase the risk associated with loan capital, since the earnings of an enterprise may not keep pace with inflation. Long-term loans may be available only if the interest rates include a substantial inflation premium or vary with the current cost of borrowing, or if the loans are indexed to changes in the value of money. The impact of inflation on financial risks is greatest when only short- or medium-term loan funds are available and the enterprise is therefore exposed to the risk of having to pay higher interest rates to refinance the loans at maturity.

Equity investors, because they are subject to the prior claims of lenders and have no fixed promise of returns, will usually expect a higher return on their capital than lenders. Like lenders, they will accept lower returns when they judge the risks to be low; and they will consider their risks to be low when equity is high in relation to debt.

An appropriately balanced capital structure is desirable for public as well as private enterprises. It would be possible to provide all the capital of a public enterprise as equity and thus spare it any financial risk; however, this would remove the financial discipline associated with the obligation to service debt. Although the provision of public funds to a public enterprise as equity capital is sometimes viewed as entailing no financial cost to the government, it does have an opportunity cost since the funds could be used elsewhere. External aid agencies, in most instances, provide their financial assistance in the form of debt rather than equity.

Capital structure tests generally take the form of a limit on long-term borrowing; this limit may be an absolute amount or it may depend on annual cash flow or the value of equity capital. The preferred form of test is *debt-service coverage*, since it relates the borrowing capacity of the enterprise to the terms of the debt as well as to its amount. The debt-service coverage test, which is applied each time a new long-term loan is contemplated, compares the internal cash generation (defined as gross revenues less operating expenses before depreciation and interest) with the maximum future debt service for principal and interest, including service of the proposed debt, in any year. If the maximum coverage specified in the test is not met, the ability of the enterprise to service the proposed borrowing is brought into question, and the debt should not be incurred without prior approval from a designated authority.[6]

Fixing the appropriate level of debt-service coverage is, as is so often the case, a matter of judgment. The coverage most frequently prescribed in World Bank loans is 1.5, but it may vary from as low as 1.3 to as high as 2.0 or more depending on how stable or volatile the earnings of the enterprise are expected to be.

The second most common form of debt limitation is based on the *debt-equity ratio*. This ratio expresses the relative proportions of long-term debt and equity in the capital structure. The debt-equity ratio is simple to understand and administer and is consistent with the need for maintaining a sound capital structure without unduly restricting the enterprise's ability to make routine financial decisions without prior approval from some authority. Its principal shortcoming—a significant one—is that it disregards the terms and conditions of the debt and their impact on the debt-service burden. It is used most often for new enterprises, such as a "greenfield" industrial plant, for which the debt-service coverage test is not applicable because of the absence of an earnings record. In such cases, the debt-equity ratio helps to ensure a satisfactorily balanced financing plan in the early years. The debt-equity ratio is also used in connection with financial intermediaries such as industrial and agricultural finance companies which, because of the nature of their business and the composition of their assets and liabilities, can safely operate with a relatively high proportion of debt.

The considerations determining the appropriate magnitude of the debt-equity ratio are the same as those discussed for debt-service coverage. A maximum debt-equity ratio of 60:40 has been used for many years in World Bank loans, with generally satisfactory results. A 70:30 ratio has sometimes been accepted for entities with very dependable earning power, while lower ratios are preferable for those whose earnings are subject to wide fluctuations. For financial intermediaries, the proportions are quite different and can range from a low of 75:25 (more frequently expressed as 3:1) for new intermediaries to a high of 90:10 (9:1) for experienced ones with a proven record of satisfactory earnings. Other types of restrictions (for example, on the amount of equity investments that the intermediary can make or on the proportion of its total investment that can be placed in any one enterprise or sector) are also used to guide its financial performance.

For a public sector enterprise with a high proportion of debt held by

6. There are two versions of the debt-service coverage test, one based on actual earnings (cash generation) for the latest fiscal year or a more recent twelve-month period and one based on a forecast of future earnings. The former is generally to be preferred since it is more objective and certain.

the government, it is sometimes felt that the debt-equity ratio loses some of its importance: it is presumed that the debt can readily be renegotiated if circumstances require. This reasoning disregards the fact that the government typically is hard pressed for funds and can ill afford continued injections of funds, whether of debt or equity, into financially weak ventures. Public sector enterprises should normally be expected to meet the same standards of financial performance as private enterprises, including a satisfactory capital structure.

A third test of capital structure is the *absolute debt limit*; it stipulates the amount of debt that can be incurred annually without prior authorization. Because of its inflexibility, it is used only when it is not feasible to apply either of the other capital structure tests. The typical case is that of a public utility with a capital structure that, as a statutory requirement, consists entirely or predominantly of debt. A different and more common type of limitation is for creditors, particularly external lenders, to restrict the amount of dividends that may be paid to shareholders as a means of safeguarding the enterprise's capital base.

Liquidity Standards

Achieving and maintaining an adequate level of liquidity is the third of the major objectives of financial performance. Liquidity tests are designed to ensure that there is sufficient current or working capital—defined as the surplus of current assets over current liabilities—to meet obligations in a timely manner. These tests are most frequently used for industrial and agroindustrial enterprises, whose working capital needs tend to be large, and seldom for utilities and railways, whose needs are small. In the absence of adequate coverage of current liabilities, the enterprise would be forced into expedients such as expensive short-term borrowing, delayed payment of obligations, or deferral of essential maintenance in an effort to stave off insolvency.

The *current ratio*, which is current assets divided by current liabilities, is the generally accepted measure of the adequacy of working capital, since it indicates the extent to which short-term obligations are covered by assets capable of being converted into cash in a period roughly corresponding to the maturity of the obligations. Current assets normally comprise cash, marketable securities, accounts receivable, and inventories; current liabilities comprise accounts payable, short-term notes payable, accrued taxes and expenses, dividends payable, and long-term debt maturing within the year.

The appropriate magnitude of the current ratio depends on the type of production and selling operations and on the characteristics of the market for the product. A current ratio of less than 1:1, or one that is declining toward that level, is not likely to be acceptable in most circumstances, and ratios in the range of 2:1 to 4:1 are more common. A company with a rapid turnover of inventory and with receivables that are easy to collect can have a relatively low ratio; one subject to seasonal or fluctuating demand for its output will need a higher ratio.

Advantages of using the current ratio are that it is simple and easy to understand, that it is an objective test, and that it can be based on readily defined accounting principles and calculated from standard financial statements. It is, of course, only as good as the underlying accounts and requires close and consistent monitoring lest unacceptable management and accounting practices (such as inadequate provision for bad debts) be used to give the appearance of compliance.

Inventories deserve particular attention: they are the least liquid of current assets and those on which losses are most likely to occur if borrowing conditions are adverse. In a period of declining sales, it may be difficult to convert them into cash at reasonable prices.

An alternative and more rigorous test of liquidity designed with this problem in mind is the *quick ratio*. It excludes inventories and therefore compares only highly liquid current assets with total current liabilities. In other respects, it has the same advantages and disadvantages as the current ratio. A quick ratio of at least 1:1 (sometimes expressed as 1.0) is usually prescribed.

Finally, a *dividend limitation* can also be applied to secure the solvency of the enterprise. It prevents the entity from declaring a dividend when doing so would cause the current ratio (or quick ratio) to fall below a specified minimum. Payment of the dividend is deferred until the enterprise has taken further measures to establish and maintain the liquidity required for its operations.

FINANCIAL STATEMENTS

Measuring progress in meeting the various tests of financial performance requires an up-to-date system of financial accounts and reports. The three principal financial statements employed in financial analysis are

- The *balance sheet*, which presents the assets and liabilities of the enterprise at the end of each accounting period, usually a year
- The *income (profit or loss) statement*, which summarizes the revenues and expenses of the enterprise during the accounting period
- The *sources and uses of funds statement*, which depicts the flow of financial resources (depreciation not being included) into and out of the enterprise during the accounting period.

For project purposes, these statements need to be prepared, analyzed, and forecast for the full implementation period and for at least the first several years of full-scale operation. The statements can be made more useful for comparative purposes by including corresponding data for several previous years. For other financial planning purposes, different time spans will be appropriate. An independent auditor should provide a report and opinion on the extent to which the statements provide a true and fair view of the financial condition of the enterprise. If the present system of financial accounts (and their external audits) is inadequate, as is frequently the case, technical assistance may be available from aid agencies to improve it or to establish a new system.

Measuring progress toward achieving financial objectives requires the use of an integrated system of management information including budgeting, accounting, internal control, and financial reporting. These tools are intended to provide management with data for planning and directing operational and financial performance. For lenders, investors, and other external parties, the final output of this system is a set of financial statements that should present a clear picture of an enterprise's financial performance and status. During project preparation and appraisal, this system should be examined to make sure that effective control exists throughout the enterprise and that reported results are reliable.

The budgeting process provides an effective discipline for periodically reviewing and adjusting the operating policies of an enterprise. Preferably, this process should be split between long-term budgeting and planning, on the one hand, and short-term control of operations through the annual capital and recurrent budgets on the other. Involving all levels of management in the process of budgetary planning, coordination, and control is a way of ensuring their knowledge of and commitment to the prevailing policies. Other components of the management information system (production, sales, administration, and accounting) can be linked with the budget through common classifications or descriptions of the activities subject to control.

The accounting system, a principal element in an enterprise's management information system, should generate accurate, timely data for decisionmaking. This will also make possible the early publication of financial statements for external use. The system should incorporate consistent, prompt recording of quantities and values of fixed assets, working capital, debt transactions, operating income, and expenditures. A standardized system of costing should be integrated with the accounting system to provide operational unit costs to line managers and policymakers.

Harvesting irrigated rice, Sri Lanka

22

Social Analysis

DEVELOPMENT PROJECTS engage people in a variety of roles—as beneficiaries, producers, consumers, and even, on occasion and unintentionally, as victims. Some projects—in such fields as rural development, education, and health—are clearly people-oriented; others—such as those that provide infrastructure—are less so. But even a project for a petrochemical or cement plant can get into serious difficulties or fail to achieve its economic development objectives if it is not able to motivate a work force or build a viable community for workers and their families. The sector chapters in part II contain abundant evidence that a project has little chance of success if it runs counter to or ignores the traditions, values, and social organization of the intended beneficiaries, or if its objectives are too abstract to be understood by them or too remote from their everyday concerns.

Project design is sometimes influenced more by the cultural orientation of the planners than by that of the people directly affected (the so-called project population). Moreover, project design has usually tended to emphasize technical solutions to development problems, to the neglect or exclusion of broad social issues. The purpose of social analysis is to consider the suitability of the proposed design to the project population, to suggest ways to improve the "fit" between the two, and to fashion strategies for project implementation that can be expected both to win and hold people's support and to achieve project goals by stimulating changes in social attitudes and behavior.

Social analysis should take its place alongside the other dimensions of project analysis—technical, economic, financial, and so forth—all of which, as we have stressed, are essential components of an integrated approach to project work. Like the other dimensions, social analysis should begin at the outset of project identification and continue through each stage of the project cycle. The World Bank has for many years taken some account of social issues in its project work. But it has only recently come to recognize the importance of doing so systematically for all people-oriented projects—which constitute a large proportion of its portfolio—and of including sociologists on the interdisciplinary teams working on these projects.

The Bank is, therefore, still in the process of devising appropriate techniques for social analysis and of learning from the consequences of the earlier lack of attention. This chapter, accordingly, relies more on anecdotal evidence from Bank-assisted projects than do most of the others. But enough experience has been gained to confirm the importance of social analysis. A recent review of evaluation reports for fifty-seven Bank-assisted projects—purposively selected for the quality, detail, and depth of material on social issues in the reports—found that failures or disappointing results were often attributable to neglect of the social environment.[1] Conversely,

1. Conrad Kottak, "When People Don't Come First: Some Sociological Lessons from Completed Projects," in Michael Cernea, ed., *Putting People First: Sociological Variables in Development Projects* (New York: Oxford University Press for the World Bank, forthcoming). This chapter draws extensively on Kottak's article.

a deliberate effort to take that environment into account clearly contributed to project success. Moreover, the economic rate of return of the thirty projects found to be compatible with the social environment was more than twice that of the others.

ELEMENTS OF SOCIAL ANALYSIS

Social analysis makes it possible to test the validity of planners' assumptions about social conditions and adjust them as necessary, to express project goals in terms that have meaning for both the project population and the implementing agencies, and to design practicable ways of achieving those goals that depend on social change. More concretely, social analysis focuses on four principal areas:

- The sociocultural and demographic characteristics of the project population—its size and social structure, including ethnic, tribal, and class composition
- The way in which the project population has organized itself to carry out productive activities, including the structure of households and families, availability of labor, ownership of land, and access to and control of resources
- The project's cultural acceptability; that is, its capacity both for adapting to and for bringing about desirable changes in people's behavior and in how they perceive their needs
- The strategy necessary to elicit commitment from the project population and to ensure their sustained participation from design through to successful implementation, operation, and maintenance.

Sociocultural and Demographic Characteristics

The first step in social analysis is to identify the project population, its size, and its composition. As we have seen earlier, the point of departure for initial project design is often the choice of a technology for, say, irrigation or road construction. But planners must focus even at this early stage on the characteristics of the project population lest faulty assumptions about that population lead to serious—and often costly—mistakes in project design. Since the way of life of those to be served by a project often differs considerably from that of the planners, the risk is high that the project will prove inappropriate to local social conditions unless the planners make a conscientious effort to avoid such mistakes.

For example, it is frequently assumed that the project population is homogeneous. In fact, it is almost always diverse and stratified with respect to wealth, influence, ethnic identity, occupation, educational level, family system, and mobility. If account is taken of these diversities, project components can be designed to meet the specific needs of different segments of the population. Identifying disadvantaged or minority groups may require a special effort if project designers are unfamiliar with the local situation. Interviewing a few local leaders or spokesmen about conditions in the project area is unlikely to be sufficient, since the views of some of the poorest members of the target population, such as the landless, may not be represented. Other techniques are needed to reach those who are least accessible.[2]

Arriving at correct assumptions about household composition, both urban and rural, may also require a special effort. In urban projects, for example, planners have sometimes incorrectly assumed that households are composed of isolated, nuclear families that have largely severed their ties to the extended social networks that play such an important role in rural areas. In fact, poor urban households are often fluctuating social coalitions, the membership of which varies with changes in the economic and political environment. Children move from one household to another to gain access to educational opportunities, family members move from poorer to better-off households, and people from rural areas move in with relatives in the city while seeking work. These fluctuations require housing that can be adapted to changing household composition.[3]

A low-cost urban housing scheme in Indonesia, for example, was designed on the assumption that the households of the intended beneficiaries were organized as nuclear families; in fact, the households were structured as extended families, and these families lost out to middle-class groups for whom the shelter units were more appropriate. A rural settlement project in Senegal assumed erroneously that nuclear families would settle on small family farms in the project area; again, the unit of social organization proved to be the extended family. But in the second case, the project population was given scope to use project resources in its own way. The early settlers took advantage of this flexibility to have other members of their extended families join them, thus reestablishing their kinship networks in the new area. In the end, twice as many individuals were located on the project land as had been estimated, and the economic return was very favorable.

Designing facilities for extended, as distinct from nuclear, families when appropriate also makes possible more realistic projections of the capacity of beneficiaries to pay for services and to mobilize resources for investment. Many urban households receive a significant portion of their income through transfers from relatives, friends, or neighbors. In this way, informal social security networks have been developed to maintain a basic level of consumption and to ensure access to resources in times of crisis.[4]

Consideration of sociocultural and demographic characteristics is essential when a project requires resettlement of people. Involuntary resettlement creates special social problems: it engenders feelings of

2. Several field techniques known collectively as "rapid rural appraisal" provide discriminating, cost-effective approaches to the diagnosis of rural poverty. See Robert Chambers, "Shortcut Methods in Social Information Gathering for Rural Development Projects," in Cernea, ed., *Putting People First.*

3. Michael Bamberger and Scott Parris, "The Structure of Social Networks in the Zona Sur Oriental of Cartagena," World Bank Water Supply and Urban Development Department Discussion Paper no. 50 (Washington, D.C., 1984).

4. Daniel Kaufman and David L. Lindauer, *Income Transfers within Extended Families to Meet Basic Needs: The Evidence from El Salvador,* World Bank Staff Working Paper no. 644 (Washington, D.C., 1984).

helplessness and alienation and tends to reduce social cohesion and the potential for productive group action. Design of resettlement components—including the type of dwellings, compensation for those displaced, and creation of substitute employment—should seek to ensure that those resettled will be no worse off, and if possible better off, than before. When adequate attention has been paid to these considerations during the design stage, the conclusion has in some cases been that, in view of the resulting cost estimates or the administrative requirements, the project should be scaled down or abandoned. In most cases, however, if resettlement is carefully planned and implemented, its cost can be borne without jeopardizing the economic viability of the project. Positive examples include the Accra-Tema water supply project in Ghana, the Itumbiara and Sobradinho hydroelectric projects in Brazil, and the Ban Chao Nen hydroelectric project in Thailand.

Social analysis is especially necessary—and the task especially difficult—when tribal societies are relocated or otherwise affected; the risk of project failure and the social costs are very high. In the absence of special precautions, tribal societies have been destroyed or, at the least, severely disrupted and their members reduced to destitution.

Social Organization of Productive Activities

Most project populations, particularly in rural areas, have organized themselves for productive activities in ways that reflect available resources and constraints. Most fundamental are the rights relating to ownership and use of land and water. Other arrangements include individual and communal ways of managing resources during the annual production cycle, access to capital, availability of labor during the different seasons, ways of organizing work units, division of labor and rewards, types of local productive associations, relations with commercial and government institutions, and access to government services. Whatever their limitations, these arrangements must be understood; they provide the foundation on which a project must be built.

Tenure arrangements for land, water, forest, and pasture—the mix of ownership, user rights, and control—are an important even if invisible aspect of the social organization of productive activities. If a project design team makes field surveys in the dry season, it may learn little about the full annual cycle of local land and water resource management. In a project in Indonesia, 2,500 cattle were placed on hills believed to be no longer devoted to grazing. Project costs rose steeply in the wet season when local farmers drove an additional 5,000 cattle up onto the hills. It had been overlooked that farmers grazed their cattle on rice stubble in the plains during the dry season but moved them to the hills when the rains began and the plains were planted with rice.

Ignorance of local land and water use practices, individual or communal, not only adds to a project's cost but can lead to its failure. In several forestry projects, trees were planted on what was believed to be public land. But the land was locally recognized as communal, and the local population pulled up the trees so they could resume their previous use of the land. Similarly, a cattle ranching project in Madagascar was located on land regarded by the implementing agency as government property, but which included within its boundaries areas long used for communal grazing; thousands of local inhabitants soon began to tear down fences, burn pasture, and steal the project's cattle to clear their ancestral lands. If irrigation projects are to reach all of the intended beneficiaries, the existing pattern of landownership and water use, and even the structure of political power and influence in the community, have to be studied, and in some cases new ways devised of organizing farmers to secure their access to water.

Another frequent misapprehension concerns how farming is organized and carried out. In particular, the amount of seasonal labor that could be made available for project purposes has often been seriously overestimated; sound estimates require a realistic assessment of population density, seasonal migration, and the timing of peak labor demands. Farmers in India could not take advantage of the new crops promoted by an agricultural development project because the peak labor demand conflicted with that of the rice harvest. Similarly, in a sizable number of Bank-assisted agricultural projects in tropical Africa, farmers could not adopt the recommended double-cropping because population density in the project area was low, and therefore labor was too scarce. Road-building projects in rural areas have often been delayed when construction during the dry season coincided with the peak use of labor in farming activities.

People behave rationally within their own systems of material incentives and social organization. These can often be modified in the course of development, but project designers must take into account and accommodate the initial conditions. A settlement scheme to transform Afar pastoralists in Ethiopia into sedentary cultivators ignored their system of positive and negative incentives, including their traditional land rights, their long experience in communal grazing but lack of experience in family farming, their probable reaction to the contemplated change, and their independence; consequently, the project had to be canceled and a new one planned. By reinforcing positive incentives and building on existing forms of social organization when they are effective, simple social design features can hold down project costs and facilitate the process of social change.

Cultural Acceptability

For a project affecting large numbers of people to succeed, those people must understand and agree to its various features. Design and implementation arrangements must, therefore, take account of the population's values, customs, beliefs, perceived needs, and goals. This may require particular care to ensure that the role of women is adequately considered, as discussed later in this chapter.

Forecasts of project results have often been unduly optimistic because planners overestimated the extent to which the intended beneficiaries appreciated the aims of the project and recognized its relevance to their needs.[5] National goals may be too far removed from the daily concerns

5. Heli Perrett and Francis J. Lethem, *Human Factors in Project Work*, World Bank Staff Working Paper no. 397 (Washington, D.C., 1980).

of the local populace to attract their support, or the two may conflict: hillsides may be deforested in the search for fuel or a communal range overgrazed by individual herdsmen. The likelihood of project failure is compounded when people find the goals of a project inimical to their way of life. Thus, the abstract aims of a livestock project in Papua New Guinea, "development of individual initiative" and "evolution of private land rights," were not only remote from but also incompatible with the local pastoral system of widespread kinship groups and communal grazing lands. Social analysis might have suggested a design that, by building on local experience and practice, would have linked project objectives and broad national goals to the personal goals of the project population.

One of the most prominent areas in which cultural attitudes may affect the attainment of national (and project) goals is that of family planning. As noted in chapter 10, Population, Health, and Nutrition, the benefits of family planning may accrue to the nation before they are realized by the individual family. Social analysis can increase planners' sensitivity to the existence of or potential for important differences between private and collective goals so that information and incentive programs can be devised to modify attitudes and encourage a positive response. The first Bank-assisted population project in Jamaica was designed to implement the official policy of slowing population growth. The response of individual poor Jamaicans, however, was influenced by their perception that significantly greater respect was accorded to women who were mothers, their belief that having children enhanced the stability of informal unions, and their association of fatherhood with virility. Once the problem was correctly identified, the second population project in Jamaica incorporated an information, education, and communication program that emphasized the advantages to be realized through smaller family size.

Poverty, through its influence on customs and practices, can undermine programs to reduce family size. An experimental project in India was designed to persuade parents that, by having fewer children, those children they did have would be better fed and more likely to survive and thus to provide security for them in their old age. Supplementary food was supplied only for children below the age of two; project planners expected that the greater weight and better health of these children would be apparent. Yet, because so little food was otherwise available, most mothers did not reserve the supplementary supply for children in the target age group but divided it among all their children. There was, therefore, no measurable improvement in the condition of the youngest. Designers of a subsequent phase of the project made food supplements available to all children of family planning acceptors as well as to any severely malnourished child.

Health is another area in which project results may be contingent on the ability of people to appreciate the connection between the project and its intended benefits. In a Guatemalan village, gastrointestinal diseases related to contamination of the water supply were among the chief causes of death, particularly of infants. Most villagers believed that if water looked clean, its quality was good. Three latrine-building projects accomplished little in the way of reducing disease. When villagers finally did show interest in latrine facilities, it was not out of concern for sanitation; rather, they wanted privacy and the convenience of having facilities close by. Taking advantage of the interest expressed, the implementing agency responded by letting the villagers, through their leaders, select the type of latrine to be constructed and decide where to place the demonstration model. Instead of importing a model, one was built by local carpenters using local materials. Thereafter, meetings were held with villagers and pamphlets distributed to explain how use of a latrine could protect the water supply. At the time the project was studied, it was too early to determine whether this effort would succeed, but the outlook had become more favorable.[6]

Eliciting Commitment

In the preceding sections we have seen how the demographic and other characteristics of the target population, their forms of social organization, and their cultural attitudes influence the process of social change and hence the outcome of development projects. An additional and closely related condition for success is to find means to enlist the commitment, support, and active participation of the target population and, in doing so, to build up the capacity of local people and their organizations to operate and maintain the project.

Participation

The Guatemalan latrine project mentioned earlier illustrates how active involvement of the intended beneficiaries may improve the prospects of a project. Such participation is very important in projects that seek to bring about social change; people must be convinced that the risks of change are worth taking and that a sustained effort to reach the project's goals is worthwhile. Participation can—and should—characterize all stages of the project cycle. It can assume a variety of forms, such as giving advice on selecting and planning investments, contributing labor, materials, or cash, and monitoring project execution. When intended beneficiaries participate actively, they increase the chance that they will benefit from the project on their own terms. Such participation also enables the project authorities to extend the benefits to more people for the same expenditure of funds.

Consultation before taking steps that affect people's lives helps to forestall or minimize opposition, mobilize support, and increase the positive impact and sustainability of projects. As noted earlier, farmers are a source of much relevant information for project design, from production patterns and market conditions to environmental aspects. Small diversion dams constructed in the Philippines, Mexico, Nepal, and elsewhere without the benefit of farmers' advice and experience with local soil and flooding conditions have sometimes washed out.[7] In the Philippines, to avoid such costly consequences, staff of the National

6. Mary Elmendorf and Patricia Buckles, *Sociocultural Aspects of Water Supply and Excreta Disposal*, Appropriate Technology for Water Supply and Sanitation Series, vol. 5 (Washington, D.C.: The World Bank, 1980).

7. Norman Uphoff, "Participation in Development Initiatives: Fitting Projects to People," in Cernea, ed., *Putting People First*.

Irrigation Administration responsible for communal irrigation projects now walk the fields and ditches with farmers in an iterative process of design, consultation, and redesign. Moreover, provincial irrigation staff—engineers and community organizers—and farmers from communal irrigation projects attend training sessions together. These procedures not only mobilize support, they also provide an occasion for people in the community to raise questions and for project staff to deal with them.

Few projects have put as much effort into studying the conditions, constraints, and results of local participation as the Programa Integral para el Desarrollo Rural, or PIDER, a program established in Mexico to channel resources into low-income, underdeveloped rural areas. A methodological study based on work with more than 9,000 communities with some 12 million inhabitants states:

> Without active participation of beneficiaries, projects in the communities do not achieve planned objectives and targets and, in the best of cases, operate poorly. In addition to being a waste of available resources, such poor results cause the communities to become discouraged and to lose interest and confidence in the efforts of government agencies to benefit them. Community passivity also compromises the objectives of PIDER: if beneficiaries are not involved in projects, the program will do no more than build works and will make no contribution to promoting the self-sustaining development required to ensure that community members attain a more decent standard of living.[8]

In the first stage of PIDER, there was greater participation in building and maintaining roads, activities which were introduced with the help of village committees, than in installing and maintaining water supply systems, which were introduced unilaterally by a government agency. The consequences of the difference in approach were recognized by the agency; as a result, in the second stage of the program, the agency drew heavily on the experience gained in the road projects and worked to elicit interest and participation in water supply construction and maintenance. Both project staff and beneficiaries were given practical orientation and training either separately or jointly.

Project staff and beneficiaries can learn much from each other. Benefits have been lost or costs increased when project designers have underestimated the technical capacity of local people. The Bank's appraisal team for the first irrigation project in Burma concluded that large central maintenance shops should be established for pump repairs. Not until the project was under way did the highly developed skills of the local mechanics become apparent. Farmers were patronizing these mechanics, at much less cost to themselves, rather than the more distant and expensive central maintenance shops. In contrast, the appraisal missions

---

8. "Lineamientos metodológicos para el programa de apoyo a la participación de la comunidad rural" (Mexico D.F., Mexico: Secretaría de Programación y Presupuesto, Dirección General de Desarrollo Rural Integral, January 1982), quoted in Michael Cernea, *A Social Methodology for Community Participation in Local Investments: The Experience of Mexico's PIDER Program*, World Bank Staff Working Paper no. 598 (Washington, D.C., 1983), p. 85. Material on PIDER in this chapter is drawn primarily from this paper.

for road maintenance projects in Liberia and Madagascar did address the question of local capacity. They found that, while it would be necessary to make provision for materials and supervision, the requisite maintenance skills were widely available locally.[9]

It is advisable to discuss with community representatives the terms for participation to make sure that these are acceptable and not regarded as inflexible or coercive. In the PIDER program, villagers' contributions, which vary with the type of project, are negotiated at an early stage during planning meetings. Participants are told how the proposed amount and nature of their contribution were determined, what public resources are available, and how these resources compare with the need. The importance of community cost-sharing to increase the impact of the government investment is stressed. Once agreement is reached, the intended beneficiaries sign a contract with the government setting out the obligations that each side has undertaken. This formalization of community and government obligations extends the consultation process to a more concrete kind of participation and is a step toward institutionalizing the participatory approach.

Participation of the local community in mobilizing resources and helping with the work is sometimes carried even further through what is called assisted self-reliance. Local groups are encouraged to exercise autonomy in using resources, with the government providing technical assistance, training, and supervision. An effective rural water supply program, based on assisted self-reliance, has been developed in Malawi.[10] Given the large gap that usually exists between resource availability and development needs, this approach can greatly reinforce development efforts. Some governments, however, have been reluctant to adopt this approach out of a concern that local organizations will become too independent or powerful and may even become targets for or channels of dissidence, especially in remote regions or among minority groups. It is nonetheless desirable that the leaders of the local community be involved and their support ensured, whatever the risk that they may co-opt project ideas and benefits and thereby compromise the participatory approach. Since it is difficult in practice to bypass community leaders, it is more sensible to emphasize their accountability to the local population than to attempt to ignore them.

Planning for participation is, of course, easier than achieving it, especially in stratified societies. Among the many constraints are the size of the country's bureaucracy and its resistance to innovation, the likelihood that local vested interests will be reluctant to share authority, and the absence or inexperience of local community-based organizations. Designers of a rural development project in Nepal expected that planning would be carried out at the district level, but that did not happen. Instead, decisions were made in or directed from Kathmandu; local officials and the intended beneficiaries had little opportunity to propose changes. Owing to the centralized and inflexible administration, project implemen-

9. Cynthia Cook, "Social Analysis of Rural Roads Projects," in Cernea, ed., *Putting People First*.

10. Colin Glennie, *A Model for the Development of a Self-Help Water Supply Program*, World Bank Technical Paper no. 2 (Washington, D.C., 1982).

tation was long delayed.[11] In contrast, a rural development program in Colombia gave local committees the authority to make routine decisions; in addition, the provincial representative of the national planning office could authorize any adjustments to programs and budgets that were requested by beneficiaries and endorsed by their local committees.

Project monitoring and evaluation are usually considered management tools. Nevertheless, beneficiaries can play a role in these aspects of project work as well, although there is likely to be considerable resistance on the part of both technical agencies and the local power structure to this approach. In the PIDER program, the monitoring system has not yet been fully developed, but a review of the experience in the state of Guerrero suggests that participation of community representatives in informal monitoring has been effective; moreover, communities are increasingly being given formal monitoring rights to assist them in carrying out this function. Beneficiaries, being on the spot, are well situated to check on construction and equipment delivery, to determine whether reports of performance by technical agencies are accurate, and to suggest ways of dealing with problems.

Building Local Capacity

An effective strategy for strengthening the capacity of people, particularly the poor, to participate in the development process often depends on their having an association through which to define, declare, and promote their interests. In the early years of an integrated rural development project in Ghana, there were only three farmers on the project's thirteen-member decisionmaking board, with the result that little consideration was given to farmers' concerns. Subsequent establishment of forty-two farmers' committees gave farmers a voice in decisionmaking and led to their extensive participation in the project. Among other things, service center facilities were built by farmers themselves rather than by contractors, as originally planned. Thus, participation increased the farmers' capacity to undertake development efforts on their own.

Organizational and technical capacity expands with experience. These skills are likely to grow slowly at first, and short-term costs may be high; but progress often accelerates later, with economies realized over the long term. In irrigation projects, where development has traditionally focused on technical design and construction, there have often been long periods of inefficient operation while water management skills slowly improved. To avoid this, the National Irrigation Administration in the Philippines employs community organizers to strengthen water users' associations before irrigation systems are built and to involve them in the planning and construction stages. The result is that the irrigation systems are meeting local needs more rapidly since users' associations are competent to assist in water allocation as soon as the physical structures are completed. Moreover, development of organizational capacity has been integrated with technical training to prepare the farmers' groups for a series of tasks associated with operating and maintaining the system.

11. Uphoff, "Participation in Development Initiatives."

Because building local institutional capacity is a slow and difficult process, the presumption is in favor of relying on existing organizations. A weak organization can usually be strengthened by staff training and other measures; the very fact that it has persisted suggests that it may be serving a local need and has acquired some credibility. A recent review of Bank-assisted irrigation projects found that newly formed cooperatives and associations tended to perform badly, while already existing groups proved more effective. Tertiary canals in Korea, the Philippines, and Peru have been well managed by local water users' associations, which were small, were linked with extension activities, followed clear rules of operation, and had strong leadership. In projects where the irrigation system was more complex, it was necessary to strengthen the associations and to provide closer links with extension activities, as well as to formulate the rules of operation more precisely. The review also found that when new users' associations had been formed without any attempt at building their organizational and technical capacity, they existed mainly on paper. The consequence was poorly maintained tertiary canals and inequitable water distribution, with water shortages for many downstream farmers.

When an existing organization is assigned new functions, it is advisable that these functions be as similar as possible to those it has performed in the past and that they not be expanded too rapidly. The communal water users' groups in the Philippines, for example, moved gradually from learning how to work closely with technicians, to providing advice on location and types of water structures, to checking and auditing construction expenditures, procurement, and quality of materials, to inspecting construction, to learning how to operate and maintain the system, to training in water management.

Although it is generally advantageous to rely on an established local organization, that does not mean that a new group cannot be successful; all existing groups were once new. The likelihood of success will depend, among other things, on whether the new group meets a real need, on the quality of training provided to its members and staff, and on the establishment of a realistic time frame for building its capacity. In Benin, growers initially sold their cotton through an arrangement that provided opportunities for purchasing agents to tamper with weights and prices on the cotton received, taking advantage of the fact that most growers could not read. The project managers, therefore, organized informal associations of growers and offered them literacy programs and training in cotton weighing. During the first year, half the crop was weighed and recorded by association representatives; the associations also purchased cottonseed and maintained credit accounts for their members. Some associations later organized the production and sale of marketable household goods and were able to invest in rural community facilities such as schools and wells.

Similarly, in an education project in Burkina, special village councils were elected to guide the training of illiterate and semiliterate youths. During project implementation, the councils provided a check on possible misappropriation of funds and made loans for inputs; they also assisted in acquisition of land, construction of buildings, and recruitment of pupils. Villagers' interest in the program was encouraged by this participation of councils responsible to them. But the councils were not doing what they had been set up to do: influence the curriculum. Gradually, however, as they learned what they were expected to do and how to do it and as they gained experience in exercising influence, they became more confident and took on this task as well.

ROLE OF WOMEN IN DEVELOPMENT

For the most part, we have been discussing people in this book as though there were no differences in gender when it comes to participating in projects and sharing in their benefits. It is important to recognize, however, that women have not been equal partners in the process of economic development, although they constitute half the world's population. Development planning has tended to ignore women's interests and needs; certainly it has often failed to deal with them adequately or systematically. Many types of projects, if they are to succeed, cannot afford to be blind to the differing roles of men and women.

The principle of equity argues strongly for considering, at the stage of project design, whether and how the project may affect women and for expressly seeking to improve women's status or, at the very least, for ensuring that the project will not affect them adversely. Only recently has it been understood that there is also a high economic cost to society in failing to use effectively the resources that women represent. The equity and economic arguments go hand in hand and are mutually reinforcing.

The contribution of women to economic activity is already substantial, although by and large undervalued. Women provide an estimated 50 to 80 percent of agricultural labor, depending on the region: they produce most of the subsistence food and often help to produce cash crops. In farm families, more women than men do agricultural work, and it is common for them to work more hours a week. Women participate in production, harvesting, marketing, and storage; in some societies, they carry out all agricultural functions except initial land clearing and heavy plowing. Whatever cash income they earn, whether by selling food crops or by working in the informal sector in cities, supplements the family budget.

Women also perform many of the activities that affect a family's health: they prepare and allocate food, inculcate sanitation and hygiene habits, and provide initial medical care. Educating girls may, therefore, be one of the best investments a country can make in future economic growth and welfare—even if they never enter the labor market. The inverse correlation between women's education and fertility has been commented upon previously (chapter 10, Population, Health and Nutrition): as women become better educated, health and nutrition practices improve, infant morbidity and mortality decline, marriage and childbirth are delayed, and birth rates fall. Preferences for smaller families emerge and women are more receptive to family planning. This is particularly true when girls remain in school beyond the primary level. It is shortsighted, inefficient, and wasteful of both human and capital resources to ignore women's capacities and to miss opportunities for enhancing their productivity and enabling them to contribute as fully as possible to economic growth.

Constraints on the Role of Women

Implicit in the tendency to overlook the role of women has been the assumption that social change will automatically benefit them. Often this is not the case. Although the particulars differ from country to country, women in developing countries are subject to constraints different in kind and degree from those applicable to men.

Education

Despite the importance of expanding educational opportunities for females, they are, on the whole, less educated than males, as table 22-1 shows. More boys than girls attend school, and even when female enrollment is relatively high, the percentage of girls completing school tends to be much lower than it is for boys—only half as much in some countries. Girls' access to schooling is limited for a variety of reasons: parents perceive less immediate, or even negative, economic returns from educating daughters and cannot afford what they consider the luxury of sending them to school; girls are required to help in the household or to perform agricultural tasks; schools are too few or too distant; the culture precludes male instructors for female students, but there are too few female teachers. Girls' potential for gainful employment is further re-

Table 22-1. *School Enrollment*

	Ratio of adult male to adult female literacy, 1980	Number enrolled in secondary school as percentage of age group, 1981		Percentage aged 15–49 ever enrolled in primary school, 1980	
		Male	Female	Male	Female
Low-income economies					
Burma	1.4	..	..	..	..
India	1.9[a]	39[a]	20[a]	84	48
Rwanda	1.6	3	1	75	49
Burundi	1.6	4	2	32	14
Sri Lanka	1.1[a]	49	54	100	92
Kenya	1.7	23	15[a]	74	48
Afghanistan	5.5	17	4	..	..
Lower middle-income economies					
Ivory Coast	1.9	25	9	..	..
Guatemala	..	17[a]	15[a]	57	46
Turkey	1.6	57	28	100	77
Upper middle-income economies					
Korea	..	89	80	100	97
Panama	1.0	60	69	100	99
Mexico	1.1	54	49	97	92
Singapore	1.2	65	65	100	100

Note: Countries are listed in ascending order of 1982 income per capita, except that GNP per capita cannot be calculated for Afghanistan.

.. Not available.

a. For years other than specified.

Source: World Bank, *World Development Report 1984* (New York: Oxford University Press, 1984), Population Data Supplement, table 5.

duced by school programs or training limited to traditional women's occupations such as handicrafts and gardening. Too often girls are not offered courses in science, accounting, or other fields that would equip them for work in the modern sector.

Command over Resources

Women's access to productive resources and to services, like their access to education, is frequently more limited than that of men. Their mobility may be constrained by economic considerations, by demands of household and child care, or by custom. In addition, they often face legal restrictions. Generally, women do not own pledgeable assets and so are ineligible for formal credit, and their husbands or male kin may be reluctant to borrow on their behalf. Women's access to other types of productive resources may be impeded by law, which may prevent them from holding title to land; by custom, which may allow them to use land only with the permission of male family members; or by their limited literacy and numeracy and lack of skills and training.

Location of facilities is often a critical determinant of women's use of them. Limited mobility may preclude women from using distant health centers, even if there are no other constraints, such as cost or lack of female personnel. The placing of standpipes may make the difference between women using them or not. The same may be true of sanitary facilities if, for example, they are located—for reasons of economy—outside the compounds where families live and if women, by social custom, are not allowed to leave the compound after dark. Women who are household heads are often discouraged from applying for urban housing if it is not located close enough to their place of work.

Other Constraints

Time itself, or rather its insufficiency, may be a serious constraint. This is especially true in rural areas, where agricultural tasks and household duties—cleaning, preparing food, gathering fuel, collecting water, and caring for children—combine to produce the typical "double work day" of women throughout the developing world. On the average, 80 to 90 percent of the time spent carrying water and fuel and gathering crops from the fields is accounted for by women. This phenomenon is not confined to rural areas, however. From an early age, girls—whatever the setting—devote more time to family and household activities than do boys.

The commercialization of agriculture may increase, rather than ease, the work load borne by women. Cash crops are usually the province of men. Expansion of cash crop acreage may add to family income, but it will often mean that women must assist their husbands while still expending their own unpaid labor on subsistence crops. Women will not necessarily be compensated for their cash crop labor; even when they have performed such tasks as seedbed preparation and transplanting, all of the sales income may go to the men. In many places where women work alongside men as day laborers, their earnings are paid to the men; even if this is prohibited by law, they are usually paid at a lower rate.

Extension services tend to be biased toward serving men and make little or no effort to address women. Under a project in the Bolivian Altiplano, where women have responsibility for livestock, training in livestock care was nevertheless given to the men, who passed the information on to their wives with inevitable and costly omissions. To further complicate the situation, in some cultures women may not take part in any public gathering or meet with men outside their households; unless specific provision is made for female extension agents, women will have no access to the services. This may also prevent them from benefiting from credit programs when information about these programs is disseminated through the extension service. Similarly, women may not avail themselves of health services if the health center staff are male. Thus, selection of an inappropriate channel for information or service may frustrate project implementation or make it less effective.

Not only do men have preferential access to training and extension services in agriculture, but on-the-job training and job upgrading activities in industry are generally designed for male workers, on the assumption that men will not waste the training by leaving the labor market. This ignores the extensive migration of male labor abroad from some countries, as well as the fact that there are many households in both urban and rural areas in which women are the primary income earners. Male migration leaves behind women who frequently are ill-prepared to take over the jobs previously performed by men, whose productivity in the new tasks is limited by the factors mentioned above, and who must incorporate the additional tasks into an already overcrowded day.

Approaches to Project Design

If these constraints on the participation of women in the development process are to be relieved, project designers must acquaint themselves with the extent to which relevant activities of the project population are gender-specific: what is done by each sex, how, when, and why. They should also consider whether there are any potential impediments—cultural, legal, physical, or financial—to the participation of women in project activities or to their enjoyment of its benefits. In conducting this enquiry, account must be taken of regional and country variations. For instance, in Senegal, women are responsible for cultivation of swamp rice; in Sierra Leone, men are responsible, while women cultivate upland rice. With such information, it should be possible to avoid designing projects that rest on misconceptions about male and female roles and to make provision, where appropriate, for training both sexes.

Much of what women do is invisible in the sense that economic statistics take no account of it. This is true especially of self-employment and uncompensated family work, whether in the agricultural sector or the informal urban labor market. Women themselves, therefore, are likely to be the best source of information concerning their practices, preferences, and needs. By consulting and involving women at the planning stage and determining their probable reactions as participants or beneficiaries, planners should be able to avoid a negative or counterproductive result and to enhance women's understanding of, and commitment to, project objectives. For some tasks women may be more productive than men. In rubber plantation projects in the Ivory Coast, for example, women were found to be better tappers than the average male; since output was suffering from high turnover among the labor force of single males, a deliberate policy of recruiting and training couples was introduced. Yet project designers have more often than not thought of the farmer as "he," and have ignored the traditional division of labor according to tasks or crops between men and women.

It is often simple to accommodate a project's design to the respective roles, tasks, and circumstances of men and women. Sometimes, a better definition is all that is needed, as illustrated in the El Salvador sites and services project described below in the section on "Applying Social Analysis." When, on the assumption that household heads are male, a sites and services project requires an in-kind contribution in the form of construction labor, urban families headed by women are likely to be disqualified. A rural development project in Senegal defined "family" as a man and all his wives, and allocated one farm plot to each family. Applications from wives living in separate households were accordingly rejected until the selection criteria were modified.

Technological Change

Improved technology—such as the introduction of better planting materials, fertilizers, and pest and disease controls—has generally been applied to those parts of the agricultural cycle for which men are responsible, while traditional methods are retained for those processes such as weeding and harvesting that are done by women. Unless this disparity is specifically addressed, the potential of new technology to increase yields may be offset by slow procedures in the women's part of the work. In a smallholder project in Zaire, new technologies reduced the input of labor per ton of maize in preharvest operations but created a bottleneck in harvest and postharvest processing, which tended to be done by women using traditional methods.

If new technologies are applied to predominantly female activities without being carefully designed, women's situation—far from improving—may be altered for the worse as the higher status conferred on the work leads to its being taken over by men. When tractors were first introduced into India, it was the males in the family who were taught to drive them; the tractors displaced women in some of the activities for which they had been responsible. When modern laundries were installed in connection with a Bank-assisted tourism project in Mexico, men were employed to operate the facilities; the women who had washed and ironed tourists' laundry by hand lost their livelihood. Throughout the developing world, products hand-made by women at home are being replaced by products made in factories by a predominantly male labor force. ("Offshore" industries owned by multinational corporations and manufacturing for export are an exception: their labor force is often made up mostly of women, and one criterion for their location appears to be the availability of a pool of unskilled, cheap, docile female labor.) Given their characteristically low level of education and lack of skills, the displaced women cannot readily find other work. They need to be given training in the modern tools or machinery used under the project or else trained for substitute employment.

Project experience demonstrates the importance of designing equipment and tools that women are willing and able to use. Efforts in several countries to introduce improved stoves under Bank-assisted projects have been unsuccessful; although the stoves used fuel efficiently, they did not satisfy women's requirements. Recent forestry projects, including several in India and Nepal, use male and female extension agents to develop, adapt, and demonstrate these improved stoves, in association with village women.

Need for Incentives

It was noted above that women in developing countries have little, if any, spare time. That being so, even when a project takes specific account of women, they may prove unreceptive or unable to find the time to avail themselves of proffered training or to put into practice what they have been taught. It may be necessary to provide an incentive for them to participate; adding to their income or that of their family is particularly effective. For example, to induce women to assist with cash crops, an irrigation and land settlement project in Kenya required that some of the income from cash crop sales be paid directly to the farm wife. Alternatively, the incentive may take the form of a labor-saving or efficiency-promoting feature, such as providing improved tools and equipment to facilitate and shorten the time consumed by women's traditional tasks. Rural development projects in the Yemen Arab Republic, a country that has experienced heavy male emigration, include provision of labor-saving technologies for women's traditional activities to release time for farm work. Population and family planning projects in Bangladesh offer women vocational training and employment opportunities as well as improved health care and family planning services. They seek to raise women's socioeconomic status, thus making them less dependent on the labor of their children and more receptive to the idea of limiting the size of their family.

Access to Services

Project design may have to give explicit attention to providing access for females. In Bangladesh, where women's mobility is constrained by the cultural prescriptions of purdah, a rural development project established cooperatives of poor women and provided them with collective credit and advice on economic activities. Since parents are often unwilling to allow their daughters to travel far to school, a project in Jordan (where schools are segregated by sex) has built smaller and more dispersed vocational schools for girls; these are located closer to their homes than would be possible with larger, more centralized facilities. A project in Swaziland uses the criterion that primary school pupils should not walk more than five kilometers to reach their school, thereby making education more accessible to girls.

Competition between schooling and farm work can be reduced by adapting the school calendar to the agricultural cycle, in recognition of demands made on children, including girls, to help in the fields during the planting and harvesting seasons. In Paraguay, the school year was changed so that vacations coincided with periods of maximum demand for agricultural labor. A project in Ecuador provides classes on weekends for girls whose responsibility for animal herding keeps them from school during the week.

Other projects provide training for female teachers when they are needed if girls are to attend school. Curricula can be designed to include courses that help to prepare girls for income-generating employment; this is an incentive for continued attendance and helps to reduce parental resistance by making girls more of an economic asset to the family. Many Bank-assisted rural development projects incorporate training programs which go beyond skill development to literacy, numeracy, and health and nutrition training. Water supply and sanitation projects also provide for health education; many are directed to women in recognition of their crucial role in inculcating better health and sanitation habits in the young.

Specific Components

Projects or components of projects designed specifically for women are often limited in scope and impact. Perhaps more important, they tend to isolate women as a group, depriving them of the opportunity to benefit from or participate actively in those aspects of a larger project which are not gender-specific. For example, a rural development project in Brazil included a social extension component addressed to women, dealing with health, nutrition, and hygiene. As a result, women were excluded, implicitly but effectively, from participation in the project's principal, production-oriented elements. The women's component was later corrected to make it an integral part of the project and relate it to the broader objectives; among other changes, provision was made for joint training of female social extension workers and male agricultural extension agents. The former came to understand the agricultural changes being promoted and were able to explain these to the women. The women then encouraged and assisted their husbands in making the changes, whereas earlier their resistance (owing to lack of understanding) had inhibited attainment of the project's objectives.

A similar experience was noted in the Bolivia rural development project mentioned above. Initially, the women's component was irrelevant to the main objectives of the project; women were excluded from training and from participating in the project's livestock activities, in which they have traditionally had the significant roles of herding and shearing the animals and collecting, washing, and spinning the fleece. The project was later reorganized to promote women's participation and at the same time to train them in health, nutrition, child care, basic literacy, and simple arithmetic. The project includes credit and technical assistance for development of woolen handicrafts, which can generate income during slack periods in the agriculture cycle; women will be trained to produce and market these products as well.

If there is to be a women's component, it is important that it be designed as an integral part of the project from the outset, and that its implementation be carefully monitored. To reach poor women, provision should be made for them to earn additional income, both to finance their participation and as an incentive for them to participate.

Applying Social Analysis

A brief discussion of three Bank-assisted projects, each in a different country and in a sector that has not figured prominently in this chapter, may help to illustrate further how the achievement of specific development objectives, including the integration of women, can be made more effective, and some pitfalls avoided, by application of the principles we have been discussing.

Mexico: Steel

A steel project in Mexico demonstrates that even when a project is not primarily people-oriented, it may encounter serious difficulties if it cannot mobilize and motivate its workers and provide them with adequate community services. Faced with extremely rapid growth of urban centers, the government of Mexico decided to locate a large steel plant in an unpopulated coastal area (Lázaro Cárdenas) rich in iron ore, in the expectation that this might encourage other industries to locate there as well. It was assumed that development of the area would require only the establishment of a strong economic base, and that housing and urban services would come into being without the kind of design and implementation efforts that had been devoted to the steel plant.

As it turned out, however, unskilled workers who came to work in the plant became squatters, while skilled workers and middle management found a dearth of housing, water and sewerage facilities, power infrastructure, and schools. The consequence, during the plant's early years, was an extremely high rate of labor turnover, more than 30 percent annually at all levels. The cost of this turnover, coupled with strong demands from management and technical staff that their personal needs be met, led state agencies to undertake community-building efforts in conjunction with a Bank-assisted regional development project. The effort succeeded: Lázaro Cárdenas was transformed from a frontier settlement into a town with adequate housing and medical, educational, and recreational facilities, and turnover at the plant fell to about 10 percent annually.

Indonesia: Nutrition

When Indonesian officials recognized that high levels of anemia prevailed among adult male workers and contributed to their low productivity, a project was designed to arrest the problem at an early stage by raising the nutritional level of poor rural children through an educational program to change mothers' habits. A pilot project was directed toward some 40,000 households in sixty villages in three provinces. Pregnant or nursing mothers with malnourished children under two years of age were targeted as beneficiaries. A team of nutrition and education specialists was organized at each administrative level, while villagers selected volunteers for training in weighing children and giving practical nutritional advice to mothers. In each province, moreover, an investigating team was trained to determine current nutritional practice through interviews, at which modest changes in food habits were also recommended. In follow-up sessions, mothers' reactions were discussed and recorded for purposes of subsequent training of the volunteers.

Since no funds were available for food distribution, project efforts emphasized close collaboration with mothers to collect and analyze information on nutrition; the advice given could then take into account local differences in diet. An evaluation of the project showed a striking result: infant malnutrition was reduced by 50 percent. It was concluded that the mothers' positive response was related not to their educational level but to their acceptance of advice adapted to local conditions, particularly regarding preparation of weaning foods. The services offered by volunteers at the village level appeared to be more efficient and equitable in reaching rural women than comparable services offered at subdistrict health centers.

The strategy of this project effectively translated a national goal into terms that rural women could understand and act upon through their daily habits. Project staff paid careful attention to the minutiae of everyday life (for example, they changed the measure of ingredients to tablespoons when they learned that the women did not own teaspoons). Although concerned about their children's health, the women did not at first believe they could improve it (or their own health) through recommended nutritional practices, given their meager resources. The periodic weighing of infants, however, convincingly demonstrated the health improvements brought about by such practices; the link was reinforced by posters, radio messages, and other informational material.

El Salvador: Sites and Services

In El Salvador, it was found that only about 40 percent of urban families could afford public housing. A private foundation initiated a housing program supported by the government and the Bank and based on the sites and services approach (see chapter 12, Urbanization). The project had four principal objectives: to demonstrate a viable, low-cost alternative to public housing; to include among the options housing affordable by families with a monthly income of as little as $40 (in 1970 dollars)—which covers about 80 percent of all urban families; to demonstrate that the private sector had a role to play in providing very low-cost housing; and to develop mutual-help groups capable of building housing and establishing community organizations. The government was particularly concerned with the first three objectives; the private foundation was interested in all four; and the project population—initially—was interested only in the second. However, the mutual-help and organization-building features became increasingly important to the participants, both as an immediate benefit and in connection with broader needs that evolved.

The project fashioned a strategy that provided participants—both individuals and groups—with significant incentives that could be used flexibly. The main incentives were made contingent on active participation. Housing costs were substantially reduced through contributions of construction labor on weekends. The requirement of a 10 percent down payment could be avoided, and essential training could be acquired, by joining a mutual-help group. In general, all beneficiary families had to participate in construction. The opportunity cost of providing free labor was very high, however, for families at both extremes of the income spectrum. Weekends were one of the highest earning periods for many skilled workers and small businessmen, while some of the poorest house-holds could not afford to sacrifice whatever they might be able to earn on weekends, however little. Some exceptions were made for those with weekend employment to allow them to pay outsiders to complete the construction. More careful social analysis might have introduced additional flexibility into the organization of work groups as a way of dealing with this problem.

The project also illustrates the importance of planning specifically for the needs of women. The income eligibility test was initially expressed in terms of "earned income." As a consequence, many households in the project area were unable to qualify; they were headed by women, who derived most of their income from nonformal employment, not from wages. Substitution of "total income" as the test opened up the project to this group of intended beneficiaries.

Other components of the project improved the technical and organizational capacity of the participants. As community organizations gained experience, they became confident of their ability to negotiate for government services. The two-way flow of information through a board representing the community helped to keep the project responsive to community needs and preferences and to make the participants aware of resource limitations. The general success of the strategy is evidenced by its results and by the extent of beneficiaries' satisfaction with the project: there was a very low rate of dropout from the program and a very high rate of loan repayment, one of the highest in any Bank-assisted shelter project.[12]

A PROFESSIONAL APPROACH TO SOCIAL ANALYSIS

The examples cited in this chapter have illustrated a variety of situations in which social issues have arisen at different stages of the project cycle. They have shown the need not only to adapt project designs to the traditions and mores of the population to avoid adverse effects, but also to organize and plan ways of mobilizing the energies of people to foster the process of social change. Many of the social aspects of projects prove fairly simple to handle once they are identified and understood. In some cases in which project staff did not do so, it would in fact have been relatively easy to conduct the necessary field investigation—to establish urban and rural household composition or farm size, for example. Investigation of other social conditions, such as seasonal labor availability, subsistence requirements, and land tenure and water arrangements, requires more extensive field observation.

The evidence suggests that professional training and experience in social analysis are very helpful in recognizing potential social problems; in appreciating social issues that would not be apparent to most outsiders—

12. Michael Bamberger and others, *Evaluation of Sites and Services Projects: The Evidence from El Salvador*, World Bank Staff Working Paper no. 549 (Washington, D.C., 1982); and Michael Bamberger and Alberto Deneke, "Can Shelter Programmes Meet Low-income Needs? The Experience of El Salvador" in G. K. Payne, ed., *Low-Income Housing in the Developing World* (New York: Wiley, 1984).

sometimes not even to local people, who are inclined to take familiar patterns for granted and not to appreciate their significance for project design; and in adapting project resources to local conditions once these are identified. Nevertheless, individuals who lack such training or experience but who are sensitive to local conditions, as well as individuals who are familiar with the project population, have done useful work in many projects. When trained specialists are not available, therefore, it is better to build on studies carried out by generalists than to have none at all.

In many projects, however, skilled social analysis could have saved much more than it would have cost. Governments are increasingly recognizing the importance of engaging trained, experienced personnel whose professional skills can help to ensure that projects work effectively with and for people. More sociologists and anthropologists are available in many developing countries than are being employed in project analysis. It is anomalous that livestock departments in agricultural ministries throughout the developing world are staffed with veterinarians to deal with the cattle but lack any professional staff to deal with the owners of the cattle, with the social organization of animal husbandry, or with pastoral populations.[13] It would not be farfetched to conclude that some correlation exists between this situation and the poor performance of livestock projects in many developing countries (see chapter 6, Agriculture).

The project examples reviewed in this chapter demonstrate clearly that effective project design and implementation require bottom-up participation by local people as well as top-down activity by the government.[14] The successful and cost-effective projects cited have mobilized people around one or more of their own goals and trained them to act with greater self-reliance. People's understanding of their situation and their active efforts to improve it are essential conditions for progress. No less essential are adequate funding, knowledge, and the technical and organizational resources of a competent government agency. Development projects must balance these two sometimes conflicting but interdependent requirements. Social analysis can help to provide the link.

Predicting future social behavior is even more uncertain than forecasting financial or economic behavior, and designing effective organizations and approaches for bringing about changes in social behavior is more problematic still. Social analysis can, however, improve both forecasts and project design by applying lessons from comparable projects, backed by the training and broad experience of the analysts. Project planners have repeatedly made unduly optimistic assumptions about the likely outcome of projects by overestimating the local people's interest in a project, their recognition of a need for it, the resources available to them for implementing the project, the economic and social incentives to do so, and the rate at which change in their social condition can take place. By enabling more informed judgments of people's likely responses, social analysis can contribute to better project design and implementation.

13. Michael Cernea, "Sociological Knowledge for Development Projects," in Cernea, ed., *Putting People First.*
14. Uphoff, "Participation in Development Initiatives."

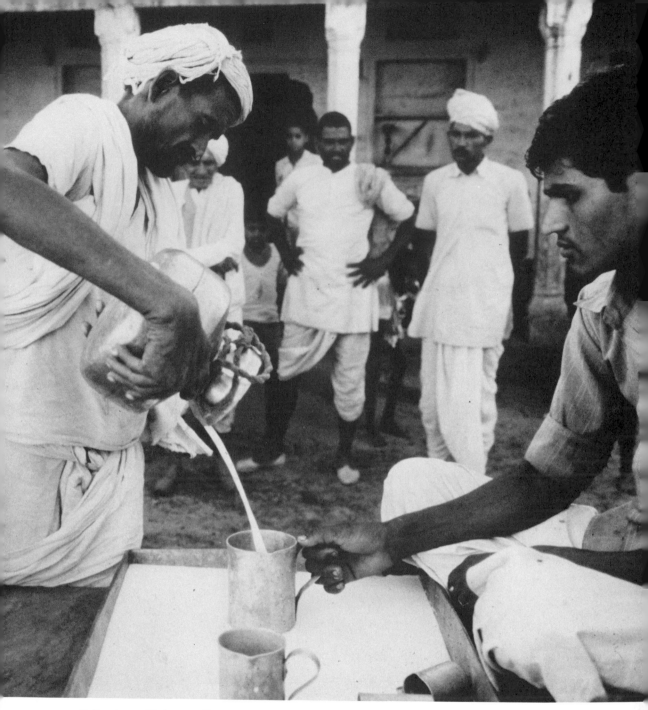

Collecting milk from villagers in dairy cooperative, India

23

Institutional Analysis

THE OUTCOME of development projects is dependent on the quality of the institutions responsible for them. This applies not only to the organizations that implement and operate projects but also to the sector and government institutions that affect project success: ministries, development banks, research organizations, and so on. But institutional development—in the sense of increasing the ability of institutions to set clear development objectives and work effectively with their human, financial, and other resources toward meeting them—is difficult for many developing countries, as is abundantly evident in the sector chapters of part II. Institutions in agriculture, education, health, water and sanitation, and other sectors typically suffer from serious shortages of skilled and experienced staff, an excessive number of untrained staff, overloaded services and facilities, inadequate wages and salaries, and a counterproductive policy environment. These problems are particularly acute in institutions in the public sector, and a large part of this chapter will be devoted to issues of public sector management.

The institutional dimension of project analysis—like the social dimension—has until recently received less attention from development practitioners than the technical, economic, and financial ones. Less is known about what does or does not work in particular circumstances. There is no outside body of established knowledge on which to draw, and there are few reliable and readily transferable institutional models from either developed or other developing countries, especially in circumstances of rapid economic and social change. Developing countries and aid agencies, including the World Bank, have had to invent and adapt institutional solutions to suit conditions that are often very demanding. In some countries—particularly in sub-Saharan Africa—the failures and mistakes threaten to outweigh the lasting successes.

Although about three-quarters of Bank-assisted projects during the past decade have included an investment component for long-term strengthening of project institutions, this component has accounted on the average for only about 2 percent of total project costs. (This estimate excludes projects designed solely to provide technical assistance, in which institutional development, by some definitions, may account for 100 percent of the investment.) The institutional factor is, however, a much more important variable in project success than this low figure suggests. As we have seen in chapter 17, Project Implementation, of the problems that arise in executing Bank-assisted projects, managerial or institutional difficulties (the terms are used interchangeably) are frequently cited as the most important cause. The experience of governments and of other development agencies underscores this finding.

Developing strong institutions, then, is a primary means of ensuring efficient implementation of projects and of safeguarding the hard-won national and international resources committed to them. But the significance of strengthening the institutions associated with an investment transcends the efficient execution of that investment, just as institutional shortcomings in a single project can have serious repercussions well beyond the project itself. Careful attention to the quality of institutional performance in a series of projects can help to build up managerial capacity and hence development potential in an entire industry or sector. In Tunisia, to take one example, a series of Bank-assisted investment projects in water supply and waste disposal have established and supported effective sector institutions with capable staff. These institutions have been able to expand service coverage progressively to the poorest groups while maintaining financial solvency, and they have acquired a capacity for technological innovation in the face of severe physical constraints.

Institutional problems do not, of course, always occur in the same form; they tend to change over time and to differ among sectors as well as countries. Whereas many developing countries were preoccupied two decades ago with putting in place the fairly simple organizations needed for rudimentary productive facilities and services, they now possess institutional structures that are more fully articulated and integrated into the modern economy. These institutions have to respond to more complex technological demands and are more exposed to the broad economic environment.

In developing countries, policymakers and managers alike must strike a balance between applying the generalized lessons of experience (such as this book tries to recount) and devising innovative solutions to suit their unique requirements and problems. That balance is particularly difficult to achieve, and particularly important, in the design and management of development institutions. Nevertheless, some common problems are identifiable across a wide range of countries as well as sectors. Likewise, some general lessons can be drawn from the experience of countries at different stages of development about what to encourage and what to avoid in designing and managing the institutions that are charged with the task of development. This chapter is concerned with sharing these lessons of experience.

The countries that have been most successful in recent decades in establishing strong institutions cover a wide spectrum—Japan, India, and Brazil would be on most lists. Although they still have many institutional shortcomings, these countries have devoted strong and sustained efforts to building up the capacity of their institutions to manage high-priority activities, and all of them have recognized that institutional development entails a lengthy process of experiment and adaptation that does not take place spontaneously, even in response to market forces.

Recently, development projects—and the institutions responsible for them—have become more vulnerable as the international recession has led to a decline in foreign demand for many products and to a shortage of foreign exchange and budgetary resources for investment, operation, or maintenance. Many African countries have experienced a marked deterioration in institutional effectiveness for a combination of these reasons; even their model development institutions are suffering. It is important, therefore, to learn from experience not only what is appropriate for long-term institutional development but also what will benefit hard-pressed managers and projects in the short run.

COMMON PROBLEMS FACING PROJECT INSTITUTIONS

Institutional problems are sometimes identified in superficial terms, which may misdirect the search for solutions. A project in difficulty will be described as having "weak management," while success may be attributed to a "dynamic project manager." Financial control problems are often claimed to be caused by a lack of microcomputers for accounting, while inadequate staff performance is readily ascribed to lack of training.

The solutions proposed for these immediate difficulties, however, are sometimes merely an expensive way of uncovering the next layer of problems. Good managers are indeed essential. But if managers are not, in fact, incompetent but rather faced with conflicting requirements and inadequate authority, then the costly and time-consuming process of replacing them is likely to result in little improvement—and the new managers may leave in frustration in a short time. Likewise, if the real problem is not automation of accounts but instead the flow and accuracy of information, computers are likely to be an expensive diversion, or at best helpful only after other measures have been put in place. In Kenya, for example, the introduction of microcomputers into the Ministry of Agriculture's budgetary procedures has been successful not merely because it enlarged and speeded up processing capacity, but because it was taken as an opportunity by management to redefine the information system itself. As a result, reporting procedures were simplified and accelerated from weeks or months to days, and a system for evaluating more clearly the consequences of different types and levels of expenditure could be installed.

Similarly, lack of training, although doubtless important, may in some circumstances be a minor cause of inadequate staff performance compared with poorly designed tasks and incentives and inadequate opportunities for career development. In any event, the effectiveness of training may often depend on changes in the organization, content, and career prospects of the job to which the trainee is subsequently assigned. Without these changes, an expensive training effort may well be a wasteful investment.

In short, many of the institutional problems commonly encountered in implementing projects have deeper causes, which must be understood before successful long-term solutions can be designed. Many of these difficulties will take decades to overcome, since they reflect general economic and technical backwardness as well as social and cultural constraints. New institutions have to take root in their societies and adapt their plans for change and modernization to their cultural milieu. Technical and managerial competence must be improved gradually, to bring about effective policy planning, work programming, financial and personnel management, and all the other essential functions of modern organizations. For development projects specifically, building institutional capability is often hindered by three sets of problems: a counterproductive policy environment, the complex objectives fixed for projects, and overemphasis on the short-term implementation of new investments.

The Policy Environment

All development projects, whether in the public or private sector, are intimately affected by the government's macroeconomic policies and by the legislative and regulatory framework embodying those policies. It is often difficult, therefore, to separate the impact of government action on institutional performance from its impact on project performance in general. However, if institutions are forced to spend time and effort to counteract the effects of government policies and interventions, they cannot build long-term capacity very effectively.

To repeat a familiar theme of this book, political commitment matters—especially in the long term. High-level government interest has often declined sharply once project funds have been disbursed (or even once they are committed), and project managers find themselves starved for operating resources and without access to decisionmakers who have the authority to respond to their requests. Shifting political forces—or even a change of individuals at the ministerial level—can also drastically affect the fortunes of a project and the capacity and morale of its staff.

Institutional problems multiply rapidly when government policies seriously distort the economic environment of a project. Inappropriate exchange rate and trade policies may affect not only the financial and economic returns of the project; they may also necessitate an inefficient shift of institutional resources toward, for example, chasing spare parts or dealing with the import-export bureaucracy. Just as pricing policies can send the wrong signals to project managers, so too can government tax policies. In Sri Lanka, for example, the publicly owned plantations producing the major treecrops upon which the country depends for its foreign exchange earnings faced export duties on tea and rubber production in 1978–82 averaging 37 percent and 50 percent of export values, respectively. The very narrow or sometimes negative profit margins that resulted (since these crops face a high degree of international competition) probably account for much of the production decline of recent years, and for the tendency of individual producers and plantation managers to try to maximize their returns by benefiting from the subsidies on inputs rather than by expanding output. An even more striking example is that of cocoa in Ghana (described in chapter 3, Pricing Policy): exchange rate policy and the abuse of the taxing powers of the Cocoa Marketing Board produced a steep, long-term decline in returns from cocoa—and a consequent disastrous decline in production as farmers switched to other crops with much lower real returns to the economy.

In these and similar cases, the most obvious effect of price and fiscal policies is on the economic and financial performance of projects. At the same time, these policies divert attention from the institutions' development functions or undermine incentives, morale, and management capacity in the institutions themselves. It becomes impossible to evaluate managerial or staff performance meaningfully, since an institution's poor performance can always be blamed on the policy environment that keeps it from carrying out its appointed tasks effectively.

Another example is afforded by power utilities, which traditionally have been among the more effective institutions in many developing countries. A World Bank review covering sixty countries indicated widespread failure by governments during the 1970s to permit the utilities to pass on to consumers increases in energy and capital costs. By 1980, half of the institutions had returns on capital of less than 4 percent, and some were incurring losses. Their capacity to attract and keep competent staff and to fulfill their strategic development functions was correspondingly damaged, and once-strong institutions were progressively being eroded.

These broad effects of the policy environment are reinforced in many countries by detailed government regulations, controls, and direct interventions, especially for public sector institutions. Sector and finance ministries have a legitimate interest in overseeing the operation of these institutions, which are often charged with fulfilling important national development responsibilities. Unless carefully designed and implemented, however, government interventions or controls can have two damaging effects. First, because they may be inconsistently applied, often by several different agencies, they may interfere with the ability of managers to carry out their responsibilities and may make them uncertain and defensive. Second, extraneous requirements may be imposed on project institutions to promote social welfare objectives or to serve political advantage or bureaucratic convenience, but without the institutions being compensated for the attendant costs. One of the most common forms of this interference is the use of public sector institutions to boost employment, often with scant regard for the financial health or operational efficiency of the institutions. Irrespective of the merits of these social goals, such interventions can be counterproductive in the short run and may seriously undermine the performance of institutions in the long run. We shall return to this subject in the discussion of public enterprise reform below.

Complex Objectives

Many of the managerial and organizational difficulties that projects in developing countries encounter result from a broadening vision of the development process itself. As development projects have extended beyond construction of transport facilities, public utilities, and industrial plants, novel institutional problems have arisen.

To begin with, it is often difficult to define precisely the objectives, and the instruments for achieving them, in socially oriented projects or in projects integrating multiple components for delivery to large numbers of users or beneficiaries. Compare, for instance, investment in education and in fertilizer production. Producing educated and adaptable human beings is clearly an objective less susceptible to exact assessment than producing a given tonnage of fertilizer with specified chemical characteristics. The means of reaching the objective in the case of education are also much more complex and uncertain. In other types of projects, the objectives facing institutional managers may be specific enough but there may be too many of them, with uncertain tradeoffs. Institutions running integrated rural development projects, for example, will characteristically have objectives that include raising agricultural production (often with targets for increasing specific crops and for reaching specific groups of farmers), developing infrastructure such as minor roads and water supply, extending social services, and changing cultural practices affecting child care and nutrition. A common feature of social or people-oriented projects in recent years has been that large numbers of components, often well beyond the coordinating or executing capacities of the agencies concerned, are tacked onto projects in an attempt to address all these objectives simultaneously.

Second, social and poverty-focused projects deal with large numbers of people whose compliance the institution cannot command. Whereas the manager of a power plant has direct authority over employees, for example, the manager of a rural development project has few direct means for inducing desired behavior in independent smallholders. He must rely, instead, on such material incentives as the project may offer, plus a gradual process of education and persuasion.

Another problem is that these newer areas of development are relatively uncharted. Knowledge of the economic, social, and cultural characteristics of small farmers, disadvantaged tribal peoples, or urban squatters is still rudimentary in many countries, despite an impressive gain in the past decade. Devising management and institutional techniques appropriate for projects that deal with these groups is at a still earlier stage and presents particular difficulties—the more so since management as a discipline has been formulated and applied predominantly in industrial countries and in industrial-type institutions in developing countries.

Standard and Pilot Projects

Executing infrastructure, public utilities, or large industrial projects, therefore, has certain institutional advantages. Appropriate institutional arrangements are familiar and usually can be specified closely, cultural factors do not strongly influence the outcome, and well-tested technologies are available. In agriculture, some of the most successful schemes for small farmers have been those where standardized technologies, traditional crops, and adapted forms of factory-type operation were possible, based on institutional models that were well established. Plantation and outgrower schemes for rubber and oil palm in Malaysia and Indonesia and the reorganization of the tea business in Kenya are examples. The Kenya Tea Development Authority has become the world's largest exporter of black tea by integrating some 45,000 smallholders into a tightly managed institution that provides extension services, buys and transports leaf, processes the leaf in its own factories, and markets the tea internationally.[1]

In many people-oriented projects, however, standardized technologies and institutional approaches are not likely to be available. This puts a high premium on an institution's adaptive capacity. Because of cultural differences, what has worked well in one country, or even one province, may not work in another; but the only way to find out may be to start the project and then make adjustments as the results dictate. This adaptive approach often poses formidable difficulties for large bureaucracies—not to speak of international aid agencies—because of their obligation to account for planned expenditure and their tendency to overdesign projects, partly to avert risk. In some cases, it may be preferable to embark on a series of pilot projects, to be expanded according to a set timetable if specified results are achieved, rather than on a larger project with its heavier institutional and logistical demands. This was the strategy adopted in the Indian program of dairy development through village milk

---

1. Geoffrey Lamb and Linda Muller, *Control, Accountability, and Incentives in a Successful Development Institution: The Kenya Tea Development Authority*, World Bank Staff Working Paper no. 550 (Washington, D.C., 1982).

cooperatives linked to the National Dairy Development Board, although the success of the project since its inception in 1974 has made very rapid expansion possible. The lessons from the operational experience of pilot projects often could not have been learned from feasibility studies.

An alternative to such pilot projects is to subcontract small schemes to voluntary agencies, with the government providing funds and technical assistance without major bureaucratic commitment. Yet another variant is to include in a larger investment project an experimental component in which new approaches can be tested. The Philippines National Irrigation Administration, for example, has been experimenting since 1976 with pilot projects to promote small irrigation systems, with farmers participating in planning and constructing such systems through local water users' associations.

Coordination Problems

Another way to get around the institutional—as well as other—constraints of large-scale projects (as discussed more fully in chapter 16, Project Preparation) is to simplify such projects, that is, to identify which activities are central to the project's primary purpose and to concentrate scarce institutional resources on them while deferring desirable but difficult or secondary objectives until the primary function is well established. This strategy is not always possible, but when it is, such phasing can put projects on a sounder managerial footing.

Similar scrutiny should be directed to the coordination requirements of the project, since coordination among different agencies can be time-consuming and unproductive. Kenya, for example, decided that the difficulties of coordinating the country's integrated agricultural development program made it more sensible to have a series of administratively separate projects for credit, extension, and so forth, rather than to promote coordinated arrangements. Where coordination remains essential, as it often does, careful design is needed to make sure that it takes place at the right operational level, with the authority for getting particular tasks done very clearly demarcated. Incentives can be provided for staff and agencies to cooperate. For example, creation of small working groups at the operational level that have control over minor but valued resources (such as vehicle use) can often be a more productive coordination mechanism than the ritual of a coordinating committee made up of more senior staff.

Improving Management Controls

The difficulties of evaluating output and performance in people-oriented projects can be reduced by disaggregating project activities as far as possible into discrete functions that can be monitored and managed more closely. For example, the function of financial management in these projects is often given much less attention than would be the case in an industrial project. But accounting for financial flows—now greatly facilitated by inexpensive and accessible computer technology—can reduce the uncertainties in such projects and improve management control, as well as help to ensure financial propriety. Moreover, properly organized financial management can form the basis of a streamlined management information system. Careful design of such a management information system with a well-established accounting function at its core, clear definition of the scope of management's decisionmaking authority, and set procedures and criteria for those decisions that lie outside management's control are essential ingredients for efficient management of socially oriented projects no less than for more traditional projects.

A similar emphasis on rigorous organization and close attention to results can be applied in managing staff. Too often, the personnel engaged in projects that provide services to large numbers of beneficiaries are demoralized by a general laxity of administration deriving from the inherent uncertainties and political susceptibilities of the project. Even in such a difficult field as agricultural extension, however, it has proved possible through the training and visit system (see chapter 6, Agriculture) to improve discipline and morale by strict programming of fieldwork, careful record keeping and debriefing, and close managerial control within an administrative structure of clearly defined responsibilities.

None of these approaches offers a complete answer to the institutional problems that have multiplied as broader development objectives have been addressed through project work. They do emphasize, however, that substantial benefits accrue from deliberately expanding the capacity of institutions to experiment, learn, and adapt; from using beneficiaries as a source of inputs and ideas; from simplifying design; and from maximizing the number of project activities that can be objectively assessed and tightly managed.

Neglect of the Postinvestment Phase

Despite the difficulties that arise in the construction of projects—or perhaps because of them—project implementation does not always get the high-level attention it deserves. There is, nevertheless, often greater concentration, by decisionmakers and project institutions alike, on the investment phase than on the subsequent phases of operation and maintenance. The consequences of this neglect show up as lower returns on scarce resources, a deteriorating capital stock, and serious financial and managerial constraints on institutional development. A powerful set of protagonists can be lined up who have an interest in the execution of a project: external sources of capital, policymakers, companies and unions that will benefit from construction contracts and jobs, and so forth. Once a project is completed, however, it is more difficult to obtain the flow of resources and the institutional incentives needed for effective operation— or even to get the relevant authorities to address the problems.

One aspect of the neglect of postinvestment performance is that too little attention is paid, in institutional design, to the costs and benefits of maintenance, conservation, and rehabilitation or improvement of capital stock. The difference that adequate attention can make is illustrated by some South Asian irrigation systems: improvements in the institutional arrangements for canal maintenance and also for the management of water distribution have produced dramatic increases in water availability in some areas and greatly increased the productivity of the original investment with only small additional outlays.

Similar instances are found in the institutional arrangements through which highway maintenance, school building maintenance, and similar activities are organized and carried out. In road maintenance—probably the paradigm case—Argentina and other countries have subcontracted stretches of highway to private sector maintenance companies, with specified standards and rates of payment, to good result. A different but also effective approach has been followed in some African countries, where highway maintenance remains the responsibility of a public agency but is allocated to foremen and crews from "training production units" who are responsible for specific stretches of road and are judged by the results. Whatever ingenious institutional mechanism is adopted, however, adequate budgetary support (or, alternatively, cash flow from operations) is essential.

A second consequence of neglecting the postinvestment phase of a project is that the recurrent costs of investments are insufficiently analyzed; moreover, there is little planning of where the resources to meet these costs will come from. This is not only a budgetary question, but also a failure to design project institutions that maximize the possibilities of self-financing. Legal status, location within the bureaucracy, and design of service delivery modes, for example, may in different ways significantly affect the capacity of the project institution to generate income through control of the cost of its inputs or the prices charged for its services.

Public Sector Management

In many developing countries the public sector constitutes the largest, and often the most important, aggregation of institutions. These can be subdivided into the government ministries and core agencies forming the public administration or civil service, and the state-owned enterprises or parastatals. While the two groups share some problems, they are sufficiently distinct to warrant separate discussion.

Public Administration Reform

Public administration is an activity to which the international donor community has only recently turned its attention. World Bank lending to support institutional and policy reform of public administration is of relatively recent origin and limited scope. Between 1980—when a systematic effort began—and 1984, the Bank addressed problems of public administration in seventeen countries through a combination of diagnostic studies and technical assistance. It is still too early to draw many conclusions, but not too early to point to some important issues that have surfaced. Experience has already confirmed, if confirmation were needed, that how well the public administration functions has a great impact not only on the efficiency of public and private investment but on virtually all aspects of economic activity.[2]

Comprehensive or Selective Approach?

A comprehensive reform of the civil service—however badly needed— is a highly ambitious undertaking, and few countries, developed or

2. Selcuk Ozgediz, *Managing the Public Service in Developing Countries: Issues and Prospects*, World Bank Staff Working Paper no. 583 (Washington, D.C. 1983).

developing, have been able to carry it out successfully. Establishment of a civil service reform commission with a mandate to review the workings of the civil service as a whole and to recommend solutions has been an initial step in several countries, but commissions of this kind have had a chequered history and their impact has usually been quite limited.

However the reform effort is approached, a careful diagnosis of the main problems of public administration and a delineation of possible solutions is a prerequisite to concrete action. Outsiders can sometimes act as catalysts or provide a useful perspective, but the prime movers must clearly come from within the government. While general studies are desirable to establish the overall strategy and direction for change, the magnitude of the problems in most countries is too great and the time needed for institutional development too long to allow progress on more than a few fronts at any time. A prudent course is warranted; major political and bureaucratic interests are often at stake, and the short-term political costs of attacking vested interests may loom larger in the eyes of government than the long-term gains from improving institutional performance. It is usually desirable, therefore, to adopt a selective approach, beginning with modest efforts to address only a few of the more critical problems. The criteria for selecting which problems to tackle first should be that

- The problem is a serious constraint on the performance of the public service
- The solution is within the capacity of the public administration to carry out
- The climate is favorable for sustained action (that is, public support can be mobilized and maintained).

In one country, this process of selection might result in efforts to reform the tax system, including improving the data base, streamlining procedures and forms, strengthening the institutions responsible, and improving tax enforcement and collection. In another, budgetary reforms might be sought, such as the introduction of program budgeting, better analysis of the implications of capital expenditures for recurrent costs, more comprehensive budgets that include transfers to and from state enterprises, and better control over budget execution. In a third country, stronger investment planning might be attempted through the introduction of more flexible plans, stronger links between the investment plan and the budget, stronger planning institutions, and more accurate, timely, and relevant data for planning. In countries that have relatively weak public institutions—often of recent origin—as in sub-Saharan Africa, a prolonged process of institutional development may have to precede efforts at reform. In countries with a more robust and resilient public administration, institutional reforms may be most productive when linked to particular policy reforms.

Civil Service Staffing and Compensation

At the heart of the performance of the public administration lie issues concerning the efficiency, competence, and morale of civil servants. It is common in the poorer developing countries, especially in Africa, to find the public service grossly overstaffed at lower levels, while salaries and benefits at the higher levels are inadequate to attract, retain, and motivate competent professional staff. In a number of countries, real wages in the public sector have fallen over the last decade, with managers' salaries falling particularly sharply compared with what the private sector pays. Administrative regulations and procedures, often inherited or transplanted from developed countries but ill-suited to local circumstances, may further reduce the efficiency of the civil service, sometimes drastically. Bank-supported efforts to improve these aspects of public administration have included:

- Strengthening personnel management by conducting diagnostic studies, by training the staff of the agency that has oversight responsibility for the civil service, and by reforming rules and regulations
- Reducing staff on the government payroll by identifying redundant workers and helping to retrain and relocate them, and by designing programs to control public employment
- Selectively raising civil service compensation, when this is necessary to bring it more closely in line with that of competing positions in the private sector
- Changing the organization and procedures of public agencies to improve efficiency, generate timely and more accurate information, and make the agencies more responsive to their public
- Improving training programs for government personnel.

In Jamaica, for example, the government decided that raising the salaries of senior civil servants was an essential first step toward revitalizing the public administration. Ways of changing organization, procedures, and staffing have also been identified through a series of special studies. One country, with technical assistance from the World Bank, is concentrating on getting rid of redundant and "ghost" employees (at some risk to the expatriate consultant, whose house was attacked by a mob). A principal objective of a Bank-assisted project in Mali is to reduce overstaffing, and the government has decided to change its policy of guaranteeing public service employment to all university and secondary school graduates (a policy pursued in some other countries as well). A public sector management project in Peru includes a component to raise compensation for senior government officials through the establishment of a senior executive service. In Uganda, the government is trying to rebuild the civil service's capacity for personnel and organization management and, in the process, to contain unproductive growth of employment in the public sector, which is imposing an unsustainable burden on the budget.

Public Sector Investment Program

As mentioned in chapter 4, Public Investment Programs and Budgets, deficiencies of government agencies in managing investment programs frequently are a drag on public sector activities and hence an important area in need of attention. Programs and activities with which the Bank has been associated have sought to improve the decisionmaking process so as to curb inappropriate or excessive investment, ensure the most economic use of public resources, and improve the speed and efficiency with which decisions are made. To accomplish this, the programs support better coordination between economic and financial agencies and a clearer definition of responsibility for evaluating and monitoring investment, combined with improvement in the government's ability to identify new investments and to set priorities among them.

Substantial change along these lines has been achieved in several countries—notably Jamaica, Ivory Coast, and Turkey—as a result of sustained, high-level political attention. In other countries, reform is proceeding step by step through the introduction of such procedures as the painstaking review of proposed investment projects followed by improvements in the investment decisionmaking system. Another approach is to recast budget procedures to capture within the budget all investment expenditures and to display recurrent expenditures as well. Such changes have been instituted with Bank assistance in countries in Africa and Latin America, in particular. But not surprisingly, attempts to improve the management of the public investment program in the short term have generally proved quite difficult. Even when governments were prepared to make significant adjustments to investment policies, problems were often exacerbated by the severity of the recession of the early 1980s. In several countries, the institutions dealing with public investment proved weaker, more poorly organized, and slower to react than anticipated. Staffing weaknesses, poor interministerial coordination, the resistance of line agencies to any curtailment of their investment programs, and inadequate information on which to base decisions or guide actions have also slowed progress.

Consultants and Training

In many countries, responsibility for devising and carrying through the institutional and policy reforms of the public service falls on the shoulders of a very small group of senior decisionmakers. These officials have many other responsibilities, and in any event cannot directly supervise the implementation of complex reform programs. Specialized skills from outside the public sector, or from outside the country, may therefore be needed. The World Bank has relied heavily on consultants both for its diagnostic studies and for its lending work in conjunction with administrative reform. It has usually looked for people who are familiar with the country (or at least the region) and already known to the government. The standing and credibility of consultants tend to weigh heavily when their recommendations come to be considered; governments are unlikely to be impressed by advice that is not backed by relevant experience. Consultants new to a country may have to be educated at the government's expense, as has happened in more than one case. The multifaceted nature of work on public administration often calls for a combination of expatriate and local consultants, generalists and specialists, on long- and short-term assignments. There are, however, few consulting firms or organizations that can yet provide the mix of reputation, technical skills, and international experience that is needed.

The political sensitivity of the subject and the lack of ready-made technical solutions add to the risks in seeking advice or technical assistance from abroad. When expatriate consultants are used, two additional but important tasks should be assigned to them: helping to build up a local consulting capacity, and training local officials as counterparts to the foreign advisers.

In sum, institutional reform of the public administration is a difficult and lengthy process; progress is likely to be slow and subject to frequent reversals as political fortunes change. At times there may be a danger of substituting form for substance: studies may be completed, committees established, legislation passed, or regulations issued without any real change in performance occurring. Yet in many countries, the weaknesses of public administration remain such a serious obstacle in the path of development that the cost of failing to come to grips with them—or at least to make a start and persist in the face of setbacks—is high.

Public Enterprise Reform

State-owned enterprises (also known as parastatals) have proliferated in recent years; they present an especially acute set of institutional problems. Much of what has been said about public administration reform applies with equal force to these enterprises. There are some differences of approach, however, which reflect the fact that parastatals are engaged in the production and sale of goods and services and accordingly should be (though they usually are not) subject to less government intervention. A principal reason for government intervention is that many state-owned enterprises have large operating deficits and consequently impose a heavy burden on the public budget.[3]

Although experience with public enterprises varies widely from country to country, some broadly applicable lessons are emerging. One is that the government's legitimate responsibility often needs to be defined more precisely. The most appropriate role for government is to set the broad strategies and policy directives for public enterprises as well as the operational and evaluation framework and then, as far as possible, to hold them publicly accountable for their performance—all the while keeping them at arm's length rather than in an intimate embrace.

A second lesson is that governments could often make better choices than they do about which fields are appropriate for public enterprise activity. Although political and historical factors will always play a powerful role, it is important to tailor public ownership to the management capacity of the public sector and also to concentrate it where it is most needed and likely to make the greatest contribution. Caution should be exercised, therefore, when choosing public ownership, even when the choice is based on the traditional grounds of natural monopoly, national security, or public interest.

In operational terms, action is needed in most countries at two levels. First, at the national level, governments need to improve the policy and operating environment within which state-owned enterprises function, a point we have discussed with respect to project institutions in general earlier in this chapter. Second, at the level of individual enterprises,

3. Mary M. Shirley, *Managing State-Owned Enterprises*, World Bank Staff Working Paper no. 577 (Washington, D.C., 1983).

reforms are needed in management, employment conditions and incentives, operational autonomy, and the competitive environment. Experience indicates that changes instituted at one level will rarely be fully effective without complementary action at the other. The objective of both sets of reforms is greater efficiency: to improve the performance of state-owned enterprises by removing, as far as possible, the special restrictions—and special privileges—which government ownership characteristically entails, and by clarifying the objectives of enterprises and the yardsticks by which they are judged.

Improving Information

In practice, the first priority for reform-minded governments is often to obtain better information about public enterprises as a whole—about their finances (profits and losses, foreign borrowings, payment arrears among enterprises and between enterprises and government), investment plans, trends in operational efficiency, effectiveness in meeting public objectives, and so forth. Although sector ministries are, in principle, knowledgeable about the enterprises under their tutelage, their information is often sketchy or out of date, and what information they do have is not communicated reliably to the decisionmakers charged with central economic policy, such as the finance and planning ministries.

Some countries have found it useful, therefore, to concentrate initially on strengthening the agency that supervises state enterprises through improvements in the information system. In some cases, this has meant setting up small special units to collate and analyze data from enterprises in all sectors. This approach has been adopted with some success in Pakistan, where the Ministry of Production has established an expert advisory cell that analyzes computerized information on the financial and operational performance of a large number of enterprises. Performance is evaluated by the criterion of public profitability: that is, profit figures are adjusted to exclude elements deemed irrelevant from a national point of view (such as tax avoidance) and also to compensate enterprises for actions taken in accord with noncommercial objectives imposed by government policy. A comparable initiative is under way in Korea, where the public enterprise division of the Budget Bureau was reorganized in 1984 to concentrate on evaluation of enterprise performance.

Rationalizing the Rules of the Game

Even in advance of obtaining detailed knowledge of this kind, however, some desirable directions for reform are usually readily apparent. One often obvious reform is to curtail direct state ownership (and especially the granting of monopoly power) in activities where public enterprises are characteristically least effective. Many countries have fostered a large expansion of public manufacturing enterprises, which often enjoy preferential treatment from the government but operate at high cost to the consumer and use capital wastefully. Similarly, parastatal agricultural marketing organizations have often operated inefficiently and provided poor service to farmers without any compensating benefits through improved export earnings or food security. State road transport enterprises, too, have generally had a very poor record. In these sectors in particular, most countries have highly competitive private alternatives that can be tapped, often with results that are superior in efficiency and equity. This is true even in countries with an overall commitment to public ownership, as experience in Yugoslavia, Hungary, and China demonstrates.

More broadly, decisive action is usually needed to rationalize the "rules of the game" under which public enterprises operate. One way of clarifying the respective roles of government and these enterprises is by reaching an explicit agreement between the two parties. Such an approach is at the heart of the contract plan *(contrat plan)* derived from French experience, in which several developing countries have shown interest. In Senegal, for example, the government has been experimenting—with Bank assistance through both project and structural adjustment lending—with the contract plan as a method of regulating the relationship between government and enterprises. Such plans, which have been or are being negotiated with ten important state enterprises, compel both the government and the enterprise to concentrate on the sources of deficits, to articulate operational objectives and investment priorities, and to identify the main obligations and constraints on each party—such as pricing and employment constraints. The enterprise's managers are then given more autonomy to implement measures to reach specified objectives, and they are held publicly accountable for the results.

Most of the contracts resulting from this joint planning and negotiating process in Senegal have produced measurable improvements in performance, even in the short term. The Dakar state bus company, for example, was able within the first year of the contract plan to improve its cash flow to the point that it could eliminate its bank overdraft and pay off 30 percent of its arrears to suppliers. Such plans must be carefully drawn; the short-term effects on the budget have been uncomfortable for the Senegalese government, which found itself committed under the contracts to an unrealistically high level of financial support. Also, the question of sanctions for noncompliance by an enterprise (or by the government) remains to be resolved. But the approach has helped to stabilize the policy framework within which the enterprises operate and to identify more clearly the costs and benefits of the noncommercial responsibilities with which the enterprises are charged. It has also been valuable in providing a forum for constructive dialogue between enterprises and the government. Variants of this approach are currently being developed in some other African countries, among them Togo, Congo, and Burundi.

In other countries, techniques familiar from private sector experience are being employed. Thailand is introducing corporate plans for all public enterprises as a means of compelling them to commit themselves to acceptable levels of efficiency, while Turkey recently enacted legislation establishing a holding company structure as a means of rationalizing the vast state enterprise sector and making its management more closely accountable. A somewhat comparable holding company scheme is employed in Peru.

Whatever approach is followed, improvements in the rules of the game are likely to include

- Pricing policies that give managers of state-owned enterprises more freedom to set prices so they can earn a reasonable rate of return
- Credit policies that require the enterprises to pay market rates of interest and compete fairly with private enterprises in credit markets
- Labor policies that give enterprise managers greater discretion in personnel decisions, wage determination, and reduction of surplus labor.

Monopolistic Enterprises

Although it is desirable for some purposes to treat public enterprises as a single category, this should not be allowed to obscure important technical and economic differences. Thus, for instance, increasing operational autonomy and competitive pressure is an appropriate policy toward state-owned manufacturing industries, as discussed in chapter 9, Industry. Commercial trading enterprises can also be exposed to greater competition. But some state-owned enterprises are inherently monopolistic. The absence of competition requires that regulatory agencies—which are simultaneously weak and highly interventionist in many countries—be strengthened and their methods of supervision improved. This is all the more important since, despite their monopoly position—or perhaps because of it and the consequent absence of competitive pressure—these enterprises often operate inefficiently and with large deficits.

In addition to improving the flow of information and strengthening financial control, benchmark criteria can be established by supervising agencies against which future performance may be judged—such as billing ratios and physical loss rates (for example, of pumped water) for utilities, and unit cost or other productivity measures more generally. In some cases, it may be appropriate to decentralize or to break up large monopolies—especially when economies of scale are not an overriding consideration—thereby introducing the possibility of some competition and making the enterprises more responsive to their clientele. Encouraging these enterprises to compete in export markets, where feasible, also provides a stimulus to greater efficiency.

Improving Enterprise Management

Reform of the policy framework, agreement on objectives, and establishment of performance criteria may be ineffective, however, in the absence of direct action to improve management at the enterprise level: its quality, degree of autonomy, accountability, and incentives. The contract plan provides one explicit way of specifying management obligations and measuring management performance. Pakistan, using another approach, has established a signaling system designed to set clear and reasonable goals for state enterprise managers, measure actual performance, and reward managers according to how well they achieve their goals—although the system has yet to be used for this last purpose. Whatever the approach, it is useful to improve basic functions such as accounting, which are often deplorably weak even in large, strategic enterprises.

Such institutional initiatives may be a promising beginning, but they need to be complemented by action on other fronts. In many countries, for example, senior managers are frequently changed on quasi-political grounds, while boards are dominated by politicians and civil servants lacking relevant expertise. Indeed, in some countries, directorships on the boards of state enterprises are a recognized perquisite for underpaid senior government officials. Governments, therefore, need to repose greater authority in the executive officers of the companies and to take action gradually to professionalize boards of directors so that they articulate the broad national interest in having the enterprise operate successfully rather than a narrower political or bureaucratic agenda. Appointing representatives of consumers to the boards can also help to sharpen the focus on serving the public interest. To do this requires both political courage on the part of the government and a continuing program of management development in state enterprises so that they can attract and retain leaders of high caliber. Some further means of strengthening management, which apply to institutions of all kinds, public and private, are discussed in the final section of this chapter.

Divestiture and Liquidation

None of these objectives is easily accomplished, and all of them call for sustained action on the part of both the central government and public enterprises. They will be particularly difficult to accomplish if government attention is preoccupied with the affairs of state-owned enterprises that are a major financial drain, that absorb a disproportionate share of scarce managerial skills, or that operate very inefficiently in fields of activity where public ownership is not essential. In recent years some governments have sought to rationalize the size of the public sector and divest or liquidate some enterprises. Since the human and political costs can be high, liquidation has been undertaken mainly when past investments have been grossly inappropriate or unsustainable. Examples are provided by the Ivory Coast and Panama, where overcapacity and large financial losses have led to the closing of sugar factories. In other countries, the authorities have closed small uncompetitive enterprises, or they have terminated peripheral operations of larger concerns to preserve the main business. Few developing countries, however, have undertaken the kind of major contraction of state-owned basic industries that is under way in some OECD countries, such as Great Britain.

With respect to divestiture, experience indicates that governments need to be flexible and creative in their approach if substantial benefits are to be reaped, since enterprises that sustain losses are unlikely to attract investors. Some countries, among them Liberia, Ethiopia, Uganda, and Thailand, face the additional complication that some state enterprises are the result of past confiscation of private firms, which entails legal and political problems. Apart from outright sale to private interests, alternatives that governments need to consider include contracting out particular activities, leasing arrangements, and management contracts. The last technique involves private management in the running of enterprises but provides the "insurance" of having the government share the risk. It is widely used in the hotel industry in many parts of the world and is also being employed in other activities in some African and Latin American countries. While contracts have to be carefully negotiated (for example, to establish clear performance criteria for rewarding the private managers), the contracting technique may offer a politically acceptable mode of partial divestiture in many countries.

A Systematic Approach

Developing countries are acquiring an array of techniques for improving the performance of public enterprises, as this discussion has shown. Collectively, these techniques offer governments the chance to bring a greater measure of financial order and efficiency into the affairs of public enterprises. Except for those few countries where one or two enterprises dominate the scene, what is needed is a systematic approach that includes

- A careful definition of the problem (for example, classifying enterprises by their economic function and strategic importance, as has been done in Thailand and Peru)
- A sustained effort to build up the government's information system and analytical capacity
- An emphasis on selectivity as the watchword for public ownership, along with a creative program to rationalize the sector, including divestiture where necessary
- A different approach for competitive and for monopolistic enterprises, with reliance on market or regulatory pressures to enhance the productivity of each type of enterprise
- Clarification of the respective obligations and prerogatives of the government and of enterprise management, with the objective of increasing the autonomy and accountability of management
- Improvement in the performance of enterprise management through more stable appointment policies, more professional boards of directors, and additional resources for basic functions such as financial control.

PLANNING, MANAGEMENT, AND STAFF DEVELOPMENT

Project institutions need to be planned as part of an articulated institutional development strategy for the parent agency, for the sector, and indeed for the country. We have referred on several occasions to the proliferation of independent project units, the main justifications for which are the availability of resources for new investments and the weakness of existing institutions. As a general rule, creating new organizations in fields where old ones are already in place should be done sparingly. The new institutions may take years to gain local credibility and become effective, and they may not be immune to whatever administrative, political, or other forces have weakened the existing institutions. Instead, maximum emphasis needs to be placed on improving the capacity of existing line agencies, with independent project units being used mainly to develop new types of activity, to coordinate activities, or to serve as a training ground for agency staff. Even in these cases, reintegration of the units into the main institutional structure should be anticipated and planned from the outset.

Planning units within agencies and ministries can often be usefully deployed to make careful assessments of present managerial capacity and to plan a strategy for improving general competence as well as carrying out specific projects. The Jamaican government, for example, began a series of such management assessments (or audits) of its core ministries in 1982 and plans to extend them to all ministries and to the major public corporations.

The importance of management and staff development to the effective functioning of project institutions is a leitmotif of this book. It is a large and complex theme, since the pervasive shortages of managers and skilled staff are an almost universal characteristic of underdevelopment. But the leading issues can be identified. The primary one is incentives—for all staff, but particularly for managers and technicians whose performance has the most decisive impact on institutional efficiency. This is a difficult problem in the public service, since financial incentives cannot normally match those in the private sector, but much can be done. Gross disparities can be narrowed; easier lateral entry and exit can encourage public service as a regular part of a career; "super-grades" outside the normal system may be considered to meet extreme needs. Elements of the financial package other than salaries can be made more attractive—watching out, however, for perverse effects. (For example, extension officers in one Asian country were paid an overnight allowance if they needed to visit farmers more than 25 kilometers from the duty station. As a result, few farmers within 25 kilometers of extension stations ever saw an extension officer.) Career development paths can be improved for staff working in project units or elsewhere outside the regular hierarchy of the line ministry.

Managers and staff respond to work incentives as well as material incentives: to being given responsibility, to being judged fairly on their performance, and to working in a good institution. In that sense, staff development is circular; as in the Kenya Tea Development Authority or the Indian National Dairy Development Board, staff are highly motivated in part because their institution performs well. Nevertheless, decision-makers can encourage positive trends by increasing managerial autonomy, by involving staff in designing tasks and organizational solutions, and by instituting performance appraisal and promotion systems.

The counterpart to improved management and staff incentives is improved accountability. As we have seen, this is the thrust of various public enterprise reform programs, and it is a feature of many successful institutions. The general manager of the Ethiopian Telecommunications Authority, for example, is held accountable by its board for the enterprise's performance but is given a degree of operational autonomy commensurate with his responsibility. At other levels within an institution, too, there is often an opportunity to redefine tasks and reorganize work groups to clarify who should do what—and be held responsible for the outcome.

Finally, management and staff need training and skill development. We say "finally," not because it is the least important aspect of institutional development—far from it—but because training in the absence of the other factors discussed has limited utility. At times, training becomes a remote and irrelevant activity, with little apparent impact on performance and with considerable waste of resources. However, the need for skilled people remains urgent, and so the search for training strategies relevant to institutional needs must continue. In recent years, some countries have experimented with "action-learning" or "action-research" approaches to training. These try to break down the artificial barriers between training and work by giving trainees practical problems in real organizational settings to solve, review, and discuss collegially. This approach has been used in India, Bangladesh, Egypt, and the Philippines, and has proved particularly useful for entry-level staff.[4]

In other cases, more resources are being devoted to management education for middle-level and senior personnel in midcareer; often both civil service and public enterprise staff are covered. Occasionally, programs for public sector managers are integrated with those for private sector managers. The emphasis is increasingly on participatory and problem-solving approaches and on developing the ability of managers to relate specific operational solutions to broader strategic objectives. Regional and national management institutions are slowly being strengthened, with some—such as the Indian Institute of Management, the Central American Institute of Business Management, or Malaysia's National Institute of Public Administration—gaining an international reputation. In contrast with many training institutions that have acquired a reputation for low standards and irrelevance, such innovative institutions are deliberately becoming more accountable to their client agencies, more willing to market their services, and more concerned about exchanging their personnel with client institutions to keep up with on-the-job developments. A related and promising approach is to decentralize training budgets, a move which gives managers at all levels the resources to develop their human capital but also imposes the obligation to reflect and decide, within guidelines, on the types of training to which they wish to allocate staff time and money.

The training of its personnel is something of a gamble for an agency or institution because of the frequent loss of people, once they are trained, through resignations, transfers, promotions, and the like. Bonding the staff to serve for a specified time after their training may help, but it is not a long-run solution and may be difficult to enforce. A better way to cope with this type of attrition is to recognize the problem explicitly and to plan for it by training more staff than are immediately required. It is true that this augments the problem of finding suitable candidates and relieving them from their existing duties for training, but it also spreads the benefits of training more widely through the economy and in that way contributes to the overall development effort.

4. Samuel Paul, *Training for Public Administration and Management in Developing Countries: A Review*, World Bank Staff Working Paper no. 584 (Washington, D.C., 1983).

Family collecting firewood, rural Mexico

24

Environmental Analysis

UNTIL THE 1970S, developing countries generally regarded environmental quality as a luxury that could be afforded only after they had attained a considerably higher level of economic development. Views have changed dramatically in the past decade. Many development planners now recognize that sound management of the environment is a necessary component of economic development, not an obstacle to it. In 1982, 111 countries—most of them developing—had environmental ministries or their equivalent, compared with only eleven in 1972. But despite this increased attention to environmental management, many developing countries are still not able to deal effectively with the serious environmental problems they face.

Environmental concerns encompass a broad range of issues, including public health and occupational safety; control of air, water, and land pollution; sound management of renewable natural resources;[1] more efficient use of natural resources through multiple use, recycling, and erosion control; conservation of unique habitats, especially for rare or endangered species; and cultural preservation. Virtually all the environmental problems faced in developed countries are found also in developing countries, their relative importance depending on local circumstances, the country's state of development, and the resource base. The problems often differ more in degree than in kind. Thus, industrial pollution is more pervasive in industrial countries, although it is also a major problem for many cities in the developing world—Mexico City or São Paulo, for example. Soil erosion and deforestation, in contrast, are more acute in developing countries. An important difference in kind is that many developing countries have tropical environments, which are much more complex than temperate environments—and about which much less is known. Damage to the environment is likely to be more difficult to remedy in the tropics.

ENVIRONMENTAL TRENDS

We begin this chapter by describing some of the main environmental problems and trends in developing countries. Since indicators of environmental quality are not yet systematically calculated for most of these countries, it is not possible to obtain more than a very general picture of what the trends are. The evidence that is available strongly suggests that environmental quality is deteriorating in developing countries and that this is adversely affecting human welfare and posing significant barriers to sustainable economic development.

Among the most urgent environmental problems in most developing countries are those relating to land. Overgrazing by livestock and cultiva-

---

1. Renewable natural resources include living resources (plants and animals) and other natural resources (particularly soil and water) that create or sustain life and that are self-renewing if not overexploited or otherwise mismanaged. Nonrenewable natural resources include minerals (which can often be profitably recycled in subsequent uses) and fossil fuels (which cannot). Care is required in extraction and processing of nonrenewable resources to prevent unnecessary damage to renewables.

tion of unsuitable soils are causing desertification in semiarid areas; worldwide, an estimated 6 million hectares (an area almost the size of Ireland) are lost to desertification each year. In addition, valuable cropland and grazing land are being irretrievably lost to soil erosion.

Deforestation is rapid in many developing countries: Haiti and Nepal, for example, have already lost the bulk of their forest cover. Annual global losses in tropical areas are estimated at about 10 million hectares or 1 percent of the remaining stock, with the percentage considerably higher in some countries. Loss of forests entails loss of their effect on stabilizing soil and slowing water runoff; the result in some cases is floods and landslides during the rainy season as well as rapid sedimentation of hydroelectric reservoirs, irrigation canals, and harbors. Loss of forests can also make it difficult for developing countries to meet their growing demands for paper, building materials, and, most serious of all, fuelwood. It could take hundreds of years to reverse some of these forms of environmental degradation. And the climatic changes, global or regional, induced by large-scale deforestation could prove to be irreversible.

Other environmental conditions have a directly harmful effect on living creatures. Fisheries, a vital source of protein and of foreign exchange earnings for many developing countries, are being damaged by overfishing and destruction of critical fish breeding habitats, as well as by pollution from industrial or agricultural sources. Biocides intended to protect crops against insects or other pests are in some cases creating new production problems for agriculture by destroying natural predators and the pollinators of crops, as well as by encouraging the rapid evolution of resistant varieties of pests; if improperly applied, biocides may also kill fish and even poison agricultural workers. Excessive use of fertilizer can contaminate bodies of water, with adverse consequences for wildlife, and cause the accumulation of nitrites in drinking water, with harmful effects on humans. Air and water pollution can injure the health of the urban population and may even necessitate expensive and administratively difficult decentralization of industry.

The stock of wildlife, one of the most valuable sources of foreign exchange earnings (from tourism) in some countries, is declining under a variety of development-related pressures. Furthermore, the rate at which species are becoming extinct because of man's actions is believed to be rapidly accelerating. The best available estimates suggest that if current trends continue, some 15 to 20 percent of the world's millions of plant and animal species may become extinct between 1980 and the year 2000. The implications go beyond ethics and aesthetics: many poorly known, even unknown, species are potentially important as renewable sources of energy, as industrial products or medications, as genetic inputs to agriculture, and as material for applied biological research.

Ironically, these types of environmental degradation are generally more severe in developing countries, where most people make their living directly from the land, than in developed countries. Environmental damage often affects the poor to a disproportionate degree. Poverty, inequities of land tenure, unemployment, and population pressures often compel the poor to use unsound farming, grazing, or fishing methods or to settle on ecologically fragile, marginal lands. A vicious cycle of increased poverty and further ecological degradation often follows, in which potentially renewable resources, including topsoil and fuelwood, are depleted for current use.

Especially difficult problems arise when tribal people or vulnerable ethnic minorities are involuntarily resettled or their traditional patterns of life otherwise radically altered. Unless interfered with, these people live sustainably in environments that are marginal for development. When their societies are severely disrupted, they often plummet to the ranks of the indigent burdening the state. This may also lead to the loss of economically valuable information acquired by tribal people over many generations, concerning practical uses of little-known plant and animal species.

How can developing countries deal with these problems? What should be their objectives? What has been their experience in incorporating environmental safeguards into development projects and programs, and with what costs and benefits? What are the major difficulties—technical, political, and conceptual—and how have these been overcome in typical cases?

OBJECTIVES

In broad terms, the overriding issue is how to avoid environmental damage or reduce it to an acceptable minimum without slowing the pace of development. The environment constitutes "natural capital"; its benefits and services—water flow, soil protection, breakdown of pollutants—support and enhance economic development. When poorly planned, development may contribute to the depreciation of a country's national capital. Even when carefully planned, the process of economic development inevitably causes some modification of natural ecological systems and generates wastes and pollutants. The objective of environmental management should be to achieve a balance between human demands on the natural resource base, from future as well as present generations, and the environment's ability to meet these demands. There may be circumstances in which a different choice may be made by (or forced upon) a society, but in general the objective of development policy should be to manage a country's renewable resources so as to yield the greatest present benefits possible without reducing their potential to meet future needs, that is, without reducing the "carrying capacity" of the environment.[2]

Maximum Sustainable Yield

The management of renewable resources should be based on the concept of maximum sustainable yield, which is defined as the maximum

2. Carrying capacity refers to the maximum number of organisms that can be supported in a given environment indefinitely at a given level, allowing for seasonal and random changes, without any degradation of the environment that would diminish this maximum number in the future. Carrying capacity may be increased—or decreased—by a change in technology employed. The concept is exemplified by the sustainable stocking rate of, say, cattle per hectare of given pasture. Similarly, the density of the human population at a given standard of living is a function of carrying capacity (which may be augmented by inputs of energy, food, and so on, as in a city).

rate of exploitation that can be sustained without depleting the future supply. An example is the level of waste discharge that is within the environment's natural assimilative capacity and can therefore be sustained without further pollution. It is simply another way of looking at the carrying capacity of a particular ecosystem. Since the supply of at least some renewables can be enhanced by appropriate investments (aquaculture for fisheries, afforestation for wood supply), the objective of a "sustainable" development policy may relate not to a fixed level of exploitation but to an expanded one. Obviously, the maximum sustainable yield is not a constraint with regard to such renewable resources as solar and hydropower, the future supply of which is not likely to be affected by the rate of current exploitation.

Some nonrenewable resources are in varying degree substitutes for renewable ones—for example, oil, gas, and coal for fuelwood, solar power, and hydropower. Also, some renewables are substitutes for each other; thus, meat, fish, and dairy products are alternative sources of protein. The concept of maximum sustainable yield should be viewed broadly to include resources that are close substitutes; that is, governments should look at the maximum sustainable yield of energy in general rather than of a particular fuel, or of all protein rather than of meat or fish alone. There are, of course, practical limits to substitution. For example, few feasible alternative sources of food or other necessities are available to herdsmen where overgrazing has led to desertification, or to farmers in hilly areas where deforestation and erosion are causing losses of arable land. Even if a country could afford to import kerosene to substitute for fuelwood, the rural poor most in need of the alternative fuel usually would not have the money to buy it. Consumers may adapt more readily to alternative protein sources than fishermen can convert to livestock production. Such limits may rule out substitution in some cases, except over a very long time.

Nonrenewable Resources

The rate of exploitation of nonrenewable resources is not, strictly speaking, an environmental question. The recovery, processing, or use of such resources may, it is true, have profoundly important environmental effects—as when the burning of fossil fuels and smelting of ores release sulfur and nitrogen oxides into the atmosphere and create acid rain. The resulting damage may lead to pressures for investment in technology to reduce unwanted emissions, to changes in relative prices that make environmentally undesirable resources more expensive, and so on. In any event, the rate of exploitation of nonrenewables—the basic decision whether to mine them or to leave them in the ground—is determined primarily on the basis of an economic cost-benefit calculation that takes into account such factors as expected growth of demand in the future, extent of known reserves (and possibilities of increasing them), potential for expanding output and for technological change, expected changes in relative prices, and so on. Most governments will discharge their responsibility to future generations by seeking to invest the proceeds from sales of an exhaustible resource in a way that increases permanently the productive base of the economy.

For optimum management of a country's natural resources, therefore, these resources must be viewed as a whole. There may be circumstances in which a country considers it advisable to allow a renewable resource to be exploited beyond its maximum sustainable yield—for example, to use up its fuelwood if it has great reserves of oil or coal. A country with vast forest resources may not worry about the rate of exploitation or the rate at which forest land is being converted to cropland or other uses. A country in a strong export position—for example, in oil—may rely on imports for some time to supplement or substitute for its domestic natural resource base. In most cases, however, such approaches are feasible only in the short or medium term. While nonrenewables, which by definition have no sustainable yield, are exhaustible, renewables, most of which are of a life-supporting nature (topsoil, clean water, and so on) can be overexploited in the long run only at a country's peril.

DEALING WITH ENVIRONMENTAL CONCERNS

In both developed and developing countries, the objective of sustainable development can be effectively pursued only if there is a considerable change in attitudes toward the environment that is reflected in national policies. The governments of many developing countries are beginning to identify national development strategies that are ecologically sustainable. But progress is slow and uneven.

Policy Changes

In environmental work, prevention is more important and virtually always less costly than remedial action, which sometimes may not be feasible at all. Accordingly, national policy should require that every proposed development project or program with a potentially significant impact on the environment be analyzed to determine what its effects are likely to be. When these effects are seriously adverse, the project should be redesigned. If redesign cannot sufficiently reduce the hazards, the project should be dropped—unless it can be clearly demonstrated that, because of special circumstances, its overall long-term benefits clearly outweigh the long-term costs, including the environmental costs.

For such analysis, many countries will need to prepare a much more comprehensive assessment of their environmental and natural resource base than they now have. Project planners need to be equipped not only with natural resource inventories, but also with "environmental indicators" showing trends in use (or overuse) of renewable resources. Assistance in such efforts is available to developing countries from a number of agencies, including the UNEP, the UNDP, the World Bank, and others. Such indicators would permit environmental monitoring on a broad scale. For example, grazing land can sustain no more than a certain number of livestock indefinitely. Although a further increase in stocking densities can add to the short-run economic return, it can do so only at the cost of long-run degradation and lower carrying capacity. Lack of data may make it difficult, however, to determine just what the carrying capacity is at a given level of technology. Environmental monitoring should cover biological trends (such as the number and location of wild and domesticated animal and plant populations), human health concerns (such as the effects of air and water pollution), and the supply and quality of various natural resources (such as topsoil and firewood). It should provide an early warning system of potential or actual environmental damage and suggest needed corrective action. Like data on foreign trade, tax revenue, or agricultural production, data on the environment should become a regular input into development planning, both for specific projects and for national development strategies.

With regard specifically to renewable resource conservation, a World Conservation Strategy was set forth in 1980 by the International Union for the Conservation of Nature and Natural Resources, with cooperation from the FAO, the UNEP, Unesco, and the World Wildlife Fund. It was endorsed by more than a hundred governments and by international agencies including the World Bank. It suggests pragmatic approaches to help developing countries ensure that the lack or misuse of renewable resources does not thwart their development efforts. Governments should consider formulating national conservation strategies, modeled loosely on the World Conservation Strategy but tailored to local needs. Among developing countries, Sri Lanka, Zambia, Nepal, and the Dominican Republic have begun to develop such national strategies.

Project Design

Giving adequate consideration to the environment when designing a project requires more than an improved data base and monitoring system. It also requires identification of appropriate standards for any project affecting the environment and the incorporation of safeguards to ensure that such standards are met.

Safe Minimum Standards

As more has become known about the impact of development on the environment, safe minimum standards with which a project must comply if it is to be socially and environmentally acceptable have been increasingly adopted by the international community. These relate to such matters as setting standards for public health and safety, protecting specially designated natural areas (parks and natural preserves), and safeguarding plant or animal species in danger of extinction. Projects should not contravene any applicable international agreement on the environment. Nor should they adversely affect the environment of a neighboring country without its consent, although this principle is not yet widely accepted or observed.

A few environmental criteria are virtually absolute; most are relative. Usually, these are readily distinguishable at the extremes, but in between lies a large gray area where values are changing. Some environmental degradation may be acceptable: for example, it may be more cost-effective, and preferable to those affected, to compensate people for a project's unwanted environmental effect—such as the noise of a railway routed near a village—than to eliminate the effect at great expense by rerouting the railway or soundproofing houses. Similarly, resettlement of some inhabitants may be considered an acceptable and necessary cost of providing the benefits of hydroelectric power to a large group of consumers. What is important is that such tradeoffs be recognized and explicit judgments made about how to deal with them.

The costs of modifying a project to meet appropriate environmental criteria should be regarded as normal project costs. In relatively few cases will such costs be appreciable (see the discussion below); in any event, as indicated earlier, it must be determined whether the total benefits are worth the total costs and whether the project should proceed. Such a decision should take into account both quantifiable and nonquantifiable costs and benefits.

Environmental Safeguards

Safeguards that need to be incorporated to prevent, minimize, or compensate for a project's adverse environmental consequences are sometimes very simple, requiring only minor redesign, and sometimes more complex. The World Bank's experience in this regard is instructive. In 1970, the Bank began examining every project considered for financing to identify likely environmental, health, and related problems and opportunities. A review of the work done from July 1971 through June 1978, covering a total of 1,342 projects in industry, agriculture, energy, education, health, transport, and telecommunications, showed that the majority of projects—845 (63 percent)—had no apparent or potential environmental problems. In 22 projects (2 percent) some other agency—such as the UNDP or WHO—had already identified the problem, and action had been taken to incorporate necessary safeguards. In 365 projects (27 percent) there were relatively simple environmental problems, which were dealt with by the borrowing governments and Bank staff, mostly through improvements in project design or operation. The remaining 110 projects (8 percent) had environmental problems sufficiently serious to require special studies by consultants to design and incorporate safeguard measures.

From these figures it can be seen that, of the projects requiring attention, roughly three-quarters could be dealt with through relatively simple design changes. In very few cases was it necessary to abandon the project for environmental reasons. It was found that the cost of incorporating environmental protection components into nonenvironmental projects (that is, all projects except primarily environmental ones such as pollution control, water supply and sewerage, and reforestation) ranged from 0 to 3 percent of total project costs, with the higher figure usually the result of adding protective measures after the project design was already well advanced.

These cost relationships may not apply in the future, since many expenditures for environmental protection are being incorporated into the basic technology for projects and so will become increasingly difficult to distinguish from other project costs. As economic development continues, however, developing countries are likely to face increasingly serious environmental conditions and to be forced to adopt higher standards. Worsening air pollution in Mexico City, São Paulo, Ankara, and many other cities indicates that environmental controls will have to be tighter on new projects; they will be both expensive and technically complex.

The cost of removing additional amounts of pollution from a waste flow is generally proportional to the amount already removed. This trend will produce higher costs—undoubtedly higher than 3 percent—for incremental improvement. Overall, however, a figure of about 5 percent for most projects in most sectors seems to be a likely ceiling.

For maximum effectiveness, environmental concerns should be reflected in project design at the earliest possible stage, when they can be accommodated at least cost. As part of project identification and preparation, an environmental reconnaisance should identify risks and opportunities and draw up appropriate plans, using environmental specialists such as ecologists and environmental lawyers.[3] The plans for project design, implementation, and evaluation should specify the environmental impact expected and the safeguards to be incorporated. For projects with important environmental implications, establishment of a small environmental unit within the principal project implementing agency is often an effective measure. Environmental impact should be closely monitored during project implementation and examined when evaluating completed projects to assess the efficacy of environmental components and to guide the design of subsequent projects.

Among the most common measures needed are controls on air and water pollution to reduce emissions and effluents to acceptable levels. Large steel production facilities, for example, are notorious for generating huge amounts of pollutants. In one developing country, initial plans for the expansion of a large integrated steel mill located near a commercial harbor, a major international fishing industry, and a town of 28,000 inhabitants were completely inadequate to deal with existing pollution, to control increased pollution stemming from the expansion, or to mitigate threats to workers' health and safety. With the World Bank's assistance, stringent controls were introduced for the existing plant as well as for the new facilities to protect both the town and the fishing industry; the expense was moderated by providing for recirculation of waste water and recovery of materials.

In another case, plans for a new sugar plantation and refinery included an irrigation system that could have aggravated the already serious problem of schistosomiasis and contaminated a nearby river and lake. To control the snails that carry schistosomiasis, molluscicides were dripped in flowing canals and sprayed in stagnant irrigation areas. Medical surveillance and treatment, as well as proper sanitary facilities, were also made part of the project. To prevent contamination of the river and lake, the project set limits on the use of fertilizers and biocides and called for liquid effluent to be discharged into spillproof evaporation ponds. A smokestack was constructed high enough to disperse gaseous emissions, and housing and associated services were located upwind from the exhaust.

New highway construction may unintentionally encourage colonization of ecologically fragile areas and thereby lead to deforestation and accompanying erosion, sedimentation of waterworks, flooding, and land-

3. The World Bank's Office of Environmental Affairs has produced standard terms of reference for particular kinds of projects—hydroelectric, highway, and so on—that specify the minimum information required.

slides. This outcome can be prevented, however, as it was in Costa Rica, where the boundaries of a national park were extended to encompass an area of vulnerable rain forest on steep slopes bisected by a new highway. In an irrigation project in Indonesia, deforestation of the watershed above the irrigation works was forestalled by establishing a 2,700 square kilometer national park. For less than 1 percent of total project cost, this component protects the irrigation investment by reducing sedimentation and thus maintenance costs and by helping to ensure the steady, year-round flow of water necessary for optimal rice production. The park also preserves much of the rich flora and fauna unique to the island of Sulawesi.

An asbestos mining and processing facility in a Latin American country posed serious health hazards because of the amounts of asbestos fiber in the air. The company agreed to comply with stringent standards specifying maximum exposure levels for employees. This required a number of engineering controls to reduce the amount of fine asbestos particles and dust in the air. The company also undertook to conduct yearly medical examinations, including an X ray and respiratory tests for each employee, to supply respirators, and to launder asbestos-contaminated work clothes.

Another technique to contain environmental damage is to limit the physical area adversely affected by a project. For example, selection of hydroelectric reservoir sites should take into account the ratio of hydropower generated to the area inundated. Dam sites should also avoid flooding unique ecological areas.

Analysis of Tradeoffs

Environmental considerations can play an important part in the evaluation of tradeoffs among alternatives that is central to sound project identification and preparation. For example, axial tube turbines and other low-head or no-head hydropower facilities do not flood extensive areas, but they generate less power than large dams. Similarly, reclamation of coastal mangrove swamps to grow salt-tolerant rice varieties is likely to diminish offshore catches of fish and shrimp, which depend on mangroves as a nursery. Prudent environmental management can reduce the need for such tradeoffs, for example, through land use planning that protects important wetlands. It can also suggest ways in which one sector can benefit another. Thus, aquaculture (fish farming) can recycle many agricultural or livestock wastes as fish food, thereby turning a nuisance or pollutant into a valuable resource.

Comprehensive Approach

In the early stages of the technology of environmental control, the emphasis was on treating pollutants and waste matter before they entered the environment. Experience has shown the need for a more comprehensive approach, especially in large urban areas of developing countries. In these areas, rapid industrial and population growth typically gives rise to environmental, health, and social problems associated with air and water pollution, poor sanitation, congestion, noise, and lack of open spaces and recreational areas. Since the mix and intensity of these problems vary among cities, solutions must be designed for each setting.

The rehabilitation of Sarajevo, Yugoslavia, a city of roughly half a million people, demonstrates what can be accomplished. Deep in a valley surrounded by high mountains, Sarajevo is subject to extended periods of temperature inversion, in which relatively warm air caps cooler air beneath, trapping atmospheric pollutants. Compounding the problem, the city has relied on lignite, a low-grade coal with 3 percent sulphur content, for heating. In winter, as temperatures dropped and heating requirements rose, the release of pollutants, particularly sulphur dioxide, shot up markedly. The result was a high level of air pollution, with attendant health hazards. In addition, the city's water system was able to supply water for only six hours a day. When no water was available, sewage spilling from broken pipes was back-siphoned into the water supply system; the pollutants were conveyed to water users in the next day's flow. With the help of a World Bank–assisted project, Sarajevo began in 1981 to enjoy a reliable and safe water supply and sewage collection system, including a new treatment plant; a sanitary landfill system for solid wastes; and a significant abatement of air pollution through use of piped natural gas (which burns cleaner than lignite) and a new traffic system that routes vehicles around rather than through the city.

Projects whose purpose is primarily environmental are often justified in nonurban areas as well. For example, wildlife conservation in Kenya is critical to the continued success of tourism, a major foreign exchange earner. A project to improve planning and protection of national parks and other protected areas, along with antipoaching measures, wildlife studies, and training of personnel, was estimated to have an economic rate of return of more than 15 percent.

Many other types of projects are heavily environmental and call for a comprehensive approach, among them reforestation and soil conservation; management of rangelands, wildlands, and watersheds; management of fisheries and water resources; slum upgrading and related urban improvements; expansion of water supply and sewage systems; development of renewable energy resources; prevention of desertification; and safeguarding of public health.

Economic Analysis of Environmental Protection

With careful environmental management, the pace of economic and social progress need not be slowed. In virtually every sector of the economy, projects have demonstrated that incorporating environmental safeguards (whose costs, as we have seen, are usually very modest) enhances economic and social benefits, or reduces economic and social costs, when compared with the risk of irreversible damage or the expense of subsequent remedial measures. In some cases, such components may improve a project's technical as well as economic performance; for example, a watershed management component of a hydroelectric project that minimizes reservoir sedimentation will extend the dam's useful life and enable turbines to operate at full capacity.

Environmental projects often do not lend themselves to the straightforward application of economic cost-benefit analysis. In principle, the methodologies and evaluation criteria applicable to projects with environmental aspects are similar to those for other kinds of projects: the proposed project should be the least-cost way to achieve the desired objectives, and the discounted costs and benefits, when the "with" and "without" cases are compared, should yield an economic rate of return greater than the opportunity cost of capital (see chapter 20, Economic Analysis). This applies to environmental components of other projects as well, the benefit of which may often be the avoidance of environmental damage. Problems arise, however, because the environmental costs and benefits, which often occur over a relatively long time, are difficult to forecast and to measure.

Measurement Difficulties

The natural environment, as noted earlier, provides not only specific resources, but also a wide range of environmental services such as maintenance of water flow patterns, soil protection, breakdown of pollutants, recycling of wastes, and even regulation of climate. These services are frequently overlooked or their value underestimated because they are almost always public goods, not priced in the marketplace. Consequently, the costs of damage to these services are difficult and sometimes impossible to quantify.

When the extent and character of environmental change can be predicted, existing markets and prices can often provide a reasonably unambiguous measure of the monetary value of some of the effects. The value of fish protein gained or lost through a change in water quality can usually be measured in this way, for example. Repair and maintenance costs of physical structures subject to air and water pollution or to siltation from deforestation upstream can be measured directly or estimated closely.

The health effects of a change in the amount of air pollution or the quality of drinking water are more difficult to measure. To the extent that these health effects can be identified, hospital data and physicians' fees will measure some of the costs; the cost of relocation for those who must move can also be measured. But many other costs will go unmeasured, and victims of the adverse effects will rarely, if ever, be compensated.

Cost-benefit analysis often measures benefits in terms of what consumers are willing to pay for goods or services. Although an attempt should usually be made to estimate the value of benefits that accrue to individuals, the appropriateness of using people's willingness to pay as a measure of environmental benefits may be limited by several factors, including the way that national or individual wealth is distributed. The poor, who often suffer most from environmental damage such as pollution, should be protected even though the costs of protection may exceed their capacity to pay. The willingness to pay for environmental benefits is also a function of cultural preferences and tastes. People's decisions as consumers are not always consistent with their best interests as citizens. If the benefits of environmental management are poorly understood or inadequately appreciated, countries or individuals will underinvest in environmental protection, to their ultimate detriment.

In the measurement of environmental costs and benefits, indirect methods must often suffice. For example, if no market exists, the value of benefits may sometimes be estimated by noting anticipated changes in prices of other, marketed goods. In a sewerage project in Brazil, the monetary value of some of the aesthetic and health benefits associated with a cleaner river was estimated on the basis of a predicted increase in nearby land values, presumed to result from those benefits.

Especially difficult is the task of quantifying the cost of irreversible damage and foreclosure of future options. Many complex natural habitats and their ecological services are now thought to be basically nonrenewable, at least within the life span of human civilization. The world's wildlands harbor millions of yet unstudied species, the scientific and economic value of which is impossible to estimate. This is particularly true in the tropics, where the diversity of species is greatest and scientific knowledge poorest. If economic values cannot be assigned, a judgment must be made about where the long-term interests of society lie.

Time Horizon and Discounting

A particularly intractable problem in cost-benefit analysis of projects with significant environmental impact arises out of the use of a discount factor to obtain the net present value of future costs and benefits. The discounting process relates future costs and benefits to an investment decision made in the present. But many of the important benefits of environmental management may accrue to future generations and become discernible only after the time at which standard cost-benefit analysis discounts future benefits virtually to zero. Presumably, future generations would pay or otherwise encourage present users of the natural environment to conserve more of it, in quantity and quality, were it possible to take their interests into account.

The reasons for using a positive discount rate in project analysis—one that approximates the estimated opportunity cost of capital in the economy—are described in chapter 20, Economic Analysis. The concept of the time value of money means that a dollar spent today represents a greater sacrifice or cost than if spent a year from now, because in the latter case it could be invested in the meantime and earn a return. Thus, benefits received earlier are worth more and costs incurred later represent a smaller sacrifice. The strength of the decisionmaker's preference for late rather than early costs is measured by the level of the discount rate. A high discount rate means that the yield of alternative investments is high or, to put it another way, that the opportunity cost of investments forgone is high.

The use of a discount rate can help decisionmakers to apply their time preferences in choosing among projects in which the streams of costs and benefits vary over time so that the preferred choices are not obvious. In projects without a significant environmental impact, use of a positive discount rate encourages an efficient allocation of resources—screening out projects with a low return and favoring more beneficial ones. Yet the uncomfortable fact remains that positive discount rates discourage investments with long-term benefits while encouraging those with long-term costs.

Expectations about future living standards also influence the choices made. Decisionmakers generally assume that consumption levels and living standards will be higher in the future, so they assign a positive discount rate to present consumption. Many environmental analysts, however, fear that not only nonrenewable but also renewable resources will become scarcer in the future because of today's environmental degradation, and that consequently consumption standards will be lower despite improved technology and other factors. They favor using a low or even a negative discount rate that places a premium on future benefits and weighs future costs heavily. Neither of these views can simply be dismissed. Since any positive discount rate, however low, is a numerical way of expressing the view that after a given number of years future costs and benefits are worth close to zero, the methodology is not neutral; it embodies a judgment about the future. For several reasons, however— because money has a time value, because a low discount rate could admit projects with a low return, and because use of different discount rates for environmental and other projects could distort investment choices—the conventional method of using a positive discount rate appears the only feasible approach at present. But further innovative work is needed to combine, within the framework of cost-benefit analysis, a positive discount rate for most project components and a means of weighing adequately the long-term benefits and costs of environmental components. In the meantime, to do what the marketplace (and standard cost-benefit analysis with a positive discount rate) will not do to reflect the interests of future generations, governments must step in with policies and regulations to ensure that environmental impact is properly taken into account.

Qualitative Analysis

When some of the costs and benefits cannot be quantified, as is often the case, the effects of alternative courses of action may be evaluated in qualitative terms. It will be easier to decide whether to proceed with an air pollution control project for an industrial city if a qualitative statement of the benefits (or costs) of reducing (or increasing) the level of sulphur dioxide accompanies the other, quantitative data on project costs and benefits. Such a statement should cover all aspects of pollutant effects— on sight, smell, taste, health, corrosion, recreation, and animal and plant life. The qualitative presentation, like the quantitative one, should show the difference between the "with" and "without" cases as well as the differences among project alternatives.

An approach sometimes found useful when only some of the project benefits are quantifiable is to ask what the value of the (residual) nonquantifiable environmental benefits would have to be in order to justify the project. Given the cost stream, discount rate, and value of directly quantifiable benefits, the value that the residual benefits must have to equalize total costs and total benefits can be calculated and provide the basis for a more informed judgment. This kind of analysis has also been useful in dealing with intangible gains or losses, including aesthetic values or recreational opportunities, and is especially relevant to situations that threaten the loss of unique natural or cultural assets.

Enforcement and Cost Recovery

Normally, project costs should be recovered from the beneficiaries rather than paid for out of general revenues, particularly in countries with limited possibilities for raising such revenues (see discussion of cost recovery policies in chapter 21, Financial Analysis). For costs of environmental components, however, it may not be practicable or even desirable to do this, for two reasons. First, it is difficult to identify the ultimate beneficiaries. For example, those who benefit from an air pollution control project will be widely scattered in space and time; they may include people outside the country as well as members of future generations. Second, the ultimate benefit of environmental safeguards is often the restoration of the environment to its earlier condition, or avoidance of damage to it, rather than the realization of a net gain. For example, it does not make sense to charge the people living in the vicinity of a steel plant for protection from its pollutants; presumably the firm, and in the final analysis the steel users, should pay. In contrast, flood control costs are normally charged to general revenues since the causes of floods are seldom attributable to specific acts of man but are considered as acts of God or nature.

Subsidies

As a general rule, those who are responsible for imposing costs on others should be required to pay for them. Yet many governments do not, for example, charge polluters the full costs of environmental safeguards; in fact, they often provide subsidies to help existing enterprises meet the cost of installing control equipment or to compensate them for the increased cost of complying with new or revised standards. One problem with this approach is that the regulatory agency must be able to distinguish costs incurred for purely environmental purposes from those that would be incurred routinely to increase production or improve efficiency. Moreover, the availability of subsidies may encourage inefficient investment decisions: an enterprise may decide to invest in "end-of-pipe" treatment facilities rather than change an internal process—which might be cheaper—because the former can more easily be demonstrated to be an antipollution device and hence eligible for a subsidy.

Although these distorting effects are well known, subsidization is common. It is defended on the grounds that industry would not otherwise cooperate in achieving environmental goals. When emission standards are set by the government and applied to all enterprises, however, pollution control becomes another cost of production, like wages and interest. Subsidies may, nevertheless, be provided to existing enterprises that must incur appreciable costs to adapt their facilities to comply with the new regulations.

Regulation, Standards, and Licenses

Pollution control may also be addressed through such regulatory mechanisms as licenses or permits that allow a given volume and concentration of effluent discharge per unit of time, that establish minimum standards of water or air quality, or that specify the treatment equipment to be used. A regulation that is uniformly applicable is easiest to devise and, in theory, to enforce. But the advantage of administrative simplicity may be outweighed by the economic inefficiencies that can result. For example, uniform effluent standards do not permit enterprises to take advantage of local absorptive or regenerative capacities and variations in the costs of pollution at different sites. Furthermore, uniform standards ignore the fact that the marginal cost of adjusting the quantity or quality of effluents differs among enterprises.

Alternatively, effluent standards may be tailored to each enterprise; they may require, for example, varying reductions in pollution, set to achieve the level desired for the region—provided all the enterprises comply. Ideally, the marginal cost of an additional unit of reduction would be equalized for all enterprises. However, the administrative cost of obtaining the information required to institute such a system is often excessive for developing countries. Furthermore, appeals or litigation may cause even more delay when individual standards are set than under a uniform system. Nevertheless, individual standards have often been adopted in World Bank–assisted projects.

Effluent Charges

Another technique is a system of effluent charges based on the total amount of pollutant discharged. A well-calculated unit effluent charge will achieve a desired reduction in effluents at a lower total cost to the economy than will a regulation that sets quality standards. Self-interest may lead each enterprise to maximize profits by investing in process changes or effluent treatment up to the point at which the cost of a unit reduction in effluent is equal to the amount of the charge. Enterprises with different cost characteristics are therefore likely to respond differently.

Because their absorptive or regenerative capacities, and therefore the harm caused, will vary for different watersheds or airsheds, effluent charges should be set on a regional basis. The level of the initial charge is not critical, since it may be raised or lowered subsequently to bring results in line with the target. When pollution is excessive and the first steps toward improvement are being taken, the difference in results between a system of individually specified standards and a system of effluent charges may be minimal. As greater environmental improvement is desired, however, marginal costs typically increase, and the economic case for a rigorous system of charges becomes stronger.

Training

Lack of trained manpower is a major constraint to environmental management in most developing countries. Projects incorporating environmental technology should routinely provide for any necessary training to operate and maintain the technology and to monitor environmental quality. Projects with a major environmental component need one or more environmental specialists, starting at the project preparation stage, to assist with study, design, and implementation. Although a temporary solution may be to engage local or expatriate consultants, the implementing agency should arrange for intensive training of staff to take over from them—as well as for long-term training of younger agency staff and university graduates. Training in the implementing agency can usefully be paralleled in a country's environmental ministry or equivalent agency. When environmental specialists are assigned to an agency other than the one implementing the project, special measures to ensure cooperation

between the two agencies may be necessary. For example, in Bank–
assisted projects in Brazil, Indonesia, and Thailand, the project agency
created in-house environmental units and arranged for the federal environmental agency (and others) to oversee its activities.

Transition to a Sustainable Society

In the relatively unpopulated world of earlier times—one with underutilized natural carrying capacity—a system of "frontier economics" may
have been appropriate. The natural resource base was diminished and the
resulting revenues were invested in economic growth. Land and forest
were exploited with little restraint because the frontier seemed endless.
Wastes were discharged freely because the absorptive capacity of air and
water was great.

That carefree era is largely over for most countries, even those with
low population densities. (Largely unsettled areas have usually remained
so for compelling reasons, including infertile soils, pests, or other environmental constraints—as in Brazil's Amazonia or in some of Indonesia's
Outer Islands.) Land, fresh water, petroleum, and other natural resources
are no longer relatively abundant. As a result, human societies are having
to shift from "frontier" economics to "finite" or "spaceship" economics
and adjust to the limitations of the planet's natural resource base and of
its capacity to assimilate wastes. A sustainable society is one that can live
indefinitely within its means—its natural as well as human and financial
resources. The success of efforts to increase the well-being of a society or
the quality of life is not necessarily measured by growth in GNP. What is
essential is that developed and developing countries alike improve the
way in which natural resources are managed, rather than simply promote
higher rates of resource consumption.

Inspecting equipment at a petrochemical plant, Brazil

25

Procurement

MANAGING THE PROCUREMENT PROCESS is a central aspect of project implementation for all kinds of projects. Delays in procuring the necessary goods and works are likely to be compounded into further delays and increased costs for the project as a whole. Since the number of possible ways in which things can go wrong in procurement is seemingly endless, and "Murphy's law" (when it is possible for things to go wrong, they generally will) appears to be particularly applicable, procurement has to be thought of as a process to be planned, organized, and managed. The critical path network approach (see chapter 17, Project Implementation) is very well suited to dealing with the numerous administrative and procedural steps that procurement entails.

Procurement must be managed to serve three objectives. First, it must help ensure the efficient and economical execution of the project. In this regard, it is sometimes (mis)stated that the goal of procurement is to acquire the highest quality of goods or works at the lowest possible price and with the best delivery time. In practice, of course, there will be tradeoffs among these three elements, not all of which can be maximized simultaneously. Analysis, evaluation, and judgment are all needed to obtain the composite package that is most advantageous. Second, procurement in the public sector can be used to promote national goals for the development of domestic industry, for balanced regional development of industry, or for expansion of small-scale enterprises. Third, procurement must comply with the requirements of any external agencies assisting with the project. These three objectives, which overlap, figure with varying degrees of prominence throughout the discussion of the procurement process that follows. Departing from our approach in most of this book, we shall describe the World Bank's procedures in some detail.[1] These procedures, which are followed to a large extent by other external aid agencies, are mandatory for Bank-assisted projects. Compliance with them has had an important bearing on how well these projects have been implemented.

This chapter is concerned especially with procurement by or on behalf of agencies in the public sector. Private firms should be no less motivated by interests of economy and efficiency, but they normally operate under their own simpler rules and procedures except insofar as they are the beneficiaries of public funds or subjected to public regulation of their procurement practices. In general, their self-interest can be expected to lead to economical procurement.

METHODS OF PROCUREMENT

A wide variety of procurement methods is used in developing countries, ranging from direct placement of a contract or the use of the agency's own work force at one end of the scale to full-fledged international

1. The procedures are set forth in the World Bank, *Guidelines for Procurement under IBRD Loans and IDA Credits*, 2d ed. (Washington, D.C., 1984).

competitive bidding at the other. Which method is most appropriate will depend on the size and nature of the project, the particular goods or works to be procured, and the requirements of lending agencies.

International Competitive Bidding

International competitive bidding is the method of procurement that has generally proved to be the best means of satisfying the three basic considerations underlying the Bank's procurement policy:

- The need for economy and efficiency in project execution
- The Bank's interest, as a cooperative international institution, in giving qualified firms in all its member countries (as well as in Switzerland and Taiwan, China) an equal opportunity to compete
- The Bank's interest in encouraging the development of local manufacturers and contractors in the borrowing country, through the use of preferential measures in bidding and contracting.

Moreover, international competitive bidding, with its emphasis on a broad, open, competitive tendering process as described below, has also proved to be an important safeguard against the waste, corruption, and discrimination that can occur in procurement by public bodies.

Other multilateral aid agencies and some bilateral agencies have modeled their procurement regulations on the Bank's guidelines, with minor variations—notably with respect to the countries eligible to bid and to the degree of preference, if any, for manufacturers and contractors in the borrowing country or in other developing countries. Many developing countries have also relied on international competitive bidding for large-scale purchases from abroad by public agencies—albeit with simplified procedures for notification and invitation to bid—essentially for the same reasons of economy, efficiency, and fairness.

There are many detailed features of international competitive bidding, but three are fundamental. The first is widespread *notification* of the opportunity to submit bids, so that all interested and qualified firms in all eligible countries can participate. The notification can take place in a variety of ways, which are often used in combination: publication in an official gazette, advertisement in local newspapers, notification of embassies in the nation's capital, and—for large, specialized, or important contracts—advertisement in newspapers of international circulation or in relevant trade journals or technical magazines. In addition to the use of periodicals or newspapers, the World Bank, the Inter-American Development Bank, the Asian Development Bank, and the United Nations Development Programme now require that the procurement opportunity be publicized through a General Procurement Notice in the United Nations Development Forum, Business Edition.

Second, the technical *specifications* of the goods to be purchased or works to be performed need to be stated fairly (that is, neutrally) to ensure the widest possible participation of qualified firms of differing nationalities. If national standards with which equipment or materials must comply are cited, the specifications should state that other but equivalent standards will also be accepted. Similarly, specifications should be based on performance requirements, and reference to brand names or the like should be avoided.

Third, the award should be made, in accordance with the *evaluation* criteria specified in the tender documents, to the qualified bidder whose tender is evaluated to be the lowest. Although this rule is essential to ensure that the competitive process works fairly, it poses problems to the evaluator, as described more fully below, and is the most difficult of the three features to apply in practice.

International competitive bidding is best suited for procurement of large equipment items (such as turbines, locomotives, and telecommunications hardware) and large civil works (such as dams and major highways) in which firms of different nationalities will be interested in participating. International competitive bidding is sometimes criticized on the grounds that its procedures are too formal, elaborate, and therefore time-consuming. Although the procedures do result in a somewhat longer bidding process than typifies the other methods described below, the time differential can be narrowed by suitable advance planning and by carrying out individual procedures in parallel rather than in sequence whenever possible. Even if it takes more time, however, in the Bank's experience international competitive bidding is generally the best way for countries to achieve the objectives of procurement in those cases in which it is applicable.

Limited International Bidding

Limited international tendering is a modified form of international competitive bidding in which qualified bidders are invited to bid without open advertisement. It may be appropriate if the contract amounts are small, if the number of suppliers is limited, or if other reasons (such as the need for early delivery) justify a departure from international competitive bidding. Bids should be sought from a group of suppliers broad enough to ensure competitive pricing. Without sufficient competition, the savings in time and effort may be offset by higher bid prices. In the case of commercially traded commodities such as metals, cereals, or fibers, purchases through organized international commodity markets (for example, the London metal market) can meet the requirements of competitive bidding.

In addition, in some large and complex industrial projects such as petrochemicals, potential bidders may be few and the cost of preparing a bid high. Tendering may then be limited to, say, four qualified firms from three countries in order to save time and also to get better proposals, since each firm has a better chance of winning the contract.

Local Competitive Bidding

Local competitive bidding, as the name implies, is carried out through local advertising only and in accordance with local bidding procedures. It may be favored by government regulations in cases in which foreign participation is not required or expected. It may also be accepted by external aid agencies for goods and works not suitable for international competitive bidding, as long as appropriate procedures are followed. Foreign contractors are not likely to be interested, for example, in bidding for works that are individually small and dispersed (such as the construction of small schools, rural markets, or health clinics or the lining of canals in a number of different locations). Similar considerations may apply to goods manufactured or readily available in the country (such as small electric motors, pumps, or school furniture) and purchased in small quantities. The size of the contracts, the possibility of combining them into larger packages, and the competitiveness of local industry will all be factors determining where the line between international and local competitive bidding should be drawn.

The choice of local bidding procedures may arise naturally from the process of project design, as when structures designed for labor-intensive methods of construction are chosen to provide local employment. In addition, local competitive bidding may be favored when it clearly offers substantial savings of time and money in procurement and when these savings will significantly improve project implementation. There will be few cases, however, in which such savings are real and capable of offsetting the distinct advantages of international competitive bidding. If providing spare parts and service facilities locally is an important feature of the project—as it may be for, say, farm machinery—procurement may be limited to suppliers offering such services (who may often be local representatives of foreign firms).

Local procurement procedures and regulations may differ in some respects—such as the process of notification and the use of local language and local currency—from those specified for international competitive bidding. The same considerations of fairness, economy, and efficiency should guide the process, however, in either case.

A clear advantage to the country of local competitive bidding is the opportunity to develop local industry. Its principal disadvantage is that there may be an insufficient number of local firms to avoid collusion among them and ensure competitive pricing. Some of the other shortcomings that have commonly been observed in local procurement are:

- Formal or informal negotiations on prices with bidders after the bids have been opened or the use of evaluation criteria other than those publicly disclosed, with the resulting danger of corruption or collusion
- Excessive delay in processing and evaluating bids, which ultimately increases the cost
- Excessively detailed review of proposed awards by a central tender board or equivalent agency
- Inadequate training of managers and staff responsible for procurement
- Failure to provide foreign exchange and import licenses more or less automatically when goods or components have to be obtained from abroad, giving rise to further delays.

Although many local procurement procedures have been inspired by a commendable desire to safeguard the use of public funds, care must be taken to ensure that their practical administration does not yield the opposite result. Possible ways of strengthening local procurement procedures include:

- Insistence on public opening of bids
- Delineation of streamlined procedures for review and approval, with

fixed intervals for the various stages, greater delegation of authority to line agencies and operating units, and more selective review in recognition of the typical profile of contracts (80 percent of the value of contracts are accounted for by 20 percent of the number)

- Use of outside technical experts for difficult or controversial contracts
- Specialized training for procurement staff.

International and Local Shopping

Shopping is a procurement method based on comparing price quotations obtained from several foreign or local suppliers, usually at least three to ensure competitive prices. It requires no formal advertising or bidding documents and is an appropriate method for procuring goods that are readily available "off the shelf" or commodities whose specifications are standardized and whose value is low. It may also be appropriate for very small, simple works.

Projects involving loans to industrial or agroindustrial enterprises or to individuals through financial intermediaries present a special case. Typically, loans are made to a large number of beneficiaries (farmers, small or medium-size enterprises) for the partial financing of subprojects. Procurement is usually undertaken by the beneficiaries in accordance with established commercial practices, which should provide the buyer with the opportunity to choose from several alternative suppliers. The intermediary institution is expected to ensure that acceptable practices are followed, but reliance is placed primarily on the self-interest of the beneficiaries to obtain the most advantageous terms. Sometimes a central agency may use a competitive bidding process to select a number of alternative models of an item (for example, a tractor) from which the beneficiaries can then make their choice.

Direct Purchase

Contracting directly with a single supplier or contractor may be appropriate in certain circumstances. Extension of an existing contract, preferably one entered into originally on the basis of a competitive tender, may result in lower prices and shorter delivery time for equipment by obviating the need for retendering; or it may take advantage of a contractor who is already on-site and does not require time and money to mobilize his construction forces. The buyer should be sure that prices on the extended contract are reasonable and that it is unlikely better results could be obtained from further competitive bidding. When in doubt, it is better to put the existing contractor or equipment supplier to the test of the competitive market. A single source is also used when the item to be acquired is proprietary in nature and must be purchased from the sole manufacturer. Items that are so critical to the successful operation of the project that a cost premium is justified to ensure early delivery or satisfactory performance may also be purchased directly from a qualified supplier.

Standardization of equipment or spare parts so that they are compatible with existing equipment may be another reason for purchasing directly from the original supplier. Although standardization on a limited number of makes or models may have clear advantages when it comes to maintenance costs, training of personnel, inventories of spare parts, and so on, there may be countervailing advantages to having alternative models, sources of supply, and competitive prices. The optimum number of models depends on several factors, including the total size of the equipment fleet. It is sometimes possible to analyze the alternatives and to quantify the premium, if any, that should be given to the standardized equipment. Competitive bidding can then be open to all potential suppliers, with the premium for standardization specified in the tender documents.

Government Contracting and Force Account

In centrally planned economies and some others, a government-owned contracting organization may execute works on the basis of established or negotiated prices. The disadvantage of this form of procurement is the absence of competition and market discipline; the contractor may be unresponsive to considerations of time, price, and quality. Circumstances permitting, it would be preferable to form several parastatal enterprises, organized under autonomous management and obliged to compete with each other for procurement contracts. Properly organized and managed parastatal construction companies have successfully participated in international competitive bidding under Bank-assisted projects.

More widespread is the practice, in all types of economies, of having government departments execute works using their own work force. This is customarily referred to as *force account*. Force account may be the most economic and efficient way—sometimes the only way—of executing

- Works that cannot be measured accurately in advance, such as rehabilitation of irrigation canals that must first be drained
- Small works, such as village wells and rural roads, located in remote or insecure areas or on widely scattered sites
- Works that must be coordinated with ongoing operations, such as maintenance of a railway line
- Works requiring special expertise that general contractors may lack, as in the transport or energy sectors
- Works for which social objectives, such as the need to utilize unemployed local labor, are considered of overriding importance.

This form of organization may also be a valuable training ground for supplying managers and skilled workers to the construction industry at large.

Force account work has inherent disadvantages, however, the most serious of which are the risks of political interference, bureaucratic overstaffing, and lack of financial discipline. These conditions can lead to higher costs and inefficient use of resources, often disguised by inadequate accounting that does not measure the full costs of the operation. Some of these drawbacks can be mitigated, for example by the establishment of incentive payments and adequate cost and performance controls. But excessive reliance on force account can inhibit the growth of a viable domestic construction industry, public or private, itself one of the important ingredients of economic growth. It is best to confine the use of force account to the special cases referred to above and to the maintenance of a minimum capacity needed permanently for routine operations, for emergencies, and for training staff.

COMMON TYPES OF CONTRACT

For all civil works procurement other than by force account, three types of contract normally apply: lump sum, cost plus, and unit price. Lump sum or cost plus contracts may be preferable for certain specific situations (lump sum when it is important to know in advance the cost of the works, cost plus when circumstances make it difficult to estimate costs), but they have inherent disadvantages. By far the most common form of contract is based on unit prices quoted by the contractor for a designated "bill of quantities" that states all the items of work to be performed together with the estimated quantity of each item. Its principal advantage is that it readily accommodates changes in the quantity of work as that work goes forward; moreover, in multiyear contracts, the unit prices fixed on a certain date can be modified through a price adjustment formula to reflect changes in the cost of inputs.

STEPS IN PROCUREMENT

For all types of procurement that use bidding procedures (that is, procurement other than by direct contract or force account), the steps are essentially the same. The timing will differ according to the method followed, but the general injunction still applies: procurement is a process that must be planned, and the time required to carry it out properly should not be underestimated.

The principal steps in the procurement process, in the sequence in which they occur, are:

- Preparation of tender documents
- Advertising, prequalification, and issuance of tender documents
- Bid preparation
- Receipt and opening of bids
- Evaluation of bids and recommendation and review of award
- Contract finalization with winning bidder
- Contract execution.

Preparation of Tender Documents

Preparation of tender documents is the first and at the same time the most difficult and important step in the procurement process. The tender documents (also called bidding documents) are the principal means of communication to the bidders and form the basis for preparation of the bids and their subsequent evaluation. Problems that arise at the other critical stage in the process—bid evaluation—can be attributed more to faulty preparation of tender documents than to any other cause. This is another instance in which there is no substitute for being right in the first place. Preparation should therefore not be hurried, and it should command the attention of experienced staff. If consultants have been employed to do the detailed engineering, they are often retained to prepare the tender documents as well.

The Bank's guidelines spell out the process:

- The bidding documents should furnish all information necessary for a prospective bidder to prepare a bid for the goods and works to be provided. While the detail and complexity of the documents will vary with the size and nature of the proposed bid package and contract, they should generally include an invitation to bid, instructions to bidders, form of the bid, form of the contract, general and special conditions of the contract, technical specifications, and a list of goods or bill of quantities and drawings.

- The bidding documents should clearly define the scope of work to be performed, the goods to be supplied, the rights and obligations of the procuring agency and of the contractor or supplier, and the functions and authority of the engineer or architect if one is engaged to supervise and administer the contract.

- The bidding documents should set forth clearly and precisely the work to be carried out, the location of the work, the goods to be supplied, the place of delivery or installation, the schedule for delivery or completion, and the warranty and maintenance requirements, as well as any other pertinent terms and conditions. In addition, the bidding documents, when appropriate, should define the tests, standards, and methods that will be employed to judge the conformity of equipment as delivered, or works as performed, with the specifications. The bidding documents should specify any factors to be taken into account in addition to price in evaluating bids, and how such factors will be quantified or otherwise evaluated.[2]

Advertising, Prequalification, and Issuance of Tender Documents

The advertising procedures that generally apply to competitive bidding have already been described. Prequalification in advance of bidding is normally advisable for large and complex civil works, and occasionally for equipment, to ensure that invitations to bid are confined to capable firms. Although prequalification takes more time, it is justified when the cost of preparing bids is large or when some special reason exists for limiting the number of bidders. It has the further advantages of testing the interest of the contracting industry in the work and of assuring competent contractors that only qualified firms will be allowed to bid, thereby making them more willing to participate. If prequalification is used, all firms that meet the requirements should be allowed to bid. The award can then be made to the bidder with the lowest evaluated cost, as explained below.

---

2. There is considerable merit in using a standard set of general conditions. Perhaps the one most frequently used is that of the Fédération Internationale des Ingénieurs-Conseils (FIDIC). The World Bank, in cooperation with the Inter-American Development Bank and the Asian Development Bank, has prepared sample bidding documents for the procurement of goods and works through international competitive bidding.

Prequalification should be based entirely on the ability of the interested firm to perform the requisite work satisfactorily, with account taken of the firm's experience and past performance on similar contracts; capabilities with respect to personnel, equipment, and plant; financial resources; and current work commitments. Prequalification should be timed so that bidding documents are available for distribution as soon as the process is completed.

One means of developing the local contracting industry is to encourage foreign contractors to make maximum use of local firms through joint ventures. If there is adequate capacity to perform some of the work locally, the tender documents should explain the proposed joint venture arrangement and ask foreign contractors to find suitable partners; the joint venture would then be prequalified as a unit. (Under World Bank procedures, such joint ventures, while encouraged, cannot be made mandatory.)

For smaller and less complex works and equipment, prequalification is not necessary; tenders can be accepted from all bidders who consider themselves capable of executing the contract as specified. In the absence of prequalification, a letter of invitation to bid, accompanied by the tender documents, should be furnished to all eligible applicants who respond to the advertisement. Once it is determined which bid has the lowest evaluated cost, a postqualification of the successful bidder can then establish whether he is capable of doing the work.

Bid Preparation

When bids are invited, sufficient time has to be allowed for interested firms to visit the project site, if desirable, and to prepare and submit their bids. For international bidding, the time given should be at least 45 days in the case of standard goods and at least 90 to 120 days for a major industrial plant or complex civil works. Efforts to economize by reducing the time are likely to prove illusory and could result in higher rather than lower costs.

The bids submitted are valid for a period that is specified in the bid invitation and that should be sufficient to enable the procuring agency to finish evaluating the bids and secure the necessary review and approval by higher authorities. Ninety days is typically specified but is often inadequate. Every effort should be made to complete the process within the original period of bid validity, which must therefore be realistic; extending this period, although frequently done, can entail further complications as bidders seek to withdraw or revise their bids.

A bid bond or guarantee is often required on large contracts, in which case it should be specified in the tender documents. While the bond or guarantee should be sufficient to afford reasonable protection against frivolous bids, it should not be so high as to discourage bona fide bidders; 1 to 2 percent of the estimated contract value is generally appropriate. The successful bidder, notably in civil works contracts, is required to submit a performance surety to protect the procuring agency should he not fulfill his obligations. Performance sureties come in two principal forms: a bank guarantee, typically for 10 to 15 percent of the contract value, which can be called by the procuring agency at any time if it determines that the contractor is in default; or a bond, usually for the full value of the work, issued by a surety company, which undertakes to have the work completed, up to the value of the bond, should the contractor be found (by a third party) to have failed to do so. The latter is in use primarily in North America.

Receipt and Opening of Bids

Two issues frequently arise during this phase of procurement. One is whether the opening of bids, at the time and place stipulated, should be done in public, or at least with representatives of all bidders present. Philosophy and practice vary widely. Some governments favor secret bid opening, primarily on the grounds that, if bid prices are made public, pressures will be brought to bear that will make an objective evaluation more difficult. Nevertheless, legislation in many countries, and the loan agreements of international lending institutions, call for public bid opening. The World Bank normally requires it as the best means of assuring all bidders and the public at large of the integrity of the bidding process.

The second issue is whether and under what circumstances a bid should be rejected, either before opening if it has not been delivered at the stipulated place and time or after opening if a preliminary examination indicates that it is not substantially responsive to the specifications and conditions of the tender documents. This is often a matter of judgment rather than of set rules. In the long run, however, barring exceptional circumstances, the procuring agency's reputation for fairness can best be enhanced by close adherence to contract specifications and procedures. This is the course of action most likely to avoid controversy and to secure the benefits that come from the continued willingness of firms to compete and to bid at reasonable prices.

Bid Evaluation, Recommendation, and Review

Evaluating the bids, reviewing the recommended award with the appropriate authorities within and, if necessary, outside the country, and awarding the final contract comprise the "bottom line" of the procurement process. It is not surprising, therefore, that it is the part that most frequently gives rise to contention.

Much of the difficulty—and controversy—arises from the fact that the award should be made not to the bid that is *priced* lowest, but to the bid that is *evaluated* to be lowest in terms of total cost—hereafter referred to as the *lowest evaluated bid*. Price, while obviously important, is only one aspect of the total cost. The objective of the evaluation should be to determine which responsive bid will provide the lowest total cost. Although this criterion is clearly in the best interest of the procuring agency, it is almost axiomatic that the lowest-priced bidder will lodge a strong protest and exercise pressure if the ultimate award is not made to him.

Among the factors other than price that may have to be taken into account in comparing bids are time of delivery, schedule for completion, commercial terms of the contract, operating and maintenance costs, efficiency or productivity of equipment, reliability of construction methods, availability of spare parts and service facilities, need for operator and mechanic training, and useful life of the equipment. While the relevant criteria and the method of their application should be set forth in the tender documents, and can to some extent be quantified, some judgment will nonetheless have to be exercised in applying them, particularly when differences in quality of performance are involved. ("Life cycle costing" of equipment, under which all relevant costs over the useful life of the equipment are taken into account, is a worthwhile approach but requires more information than many bidders can readily provide.)

Two areas of particular difficulty in the evaluation process are the degree of responsiveness of bids and the extent to which modifications may be permitted after bid opening. Bids should be rejected at the time of bid opening only if they are clearly nonresponsive in one or more significant respects (such as failure to submit the bid bond, to accept the basic technical design, or to use the prescribed price adjustment formula) since there is limited time on that occasion to examine the bid documents or obtain a legal opinion, and a decision to reject may be difficult to reverse. In general, judging whether a bid is responsive should be left to the more careful and thorough review that is the heart of the evaluation process. Some cases are simple; but for large, complex civil works or procurement of sophisticated equipment (such as telephone networks or locomotives) every bid may be nonresponsive in at least some detail. The evaluators then have the challenging task of determining whether the deviations from the specifications are significant or whether the bid remains substantially responsive and lends itself to proper evaluation and comparison with other bids. Moreover, what may be significant in one set of operating circumstances or conditions may not be so in another. If the bid is not rejected, some adjustment should be made to its cost as originally presented to allow for the deviations and make it comparable with the other bids. These adjustments can very readily give rise to dispute.

In the same spirit, no bidder should be *allowed* to substantially alter a bid after it has been opened, since this would clearly be unfair to the other bidders; nor should one or more of the bidders be *required* to modify their bids, as for example through a practice sometimes referred to as a "Dutch auction," in which the procuring agency seeks to negotiate reduced prices from several of the bidders sequentially. This practice may result in lower prices in the short run, but it will eventually discourage firms from participating in bidding in countries or with agencies known to follow it. Some clarification of the bids is frequently necessary, however, and the line between a clarification and a substantive modification of the bid may be a fine one for the evaluator to draw. Absence of factual information should normally be remedied by a request for clarification.

Experience offers little precise guidance on how to handle these delicate matters, the details of which vary from case to case. The award of multimillion dollar contracts may often hinge on matters of judgment. Objectivity, quantification of factors whenever possible in accordance with specified criteria, consistency with the specifications of the tender documents, and equality of treatment for all bidders should be the primary considerations. Thus, if one of the bids reveals a deficiency in the tender specifications, a not infrequent occurrence, all bidders should be permitted to modify their bids, or the contract should be retendered.

Once the technical staff of the procuring agency has completed its evaluation and arrived at a recommendation, that recommendation is likely to be subject to approval by a contract review board in the agency or by a central authority. This review may be important to ensure consistency of treatment and adherence to established procedures and to avoid some of the dangers of collusion. The board, however, should resist the temptation to substitute its judgment for that of the staff on technical matters.

In the case of the World Bank, which reviews all important contract evaluations prior to the award, the purpose of the review is not to second-guess the borrower. Instead, the Bank determines whether or not the borrower has acted reasonably and in accordance with the Bank's guidelines in making the evaluation. In matters of judgment on which reasonable men may disagree, the Bank may accept the borrower's recommendation even if it might have decided the matter differently had it been responsible, as long as the principles and procedures of the guidelines have been respected.

Although bids should preferably be opened in public, the ensuing process of bid evaluation and review must be kept confidential until the selected contractor has been notified of the award. Bidders on important contracts somehow manage to keep themselves well informed, but the principle of confidentiality is nonetheless essential so that those responsible can carry out their duties without undue interference from interested parties.

Contract Award

The contract should be awarded to the responsive bidder whose bid has been evaluated by the appropriate authorities to be the lowest in total cost and who meets the standards of capability, experience, and financial solvency established through pre- or postqualification. Perhaps the principal point that needs to be made about this stage is that it should not be the occasion for negotiations with the successful bidder to pressure him to lower the price, change other contract terms, or undertake additional work not specified in the tender documents as a condition of the award. Although there may often be a number of open questions that need to be resolved with the successful bidder on a complex project prior to contract finalization, obliging him to modify his bid under the threat of loss of the contract to another bidder would invalidate the whole procurement process.

ENCOURAGEMENT OF DOMESTIC INDUSTRY

One of the ways in which procurement can be used to help develop the local construction industry—participation in joint ventures with foreign firms—has already been mentioned. Similarly, subcontracting can be encouraged in the tender documents when it is known that there is a local capability to provide some of the equipment and materials or to execute some of the works. Another contracting procedure, sometimes described as "slicing and packaging," is also designed in part for this purpose. Civil works are divided (sliced) into a number of individual contracts small enough to enable small local contractors to bid on them. Larger contractors, local or foreign, can bid on packages of these contracts. The tender documents generally indicate that the award will be made to the firm, or combination of firms, whose bids result in the lowest price for a package or a group of packages.

For contracts funded entirely with its own resources, a country must decide whether or not foreign firms will be permitted to bid. It must balance the desirability of promoting local industry against the desirability of fostering competition and securing the lowest prices and best conditions for the project. Most but by no means all countries have resolved this choice in favor of permitting foreign participation, although foreign bids may be subject to tariffs or other measures favoring local enterprises.

Some international lending institutions also permit a preference for domestic contractors as part of international competitive bidding. For World Bank–assisted projects, domestic manufacturers of equipment are eligible for a preference of 15 percent or the prevailing level of customs duties, whichever is lower. (Domestic manufactures are defined as those with a local value added of at least 20 percent.) The 15 percent level has not been established through any highly refined analysis, but reflects a working compromise between the interests of the developed and developing member countries of the Bank. A preference of 7.5 percent is accorded to local civil works contractors, but only in developing countries with a per capita income below a designated level. To qualify, a contractor must have a majority of local ownership. The lower preference for civil works reflects two considerations: the natural protection which domestic contractors already enjoy through greater familiarity with local conditions, labor regulations, and so on; and the fact that the difference in local value added between foreign and local construction firms, to which the preference is in principle addressed, is relatively small since both groups of firms use local labor and materials and some local equipment. The degree of effective protection provided by the 7.5 percent preference is, therefore, quite large.

The practice of other external agencies varies. Some follow the World Bank's rules, in some instances with small differences in the amount of the preference or the way it is applied; some extend the preference to firms in other developing countries as well; others, perhaps the majority, have no stated preference. Some accept the procurement arrangements, including any customs duties or quotas, of the national authorities.

There are many other means of developing local industry, particular branches of industry, or small enterprises in general. Some of these are related to procurement (such as reserving part of the domestic market for designated sizes or classes of firms or requiring large firms to subcontract with them), but most of them transcend the procurement process and merge with the broader issues of industrial development policy discussed in chapter 9, Industry.[3]

---

3. For a discussion of measures to develop the local construction industry, see Ernesto E. Henriod, *The Construction Industry: Issues and Strategies in Developing Countries* (Washington, D.C.: The World Bank, 1984).

Trainees from Ghana and Nigeria inspecting sorghum at International Crops Research Institute for the Semi-Arid Tropics, Hyderabad, India

26

Use of Consultants

PROCUREMENT OF CONSULTING SERVICES, like other types of procurement discussed in the preceding chapter, can have an important bearing on the outcome of a project. The product supplied by consultants differs in several respects from equipment or civil works and so, as a consequence, does the procurement process. In procuring goods and works, objective criteria such as price and measurable differences in quality dominate the evaluation. With consultants, it is difficult to specify performance levels in quantitative terms, yet differences in the quality of service may have a very large impact on project results.

WHY USE CONSULTANTS?

Consultants are commonly used in project work for four main tasks, the substance of which is discussed in various other chapters of this book. As described in the World Bank's guidelines for the use of consultants,[1] these tasks are:

- *Preinvestment studies*—the investigations that normally precede a decision to go forward with a specific project. These studies may have as their objectives the establishment of investment priorities and sector policies, the determination of the basic features and the feasibility of a project, or the identification and definition of changes in government policies, operations, and institutions necessary for the successful implementation or functioning of development programs and investment projects.

- *Preparation services*—the technical, economic, or other work required to define a project fully and prepare it for implementation. These services normally include preparation of detailed capital and operating cost estimates, detailed engineering, and tender documents required for invitation of bids for construction work and equipment. In addition, they often include work in connection with preparation of procurement documents, determination of insurance requirements, prequalification of licensors and contractors, and analysis of bids and presentation of recommendations.

- *Implementation services*—construction supervision and project management, including inspection and expediting, certification of invoices submitted by contractors and suppliers, and technical services connected with the interpretation of contract documents. These services can include assistance in procurement, coordination of inputs by various contractors and suppliers engaged on a single project, and the start-up of facilities and their operation for an initial period.

- *Technical assistance*—a wide range of advisory and support services, such as national and sector planning and institution building,

---

1. World Bank, *Guidelines for the Uses of Consultants by the World Bank and its Borrowers* (Washington, D.C., 1981).

including organization and management studies, staffing and training studies, and assistance in implementation of study recommendations.

Insofar as possible, these tasks should be assigned to local personnel. Creating and strengthening local capability to conceive, design, and carry out projects on a sound basis is an important part of the development process. Without such capability, a country may not control fully its economic and social development, and even its ability to make the best use of financial, technical, and human resources from abroad may be impaired. Furthermore, the effective transfer of skills and the development of technology appropriate to local conditions are facilitated by the understanding of local conditions and the insights that local staff can usually best provide.

The first step is to develop such capability within the department, agency, or other entity responsible for the project. In the long run, this can be done through the educational system or through different forms of on-the-job training or study abroad. In the short run, it may be necessary to choose between the need to design and implement a high-priority project promptly and efficiently and the need to build up local capability; the second objective may have to be subsumed under, and made a part of, the first. Bank experience has demonstrated that much can be accomplished in this way; over the years many of the Bank's borrowers, beginning with relatively simple tasks, have strengthened their capacity to design and implement their own projects, eventually with little outside help.

Few agencies in developing countries, however, can afford the luxury of retaining on their staff persons who are versed in all the areas of specialization necessary for project work. An agency will generally have personnel who are able to perform some of the tasks, but they may be partially or fully occupied with other duties. In some countries, inadequate salaries may mean that staff are not available on a full-time basis because they hold more than one job. Or the task to be done may entail temporary work for which the agency may not wish to hire staff on a permanent basis. Any institution is likely, therefore, to find it advantageous to hire outside consultants at one time or another, and some will want to do so on a regular basis.

LOCAL OR FOREIGN CONSULTANTS?

When in-house capacity is inadequate to meet the demands of the project, the next-best choice is the use of local consultants or, failing that, consultants from another developing country, provided they are qualified to perform the assignment and have the relevant background and experience. Local consultants are naturally preferred, and they offer genuine advantages, mainly because of their knowledge of local conditions, procedures, and customs. Moreover, costs are likely to be lower than when foreign consultants are employed, and a greater proportion of the costs are incurred in local currency; the higher cost of expatriate consultants and the higher living standards they enjoy can present practical, and even political, obstacles to their acceptance in the country. Nevertheless, there are occasions when it makes sense to use foreign consultants because they are perceived to be more independent of local pressures, because they can act as a lightning rod for controversial recommendations, or because they make available a technology with which the country is not familiar. Also, only a few developing countries (such as Brazil and Mexico) have a local consulting industry capable of providing most of the wide range of services called for in project work, and many countries have hardly begun the process. For some assignments, only consultants from developed countries may be qualified—assignments requiring the "hard" skills (engineering) and pertaining to large and complex projects (major dams, expressways, fertilizer plants, airports), for which consultants may sometimes be employed even in developed countries. In such cases, the higher price that expatriates command will be more than offset by the unique contribution they can make to the success of the project.

Establishing a local consulting industry has important long-term advantages: helping to build local technological capacity, providing some competitive spur to agency staff, and supplying the more specialized or expert services that an agency needs only on occasion. How can a government foster a domestic consulting industry? One of the most effective ways is through joint ventures with foreign firms, as discussed below. The most important impetus, however, is strong support from the government through a steady volume of work. Local firms can be expected to be formed almost spontaneously by individuals who have worked for foreign consulting firms or for government agencies if they perceive that an opportunity exists. This is an area where the market will respond—as it has in Indonesia and the Philippines, for example—if demand (a regular source of work) and supply (trained staff) exist. Recurrent assignments on which a local consulting industry can grow include those associated with irrigation canals, roads, public buildings, power distribution systems, and water and sewerage networks.

INDIVIDUALS OR FIRMS?

Consultants may be hired as individuals or as a firm. Although the latter approach is more common and usually preferable, individual consultants can be used when they are expected to work independently and not as part of a team, when no additional outside professional support is required, and when the experience and qualifications of the individual are paramount. Individual consultants entail less out-of-pocket costs to the employing agency, since the substantial overhead costs of a consulting firm are reduced or avoided. But some of these costs are, in effect, absorbed by the agency as part of its own overhead. Recruitment of individuals with the appropriate skills and experience can be difficult, and consulting firms are understandably reluctant to release their staff to serve in an individual capacity. Public advertising is likely to induce a flood of applicants whose qualifications will be difficult to assess.

When three or more individuals are expected to work together as a team, the task of recruiting, administering, coordinating, and ensuring collective responsibility becomes formidable. In practice, recruitment of individuals to work as a group has seldom been successful. This applies to individuals seconded by external aid agencies as well as to those recruited directly. In these circumstances, the use of a consulting firm is desirable if not essential. Consulting firms may also have difficulty in putting together a team with the required skills to match the job requirements, but they start with an established staff and with greater experience in recruiting individuals from outside.

ONE FIRM OR A LIST?

When the need for a consulting firm has been identified, the question arises whether to contract directly with a particular firm or to seek proposals from a number of firms. If a firm known to the agency has the required competence and has established a satisfactory relationship, usually as a result of past or current service, there is good reason to continue with it. The consultant-client relationship is a close, personal one; when it is working well, it is eminently sensible not to disturb it.

Another reason for engaging a specific firm is to ensure professional continuity at the successive stages of the project cycle. If a firm has carried out preinvestment studies for a project and is technically qualified to undertake the subsequent preparatory work, continuing to use its services will ensure consistency in the basic technical approach and a commitment to the project cost estimate on which the investment decision was based. If a different firm were retained for the detailed engineering, it might wish to make its own review of the preliminary design work and cost estimate. Similar arguments of continuity and consistency apply to implementation and supervision work. It is desirable, however, to enter into separate contracts for the successive project stages, or at least to provide for a formal review at the end of each stage with the right of contract termination, so that the agency is free to dismiss a firm that has not performed to its satisfaction. Such a review is also desirable to counteract the natural—if unfortunate—bias of a consultant to come up with positive findings at the feasibility study stage in order to secure the larger volume of business associated with the subsequent stages of project preparation and implementation.

One type of continuity that should not be encouraged is the use of consulting firms that are part of, or affiliated with, other commercial activities such as construction firms or equipment manufacturers. To ensure impartiality and avoid a potential conflict of interest, if such firms are used as consultants they should agree to limit their role to the provision of these services and to disqualify themselves, and their associated organization, from participating in the supply of equipment or works under the project. (This rule need not apply to turnkey contracts that consist of consulting services, the supply of equipment, and the construction of related works in a single package.)

The World Bank and most other international financial institutions, recognizing the fundamental differences between the procurement of consulting services and of goods and civil works, recommend but do not require competitive proposals for such services. They will accept direct contracting with a firm, including a local firm, subject to their approval of the firm's qualifications. Bilateral aid agencies are more likely to require a consultant of their own nationality if no capable local firm exists, and some require it in any case.

When the choice of a suitable partner is not obvious—and it often is not—proposals from several firms should be solicited. Again in contrast to the procurement of goods, all potential candidates need not be included. The cost to a firm of submitting a proposal is high and the agency's task of evaluating proposals arduous. A short list is, therefore, appropriate: the World Bank usually recommends no less than three and no more than six firms. Even with a short list, it is desirable to seek a wide geographical spread among the firms, language requirements permitting, with no more than two firms of the same nationality. Qualified local firms and those from other developing countries can be included in the short list.

Some agencies lack experience in how to draw up a short list, especially for difficult assignments. In practice, it can be derived in a number of ways. One procedure is to publish an open invitation describing the work to be undertaken and the qualifications sought. The respondents are then narrowed down to a short list by taking into account geographical or national diversity in addition to experience and other qualifications. This process can be time-consuming, however, and such an advertisement is likely to inundate the agency with written responses and personal visits by representatives of interested consulting firms. Approaches to foreign embassies or to professional associations may also give rise to a spate of responses that will have to be evaluated.

A more promising procedure is to ask for recommendations from other officials in the country or in neighboring countries who have had experience with similar assignments. Assistance is also available from some multilateral lending institutions. The consulting service office of the World Bank gives borrowers access to its computerized files and provides, on an exceptional basis, a short list of firms that appear to have the relevant experience and qualifications.

Joint Ventures

The short list can include a joint venture between a local and a foreign firm, or between local firms, in cases where a local firm by itself is not qualified to perform the full range of services required. Such a joint venture, in which two or more firms agree to associate for the purpose of performing a specific assignment, may be an excellent way to develop domestic consultant capacity. The consulting professions in Colombia and the Philippines developed largely through joint ventures. Foreign firms often welcome these arrangements to overcome such handicaps as a lack of familiarity with the local situation or language difficulties. Responsibility is a major issue in a joint venture, however, and the contractual arrangements should clearly define the responsibility (and liability) of each firm.

When each of the two firms has something to contribute, wishes to transfer or receive knowledge, and can collaborate productively, a joint venture can work very well. But it is not without risks. It has happened that the local partner has been little more than an empty shell, receiving a portion of the fee merely for lending its name to the effort. This only serves to increase costs, while doing nothing to develop local capacity. Conversely, a foreign firm has sometimes been brought in to lend prestige to a local firm that could not qualify on its own, but the foreign firm has later pulled out or was not used as proposed. For joint ventures to succeed, they should result from the voluntary association of willing partners and not from a "shotgun wedding" arranged by the agency employing them and acquiesced in by the two parties in order to secure a contract. Such freedom of choice may be required by external lenders if they are to finance the contract.

TERMS OF REFERENCE

In the invitation to consulting firms to submit proposals, the terms of reference of the assignment play the same central role as do the tender documents used for the procurement of goods and works. They serve three main purposes:

- To confirm the agreement between the agency and others concerned (such as external lenders) on the objectives and intended scope of the proposed assignment
- To inform the consultants of the objectives, scope, and timing of the work and of the inputs to be provided by the agency
- To define the consultants' services—including the output (reports, drawings, and so on)—as they will be formulated in the contract eventually to be negotiated with the firm selected.

The terms of reference should be as clear and specific as the nature of the assignment permits. This is particularly important for preinvestment studies, in which the scope and character of the assignment are open to different interpretations and require sharp definition. It is sometimes thought that broadly defined terms of reference will encourage the firms submitting proposals to develop more imaginative approaches to the problem. Although this may have merit in certain situations, it has generally been found useful to specify precisely the nature of the problem to be addressed and the scope of the assignment, not only to give focus to the consultants' work in preparing the proposals and to channel it in the right direction but also to make a comparison of the proposals possible.

The documentation should also contain a realistic description of the working conditions, the data and information available and their shortcomings, the kind of support to be provided to the consultant by the employing agency or others, tax liability, and so forth. In its own interest, the agency should be open and frank about difficulties in carrying out the terms of reference. The procedure for comparing and evaluating proposals, including the role of price, should be mentioned. It is essential to provide sufficient time for consultants to prepare their proposals in a considered manner. A joint meeting with all the interested consultants, similar to a prebid conference in major civil works construction, may be useful for complex assignments.

If training is one of the objectives, it should be specifically provided for in the terms of reference and in the budget for the consulting assignment. Granted that some transfer of knowledge inevitably takes place through working together, it is nevertheless most effective when carefully planned beforehand and agreed upon during negotiations with the consultants.

The availability of interested and qualified trainees is essential and should be ensured before the assignment begins. Moreover, both parties must recognize that the trainees are there to be instructed and not to act as low-paid assistants or errand boys.

EVALUATION AND SELECTION

Technical Qualifications

The starting point for evaluating the proposals submitted by the firms on the short list should be their technical merit. Three principal factors need to be taken into consideration:

- The firm's general experience in the field of the assignment
- The adequacy of the proposed work plan and approach in responding to the terms of reference
- The qualifications and competence of the personnel proposed for the assignment.

The relative importance of these factors will vary with the type of assignment. As a guide in evaluating proposals, it is convenient to use numbered ratings for each category. For preinvestment studies, the firm's general experience might be given a weight of 10 to 20 percent, the work plan 25 to 40 percent, and the key personnel 40 to 60 percent. For detailed engineering, greater weight might be given to the experience of the firm and less to personnel.

In assessing personnel, relevant factors include their academic preparation, work experience, familiarity with similar conditions, and knowledge of the local language. It is, unfortunately, difficult to assess a curriculum vitae with confidence. Apart from the degree of exaggeration common to such statements, it is usually not possible to know how well past jobs were performed or how thorough or successful past training or study has been. For this reason, interviews with key personnel and direct verification of their references are desirable for important assignments.

The comparison of proposals should be done as objectively as possible and preferably by several individuals working independently who, among them, cover the range of professional expertise called for by the assignment. It must be recognized, however, that the comparison and final selection is an art and not a science. The numerical values serve to bring order into the process and to organize and give relative importance to the qualitative judgments that must be made, but they cannot substitute for those judgments.

Price

An issue of growing importance and controversy is the extent to which price should be taken into account in the evaluation process. The cost of consulting services can vary widely, especially among firms of different nationalities. Unlike the qualitative factors mentioned above, price differences can readily be quantified and therefore evaluated, and a number of countries have adopted regulations requiring that price be one of the determining factors.

In appropriate cases, some of which are identified below, price comparisons can lead to substantial cost savings to the employer without impairing the quality of the work performed. In general, however, the Bank's experience strongly suggests that the selection process, whether or not any weight is given to price, should maintain quality as the paramount consideration. The cost of consulting services is usually only a small fraction of total project costs, and differences in the quality of the work performed can have a great impact on the final outcome. In most circumstances, the consultant who is most costly to the project is the one who does the job least well.

Three characteristics of consulting services affect the extent to which price may appropriately be considered in the selection process:

- The complexity of the assignment
- The impact of the assignment on the success of the project
- The comparability of the proposals submitted.

A technically complex assignment would be, for example, a multisectoral feasibility study (such as an urban master plan), the design of an offshore oil production platform, or a community action program calling for changes in social attitudes and behavior. At the other end of the scale, tasks of a straightforward technical nature would include the detailed engineering of secondary roads or of a simple water supply system. Assessing the impact of the assignment on the end product is largely subjective, but it can be done on the basis of the adverse consequences (additional costs or forgone benefits) that would ensue if the assignment were not performed satisfactorily. Thus, the collapse of a major dam would be of far greater significance than leakage from a defective water pumping system, and small differences in the quality of policy advice could have substantial financial or economic consequences. With respect to comparability, assignments of a clearly defined technical nature, such as routine detailed engineering or construction supervision, are more likely to give rise to proposals that can be directly compared than are assignments related to management advice, training, or sector and policy studies.

Price should not be used as a selection factor if the assignment is complex or difficult to specify precisely enough to ensure comparability of the proposals, or if small differences in the quality of the services performed could have a large impact on the ultimate success of the project. In the majority of cases, the quality of the consultants' services is likely to be the primary consideration.

When price is taken into account, it should be done in a way that does not undermine the technical evaluation. If prices are known in advance and price differences are substantial, the pressure on the evaluators to select the lowest-priced proposal rather than the one with the greatest technical merit can be well-nigh irresistible. Consequently, the technical evaluation should be made independent of price. This can be done through a two-stage procedure. Technical proposals are submitted separately and evaluated first; the financial proposals, including prices, are kept in sealed envelopes and opened only after the technical appraisal has been completed. What weight to give to price differentials in the final evaluation will be a matter of judgment. The mechanical application of a quantitative formula giving specific weights to price and technical factors is not likely to be satisfactory, since different things are being compared: a 10 percent difference in price, for example, is not necessarily equivalent to a 10 percent difference in technical quality.

This two-stage procedure for technical and price evaluation should not be confused with the so-called "two-envelope" procedure that enjoys a surprising vogue. As in the former procedure, both technical and financial terms are called for at the same time, with the financial terms in a separate sealed envelope. A technical evaluation is undertaken, but only the envelope containing the financial terms of the firm that is rated highest technically is opened. If the negotiations with this firm are successful, all other financial envelopes are returned unopened to the unsuccessful bidders. The intent is to prevent the selected firm from increasing its price to take advantage of its negotiating position. Whatever the theory, in practice all of the second envelopes are often opened at the same time and compared with the technical proposals in what is in effect a one-stage procedure. Indeed, if the two-envelope procedure were rigorously followed and the firms submitting proposals believed that only the price envelope associated with the best technical proposal would be opened, it is difficult to see how it would have a restraining influence on the prices they proposed. In short, this procedure has little to commend it.

Negotiations, Signature, and Implementation

Negotiations on price with the firm whose proposal has been evaluated as the best are customary when selection has been made solely on a technical basis. The employing agency generally enjoys a strong bargaining position, since the selected firm risks the loss of the contract to the second-best firm, which may be waiting in the wings. Care must be taken not to press the negotiating advantage too strongly, however, lest the consultant be forced to cut corners unduly in order to protect both his profit and his opportunity to close the contract. When price has been a factor in selection, there is normally little room for negotiation, and any reduction in price is likely to be at the expense of quality. If the best technical proposal is not the lowest in price, giving the best proposal to the lowest bidder and asking him to adapt it to his low price, or asking the bidder with the best technical proposal to do the work for the lowest price, are both practices that should be discouraged.

Given the great weight assigned to the qualifications and competence of the personnel in evaluating proposals, changes in the team at the time of negotiation or afterward are properly viewed with suspicion. If negotiations are entered into within the time limit set out in the request for proposals, the agency is entitled to resist any changes in the personnel to be assigned to the job in the absence of persuasive reasons. Unfortunately, the selection process often takes longer than anticipated, in which event it is unreasonable to expect the consultant to have kept the team that was originally proposed on indefinite standby; some substitution may be necessary. The agency can only satisfy itself that the substitutes are adequate replacements, using the same criteria as in the original evaluation.

A draft of the proposed contract should have been included in the request for proposals. It should set out the contractual obligations of both parties in a clear and balanced manner. There are a number of model documents, including several prepared for different types of assignment by the Fédération Internationale des Ingénieurs-Conseils (FIDIC).

The office space, secretarial staff, transport, housing, import licenses, and work permits promised to the consultant in the request for proposals or during negotiations must be provided if the consultant is expected to perform his contractual obligations. Failure to do so can quickly lead to frustration on both sides and impair the relationship in ways that will jeopardize the final product.

The same applies to the counterpart staff assigned for technical or administrative support to the consulting firm or for training by it. This often presents a problem. Almost by definition, qualified personnel will be in short supply and assignment of good trainees or effective support staff will mean taking them from important current assignments. This becomes a question of weighing the long-term benefits of better skilled staff against the short-term losses. Sources for temporary replacements might be (local) consultants, bilateral aid agency staff, retired personnel, and staff temporarily rotated from other government ministries or agencies.

Once employed, a consultant may be asked to undertake work not specified in the contract. The extent to which such requests should be made and accepted without contractual modifications or additional fees is always a delicate matter. Spontaneous advice and minor extra work are usually provided as a gesture of goodwill or as a business promotion, and more readily accommodated if promised support has been forthcoming and payments made reasonably on time. Significant added work can be undertaken only if additional payment is made or some reduction in the original scope of work agreed upon.

Last, but by no means least, the work of the consultants needs to be closely supervised by the employing agency throughout the period of the contract. When consultants have been recruited at the urging (or perhaps insistence) of an external lender, there may be an unfortunate tendency to look upon them as working for the lender rather than the borrower. Even if the services being provided are highly specialized and beyond the technical capacity of the agency, a close relationship between the consultants and the agency needs to be maintained if the work is to be performed in a manner consistent with the broader interests of the project.

PART V
Summary and Conclusions

Kneading clay for pottery, a handicraft industry, rural Mexico

27

Highlights of Experience

IT HAS BEEN SAID that to govern is to choose. In the economic arena, the most basic choice that all societies must face in allocating resources is between current consumption of goods and services and investment in future growth. In developing countries, the choice must be made in the face of the deplorably low, often subsistence, level of consumption of a large proportion of the population and the urgent need to invest as the best hope of achieving higher living standards. When the choice is made in favor of investment, it is imperative that the scarce resources be deployed to obtain the maximum benefit. Packaging these investments into projects through the disciplined approach described in this book can be a very effective means toward this end. In this concluding chapter, we highlight some of the principal lessons that can be drawn for the benefit of developing countries from the World Bank's more than thirty-five years of experience with the project approach.

At the beginning of the book, we described economic development and the project work which is an integral part of it as a long, slow, and often painful process of learning from experience. Investing in development through projects is subject to all the vicissitudes and constraints that hamper development generally. Projects take years to prepare and implement. Throughout this time, project managers must confront and deal with the scarcity of human skills and material resources that are synonymous with underdevelopment, with a chronic shortage of funds, and with shifts in political support. They must operate within often fragile economic structures that are exposed to the worldwide forces of inflation and recession and to the unpredictable forces of nature.

Project work is thus highly demanding, and it sometimes seems to demand most from those countries with the least capacity to respond. It is more difficult, but also more important, to do project work well when there is little or no cushion to absorb the effects of unsound policies, weak public administration, or unskilled project management. This is true of all types of projects, particularly those intended to alleviate poverty and raise the living standard of large numbers of people.

Fortunately, the rewards of project work are commensurate with the demands. Done well, project work pays high dividends. In the postwar era, it has become one of the most potent instruments for promoting economic growth. By setting investment priorities within a national and sectoral strategy, getting the policies right, and combining investments with technical assistance to strengthen institutions and train people, the project approach can enable countries to take more rapid strides along the path of economic development.

Doing project work well is as much an art as a science. Drawing on the wealth of World Bank experience, we can identify many of the ingredients of success as well as many of the pitfalls. Developing countries can profit from this experience and thereby telescope the learning process. Some may be able to achieve in decades the economic progress that took generations in the now developed world .

In reviewing the lessons of the Bank's experience, we have been struck again and again by how obvious many of them seem to be. They often read like little more than the dictates of common sense. But to say that something is obvious does not mean that it is simple. Perhaps simple to understand—except for a few esoteric subjects such as cost-benefit analysis—but not simple to put into practice. If the lessons of experience have not yet been learned, it is not because of irrationality or obduracy, but rather because a powerful constellation of forces makes things what they are and serves as a formidable obstacle to change. Moreover, economic development, as we have repeatedly observed, is a long-term process; when governments change frequently, the continuity of effort that is a sine qua non of development is soon broken. Even in reasonably stable political conditions, public officials are often and understandably preoccupied with more immediate considerations. They are more likely to suffer the short-term political penalties of policy changes such as raising the prices of basic commodities than to reap any political rewards from their long-term benefits.

To take just one example of the difficulty of applying a simple lesson of experience: it is by now widely accepted that developing countries should use the technology most "appropriate" to their circumstances. These circumstances usually include a surplus of low-cost, unskilled labor and a shortage of capital—facts which suggest that the technologies adopted should be relatively labor-intensive. The point seems obvious; which government would knowingly or willingly espouse an "inappropriate" technology? Yet in countless instances—and this book cites a number of them—developing countries have adopted or retained technologies clearly unsuitable to their circumstances.

Why does this happen? Foreign consultants or advisers may advocate the technology with which they are most familiar. Local engineers, if educated abroad or the heirs of a colonial legacy, may have acquired a similar bias in favor of advanced technology, or they may simply presume, as do their superiors, that what is most modern is best. Special interest groups may favor a particular technical approach, while those who would benefit most from some other approach may be either unaware of the choice or politically disenfranchised. Deep-seated customs and traditions may favor certain solutions and make others unacceptable. Economic policies that overprice labor (through minimum wage or other legislation) or underprice capital (through subsidized interest rates or an overvalued currency) may send distorted signals to decisionmakers. A simple lack of knowledge or reluctance to experiment may limit the range of choice. Bilateral lending agencies may themselves be part of the problem; when aid is tied to the supply of equipment from the donor country—a policy as widely practiced as it is deplored—freedom to choose an appropriate technology may be compromised. With so many factors at work, it is not surprising that a "simple" lesson—such as selecting an appropriate technology—may prove far from simple to apply.

Trying to summarize the lessons of the World Bank's experience in a single chapter is a daunting task. We can only highlight the more important lessons, with no expectation of doing justice to the many issues and problems that these lessons raise. The presentation generally follows the sequence in which the book is organized: national investment management, sector analysis and management, the project cycle, and the various dimensions of project analysis. The sector chapters of part II are not referred to as such, since the broader lessons emerging from them underlie the points discussed in parts III and IV.

No attempt is made to indicate the relative importance of these lessons, although some are clearly more important than others. Not getting prices right, for example, or not providing adequate recurrent funds to operate and maintain project investments can have more far-reaching consequences than not regularly evaluating completed projects. Since the lessons relate to different aspects of investment planning, sector analysis, and project work, it should be possible, at least in theory, to apply them all. But to many officials in developing countries, they may appear to constitute a formidable agenda. It is for each official, knowing the local circumstances, to establish priorities for action at any time. Progress may often be slow and partial, but responding flexibly to changing circumstances, combining rational economic choice with informed political judgment, avoiding the more egregious mistakes, and maintaining a steady pace are the best way to keep the country on the path to sound economic development.

National Investment Management

Project work in its broadest sense takes place at three levels:

- At the national level, where national investment plans are formulated, priorities among sectors are established, and the macroeconomic framework of policies for economic growth is put in place
- At the sector level, where priorities for investment within each sector are determined and the issues and problems affecting the development of the sector are addressed
- At the project level, where individual projects are identified, prepared, and implemented and attention is given to their technical, economic, financial, social, institutional, and other dimensions.

Only in the abstract can the project process be described as a sequence of steps proceeding in logical order from the national to the project level. Project work is in fact a continuum; decisions or actions affecting individual projects may take place at each of the three levels simultaneously and in interactive ways.

Development planning. At the national level, the surge of enthusiasm for comprehensive development planning, which reached a peak in the 1950s, was followed by disenchantment with its limited accomplishments. No clear association could be found between a comprehensive planning effort and sustained economic growth. The elaborate and data-hungry models employed were unable to cope with the complexity and rapid change that characterize the process of development; nor did most developing countries have the administrative capacity to implement comprehensive plans. The technical and administrative deficiencies of comprehensive planning proved to be inherent in the process and, therefore, unlikely to be overcome by more strenuous efforts to improve the planning machinery.

Planning is therefore being directed increasingly toward new goals. Countries covering a wide political and economic spectrum no longer seek to rely on positive commands and negative controls to carry out a long-term plan that targets inputs and outputs for all sectors of the economy. Instead, they have turned to a strategy that focuses on two elements: a macroeconomic framework of policies to spur economic growth and elicit desired behavior from both public and private entities; and a public sector investment program that allocates scarce resources to high-priority public needs. The success stories of postwar economic development come from those countries that have managed these two tasks effectively.

The macroeconomic policy framework—comprising fiscal, monetary, exchange rate, wage, and trade policies—affects all aspects of economic behavior, including resource allocation, capital accumulation, balance of payments equilibrium, and, ultimately, the pace of economic growth. No single set of policies, and no specific institutional arrangement for managing those policies, are appropriate to all countries in all circumstances; what is appropriate varies with a country's natural and human resources, level of development, and development strategy and objectives.

Pricing Policy. Central to any policy framework, however, is pricing policy. Many of the macroeconomic policy variables—interest rates, wage rates, exchange rates—are prices. Whether determined in free markets, or established by a central planning agency, or modified by government intervention, prices strongly affect a country's rate and pattern of development. The importance of "getting the prices right" is therefore a fundamental lesson of development experience. The basic pricing rule for obtaining the most efficient use of an economy's resources is to set the price of each good or service at its marginal cost—a result that a free competitive market would achieve and that public pricing policy should, in principle, emulate. In the real world, however, actual market conditions nearly always diverge from the competitive ideal. Moreover, in pricing public sector goods and services (power, water, rail transport, and so on), public agencies must take into account not only the objective of economic efficiency but also other objectives such as achieving a more equitable distribution of income or generating additional revenue. These considerations may justify departure from a rigorous marginal pricing rule (a point we return to in the discussion on cost recovery below) and may call for carefully designed intervention in the market to achieve both social and economic objectives. It is important that such intervention be devised to make use of market forces rather than to supplant them.

In many developing countries, however, a persistent and often massive distortion of prices has resulted from a multiplicity of government interventions, many of them poorly conceived or mutually incompatible. These distortions have reduced the efficiency of investment and slowed economic growth. The countries that have enjoyed relatively high growth rates are those that have managed to avoid significant price distortions; specifically, they have

- Avoided an overvalued exchange rate
- Kept the rate of effective protection for manufacturing industry relatively low and uniform among products
- Avoided underpricing of agricultural products and other disincentives to farmers
- Kept interest rates and hence the price of capital positive in real terms
- Avoided real wage increases not justified by rising productivity
- Applied cost recovery principles in pricing infrastructure services
- Avoided high inflation.

Many examples from the developing world in the past twenty years demonstrate how critical the proper management of this interconnected system of prices and incentives is for economic progress. Furthermore, the effects of macroeconomic policies are felt with full force at the project level. Thus, another fundamental lesson is that it is virtually impossible to have good projects in a bad policy environment.

Public investment programs and budgets. In formulating public investment programs, detailed and overly sophisticated forecasting exercises have generally proved counterproductive because of inadequate data and limited understanding of how sectoral investments and outputs are linked. Analytical efforts should therefore concentrate on designing investment programs in key infrastructure sectors, where the market alone cannot guide investment decisions, and on checking the consistency of these programs with the likely requirements of the productive sectors. Governments also need to be selective; they can effectively address only the most important public investment issues at any one time.

Experience has further shown that it is advantageous to combine the programming of public investment with indicative forecasting (not targeting) for the private sector. Emphasis should be placed on coordination and consultation—between departments of government as well as between government and the private sector. Governments also need to develop the capacity to respond quickly to changing events by modifying their policies and programs; this will usually require a much improved data base and information flow as well as centralized responsibility for policy coordination.

Establishing investment priorities among sectors—the attention to be given, for example, to programs in health, education, or housing relative to the productive or infrastructure sectors—is particularly difficult and ultimately entails political choices. Economic analysis can make only a limited contribution to this process, but it may still be crucial in clarifying the costs of alternatives and providing data on which informed judgments can be based. In establishing investment priorities within a sector, however, cost-benefit analysis can be very helpful in improving choices.

Experience has taught a number of other lessons about formulating and implementing public sector investment programs.

- Care should be taken that the investment plan is not too ambitious given the available resources. There is a widespread tendency to underestimate the cost of implementing specific projects and the time required. When too many projects are started at the same time, available skills are dispersed, project implementation is slowed, and economic and financial returns from the investments are reduced.

- New projects should not be started at the expense of adequate funding for those projects already under way. Completion of ongoing projects, if they are still justified given the incremental costs and benefits, should have a high priority for funding, as should the operation and maintenance of completed projects.

- The "free" resources left after the needs of ongoing and completed projects have been met should be calculated. This makes possible rational decisions about how much funding can be devoted to new projects in any budget year.

- Planning agencies need to strengthen their project appraisal capacity and to make greater use of cost-benefit analysis to identify and screen out projects with low rates of return.

- Investment plans need to be kept flexible and modified as circumstances change. In addition, a "core program" of investments should be identified so that cuts in programs made necessary by a shortfall in resources can be determined by priorities established in advance. Another technique found useful in many countries is to have a rolling investment program—usually a three-year program—that is updated annually or more frequently if circumstances warrant.

The government budget is the principal administrative instrument for translating public investment programs into concrete action. But the link between the two needs to be made much stronger in most developing countries. Many countries do not have a consolidated public sector budget, which is essential if the government is to obtain a full picture of both resource mobilization and expenditure. When such a budget is prepared, it will reveal whether public funds are being invested in activities or in proportions that are not in accord with the public sector investment program, and whether a substantial redirection of resources is desirable.

In fulfilling its budgetary responsibilities, a government must also concern itself with

- Organization and location of the budget and planning functions (although recruitment of qualified staff and establishment of proper procedures for reviewing investment proposals may be no less important)

- Budget classifications that will facilitate planning and management and improve the integration of budget appropriations with the investment program

- Monitoring and evaluation of the budgetary outcome, with emphasis on the accomplishment of programs and projects in addition to the traditional concern for financial propriety.

Even when investment requirements are appropriately matched with financial resources, two budgetary shortcomings common to many developing countries have adverse effects on projects. First, budgets often fail to provide sufficient recurrent funds to operate and maintain projects once the investment phase is over. Second, tight central budgetary controls, by frequently delaying the provision of funds to project managers, have plagued the implementation of investments. In most countries, there is a clear need to give spending agencies greater operational freedom to carry out their assigned tasks. The corollary—that spending agencies should be held more accountable for results—has encouraged the search for new systems, such as program and performance budgeting, which seek to make evaluation of results an integral part of the budgeting process. Implementation of such systems, however, has proved difficult; experience suggests that the way to more effective budgetary management in a developing country is probably through careful identification of specific problem areas, followed by adaptive and evolutionary change, rather than through the large-scale import and installation of new systems.

SECTOR ANALYSIS AND MANAGEMENT

Sector analysis bridges the gap between the macroeconomics of national investment management and the microeconomics of individual projects. It is indispensable for resolving questions of choice, of priority, and of interrelations among projects. Yet it is a neglected activity in many countries. Compared with the elaboration of theories and models for national investment planning or of cost-benefit and other techniques for project analysis, theoretical and practical guidelines for the conduct of sector analysis are much less developed. Nevertheless, many sectoral issues are amenable to analysis, analytical capability is growing with experience, and the number of countries carrying out systematic sector work is steadily increasing.

Sector analysis is clearly useful to external lending agencies—including the World Bank, which has helped to introduce it to many of its member countries—in guiding project selection and design. But it is no less important to officials of ministries and operating agencies in developing countries, who can understandably lose sight of the broad objectives, needs, and priorities of a sector amid the day-to-day tasks of administering regulations and managing crises.

Sector analysis serves several purposes:

- It provides a better understanding of development policies and issues in the sector. This is useful both in enhancing the contribution that the sector can make to the overall strategy for economic development and to the planning of public investment, and in ensuring that the framework for sector policy, no less than that for macroeconomic policy, is conducive to sound project work.
- It makes possible the determination of investment priorities in the sector, which guide the identification and selection of specific projects.
- It evaluates the capacity of the principal institutions in the sector to implement desired policies, programs, and projects.

Most sector analysis falls into one of two broad categories: comprehensive surveys of an entire sector (or important subsector) and special studies of particular topics within a sector. Because the former tend to yield a low return for the heavy investment of manpower and other resources, governments are generally well advised to devote most of their sector work to a program of sharply focused special studies of high-priority issues. Much painful experience argues for keeping the reports on these studies brief and concise, in line with their operational purposes. Good sector analysis requires that qualified staff and other resources be made available for long periods, and this in turn requires that there be sustained commitment from high-level authorities. When these are not forthcoming, the quality of project work also suffers.

Each of the main sectors that we have discussed in part II has distinctive characteristics as well as differing objectives and development issues. No effort is made to summarize them here. At the same time, the sectors share three basic areas for action: policy improvement; institutional strengthening; and better selection, design, analysis, and management of investment projects. The main lessons of experience in these areas are highlighted in the following sections on the project cycle and project analysis.

THE PROJECT CYCLE

It is convenient to think of project work as comprising several distinct stages, commonly referred to collectively as the *project cycle*. The idea of a cycle underscores the point that the stages are closely linked and follow a logical progression, with the later stages providing the basis for a renewal of the cycle. The principal stages of the cycle are the identification of a project; its design, preparation, and appraisal; its implementation; and its evaluation once the investment phase has been completed.

Project identification. The project cycle begins with the identification of project ideas that appear to represent a high-priority use of a country's resources to achieve important development objectives. The identification and preliminary screening of ideas is a critical part of the process. Decisions made at this stage, either explicitly or by default, have a far-reaching impact on the final outcome of the project. It is particularly important at the outset to consider as wide a range of alternative approaches as feasible. All too often, project ideas are put forward and accepted without adequately weighing alternative, and possibly cheaper or more effective, means of achieving the same objectives. Whether the result of vested interests, political pressures, or simply lack of information about viable options, the consequences are the same: opportunities lost at this stage can seldom be recaptured. There is no substitute for being right in the first place.

Explicit attention should be paid to defining a project's objectives at the earliest stage and to ensuring that all the parties concerned, including external lending agencies, agree on those objectives and on the strategy for achieving them. The intended beneficiaries of the project must be consulted when their participation in designing and implementing the project is important to its ultimate success—as it is, for example, in rural and urban development. Failure to reach an understanding about objectives and to secure a firm commitment from all those concerned has often generated friction later and resulted in poor project implementation.

A project can be considered to have passed the identification test when

- Major options and alternatives have been identified and some initial choices made
- The principal policy issues affecting project outcome have been identified and appear to be amenable to solution
- The project options selected are likely to be justified, given rough estimates of the expected costs and benefits
- It appears that the project will have adequate support both from the political authorities and from the intended beneficiaries
- The prospects are reasonable that adequate funding will be available from local and, if needed, external sources
- A specific plan for preparation of the project has been established.

Project preparation. At the next stage, that of project preparation, a feasibility study should be undertaken for all but the simplest and most routine projects. As the term implies, its purpose is to establish the feasibility or justification of the project, both as a whole and in its principal dimensions—technical, economic, financial, social, and so forth. Each dimension must be analyzed both separately and in relation to all the others. This is done in a series of approximations that test, for example, different technical approaches for their economic benefit and financial viability. The purpose of the analysis is not to determine whether a particular project idea is good enough to proceed with, but to arrive at the best one possible under the circumstances. Although the feasibility study should be designed with due regard for cost, this is not the place to skimp; if done well, the study is bound to pay for itself many times over through cost savings or increased benefits.

Good project preparation reduces the likelihood of difficulties during implementation by anticipating the problems that may arise and devising measures to deal with them. For most types of projects, detailed engineering should be completed, cost estimates made relatively reliable, institutional arrangements specified, and financial plans worked out before funds—whether from an external lender or from the domestic budget—are committed. One of the common causes of delayed or poor implementation of Bank-assisted projects has been inadequate or incomplete project preparation.

A pervasive shortcoming of preparation work, as already noted, has been to underestimate the cost of implementing projects as well as the time required. This optimism on the part of planners is found in all projects, large and small, complex and simple, and in virtually all countries. The cost overruns that ensue can have adverse effects on both the financial and economic viability of projects. Including physical and price contingencies as an integral part of the cost estimates helps to improve their accuracy.

One of the thorny issues of project design is how to achieve the right balance between simplicity and complexity. Projects that have a few, well-defined objectives and are based on proven technologies or approaches stand a better chance of being implemented successfully than projects that embody many objectives or unproven methods. Given the scarcity of trained staff, managerial skills, and administrative capacity in developing countries, special efforts to simplify objectives and to select technologies and approaches that have a high probability of working in a particular environment have paid off very well.

At times, however, projects suffer from being too restricted in scope. There are countless examples of projects that did not yield their full benefits, or even failed, because the need for complementary investments and activities had not been recognized and met. This is true of many kinds of agricultural projects (in which research, extension, credit, inputs, marketing, processing, and storage may all be necessary elements), of urban and regional development projects, and of highway maintenance projects, among others. Projects can be too simple as well as too complex; indeed, the swing of the pendulum in recent years toward greater complexity reflects the unimpressive results of projects that were too simple.

There is, however, a middle ground. Even when a multicomponent approach, with its inherent complexity, is necessary, it is possible to concentrate efforts and resources on those elements that are essential to achieving the primary objectives and to leave desirable but secondary objectives to subsequent projects or to parallel operations outside the project. Adjusting the scale of a project or the timing of its components can be another way of matching complex project design with limited implementation capacity. Furthermore, the administrative capacity of an agency can be expanded under a project through well-designed technical assistance.

Project implementation. All project identification and preparation work is directed toward facilitating project implementation and helping to ensure its success. In turn, the lessons learned during project implementation are fed back into the planning and design of the next generation of projects. Ideally, if all the preceding work has gone well, project implementation should hold few surprises. But events seldom go according to plan; circumstances change, and implementation therefore becomes a critical stage of project work.

Projects should be designed with a view to how they will be implemented. There must be a close match between a project's objectives and the capacity of local institutions to implement, operate, and maintain it. Also, projects should be prepared in as much detail as is feasible under the circumstances. Since experience shows that projects are seldom implemented exactly as designed, sufficient flexibility must be preserved so that management can change course, sometimes drastically, during implementation if this becomes necessary.

Particular attention should be paid to the start-up period, before implementation has reached full stride. Use of critical path analysis, monitoring and evaluation techniques, and management information systems can facilitate this and later phases of the implementation process.

How to organize the management of project implementation and how to ensure effective coordination among the various parties can be vexing questions. There has been a tendency, fostered in part by external lending institutions, to assign responsibility for the management of projects in the public sector to special project implementation units established outside the regular line ministries. Such "enclave" units have helped to insulate project implementation from some of the bureaucratic, staffing, and salary weaknesses of the traditional ministries, thereby contributing in some instances to better implementation. But they have been without lasting institutional benefit, since they have operated under conditions that could not be replicated by the line agencies. Project implementation units should be confined to such special cases as projects that embody innovative or very large-scale activities. Even then, arrangements should be made to reincorporate the units as soon as possible into the agencies that bear permanent responsibility for such activities, in accordance with a strategy for strengthening the capacity of those agencies.

Ensuring effective coordination when several agencies or organizations are responsible for different components of a project is inherently difficult. Unless well planned, it can be very time-consuming and unproductive. Some coordinating mechanism must be found; the basic requirements are a clear definition of the responsibilities of each of the participating agencies and adequate incentives for them to cooperate in achieving the project's objectives. If a coordinating committee is used, its authority needs to be clearly demarcated, and its members should be as close as possible to the operating level. Committees composed of ministers or other high-level officials with many other responsibilities have rarely performed well.

The Bank is continually reviewing its experience with project implementation to determine the principal factors that account for the success or failure of projects. Several factors emerge as essential ingredients of successful implementation.

- Probably the most important reason for the success of a project is strong commitment by the government to its objectives. A coalition among the interested agencies and principal actors needs to be formed early in the planning stage and continued throughout implementation. When financial resources allocated to a project dry up, tariffs are not increased on time, or prices and other incentives become distorted, lack of effective support may be the cause. Similarly, mutual commitment and support is needed between the government and any external financing agencies.

- Appropriate design and adequate preparation—both already alluded to—are essential. The objectives and design of projects need to be adapted to local political, administrative, economic, and cultural conditions, particularly if success hinges on changing behavior. When technologies and approaches have not been fully worked out, a pilot project to test them can save both time and money.

- There is a close correlation between good managers and good projects. Many examples can be cited of projects in serious difficulty that were turned around by the appointment of a particular individual; in others, performance declined markedly when a good manager departed. This does not gainsay the importance of the policy environment, but it does affirm that good managers make a difference.

The underlying reasons for success and for failure are largely mirror images. But some of the specific difficulties that projects typically encounter during implementation deserve special mention.

- Managerial problems are the most pervasive. Weak public administration and weak management at the enterprise or project level are often at the root of delays and cost overruns. Such weaknesses are manifested in inadequate planning, delays in land acquisition, protracted bidding and contracting procedures, insufficient project supervision, slow response to changes in the policy environment, and low staff morale and productivity.

- Financial difficulties are common. They can arise from an imbalance between the national investment plan and available resources, which leads to underfunding of publicly supported projects across-the-board; from worldwide or domestic inflation; from a government's reluctance (heightened during inflationary periods) to authorize tariff increases for public services or basic commodities; or from bureaucratic delays in providing funds or even in paying the government's bills. Whatever the reasons, the consequences are the same: physical delays in project implementation, cost overruns, reductions in the scope of the project when this is possible, and deferred implementation of institutional and policy reforms. Cost overruns are a barometer of the implementation process since practically all of the problems encountered result in additional costs as well as delays.

- Technical problems arise continually. These can include difficult or unexpected soil conditions, materials of poor quality, design defects, and unsuitability of imported equipment for local conditions. In agriculture, inadequate technical packages or disappointing results from newly introduced technologies are common. In people-oriented activities such as health delivery systems or education, well-tested approaches to the particular circumstances of a country or region may be lacking. It often takes longer than expected to ease institutional bottlenecks and to develop the services necessary to provide new technologies and to persuade beneficiaries to adopt them. But in most instances, solutions are worked out eventually. Technical problems tend to be less intractable than financial or managerial ones.

Ex post evaluation. The project cycle does not end when implementation is completed and the project goes into operation. There remains yet another stage, that of ex post evaluation, so called to differentiate it from the monitoring and evaluation that should be a regular part of project implementation. Actual results are viewed with the advantage of hindsight. The main purpose is to learn lessons for the design of future projects that supplement those gathered during the course of implementation. A second purpose is to help ensure accountability, whether of international aid agencies to their government shareholders or of national agencies and enterprises to their government and people.

Ex post evaluation should provide a comprehensive and detailed review of the elements of success and failure of the project: what went well and deserves to be repeated; what went wrong and why; how to avoid similar mistakes next time. It normally takes place shortly after the investment phase of the project is completed, at which time the construction costs are known but, for many types of project, a large portion of the benefits still lies in the future. It may be desirable, therefore, to undertake a second evaluation some years later; such a "second look" can yield fresh insights into projects that undergo significant changes while in operation.

The World Bank has a well-established procedure for evaluating completed projects, based on the principles of close involvement of operational staff, objectivity, full disclosure of results, and comprehensive coverage. The process has resulted in a gold mine of information, on which this book has drawn heavily. Developing countries have been slow to take up the Bank's example, in part because of shortages of trained staff and the need to give priority to the operational stages of project work. Those countries that do have an ex post evaluation system, however, are discovering that systematic efforts to learn from experience are invaluable for enhancing the developmental impact of project work.

PROJECT ANALYSIS

Throughout the several stages of the project cycle, various dimensions of project work are addressed, both separately and in relation to each other, and in varying degrees of detail.

Technical analysis. Of these dimensions, technical analysis is perhaps the most familiar. Among the issues of technical design are size, location, timing, and choice of a technology package. We have already alluded in this chapter to the need to select a technology appropriate to the circumstances of the country and the requirements of the project. The point bears repeating in any list of lessons. "Appropriateness" is a relative concept. It generally means that the technology should be determined in relation to the objectives of the project, to the impact on intended beneficiaries, and to local conditions, including the availability and cost of capital, raw materials, and labor, the size of markets, and the present and potential capacity for planning and implementation.

Numerous tradeoffs are implicit in these considerations; for example, a technology may often have to be reduced in complexity to fit the capabilities of local institutions or the sociocultural traditions of the beneficiaries. The range of choice is very wide, from sophisticated, high technology for long-distance telecommunications even in the least developed countries to a labor-intensive approach for maintenance of rural roads, schools, or tertiary irrigation canals even in middle-income countries. Whatever the choice, it is important that it not be unduly biased by government interventions or price distortions of the kind referred to earlier.

Technical analysis also provides an opportunity to consider how a country can best take advantage of its investment plan, policy framework, and development projects to build a capacity to use science and technology effectively throughout the economy. Both trained people and institutions capable of utilizing their skills are required. In the early stages of a country's development, the emphasis should be on building local capacity to import technology from abroad knowledgeably and to adapt it to local conditions. At later stages, the emphasis should shift to the development of local technology and its integration with imported technology, and to the encouragement of local research and innovation.

Economic analysis. The basic question that economic analysis addresses is how to allocate scarce resources among many competing uses. It
seeks to determine not only whether a project can be expected to provide
a satisfactory return to the economy, but also whether there is an
alternative way of achieving the same objectives that would offer a higher
return. The analysis entails a comparison of costs and benefits with and
without the project, both discounted to present values, through the use
of analytical techniques that by now are highly refined—though no more
accurate than the underlying data. The central concept—that, for purposes of economic analysis, resources should be valued in terms of their
opportunity cost to the economy in their best alternative use—is applicable to all economic systems, whether market-oriented, centrally
planned, or a combination of the two.

Most lending agencies use cost-benefit analysis to assess the projects
they help finance, and many developing countries are applying this
analysis in one form or another to projects that they fund from public
resources. Private industrial enterprises also use cost-benefit analysis for
major investments. If done properly, it can be a powerful tool for guiding
investment choices.

Cost-benefit analysis encounters some practical problems, among
them: how to define the situation "with" and "without" the project
(which should not be confused with the situation "before" and "after"
the project); how to handle sunk costs incurred before the analysis (the
short answer is to disregard them); how to establish the shadow (that is,
opportunity) prices for labor and capital when market prices are distorted
for various reasons; and how to deal with nonquantifiable benefits. For
most of these problems of definition or measurement, reasonable approaches can be found that are consistent with the reliability of the
available data. The results of the analysis can be presented as a measure
of net present value, as an internal rate of return, or as a cost-benefit ratio;
each has its particular uses.

Not all types of project are amenable to cost-benefit analysis; it is not
customarily used, for example, in evaluating education or health projects.
Nor does it have the same meaning in different sectors. In power and
water, for example, where prices are publicly administered rather than
fixed by the marketplace, the economic rate of return is a minimum
estimate, more indicative of the appropriateness of the regulated tariffs
than of the real return to the economy. Cost-benefit analysis, therefore,
is not very useful in comparing the merits or relative ranking of projects
in different sectors. Much depends on the common sense, judgment, and
even ingenuity of the analyst. Whim, bias, and intuition will also inevitably play a part. These caveats notwithstanding, economic evaluation
can introduce rationality into the decisionmaking process, identify and
measure risks, and avoid some of the more serious mistakes that can
occur even in the best-laid investment plans.

Financial analysis. Issues of financial analysis arise in the course of
project design in several ways. The first and most universal concern,
applicable to all types of projects, is that there be sufficient funds both to
complete the project and to operate and maintain it subsequently. This
sounds obvious, but far too many development projects have been

launched without adequate consideration of the future availability of funds. This is notably true for education projects, in which recurrent costs for teachers' salaries may quickly exceed the capital costs of the facilities; or for projects in irrigation, roads, health, water supply, and other infrastructure, in which facilities once completed may deteriorate rapidly for want of adequate maintenance. This reluctance to provide adequate recurrent expenditures reflects in part the greater political appeal of new investments and in part the unwillingness of most external lenders to finance such expenditures.

A second financial concern is to recover an appropriate portion of the costs from the beneficiaries or users. A cost recovery policy has three separate but related objectives:

- *Economic efficiency.* The resources provided under a project are used most efficiently when they are priced in accordance with their marginal or opportunity cost. The extent to which efficiency prices can be applied, however, varies widely from sector to sector.

- *Income distribution.* In the interests of equity, the prices or other charges levied to recover costs should take into account differences in income levels (as affected by the project) and in ability to pay.

- *Revenue generation.* Governments in developing countries, being short of resources, need to generate revenue from projects. In addition, revenue-earning enterprises need to be made or kept financially viable. If rural and urban development, water supply, and other projects are to be replicable on the scale necessary to reach the large numbers of potential beneficiaries, a substantial contribution from the initial beneficiaries will often have to be secured.

Difficult tradeoffs may be required among these sometimes conflicting objectives, and the poorer the country the more painful the choices may be. Cost recovery for basic services can be an explosive political issue. This fact, together with administrative considerations, will determine what can be accomplished and how quickly. Two important rules to follow are that new or increased levies should be related to benefits as they materialize and imposed in small but regular increments, and that similar situations should be treated similarly to avoid the appearance of discrimination.

The financial viability of revenue-earning enterprises—electric and water utilities, public and private industries, railways, telecommunications entities, and so on—can be translated into three subsidiary objectives or tests of performance:

- Will the enterprise have sufficient revenue to earn a reasonable return on its invested capital? As part of the test of "reasonableness," will it be able to generate enough funds internally from its operations to make a satisfactory contribution to its future capital requirements?

- Will the capital structure of the enterprise enable it to meet all of its capital obligations, including the service of its debt, in a timely manner?

- Will there be adequate liquidity, that is, sufficient working capital to cover all current operational requirements?

Insistence on financial viability is an important means of imposing discipline on an enterprise and encouraging efficient management and use of resources. There is almost always some scope for improving financial performance by raising operating standards and reducing waste. Achieving financial viability will, however, ultimately throw issues of tariff policy into bold relief. In many cases, increases in prices—often substantial—will be necessary to reach the financial objectives. To raise the price of a basic product or service that figures prominently in the cost of living is an act of political courage. But not to raise the price may, in the long run, have even more adverse economic, and therefore political, consequences. During an inflationary period, governments are especially reluctant to increase the cost of basic goods and services. This is understandable, but failure to raise prices may also have an inflationary impact if the government must borrow to cover the deficits.

One means of easing the bureaucratic and political pain of raising the price of public services, as we have noted, is to adjust prices in small increments and at regular intervals. Another is to make price increases automatic or quasi-automatic, as when fuel costs are passed on to users through equivalent increases in electricity prices without the need for government approval each time.

Social analysis. The role of social analysis, which deals with the impact of projects on people, is to consider the suitability of the proposed project design to the people it is intended to serve, to make proposals for improving the "fit" between the two, and to fashion strategies for project implementation that can be expected both to win and hold people's support and to achieve project goals by inducing changes in social attitudes and behavior. Some projects—in such fields as rural development, education, and health—are clearly oriented toward people. Infrastructure projects are less so, but even these may have to deal effectively with people, as workers or consumers, in order to achieve their objectives. A project that runs counter to or ignores the traditions, values, and social organization of the intended beneficiaries, or that is based on objectives which they do not share, has little prospect of success.

Social analysis is a relative newcomer among the dimensions of project analysis. It focuses on four principal areas:

- The sociocultural and demographic characteristics of the project population
- The way in which the project population is organized to carry out productive activities
- The project's cultural acceptability, including its capacity both for adapting to people's behavior and perceived needs and for bringing about changes in them
- The strategy necessary to elicit commitment from the project population and to ensure their sustained participation throughout the project cycle.

Predicting social behavior is even more uncertain than forecasting financial or economic behavior. Project planners have often made unduly optimistic assumptions about local people's interest in and need for a project, the economic and social incentives for them to participate, and the rate at which change in their social condition can be brought about. Social analysts with professional training and broad experience can improve the projections, however; more important, they can make a significant contribution to a project's success by helping to design effective organizations and approaches to achieve desirable changes in social behavior.

Social analysis of projects has frequently failed to take adequate account of the particular interests and needs of women. Although they constitute half the world's population, women have reaped far less than their share of the benefits of development. Women tend to have less schooling than men, their mobility is constrained by economic and social considerations, and they often face legal barriers to their ownership of assets or access to credit. Yet women play a key role in the development process, both as producers and consumers; for example, they provide most of the agricultural labor used in production, harvesting, marketing, and storage. Moreover, the central position of women in family life profoundly influences attitudes and decisions on education, nutrition, health, and family size. Thus, even if women never enter the formal labor market, ensuring that they receive an adequate education may be one of the best investments a country can make.

Failure to appreciate the role of women and introduce it into the way projects are designed and implemented is not only inequitable but also retards the pace of economic growth. Decisions about which technologies to use and about how to provide a wide range of services must be made with full regard to women's needs and constraints; otherwise, project benefits will be reduced and the position of women made even worse. In many respects, women are the largest underutilized resource for development.

Institutional analysis. In recent years, institutional analysis has become one of the important dimensions of project work. The outcome of development projects depends on the quality of the institutions responsible for them. Yet institutions in developing countries typically suffer from an acute shortage of experienced managers and staff, an excess of untrained staff, overstrained services and facilities, low wages and salaries, inadequate data and information systems, and an inimical policy environment. There are no standard solutions and few readily transferable institutional models from either developed or other developing countries. Institutional development must be seen as a lengthy process of experiment and adaptation, subject to many reverses when political or economic fortunes change. Still, when strong institutions have been forged, they have played a key role in development.

The overall policy environment affects the performance not only of projects but also of the institutions responsible for them. If managers of these institutions are compelled to spend time and effort counteracting the impact of government economic policies (such as a critical shortage of foreign exchange for spare parts owing to an overvalued exchange rate), they cannot build long-term capacity effectively. Institutional problems multiply rapidly when government policies seriously distort the economic environment or when government regulations impose extraneous requirements, such as the employment of extra staff for political or social reasons.

Institutional problems have been compounded as more complex development objectives have been assigned to projects. Executing multicomponent projects or projects focused on alleviating poverty or upgrading social services has placed heavy demands on institutions. Knowledge of the economic, social, and behavioral characteristics of small farmers, urban squatters, or disadvantaged tribal peoples is still rudimentary. Understanding of the management and institutional techniques for dealing with such projects is also at an early stage.

Institutions in the public sector present a particular challenge, both because of their importance and because of the many problems they characteristically confront. A comprehensive reform of the public administration—however badly needed—is a very ambitious undertaking. Few countries, developed or developing, have successfully carried out such a reform in the face of the strong resistance that these efforts generate. While careful diagnosis of the problems of the public service is a necessary first step in establishing an overall strategy for change, implementing the strategy will almost invariably call for a selective approach. The best results have been achieved by concentrating on a few of the more critical problems. The ones to tackle first are those that seriously constrain the performance of the public administration and that are within its capacity to solve; in addition, it should be possible to mobilize and maintain public support for the reform effort.

Parastatals and other forms of state-owned enterprise have proliferated in recent years. Their performance has at best been mixed, and concern has been growing about the need to increase their efficiency, reduce their deficits that burden the public budget, and avoid political interference in their affairs. Given the preponderance of public enterprises in the economies of many developing countries, reforming them has repercussions going far beyond improved project performance. Some governments, in fact, are beginning to devote considerable effort to limiting the spread of public enterprises and to transferring ownership of some of these enterprises to the private sector. The legitimate demands on the public sector are very large, and the capacity for public management is among the scarcest of development resources. This capacity should, therefore, be reserved for use where it is most needed and most likely to be efficacious; governments should exercise great caution in deciding which fields are appropriate for public ownership.

For those agricultural and industrial parastatals carrying out processing, manufacturing, or marketing operations that private producers and merchants can do efficiently, the simple answer may be to abolish them. For others, reducing the number of staff, rationalizing their structures, and appointing and promoting staff on the basis of merit are among the measures that are needed. In several countries, policy reforms are being tried that will improve the "rules of the game" under which the enterprises operate. This reform has two objectives: to give public enterprises greater authority and autonomy to carry out their activities in accordance with broad goals and specific performance targets agreed on with the government; and to hold the enterprises accountable for their results, while improving the flow of information to government about their performance.

A widespread weakness of development institutions, particularly but not exclusively in the public sector, is the shortage of qualified managers at the middle and upper echelons and of experienced specialists such as accountants and engineers. This is a basic characteristic of underdevelopment that can change only gradually. In the long run, the educational system in all its forms—from primary education through universities, vocational schools, and management institutes—must provide the solution. But some steps can be taken immediately. Expatriate managers and consultants can be used to free bottlenecks in the short run—as long as care is taken that this does not delay the development of local managerial capacity, but rather fosters it through counterpart and on-the-job training. Whatever the source of management, greater attention to organizational questions and improved management, accounting, and information systems and procedures can enhance effectiveness. Continuity of management is also important; frequent changes for political reasons are highly disruptive.

One fruitful approach to strengthening management in the public service is through improved incentives. Salary and other financial incentives for public officials cannot normally match those in the private sector, but disparities can be narrowed. In particular cases, elements of the financial package other than pay can also be improved without disturbing prevailing standards in the public service. Establishing "super-grades" outside the normal system may be a way to meet special needs, while making lateral entry and exit easier can encourage managers to view public service as a natural stage in a career.

Programs for training managers and staff also deserve much more attention. The potential contribution of such programs is very large, yet experience shows that too often they have little effect. Training programs cannot be added to projects at the last moment, but must be planned carefully in advance and properly executed. Adequate resources must be provided and skilled trainers recruited. As a general rule, the closer training is to the workplace in which it will be used, the more effective it is likely to be. This argues for on-the-job training when feasible.

Environmental analysis. It is now widely recognized that environmental analysis is necessary for a country to ensure the sound management and use of its natural resources as an integral part of its strategy for economic growth. Desertification, deforestation, soil erosion, overexploitation of such renewable resources as fisheries, and air and water pollution are lowering the carrying capacity of the environment. Usually the poor are disproportionately affected by environmental degradation. The objective of environmental management should be to achieve a balance between human demands on the natural resource base and the ability of that resource base to meet these demands on a sustainable basis in the interests of future generations as well as those alive today.

With careful environmental management, the pace of economic and social progress need not be slowed. In environmental work, the "ounce of prevention" is almost always more important and less costly than the "pound of cure." Sometimes remedial action may not be feasible at all. All proposed development projects should be screened to detect those with a potentially harmful impact on the environment. Most environmental problems, if properly anticipated, can be dealt with at relatively small cost—usually less than 5 percent of total project cost. Analysis of the tradeoffs between different design features and their environmental impact should be a routine part of project work; the analysis is complicated, however, by the fact that the standard time-discounting methodology gives insufficient weight to environmental costs and benefits because of their long-term nature.

Procurement. For all kinds of projects, managing the procurement process is an important aspect of project implementation. Delays in acquiring the necessary goods and works are likely to be compounded into further delays and increased costs for the project as a whole. Procurement is therefore a process to be carefully planned, organized, and managed, the more so since the number of ways things can go wrong sometimes appears endless.

Procurement must serve three objectives. The first is to help ensure the efficient execution of the project by acquiring goods and works with the optimal combination of quality, price, and delivery time. The second is to promote such national goals as the development of local industry, the balanced regional development of industry, or the support of small-scale enterprises. The third is to comply with the procurement regulations of any external lending institutions helping to finance the project.

There are a wide variety of types and methods of procurement. Which is the most appropriate depends on the size and nature of the project, the particular goods or works to be procured, and the regulations of lending agencies. For large projects, international competitive bidding is generally the best way of ensuring efficient procurement, safeguarding against waste or corruption, and satisfying the interest of lending agencies that all qualified firms be permitted to bid. Local competitive bidding is more appropriate for small-scale procurement of goods and works in which foreign firms will not be interested; changes in procedures may be necessary to ensure effective competition among local firms.

Use of consultants. Procurement of consulting services raises different issues. There is, first, the question of need. Most of the services for which consultants might be recruited can, in principle, be done by local staff of the project agency if they are competent, experienced, and available. When such in-house capacity does not exist (as may often be the case) and cannot be put in place by additional training soon enough to meet the demands of the project, the next best choice is the use of local consulting firms. Establishing a local consulting industry is desirable both to provide some competition to stimulate agency staff and to supply more specialized skills or expert services. When local services are not available, firms from other developing countries may offer the dual advantages of better knowledge and understanding of comparable local conditions and relatively low costs. There will, however, remain some assignments—especially for large or complex projects and those requiring highly technical knowledge—for which only expatriate consultants from developed countries are qualified. Joint ventures between foreign and local consulting firms, if entered into voluntarily, are often a good way of developing local capacity.

The consultant-client relationship is a close, personal one; when a satisfactory partnership already exists with a particular firm, it may be eminently sensible to continue it. When no such relationship exists, or when for other reasons it is desirable to invite proposals from a short list of qualified firms, the selection process should ensure that price considerations are subordinated to a concern with quality. The cost of consulting services is usually only a small fraction of total project costs, but the quality of the work performed can have an impact on the final project out of all proportion to the cost.

These, then, are some of the principal lessons that the World Bank has learned in more than thirty-five years of assisting its member countries in managing their investment resources. We offer them not in the belief that they provide final answers to the formidable problems of development, but in the conviction that better national investment planning, macro-economic and sector policies, and project work can ease the path of development, bring its benefits to people sooner, and distribute them more equitably.

Enjoying water provided under urban improvement program, Calcutta, India

Index of Place Names

Abidjan, 276, 291, 299
Addis Ababa, 293
Afghanistan, 100
Africa, 39, 85, 87, 104, 113, 122, 123, 126, 127, 129, 137, 139, 149, 161, 189, 212, 219, 232, 237, 248, 259, 275, 276, 278, 279, 293, 305, 317, 321, 358, 369, 370, 374, 400, 406, 459, 477, 500, 507, 508, 510, 513, 515. *See also* East Africa, North Africa, Sahel, Southern Africa, Sub-Saharan Africa, West Africa
Algeria, 371
Ankara, 529
Argentina, 22, 34, 40, 42, 246, 255, 259, 260
Asia, 19, 85, 87, 122, 123, 127, 149, 212, 248, 276, 297, 399, 400, 517. *See also* East Asia, South Asia, Southeast Asia

Bahamas, 61
Bahrain, 61, 64
Bamako, 300
Bangkok, 275, 317
Bangladesh, 22, 26, 35, 55, 56, 57, 63, 86, 91, 100, 158, 203, 419, 489, 518
Barranquilla, 289
Beijing, 275
Benin, 483
Bogotá, 291
Bolivia, 40, 53, 123, 261, 487, 490
Bombay, 289
Botswana, 19, 26, 54, 57, 292
Bouaké, 276
Brazil, 25, 26, 40, 60, 61, 95, 100, 127, 158, 166, 167, 169, 176, 189, 222, 255, 259, 275, 299, 315, 350, 405, 406, 476, 490, 500, 534, 538, 561. *See also* Ponta Grossa, Recife, São Paulo
Burkina, 262, 268, 280, 286, 370, 483
Burma, 480
Burundi, 152, 513

Cairo, 277, 286, 300
Calcutta, 256, 289, 300
Caribbean, 19
Cartagena, 475, 482, 563
Chad, 371
Chile, 8, 25, 34, 40, 42, 61, 189, 222, 253, 419
China, 24, 41, 42, 85, 86, 87, 100, 122, 153, 156, 157, 184, 237, 244, 275, 305, 309, 325, 387, 513. *See also* Beijing, Shanghai, Taiwan

Colombia, 22, 40, 127, 131, 189, 193, 222, 259, 284, 387. *See also* Barranquilla, Bogotá, Cartagena, Medellín
Congo, 513
Costa Rica, 60, 531
Cyprus. *See* Nicosia

Dakar, 276, 513
Dar es Salaam, 247, 323
Dominican Republic, 528

East Africa, 60, 112, 258, 292, 305, 352
East Asia, 19, 86, 184, 189, 190, 275
Ecuador, 286, 490
Egypt, 60, 99, 189, 244, 518. *See also* Cairo
El Salvador, 293, 475, 488, 492–93
Ethiopia, 22, 97, 145, 370, 477, 515, 517. *See also* Addis Ababa

France, 196

Gabon, 315
Ghana, 22, 36, 37, 40, 136, 193, 214, 228, 370, 476, 482, 502
Greece, 189
Guatemala, 145, 319, 478, 479
Gujarat, 323
Guyana, 64

Haiti, 100, 145, 524
Honduras, 399, 400
Hong Kong, 20, 189, 252
Hungary, 24, 26, 42, 255, 513

India, 19, 22, 24, 26, 36, 56, 57, 62, 63, 64, 65, 85, 86, 87, 95, 100, 101, 106, 123, 156, 157, 222, 233, 234, 237, 238, 244, 275, 286, 298, 319, 320, 323, 350, 401, 404–06, 419, 477, 478, 488, 489, 500, 504, 517, 518. *See also* Bombay, Calcutta, Gujarat, Madras, Punjab
Indonesia, 65, 86, 95, 101, 121, 123, 136, 139, 193, 203, 214, 222, 233, 235, 237, 297, 298, 313, 352, 401, 475, 476, 491–92, 504, 531, 538, 561. *See also* Jakarta
Iran, 370
Israel, 169, 189
Istanbul, 256

Subject Index

Accounting system, 467–68. *See also* Financial information systems
Agrarian reform, 98–99
Agricultural marketing organizations, 94–96, 512. *See also* Cocoa Marketing Board (Ghana)
Agriculture: cost-benefit analysis and, 443, 444; cultural and political issues and, 109–10; development objectives and, 89–90; economic aspects of, 84–85; energy and, 150; financial aspects of, 87–88, 107–09; food security and, 96–97; general characteristics of, 83; income distribution and, 92; infrastructure and, 93–96; institutional aspects of, 88–89, 110–12; investment issues and, 112–15; land management and, 97–100; prices and, 35–37, 90–92; private sector in (Bangladesh), 56; productivity and, 84; project outcome and, 114–15; sector definition and, 71; social aspects of, 85–87, 109; technical problems and, 374; technological change and, 103–07; tractor use and, 404–05, 488; water management and, 100–03; women and, 109, 484, 486, 490. *See also* Farmers
Air pollution, 530, 533
Air transport, 248; facility usage and, 260; planning of projects for, 266–67
Alternatives, consideration of project, 341, 421, 422, 581; energy, 173; environmental, 531
Annual Review of Project Performance Audit Results (World Bank OED), 384
Asian Development Bank, 544, 550
Automobiles, 254, 260; tax on, 284, 299

Balance of payments, 34; energy and, 150–51
Banks: implementation problems and, 372; industry and, 186, 194–95; rural finance and, 107–08
Benefit-cost ratio, 432. *See also* Cost-benefit analysis
Bids (procurement), 592; contract award and, 545, 552, 553, 554; evaluation of, 552–54; preparation of, 551–52; types of, 544–47
Biocides, 524, 530
Bretton Woods conference (1944), 6, 7
Budgets: controls and, 62–63; coverage of, 60–61; educational expenditures and, 122; evaluating results of, 64–65; item classification and, 61–62; national

investment management and, 59–65, 578–79; performance review (financial) and, 468; planning and, 61; project finance and, 450–51; public expenditures (urban) and, 284–85; trimming investment, 432–33
Bureaucracy, 413, 414, 583, 588; political problems with, 375; price adjustments and, 463
Buses, 246, 250, 254; in Calcutta, 256; special lanes for, 260; technical assistance and, 299

Cadastral services, 287
Canals, 103, 450
Capital: financial performance and structural standards for, 464–66; industry and, 192, 199–200; policies and, 31; rate of return on, 460–61; road projects and, 266; system expansion and, 33; underpricing of, 37–38; venture, 414–15
Carrying capacity, 525–26, 538
Case studies: of public investment, 58–59; of social analysis, 491–93; of technical design, 396–406
Cash generation (performance test), 461–63
Centrally planned economies, 6, 19, 24, 32, 42
Children: agricultural sector and, 109; food supplement program for, 478; health services for, 215; mortality rates for, 211; training of illiterate, 483; water supply and, 315; women's education and number of, 484
Cities. *See* Urbanization; Urban sector
Civil works: case study of, 398–401; cost estimation, 408. *See also* Construction
Class size (student-teacher ratio), 121, 135–36
Coal, 152, 153, 158, 160, 177
Cocoa Marketing Board (Ghana), 36–37, 502
Community involvement: building local capacity and, 482–84; education and, 128, 129; health services and, 236–37; health workers and, 225–26, 236; project participation and, 479–82; urbanization projects and, 293–94; water and sanitation and, 319–20
Competition, 23, 32, 33, 194, 514; public enterprises and, 196, 512–13, 514, 516; railways and, 245; transport and, 250, 256–57